Hard-to-Survey Populations

Surveys are used extensively in psychology, sociology, and business, as well as many other areas, but they are becoming increasingly difficult to conduct. Some segments of the population are hard to sample, some are hard to find, others are hard to persuade to participate in surveys, and still others are hard to interview.

This book offers the first systematic look at the populations and settings that make surveys hard to conduct and at the methods researchers use to meet these challenges. It covers a wide range of populations (immigrants, persons with intellectual difficulties, and political extremists) and settings (war zones, homeless shelters) that offer special problems or present unusual challenges for surveys. The team of international contributors also addresses sampling strategies including methods such as respondent-driven sampling and examines data collection strategies including advertising and other methods for engaging otherwise difficult populations.

ROGER TOURANGEAU is a Vice President at Westat

BRAD EDWARDS is a Vice President and Deputy Area Director at Westat

TIMOTHY P. JOHNSON is Director of the Survey Research Laboratory and Professor of Public Administration at the University of Illinois at Chicago

KIRK M. WOLTER is Executive Vice President, NORC at the University of Chicago, and Professor, Department of Statistics, University of Chicago

NANCY BATES is a Senior Researcher for Survey Methodology at the US Census Bureau

Hard-to-Survey Populations

Edited by

ROGER TOURANGEAU,
BRAD EDWARDS,
TIMOTHY P. JOHNSON,
KIRK M. WOLTER, AND
NANCY BATES

CAMBRIDGE
UNIVERSITY PRESS

University Printing House, Cambridge CB2 8BS, United Kingdom

Cambridge University Press is part of the University of Cambridge.

It furthers the University's mission by disseminating knowledge in the pursuit of
education, learning and research at the highest international levels of excellence.

www.cambridge.org
Information on this title: www.cambridge.org/9781107628717

© Cambridge University Press 2014

First published 2014

Printed in the United Kingdom by Clays, St Ives plc

A catalogue record for this publication is available from the British Library

Library of Congress Cataloguing in Publication data
Hard-to-survey populations / edited by Roger Tourangeau, Brad Edwards, Timothy P. Johnson,
Kirk M Wolter, and Nancy Bates.
    pages   cm
ISBN 978-1-107-03135-7 (hardback)
1. Demographic surveys.   2. Social surveys.   I. Tourangeau, Roger.
HB849.49.H367   2014
001.4′33–dc23

                                                                              2014002761

ISBN 978-1-107-03135-7 Hardback
ISBN 978-1-107-62871-7 Paperback

To our partners – KAREN TOURANGEAU, ALAN LOPEZ, LUELLEN DOTY, MARY JANE WOLTER, AND MONA ALCAZAR

Contents

Figures

xi

Tables

Boxes

Contributors

OWEN ABBOTT
Office for National Statistics, UK

KEITH ATTERBERRY
Survey Research Laboratory, University of Illinois at Chicago

WILLIAM G. AXINN
University of Michigan

NANCY BATES
US Census Bureau

KIRSTEN BECKER
RAND Corporation

ERAN BEN-PORATH
Social Science Research Solutions

SANDRA H. BERRY
RAND Corporation

MOLLYANN BRODIE
Kaiser Family Foundation

ANNE MARIE BROOKS
Department of Children and Youth Affairs, Republic of Ireland

ANNA CHAN
US Citizenship and Immigration Services

KRISTEN L. CIBELLI
University of Michigan

ROBERT GRAHAM CLARK
University of Wollongong

GARNETT COMPTON
Office for National Statistics, UK

A. RUPA DATTA
NORC at the University of Chicago

IAN DAVIES
Central England People First, UK

CLAUDIA DEANE
Kaiser Family Foundation

YASHWANT DESHMUKH
Cvoter, India

BRAD EDWARDS
Westat

ERIC EMERSON
Lancaster University, UK and University of Sydney, Australia

W. DOUGLAS EVANS
George Washington University

DIRGHA GHIMIRE
University of Michigan

IRENE GLASSER
Center for Alcohol and Addictions Research, Brown University

PATRICK P. GUNN
Cooley LLP

MARIEKE HAAN
University of Groningen, Netherlands

ELIZABETH C. HAMEL
Kaiser Family Foundation

SINÉAD HANAFIN
Visiting fellow, Trinity College Dublin

JANET HARKNESS
University of Nebraska–Lincoln

STEVE HEERINGA
University of Michigan

MELISSA HERRMANN
Social Science Research Solutions

ERIC HIRSCH
Providence College

ALLYSON L. HOLBROOK
University of Illinois at Chicago

JENNIFER HUNTER CHILDS
Center for Survey Measurement, US Census Bureau

LILLI JAPEC
Statistics Sweden

TIMOTHY P. JOHNSON
Survey Research Laboratory, University of Illinois at Chicago

GRAHAM KALTON
Westat

CECILY C. KELLEHER
UCD School of Public Health, Physiotherapy and Population Science, Dublin

JENNIFER KELLEY
University of Michigan

PIERRE LAVALLÉE
Statistics Canada

SUNGHEE LEE
University of Michigan

STEPHEN LUBKEMANN
US Census Bureau

LARS LYBERG
Stockholm University

TYLER H. McCORMICK
University of Washington

PATTY MAHER
University of Michigan

SALLY MALAM
TNS BMRB, UK

DOUGLAS S. MASSEY
Princeton University

BAIRBRE MEANEY
Department of Children and Youth Affairs, Republic of Ireland

ZEINA N. MNEIMNEH
University of Michigan

PETER MOHLER
University of Mannheim, Germany

MARY H. MULRY
US Census Bureau

IDES NICAISE
HIVA – Research Institute for Work and Society, University of Leuven, Belgium

TIMOTHY P. OLSON
US Census Bureau

YFKE ONGENA
University of Groningen, Netherlands

NATE ORR
RAND Corporation

YULING PAN
US Census Bureau

BETH-ELLEN PENNELL
University of Michigan

JUDY PERLMAN
RAND Corporation

BRIGID QUIRKE
UCD School of Public Health, Physiotherapy and Population Science, Dublin

GILLIAN ROCHE
Central Statistics Office, Republic of Ireland

MOHAMMAD SALIH ALKAISY
IBN Cena Teaching Hospital Mosul, Iraq

INGRID SCHOCKAERT
HIVA – Research Institute for Work and Society, University of Leuven, Belgium

LAURIE SCHWEDE
Center for Survey Measurement, US Census Bureau

TOM W. SMITH
NORC at the University of Chicago

MATHEW STANGE
University of Nebraska–Lincoln

INEKE STOOP
The Netherlands Institute for Social Research/SCP

ROBERT TEMPLETON
New Zealand Ministry of Health

RODNEY TERRY
Center for Survey Measurement, US Census Bureau

STEVE THOMPSON
Simon Fraser University

DAN TOMLIN
University of Michigan

ROGER TOURANGEAU
Westat

RICHARD VALLIANT
University of Michigan

ARTURO VARGAS
National Association of Latino Elected and Appointed Officials Educational Fund

JAMES WAGNER
University of Michigan

JEROME D. WILLIAMS
Rutgers Business School

KIRK M. WOLTER
University of Chicago

TING YAN
University of Michigan

TIAN ZHENG
Columbia University

Preface

Between rising costs and falling response rates, surveys certainly seem to have their problems these days. Yet, it also seems that surveys have never been more popular as a research tool than they are now. Every year, more and more federal surveys are done (Presser & McCulloch, 2012) and the rate of growth has, we suspect, been even faster for academic and commercial surveys. And it also seems to us that surveys are being done with an ever-wider array of groups and in an ever-wider range of settings than ever before. Groups that may once have been deemed impossible to survey – groups like the homeless, prostitutes, war refugees, victims of natural disaster, and persons with serious physical or mental disabilities – are now the target populations for surveys – maybe not routine surveys, but surveys nonetheless. This volume tries to capture the experiences and lessons learned that have accumulated over the years in doing surveys with such hard-to-survey populations. We hope that presenting some of the best of the recent work here will spur the development of methods for surveying these groups, moving the field beyond stories about individual experiences and toward a more systematic understanding of the problems and solutions.

The book is divided into five parts. The chapters in the first section, edited by Roger Tourangeau, develop an overall conceptual framework for surveys of challenging populations, examine such populations across nations, recount efforts to reduce and measure these difficulties in national censuses, and describe quality control and quality assurance issues for such surveys. The next two parts look at settings and populations that make surveys hard to do. Part II, edited by Brad Edwards, examines surveys done after disasters, in war zones, and with homeless and itinerant populations. Part III, edited by Timothy Johnson, looks at a range of hard-to-survey populations, including difficult groups in European surveys, linguistic minorities, immigrants and other hard-to-count groups in the US, children and young people, persons with intellectual disabilities, vulnerable and stigmatized groups, and political extremists. Part IV, edited by Kirk Wolter, looks at the issues in sampling hard-to-survey populations. This part includes chapters on traditional methods for sampling rare populations, more recent techniques for such populations, indirect sampling, methods for finding special populations from existing lists or census data, network methods, and link-tracing and respondent-driven sampling. The final part of the book, edited by Nancy Bates and Brad Edwards, looks at the tactics researchers have used to carry out surveys of hard-to-survey groups, including media campaigns, methods for reaching and retaining the poor in surveys in the EU, tailoring the survey to the population, ethnographic studies of interviewer–respondent interactions in surveys with language minority groups, mobilizing members of a hard-to-survey population to participate, and finding members of such populations.

Planning for this volume was closely coordinated with the International Conference on Methods for Surveying and Enumerating Hard-to-Reach Populations (H2R), held in New Orleans from October 31 to November 3, 2012 (www.amstat.org/meetings/h2r/2012). New Orleans was chosen as the site in part to signal our support for the city's rebirth after the devastation of Hurricane Katrina in 2005. (The difficulty of surveying New Orleans residents after Katrina is a major focus of Chapters 6 and 9 in this book.) Seeds for both the book and the conference were planted in 2008 at the US Census Bureau, as it prepared for the 2010 Decennial Census, and the conference was timed to coincide with early release of research with hard-to-survey populations in that census. Invited papers presented at the H2R conference were candidates for book chapters in this volume.

The conference was organized by a committee chaired by two of the editors of this book, Nancy Bates and Brad Edwards. In developing plans for the conference and the book, Bates drew heavily on the prior experience of her colleague, Jennifer Rothgeb. Bates also received early encouragement and advice from Lars Lyberg. We gratefully acknowledge their help and support. Besides the other three editors (Johnson, Tourangeau, and Wolter), the organizing committee included Siobhan Carey from the Office of National Statistics in the UK; Linda Jacobsen from the Population Reference Bureau in the US; Frauke Kreuter from the Joint Program in Survey Methodology at the University of Maryland and the Institute for Employment Research (IAB) in Germany; Pierre Lavallée from Statistics Canada; Mary Mulry from the US Census Bureau, USA; and Gordon Willis from the National Institutes of Health in the US. The organizing committee was crucial to the success of the conference and the success of this book.

And, by any measure, the H2R conference was a big success. Despite Hurricane Sandy, the major storm that hit the northeast coast of the US the day before meetings began, stranding many travelers, more than 300 researchers made it to Louisiana for sessions that included three short courses (given by Reg Baker, Peter Mohler, and Matthias Schonlau), 144 papers, 18 posters, and a plenary, for a total of 166 presentations. Presenters came from more than twenty countries on five continents (and some islands) and included some students and other researchers from less developed parts of the globe who received travel scholarships. To circumvent Sandy, some authors presented papers remotely, with technical video support in New Orleans. The plenary session showcased the authors of Chapter 10 in this volume, describing a landmark study of Irish Travellers conducted in two countries and illustrating virtually every aspect of difficulties in (and strategies for) surveying the hard to survey. The Irish Travellers Health Survey used innovative methods to identify and systematically study a population that was highly mobile or nomadic, with low literacy rates, a unique language and isolated culture, and subject to high levels of stigmatization. The survey design was created with a high level of participation from the study population, and the data collectors were all members of the group. Innovative methods were developed to allow interviewers with low literacy levels to conduct computer-assisted interviews.

There was a session in memory of Janet Harkness, who died in late May of 2012 and who co-authored several conference papers and two of the chapters in this book. We mourn the passing of this distinguished survey researcher. Apart from the papers published in this book, additional papers from the conference will be published in upcoming special issues of the *Journal of Official Statistics* and *Survey Practice*.

The conference would never have happened without the support it received from a number of organizations – the American Association for Public Opinion Research; the Survey Research Methods, Social Statistics, and Government Statistics Sections of the American Statistical Association (ASA); the National Science Foundation; the Institute for Employment Research in Germany; and the World Association for Public Opinion Research. Beyond these key sponsors, there were three other levels of support: contributors (who gave funds but who did not assume any financial risk), partners (who contributed in-kind support), and additional sponsorships (for specific activities or events). Contributors included GfK, the International Association of Survey Statisticians, the National Agricultural Statistical Service, NORC at the University of Chicago, the Office of National Statistics in the UK, the Population Association of America, the Survey Research Center at the University of Michigan, the US Bureau of the Census, the US Bureau of Labor Statistics, and Westat. Partnering with H2R were Statistics Without Borders and the US Census Bureau's five Race and Ethnic Advisory Committees (African-American; Native Hawaiian and Other Pacific Islander; Asian, Hispanic; and American Indian and Alaska Native). The additional sponsors were Abt SRBI, American Institutes for Research, Headway Workforce Solutions, Mathematica Policy Research, NORC at the University of Chicago, RAND Corporation, and RTI International. We gratefully acknowledge these supporters, without which neither the conference nor the book would have come about.

The ASA also provided an institutional home for the conference and the ASA meetings department helped immensely in putting the conference together. Our special thanks go to Naomi Friedman, Donna Arrington, Joyce Narine, Kathleen Wert, Kathryn Wright, and others at ASA for their hard work on the conference. In addition, we thank Margo Kline for her help in getting the authors to sign their contracts and copyright forms and to Margo Tercy, Jerri Brown, Ben Engelbach, Alex McIntosh, and Phyllica Sookhar for their help in getting the files ready for the publisher. Finally, Patty Kelley did the index, with assistance from Cat Tourangeau and Margo Tercy. We are very grateful for their excellent work on this difficult chore.

References

Presser, S., & McCulloch, S. (2012). The growth of survey research in the United States: government-sponsored surveys, 1984–2004. *Social Science Research*, 40(4), 1019–24.

PART I

Introduction

1

Defining hard-to-survey populations

ROGER TOURANGEAU

1.1 Introduction

This book is about populations that are hard to survey in different ways. It focuses on populations of people rather than establishments or institutions. In an era of falling response rates for surveys (Brick & Williams, 2013; Curtin, Presser, & Singer, 2005; de Leeuw & de Heer, 2002), it may seem that *all* household populations are hard to survey, but some populations present special challenges of various sorts that make them harder to survey than the general population. Some of these hard-to-survey populations are rare; others are hidden; some are difficult to find or contact; still others are unlikely to cooperate with survey requests. This chapter tries to distinguish the major challenges that make populations hard to survey and reviews attempts to quantify how hard to survey different populations are.

One way to classify the various sources of difficulty is by what survey operation they affect. In this chapter, we distinguish populations that are *hard to sample*, those whose members who are *hard to identify*, those that are *hard to find or contact*, those whose members are *hard to persuade* to take part, and those whose members are willing to take part but nonetheless *hard to interview*. These distinctions reflect the main steps in many surveys. First, a sample is selected. Often, the next operation is identifying members of the target population, for example, through screening interviews. Then, the sample members must be found and contacted. Once contact is made, sample members have to be persuaded to do the survey. And, finally, the willing respondents have to have whatever abilities are needed to provide the requested data or special steps have to be taken to accommodate them. As we shall see, with any given population, problems can arise with each of these operations, making the population hard to survey. And, as will become clear, some hard-to-survey populations present combinations of several kinds of trouble.

1.2 Hard-to-sample populations

In the ideal case, there is a complete and up-to-date list of the target population and the sample can be drawn from this list. Unfortunately, this ideal is rarely realized in practice; for most populations of interest in surveys, there is no list frame and sampling begins with some general purpose sampling frame, such as an area, address, or random digit dial

3

(RDD) frame. Problems arise when the target population represents a small fraction of the frame population. Kalton (2009; see also Chapter 19 of this volume) distinguishes major subgroups or domains (constituting more than 10 percent of the total population), from minor subgroups (1 to 10 percent) and from mini-subgroups (less than 1 percent of the total population). To pick out the members of the target population from the other members of the general population, surveys often begin by administering a short battery of screening questions. In the absence of a special frame or frames, then, one reason that a population can be hard to sample is that its members are rare, representing a small fraction of the larger frame population, often the general population. (Another source of difficulty, to which we return later, is that it may be hard to identify the members of the rare population in a short screener.)

Discussions of the issues involved in sampling rare populations (e.g., Chapter 19; Kalton & Anderson, 1986; Sudman, Sirken, & Cowan, 1988) often point to two other population characteristics, apart from overall prevalence within the general population, that affect the level of difficulty in finding members of the population in a screening survey. The first is the level of variation across areas or sampling strata in the prevalence of the rare subgroup. It is sometimes possible to increase sampling efficiency by oversampling strata where the prevalence of the rare subgroup is relatively high and undersampling areas where the prevalence is relatively low. It is easier to find members of the rare population when a substantial proportion of them is concentrated in a small number of areas or strata that can be identified prior to sampling. For example, a recent experiment in the National Household Education Survey attempted to boost the number of Hispanics in the sample by targeting census tracts in which at least 13 percent of the population was Hispanic (Brick, Montaquila, Han, & Williams, 2012).

The other variable affecting the difficulty of locating members of a rare population is the cost of a screening interview relative to the cost of the main interview. If screening interviews are relatively cheap (for example, only a few questions are needed to identify members of the target population), then having to carry out a lot of them will not affect the final data collection costs so much as when screening is relatively expensive. Consider a situation in which members of the rare population constitute 5 percent of the total population. If we ignore the effects of nonresponse to the main interview, this implies that twenty screeners will have to be done for each main interview. However, if the screening interviews cost only one twentieth of the main interview, then the total costs per case are only doubled by the screening costs (that is, twenty screeners plus one main interview cost twice as much as a main interview alone). But if the screening interviews are expensive – say, half the cost of the main interview – then the need to complete twenty screenings per main interview will drive up the total cost per case by a factor of 11. Screening costs can be high if medical tests or a long series of questions are needed to identify members of the target population or if it is difficult to get people to complete the screener. Some surveys use a two-phase screening process, where the first-phase screener casts a broad net and the second phase screener applies more stringent criteria. Clearly, sampling efficiency matters more when the screening process is expensive.

Kalton (2009) provides a measure (R) of the gains in sampling efficiency that can be achieved with a disproportionate allocation of the initial sample across strata that vary in the prevalence of the rare population:

$$R = \frac{\left[\Sigma W_h \sqrt{P(c-1) + P/P_h)}\right]^2}{P(c-1) + 1}, \tag{1.1}$$

in which W_h is the proportion of the rare group in stratum h, P is the overall prevalence of the rare group, P_h is its prevalence within stratum h, and c is the ratio of data collection costs for a member of the rare population to the costs for the nonmembers (that is, for cases who screen out).

One way to measure the difficulty of sampling members of the rare population is by the added cost per case due to the need to conduct screening interviews. With a proportionate allocation of the screening sample, the added cost (Δ_c) per case, expressed as a proportion of the total cost per case, depends on the prevalence (P) of the rare group and the cost ratio parameter (c) described earlier in Equation 1.1:

$$\Delta_c = 1 + c/P.$$

Under an optimal allocation across strata, the added cost would be $R \times \Delta_C$, where R is the efficiency gain factor defined in Equation 1.1. For example, if the efficiency factor was .8 and screening increased the data collection cost per case by a factor of 1.5, the net effect would be an increase of 20 percent (that is, $.8 \times 1.5 = 1.2$). Δ_C and $R \times \Delta_C$ provide measures of the sampling difficulty associated with a rare population. In summary, then, a population is harder to sample as its overall prevalence becomes lower, as its prevalence varies less across the sampling strata, and as the screening costs increase relative to the cost of a main interview. In the best case, most of the rare target population falls within a few strata or a single high prevalence stratum and the screeners are relatively inexpensive.

A related situation involves selecting the sample from two frames – a general purpose frame with low prevalence but high coverage of the rare population, and a special frame with higher prevalence but less complete coverage of the rare population. The latter might be a list of known members of the rare population. The dual frame sample yields the highest gains compared to the general purpose frame alone when the special frame has a much higher prevalence than the general purpose frame and when it includes a large fraction of the rare population (e.g., Lohr & Rao, 2000).

Another type of population that presents particular difficulties for sample designers are mobile or "elusive" populations. These are populations, such as the homeless and similar groups (e.g., migrant workers), that are not easily linked to any one place. Here, the best sampling strategy often involves sampling places where the members of the elusive population are likely to be found rather than sampling the members of the population directly. Kalton (2009; see also Chapter 19 in this volume) describes this approach as "location sampling." Examples include sampling homeless shelters and soup kitchens as a strategy for capturing the homeless (e.g., Ardilly & Le Blanc, 2001) or sampling oases or waterholes to capture nomadic herdsman. Sampling is likely to continue for some period of time and, precisely because such populations are mobile, members may have multiple chances for selection. Moreover, the frame of locations is likely to be incomplete; thus, elusive populations may well be undercovered even when a location sample is selected. If the main goal of the survey is to estimate the size of the population, capture-recapture methods can be used. These methods, initially developed for estimating the size of nonhuman populations, are now used in estimating the coverage of censuses of human populations (see Mulry, Chapter 3 in this volume). Two samples are taken; in the best case, the samples are completely independent. (With the census, one of the samples is the post-enumeration survey sample; the other is a sample from the census enumerations.) The estimate of the size of the population reflects the proportion of cases found in both samples. A potential problem with this method is "correlation bias" – that is, the violation of the assumption that the capture and recapture probabilities are independent. When members of the rare population systematically vary in their elusiveness (or when they vary in their elusiveness within sampling strata), this variation will produce correlation bias. Imperfections in the sampling frame can also lead to correlation bias. For example, if the frame for a survey of the homeless omits certain sites, then the homeless linked only to those sites are likely be missed in both the initial and recapture survey.

Mobility presents challenges not only for sampling a population, but also for locating the members of the group. We have more to say about these problems in Section 1.4 below.

1.3   Hard-to-identify populations

A screening survey is predicated on the assumption that the respondents are both willing and able to answer the screening questions accurately. Screening data are often provided by household informants, who provide information about themselves and about the other members of the household. In some cases, a neighbor may be used as a last resort when screening is based on age, race, or some other visible characteristic. And, in network samples, screener respondents may be asked not only about their own households but also about the members of linked households (e.g., the households of their siblings; see Sudman *et al.*, 1988, and Chapters 23 and 24 in this volume, for discussions). Regardless of the exact method of screening, the accuracy of the screening data will depend on the screening respondents knowing the relevant characteristics of each person they are asked about and their willingness to report that information. Unfortunately, these conditions may not always be met, creating a second type of hard-to-survey population.

1.3.1   *Stigma, sensitivity, and motivated misreporting*

Consider the difficulties in identifying the members of some cultural or religious minority, such as immigrants (see Massey, Chapter 13 in this volume), men who have sex with men, or Muslims (Keeter, Smith, Kennedy, Turakhia, Schulman, & Brick, 2008). Members of a highly stigmatized population, such as illicit drug users, may keep this characteristic secret even from other household members. And household informants may be reluctant to identify persons with the relevant characteristics to outsiders.

Even when the characteristic of interest is not sensitive (for example, when the population of interest is a specific age group), screening interviews often miss members (Horrigan, Moore, Pedlow, & Wolter, 1999; Judkins, DiGaetano, Chu, & Shapiro, 1995). Although almost all surveys are prone to *some* undercoverage (see, for example, Shapiro, Diffendal, & Cantor, 1993, on the coverage of the Current Population Survey, or CPS), the undercoverage in screening surveys seems to be worst for the very groups targeted by the survey. One of the best documented instances of such underreporting involves the National Longitudinal Survey of Youth, 1997 Cohort (NLSY-97). The eligible population for this survey was young people, aged 12–23. Horrigan and his colleagues (Horrigan *et al.*, 1999) compared the numbers of persons found in the NLSY-97 screening effort with the expected numbers based on CPS figures for the different age groups. The NSLY screening data show roughly the same numbers as expected for the age groups above 23 and slight undercoverage for those below 12 (roughly 90 percent coverage relative to the CPS). For the age range targeted in the screening effort (12–23 years old), however, the coverage dropped to about 70 percent. Similar problems have been found with several other national surveys (see Judkins *et al.*, 1999); in each case, undercoverage was considerably worse for the survey's target population than for other groups. To avoid the biases produced by this sort of underreporting, surveys sometimes retain some of the households that screen out for further data collection. Of course, this increases data collection costs.

Tourangeau, Kreuter, and Eckman (2012) argue that the underreporting of eligible household members in screeners is an example of *motivated misreporting*, in which respondents, interviewers, or both, shade the answers to minimize the work they have to do (see also Kreuter, McCulloch, Presser, & Tourangeau, 2011). When eligible households screen out, they do not have to complete the main interview, reducing the burden for both the potential respondent and on the interviewer. My co-authors and I carried out an experiment in which we varied how much the screening questions in a telephone survey disguised the target population (Tourangeau *et al.*, 2012). Some households got questions that asked directly about the eligible population ("Is anyone who lives there between the ages of 35 and 55?"); a second group of households got questions about younger and older age groups ("Is everyone who lives there younger than 35? Is everyone who lives there older than 55?"); a final group got a series of questions for each member of the household, including their sex, race, and age. The last method is known as the full roster approach. The full roster clearly beat both the direct questions and the complement questions for finding members of the target population. With the full roster version of the screening questions, 45 percent of the households screened in versus 32 percent with the direct questions and 35 percent with the complement questions. We knew from the frame data that some of the sample households included an eligible household member; the full roster led to the least underreporting within these households.

The downside was that the full roster also produced the lowest overall response rates (24 percent versus 32 percent for the direct question group and 29 percent for the complement question group); these response rates reflect nonresponse to both the screener and the main interview. Both interviewers and nonrespondents seem to contribute to the shortfall in eligible household members. There was a highly significant negative correlation (-.58) across interviewers between their screener response rates and their screener eligibility rates. The interviewers with the highest response rates to the screener also found the lowest proportions of eligible households.

So, there is clear evidence that members of even nonstigmatized groups can be hard to identify in screening interviews. It seems quite likely that the undercoverage of members of stigmatized groups will be even worse. At least one line of evidence provides support for this conjecture. Tourangeau, Kearney, Shapiro, and Ernst (1996) carried out an experiment that varied the procedures used to roster the members of sample households. We found that an anonymous rostering procedure led to better coverage of young Black males, a group often underrepresented in surveys and censuses. This study was done mainly in poor neighborhoods, where coverage is often low. The respondents in our screening sample may have deliberately omitted some household members (especially Black male members) because they were worried about losing welfare benefits or incurring some other penalty if they included them. Such concerns may lead to concealment on the part of respondents; my colleagues and I argued that the anonymous rostering procedure helped allay such concerns and reduced omissions from the rosters. These results suggest that omissions may occur more often the more respondents that are worried about the potential costs of reporting a member of the target population.

1.3.2   Metrics for the hard to identify

There are several ways to quantify the level of difficulty in identifying members of a given population. My discussion of the prior work in this area has already mentioned some of these potential metrics.

The most commonly used measure of the difficulty of identifying members of a specific population is its *coverage rate*. The coverage rate is the estimate of the size of the population from the survey to the estimated size based on some benchmark survey or the census:

$$CR = \frac{\hat{N}_i}{N_{Bi}},\tag{1.2}$$

in which $\hat{N}_i$ is the estimated size of population group i from the survey (typically, the sum of the weights for the respondents in that group after any nonresponse adjustments) and N_{Bi} is the benchmark for that group (such as the estimate of the subgroup's size from the American Community Survey).

The coverage rate reflects the joint effects of all sources of error (including frame problems, screener nonresponse, and so on), not just misreports in the screening interviews;

in addition, it captures the net impact of all these forms of error. That is, overreports and underreports can cancel out so that a coverage rate near 1.0 may mask a high level of offsetting errors (see Mulry, Chapter 3 in this volume, who describes additional measures used to assess coverage in a census). The screening classifications can sometimes be compared to more accurate measures of the relevant characteristics. This allows the proportion of those who should have screened in but were incorrectly classified as ineligible to be computed (this is the *false negative rate*); similarly, it also allows the proportion of those who screened in but should have been classified as ineligible (the *false positive rate*) to be computed. False negatives are generally more problematic than false positives, since the latter can be removed once they are identified in the main interview.

1.3.3   Other methods for hard-to-identify populations

Snowball sampling, and its more recent outgrowth respondent-driven sampling (RDS; see Chapters 23 and 24 for discussions), are methods intended to reduce the problems of identifying members of rare or stigmatized populations. As Goodman recently pointed out (Goodman, 2011), snowball sampling was originally introduced by Coleman (1958–59) as a method for selecting a sample of the members of a social network, such as groups of friends at a school. Coleman started with a random sample of network members and used this initial sample to identify other members of the network. As Goodman noted, his method yielded a probability sample. Over time, however, snowball sampling has come to mean recruiting a convenience sample of members of some population, typically members of a "hidden" population (such as illicit drug users or illegal immigrants); these initial "seeds" then recruit additional members of the population, who then recruit additional members, and so on. In a series of papers, Heckathorn (1997, 2007, 2011) has explored the statistical properties of RDS and introduced several estimators that can be used with such samples. Under certain assumptions, Heckathorn argues, the estimators are unbiased. For our purposes here, three of the assumptions underlying RDS are crucial (these quotations are all taken from Heckathorn, 2011, p. 363):

(1) "Respondents know one another as members of the target population, as is typical of groups such as drug users or musicians";
(2) "The network of the target population forms a single component"; and
(3) "Respondents can accurately report their personal network size, i.e., the number of those they know who fit the requirements of the study such as drug injectors or jazz musicians."

If these assumptions are met, the members of the hidden population are not hidden to each other, but only to members outside the population. Of course, even if members of the hidden population know each other, this does not mean they are willing to reveal each other to the researchers. (Consider using RDS to recruit a sample of illegal immigrants.) It remains to be seen how often these and the other assumptions on which RDS rests are met in practice and how robust the method and associated estimators are when its assumptions are violated (see Chapter 24).

1.4   Hard-to-reach populations

So, some populations are rare or elusive and, as a result, hard to sample. With other populations, the challenge is picking out the members of the target group from some larger population (such as the general population), particularly when the members of the target group do not want to be identified. But there is still another source of difficulty that can make a population hard to survey – the members may be hard to locate or hard to contact. For example, Kelleher and Quirke (Chapter 10) describe a survey of Irish Travellers, a group that is hard to survey for several reasons, not the least of which is their mobility.

1.4.1   The hard to locate

There are at least four types of mobile populations that may be hard to locate:

- Members of traditionally nomadic cultures (such as the Bedouins of Southwest Asia and the Tuareg of North Africa);
- Itinerant minorities (such as the Romani in Europe or the Travellers in Ireland);
- Persons who are temporarily mobile or displaced (recent immigrants, homeless persons, refugees); and
- Persons at a mobile stage in their life cycle (college students).

Some of these populations are quite large. Passel (2006) estimates that there are 11.1 million "unauthorized migrants" in the United States (although these are probably mostly in households and thus not especially mobile) and estimates of the size of the Romani population in the US range up to a million. Mobility can make the members of some populations hard to locate. As we noted earlier, one strategy for capturing the members of mobile populations is to sample places where they are likely to be found. For example, in the United States, the 2010 Census sent enumerators to migrant worker camps, soup kitchens, and homeless shelters in an effort to count these mobile populations.

Mobility can also be a problem for longitudinal, or panel, surveys. There are a few papers on movers in such surveys (e.g., Couper & Ofstedal, 2009; Lepkowski & Couper, 2002). Couper and Ofstedal examined sample members who moved between rounds of the Panel Study of Income Dynamics (PSID) and the Health and Retirement Survey (HRS). They note that some 13.7 percent of the US population moved in 2004; the corresponding rates in Western Europe were somewhat lower. Both of the surveys that Couper and Ofstedal looked at were quite successful at finding sample members who had moved. The PSID located 96.7 percent of the 1,441 cases that needed to be tracked for the 2003 round and the HRS located 98.7 percent of its 1,294 movers for the 2004 round of that survey. Still, although these tracking efforts were very successful, they also required considerable resources. On average, it took 10.2 tracking calls to find the movers in the PSID and 7.4 tracking calls to find the movers in the HRS. Still, as these results suggest, the vast majority of movers are eventually found.

The correlates of being found, according to Couper and Ofstedal (see also Lepkowski & Couper, 2002) are, not surprisingly, related to the person's level of attachment to a specific place. People who are married, employed, older, and engaged in community activities are more likely to stay put and are easier to find if they do move. Despite a tendency to change their surnames, women seem to be easier to track than men are. In general, populations that are only loosely attached to a specific home or place are difficult to find. Thus, the homeless are notoriously difficult to count and to interview and they are missed by virtually all general population surveys (although see Chapter 9 in this volume). A less extreme case involves persons with weak attachments to several households. They are at risk of being omitted from household rosters and thus missed by surveys; Martin (1999) estimated that some 4 million persons in the United States might have such tenuous connections to a household. And people displaced by storms, other natural disasters, and wars can require extraordinary efforts to find and interview (see Chapters 6, 7, and 8 in this volume).

1.4.2   Barriers to access

Even when sample members can be found, it may still be difficult to contact them. One long-term trend that has probably contributed to the decline in response rates throughout the developed world over the last two decades is the widespread adoption of lifestyles and devices that shield people from unwanted solicitations. More and more Americans live in gated communities, locked apartment buildings, or other residential settings in which they are protected by gatekeepers, and the trends are similar in Western Europe. By the mid-1990s, nearly 40 percent of new residential developments in the US were gated (Blakely & Snyder, 1997). Even before cell telephones became popular, Americans used caller-ID and answering machines to screen out their telephone calls; now, as the population shifts to cell telephones, almost everyone is able to filter his or her calls.

It is not clear whether this shift to cell telephones has made it harder or easier to reach potential respondents. According to Blumberg & Luke (2012), about 25 percent of the adult population in the US was cell-only by mid-2010. Hispanics, young adults (18–34 years old), people living with roommates, poor people, and renters were more likely to be cell-only than the rest of the population. The figure for Hispanics was nearly 35 percent; for 25–29 year olds, it was more than 51 percent; and for adults living with unrelated adults, it was 69 percent. Although cell phones do encourage the screening of incoming calls, they are mobile devices and many cell users have their telephones with them all the time. In general, though, it seems that many of the same groups that are hard to survey for other reasons (such as young adults) are also getting harder to contact; these groups seem to be overrepresented in the cell-only population. At the other end of the spectrum, Groves and Couper (1998) suggest that two groups are relatively easy to contact – the elderly and parents with young children. Members of both of these groups are more likely to be at home than members of other subgroups of the general population. On the other hand, access to elderly in assisted-living settings may be limited by gatekeepers.

1.4.3   Metrics for contactability

Many survey researchers routinely distinguish between various forms of nonresponse, including the failure to locate the sample person, failure to make contact, and failure to persuade the sample person to take part (which we discuss further in the next section). Lepkowski and Couper (2002) present a model in which the overall response propensity for a given sample member is the product of his or her likelihood of being located, being contacted, and agreeing to take part. Thus, a natural metric of a population's difficulty on each of these scores is the complement of their average propensities – that is, the observed or modeled proportion of the population that could not be found, that could not be contacted given that they were found, or that could not be persuaded to take part given that they were contacted. Another statistic commonly used to measure the level of difficulty in contacting sample members is the average number of contact attempts or calls until contact was made. Hard-to-contact populations are those where relatively high proportions are never contacted and those whose members require high numbers of contact attempts to reach.

1.5   Hard-to-persuade populations

Once the sample person is reached, there is still the problem of getting him or her to agree to do the survey. As response rates have fallen in the US and elsewhere, survey researchers have increased their efforts to find sample members and to make contact with them; as a result, the rise in nonresponse rates mostly reflects rising levels of noncooperation (Groves & Couper, 1998, pp. 160–63; Steeh, Kirgis, Cannon, & DeWitt, 2001). In addition, the distinction between noncontact and noncooperation may be breaking down. Screening one's telephone calls or choosing to live in a gated community may be a means of preemptively fending off unwanted requests, including unwanted survey requests.

Two variables are often singled out as potential sources of general resistance to surveys – the sense of busyness that seems to pervade contemporary life and falling levels of civic engagement (Brick & Williams, 2013; Groves & Couper, 1998, ch. 5). Abraham, Maitland, and Bianchi, (2006) pitted these two explanations against each other in a study of non-response in the American Time Use Survey (ATUS). Several features of the ATUS make it particularly useful for studying nonresponse. First, the sample consists of respondents to the CPS and so detailed information is available for the ATUS nonrespondents as well as for the respondents. Second, for a survey conducted by a federal agency, the ATUS has a relatively low response rate (in the high 50s). Finally, if the busyness hypothesis were true so that busier people are less likely to respond to the ATUS than less busy people, then this would introduce noticeable biases into ATUS estimates, which concern how people spend their time. Abraham and her colleagues found more support for the civic engagement hypothesis than for the busyness hypothesis; in particular, they found that ATUS sample members with lower levels of community engagement were less likely to be *contacted* for their ATUS interviews than those with stronger community ties. This was somewhat surprising since community ties are usually seen as linked with willingness to participate.

Several other studies find that various forms of community involvement are related to survey participation. Groves, Singer, and Corning (2000) showed that respondents who reported high levels of civic involvement in one survey were much more willing to complete an unrelated mail survey later on than those who had reported low levels of involvement, at least when neither group was offered a monetary incentive. The difference in response rates to the mail survey was substantial – nearly 30 percentage points (50 percent for the high involvement group versus 21 percent for the low). Tourangeau, Groves, and Redline (2010) found that voters were more likely to complete a survey than nonvoters, and this difference was apparent even when the survey topic was not political. Finally, Abraham, Helms, and Presser (2009) found that nonresponse in the ATUS was affected by sample members' volunteering behaviors. They showed that sample members who reported in the CPS that they had done volunteer work in the past year were much more likely to become ATUS respondents than sample members who did not report any volunteer work. ATUS respondents were almost twice as likely as ATUS nonrespondents to have reported volunteering in the CPS. Activities such as community involvement, voting, and volunteering may reflect a generalized willingness to help others, clearly a characteristic related to willingness to take part in surveys.

These findings contain hints about populations that are likely to exhibit high levels of resistance to surveys in general. Persons who are socially isolated or who are low on altruism may be hard to recruit for surveys or may require special incentives to get them to take part (see Groves *et al.*, 2000). Many surveys are conducted by government agencies or academic researchers so that groups with hostile views toward the government or toward social science in general may be less likely to cooperate in a range of surveys.

This is not to say that the specifics of the survey do not matter. According to Groves *et al.* (2000), people decide whether to participate in a survey based on their evaluations of whatever features of the survey happen to be salient at the time they make their decisions. The topic of the survey, its sponsor, its length, or the incentives it offers may all affect who cooperates with a specific survey request and who refuses, although the effect of topic interest on cooperation rates has turned out to be surprisingly hard to demonstrate (Groves, Presser, & Dipko, 2004; Groves *et al.*, 2006). Still, the leverage-salience theory of Groves *et al.* (2000) indicates that groups that are easy to persuade for one survey may be hard to persuade for another. Indeed, the decision whether to take part may have a large chance component, reflecting whatever features of the survey momentarily draw the sample person's attention.

The natural metric for assessing how hard the members of a given population are to persuade to take part is its refusal rate – that is, the proportion of those who were contacted but who declined to take part. Additional indicators of reluctance are the proportion of population members who required refusal conversion, special incentives, or other extraordinary measures to obtain their cooperation. Ideally, one could compare populations on their average rates of refusal, need for conversion efforts, and so on across a range of surveys.

1.6   Hard-to-interview populations

There are at least three additional reasons why some populations may be difficult to survey:

- They may be vulnerable populations (such as prisoners or young children), requiring explicit consent from a caretaker, parent, or guardian to interview;
- They may have cognitive or physical impairments that makes them difficult or impossible to interview at least under the standard survey protocols; or
- They may not speak (or read) the language in which the survey questionnaire is written.

In all three cases, it may be difficult to collect the survey data of interest – difficult but not necessarily impossible. Children often take part in surveys (for example, in surveys of students), although parental consent is generally required and data may be gathered both from the sample children directly and from other informants (such as teachers or parents). For example, the Early Childhood Longitudinal Survey – Kindergarten Cohort (ECLS-K) collected cognitive assessment data from kindergartners as well as getting additional information about the children from their parents, teachers, and school principals (West, Denton, & Germino Hausken, 2000). Chapter 15 in this volume presents a more general discussion of surveys of children and young people.

Surveys are generally designed for respondents who are in reasonably good health, who have intellectual abilities in the normal range (or above), and who are not suffering from serious sensory impairments. Thus, people who are very ill, who have extreme intellectual handicaps, or who are deaf (in the case of surveys administered aurally) or blind (in the case of surveys administered visually) are left out of many surveys. This may not be a major problem for surveys of the general population, since the conditions like these that prevent participation are likely to be rare. In the CPS, for example, all of these sources of difficulty (including language barriers) account for less than 8 percent of the nonresponding households (vs. 53 percent for refusal; see US Census Bureau, 2006) and less than 1 percent of all eligible households. Although the CPS is a household survey and can collect information from anyone in the household who is at least 15, our impression is that physical, cognitive, and linguistic obstacles are generally relatively minor contributors to nonresponse in most surveys of the *general* population.

The picture changes, though, for surveys aimed at population subgroups where these problems are common. In surveys of immigrants, for example, linguistic issues are likely to loom larger. For some states within the US, non-English speakers constitute substantial minorities. Reflecting the makeup of California's population, the California Health Interview Survey conducts interviews in five languages – English, Spanish, Chinese, Korean, and Vietnamese (Edwards, Fraser, & King, 2011). Translating the survey questionnaire is only one of the accommodations that a survey may offer to reduce the impact of physical, cognitive, or linguistic barriers to participation. The ECLS-K study designed and fielded cognitive assessments that did not require the children to read (West *et al.*, 2000). Chapter 16 describes a national survey of people with intellectual disabilities. And some telephone surveys use text telephone (TTY) to accommodate the deaf.

Another tactic for getting around the problems presented by the sample person's limitations is to collect the data from someone else. Parents are often used to provide information about sample children, especially young children, rather than having children provide the data themselves. Similarly, caretakers, spouses, or other proxies may be asked to provide information about frail or severely disabled sample persons. Most researchers regard self-report data as superior to proxy data (for example, Moore, 1988), at least when the sample persons are old enough and healthy enough to respond for themselves. Self-reports are more likely to be based on first-hand experiences than proxy reports and the answers of self-reporters are more likely to be based on recall rather than on estimation or guessing strategies (Tourangeau, Rips, & Rasinski, 2000, pp. 65–67). However, when the topic is the sample person's impairments, self-respondents may minimize their problems relative to proxy reporters (Lee, Mathiowetz, & Tourangeau, 2007). The question naturally arises as to how to determine whether a proxy is needed in a particular instance. One survey, conducted on behalf of the Social Security Administration, used a three-item screener to identify cases with cognitive impairments so severe that a proxy was tapped to provide the data (Skidmore, Barrett, Wright, & Gardner, 2012).

We are not aware of any existing metrics for assessing the level of difficulty of conducting interviews with the members of a given population, but at least two obvious measures suggest themselves. One is the proportion of persons who are unable to provide the survey data (or at least to provide the data without some special accommodation). That is, members of one population or subgroup are harder to interview than members of another population to the extent that a higher percentage of them cannot provide the data at all or can only provide data under special data collection procedures. If proxies are allowed, then a simple measure of difficulty at the interviewing stage is the percentage of cases for which proxies were needed. A second possible metric is the added cost per case associated with hard-to-interview sample members of the population or subgroup, a measure similar to Δ_C described earlier in Section 1.2.

1.7   General metrics for difficulty

So far, this chapter has looked at individual components of survey difficulty, ranging from problems in sampling to problems in collecting the data. This section looks at attempts to create overall measures of difficulty. Both the US Census Bureau and the UK Office of National Statistics have created hard-to-count indices to classify areas for their population censuses. We focus on the US efforts here; Chapter 4 describes the parallel effort in the UK, where a hard-to-count (HtC) index was used to stratify areas for inclusion in the sample for the post-census coverage survey (see also Brown, Diamond, Chambers, Buckner, & Teague, 1999).

Bruce and Robinson (2003) describe the hard-to-count measure created in the US. It encompasses twelve tract-level variables known to be associated with mail return rates in the 2000 Census. The twelve area-level percentages used to calculate the scores were:

(1) Percent of dwelling units that were vacant;
(2) Percent that were not single-family units;
(3) Percent of occupied units that were occupied by renters;
(4) Percent of occupied units with more than 1.5 persons per room;
(5) Percent of households that were not husband/wife families;
(6) Percent of occupied units with no telephone service;
(7) Percent of persons below the poverty line;
(8) Percent of households getting public assistance;
(9) Percent of persons over 16 who were unemployed;
(10) Percent of households where none of the adults (over 14) spoke English well;
(11) Percent of households that moved in the past year; and
(12) Percent of adults without a high school education.

Each census tract received a score ranging from 0 to 11 on each of these indicators, depending on which of twelve categories the tract fell into for each variable, with overall scores ranging from 0 to 132. This hard-to-count index correlated .77 with the tract mail return rate in the 2000 Census. The twelve variables reflect a mix of the sources of difficulty that are thought to contribute to nonreturn of census forms, including complex living arrangements, lack of trust in the government, low socioeconomic status (SES), mobility, and nontraditional addresses (Robinson, Johanson, & Bruce, 2007). The British HtC index, similarly, is based on variables that reflect the area's SES, the percentage of the population who are young or minority group members, and the number of persons per dwelling (see Abbott and Compton, Chapter 4 in this volume).

Bates and Mulry (2011) reanalyzed the data from Census 2000, using a cluster analysis procedure to group the population of census tracts into eight clusters. One variable that differentiated four of the clusters from the remaining four was the percentage of occupied units occupied by homeowners as opposed to renters. The four clusters that included a high proportion of homeowners differed in SES (one cluster was economically advantaged, one was average, and one was economically disadvantaged) and in ethnic makeup (one cluster had especially high levels of non-English speakers, among other characteristics). The clusters with high proportions of renters paralleled those with high percentages of home-owners, with one exception. There was no cluster corresponding to the economically advantaged homeowners; instead, there was a cluster of tracts with high proportions of unmarried renters living in multiunit structures. The cluster with the lowest census return rates in both 2000 and 2010 were the tracts dominated by economically disadvantaged renters, with a 58 percent return rate in Census 2000 and a similar return rate in 2010. In terms of the distinctions presented here, census nonreturn probably results mainly from unwillingness to take part and linguistic barriers to participation. Apart from their practical value, these results on hard-to-count areas in the US Census are useful in highlighting many of the groups that are traditionally thought to be hard to survey – renters (especially those in large buildings), persons who are low in education or economic resources, movers, and unmarried people.

1.8   Conclusions

Although researchers try to tailor their surveys to the population of interest, surveys as a method are often better suited to some populations than to others. The populations that are hard to survey (or at least relatively hard) are those that are hard to sample, hard to identify, hard to find or contact, hard to get to cooperate, hard to interview, or that offer some combination of these difficulties. Populations are hard to sample when there is no good list of the population members and when the members of the population represent a small fraction of the units on the available general population frames. They are hard to identify when membership in the target group is based on characteristics that are hidden or sensitive or when household informants mistrust the researchers. Populations are hard to find when their members are mobile or when they erect barriers to access. They are hard to persuade when they have low levels of engagement in the community and are unwilling to help the sponsors and researchers out. They are hard to interview when the researchers must first get consent from third parties to carry out data collection, when the sample persons do not have the requisite cognitive and linguistic skills, or when they are not healthy enough. There are sizable literatures on many of the dimensions that contribute to being hard to survey. For example, Groves and Couper (1998) examine a number of variables that affect how hard it is to contact a given household for a survey and how likely they are to cooperate if they are contacted.

Many hard-to-survey groups present more than a single form of difficulty. Imagine trying to conduct a survey of survivalists living in isolated areas around the United States. Certain ethnic minorities, such as the Romani, are rare, hard to identify, hard to locate and contact, and likely to resist taking part in surveys once they are found. In the US, unmarried young men living in apartments with roommates are generally hard to survey and these problems are even worse for young African-American males.

The implications of a group's being hard to survey depend in part on the purposes of the survey. If the survey is attempting to characterize some larger group, then members of hard-to-survey subgroups of this population are likely to be underrepresented in the survey, thus biasing overall estimates. The size of any bias will depend on the size of hard-to-survey subgroup, the level of underrepresentation, and the degree that members of the subgroup differ from members of more easily surveyed groups on the variables of interests. If a survey takes special pains to increase the representation of hard-to-survey subgroups of the target population, these steps may drive up the data collection costs. But the consequences of a group's being hard to survey are likely to be even worse when the goal is to characterize the hard-to-survey group. As we shall see in later chapters, it is in this situation that has driven researchers into devising innovative strategies for sampling, identifying, locating, contacting, and interviewing populations that offer unusual obstacles to conventional survey methods.

References

Abraham, K. G., Helms, S., & Presser, S. (2009). How social process distort measurement: the impact of survey nonresponse on estimates of volunteer work in the United States. *American Journal of Sociology*, 114(4), 1129–65.

Abraham, K. G., Maitland, A., & Bianchi, S. M. (2006). Nonresponse in the American Time Use Survey: who is missing from the data and how much does it matter. *Public Opinion Quarterly*, 70(5), 676–703.

Ardilly, P., & Le Blanc, D. (2001). Sampling and weighting a survey of homeless persons: a French example. *Survey Methodology*, 27(1), 109–18.

Bates, N., & Mulry, M. H. (2011). Using a geographic segmentation to understand, predict, and plan for census and survey mail nonresponse. *Journal of Official Statistics*, 27(4), 601–18.

Blakely, E. J., & Snyder, M. G. (1997). *Fortress America: Gated Communities in the United States*. Washington, D.C.: The Brookings Institute.

Blumberg, S. J., & Luke, J. V. (2012). *Wireless Substitution: Early Release of Estimates from the National Health Interview Survey, July–December 2011*. Atlanta, GA: Centers for Disease Control and Prevention, National Center for Health Statistics.

Brick., J. M., Montaquila, J. M., Han, D., & Williams, D. (2012). Improving response rates for Spanish speakers in two-phase mail surveys. *Public Opinion Quarterly*, 76(4), 721–32.

Brick, J. M., & Williams, D. (2013). Reasons for increasing nonresponse in U.S. household surveys. *ANNALS of the American Academy of Political and Social Science*, 645, 36–59.

Brown, J. J., Diamond, I. D., Chambers, R. L., Buckner, L. J., & Teague, A. D. (1999). A methodological strategy for a one-number census in the U.K. *Journal of the Royal Statistical Society: Series A (Statistics in Society)*, 162(2), 247–67.

Bruce, A., & Robinson, J. G. (2003). *Tract Level Planning Database with Census 2000 Data*. Washington, DC: US Census Bureau.

Coleman, J. S. (1958–59). Relational analysis: the study of social organizations with survey methods. *Human Organization*, 17(4), 2–36.

Couper, M. P., & Ofstedal, M. B. (2009). Keeping in contact with mobile sample members. In P. Lynn (ed.), *Methodology of Longitudinal Surveys* (pp. 183–203). Chichester: John Wiley & Sons.

Curtin, R., Presser, S., & Singer, E. (2005). Changes in telephone survey nonresponse over the past quarter century. *Public Opinion Quarterly*, 69(1), 87–98.

de Leeuw, E. D., & de Heer, W. (2002). Trends in household survey nonresponse: a longitudinal and international comparison. In R. Groves, D. A. Dillman, J. L. Eltinge, & R. J. A. Little (eds.), *Survey Nonresponse* (pp. 41–54). New York: John Wiley & Sons.

Edwards, S., Fraser, S., & King, H. (2011). *CHIS 2009 Methodology Series: Report 2 – Data Collection Methods*. Los Angeles, CA: UCLA Center for Health Policy Research.

Goodman, L. A. (2011). Comment: on respondent-driven sampling and snowball sampling in hard-to-reach populations and snowball sampling not in hard-to-reach populations. *Sociological Methodology*, 41(1), 347–53.

Groves, R. M., & Couper, M. P. (1998). *Nonresponse in household surveys.* New York: John Wiley & Sons.

Groves, R. M., Couper, M. P., Presser, S., Singer, E., Tourangeau, R., Acosta, G. P. *et al.* (2006). Experiments in producing nonresponse bias. *Public Opinion Quarterly*, 70(5), 720–36.

Groves, R. M., Presser, S., & Dipko, A. (2004). The role of topic interest in survey participation decisions. *Public Opinion Quarterly*, 68(1), 2–31.

Groves, R. M., Singer, E., & Corning, A. (2000). Leverage-salience theory of survey participation. *Public Opinion Quarterly*, 64(3), 299–308.

Heckathorn, D. D. (1997). Respondent-driven sampling: a new approach to the study of hidden populations. *Social Problems*, 44(2), 174–79.

   (2007). Extensions of respondent-driven sampling: analyzing continuous variables and controlling for differential recruitment. In Y. Xie (ed.), *Sociological Metholodogy* (pp. 151–207). Boston, MA: Blackwell.

   (2011). Comment: snowball versus respondent-driven sampling. *Sociological Methodology*, 41(1), 355–66.

Horrigan, M., Moore, W., Pedlow, S., & Wolter, K. (1999). Undercoverage in a large national screening survey for youths? In *Joint Statistical Meetings Proceedings, Survey Research Methods Section* (pp. 570–75). Alexandria, VA: American Statistical Association.

Judkins, D., DiGaetano, R., Chu, A., & Shapiro, G. (1999). Coverage in screening surveys at Westat. In *Joint Statistical Meetings Proceedings, Survey Research Methods Section* (pp. 581–86). Alexandria, VA: American Statistical Association.

Kalton, G. (2009). Methods for oversampling rare subpopulations in social surveys. *Survey Methodology*, 35(2), 125–41.

Kalton, G., & Anderson, D. W. (1986). Sampling rare populations. *Journal of the Royal Statistical Society: Series A (General)*, 149(1), 65–82.

Keeter, S., Smith, G., Kennedy, C., Turakhia, C., Schulman, M., & Brick, J. M. (2008). Questionnaire and fieldwork challenges in a probability sample survey of Muslim Americans. http://surveypractice.wordpress.com/2008/08/23/questionnaire-and-field work-challenges-in-a-probability-sample-survey-of-muslim-americans/.

Kreuter, F., McCulloch, S. K., Presser, S., & Tourangeau, R. (2011). The effects of asking filter questions in interleafed versus grouped format. *Sociological Methods and Research*, 40(1), 88–104.

Lee, S., Mathiowetz, N. A., & Tourangeau, R. (2007). Measuring disability in surveys: consistency over time and across respondents. *Journal of Official Statistics*, 23(2), 163–84.

Lepkowski, J., & Couper, M. P. (2002). Nonresponse in the second wave of longitudinal household surveys. In R. Groves, D. A. Dillman, J. L. Eltinge, & R. J. A. Little (eds.), *Survey nonresponse* (pp. 259–72). New York: John Wiley & Sons.

Lohr, S. L., & Rao, J. N. K. (2000). Inference from dual frame surveys. *Journal of the American Statistical Association*, 95(449), 271–80.

Martin, E. A. (1999). Who knows who lives here? Within-household disagreements as a source of survey coverage error. *Public Opinion Quarterly*, 63(2), 220–36.

Moore, J. C. (1988). Self-proxy response status and survey response quality. *Journal of Official Statistics*, 4(2), 155–72.

Passel, J. S. (2006). *The size and characteristics of the unauthorized migrant population in the U.S.: estimates based on the March 2005 Current Population Survey*. Pew Hispanic Center Research Report. Washington, DC: Pew Hispanic Center.

Robinson, J. G., Johanson, C., & Bruce, A. (2007, July – August). *The Planning Database: Decennial Data for Historical, Real-time, and Prospective Analysis*. Paper presented at the 2007 Joint Statistical Meetings, Salt Lake City, UT.

Shapiro, G., Diffendal, G., & Cantor, D. (1993). Survey undercoverage: major causes and new estimates of magnitude. In *Proceedings of the 1993 U.S. Bureau of the Census Annual Research Conference*. Washington, DC: US Department of Commerce.

Skidmore, S., Barrett, K., Wright, D., & Gardner, J. (2012). *Conducting Surveys with Proxies: Evaluating a Standardized Measure of Need*. Working Paper. Princeton, NJ: Mathematica Policy Research.

Steeh, C., Kirgis, N., Cannon, B., & DeWitt, J. (2001). Are they really as bad as they seem? Nonresponse rates at the end of the twentieth century. *Journal of Official Statistics*, 17(2), 227–47.

Sudman, S., Sirken, M. G., & Cowan, C. D. (1988). Sampling rare and elusive populations. *Science*, 240, 991–96.

Tourangeau, R., Groves, R. M., & Redline, C. D. (2010). Sensitive topics and reluctant respondents: demonstrating a link between nonresponse bias and measurement error. *Public Opinion Quarterly*, 74(3), 413–32.

Tourangeau, R., Kreuter, F., & Eckman, S. (2012). Motivated underreporting in screening surveys. *Public Opinion Quarterly*, 76(3), 453–69.

Tourangeau, R., Rips, L. J., & Rasinski, K. (2000). *The Psychology of Survey Response*. Cambridge: Cambridge University Press.

Tourangeau, R., Shapiro, G., Kearney, A., & Ernst, L. (1997). Who lives here? Survey undercoverage and household roster questions. *Journal of Official Statistics*, 13(1), 1–18.

US Census Bureau (2006). *Design and Methodology: Current Population Survey*. Technical Paper 66. Washington, DC: US Census Bureau and US Bureau of Labor Statistics.

West, J., Denton, K., & Germino Hausken, E. (2000). *America's Kindergartners* (NCES 2000–070). Washington, DC: US Department of Education, National Center for Education Statistics.

2

Hard-to-survey populations in comparative perspective

TOM W. SMITH

2.1 Introduction

It is clear that surveying difficult-to-reach populations is a universal problem (Maranda, 2004; Statistics Canada, 2004).

It is universal in several senses. First, some populations, subgroups, and individuals will always be hard to survey. Second, there are diverse and complex reasons that populations and individuals are challenging. Difficulty is neither simple nor unidimensional. Finally, difficulty spans the globe. Wherever surveys are done, difficulties arise. But the specific mix of impediments can be society-specific and the steps needed to overcome these impediments must be geared to the realities and complications that prevail in each survey in every country.

The total survey error paradigm can be used to examine the challenges in surveying hard-to-survey populations. Major components of total survey error that specifically relate to these populations include (1) sampling problems, such as the need for special sample frames, (2) noncoverage or undercoverage, (3) nonresponse, and (4) measurement errors, such as misreporting.

First, sampling problems include subgroups that are part of the target population, but that are not covered or undercovered by available sample frames. If the subgroup is the focus of the study, an alternative sampling design often must be developed. Even if the target population is not undercovered, using a sampling frame for the general population and screening down to the targeted subgroup may be inefficient and impractical due to cost. Dual or multiple frames or various referral sampling methods will often be needed to sample adequately and efficiently rare populations (Christman, 2009; Elliott, McCaffrey, Perlman, Marshall, & Hambarsoomians, 2009; Ericksen, 1976; Johnston & Sabin, 2010; Kalsbeek, 2003; Kalton, Chapter 19 in this volume; Kalton & Anderson, 1986; Reed, 1975–76; Rothbart, Fine, & Sudman, 1982; Sudman, 1972). What can be done for a given target population will vary greatly from country to country depending on what information is available for developing sampling frames (McKenzie & Mistianen, 2009; Salganik & Heckathorn, 2004; Treiman, Lu, & Qi, 2009). For example, if a national census or administrative records fail to identity a particular subgroup or rare population, then sample frames based on those sources cannot target these groups.

Second, while nonresponse is a problem for all surveys and all population groups, it is especially difficult for many hard-to-survey populations. Some of these populations consist of groups that wish to avoid detection (e.g., sex workers, undocumented aliens), that are difficult to locate or contact (e.g., the homeless, nomads), or that are less able to do interviews (e.g., drug addicts, the mentally ill, alcoholics). These characteristics tend to lower response rates. Moreover, response rates vary notably across countries (Couper & de Leeuw, 2003; de Leeuw & de Heer, 2002).

Finally, measurement error in the form of misreports contributes to the omission of hard-to-survey respondents. Rather than refusing or avoiding interviews, hard-to-survey respondents may thwart surveys by misreporting their status. For example, sex workers may deny engaging in prostitution (Smith, 1992), bankrupts may fail to report their insolvency (Bradburn & Sudman, 1979), or undocumented aliens may report legal residence in their adopted country.

Hard-to-survey populations have some combination of these attributes: (1) small size, (2) lack of identifying information to facilitate sampling, (3) difficulty in contacting, and (4) reluctance to cooperate (either to identify themselves as members of the target population or to participate once identified; Brackertz, 2007; Marpsat & Razafindratsima, 2010). "Hard to survey" is a general term that applies to all of these sources of difficulty. The term "rare" population largely refers to the size dimension. "Hidden" populations describe subgroups that are socially concealed. In many cases, the groups are actively in hiding because of the attributes that makes them the focus of research. They would include those engaged in illegal activities (e.g., sex workers, drug users and sellers, undocumented aliens), members of stigmatized groups (e.g., homosexuals, alcoholics, epileptics), or others who do not wish to reveal their status (e.g., crime victims, especially victims of sexual assaults, Williams, 1984), the wealthy (D'Alessio & Faiella, 2002; Kennickell, 1998; Lohr, 2010). As Bates and Edwards (2010) have noted, "The concept of who qualifies as 'hard to reach' is shifting." They indicate that historical groups like racial and ethnic minorities are being augmented by emergent groups such as cell-only households, undocumented aliens, survey cynics, and linguistic minorities. For a more complete discussion of the meaning of the concept of "hard-to-survey" populations, see Tourangeau's discussion (this volume).

In considering hard-to-survey populations cross-nationally, difficulties arise at the country level, at the level of social groups, and for individuals. In particular, the attributes of countries and differences across countries in the nature and prevalence of hard-to-survey social groups and hard-to-survey individuals lead to variation in the main problems that make populations hard to survey – sampling problems, noncoverage or undercoverage, nonresponse, and measurement error.

2.2 National factors

Countries as a whole have characteristics – such as the type of government they have, their economic development, the level of violence there, the number of their linguistic minorities and their overall size – that affect the size of their hard-to-survey populations or their ability to conduct surveys with them. In addition, countries vary in the availability of censuses, registries, and other data that can be used for sampling.

First, surveys are seldom allowed in countries with authoritarian governments (Smith, 2010). As a result, people in such countries in general are hard to survey and these countries are absent from comparative studies. In some cases, such as North Korea, the ban on surveying is practically universal so the whole society is in effect a hard-to-survey population. In other cases, surveys are tightly regulated and their content is restricted (Afrobarometer Network, 2007). It may be impossible to survey specific subpopulations because the government does not allow access to them. Or targeting a subgroup may be greatly hindered by restrictions on content. For example, using a general population survey to screen for a subpopulation is not possible in countries that do not permit the topic of the screening questions to be included in surveys. Lebanon has not conducted a census since 1932 due to sensitivity over the size and political representation of sectarian groups. In other countries, such as in some conservative Islamic societies, questions about sexual orientation are not permitted.

Fortunately, the number of countries prohibiting surveys has diminished over time. This is shown by the expanding number of countries in virtually all international collaborations, such as the World Values Survey (WVS), International Social Survey Program (ISSP), Globalbarometers, and Gallup World Poll (GWP), and by the expanded representation of countries in ESOMAR and the World Association for Public Opinion Research (Smith, 2010). The ISSP expanded from 4 founding members in 1984 to 49 countries in 2012, the WVS expanded from 15 countries in 1981–84 to 46 countries in 2005–08, and the GWP grew from 129 countries in 2006 to an expected 163 countries in 2012 (Tortora, 2012).

Second, poorer countries are underrepresented. There are several reasons for this. One major problem in poorer countries is resource or capacity constraints. Most survey research is indigenously funded and poorer countries often lack the resources to develop a survey research infrastructure or to carry out much research. As a result, the major cross-national research programs heavily overrepresent developed countries and underrepresent poorer countries (Smith, 2010). Moreover, even when they are covered, poorer countries are likely to have more hard-to-survey populations because of their limited resources. In general, when surveys have fewer resources, all harder-to-survey groups and individuals are likely to be even more underrepresented than usual. Surveys with more limited resources are more likely to restrict interviewing to a single main language, reduce the number of callbacks, shorten the field period, and omit special appeals to specific subpopulations. Such limitations will reduce coverage and/or lower the response rate; they are likely to increase the underrepresentation of hard-to-survey groups and individuals. Some of the developmental divide can be overcome if there is central funding and data collection coordination. This was the case with the World Fertility Survey in the late 1970s to early 1980s (Cleland & Scott, 1987). But most cross-national studies (e.g., ISSP, WVS) rely on local resources and data collection infrastructure (Smith, 2010). In addition, even when external support is available, creating an ad hoc organization to field a survey is a daunting and costly task (Afrobarometer

Network, 2007; Feld, 2009; Hornbeck, Peng, Studner, & Jodice, n.d.; Pennell, Levenstein, & Lee, 2010).

Surveys in poorer countries are also hampered by mode constraints (Pennell *et al.*, 2010; Skjak & Harkness, 2003). Almost all surveys in poor countries have to be done face to face since coverage via other modes (telephone, Internet, postal) is not adequate to cover the general population, much less hard-to-survey populations. Telephone penetration is too low in general in many countries and is especially inadequate to cover rural, tribal, and other difficult sectors. The GWP, for example, uses the relatively less expensive telephone mode in developed countries and the more costly in-person interviews for developing countries (Tortora, Srinivasan, & Esipova, 2010). Likewise, low literacy levels hamper surveys in many countries. While a majority of countries have literacy rates of 90 percent or higher, in fourteen countries literacy is below 50 percent, and in another twenty-two countries it is between 50 and 69 percent (Feld, 2009; United Nations, 2009). This rules out postal surveys for these countries. Thus, general population surveys in poorer countries are limited to the most expensive mode – in-person interviewing. Of course, lower labor costs still make surveys in these countries inexpensive compared to the cost in developed countries.

Infrastructure limitations beyond the lack of survey capacity also hinder surveys in poor countries (Pennell, Harkness, Levenstein, & Quaglia, 2010). For example, poor transportation makes it difficult to reach respondents. In Afghanistan, it "sometimes may take 18 hours or more to walk to the targeted respondents" (Feld, 2009). Likewise, consider the following general recommendations in such areas (Pennell *et al.*, 2010, p. XII–10):

- Provide adequate transportation for staff and supplies.
- If maps are unavailable or unreliable, consider use of local guides or GPS instruments.
- Arrange to secure fuel and oil and to maintain the vehicles used by the field staff; this may present logistical problems in some . . . countries.
- Arrange for emergency transport in the event that a field team member becomes ill or injured and needs immediate medical attention or it becomes unsafe to stay in an area.
- Arrange for backup transportation.

Similarly, epidemics and poor sanitation present serious health risks to interviewers in many regions.

Third, countries experiencing disruptions are underrepresented. The disruptions include problems caused by weather, natural disasters, civil disorder, and war. These may periodically affect whole societies or major regions (e.g., civil disorder in Somalia, Darfur, and the eastern Congo, annual floods in Bangladesh, winters in countries near the Arctic Circle). Usually, such conditions simply prevent even the contemplation of doing surveys in the affected areas, but sometimes they disrupt surveys already under way and, in other cases, actually trigger special surveys. For example, in Japan after the 2011 earthquake and tsunami numerous towns and cities in nearby coastal areas could not be surveyed in the normal manner. Instead, special displaced-person surveys were carried out on these affected populations.

Disaster research is specifically designed to meet and overcome such challenges; such studies often attempt to document the aftermath of major natural disasters such as floods and earthquakes (Mneimneh, Axinn, Ghimire, Cibelli, & Alkaisy, Chapter 7 in this volume; Brodie, Deane, Hamel, Herrmann, & Ben-Porath, Chapter 8 in this volume; Norris, 2006; Rodriquez, Quarantelli, & Dynes, 2007) and conflict or "danger zone" research (Feld, 2009; Hornbeck *et al.*, n.d.; Peng, 2011) designed to cover areas undergoing civil war and related disturbances. One subtype of conflict surveys are peace polls designed to help end such conflicts (Irwin, 2011). Three peace polls were carried out in Sri Lanka from 2008 to 2010. The first two excluded the northern region where rebel activity and fighting were concentrated, but the third in 2010 was able to cover the entire country.

Another social disruption is crime. For example, in Madang, New Guinea, "interviewing in residential neighborhoods at night is too dangerous" (Hornbeck, n.d.). In Mexico, interviewers have been seized by drug gangs (WAPOR, 2011).

Fourth, countries with unique and/ or multiple languages are underrepresented. Surveys in countries with isolated languages require more local expertise and there are no economies of scale to be had by sharing questionnaires and other material with other countries using the same language. Studies in the Caribbean and Latin America are more likely to include Spanish-speaking nations and less likely to be done in Haiti with its French-based Creole. Also, countries with multiple languages in general use are harder to conduct surveys in because of the higher cost of developing instruments in multiple languages and of recruiting multilingual interviewers.

Finally, very small countries are underrepresented. For example, none of the micro-states of Europe (Andorra, Liechtenstein, Monaco, San Marino, or Vatican City) are included in European-wide surveys like the European Social Survey (ESS) or Eurobarometers. Globally, a list of 242 countries and colonies shows that the 64 with the smallest populations have not been included in cross-national surveys. Small countries are de facto excluded because they (a) typically lack a survey-research infrastructure and (b) are not considered important enough to be sought out in cross-national studies (Tortora *et al.*, 2010).

Besides these general, sociopolitical attributes of countries that relate to hard-to-survey populations, there are country-level data and sampling resources that affect the conduct of surveys and the ability to reach specific subpopulations. First, the coverage of hard-to-survey populations varies across countries because of differences in the available sample frames (Haeder & Gabler, 2003). For example, in the Scandinavian countries, there are high-quality, population registers that include not only household residents, but also members of the non-household population in assisted-living facilities; these registries also include information on the age of people on the registry. Thus, the elderly in general and the non-household elderly in particular can be directly sampled. In most other countries, dual frames or extensive screening would be needed to cover all of the elderly. In other countries, the existing data sources are problematic. For example, in China people register their residences under the "hukou" system. But an estimated 221 million people, mostly migrant workers from rural areas, actually live in other areas. As a result, the official records do not adequately represent the general population and in particular are inadequate for sampling migrant workers. In other countries such as Iraq, Afghanistan, and Lebanon, there are no recent census figures to inform sampling (Afrobarometer Network, 2007; Feld, 2009;

Peng, 2011). Often creative approaches, such as using satellite imagery are utilized to draw samples in such countries (Peng, 2011; Treiman *et al.*, 2009). Without appropriate sources, general sample frames cannot be readily constructed nor can hard-to-reach subpopulations be targeted.

Second, the statistics collected by government censuses and statistical agencies strongly affect the ability to study hard-to-survey populations. In particular, disproportionate sampling typically relies on having some information on the geographic dispersion of target groups; the more detailed and accurate the information, the more efficient the sample design can be. But often countries do not collect crucial data. In the United States, the census does not measure religion and thus it cannot be used to sample small religious groups. In Germany, no official statistics are kept on race or ethnicity.

Finally, demographic information useful for sampling hard-to-reach populations may exist, but not be shared with most survey researchers. In particular, small area and even household-level information may be available to government surveys in some countries, but denied to all other surveys. The restrictions vary greatly from country to country.

2.3   Group and individual characteristics

Besides country-level attributes, there are many social and individual-level attributes that tend to vary across countries and thus also contribute to cross-national differences in hard-to-survey populations, the specific hard-to-survey populations in a country, and what needs to be done to survey those populations.

The distinction between group and individual attributes is a fluid and artificial one, since any characteristic that individuals share might be seen as defining them as a group. But the distinction has some value. By groups, we are referring especially to major social groupings which people identity with and which are typically recognized by both in-group and out-group members.

The first set of hard-to-survey groups involves geographical or social isolation. First, there are primitive or tribal populations that are socially isolated from the main society. The extreme examples are the so-called uncontacted tribes in the Amazon and elsewhere. In Brazil, sixty-seven uncontacted tribes were recognized in 2007. It is the policy of the Brazilian government to minimize any interaction between themselves and others and the uncontacted tribes. Such groups are also common in New Guinea and in some other countries as well. Next, there are tribes and primitive groups that do interact with the main society. These may still be hard-to-survey populations due to their distinct culture (typically including wariness of outsiders), linguistic barriers, or remote location. Members of such groups often do not understand what a survey is. One survey in Kenya was associated with devil worship by some respondents (Weinreb, 2006). Even for tribal groups that are fairly integrated into the main society, special procedures are often needed. For example, in many African societies, it is considered necessary to gain approval from the village chief before attempting interviews among households in the community (Afrobarometer Network, 2007; Pennell *et al.*, 2010; Van der Reis, 1997; Weinreb, 2006).

A second set of factors that make populations hard to survey involves isolated and remote locales. Before the advent of telephone surveys, almost all public opinion polls in the United States excluded Alaska and Hawaii. But even decades after telephone polling became the standard, most polls still omitted them (Smith, 2011a). In the United Kingdom, the British Social Attitudes Survey does not interview in Scotland north of the Caledonian Canal. Similarly, Statistics Canada usually excludes remote areas in the north. For example, the Canadian General Social Survey excludes the Northwest Territories, the Yukon, and Nunavut. In effect, these hard-to-reach areas have been turned into uncovered areas. Generally, these excluded remote areas represent a very small share of the overall population (0.3–0.4 percent in Canada, Great Britain, and the US), but in a few countries such as Brazil the excluded regions cover 4 percent of the population or more.

Also, countries with a large area will have a dispersed population with some segments of that population located far away from the main population centers. Additionally, some specific locations will have limited access due to the lack of roads and other means of travel. In Alaska, for example, there are many areas routinely serviced by float plane. Other examples are Mongolia and the Saharan countries of North Africa. Large countries and those with extensive mountains, deserts, swamps, many small islands, or other inhospitable terrain have more hard-to-survey populations than compact and geographically accessible countries.

A third factor – geographic mobility – hinders interviewing. Nomads are the classic example and they are concentrated in certain less-developed countries such as North African nations and Mongolia (Kalsbeek & Cross, 1982; Pedersen, 1995). Similar examples are displaced people, such as the internal and external refugees from Darfur (Hagan, 2011). But even in developed countries, mobility can be a serious impediment for surveys involving frequent travelers, with such people as pilots, sailors, long-distance truckers, and traveling salespersons being hard to contact.

Fourth, poverty often makes populations hard to survey. This is especially true in countries with large shanty towns surrounding urban centers. Often, these settlements are not legally established and roads and addresses not officially recognized. In the *favelas* of Brazil, it is often necessary to get permission from local gang members before interviewers can conduct surveys (Young, 2012). Another group of poor people that is especially hard to interview is the homeless. Poorer countries and those without a developed system of shelters and public housing have larger homeless populations that would have to be sampled by special methods going beyond household frames (Gelberg & Siecke, 1997; Iachan & Dennis, 1993; Rossi, 1989).

The poor are also harder to survey when certain survey modes are employed. They are less likely to have telephone coverage and are thus underrepresented in phone surveys. Likewise, they are more likely to be illiterate and thus not easily surveyed by mail postal surveys. To deal with illiteracy, some modes such as computer-assisted self-interviews (CASI) may need to be replaced with audio-CASI (Hewett, Erulkar, & Mensch, 2004). Likewise, certain question formats are more difficult for less-educated and low-literacy populations (Van der Reis, 1997).

Fifth, at the other end of the income gradient, there are difficulties in interviewing the wealthy (D'Alessio & Faiella, 2002; Kennickell, 1998; Marpsat & Razafindratsima, 2010), who can be hard to contact. The wealthy can often impede access by living in gated communities or guarded buildings or by having access blocked by servants or other employees. In some countries, the risk of kidnapping for ransom is high and the well-to-do are especially leery of allowing access.

Some groups are reluctant to be interviewed. Thus, a sixth type of hard-to-survey group is illegals. Because of their illegal status, they often avoid participating in surveys. This can result from undercoverage, nonresponse, or concealing their status. There are two main groups in this category: undocumented aliens and criminals. Undocumented aliens are large segments of some countries (Kelly, 1977; Sudman, 1972; Vigneswaran, 2007). In the United States, estimates put undocumented aliens at around 11 million. Many other countries have few illegal immigrants. Criminals are undercounted both because some are incarcerated and removed from the household population and because those in the general population may be reluctant to agree to interviews. The United States has the highest incarceration rate in the world. Most other countries have rates only half or less the American level. Drug users are one major category of criminals (Des Jarlais, Perlis, Stimson, & Poznyak, 2006; Heckathorn, 2002; Kuebler & Hausser, 1997; Platt, Wall, Rhodes, Judd, Hickman, Johnston *et al.*, 2006). Sex workers are another (Elmore-Meegan, Conroy, & Agala, 2004; Johnston & Sabin, 2010; Kanouse, Berry, Duan, Lever, Carson, Perlman *et al.*, 1999; Vandepitte, Lyerla, Dallabetta, Crabbe, Alary, & Buvé, 2006). The ease of including these groups depends on the exact legal status of each group in a society, their social standing, and how the police enforce existing laws regarding illegal drugs and commercial sex.

Seventh, are uncooperative survey nonrespondents, or refusers. In most countries, this group has expanded in recent years (Smith, 2011b; Stoop, Billiet, Kohn, & Fitzgerald, 2010). The size of the group of refusers varies notably across countries. For example, in the ESS which strives to both obtain a maximum nonresponse rate of 30 percent in all countries and to minimize the range of nonresponse across countries, in round 3 nonresponse ranged from 54 percent in France down to 27 percent in Slovakia (Stoop *et al.*, 2010). In some other surveys and countries, nonresponse falls below 10 percent (Couper & de Leeuw, 2003). It is widely believed that differences in the "survey climate" (or the general propensity to cooperate and complete a survey) explain most of the cross-national variation in response rates (Billiet, Philippen, Fitzgerald, & Stoop, 2007; Loosveldt & Storms, 2008; Smith, 2007). The size of the nonrespondent group also varies by the topic of the survey. Health surveys often appear to receive the highest response rate across countries, while burdensome or sensitive topics get a lower response rate. However, what topics are seen as burdensome or sensitive varies across countries. For example, standard items in US surveys on religious beliefs and behaviors are deemed to be sensitive in China. Likewise, questions about alcohol use are generally not problematic in most Western countries, but are threatening in con-servative, Islamic nations.

An eighth category of hard-to-survey populations is busy people (Brackertz, 2007). This would include those working many hours away from home, those caring for dependents in the household (children, the ill or disabled, the elderly), those otherwise occupied with duties and obligations, and those with multiple responsibilities, such as Hochschild's second-shift women (Hochchild, 1989). Levels of participation in the labor force and working outside the home varies considerably across countries. In addition, household composition differs greatly across countries. Most European households are nuclear families with few, if any, children, while households in developing countries are more likely to involve both extended families and have dependent children.

Ninth, stigmatized and marginalized groups are underrepresented in surveys. This includes both groups that fail to identify themselves as group members (e.g., closeted homosexuals, epileptics) and group members who are more likely than the general population to be nonrespondents (e.g., undocumented immigrants, Cornelius, 1982; the Romany in many European societies, Hajioff & McKee, 2000, and Titterton & Clark, 2000; and non-Muslims in some Islamic countries). Refugees also sometimes fall in this category (Bloch, 1999). What groups are stigmatized and the degree to which they try to remain hidden from surveys varies across societies (Michaels & Lhomond, 2006).

Tenth, political extremists are a difficult group to include in surveys. What groups are extremists and how "extreme" a particular group is of course varies across countries (Johnson, Holbrook, & Atterberry, Chapter 18 in this volume). For example, groups that might be considered Islamic extremists in the United States or Europe might well be classified as mainstream in various Arab countries. Also, the more political tolerance there is in a society, the less likely extremist groups are to shun surveys in order to avoid political repression or social disapproval. This varies both across countries and across time within countries (Smith, 2011c).

Some groups are willing to be interviewed, but hard to interview. Eleventh, the incapacitated are less likely to be interviewed. This includes the mentally unable (those suffering mental illnesses and the cognitively impaired), the physically ill, those with disabled communication senses (e.g., blind, deaf, mute), and substance abusers. Often, these are groups of special interest to surveys (e.g., IDU users in AIDS/HIV studies, the mentally and physically ill in health studies). Both the size of these groups and their location in society varies across countries. For, example, malaria and HIV are epidemic in many southern African countries. Also, in developing countries the mentally ill are much more likely to live in households with relatives than in developed countries and deafness is more common in less-developed countries (Pescosolido, 2012).

Similarly, a twelfth group – linguistic minorities – are less likely to be interviewed. For countries with well-established, multiple-language populations, surveys are routinely conducted in the main languages (e.g., English and French in Canada; Dutch and French in Belgium; French, German, and Italian in Switzerland). But many minority languages groups are excluded from surveys. For example, the ESS excludes minority languages spoken by less than 5 percent of a country's population. Moreover, the problem is greater in countries with many indigenous languages (e.g., South Africa, Nigeria, or India). In addition, especially in countries with large populations of immigrants, new minority languages may not be covered. In the US, the General Social Survey was not able to add Spanish until 2006.

Currently in the US, bilingual surveys in English and Spanish are common, but except for studies focusing on immigrants or a specific, foreign ethnicity, surveys in additional languages are infrequent. About 7.5 percent of those aged 5 and older speak a language other than English or Spanish at home and many do not speak English (or Spanish) well enough to do an interview in either of those languages. In other countries with significant immigrant populations, surveys outside the national language are rare (e.g., German is usually used exclusively in surveys in Germany). The challenge is especially great when there is no written form of languages. This applies not only to less-developed countries, but also to unwritten regional dialects, such as Swiss German, in developed countries.

Finally, there as several additional barriers to surveying some groups. These include local customs that make it harder to interview specific groups (Pennell *et al.*, 2010). For example, in conservative Arab countries interviewers and respondents need to be gender matched (Benstead, 2010; Feld, 2009). In addition, in many of these countries the female interviewers need to be accompanied by a male relative. This makes surveys in general and especially surveys of females more difficult. Other customs affect other groups in different countries.

Similarly, many nonhousehold populations are often harder to interview. This includes those in eldercare facilities, the hospitalized, the incarcerated, and those in other institutions. Often, this is because there is no good sample frame for these subgroups. But in countries with high-quality population registers, the elderly and those in many other types of institutions and group quarters can be readily sampled. Also, in some countries there are good sample frames of other nonhousehold populations. What is possible varies notably from country to country. Only a few groups, like the unsheltered homeless, generally present similar problems across countries. But there are major cross-national differences in the relative size of the homeless population.

What groups are covered by household surveys varies greatly across countries. For example, work camps and worker dormitories are fairly rare in most developed countries, but are major institutions in some countries such as in the mining districts in Africa. Excluding such populations as "out-of-scope" has quite different impacts across countries and greatly affects the coverage of the labor force in surveys. Similarly, many countries exclude non-citizen from surveys. In several Persian Gulf countries, this rule would eliminate a large part of and sometimes the majority of the labor force from surveys.

Also, certain populations on the cusp of the household population are often missed when they should have been covered. Examples are residential motels with kitchens, single apartment in otherwise commercial structures, and various types of arrangements bordering on being group quarters (e.g., changing US Census definitions of how groups of unrelated people sharing a housing unit are counted).

The above factors have been presented as independent factors and each does have a demonstrable and separate impact on the ease of obtaining an interview. But in actual practice, there is considerable overlap and individuals and groups tend to be affected by multiple, reinforcing attributes that thwart inclusion in surveys. For example, small, under-developed, dysfunctional countries tend to do fewer surveys and are often omitted from cross-national surveys. Undocumented immigrants are harder to interview not only because of their legal status, but also because of language barriers and poverty. The homeless are hard to locate, require special sample designs, and are more likely than others to be mentally ill and/or substance abusers. The wealthy are more likely to live in guarded residences, more likely to be away from home, and more likely to be a member of elite groups that wish to avoid publicity.

Hard-to-reach or hidden populations may be the sole focus of a study, an important element in cross-group comparisons, or only a minor component in a broader general population study. For example, a study of nomads needs to develop a study design to sample and interview this difficult target population, while a general population study needs a study design that includes nomads along with all other segments of the general population.

Assuming that the goal is to interview a random, representative sample of a particular target population, different groups would have variable costs per case associated with them. A large group that does not have to be oversampled to get enough cases, which is well covered by a standard sample frame, has a high response rate, and no appreciable mis-reporting of its status would have a low cost and good quality data. A small group that cannot be directly sampled via some special sample frame, has a low response rate, and has a high misreporting rate would have both a high-cost and lower-quality data. Where sub-groups fall on this continuum will differ across countries.

2.4 Summary and conclusion

The size and composition of hard-to-survey populations vary across countries. First, key attributes of countries such as their political system and level of development affect the ability to do surveys in general as well as to cover specific subpopulations. Second, country-level statistical and survey-research infrastructures influence the conduct of surveys. Third, the characteristics of hard-to-reach populations differ notably across countries. Finally, the size of the hard-to-reach populations varies across countries. One needs to understand the specific challenges that are most serious in each country and the resources that exist there to deal with these challenges. One then adopts a study design that practically addresses the problems and allows the hard-to-survey populations to be sampled and interviewed. In some cases, the very latest technological innovations can be utilized to overcome barriers in least-developed countries (e.g., satellite images for sampling, GPS systems for locating sampling points, audio-computer assisted self-interviews to deal with illiteracy). A one-size-fits-all solution is not useful and careful attention to the specific needs and most viable approaches for each country and target population needs to be considered.

References

Afrobarometer Network (2007). Afrobarometer Round 4 Survey Manual.

Bates, N., & Edwards, B. (2010). International Conference on Methods for Surveying and Enumerating Hard-to-Reach Populations. Unpublished report.

Benstead, L. (2010). *Effects of Interviewer Gender and Religious Dress on Survey Responses: Findings from a Nationally-Representative Field Experiment in Morocco.* Paper presented to the Society for Political Methodology, Iowa City, IA.

Billiet, J., Philippen, M., Fitzgerald, R, & Stoop, I. (2007). Estimation of nonresponse bias in the European Social Survey: using information from reluctant respondents. *Journal of Official Statistics*, 23(1), 135–62.

Bloch, A. (1999). Carrying out a survey of refugees: some methodological considerations and guidelines. *Journal of Refugee Studies*, 12(4), 367–83.

Brackertz, N. (2007). Who Is Hard to Reach and Why? ISR Working Paper. Swinburne University of Technology.

Bradburn, N., & Sudman, S. (1979). *Improving Interview Methods and Questionnaire Design.* San Francisco, CA: Jossey-Bass.

Christman, M. C. (2009). Sampling rare populations. In D. Pfeffermann & C. R. Rao (eds.), Handbook of Statistics, Volume 29a. Amsterdam: North Holland.

Cleland, J., & Scott, C. (eds). (1987). *The World Fertility Survey: An Assessment.* New York: Oxford University Press.

Cornelius, W. A. (1982). Interviewing undocumented immigrants: methodological reflections based on fieldwork in Mexico and the U.S., *International Migration Review*, 16(2), 378–411.

Couper, M. P., & de Leeuw, E. D. (2003). Nonresponse in cross-cultural and cross-national surveys. In J. A. Harkness, F. J. R. van de Vijver, & P. Ph. Mohler (eds.), *Cross-Cultural Survey Methods* (pp. 157–77). Hoboken, NJ: John Wiley & Sons.

D'Alessio, G., & Faiella, I. (2002). Non-response behaviour in the Bank of Italy's Survey of Household Income and Wealth. Bank of Italy Report No. 462. Rome: Bank of Italy.

de Leeuw, E., & de Heer, W. (2002). Trends in household survey nonresponse: A longitudinal and international comparison. In R. M. Groves, D. A. Dillman, J. L. Eltinge, & R. J.A. Little (eds.), *Survey Nonresponse* (pp. 41–54). New York: John Wiley & Sons.

Des Jarlais, S. C., Perlis, T. E., Stimson, G., & Poznyak, V. (2006). Using standardized methods for research on HIV and injecting drug use in developing/transitional countries: case study from the WHO Drug Injection Study Phase II. *BMC Public Health*, 6, 54.

Elliott, M. N., McCaffrey, D., Perlman, J., Marshall, G. N., & Hambarsoomians, K. (2009). Use of expert ratings as sampling strata for a more cost-effective probability sample of a rare population. *Public Opinion Quarterly*, 73(1), 56–73.

Elmore-Meegan, M., Conroy, R. M., & Agala, C. B. (2004). Sex workers in Kenya, numbers of clients and associated risks: an exploratory survey. *Reproductive Health Matters*, 12(23), 50–7.

Ericksen, E. P. (1976). Sampling a rare population: a case study. *Journal of the American Statistical Association*, 71(356), 816–22.

Feld, K. (2009). Research in a danger zone. *Research World*, 9(3), 49–51.

Gelberg, L., & Siecke, N. (1997). Accuracy of homeless adults' self-reports. *Medical Care*, 35(3), 287–90.

Haeder, S., & Gabler, S. (2003). Sampling and estimation. In J. A. Harkness, F. J.R. van de Vijver, & P. Ph. Mohler (eds.), *Cross-Cultural Survey Methods* (pp. 117–36). New York: John Wiley & Sons.

Hagan, J. (2011). Voices of the Darfur genocide. *Contexts*, 10(3), 22–9.

Hajioff, S., & McKee, M. (2000). The health of the Roma people: a review of the published literature. *Journal of Epidemiology & Community Health*, 54(11), 864–69.

Heckathorn, D. D. (2002). Respondent-driven sampling II: deriving valid population estimates from chain-referral samples of hidden populations. *Social Problems*, 49(1), 11–34.

Hewett, P. C., Erulkar, A. S., & Mensch, B. S. (2004). The feasibility of computer-assisted survey interviewing in Africa. *Social Science Computer Review*, 22(3), 319–34.

Hochchild, A. (1989). *The Second Shift: Working Families and the Revolution at Home*. New York: Viking Penguin.

Hornbeck, S. (n.d.). Conducting research in Papua New Guinea. Unpublished report. D3 Systems. Retrieved from www.d3systems.com/wp-content/uploads/2010/09/aapor08_papua_new_guinea.pdf.

Hornbeck, S., Peng, D., Studner, C. & Jodice, D. (n.d.). Ensuring data quality in conflict zones. Unpublished report. D3 Systems.

Iachan, R., & Dennis, M. L. (1993). A multiple frame approach to sampling the homeless and transient population. *Journal of Official Statistics*, 9(4), 747–64.

Irwin, C. (2011). Peace polls. Retrieved from www.peacepolls.org.

Johnston, L. G., & Sabin, K. (2010). Sampling hard-to-reach populations with respondent driven sampling. *Methodological Innovation Online*, 5(2), 38–48.

Kalsbeek, W. D. (2003). Sampling minority groups in health surveys. *Statistics in Medicine*, 22(9), 1527–49.

Kalsbeek, W. D., & Cross, A. R. (1982). Problems in sampling nomadic populations. In *Joint Statistical Meetings Proceedings, Survey Research Methods Section* (pp. 398–402). Alexandria, VA: American Statistical Association.

Kalton, G., & Anderson, D. W. (1986). Sampling rare populations. *Journal of the Royal Statistical Society: Series A (General)*, 149(1), 65–82.

Kanouse, D. E., Berry, S., Duan N., Lever, J., Carson, S., Perlman, J. F., *et al.* (1999). Drawing a probability sample of female street prostitutes in Los Angeles County. *Journal of Sex Research*, 36(1), 45–51.

Kelly, C. B. (1977). Counting the uncountable: estimates of undocumented aliens in the United States. *Population and Development Review*, 3(4), 474–81.

Kennickell, A. B. (1998). Analysis of nonresponse effects in the 1995 Survey of Consumer Finances. Unpublished report, Federal Reserve System.

Kuebler, D., & Hausser, D. (1997). The Swiss Hidden Population Study: practical and methodological aspects of data collection by privileged access interviewers. *Addiction*, 92(3), 325–34.

Lohr, S. L. (2010). *Sampling: Design and analysis.* Boston, MA: Brooks/Cole.

Loosveldt, G., & Storms, V. (2008). Measuring public opinions about surveys. *International Journal of Public Opinion Research*, 20(1), 74–89.

McKenzie, D. J., & Mistianen, J. (2009). Surveying migrant households: a comparison of census-based, snowball, and intercept point surveys. *Journal of the Royal Statistical Society: Series A (Statistics in Society)*, 172(2), 339–60.

Maranda, F. (2004). Opening remarks. In *Proceedings of the Symposium 2004: Innovative Methods for Surveying Difficult-to-Reach Populations* (pp. 1–2). Ottawa: Statistics Canada.

Marpsat, M., & Razafindratsima, N. (2010). Survey methods for hard-to-reach populations: introduction to the Special Issue. *Methodological Innovation Online*, 5(2), 3–16.

Michaels, S., & Lhomond, B. (2006). Conceptualizations and measurement of homosexuality in sex surveys: a critical review. *Cadernos de Saude Publica*, 22(7), 1365–74.

Norris, F. H. (2006). Disaster research methods: past progress and future directions. *Journal of Traumatic Stress*, 19(2), 173–84.

Pedersen, J. (1995). Drought, migration, and population growth in the Sahel: the case of the Malian Gourma, 1900–1991. *Population Studies*, 49(1), 111–26.

Peng, D. (2011). *Overcoming Challenges to Sample Design in Iraq*. Paper presented at the Joint Statistical Meetings, Denver, CO.

Pennell, B.-E., Harkness, J., Levenstein, R., & Quaglia, M. (2010). Challenges in cross-national data collection. In J. A. Harkness, M. Braun, B. Edwards, T. P. Johnson, L. Lyberg, P. Ph. Mohler, B.-E. Pennell, & T. W. Smith (eds.), *Survey Methods in Multinational, Multiregional, and Multicultural Contexts* (pp. 269–98). Hoboken, NJ: John Wiley & Sons.

Pennell, B.-E., Levenstein, R., & Lee, H. J. (2010). Data collection: Cross-cultural survey guidelines. Retrieved from ccsg.isr.umich.edu.

Pescosolido, B. (2012). Personal communication.

Platt, L., Wall, M., Rhodes, T., Judd, A., Hickman, M., Johnston, L. G. *et al.* (2006). Methods to recruit hard-to-reach groups: comparing two chain referral sampling methods for recruiting injecting drug users across nine studies in Russia and Estonia. *Journal of Urban Health*, 82(Suppl. 1), 39–53.

Reed, J. S. (1975–76). Needles in haystacks: studying "rare" populations by secondary analysis of national sample surveys. *Public Opinion Quarterly*, 39(4), 514–22.

Rodriquez, H., Quarantelli, E. L., & Dynes, R. (eds.). (2007). *Handbook of Disaster Research*. New York: Springer Verlag.

Rossi, P. H. (1989). *Down and Out in America: The Origins of Homelessness*. Chicago, IL: University of Chicago Press.

Rothbart, G. S., Fine, M., & Sudman, S. (1982). On finding and interviewing needles in the haystack: the use of multiplicity sampling. *Public Opinion Quarterly*, 46(3), 408–21.

Salganik, M. J., & Heckathorn, D. D. (2004). Sampling and estimation in hidden populations using respondent-driven sampling. *Sociological Methodology*, 34, 193–239.

Skjak, K. K., & Harkness, J. (2003). Data collection methods. In J. A. Harkness, F. J. R. van de Vijver, & P. Ph. Mohler (eds.), *Cross-Cultural Survey Methods* (pp. 179–93). Hoboken, NJ: John Wiley & Sons.

Smith, T. W. (1992). Discrepancies between men and women in reporting number of sexual partners: a summary from four countries. *Social Biology*, 39(3–4), 203–11.

(2007). Survey non-response procedures in cross-national perspective: the 2005 ISSP non-response survey. *Survey Research Methods*, 1(1), 45–54.

(2010). The globalization of survey research. In J. A. Harkness, M. Braun, B. Edwards, T. P. Johnson, L. Lyberg, P. Ph. Mohler, B.-E. Pennell, & T. W. Smith (eds.), *Survey Methods in Multinational, Multiregional, and Multicultural Contexts* (pp. 477–84). Hoboken, NJ: John Wiley & Sons.

(2011a). *Lessons on Developing Laws for Studying Societal Change*. Paper presented to the European Survey Research Association, Lausanne, Switzerland.

(2011b). The report on the international workshop on using multi-level data from sample frames, auxiliary databases, paradata, and related sources to detect and adjust for nonresponse bias in surveys. *International Journal of Public Opinion Research*, 23(3), 389–402.

(2011c). Trends in support for civil liberties. *GSS Social Change Report No. 59*. Chicago, IL: NORC.

Statistics Canada. (2004). *Proceedings of Symposium 2004: innovative methods for surveying difficult-to-reach populations*. Ottawa: Statistics Canada.

Stoop, I., Billiet, J., Kohn, A., & Fitzgerald, R. (2010). *Improving survey response: lessons learned from the European Social Survey*. Chichester: John Wiley & Sons.

Sudman, S. (1972). On sampling of very rare human populations. *Journal of the American Statistical Association*, 67(338), 335–39.

Titterton, M., & Clark, C. (2000). Working with socially excluded Romani communities in central and eastern Europe: lessons from Bulgaria. *Social Work in Europe*, 7(3), 38–45.

Tortora, R. D. (2012). Personal communication.

Tortora, R. D., Srinivasan, R., & Esipova, N. (2010). The Gallup World Poll. In J. A. Harkness, M. Braun, B. Edwards, T. P. Johnson, L. Lyberg, P. Ph. Mohler, B.-E. Pennett, & T. W. Smith (eds.), *Survey Methods in Multinational, Multiregional, and Multicultural Contexts* (pp. 535–44). Hoboken, NJ: John Wiley & Sons.

Treiman, D. J., Lym, Y., & Qi, Y. (2009). *New Approaches to Demographic Data Collection*. California Center for Population Research On-Line Working Paper Series. Los Angeles, CA: University of California–Los Angeles.

United Nations. (2009). UN Development Program, 2009. Retrieved from UNDP.org.

Van der Reis, P. (1997). *Transportation Surveys among Illiterate and Semiliterate Households in South Africa*. Paper presented to the International Conference on Transport Surveys, Grainau, Germany.

Vandepitte, R., Lyerla, R., Dallabetta, G., Crabbe, F., Alary, M., & Buvé, A. (2006). Estimates of the number of female sex workers in different regions of the world. *Sexually Transmitted Infections*, 82: Supplement 3, 18–25.

Vigneswaran, D. (2007). *Lost in Space: Residential Sampling and Johannesburg's Forced Migrants*. Paper presented to the African Migrations Workshop, Accra, Ghana.

WAPOR. (2011). Pollsters missing in Michoacan, Mexico. Retrieved from http://wapor.unl. edu/wp-content / ploads/2011/08/Mexico-2011.pdf.

Weinreb, A. A. (2006). The limitations of stranger-interviewers in rural Kenya. *American Sociological Review*, 71(6), 1014–39.

Williams, Linda A. 1984. The classic rape: when do victims report? *Social Problems*, 31, 459–67.

Young, C. (2012). Personal communication.

3

Measuring undercounts for hard-to-survey groups

MARY H. MULRY

3.1 Introduction

Measuring census undercount is an important way of gaining insight about subpopulations that are hard to survey. Although such groups may be a relatively small proportion of the population, they contribute disproportionately to the overall undercount. Several methods are available for measuring census undercounts, so countries are able to choose the one that best suits their situation. The methods for estimating net undercount include post-enumeration surveys, demographic analysis, administrative record matches, and reverse record checks. Countries use these methods to make population estimates that are thought to be more accurate than the census; this estimate is then compared to the census count to give an estimate of the net undercount.

The methods have different data requirements, so not every country has the data needed to apply each one. Even when such data exist, some countries have privacy and confidentiality restrictions on how the data are used. Therefore, not all methods can be applied in all countries. Demographic analysis uses vital records in aggregate calculations. Administrative record matches and reverse record checks require high-quality records systems and laws that permit their use to measure undercounts. A post-enumeration survey is a second enumeration implemented on a sample basis after a census and then matched to the census on a case-by-case basis. One advantage of a post-enumeration survey is that is does not depend on the availability of an administrative or vital records system. Even if such records are available, their quality and the characteristics of individuals that they contain are not issues when a post-enumeration survey is done. Therefore, the method may be applied in developed or developing countries.

This chapter discusses the methods for measuring census undercount and their advantages and disadvantages. Most censuses use an enumeration methodology that involves contacting the population to collect information. However, some countries, almost all of them in Europe, take their census using a register-based methodology where the information about the population is drawn from records maintained in one or more administrative registers (Valente, 2010). The coverage evaluation methodologies discussed in this chapter are typically employed for censuses that use an enumeration methodology, but they can be

This report is released to inform interested parties and encourage discussion of work in progress. The views expressed on statistical, methodological, and operational issues are those of the author and not necessarily those of the US Census Bureau.

used for register-based censuses. Also included are results of applications in some countries to illustrate identifying groups that are hard to enumerate in censuses and surveys.

3.2   Administrative record match

An administrative record match (ARM) is an evaluation procedure in which a sample from the administrative record file is matched case-by-case to the census population or subpopulation of interest. The usual assumption is that the administrative records file is more complete than the census so the percentage in the record sample not matched to the census is a measure of the census coverage error.

For the ARM to be a viable approach, the country has to possess a high-quality records system for the population of interest, which may be a subpopulation. The administrative records used for an ARM are maintained for other purposes, but the records may nonetheless provide sufficient coverage of the population of interest.

In some cases, the country has a centralized administrative record system that contains records for nearly all the residents. In other cases, the country has to merge several administrative record systems to cover the entire population of interest. Then, the combined file is unduplicated and the final product is matched to the census to identify persons missed by the census. The need to merge records systems raises the issue of the laws governing the country's records; these laws must permit matching the administrative records for statistical purposes that include census coverage evaluation.

The ARM method of coverage evaluation has several advantages. One advantage of using administrative lists is that they do not rely on a household survey or a previous census. Therefore, this method does not have the problem that post-enumeration surveys may have of missing many of the same people that the census does. Also, an ARM allows focusing on the hard-to-survey segments of the population by obtaining lists, such as the low-income population receiving Temporary Assistance for Needy Families in the US.

The ARM method also comes with disadvantages. One disadvantage is that there is no guarantee that the administrative list or lists cover the entire population of interest. This method also requires matching to the census, with possible tracing or follow-up of non-matches. An additional complication arises when several lists must be merged. Unduplication of the lists may be difficult because some people use different names and addresses for different purposes. Conversely, common names also create the problem of different people with the same name and birthdates, who may appear to be the same person to an unduplication algorithm. However, when household structure is available, the unduplication algorithms are more effective. If each person has a unique identification number that is present on all the lists and on the census, then finding duplicates on merged lists is much more successful. A crucial difficulty with using administrative records for coverage evaluation is identifying the population for which the records are complete. If the records overcover some subpopulation, this creates problems in generalizing any results to the entire population.

The first documented ARM occurred in the early 1930s in Canada where enumerations in the 1931 Canadian Census for infants under one year of age were matched to the birth registration records in nine provinces (Marks, Seltzer, & Krotki, 1974; Tracey, 1931). The study found that 80 percent of the enumerations matched to birth records, with a range of 80 to 91 percent across the nine provinces for areas not included in the Indian Reserves and a range of 57 to 74 percent in the Indian Reserves. In the US, ARMs also started in the 1930s to evaluate the coverage of birth records (Marks *et al.*, 1974). Most states conducted clerical matches of special-purpose surveys to birth records to show their records were at least 90 percent complete and could be included in the national birth registration system. Few details are available about these studies since only two conducted by the US Census Bureau for Georgia and Maryland are documented (Hedrich, Collinson, & Rhoads, 1939). The first US ARM using census data was the match of 1940 Census enumerations of infants under four months old to birth registration records and represented a substantial advance in matching methodology, although all the matching was clerical at that time (Marks *et al.*, 1974). Over the years, the US Census Bureau has conducted matches between different administrative lists and censuses to evaluate coverage and data quality. We discuss a few examples. ARMs evaluated the coverage of 1960 Census for two groups (Marks & Waksberg, 1966). A sample of Social Security recipients was matched to the 1960 Census and estimated that the number missed was 5.1 to 5.7 percent of those enumerated. A study of the net coverage of college students drew a sample from lists of students obtained from colleges and universities. The selected students received questionnaires asking about all the addresses where they may have been enumerated. Then, the study matched the students to the 1960 Census at all the reported addresses and was able to produce an estimate of net undercoverage of 2.5 to 2.7 percent, taking into account both overcoverage and undercoverage.

Another ARM conducted in conjunction with the 1980 Census assessed the feasibility of using the 1979 Internal Revenue Service (IRS) file as a sampling frame for evaluating census coverage (Childers & Hogan, 1983). A sample from the IRS file was matched to the 1980 Census at their address in the IRS file. When the study could not find a match, the person was traced using mail and personal interviews to find addresses where the person might be enumerated. However, the study was not able to trace 22 percent of the sample and did not make estimates of census undercount.

An ARM conducted in conjunction with the 1996 Community Census Test focused on determining whether there were people in administrative records who were not listed in a census or a post-enumeration survey. The study matched the census enumerations for the 1996 Census Community Test conducted in three locations (seven tracts in Chicago, Illinois; the Fort Hall Reservation in Idaho; and the Pueblo of Acoma in New Mexico) to a file created by merging several federal records files, with the combination of files varying by site (Sweet, 1997). Post-enumeration interviews used computer-assisted personal interviews (CAPI); the computers contained the administrative records but hid them from the interviewers until after they obtained a new roster at a housing unit. When an administrative-records-only person was not on the new roster, the program prompted the interviewer to ask about the person's residency. The percentage of people from administrative records who were residents but not enumerated and not on the rosters in the post-enumeration interview ranged from 2.0 to 2.5 across the three sites.

The US has not had a single administrative records system with high coverage of the entire population. By 2000, computer database processing and storage capacity had developed to the point that the US Census Bureau attempted to create a census-like file by merging and unduplicating five federal sources of administrative records, called the Statistical Administrative Records System (StARS; Leggieri, Pistiner, & Farber, 2002). A comparison between the StARS and Census 2000 found the file covered 95 percent of the population (Judson, 2000). The methodology for creating StARS enabled an ARM to examine the validity of the estimate of 5.8 million duplicate enumerations in the Census 2000 count of 281.4 million; that estimate was based on an algorithm using only census data. Census 2000 was the first to use optical character recognition technology that enabled capturing names in electronic format so the estimate of duplicates was the first of its kind and viewed as surprisingly large. The StARS algorithm chose a "best" address for a person when more than one address appeared in the five files. However, an auxiliary file kept all the addresses for each person. A match between the auxiliary file and a sample of census enumerations provided other addresses where the sample people may have been enumerated. A search of the census file for the sample people at the additional addresses produced an alternative estimate of 6.7 million duplicates, confirming that there were a large number of duplicate enumerations in Census 2000 (Mulry, Bean, Bauder, Mule, & Wagner, 2006).

The 2010 Census presented an opportunity for further research by creating a census-like administrative records file that merged both federal and commercial data sources and then comparing the unduplicated administrative records file to census records. The results of the 2010 Census Match Study showed that 88.6 percent of the 308.7 million 2010 Census enumerations could be matched to an administrative record. The main reason for the low match rate appeared to be not being able to assign unique identification numbers to 9.6 percent of the census person records. However, the census-like administrative records file had 312.2 million records for unique persons, but the study was not able to link 10.7 million to an address on the census file (Rastogia & O'Hara, 2012). Work continues on refining methods, but the focus has turned to identifying ways administrative records can reduce the cost and improve the quality of the 2020 Census, particularly in the design of adaptive operations for the follow-up of nonrespondents to the mailout/mailback questionnaires.

Other countries have different systems, cultures, and laws that have led to administrative records systems with a high level of coverage of their population that makes the systems suitable for the ARM methodology. In some countries, such as Finland and Norway, the coverage of the population and the quality of the data in the system are so high that the country has decided to use a register-based methodology for their census rather than an enumeration-based methodology. These countries typically use their census data to inform policy decisions and not to divide political power, which is different from the U.S. where census numbers are used in the apportionment of the seats in the US House of Representatives among the states.

Finland moved to a register-based census because evaluations of censuses using an enumeration methodology showed the register-based method had quality comparable to the enumeration method. The basis of this decision was not coverage, but the finding that the data on type of activity and labor force status was comparable with the net difference in the categories considered, ranging between 0.2 and 10.0 percent (Myrskyla, 1991). Finland creates its census by combining its Central Population Register (CPR) with twelve other registers, including the Taxation Register and the Register on Wages, Salaries, and Pensions. The tradition of registers of the population goes back to the 1700s when tax collection and army recruitment used registers of births and deaths recorded in church parishes (Myrskyla, 1991). The central records systems evolved from this practice. Even when enumeration methods were used in 1970 and 1980, the goal was to collect information, not count the population. The addresses on the census mail questionnaires included the name of the resident, which indicates that registers were up to date regarding where the residents live and the purpose of the census was to collect additional information. For further discussion of the evolution of register-based censuses, see Harala and Tammilehto-Luode (1999), Redfern (1986) and Statistics Finland (2004).

Assuring that the records remain accurate enough for a register-based census is also a concern. Recommendations for validation methodology for register-based censuses may be found in a report from the UN Economic Commission for Europe (2006). The Commission also has joined with Eurostat to sponsor expert meetings on register-based censuses that include discussions of potential sources of errors and methods for validating methodology (UN Economic Commission for Europe, 2010, 2012). Interestingly, one of the concerns is that some people are listed in registers in two countries and procedures to unduplicate records between countries are not currently available.

The need to validate registers has become more apparent since the 2011 German Census Count of 80.2 million people was 1.5 million lower than the estimates based on local registers, and 1.1 million of the deficit had foreign citizenship, reducing the previously assumed number of resident foreigners to 6.2 million (German Federal Statistics Office 2013). An example of a validation of register records for a subpopulation is an evaluation of the records for immigrants and foreign-born Norwegians on Norway's CPR. Through a mail survey and other work with CPR records for 218,000 immigrants and foreign-born resident Norwegians, Statistics Norway found that 1.3 percent had emigrated or had expired work permits indicating they probably had emigrated. The conclusion was that there was a considerable delay in updating CPR records when members of this group left the country (Hendriks, 2012).

The post-enumeration survey methodology discussed in Section 3.5 usually is employed for enumeration-based censuses but also may be applied to evaluate a register-based census. Using the demographic analysis methodology discussed in Section 3.3 to evaluate a register-based census is contingent on the availability of other high-quality records independent of the records used in taking the census; this seems unlikely in most countries.

3.3 Demographic analysis

Demographic analysis uses analytical techniques applied to aggregate population data to study populations and estimate their size. As a tool for census evaluation, demographic analysis involves first developing estimates for the population in various categories, such as age, race, and sex groups, at Census Day based on various types of demographic data. Then, these subgroup estimates are combined to yield an estimate for the population size of the nation as a whole. The data used for demographic analysis estimates include: birth, death, and immigration statistics; sex ratios, life tables, etc.; historical series of census data; and data from sample surveys. Corrections are made to the data for various types of known errors, usually based on secondary sources, such as administrative records, for a specific population. However, the production of the estimates does not involve case-by-case matching of records.

The basic demographic accounting relationship is:

$$Population = Birth - Deaths + Immigrants - Emigrants.$$

To apply the demographic analysis methodology, a country has to have high-quality historical time series for each of these quantities where the consistency of the different series has been confirmed. Another requirement when the records do exist is that there are no barriers to using them in aggregate to form demographic analysis estimates. The existence of records of births and deaths is particularly important because they form the basis for demographic analysis. When the records systems exist, but not all events are entered, then it is sometimes possible to estimate the coverage error rates and to use them in making adjustments. When records of immigrants and emigrants do not exist or are not complete, alternate estimation methods and data, such as survey data, are sometimes used to make adequate estimates for these groups.

In the US, an application of the demographic method of comparing aggregated totals raised the initial concern about the coverage of the census. Prior to the 1940s, the prevailing assumption was that the census had better coverage of the population than the records systems. However, a comparison of the number of males of military age in the 1940 Census to draft registration records dispelled that notion. The study estimated there were 14.9 percent more Black males of 21 to 35 years of age registered for the draft than were counted in the census and 2.8 percent more non-Black males in the same age category. By states, the estimates for non-Blacks ranged from being 4.1 percent too high in Wyoming to 16.0 percent too low for the District of Columbia. All the estimates for Blacks were too low, ranging from a deficit of 5.4 percent in Mississippi to 40.3 percent in the District of Columbia (Price, 1947). The US and other countries saw the need for developing methods to evaluate their census coverage. This led to the development of methodology to evaluate census coverage using demographic analysis, reverse record check (Section 3.4), and post-enumeration surveys (Section 3.5).

The primary advantage of demographic analysis as a tool for evaluating a census is that it uses data sources that are independent of the census being evaluated. However, the overall accuracy of demographic analysis for a country depends on the quality of the demographic data in these data sources and the quality of the corrections for any known errors in the data.

A disadvantage of demographic analysis is that the direct estimates of population size usually are available at the national level only. Another shortcoming is that the estimates are possible only for subgroups identified in the vital records. For example, in the US, population estimates are possible for only two racial groups, Blacks and non-Blacks, because the historical records put people in only those two categories. In recent years, records have also included the category of Hispanic ethnicity, which permitted the 2010 demographic analysis estimates of the US population to include estimates for Hispanics less than 25 years of age.

The first time demographic analysis methods were used to evaluate coverage error was by Coale (1955) for the 1950 US Census. The 1960 US Census was the first to use demographic analysis as an evaluation tool (Siegel & Zelnik, 1966). Many improvements were made in the demographic analysis methodology in 1970 (US Bureau of the Census, 1974). Undocumented immigration surfaced as an issue for the 1980 demographic analysis estimates (Fay, Passel, Robinson, & Cowan, 1988) and persisted in the 1990 and 2000 estimates (Robinson, 2001; Robinson, Ahmed, Das Gupta, & Woodrow, 1993). The methodology for estimating migration for the 2010 estimates changed to one based on data from the American Community Survey (US Census Bureau, 2010).

Another issue is the lack of measures of uncertainty in demographic analysis estimates due to choices of datasets and choices of assumptions. Most of the construction of the estimates does not use probability models so the uncertainty cannot be quantified with standard statistical methods, although the introduction of survey-based estimates of immigration in 2010 is an exception. The first attempt to quantify the uncertainty was for the 1990 estimates (Robinson *et al.*, 1993). For 2010, the US Census Bureau released a range of estimates based on varying assumptions. The range was 305.6 million to 312.7 million with a middle estimate of 308.4 million that was close to the census count of 308,745,438 (US Census Bureau, 2010). Demographic analysis estimates of population size do offer a way of obtaining historical estimates of census percent net undercount, as defined by

$$Percent\ net\ undercount = \frac{Population\ size - Census\ count}{Population\ size} \times 100.$$

A negative percent net undercount indicates an overcount. Figure 3.1 shows estimates of percent net undercount for the total population, the Black population, and the non-Black population for the decennial censuses in the US from 1940 to 2010 from demographic analysis. Black and non-Black are the only two racial subgroups available in historical records for the entire period. However, the non-Black population became much more heterogeneous over the period from 1940 to 2010 so the racial and ethnic composition of non-Blacks in 1940 is not what was observed for non-Blacks in 2010.

Other countries have used demographic analysis techniques to evaluate censuses, although the US is the only one with a historical series like the one in Figure 3.1. In many instances, countries focus on the internal consistency of the census counts rather than on the level of the estimates. The tools include examining sex ratios for age cohorts and comparisons with historical values. Kerr (1998) compares the demographic analysis methods used in the evaluation of censuses in Canada, US, UK, and Australia. The relatively poor quality of some records for the older population reduces the quality of the estimates of the total

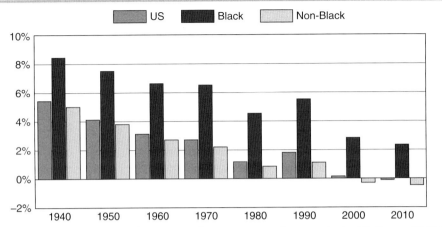

Figure 3.1   Historical estimates of percent net undercount in the US Census 1940 to 2010 based on estimates from demographic analysis.
Note: A negative net undercount denotes a net overcount.
Source: 1940–2000: Long, Robinson, & Gibson, 2003; 2010: US Census Bureau, 2012.

population in all these countries. The US addresses this concern by relying on Medicare data for those 65 years of age and older. However, all four of the countries use demographic analysis techniques to form estimates of the population for years between censuses, called post-censal or intercensal estimates, by using the census as a base and estimating the change in the population (Kerr, 1998). In addition, demographic analysis techniques are used to form estimates of the size of the population in other countries, including developing countries (Brass, 1996).

3.4   Reverse record check

A reverse record check (RRC) is a census evaluation program in which a sample of the population is drawn from records that existed before the census, traced forward to the time of the census, and matched to the census. The frame is usually composed of people enumerated in the previous census, persons missed in the previous census, births, and immigrants. This method differs from the ARM approach since the records from the last census (including the records of people identified as missed in the evaluation of the last census) are not generally classified as administrative records. This type of records sample, if well executed, is likely to have better coverage than a census. The sample for the RRC is composed of separate samples selected from each source. The proportion of the sample that is unmatched provides an estimate of the proportion of the population that was missed in the census. To obtain an estimate of net census coverage error, an RRC has to be supplemented with a separate sample of census enumerations and a validation operation in order to measure erroneous enumerations, which tend to be mainly duplicate enumerations. Then the resulting estimate of population size is

Population size = census count + number missed − number of erroneous enumerations.

A key requirement for implementing a RRC is the availability of current addresses for the people in the records samples; this usually means matching these samples to a high-quality administrative records system. The existence of a unique identifier number assigned to each resident facilitates the matching between the samples and the administrative records. The need to update addresses for the sample from a previous census and the sample of people missed by the previous census is obvious. However, even if records of births, deaths, immigration, and emigration are available for selecting the sample, the addresses at the time of the event that generated the record may be out of date by the time of the census.

A second requirement is that the privacy policies permit interviewers to ask for a person by name at an address found in administrative records. In the US, for example, the privacy policy governing the tax records held by the IRS does not permit revealing a person's name on a tax return or even that the person filed a tax return. Therefore, matching to IRS records and then asking for the person by name at the address found in the IRS records would not be approved by IRS for a statistical program. Research projects may apply for permission to ask for people at their address found in the IRS records, but few are approved (Childers & Hogan, 1983; Sweet, 1997).

A RRC takes advantage of changes over time in the probability that a particular person can be found. For example, except for the very youngest, children are easier to enumerate than young adults, who tend to be highly mobile. Canada, which uses the RRC methodology, provides an illustration. It conducts a census every five years. The sample of people enumerated in the previous census will include some children and in particular, children ages 12 to14. The RRC will be able to determine if they are missed in the next census when they are 17 to 19, ages that have a lower probability of being enumerated. Any who are missed are included in the sample of those missed for the subsequent census. Accumulating a RRC sampling frame from census to census allows the frame to become more complete over time. After several censuses, the quality of the frame of those missed in the previous census becomes very high.

On the other hand, if several implementations are needed to create a high-quality frame of persons missed by the census, this will be a disadvantage for the first few census evaluations. Another potential disadvantage is that even if hard-to-enumerate groups are easier to sample several years before the census, this advantage may be offset to some extent by a type of correlation bias. This type of correlation bias potentially arises if those people who were traced successfully are more likely to be counted in the census than those who could not be traced. Statistics Canada first used the RRC approach to evaluate the coverage of the 1961 Census but there was no frame for people missed by the previous census (Statistics Canada, 2007). The results of the 1961 RRC provided a sample of those missed by the 1961 Census for use in the evaluation of the 1966 Census. The evaluations of the Canadian censuses since 1966 have used the RRC methodology. When censuses are done every five years it is easier to trace sample people to their new addresses than when they are done every ten years.

Canada has accumulated its RRC sampling frame from census to census, thus covering anyone counted in any of the censuses and anyone born or immigrated to Canada between censuses since the start of this effort in the 1970s. Since sample people without current records are traced, a distinction can be made between those who are missed and those who have emigrated. The result is that the Canadian RRC sampling frame has become successively more complete over time. The completeness of the frame enables researchers to estimate coverage of those missed by the census being evaluated. In addition, Canada has a centralized statistical system that facilitates accessing administrative records to find current addresses. The Canadian laws permit asking for a person by name at an address found in administrative records.

The US Census Bureau has experimented with the RRC methodology on several occasions but each time found that locating new addresses for sample members when there are ten years between censuses was more difficult than hoped. The US Census Bureau conducted an RRC to estimate the number of persons omitted by the 1960 Census (US Bureau of the Census, 1964), but the 1960 RRC failed to trace 16.5 percent of the sample, which was too much nonresponse to get reliable estimates of the miss rate. Two research projects in the 1980s indicated that a RRC would not be successful in the US. The estimated nonmatch rate from an attempt to match a sample from the 1977 Current Population Survey to the 1980 Census was 14 percent, which was twice as high as the nonmatch rate from the 1980 Postenumeration Program (Diffendal, 1986). Also, the US Census Bureau evaluated the tracing component in the Forward Trace Study (Mulry & Dajani, 1989) by selecting the four samples that would be needed for a RRC and tracing them from 1980 to 1985. The estimates of the tracing rates were significantly lower for minorities than for Whites, and overall were too low to merit a recommendation to use a RRC for evaluating the coverage of the 1990 Census. A re-examination of the feasibility of evaluating the 2010 Census coverage with a RRC based on the 2007 American Community Survey (ACS) sample augmented with samples of births and immigrants from the 2008–2009 ACS reached the same conclusion because of the difficulty of tracing sample people to their address on Census Day in 2010 (Mulry & Bell, 2008).

The most recent results available from a Canadian RRC are from the evaluation of the 2006 Census. Although there was a Canadian 2011 Census, the coverage study results are not available as this paper goes to press.

Tables 3.1 and 3.2 display estimated percent net undercount for the 2006 Canadian Census for demographic groups (Statistics Canada, 2007). Table 3.1 shows the percent net undercount by sex and age. Males have a higher percent net undercount than females, and young adults ages 18 to 34 have the higher coverage error rates than the other age groups. Males in this age range have the highest percent net undercount of any age–sex group.

Table 3.2 shows the percent net undercount by sex and marital status for people 15 years of age and older. Again, in these groupings males have a higher percent net undercount than females. The coverage error rates among the never married, separated, and divorced are higher than those among the married and widowed. The widowed probably tend to be older

Table 3.1 *Estimated 2006 Canadian Census percent net undercount, by sex and age*

Age and sex	Both sexes		Males		Females	
	%	SE	%	SE	%	SE
All Canada	**2.67**	**0.17**	**3.89**	**0.26**	**1.48**	**0.23**
0 to 4 years	2.72	0.65	2.89	0.94	2.54	0.92
5 to 14 years	0.86	0.45	0.79	0.63	0.94	0.65
15 to 17 years	−0.76	0.61	−0.49	0.88	−1.05	0.83
18 to 19 years	6.22	1.55	7.78	2.41	4.54	1.93
20 to 24 years	7.63	0.73	9.46	1.11	5.69	0.97
25 to 34 years	8.00	0.56	9.91	0.86	6.08	0.73
35 to 44 years	4.31	0.49	6.66	0.78	1.92	0.61
45 to 54 years	1.50	0.42	2.98	0.69	0.03	0.51
55 to 64 years	−0.29	0.53	0.83	0.76	−1.40	0.73
65 years and over	−1.39	0.39	−1.74	0.56	−1.13	0.55

Source: Statistics Canada (2007). A negative net undercount denotes a net overcount.

Table 3.2 *Estimated 2006 Canadian Census percent net undercount, by marital status and age for persons 15 years of age and over*

Marital status and sex for persons 15 years and over	Both sexes		Males		Females	
	%	SE	%	SE	%	SE
All	**2.94**	**0.19**	**4.43**	**0.30**	**1.49**	**0.25**
Never married	6.70	0.43	8.82	0.62	4.09	0.58
Married or common-law	1.00	0.21	1.37	0.31	0.63	0.29
Separated	9.75	2.26	16.84	4.58	3.63	1.88
Divorced	4.39	1.14	7.86	1.86	1.91	1.43
Widowed	−1.28	0.73	−0.38	1.85	−1.48	0.80

Source: Statistics Canada (2007). A negative net undercount denotes a net overcount.

members of the population and the never married probably tend to be younger members. The males who are never married, separated, or divorced have the highest percent net undercount.

Canada uses the percent net undercount estimates to adjust their census for fund allocation. See Royce (1992) for details about the adjustment methodology.

3.5   Post-enumeration survey

A post-enumeration survey (PES) is a survey conducted after the census for the purpose of measuring census coverage. The survey respondents are matched to the original enumeration on a case-by-case basis. Then, dual system estimation may be used to give an estimate of the population size. A comparison of the census to the PES estimate of population size yields the net undercount rate. Much of the basic development of the methodology came out of efforts associated with the United Nations to estimate population growth. The methodology and its history are described well in Chandrasekar and Deming (1949) and Marks et al. (1974).

The first attempts to evaluate a census using a PES in the US occurred after the 1950 and 1960 Censuses (US Census Bureau, 1960; Marks & Waksberg, 1966). These efforts attempted to find the truth for each household in sample, but the surveys did not find an undercount as large as the demographic analysis estimates. An attempt to conduct a PES to evaluate the 1970 Census was so flawed that a report was not produced. Dual system estimation (DSE) methodology emerged as the means to produce better estimates from a PES because its underlying assumption that the second enumeration was independent was easier to meet than the previous method's assumption that the PES had no error (that is, that the PES found the truth for every household). So, an evaluation of the 1980 Census used the DSE approach. During the 1980s, computerized matching techniques greatly improved the PES processing and these were applied first in a PES to evaluate the 1990 Census (Hogan, 1993) and in subsequent PESs that evaluated the 2000 and 2010 Censuses (Hogan, 2003; Mule, 2012). Since the 1980 implementation, the PES has produced estimates at the national level that are comparable to those from demographic analysis, differing by at most 0.2 percent (Mulry, 2007). For more details on the evolution of the PES at US Census Bureau, see Mulry (2011).

Two key assumptions underlie the PES method (Mulry & Spencer, 1991). One is that inclusion in the coverage survey is independent of inclusion in the census, which means the operations for the two cannot share information. Office and field staff for the coverage survey cannot work in the areas where they worked on the census. Census staff cannot know which blocks are in the coverage survey sample to prevent them from treating the sample areas differently from the areas that are not in sample. The other assumption is that the probability of being included in the census is not correlated with the probability of being included in the coverage survey. If these probabilities are uniform throughout the population, this assumption is met. When both assumptions are met, the basic relationship holds:

$$\frac{Number\ of\ good\ census\ enumerations}{Population\ size} = \frac{Number\ of\ matched\ people}{Number\ of\ survey\ enumerations}$$

Then with algebra, the form of the dual system estimator is

$$Population\ size = Number\ of\ good\ census\ enumerations\ \frac{Number\ of\ survey\ enumerations}{Number\ of\ matched\ people}$$

However, it is well known that capture probabilities vary. A method for addressing this problem creates separate estimates for groups thought to differ in their capture probabilities, such as age and sex groups; population estimates are made for each of these groups (post-strata) and then summed to estimate the total population size. However, some variation in capture probabilities may still exist within the post-strata, which introduces a bias in the estimate of the population size, called a correlation bias. The concern about correlation bias is that it tends to introduce a downward bias in the estimates. Methods to reduce correlation bias include a generalized form of the DSE that uses logistic regression DSE and adjusting the groups that auxiliary data indicate are underestimated (Mulry & Cantwell, 2010). The post-stratified DSE is equivalent to a logistic regression DSE when all the interactions are included in the logistic regression model. The US Census Bureau adjusted the 2010 estimates of coverage error with demographic analysis estimates of the sex ratios of males to females, which are believed to be better than those from the PES because the sex ratios for cohorts from the demographic analysis have been consistent over time (Mule, 2012). The method assumes that correlation bias affects adult males, but not adult females or children 17 years of age and under (Bell, 1993). In 2010, the demographic analysis and PES sex ratios for Blacks 18 to 29 years of age were comparable so no adjustment was made for this group. However, the demographic analysis sex ratios for Blacks 30 to 49 years of age and 50 years of age or over were 0.91 and 0.80, respectively, while the sex ratios from the dual system estimates were 0.81 and 0.74, respectively. The adjustment for correlation bias using the sex ratios in these two age groups added 926,000 Black males, increasing the estimates of Blacks from 40.073 million to 40.999 million (Konicki, 2012).

An advantage of the PES is that it does not require the country to have a records system or historical vital records, which is one reason the UN recommends it for evaluating census coverage in developing countries (United Nations Secretariat, 2010a). The implementation requires a sample of the population that is often an area sample, but the sample must be independent of the census it is evaluating. A legal requirement is that the country's laws permit matching between the independent sample and the census data. A PES is also attractive for developed countries because its design is able to provide estimates for levels of geography below the national level and for race/ethnic groups that may or may not be distinguished in the records systems and vital records. Operational independence of the implementation may be achieved by not releasing the areas in sample to the field staff until after the census.

The PES also has some disadvantages. One disadvantage is that it requires careful implementation to assure as much independence as possible between the census and the post-enumeration survey. Also, the matching between two independent lists, the PES and the census, currently requires a substantial amount of time. The matching requires that the census enumeration files be available in addition to the PES files. Matching people who move between the census and the PES interview is complicated and is one reason so much time is necessary. A technical disadvantage of the PES is that the dual system estimates may be subject to correlation bias, discussed earlier in this section.

We examine estimates of percent net undercount based on PES methodology for the US and Australia. Estimates of net undercount for the 2010 US Census use a variant of the dual system estimation approach that employs logistic regression to produce estimates of net coverage error. New methodology produces estimates of erroneous enumerations and omissions, which are not shown here but may be found in Keller and Fox (2012). Tables 3.3 to 3.5 show estimated percent net undercount for the 2010 US Census for

Table 3.3 *Estimated 2010 US Census percent net undercount, by sex and age*

Age and sex	Persons		Males		Females	
	%	SE	%	SE	%	SE
US total	−0.01	0.14				
0 to 17 years	−0.33	0.22				
0 to 9 years	0.20	0.29				
0 to 4 years	0.72	0.40				
5 to 9 years	−0.33	0.31				
10 to 17 years	−0.97	0.29				
18 to 29 years			1.21	0.45	−0.28	0.36
30 to 49 years			3.57	0.20	−0.42	0.21
50 years and over			−0.32	0.14	−2.35	0.14

Source: Mule (2012), Table 12. A negative net undercount denotes a net overcount.

Table 3.4 *Estimated 2010 US Census percent net undercount, by relationship in the household*

Relationship in household	%	SE
Nuclear family members	−0.32	0.14
Adult children	−2.91	0.38
Other household members	3.53	0.38

Source: Olson (2012), Table 7. A negative net undercount denotes a net overcount.

demographic groups (Mule, 2012). Table 3.3 shows percent net undercount by sex and age. Males have a higher percent net undercount than females, and young adults ages 18 to 49 have a higher percent net undercount than the other age groups. Adult males 30 to 49 have the highest percent net undercount. Table 3.4 shows the percent net undercount by relationship in the household. The percent net undercounts are lowest among the nuclear family members, consisting of the householder and, if present, his or her spouse and their children under 18 years of age. Adult children have a large negative percent net undercount, indicating overcoverage, probably because they tend to be duplicated. Other members of the household have the highest percent net undercount.

Table 3.5 shows the percent net undercount by whether the household lived in a bilingual (English and Spanish) mailing area and by Hispanic ethnicity. The areas that received bilingual questionnaires were known to have high rates of Spanish speakers who did not speak English well. The areas that received a bilingual questionnaire had a higher percent net undercount than the areas that did not. Also, the percent net undercount for the Hispanics in both areas was higher than for non-Hispanics.

Table 3.5 *Estimated 2010 US Census percent net undercount, by whether the area received a Spanish questionnaire and Hispanic ethnicity*

Group	%	SE
US	−0.01	0.14
Bilingual mailing area	0.80	0.40
Hispanic	1.33	0.42
Non-Hispanic	−0.15	0.50
Balance	−0.12	0.16
Hispanic	1.72	0.42
Non-Hispanic	−0.33	0.16

Source: Mule (2012), Table 16. A negative net undercount denotes a net overcount.

Table 3.6 *Estimated 2011 Australia Census coverage error rates, by sex and age*

Age	Persons %	Persons SE	Males %	Males SE	Females %	Females SE
Total all ages	**1.7**	**0.2**	**2.2**	**0.2**	**1.2**	**0.2**
0–4 years	1.2	0.6	1.2	0.8	1.3	0.7
5–9 years	1.5	0.6	1.9	0.8	1.0	0.8
10–14 years	0.4	0.6	0.6	0.7	0.2	0.8
15–19 years	2.5	0.6	2.4	0.8	2.6	0.9
20–24 years	6.9	0.8	7.8	1.1	6.0	1.0
25–29 years	5.8	0.8	7.5	1.2	4.0	0.9
30–34 years	3.0	0.7	4.1	0.9	1.9	0.9
35–39 years	1.1	0.6	2.1	0.9	0.2	0.8
40–44 years	1.3	0.6	1.2	0.8	1.5	0.8
45–49 years	0.4	0.5	1.5	0.8	−0.8	0.7
50–54 years	0.9	0.6	1.6	0.9	0.3	0.7
55 years and over	−0.1	0.2	−0.2	0.3	−0.1	0.3

Source: Australian Bureau of Statistics (2012). A negative net undercount denotes a net overcount.

Tables 3.6 and 3.7 have estimated percent net undercount for the 2011 Australian Census for selected demographic groups based on a PES. Table 3.6 shows the percent net undercount by sex and age. Males have a higher coverage error rate than females and young adults ages 20 to 34 have a higher percent net undercount than the other age groups. Adult males 20 to 29 have the highest percent net undercount.

Table 3.7 shows the percent net undercount by sex and marital status. Again, in these groupings males have higher percent net undercount than females. The percent net

Table 3.7 *Estimated 2011 Australia Census percent net undercount, by sex and marital status*

	Persons		Males		Females	
Marital status	%	SE	%	SE	%	SE
Total persons	1.7	0.2	2.2	0.2	1.2	0.2
Married	0.2	0.2	0.4	0.3	−0.1	0.2
Widowed, divorced, or separated	−0.8	0.5	−0.8	1.0	−0.8	0.5
Never married	3.7	0.3	4.2	0.4	3.1	0.3

Source: Australian Bureau of Statistics (2012). A negative net undercount denotes a net overcount.

undercount among the never married is higher than among the married and widowed, divorced, and separated. The males who are never married have the highest percent net undercount.

In countries that conduct a post-enumeration survey, the question usually arises as to whether they should adjust the census with the results. Some adjust their official census numbers, while others do not adjust the census numbers but make adjustments for other purposes such as fund allocations. A prime example of incorporating the post-enumeration survey results in the final census numbers occurs in the UK, which adjusts its enumeration-based census. A description of the UK methodology and estimates may be found in Chapter 4 of this volume (see also Abbott, 2009). Such an adjustment also has been done for a register-based census, such as the method used for the 2011 Census in Turkey (Turkish Statistical Institute, 2012). Previously, Turkey had used an enumeration-based census and conducted a post-enumeration survey for evaluation purposes (Ayhan & Ekni, 2003).

The UN continues to encourage countries to evaluate the quality of their censuses. The UN offers manuals and other materials that aid in the implementation of the PES methodology (United Nations Secretariat, 2010a; Whitford & Banda, 2001). In addition, the UN sponsors regional workshops that include lectures on various aspects of PES methodology and presentations by countries about their past experiences with PES methods and their plans for future implementations (United Nations Secretariat, 2009; United Nations Secretariat, 2010b). Some countries use their PES as an evaluation of the census and to improve operations in future censuses, while others use the results of the PES to adjust their census numbers.

3.6 Summary

Estimates of census net undercount may be made for an entire country and for subpopulations. A higher than average census net undercount rate for subpopulation indicates it is hard to count. The people who are hard to count in a census usually are hard to survey as well because the methods for census enumeration and survey interviews are similar.

We have examined four methodologies for measuring census coverage error that focus on measuring coverage on a national basis. They aid in identifying the hard-to-count portions of the population. All the coverage measurement methods provide information for operational evaluation as well as estimates of coverage at the national level. The ability to make estimates for specific subpopulations and lower geographic areas depends on the method and how it is implemented.

A country's choice of a methodology for measuring census coverage error depends on the availability of the required data and the privacy and confidentiality policies surrounding the use of the data for measuring census undercount. To some extent, the underlying purpose of the census and the purpose of coverage evaluation program also affect the choice of methodology for measuring census coverage and the methodology for taking the census. In most countries, the census collects data for policy decisions, but in the US the Constitution specifies that the census counts be used to allocate seats in Congress among the states.

When we examined estimates of percent net census undercount for the US, Canada, and Australia, we found some themes emerge about who is hard to count. These patterns appear even though the methodology of evaluating the census may differ and even though implementations of what is basically the same methodology may differ. The main conclusions are:

- Males are harder to count than females;
- Young adults are harder to count than children and older adults, with young adult males being the most difficult age/sex group;
- Nuclear family members are easier to count than other family members. Adults who have never been married are the most difficult marital status group to count.

We also found some evidence that people who are isolated from the dominant society in some way – whether the isolation is linguistic, cultural, or geographic – are hard to count. That said, the coverage measurement methods may miss very hard-to-count subgroups, such as the homeless, migratory workers, and people who are strongly anti-government. Other methods such as ethnographic techniques may be necessary to identify and contact these subgroups.

References

Abbott, O. (2009). 2011 UK Census coverage assessment and adjustment methodology. *Population Trends*, 137, 25–32.

Australian Bureau of Statistics. (2012). *2011 Census of Population and Housing – Details of Undercount*. Report 2940.0. Canberra: Australian Bureau of Statistics.

Ayhan, H. Ö., & Ekni, S. (2003). Coverage error in population censuses: The case of Turkey. *Survey Methodology*, 29(2), 155–65.

Bell, W. (1993). Using information from demographic analysis in post-enumeration survey estimation. *Journal of the American Statistical Association*, 88(3), 1106–18.

Brass, W. (1996). Demographic data analysis in less developed countries: 1946–1996. *Population Studies*, 50(3), 451–67.

Chandrasekar, C., & Deming, W. E. (1949). On a method of estimating birth and death rates and the extent of registration. *Journal of the American Statistical Association*, 44(1), 101–15.

Childers, D., & Hogan, H. (1983). Census experimental match studies. In *Joint Statistical Meetings Proceedings, Survey Research Methods Section* (pp. 173–76). Alexandria, VA: American Statistical Association.

Coale, A. J. (1955). The population of the United States in 1950 classified by age, sex, and color – a revision of census figures. *Journal of the American Statistical Association*, 50(1), 16–54.

Diffendal, G. (1986). *CPS-Census Retrospective Study*. Statistical Methods and Survey Methodology Research Report RR86-13. Washington, DC: US Census Bureau.

Fay, R. A., Passel, J. S., Robinson, J. G., & Cowan, C. (1988). *The Coverage of the Population in the 1980 Census*. Evaluation and Research Report PHC80-E4. Washington, DC: US Census Bureau.

German Federal Statistics Office (2013). *2011 Census: 80.2 million inhabitants lived in Germany on 9 May 2011*. Press release 188/2013-05-31, Weisbaden, Germany: German Federal Statistics Office.

Harala, R., & Tammilehto-Luode, M. (1999). GIS and register-based population census. In J. Alho (ed.), *Statistics, Registries, and Science* (pp. 55–72). Helsinki: Statistics Finland.

Hedrich, A., Collinson, J., & Rhoads, F. (1939). Comparison of birth tests by several methods in Georgia and Maryland. *Vital Statistics – Special Reports*, 7(60), 245–49.

Hendriks, C. (2012). Input data quality in register based statistics – the Norwegian experience. In *Joint Statistical Meetings Proceedings* (pp. 1473–80). Alexandria, VA: American Statistical Association.

Hogan, H. (1993). The 1990 Post-Enumeration Survey: operations and results. *Journal of the American Statistical Association*, 29(3), 1047–60.

    (2003). Accuracy and coverage evaluation: theory and design. *Survey Methodology*, 29(2), 129–38.

Judson, D. H. (2000). *The Statistical Administrative Records System: System Design, Successes, and Challenges*. Paper presented at the NISS/Telcordia Data Quality Conference, Morristown, NJ, November, 2000.

Keller, A., & Fox, T. (2012). *Components of Census Coverage for the Household Population in the United States*. DSSD 2010 Census Coverage Measurement Memorandum Series #2010-G-04. Washington, DC: US Census Bureau.

Kerr, D. (1998). *Alternate Methodologies in the Evaluation of Census Coverage: Canada, the United States, Britain and Australia*. Catalogue number 91F0015MPF-Number 005. Ottawa: Statistics Canada.

Konicki, S. (2012). *Adjustment for Correlation Bias*. DSSD 2010 Census Coverage Measurement Memorandum Series #2010-G-11. Washington, DC: US Census Bureau.

Leggieri, C., Pistiner, A., & Farber, J. (2002). Methods for conducting an administrative records experiment in Census 2000. In *Joint Statistical Meetings Proceedings, Survey Research Methods Section* (pp. 2709–13). Alexandria, VA: American Statistical Association.

Long, J., Robinson, G., & Gibson, C. (2003). Setting the standard for comparison: census accuracy from 1940 to 2000. In *2003 Joint Statistical Meetings Proceedings* (pp. 2515–24). Alexandria, VA: American Statistical Association.

Marks, E., Seltzer, W., & Krotki, K. (1974). *Population Growth Estimation*. New York: The Population Council.

Marks, E., & Waksberg, J. (1966). Evaluation of coverage in the 1960 Census of Population through case-by-case checking. In *Joint Statistical Meetings Proceedings, Social Statistics Section* (pp. 62–70). Alexandria, VA: American Statistical Association.

Mule, T. (2012). *Summary of Estimates of Coverage for Persons in the United States*. DSSD 2010 Census Coverage Measurement Memorandum Series #2010-G-01. Washington, DC: US Census Bureau.

Mulry, M. (2007). Summary of accuracy and coverage evaluation for Census 2000. *Journal of Official Statistics*, 23(3), 345–70.

(2011). Post-enumeration survey. In M. Anderson, C. Citro, & J.J. Salvo (eds.), *Encyclopedia of U.S. Census* (2nd edn.): *From the Constitution to the American Community Survey* (pp. 339–43). Washington, DC: CQ Press.

Mulry, M., Bean, S., Bauder, D., Mule, T., & Wagner, D. (2006). Evaluation of census duplication using administrative records. *Journal of Official Statistics*, 22(4), 655–79.

Mulry, M., & Bell, W. (2008). *Fundamental Issues with Reverse Record Check Methodology for Census Coverage Evaluation in the U.S.* DSSD 2010 Census Coverage Measurement Memorandum Series #A-30. Washington, DC: US Census Bureau.

Mulry, M., & Cantwell, P. (2010). Overview of the 2010 Census Coverage Measurement Program and its evaluations. *Chance*, 46(3), 46–51.

Mulry, M., & Dajani, A. (1989). The forward trace study. In *Joint Statistical Meetings Proceedings, Survey Research Methods Section* (pp. 675–80). Alexandria, VA: American Statistical Association.

Mulry, M., and Spencer, B. (1991). Total error in PES estimates of population. *Journal of the American Statistical Association*, 86(4), 839–54.

Myrskyla, P. (1991). Census by questionnaire – census by registers and administrative records: the Finnish experience. *Journal of Official Statistics*, 7(4), 457–74.

Olson, D. (2012). *Net Coverage Comparison with Post-Stratification*. DSSD 2010 Census Coverage Measurement Memorandum Series #2010-G-12. Washington, DC: US Census Bureau.

Price, D. (1947). A check on underenumeration in the 1940 Census. *American Sociological Review*, 12(1), 44–49.

Rastogia, S., & O'Hara, A. (2012). *2010 Census Match Study*. 2010 Census Planning Memoranda Series, Report No. 247. Washington, DC: US Census Bureau.

Redfern, P. (1986). Which countries will follow the Scandinavian lead in taking a register-based census? *Journal of Official Statistics*, 2(4), 415–24.

Robinson, J.G. (2001). *ESCAP II: Demographic Analysis Results*. Executive Steering Committee for ACE Policy II, Report No. 1. Washington, DC: US Census Bureau.

Robinson, J.G., Ahmed, B., Das Gupta, P., & Woodrow, K.A. (1993). Estimation of population coverage in the 1990 United States Census based on demographic analysis. *Journal of the American Statistical Association*, 88(3), 1061–79.

Royce, D. (1992). Incorporating estimates of census coverage error into the Canadian Population Estimates Program. In *Proceedings of the 1992 Annual Research Conference* (pp. 18–26). Washington, DC: US Census Bureau.

Siegel, J., & Zelnik, M. (1966). An evaluation of coverage in the 1960 census of population by techniques of demographic analysis and by composite methods. In *Joint Statistical Meetings Proceedings, Survey Research Methods Section* (pp. 71–85). Alexandria, VA: American Statistical Association.

Statistics Canada. (2007). *2006 Census Technical Report: Coverage*. Ottawa, Ontario: Statistics Canada.

Statistics Finland (2004). *Use of Registers and Administrative Data Sources for Statistical Purposes – Best Practices in Statistics Finland*. Helsinki: Statistics Finland.

Sweet, E. (1997). Using administrative records persons in the 1996 Community Census Test. In *Proceedings of American Statistical Association, Survey Research Methods Section* (pp. 416–21). Alexandria, VA: American Statistical Association.

Tracey, W. (1931). Reprinted from Dominion of Canada, Dominion Bureau of Statistics, *Seventh Census of Canada, 1931* (vol. II), Census Monograph No. 3. Ottawa, Ontario: Cloutier.

Turkish Statistical Institute. (2012). *The 2011 Population and Housing Census of Turkey*. Working Paper 18. UNECE-Eurostat Expert Group Meeting on Censuses Using Registers, Geneva, 22–23 May 2012. Geneva: UN Economic Commission for Europe.

(1964). *Record Check Studies of Population Coverage*. Series ER 60, No.2. Washington, DC: Author.

(1974). *Estimates of Coverage of Population by Sex, Race, and Age: Demographic Analysis*. Census Population and Housing: 1970 Evaluation and Research Program, PHC(E)-4. Washington, DC: US Government Printing Office.

US Bureau of the Census. (1960). *The Post-Enumeration Survey: 1950*. Technical Paper No. 4. US Washington, DC: US Census Bureau.

(2010). *The Development and Sensitivity Analysis of the 2010 Demographic Analysis Estimates*. Washington, DC: Author.

(2012). *Documentation for the Revised 2010 Demographic Analysis Middle Series Estimates*. Washington, DC: author.

United Nations Economic Commission for Europe. (2006). *Conference of European Statisticians Recommendations for the 2010 Censuses of Housing and Population*. Report ECE/CES/STAT/NONE/2006/4. Geneva: Author.

(2010). *Report of the Joint UNECE/Eurostat Expert Group Meeting on Register-Based Censuses (The Hague, The Netherlands, 10–11 May 2010)*. Report ECE/CES/2010/49. Geneva: Author.

(2012). *Report of the Joint UNECE/Eurostat Expert Group Meeting on Register-Based Censuses (Geneva, Switzerland, 22–23 May 2012)*. Geneva: Author.

United Nations Secretariat. (2009). *Final Report of the United Nations Regional Workshop on the 2010 World Programme on Population and Housing Censuses: Census Evaluation and Post-Enumeration Surveys (Addis Ababa, Ethiopia, 14–18 September 2009)*. New York: Author.

(2010a). *Post-Enumeration Survey Operations Guidelines*. New York: Author.

(2010b). *United Nations Regional Workshop on the 2010 World Programme on Population and Housing Censuses: Census Evaluation and Post-Enumeration Surveys (Bangkok, Thailand, 10–14 May 2010)*. New York: Author.

Valente, P. (2010). Census taking in Europe: how are populations counted in 2010? *Population & Societies,* 457. Paris: Institut National d'Études Démographiques.

Whitford, D., & Banda, J. (2001). *Post-Enumeration Surveys: Are They Worth It?* ESA/STAT/AC.84/13. New York: United Nations Secretariat.

4

Counting and estimating hard-to-survey populations in the 2011 Census

OWEN ABBOTT AND GARNETT COMPTON

4.1 Introduction

The census provides a once-in-a decade opportunity to get an accurate, comprehensive, and consistent picture of the population of the United Kingdom. Every effort is made to ensure everyone is counted. The field operation includes many different methods for attempting to count everyone within its overall strategy, and this can include targeting populations that are known to be hard to count. However, no census is perfect and some people are missed, particularly those from hard-to-count groups. These are not uniformly distributed across geography or important subgroups of the population, such as age and sex groups.

A key output from the census is local authority population estimates by age and sex. Local authorities are the 348 local government areas that vary in size from 5,000 to 1 million people. It is important that these census outputs are fit for the purposes they will be put to – for example, resource allocation where hard-to-count minority groups can be those that attract higher levels of funding. To address the likely census nonresponse, a survey-based approach is used to estimate the population that is missed, and the results are used to adjust the census dataset to include representation for that nonresponse. This approach was used successfully in the 2001 Census.

The 2011 Census program recognized the need to focus on both field and statistical methodologies in order to achieve its key strategic aims which included:

- Getting the national and local authority population estimates right;
- Maximizing overall response rates[1] and minimizing differences in response rates in specific areas and among particular population subgroups; and
- Providing high-quality, fit-for-purpose statistics that meet user needs and which are consistent and comparable across the UK.

To achieve these aims, the Office for National Statistics (ONS) outlined its overall census design in ONS (2008), its coverage assessment and adjustment strategy in Abbott (2007), and its strategy for quality assurance of the results in ONS (2009a).

---

[1] In this chapter, the term response rates relate to that obtained after follow-up and the field operations are complete.

This chapter first outlines the methodology for the 2001 and 2011 Censuses and describes how ONS delivered on its strategic aim for maximizing overall response and minimizing differences in response rates. It is this aim that guided most of the decisions on the strategies and practical procedures developed for the 2011 Census enumeration. It led to a census that focused more resources towards hard-to-count populations than previously. These interactions and change in emphasis will be highlighted throughout the chapter. Second, the chapter focuses on the operational design for collection that arose from the strategic aim, including the actions put in place for hard-to-count populations. Third, the chapter outlines the methodology for estimating the size and characteristics of the unobserved population and how this was also designed around the likely patterns of hard-to-count populations.

Finally, the chapter will summarize the results from the 2011 Census, published in July 2012. These will show the impact of the shift in strategy from the previous census and will demonstrate how well the hardest-to-count populations were counted initially and then measured a second time through the subsequent statistical process. We focus on the methodology and results for England and Wales. The 2011 Censuses in Scotland and Northern Ireland took different approaches for some parts of the implementation that are specific to their situation, but they share the same overall goals and methods for measuring nonresponse.

4.2   The 2001 and 2011 Censuses

2001 Census

The methodology for the 2001 Census was hand delivery of the forms followed by mailback; enumerators followed up nonreturns. A large post-enumeration survey (PES), called the Census Coverage Survey (CCS) was undertaken four weeks after Census Day to measure coverage, and the results were used to adjust the census database for undercount. The dataset was filled out to give representation for those missed, with the aim of producing a one-number census (ONC). This one-number methodology is not used universally. The 2001 Census was, in most respects and on the evidence available, successful. It produced robust local authority estimates across most of the UK. But for a relatively small number of local authorities, particularly some inner city ones, there is evidence that the methods used were not equal to the challenges they faced (Statistics Commission, 2004).

The response rate – defined as the census count obtained after follow-up divided by the census population estimates – was 94 percent. This was a decrease from the 1991 Census, which had a response rate of 96 percent. In addition, response rates in some hard-to-count areas were disappointing. Response in Inner London was estimated at 78 percent, while response exceeded 95 percent in almost two-thirds of local authorities in England and Wales. Nationally, it is estimated that about 88 percent of people aged 20–24 responded compared to over 97 percent among the over-55s (ONS, 2006).

In its overall evaluation of the 2001 Census, ONS (2005) describes how a higher than expected mailback rate (this is defined as the proportion of questionnaires returned by mail) caused a loss of control on the follow-up activities, leading to many unnecessary visits to householders who had already mailed their form. Pockets of extreme nonresponse were not resolved and so some areas had much lower response (after follow-up) than expected, and this was not discovered until after field work had finished.

Brown, Abbott, and Smith (2011) outlined the lessons from the 2001 ONC process that was designed to measure coverage of the 2001 Census. In the majority of cases, the process worked well, failing in only a small number of extreme cases where the estimates were revised.

2011 Census

The key issues raised in the evaluation reviews included recommendations for the 2011 Census to:

- Explore mailout methods to enable more effort to be focused on follow-up activities;
- Develop a high-quality and up-to-date address register to support questionnaire tracking and the field force;
- Adopt central control of field operations with rapid collation of management information to maximize the responsiveness of the follow-up operation and to identify low response areas early;
- Ensure greater stakeholder and local authority engagement so that any barriers to enumeration are identified and addressed at an early stage of planning;
- Review the coverage survey design to ensure it has sufficient sample in the areas likely to have lower response rates and that predicting these areas does not rely on out-of-date data.

The underlying challenges faced in 2001 would remain in 2011 but would be increased given changes over the decade:

- Increased migration;
- Changing living styles;
- More mobile population; and
- Aging population.

As a result, the 2011 Census methodology was a mailout (supported by a national address register) followed by mailback to a central location, the option of online completion, and targeted enumerator follow-up. As in the 2001 Census, a large CCS was undertaken six weeks after Census Day to measure coverage, and the results were used to adjust the census database for undercount with the aim of producing a one-number census. However, it was not called a one-number census to manage user expectations about any post-census revisions.

4.3   Maximizing response and minimizing variability in response

This chapter focuses on the strategic aim to maximize overall response and minimize differences in response rates in specific areas and among particular population subgroups.

The second part of this strategic aim was new for the 2011 Census. In previous censuses, the aim was to maximize response, with a limited focus on making sure there were no local authorities or localized areas with extremely low response, as there had never been any such occurrences. The lessons from 2001, outlined in Section 4.2, led ONS to review the aims of the field work, with a view to boosting response in the poorest areas. Alongside statistical research into improving coverage measurement methodology, including reviewing the CCS design, was an exploration of the impact of different field outcomes. Abbott (2009a) simulated the quality of population estimates (defined by the width of the confidence intervals around the estimates) given different response rate outcomes, and greater variability of response rates at lower levels of geography below local authority. The key factor was the exploration of response variation at low levels of geography. Previous models had only dealt with response rates at the local authority level (populations on average 150,000 people), whereas this model explored the impact when response varied across areas with 250 people.

The estimation process uses a ratio estimator (see Section 4.8), which assumes a linear relationship between the census count (the auxiliary) and the dual system estimate (the outcome variable). The variance of the estimator will therefore depend on both the slope of the fitted line and the residuals. The question was, in the census situation, whether it was better to try to reduce the slope of the line (i.e., the overall nonresponse) by maximizing response or reduce the residual variance (i.e., the variance of the nonresponse) by minimizing the variation in response rates.

Figure 4.1 shows the confidence interval width for the total population within five areas (each with a population of around half a million people), by the overall simulated response and the variability in response across the area. It shows that as census response increases, the

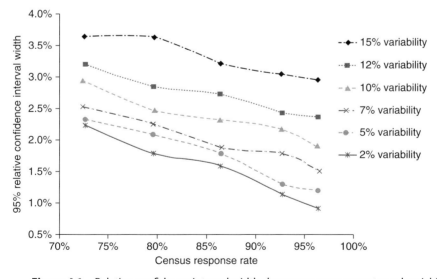

Figure 4.1 Relative confidence interval widths by census response rate and variability in response rates within a local authority

confidence interval width narrows and thus the quality of the population estimates increases. However, it also shows that it is sometimes better to have lower variation in response than a higher overall response. The variation in response therefore feeds directly into variation in the relationship and hence quality of the estimate.

These findings demonstrated a clear interaction between the variability of response achieved after follow-up and the quality of the results. If the field work could be managed to reduce the variation in response rates across small areas while at the same time increasing response, then the quality of the estimates would be maximized. For a fixed cost, this is likely to result in a lower overall response rate than under a strategy which attempts to maximize response rate. However, maximizing the overall response rate would be less likely to result in estimates which are of consistent quality, especially for local authorities, which do not have an even distribution of hard-to-count populations. As a result, the 2011 Census program adopted the aim of minimizing variability in response rates, while achieving overall target response rates, and developed an overall design to achieve those aims. These were the main components of the overall strategy:

- The hard-to-count index;
- Questionnaire content and design;
- Census collection design;
- Communications; and
- Coverage assessment.

4.4   The hard-to-count index

The hard-to-count (HtC) index was a national categorization of areas designed to predict the level of nonresponse. The index underpinned much of the census design. It was used in the allocation of field staff for the follow-up operation (Section 4.6.1), the sample design for the CCS (Section 4.8.1), and the coverage estimation process (Section 4.8.2). The HtC index was therefore an important component for controlling the variation in the quality of the estimates.

Mail return rates were predicted in order to plan follow-up. The prediction of the mail return rate in each area was based on the prevalence of factors associated with low enumeration identified from 2001. ONS (2009b) describes the area-level logistic regression models used to identify variables associated with nonresponse and to provide area-level predictions of nonresponse. The variables included:

- The proportion of people claiming Income Support or Jobseeker's Allowance;
- The proportion of young people;
- The proportion of people who are not "White British";
- The relative house price within a local authority; and
- The density of dwellings in an area.

The use of more up-to-date information addressed one of the 2001 CCS sample design problems encountered in areas of high change. The model predicted nonresponse rates for standard statistical areas called Lower Layer Super Output Areas (LSOAs) containing on average 750 households. LSOAs were grouped into five categories containing 40 percent, 40 percent, 10 percent, 8 percent, and 2 percent of the LSOAs. The design of the 40/40/10/8/2 categorization is partly driven by consistency with that used in 2001, but was more refined (the 2001 index had three levels with a 40 percent, 40 percent, 20 percent distribution and was based on information from a much smaller PES). The splitting of the top 20 percent into three groups was driven by the large variation in nonresponse rates within this group, and the choice of cut points was based on the distribution of the predicted nonresponse within the top 20 percent. In most local authorities (LAs), there were three HtC strata. The 2011 distribution provided a more localized index than the 2001 version, particularly in those harder-to-count areas.

4.5   Questionnaire content and design

Decisions about the content of the questionnaire were made with the goal of maximizing response from some of the key population groups that might be missed. As we noted, the UK Census relies mainly on a self-completion data collection instrument. It has long been recognized that such instruments need to be clear, coherent, easy to understand, jargon-free, and appealing to the general public (see Dillman, Smyth, & Christian, 2009). Having gathered user requirements, a comprehensive program of research and question testing was used to develop the design, concepts, instructions, and question wording. Throughout the development process, the emphasis was on the overall strategic aim.

This section outlines some of the key decisions and elements of the content and design.

4.5.1   Questionnaire content

An important consideration for any census is the collection base or residence rule, linking people to the places where they are to be counted. A de facto rule, in which the person is counted where he or she was on Census Day, provides no excuses for not completing a questionnaire. However, turning the results into counts based on a usual residence, or de jure, rule requires that additional questions be asked and additional processing be done. The 2001 Census used a usual residence rule, albeit without extensive instructions and limited collection of data about visitors. This might have contributed to the underenumeration. Some respondents may have misunderstood the rules and others may have actively chosen not to list themselves as usual residents.

The decision for the 2011 Census was to go somewhere between the two extremes. People were to be counted if they intended to stay in the UK for at least three months; the census also collected visitor information for those away from their usual residence on Census Night (excluding visitors in communal establishments, such as hotels). This would help to minimize those missed under a usual residence only rule, such as those who consider themselves not to have a usual residence (who were instructed to complete the questionnaire where they were on Census Night) and those who were there for less than a year (who were instructed to complete the questionnaire if they had been or intended on being there for three months or more). The explicit instructions, guidance, and publicity (see Section 4.7), enabled the respondent to recognize more easily that they were required to complete the questionnaire, thus improving response. ONS (2010a) outlined the development of the instructions and questions showing how the cognitive testing led to improvements in their design.

Information was also collected about people who had a second residence that they used for more than thirty days a year and the location of that residence. Again, this helped to make it clear to the respondent where they should be counted as a usual resident and thus improved completion rates in the right places for some residents who may have a second residence.

4.5.2   Questionnaire development

The questionnaire used in the 2011 Census was finalized following an extensive, four-year, program of consultation and testing to ensure that the questions asked met user requirements and were acceptable and understandable to respondents (ONS, 2009c).

Considerable effort was put into the design of the questionnaire. Research has shown that a well-designed questionnaire can improve response rates and the quality of answers. The questionnaire development followed standard procedures recommended for developing survey instruments for official statistics. This process included testing and iterative development of the questionnaire to ensure questions are meaningful and are understood in the same way by a wide range of respondents (Presser, Rothgeb, Couper, Lessler, Martin, Martin *et al.*, 2004). The questionnaire was tested via cognitive interviewing, which employs "verbal protocol" and probing questions to identify any difficulties with the questions or sources of potential measurement error (Willis, 1999).

4.6   Census collection design

Several aspects of the census design were implemented to address hard-to-count populations.

4.6.1   General enumeration procedures

The field strategy was designed to enable effective targeting of the follow-up process to assist and persuade nonresponders to complete the questionnaire. The 2011 Census used a mailout methodology to deliver questionnaires to all residential households, and asked households to mail back their completed questionnaire or complete the questionnaire online. The key component of the design was a targeted and flexible field force, ensuring that the follow-up resources were deployed to areas where mail return rates were lower than expected. Variation in return rates could be controlled both through the initial allocation of field staff and the quick movement of field staff during the field period as areas with low return rates became apparent. The initial allocation of field staff used the hard-to-count index described in Section 4.4 within a model which estimated the initial return rates and the difficulty of making contact with nonresponders. Households in harder areas received more field resource and hence more visits and assistance.

People living in communal establishments (such as military barracks, nursing homes, large student halls of residence, and prisons) were enumerated with traditional hand delivery of the questionnaire.

Each census questionnaire was recorded centrally as they were returned to provide daily information about nonresponding households, which told follow-up staff where to focus their efforts. In addition, these data allowed managers to identify pockets of low return and move resources to minimize return variability within their area. By design, this meant that follow-up in the highest responding areas was essentially stopped.

ONS tried to recruit collectors with the skills and experience relevant to the type of area and community they would be visiting. For example, using localized recruitment advertising aimed at particular ethnic groups. This was based on the idea that some groups of the population have more trust in people they can easily associate with, particularly for populations for which English is not their first language. Overall, the strategy was thought to be successful, with the ethnic mix of the field force broadly reflecting that of the population.

The ability of the field force to speak languages other than English was also a key element of the recruitment campaign, particularly in urban areas, where applicants were invited to provide details of other languages spoken. These language skills were used to provide additional doorstep support where language was a barrier.

4.6.2   Identification and prioritization of hard-to-count groups

Hard-to-count populations are by their nature specific and require special attention. Earlier, we described how ONS classified small areas according to their expected mail return rates. Here, we describe an additional step to increase the return rates among specific hard-to-count groups. These groups were identified and prioritized (see ONS, 2010b). Population groups were identified by size among groups that had poor response rates in the 2001 Census or through anecdotal evidence from literature reviews and engagement with local authorities and communities. Two lists of population groups were developed – those defined by their size and response rate from the 2001 Census and those groups based on anecdotal evidence.

Each group was then prioritized according to several criteria:

- The specific enumeration barriers identified for the group;
- Whether research and development work was required/planned for effective enumeration;
- Whether a multifaceted approach to targeting was required;
- And whether there was a substantial risk of poor enumeration regardless of the targeting.

Table 4.1 shows the prioritized groups identified through evidence of their size, levels of nonresponse, and characteristics that make them hard to count. Young adults were identified

Table 4.1 *Key population groups identified through evidence of size and nonresponse rate*

Priority	Group	Expected population size (millions)	Nonresponse rate in 2001 Census (percent)	Characteristics
High	Young adults aged 20–29	7.19	11.9	Accommodation variety,[a] contact issues,[b] mobility[c]
	Students	2.03	13.4	Accommodation variety, contact issues, mobility
	Short-term migrants	1.33	No data	Accommodation variety, engagement,[d] language,[e] contact issues, mobility
	Bangladeshi ethnic group	0.36	24.2	Concentrations in large cities, social and cultural perspectives,[f] language
	Black African ethnic group	0.73	29.1	Young population, concentrated in London, social and cultural perspectives, language
	Black Caribbean ethnic group	0.60	22.0	Young population, concentrated in London, social and cultural perspectives, language
Medium	Indian ethnic group	1.33	14.1	Young population, concentrated in cities, social and cultural perspectives, language
	Pakistani ethnic group	0.92	16.2	Concentrated in cities, social and cultural perspectives, language
	Chinese ethnic group	0.41	17.6	Social and cultural perspectives, language
	Long-term migrants	0.20	No data	Accommodation variety, languages, contact issues
	Multiple-occupied dwellings	1.50	17.0	Migrants, low-income populations, contact issues
Low	Pre-school	3.30	9.6	Young adult parents
	Private rented accommodation	4.65	9.8	Mobile, young adults, students, migrants
	One-person household	6.50	9.7	Young adults, contact issues
	Low-income household	9.98	No data	Unemployed, young, migrants, contact issues, engagement
	Adults aged 80+	2.84	3.6	Accommodation variety, contact issues, engagement

[a] The type of accommodation used by this group is not always of the standard type and can be difficult to find or classify.
[b] Contacting this group via mail or on the doorstep is very difficult.
[c] The population group is extremely mobile in terms of their usual residence.
[d] Engagement with this group is challenging.
[e] Language can be a barrier to enumeration.
[f] Social and or cultural issues can be a barrier to enumeration.

Table 4.2 *Key population groups identified through anecdotal evidence*

Priority	Group	Expected population size (thousands)	Characteristics
High	Gypsies/Travellers	42	Contact issues, mobility, engagement
	Illegal immigrants	430	Accommodation variety, contact issues, mobility, languages, engagement
Medium	Boarders/lodgers	Unknown	Missed at usual residence, inclusion
	People with more than one residence	241	Missed at usual residence
	Rough sleepers/homeless	2	Difficult to locate, contact issues, mobility, engagement
	Blind/visually impaired	310	Disability restricts completion
	Hearing impaired	8,978	Disability restricts completion
	Armed forces	194	Young people, missed at usual residence
	Prisoners	85	Young people, engagement, missed at usual residence
	Gated communities	Unknown	Access issues
	Caravan dwellers	Unknown	Contact issues, mobility, engagement
	Boaters	Unknown	Contact issues, mobility, engagement
Low	Visitors	Unknown	Inclusion, missed at usual residence
	Physically impaired	2,691	Disability restricts completion

as the highest priority due mainly to their size and their overlap with some of the other groups.

Table 4.2 shows the additional groups identified through anecdotal evidence gathered from census stakeholders and research. Gypsies and illegal immigrants were identified in the highest priority group due to the known challenge of engagement with government agencies.

Operational procedures or activities were put in place for each designated hard-to-count group as part of the census design. Depending on the type of population, there was one or more activities identified for that group. ONS (2010b) summarized the planned activities for each prioritized group. To provide a fuller picture of the actions actually undertaken in the 2011 Census, we provide more details for three specific groups – students in university halls of residence; the Indian population; and Gypsies and Travellers.

Students in university residence halls

The student population has traditionally been hard to count, particularly students at universities and those living in residence halls, given the complexity of their living arrangements. The concentrations of students in university towns can have a significant impact on the local census results. Recognizing the importance of these groups, the 2011 Census developed procedures specifically designed for the enumeration of students at halls of residence.

Residence halls were enumerated using the traditional method of hand delivery and hand collection. However, partnerships with universities and organizations representing students were established ahead of time to tailor the enumeration to best meet local challenges. Four tailored enumeration options were developed and universities were able to choose the option that best met their own situation. The four options were a mix of two delivery and two collection alternatives. The delivery options were for the student halls manager to deliver the questionnaires from a central point or named pigeon hole or for the student halls manager (or special enumerator) to deliver a questionnaire to each flat door or mail box. The collection options were either for the students to drop off their questionnaires at a central secure point or for the enumerator to receive access to the halls to collect the questionnaires individually.

Returns from individual students were tracked to inform the enumerator of which rooms had not returned a questionnaire. This information enabled the special enumerator to concentrate on visiting those rooms or engaging the assistance of the hall manager to encourage responses from nonresponding students.

In addition to these specific processes for students in halls of residence, engagement with the wider student community was supported by communication and other activities. These activities included:

- Student ambassadors on campus, who ran events to promote the benefits of the census;
- Advertising targeted at students in student locations, such as beer coasters and washroom posters in nightclubs;
- Competitions on some university marketing courses;
- Promotion on university television channels, radio stations, and websites.

Also, students are part of another hard-to-count population – the young. Besides the specific actions described here, additional initiatives for youth included commissioning a song from a rap artist, having a good online presence through social media, and youth magazine partnerships.

The Indian community

The UK has more than a million people who have an Indian background, and it is one of the communities that had a high nonresponse rate in the 2001 Census (around 14 percent). It was therefore identified as a hard-to-count population with medium priority.

ONS sought support and advice from national organizations including the Hindu Forum of Britain and Hindu Students Forum. Engagement with these organizations early in the census planning and the inclusion of areas with Indian communities in census tests helped foster interest in the outcomes of the 2011 Census. The development and testing of the question on ethnicity helped to ensure that engagement was ongoing.

During the field work, there were a language helpline, leaflets, and questionnaire translations that covered the many languages from the Indian subcontinent. To boost local publicity and community engagement, ONS employed seven community advisors to engage with the Indian community in areas with the highest concentrations. These advisors established geographically based community panels to engage, educate, and assist local communities and organizations. This included contacting and working with temples, luncheon clubs, and Saturday schools as well as talks to youth groups to take messages to their families.

There was also press and TV advertising targeted at Indian populations. These ads were broadcast on channels which had been recommended by the national organizations.

Travellers and Gypsies

Irish Travellers are a hard-to-count population characterized by high mobility (they live primarily in mobile caravans) and difficulty interacting with any form of authority. Although they are quite a small population (around 20,000 households), it was important to put in place a strategy for enumerating them as they tend to be clustered in particular areas.

For the first time, the question on ethnicity included a checkbox for "Gypsy or Irish Traveller." The inclusion of this category would provide better statistics for this group allowing measures of inequality.

Engagement with national organizations including the Gypsy Council was extremely important to ensure that ONS approached the enumeration in the right manner. Attendance at national Traveller events helped to raise awareness and make contact with community leaders, and ONS developed a census leaflet specific to Travellers, as well as attempting to recruit from the Traveller communities through their own websites.

Local authorities provide authorized sites for Travellers, and these were checked in advance of Census Day to establish the numbers of questionnaires to send. There are also known illegal sites, which were visited by special enumerators. The special enumerators prearranged visits to these sites, using help from local authority engagement officers to both deliver and collect questionnaires. Feedback from the census collectors indicates that the collection went well. The estimated population was 57,680 and the measured response rate was 90 percent.

4.7   Communication activities

The media tag line, "Help tomorrow take shape," was designed to invite everyone to participate in shaping the future of their local environment, in everything from key services such as health and education to local parks and facilities.

The national campaign was designed to reach the entire population in order to ensure maximum census awareness and to promote high levels of response. The challenge was to reach the target audience of 25.4 million households. The national publicity campaign used a broad mix of communication channels to attempt to expose everybody in England and Wales, at some point, to the census campaign via advertisements on TV and radio, billboard posters, online advertising, and in print. By the end of the campaign, some 86 percent of all adults had seen the advertisement(s), including 90 percent of those aged 75 or over, 80 percent of the Black and ethnic minority audience, and 77 percent of students.

All spoken languages were supported via a national helpline. Fifty-six languages were supported by written translations of the questions and web self-help leaflets. The decision about which languages should be supported was based on administrative data and data from translation services. The National Centre for Languages was also consulted. Census collectors offered these translation services where a local translator in the field team was not available.

Local authority and community engagement proved to be a real success of the communication strategy. Local authorities aided in developing and checking address lists, in promoting the benefits of the census and assisted in identifying and reaching local hard-to-count populations. Support and communication was provided via school and library activities; the census was promoted through newsletters, websites, and outreach teams; additional outdoor advertising was bought and featured census-branded templates.

These partnerships allowed ONS to cover not only the known disadvantaged groups, but also to target resource at areas known to have the characteristics associated with poor coverage.

4.8   Measuring nonresponse in the census

The 2011 Census was followed by a large coverage survey designed to measure nonresponse levels in the census with the aim of adjusting the census outputs to include the hard-to-count populations that were, despite best efforts, missed. The survey was used to estimate the total nonresponse, called the coverage assessment and adjustment process. This included all types of nonresponse, that is:

- People living in dwellings that were not included on the initial frame;
- Households who did not return a questionnaire by any means (mail, Internet, or during follow-up); and
- People who were omitted from returned questionnaires.

This is somewhat different from the approaches taken in some census-taking countries, where some imputation of responses for nonresponding households takes place prior to the assessment of nonresponse. In the US case, this is called count imputation. The strategy in the UK is to include all types of nonresponse and make a single overall adjustment.

This nonresponse represents the hard-to-count populations that the census missed. This section outlines the effort put into developing a methodology to measure nonresponse and enable the census dataset to be adjusted to include those estimated to have been missed.

Abbott (2007, 2009b) outlined the overall strategy for the coverage assessment and adjustment process in the 2011 Census. The main components of the methodology were:

(1) A Census Coverage Survey (CCS) was undertaken, independently of the census.

(2) CCS records were matched with those from the census using a combination of automated and clerical matching.

(3) The matched census and CCS data were used within a dual system estimator (DSE) framework to make estimates for large areas (known as Estimation Areas [EAs]); the DSE incorporated other reliable sources of data.

(4) Small area estimation techniques were used to make the local authority population estimates.

(5) Households and individuals estimated to have been missed from the census were imputed onto the census database, utilizing the CCS data on characteristics of those missed by the census. These adjustments were constrained to the LA estimates.

(6) All the population estimates were compared to estimates from demographic analysis, survey data, census information on visitors, qualitative information, and administrative data to ensure that the census estimates were plausible.

The following sections highlight those parts of the methodology specifically designed to tackle the hardest-to-count populations.

4.8.1   The Census Coverage Survey

The CCS is the key part of the coverage assessment methodology, providing data on those missed by the census.

The CCS begins with a sample of postcodes. A postcode is a collection of addresses defined by the Royal Mail for mail delivery purposes. They vary in size based upon the volume of mail. The CCS used a stratified two-stage sample, where the selected postcodes were independently re-enumerated. The first stage consisted of a sample of census output areas (homogeneous areas that contain around 125 households and which are used to construct the LSOAs described in Section 4.4), stratified by local authority and the hard-to-count index (obtained from the parent LSOA). The second stage selected a cluster of approximately half the postcodes from within each selected output area (see Brown *et al.*, 2011). The hard-to-count index stratification was an important aspect for controlling the variation in quality of the estimates, as the 2001 Census showed that undercount is disproportionately distributed across areas within LAs. The use of the index helped to control the spread of the sample and reduce the variance of the estimates.

The CCS sample design required a method to allocate the sample across the strata. Data on coverage patterns from the 2001 Census were used to allocate the sample. The allocation methodology, developed by Brown *et al.* (2011), used the observed 2001 nonresponse patterns to derive the expected variability of nonresponse within each stratum. This design data is used in an optimal allocation with constant costs; see Cochran (1977, pp. 98–99). A local authority that had high variability of response rates within its hard-to-count strata had a proportionally larger sample than LA's with lower variability. In addition, a local authority that had a large population or a high undercount in 2001 also had a proportionally larger sample. To ensure a conservative allocation, a minimum sample size constraint of one sampling unit within each HtC stratum of each LA was applied. This ensured representation for each LA. Finally, there was a maximum sample size constraint to ensure that areas that had extremely variable coverage did not have too large a sample.

This sample design strategy provided a design that spread the sample across different area types and also skewed the sample towards those areas where coverage was likely to be low and variable, so that the resulting estimates were based on a larger sample size.

The CCS involved an intensive re-enumeration of the population within the sample of postcodes. First, all the households were identified; then they were enumerated. The CCS questionnaire was administered by an interviewer to minimize the burden on the public. This was vital since the CCS, unlike the census, was a voluntary survey.

The survey was designed to ensure independence from the census and to obtain a high response rate. The identification of addresses did not use an address list; interviewers constructed their own frame by walking the streets, and contacting households to check their postcode. Interviewer listing was done to maximize the chance that an address missed from the census process (which used a pre-built address register) could be identified and enumerated by the CCS.

Interviewers were instructed to make as many calls as necessary to obtain an interview, and to call at different times and on different days to maximize the probability of making contact. The CCS also made use of some of the expert ONS social survey interviewers to provide assistance and advice in areas where contact rates were likely to be low or refusal rates were likely to be high.

The questionnaire included thirteen demographic questions for each individual, minimizing the length of interview so that it could be carried out on the doorstep. It included specific prompts for populations known to be missed, such as babies, people away on business, members of the armed forces, and anyone staying who had no other usual residence. In addition, there was also a self-completion questionnaire and mailback option, for households where contact was not made. This was used as a last resort towards the end of the field work and added around 6 percent to the interview rates.

Interviewer workloads were smaller in harder-to-count areas, reflecting the additional effort required to make contact in these areas. This classification of areas used the HtC index, along with information from the 2001 CCS about contact and interview rates. The workload size guidelines are shown in Table 4.3.

Table 4.3 *CCS interviewer workload size guidelines*

Hard to count	Minimum number of households	Maximum number of households
Easy	160	200
Medium	145	180
Hard	130	160
Very hard	100	120

Table 4.4 *Table of counts of individuals for dual system estimations*

		CCS		
		Counted	Missed	Total
Census	Counted	n_{11}	n_{10}	n_{1+}
	Missed	n_{01}	n_{00}	n_{0+}
	Total	n_{+1}	n_{+0}	n_{++}

Despite this, there were some areas where interview rates were lower than expected. To address this, the field work was extended and collectors moved into these areas to boost response rates (see ONS, 2012a for more detail).

4.8.2   Estimation

The census estimates were developed in three steps – the application of DSE, the derivation of Estimation Area totals, and the use of small area modeling to derive local authority totals. Some of the adjustments made to the estimates took account of the hardest-to-count population.

DSE, which was the approach used in 2001, was first used to estimate the population within the sample areas. The use of DSE required a number of conditions to be met to ensure the minimization of error in the estimates. These were fully discussed by Brown, Abbott, and Diamond (2006), and Mulry (Chapter 3 in this volume). After matching between the census and the CCS, a 2×2 table of counts of individuals was derived. This is given in Table 4.4.

This output from the matching process was used to estimate the undercount for the cluster of postcodes in each of the sampled output areas by age and sex. Given the assumptions, DSE combines those people counted in the census and/or CCS and estimates those people missed by both by a simple formula to calculate the total population as follows:

$$\text{DSE} = n_{++} = \frac{n_{1+} \times n_{+1}}{n_{11}}$$

This approach has been used widely for the estimation of wildlife populations (Seber, 1982) and for estimating undercoverage in the US Census (Hogan, 1993, 2003). It assumes that the proportion of CCS responders that were also counted in the census is identical to the proportion of CCS nonresponders who were in the census (this is the independence assumption). The full derivation of the DSE is given by Brown (2000).

Research by Brown and Sexton (2009) concluded that the application of the DSE at the cluster level (by age and sex) was relatively robust to small violations of the assumptions. However, violation of the assumptions can sometimes result in significantly biased estimates of the population. The 2001 Census showed that DSE tends to be biased downward (i.e., the estimates are always lower than they should be) due to any failure of these assumptions. Brown *et al.* (2006) developed a methodology to measure this bias and make adjustments to the dual system estimates. An updated version of that methodology was used to make corrections in the 2011 dual system estimates. This bias adjustment increased the estimated size of the "missed in both" cell of the DSE, which represent the hardest-to-count populations. The methodology was applied separately within each level of the hard-to-count index as the bias adjustment varied according to the particular population types that resided within each stratum.

A simple ratio estimator (which uses a straight line of best fit through the origin) was used to estimate the relationship in the sample between the census count and the dual system estimate for each age–sex group within each HtC stratum. The ratio estimator was not generally applied at the LA level due to sample size constraints; most LAs did not have sufficient sample sizes to allow LA-level estimates with acceptable precision. Such LAs were grouped together for estimation into Estimation Areas, formed by grouping contiguous LAs. The ratio estimator was then applied to obtain population estimates for the whole Estimation Area by the hard-to-count index and by age and sex. A synthetic estimator used the information from the whole Estimation Area to estimate LA level populations, making the assumption of identical coverage levels across LAs within the EA by HtC and age–sex strata.

4.8.3   National adjustment

When the first set of estimates for all Estimation Areas in England and Wales had been produced, the national census estimates for England and Wales were assessed for plausibility against alternative sources, such as health records, school rolls, demographic population estimates, surveys, and fertility rates. Evidence at the national level, consisting primarily of sex ratios from alternative sources, was used to assess the census estimates to examine whether there was any evidence of potential residual biases. This evidence showed that, while the numbers of females was plausible, the numbers of males aged 20–49 were outside the bounds of plausibility. As a result, age-specific sex ratios s_a were used to define an adjustment total, A_a, to the male age group estimates m_a by keeping the female estimates f_a fixed by the following procedure:

$$A_a = s_a f_a - m_a$$

A_a represents the number of missed males in age group a. The additional A_a males were allocated to EAs by HtC level, using the method outlined in ONS (2012b). The outcome was a multiplicative factor that was applied to the male age groups within each Estimation Area. Areas with high female undercount had high adjustment factors for the corresponding male estimates. This adjustment to the population estimates reflects the hardest-to-count populations that are not captured by the census and not identified adequately by the DSE.

4.8.4 Coverage adjustment

Following the production of the population estimates by age and sex, the census database was adjusted to take account of the estimated nonresponse. This was done using modeling followed by imputation. It is this process that estimates the nonresponse rates for variables other than geography and age–sex groups and provides a measure of how well the census counted hard-to-count subgroups (such as students or the Indian population).

The modeling process identified the characteristics of the nonresponding households and people based on variables other than geography, hard-to-count stratum, and age and sex; the additional variables included household tenure, household size, ethnicity, economic activity, migrant status, and marital status. These logistic regression models used the unmatched CCS records to predict the probabilities that a person with certain characteristics would be missed from the census (for example, the probability that a 20–24 year old male who was single, White, living in a privately rented house in the hardest-to-count stratum was missed). These predicted probabilities were then converted into nonresponse "weights" (by taking the reciprocal). These weights were calibrated to the population estimates at the LA level, as these population estimates were the higher-quality benchmark.

The weights were applied to the counts of individuals and these estimates drove the imputation process. For example, if there were 1,000 young males of the type noted above and the estimated weight for this group was 1.1, then we would expect the process to impute around 100 males of this type.

Modeling and imputation applied to both households and individuals. Wholly missed households were imputed, assigned a location based on the census household frame, and people within counted households were also imputed to account for those missed by the census. A similar methodology was employed in the 2001 census and the nonresponse rates in Table 4.1 were calculated from the fully adjusted database (the imputed records are equivalent to the total estimated number of people missed by the census). Table 4.1 shows how this results in different nonresponse rates for different characteristics from the 2001 Census. The 2011 Census response rates by ethnic group are shown in Section 4.9.

4.9   Response rates in the 2011 Census

A key target for the census was to achieve a 94 percent response for England and Wales overall and at least 80 percent in each local authority area. This was achieved. The person response rate for England and Wales was 94 percent, with response rates ranging from 82 percent to 99 percent by local authority.

Figure 4.2 below shows that the strategy used for the 2011 Census resulted in a reduction of the variability of person response rates across local authorities. As a result, all local authorities achieved a response rate of more than 80 percent in the 2011 Census, which was a significant improvement over the 2001 Census where thirteen local authorities had response rates lower than 80 percent. However, as expected, there were fewer local authorities with response rates over 96 percent as a result of the focus on the harder-

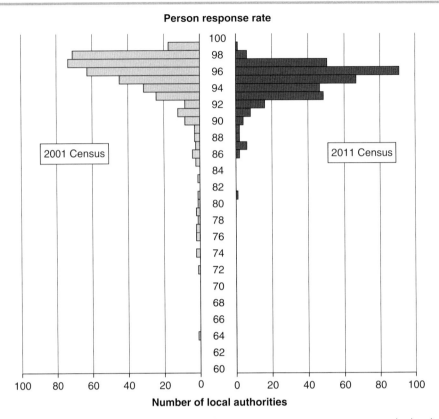

Figure 4.2   Comparison of 2001 and 2011 Census person response rates by local authorities

Note: The number of local authorities in 2001 was 376 compared with 348 in 2011.

to-count authorities. This was not an issue with stakeholders as it was made clear during engagement that this would be a likely outcome, and that overall the quality of the results would be more even.

Confidence intervals for the census population estimates were computed using a re-sampling (bootstrap) approach to provide estimates of quality for local authority total populations. Figure 4.3 shows the relative 95 percent confidence interval[2] width distribution across local authorities for the 2001 and 2011 Censuses. It indicates that the reduction in response variability, combined with the revised CCS sample design, has helped to reduce the variability in the confidence interval across the LAs in the 2011 Census. The 2011 distribution is less skewed and more evenly balanced. However, as for Figure 4.2, there were fewer local authorities with confidence intervals narrower than 1.5 percent as a result of their response rates being lower due to shifting resources from these areas into the harder-to-count authorities, and their sample sizes being smaller through the CCS sample design.

2 The relative 95 percent confidence interval is defined as the half width divided by the population estimate.

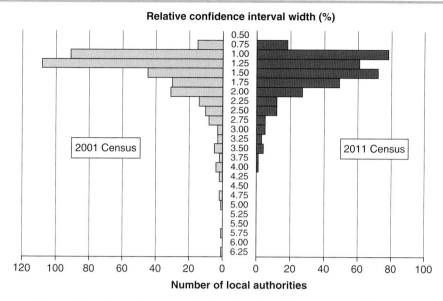

Figure 4.3   Distribution across local authorities of 95 percent confidence interval width for the 2001 and 2011 Censuses

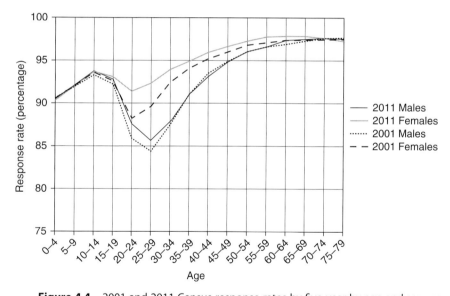

Figure 4.4   2001 and 2011 Census response rates by five year by age and sex group

Response rates by age and sex also show a similar improvement over the 2001 Census. Figure 4.4 shows the 2001 and 2011 response rates by age and sex. It shows that the 2011 Census was more successful at counting both young females and young males, especially those aged 20–29, where additional resources and priority was given to the enumeration. However, the differential response between males and females has widened in these groups.

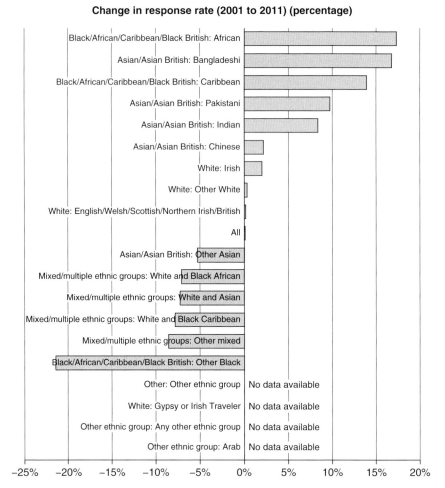

Figure 4.5   Difference between response rates in 2001 and 2011 Censuses by ethnic group

Response rates by ethnicity also show improvement over the 2001 Census. Figure 4.5 shows the change in response rates between the 2001 and 2011 Census by ethnic group. Not all categories are comparable due to differences in the question categories. It shows that for most key groups the response rates were improved, including the Indian population whose enumeration was described in Section 4.6.2. Response in the "mixed" and "other" categories was lower although these are small populations.

4.10   Conclusions

The design for the 2011 Census focused on improved methods for both counting and estimating the population of the UK. A series of measures was put in place to address the challenging enumeration of hard-to-count populations. These included language support, increased allocation of resources to harder-to-count areas, and a program of local community outreach. However, despite these efforts, it was recognized that the census would not count everyone and therefore a post-enumeration survey to measure coverage was required. For the UK, the CCS and the subsequent estimation process was an integral part of the strategy to measure the entire population, including the hard-to-count.

The 2011 Census employed a number of overlapping strategies to minimize variation in local response and maximize overall response. These overlapping activities make it difficult to evaluate the success of each activity independently. However, it is clear that differentiating areas and targeting the activities to the areas was successful. It is also clear that having a close link between the statistical and field methodology decisions, balancing the allocation of resources between easy- and hard-to-count populations, was critical to the overall success of achieving the strategic aims.

The results show that the strategy increased response rates in the hardest-to-count areas by a significant margin and provided high confidence in the estimates in these areas. This has led to results that are more uniform in quality and provide a better set of statistics for the country.

References

Abbott, O. (2007). 2011 United Kingdom Census coverage assessment and adjustment strategy. *Population Trends*, 127, 7–14. Retrieved from www.ons.gov.uk/ons/rel/po pulation-trends-rd/population-trends/no--127--spring-2007/population-trends.pdf.

(2009a). Precision of census estimates for different levels and patterns of census response. Unpublished paper. Available on request.

(2009b). 2011 United Kingdom Census coverage assessment and adjustment methodology. *Population Trends*, 137, 25–32. Retrieved from www.ons.gov.uk/ons/rel/po pulation-trends-rd/population-trends/no--137--autumn-2009/population-trends.pdf.

Brown, J. J. (2000). Design of a census coverage survey and its use in the estimation and adjustment of census underenumeration. Unpublished doctoral dissertation, University of Southampton.

Brown, J., Abbott, O., & Diamond, I. (2006). Dependence in the one-number census project. *Journal of the Royal Statistical Society: Series A (Statistics in Society)*, 169, 883–902.

Brown, J., Abbott, O., & Smith, P. (2011). Design of the 2001 and 2011 census coverage surveys for England and Wales. *Journal of the Royal Statistical Society: Series A (Statistics in Society)*, 174, Part 4, 881–906.

Brown, J., & Sexton, C. (2009). *Estimates from the Census and the Census Coverage Survey*. Paper presented at the 14th Government Statistical Service Methodology Conference, London. Retrieved from www.ons.gov.uk/ons/media-centre/events/ past-events/conference/population-estimates-from-the-census-and-census-coverage-survey-paper.pdf.

Cochran, W. G. (1977). *Sampling Techniques* (3rd edn.). New York: John Wiley & Sons.

Dillman, D. A., Smyth, J. D., & Christian, L. M. (2009). *Internet, Mail and Mixed Mode Surveys: The Tailored Design Method* (3rd edn.). Hoboken, NJ: John Wiley & Sons.

Hogan, H. (1993). The 1990 Post-Enumeration Survey: operations and results. *Journal of the American Statistical Association*, 88, 1047–60.

(2003). The accuracy and coverage evaluation: theory and design. *Survey Methodology*, 29, 129–38.

Office for National Statistics (2005). *Census 2001 General Report for England and Wales*. Retrieved from www.ons.gov.uk/ons/guide-method/census/census-2001/design-and-conduct/review-and-evaluation/evaluation-reports/general-report/index.html.

(2006). *Census 2001 Quality Report for England and Wales*. Retrieved from www.ons.gov.uk/ons/guide-method/census/census-2001/design-and-conduct/review-and-evaluation/evaluation-reports/quality-report/census-2001-quality-report.pdf.

(2008). *2011 Census: Strategic Aim and Key Research in England and Wales*. Retrieved from www.ons.gov.uk/ons/guide-method/census/2011/the-2011-census/the-2011-census-project/design-for-the-census/2011-census--strategic-aims-and-key-research-in-england-and-wales.pdf.

(2009a). *2011 Census Data Quality Assurance Strategy*. Retrieved from www.ons.gov.uk/ons/guide-method/census/2011/the-2011-census/processing-the-information/data-quality-assurance/2011-census---data-quality-assurance-strategy.pdf.

(2009b). *Predicting Patterns of Household Nonresponse in the 2011 Census*. Census Advisory Group paper AG(09)17. Retrieved from www.ons.gov.uk/ons/guide-method/census/2011/the-2011-census/processing-the-information/statistical-methodology/predicting-patterns-of-household-non-response-in-the-2011-census.pdf.

(2009c). Report of a privacy impact assessment conducted by the Office for National Statistics for the 2011 Census of England and Wales. Retrieved from www.ons.gov.uk/ons/guide-method/census/2011/the-2011-census/the-2011-census-project/commitment-to-confidentiality/privacy-impact-assessment--pia--on-2011-census.pdf.

(2010a). *Final Recommended Questions for the 2011 Census in England and Wales: Enumeration Base Questions, Usual Residence, Short-term UK Residents and Visitors*. Retrieved from www.ons.gov.uk/ons/guide-method/census/2011/the-2011-census/2011-census-questionnaire-content/question-and-content-recommendations/final-recommended-questions-2011---enumeration-base.pdf.

(2010b). *Framework for Getting the Count Right for Key Population Target Groups*. Retrieved from www.ons.gov.uk/ons/guide-method/census/2011/the-2011-census/census-consultations/working-with-communities-and-local-authorities/framework-for-getting-the-count-right-for-key-target-population-groups.pdf.

(2012a). *2011 Census Coverage Survey: Evaluation Report*. Retrieved from www.ons.gov.uk/ons/guide-method/census/2011/how-our-census-works/how-did-we-do-in-2011-/evaluation---census-coverage-survey.pdf.

(2012b). *Making a National Adjustment to the 2011 Census*. Retrieved from www.ons.gov.uk/ons/guide-method/census/2011/census-data/2011-census-data/2011-first-release/first-release--quality-assurance-and-methodology-papers/making-a-national-adjustment-for-residual-biases.pdf.

Presser, S., Rothgeb, J. M., Couper, M. J., Lessler, J. T., Martin, E., Martin, J., *et al*. (2004). *Methods for Testing and Evaluating Survey Questionnaires*. Hoboken, NJ: John Wiley & Sons.

Seber, G. A. F. (1982). *The Estimation of Animal Abundance and Related Parameters* (2nd edn.). London: Edward Arnold.

Statistics Commission. (2004). Census and population estimates, and the 2001 Census in Westminster: final report. Report no. 22. London: Author.

Willis, G. B. (1999). *Cognitive Interviewing: A Tool for Improving Questionnaire Design*. London: Sage.

5

A review of quality issues associated with studying hard-to-survey populations

LARS LYBERG, MATHEW STANGE, JANET HARKNESS,
PETER MOHLER, BETH-ELLEN PENNELL, AND LILLI JAPEC

5.1 Introduction

Some populations/groups are defined as hard to survey (H2S) in the research literature because of difficulty sampling the population, accessing the population, contacting members of the population, persuading them to participate, and interviewing group members (see Tourangeau, Chapter 1 in this volume). Reviewing the literature on populations referred to as "hard to survey" indicates the types of studies undertaken with these populations, the survey error challenges, and the methodological solutions used by researchers who study such populations. The H2S literature, however, does have limitations and research gaps exist.

The problems that complicate obtaining high-quality data from H2S populations are diverse and often interrelated. This review uses a quality assurance and quality control framework to discuss the total survey error associated with H2S studies. The discussion is based on an extensive systematic review of the quantitative and qualitative literature related to H2S, as well as our own experiences surveying these populations. (For a discussion and definition of kinds of H2S populations and the characteristics that earn them the H2S label, see Chapter 1 in this volume.)

We identify literature from various disciplines, relate these to the H2S challenges, and note which solutions are proposed or criticized. In the overview of challenges and practices, we also identify research gaps and general limitations that need to be addressed. Here, we consider types of error and survey process stages less frequently discussed or for which concrete data and solutions are sparse. We identify pertinent quality assurance/control steps to address such gaps and point to tools to remedy important measurement and documentation deficits. We hope that our systematic review can generate improved practices for surveying H2S populations.

Our literature review on H2S populations entailed searching keywords related to the topic in academic search databases, including Academic Search Premier/EBSCO, JSTOR, and

Five survey research and methodology students and three survey research and methodology professors and professionals undertook an appraisal process for this chapter. The students were Mathew Stange, A. Lynn Phillips, Nick Ruther, and Ipek Bilgen from University of Nebraska–Lincoln; Jennifer Kelley, Daniel Tomlin, and Kristen Cibelli from University of Michigan; and Olle Wredenfors from Stockholm University.

ProjectMUSE.[1] All articles were exported to RefWorks to save each citation. RefWorks was used to identify and remove duplicate articles. A copy of each article was also saved to a secure server at the University of Nebraska–Lincoln. The literature search returned 516 articles, but not all were actually relevant. A review of the articles eliminated reviews, editorials, and other articles that merely mentioned the keywords but which did not deal with H2S populations. We also dropped papers in which the target populations were not actually H2S, but are easily accessed "exotic" populations (e.g., hospital patients in Darfur; see Boccia, Guthmann, Klovstad, Hamid, Tatay, Ciglenecki *et al.*, 2006). In all, 227 articles were reviewed.

The literature search included both quantitative and qualitative research from various social and behavioral science fields and public health. The majority of articles came from the public health field. The databases returned peer-reviewed journal articles from these fields of study.

Our literature review had five specific objectives:

(1) To document how "hard-to-survey" populations are described;
(2) To identify the reasons groups are seen as "hard to survey";
(3) To identify the methodological challenges for research on such groups;
(4) To find the methodological solutions proposed; and
(5) To identify research gaps in the literature regarding methodological challenges and/or solutions.

Information from the articles was recorded in a database, including bibliographic details, review details, features of the study, H2S population description, survey error challenges, document characteristics, methodological solutions proposed or mentioned, and reviewer assessment.

5.2   The H2S survey life cycle

The survey life cycle consists of a sequence of processes where each process is a potential error source. The sequence can be described in many different ways. We have chosen a description (see Figure 5.1) that we developed to illustrate various quality assurance and quality control issues in surveys.

During each stage of the planning, there may be new insights about the feasibility of the survey design, leading to repeated revisions of the research goals, the definition of the target population, the questionnaire, sampling design, training procedures, mode choice, and so on. Once a preliminary design is agreed upon, the process steps are executed more or less in sequence, from determining the research goals to the dissemination of data.

---

1 The keywords included: "hard to reach," "hard to survey," "hard to interview," "hard to access," "hard to sample," "difficult to reach," "difficult to survey," "difficult to interview," "difficult to access," "difficult to sample," "special group(s)," "special population(s)," "elusive group(s)," "elusive population(s)," "evasive group(s)," "evasive population(s)," "hidden group(s)," and "hidden population(s)."

The Survey Life Cycle

Figure 5.1   Survey life cycle steps

   Ideally, the design chosen should be one that produces estimates with the smallest possible mean squared errors. This criterion leads to a design that takes all major error sources into account, not just, say, sampling. This implies that any organization conducting surveys must have a system for quality assurance and quality control in place (Lyberg & Biemer, 2008). The terms quality assurance and quality control tend to be used interchangeably but there is a distinction between the two. Quality assurance (QA) in a survey context means that processes are designed to deliver good products. One example of QA in data collection using interviewers is to have an interviewer training program in place. Quality control (QC) ensures that the product quality actually is good. In our interview example, this might entail monitoring of the interviewers. For each process, it is possible to define more than one QA and QC approach and often we need more than one to get good quality products. There are textbooks, such as Biemer and Lyberg (2003) and Groves, Fowler, Couper, Lepowski, Singer, and Tourangeau (2009), that list QA and QC approaches for many, but not all, of the process steps. For instance, if we want examples of QA and QC in the process of translating questions and other survey materials we would have to go to other sources, such as Harkness, Villar, and Edwards (2010). Sometimes, it is possible to do QC by collecting and analyzing process data or paradata, thereby checking whether a process is performing in a stable and predictable way (Lyberg & Couper, 2005).

An H2S survey is not any different from other surveys when it comes to the various design steps. The crucial step in an H2S survey is accessing the target population and that process is more complicated and consumes more resources than in other surveys. QA and QC approaches should basically be the ones provided in survey textbooks. What we have observed, though, is that data quality perspectives are frequently missing in the design of H2S surveys. At least, it is very unusual that quality issues besides sampling and non-response are discussed. This is not a satisfactory state of affairs. As long as H2S populations are investigated using survey methods, the fundamentals of the survey profession still apply even under the most difficult of circumstances.

5.3   The H2S literature

The H2S literature is often linked to the literature on sampling rare populations. The latter literature concerns situations where no single frame of the members of the rare population exists at the outset and examines a number of methods either to estimate the size of the rare population or to estimate the characteristics of this population. Methods proposed include screening from a larger population, disproportionate sampling, multiplicity sampling, using multiple frames, and snowballing or reputational sampling (see Kalton, Chapter 19 in this volume; Kalton, 2003, 2009; see also Kalton & Anderson, 1986; Kish, 1965; Sudman, Sirken, & Cowan, 1988). All these methods assume that a probability sample can be drawn, albeit with some coverage error. The rare trait in this literature does not necessarily have to be something socially undesirable or stigmatizing. It is just rare and could be, say, active birdwatchers in Nevada, people in Botswana with very high incomes, or Baltimore Orioles fans living in Europe. But the trait can, of course, also be a sensitive or stigmatizing one and members of the rare population might not be interested in being researched. This is when the problem of rarity goes from one of identifying and observing members of the rare population to one of actually reaching and persuading members to participate in the research. Typically, we also go from probability sampling to various forms of nonprobability sampling when we move from just "rare" to H2S. Often, these populations are called "hidden" and involve groups such as homeless people, prostitutes, men who have sex with men, people with rare diseases, migrants, and linguistic minorities. One can easily imagine that the main problems associated with this move are first to locate population members and then to study them using some kind of sampling scheme that at best resembles a probability sample. Many of the studies are not even surveys as we know them. Admittedly, there is a grey zone between these two literatures and considerable overlap (i.e., some of the rare population literature also covers issues involving hidden populations).

The research literature involving H2S populations covers a wide range of academic fields. The majority of the published literature reviewed under our search criteria comes from the public health field with many of the studies focusing on HIV/AIDS research. To a much lesser extent, articles come from the fields of sociology, anthropology, education, statistics, psychology, and survey research. The studies in these articles include surveys, program/ service evaluations, descriptions of outreach programs, and qualitative studies. Methodological studies are limited in this literature. Predominately, the H2S literature includes substantive research that sometimes discusses methodological issues, but the discussion is limited and substantive results are primary.

Both qualitative and quantitative methods are used by researchers to study H2S groups. The qualitative studies reviewed focused on understanding and describing the experiences of the groups. These studies often have small sample sizes and use convenience or purposive samples. As such, the generalizability is limited; however, the studies provide rich, descriptive information about the target populations and research questions explored. The methodological lessons to be learned from qualitative studies are relevant for understanding issues related to access, question wording, contacting groups, persuading H2S groups to participate in research, as well as issues encountered when interviewing H2S populations. Quantitative studies tend to use surveys and at least attempt to use probability sampling. Still, some survey research studies involving H2S groups as target populations use non-probability sampling methods, which limit the generalizability of the findings. But the possibility of bias is still present when probability techniques, such as venue-based sampling, are used; selecting too few venues or only venues of a certain type can bias the generalizability of the findings to the target population. However, these studies often still provide valuable information.

The characteristics that make populations more difficult to research are often interdependent. For example, undocumented immigrants have irregular legal status which can lead to distrust of researchers, particularly researchers associated with the government. Undocumented immigrants might also have language and cultural barriers that lead to being deemed H2S by researchers.

5.3.1 Methodological solutions

The methodological solutions provided in the H2S literature are to a large extent confined to contacting and sampling the members of the populations of interest. Here are some examples of solutions.

Community-based research

Using community-based methods or participant-based research is one method employed by researchers studying H2S populations (Coady, Weiss, Galea, Ompad, Glidden, & Vlahov, 2007; Garland, Spalek, & Chakraborti, 2006). Partnering with organizations involved with H2S populations can foster trust and provide access to the population (Flanagan & Hancock, 2010). Partnering with the H2S population itself is another option. For instance, Lavelle, Larsen, and Gundersen (2009) discuss partnering with American Indian organizations and tribal councils.

Innovative sampling methods

When the research goal is to estimate the size of the H2S population, the most common method is some adaptation of the capture–recapture technique originally developed to estimate the size of animal populations. For instance, in an attempt at estimating the size of the population of marijuana cultivators in Quebec, the sampling method used information on recurring patterns observed among cultivators, such as frequency of re-entry into treatment or frequency of re-arrest (Bouchard, 2007).

When the research problem is to estimate characteristics of the H2S population, the usual procedure is to use some kind of venue-based sampling. One variant used when studying men who have sex with men is called time-space sampling (Stueve, O'Donnell, Duran, San Doval, & Blome, 2001) and is conducted in three steps. First, a probability sample of venues where members tend to congregate is selected. Then, a specific day and time period associated with each selected venue is randomly chosen. Finally, selected venues are visited during the chosen time slots and members are screened and asked to participate. Another common approach is to use some kind of respondent-driven sampling, variants of which are called snowball sampling and chain-referral sampling (Heckathorn, 2007; Lansky, Abdul-Quader, Cribbin, Hall, Finlayson, Garfein *et al.*, 2007; Salganik & Heckathorn, 2004; see Thompson, Chapter 24 in this volume).

A prerequisite for these schemes is that a sample is possible since members know each other. These schemes start with a number of "seeds" that are interviewed and then asked to recruit a limited number of other members of the H2S population they belong to. New recruits in turn are asked to recruit a limited number of other members and the process continues until the desired sample size is obtained or the survey period is over. More recently, attempts have been made to recruit samples via websites. It turns out that websites can add H2S members who tend not to frequent popular venues or whose networks are limited or nonexistent (Johnston, Trummal, Lohmus, & Ravalepik, 2009).

The recurring problem with these schemes is to establish how closely they resemble probability sampling methods.

Qualitative methodologies

Qualitative methods are often used by researchers of H2S populations. These include case studies (e.g., Dunlap, Golub, & Johnson, 2003; Greenhalgh, Collard, & Begum, 2005; Jones & Allebone, 1999), focus groups (e.g., Armstrong, 2003; Horwitz, Roberts, & Warner, 2008; Vyavaharkar, Moneyham, & Corwin, 2008), and semi-structured and in-depth interviews (e.g., Dowrick, Gask, Edwards, Aseem, Bower, Burroughs *et al.*, 2009; Flanagan & Hancock, 2010; Han, Kang, Kim, Ryu, & Kim, 2007). Qualitative studies provide insight into the experiences of a population and do not require large sample sizes (Creswell, 2007). Thus, researchers can still study a group that is difficult to sample using probability techniques. Although generalizability is limited, generalizations are not the aim of most qualitative research (Creswell, 2007; Merriam, 2009). Qualitative research of H2S populations, nonetheless, can provide insight for developing quantitative studies.

Ethics and confidentiality

Adhering to ethical practices and using confidential settings are also advocated in this literature (e.g., Agustín 2007; Bodenmann, Vaucher, Wolff, Favrat, de Tribolet, Masserey *et al.*, 2009; Faugier & Sargeant, 1997; Garland *et al.*, 2006; Pettifor, 1979). Ethical considerations and confidentiality are important to help establish trust; mistrust can introduce measurement and nonresponse errors because of socially desirable responses, refusals, and break-offs.

Administrative data

Coleman, Rajabiun, Cabral, Bradford, and Tobias (2009) suggested using medical record data to obtain some information about their target population of HIV positive individuals who were at risk of dropping out of care.

Cultural awareness

When populations are H2S because of cultural and language barriers, researchers suggest making data collection instruments and outreach "culturally appropriate" (Coady *et al.*, 2007) and providing interviewers "cultural sensitivity" training (Greenfields, 2009). This can also develop trust and help overcome cultural and linguistic barriers that make some populations H2S.

Data collection

Certain tools or methods may be necessary when surveying H2S populations. A small number of the articles in the systematic review were explicit methodological studies. For example, de Leeuw, Hox, and Kef (2003) investigated the use of computer-assisted self-interviewing for special populations and their results indicate that self-administered surveys are feasible with some H2S groups. Other research by Blair and Czaja (1982) investigated the use of random digit dialing (RDD) for sampling H2S subpopulations.

5.3.2   Limitations of the H2S literature

The research literature involving H2S populations has its limitations. There is sparse documentation of methods used in research. For example, details of translation, questionnaire design, interviewer training, and even sampling are sometimes lacking. Other times, the importance of being "culturally aware" is stressed, but little is said about how this is accomplished. Qualitative research often lacks a description of the qualitative approach used and assumptions of the approach. Another criticism of the H2S literature is that general-izations are sometimes made beyond the scope of what generalizations can reasonably be made given the methods employed.

Many studies are limited in scope. Target populations are often restricted to small geo-graphical areas, such as cities, neighborhoods, and counties and they are sometimes vaguely defined, such as "HIV-infected individuals who are underserved and not in care or face risk of dropping out of care" (Coleman, *et al.*, 2009), "team leaders and practitioners from voluntary community service organizations" (Flanagan & Hancock, 2010), "low income women 40+" (Freimuth, 1995), "Spanish speaking cancer patients" (Canales, Ganz, & Coscarelli, 1995), "off-reservation Navajo families" (Hossain, 2001), and "non-English speaking women living in under-resourced and multi-ethnic boroughs" (Greenhalgh, Collard, & Begum, 2005). Some studies are extremely small with fewer than fifty partic-ipants (e.g., Hossain, 2001; Schroepfer, Matloub, Creswell, Strickland, & Anderson, 2009; Toktaş, 2006).

The client or user of the H2S research is more or less absent in the reporting of results. We are sure that the results are used but seldom are the discussions between the researchers and other stakeholders described. One might think that such discussions might lead to contin-uously improved research methods but that does not seem to be the case. Admittedly, sampling procedures have become more standardized, where the target population is thoroughly investigated and defined before any contact attempts are made (Johnston *et al.*, 2009). The National Behavioral Surveillance System that studies injecting drug users in twenty-five US Metropolitan areas (Lansky *et al.*, 2007) has many sophisticated features in place, such as formative assessment, pilot studies, literature reviews, expert consultation, standardized recruitment procedures, eligibility assessment, defined adminis-tration processes, and data management processes, and explicitly takes into account some sources of errors not usually dealt with in the H2S literature.

But a majority of studies discard the total survey error perspective. Many authors seem to have a research background with very limited survey methodology. Issues and phenomena such as social desirability bias, choice of data collection mode, interviewer training, quality control and validation, monitoring, pretesting, replication, and translation are not discussed in most studies. There are exceptions, of course. Computer-assisted self-interviewing (CASI; de Leeuw *et al.*, 2003) and audio-CASI (Cherry and Rost, 2009) are used occasion-ally to combat social desirability bias. In some situations, coverage can be extensively improved by using spatial sampling. Modern GPS can identify small units with great precision, a technique that can be suitable for minority populations (Landry & Shen, 2005). It is easy to understand the complexities of some of the research situations. The major practical problem is to access a reasonable part of the target population, one that can be sampled even though a substantial coverage problem may remain. The next problem is how to approach potential respondents. A recurring theme is that trust must be established and the moment of contact becomes crucial. Venue sampling is especially demanding for interviewers and researchers. It is not only difficult to screen and motivate respondents, the work environment is sometimes dangerous for all involved. This was the case when studying female street sex workers in Cape Town (Pauw & Brener, 2003) and men on the "down low" (Icard, 2008). In such situations, issues such as question wording and inter- viewer variance are not the first things on the interviewer's mind.

Having said that, we must emphasize that the purpose of all quantitative survey studies is to make inferences to a target population. The basic processes need QA and QC approaches. We are convinced that a lot of that work can be conducted at the planning stage and in a safe environment. A continued neglect of total survey error issues will not generate a continuous quality improvement of H2S research methods. Involving survey methodologists to a greater extent than is currently the case is one possible approach.

Qualitative studies can be improved by being more explicit about the approach used and the limitations of the research methods. Creswell (2007) and Merriam (2009) both outline the methods of different qualitative research approaches and the limitations and assumptions of each. These books on qualitative methods highlight the documentation needed in qualitative studies and how to write up the results without violating assumptions of the methods used in the research (e.g., making generalizations from case studies). In some of the qualitative studies included in our review, authors do not seem to be really clear about the purpose of the exploratory study and what the next steps should be.

Since we coded up all 227 studies, it is possible to provide a few summary statistics that underscore some of our arguments about the relatively low quality of many of these studies. Only 7 percent were specifically survey research or statistics articles. Many – 42 percent – of the studies were qualitative. A majority of the studies (54 percent) used nonprobability sampling. Probability sampling was used in only 7 percent of the studies. With the remainder, it was not really possible to understand fully the sampling procedures used.

5.4   H2S design, implementation, and quality assurance

Research studies of H2S populations involve various challenges that can lead to survey error. These include both errors related to measurement (construct validity, measurement errors, and some processing errors) and errors related to representation (coverage error, sampling error, and nonresponse error).

5.4.1   Error sources in the total survey error perspective

Construct validity (specification error)

Specification error occurs when the concept implied by the survey question(s) and the concept that should be measured in the survey differ. For instance, when faced with cultural and language barriers, H2S populations require questions to be translated or adapted to the specific context to overcome these barriers. The questions, however, might not be translated appropriately or they may not be culturally appropriate to the target population (Andresen, Diehr, & Luke, 2004; Garland *et al.*, 2006). Therefore, the intended constructs might not be measured.

Measurement error

Often, research with H2S populations involves asking sensitive questions, for example, asking sex workers and HIV-positive individuals about sexual behaviors. Misreports and social desirability biases are likely with sensitive questions asked of H2S populations (Agustin, 2007; Cáceres & Rosasco, 1999; Chavez, Edwards, & Oetting, 1989; Koné, Sullivan, Senturia, Chrisman, Ciske, & Krieger, 2000). Lack of trust of researchers, which can make the population H2S, can also lead to measurement errors (Coe, Gibson, Spencer, & Stuttaford, 2008; Stueve *et al.*, 2001). In this case, social desirability bias might be heightened if respondents are less likely to provide accurate reports because they distrust the researchers. Also other measurement errors related to the response process are common, as they are in virtually all types of surveys.

Coverage error

Coverage error is possible when relatively large parts of the target populations are missing from the sampling frames (Hidaka & Operario, 2006). Sometimes, there is no sampling frame available or the coverage of the frames is poor for H2S populations. For example, Lavelle *et al.* (2009) note that mail and telephone frames are poor for surveying American Indians. When a population is described as H2S because of difficulty identifying the population, this also leads to coverage errors. Chavez, Hubbell, Mishra, and Valdez (1997) describe this difficulty when surveying undocumented Latina immigrants in Orange County, California. Factors such as tenuous legal status and not wanting to reveal group members can produce issues in screening for a H2S population. Lack of trust of researchers can lead to misreporting when respondents are asked if an individual belongs to a group. This measurement error in turn produces coverage error.

Sampling error

Small sample sizes and nonprobability sampling techniques used in H2S populations research limit the generalizability of findings (Barkan, Melnick, Preston-Martin, Weber, Kalish, & Miotti *et al.*, 1998; Ennett, Bailey, & Federman, 1999). Bias may also arise from the sampling method used. For example, targeted location sampling (i.e., venue-based sampling) might mean people included in the sample differ on the variables of interest from people who are members of the target population, but who do not frequent the locations on the sampling frame and thus have no chance of being selected. Examples are studies of men who have sex with men using time–space sampling (Stueve *et al.*, 2001). Men sampled at places such as gay bars might be different on the variables of interest from men who have sex with men but who do not frequent the locations used for sampling in the study. In Ford, Weiss, Kipke, Ritt-Olson, Iverson, and Lopez's (2009) study of young men who have sex with men (YMSM), the venue-based sampling method produced a sample in which 89 percent of the participants reported visiting a gay bar or club in the previous three months.

This might not be representative of the general YMSM population and the method might not be feasible in locations in which the gay community is not highly visible.

Nonresponse error

Nonresponse occurs when sampled individuals do not respond to a survey (unit nonresponse) or do not respond to specific questions on a questionnaire (item nonresponse). Our review of the H2S research literature indicates that nonresponse often occurs when members of the target population are difficult to recruit or persuade to participate because they do not trust the research or the researchers. For example, not gaining response of undocumented immigrants was attributed to "mistrust" in a study by Bodenmann *et al.* (2009). Stigmatized status can also contribute to nonresponse if members of the target population do not wish to reveal their membership in the group (such as drug users or individuals with HIV). In these cases, social desirability contributes to concealing membership. Nonresponse bias would be introduced if those members of the target population who fail to respond are different on statistics of interest from members of the target population that do respond. Social desirability can also contribute to item nonresponse if respondents refuse to answer a question to avoid appearing in an unfavorable light.

Processing errors

Processing errors occur when errors are made in processes such as data capture (scanning and keying), coding of open-ended responses, and weighting of the survey data. Sometimes, statistical disclosure techniques must be administered to preserve confidentiality. By and large, though, these are error sources that are no different from those in other surveys. The important thing for H2S researchers is to know that these error sources exist and that standard methods for dealing with them must be used.

A general discussion of the total survey error paradigm is given in Groves and Lyberg (2010).

5.4.2   Organizational and operational issues

In this section, we review the various steps in the survey life cycle and comment on aspects of QA and QC that are potentially useful in H2S research.

The study aim and purpose will affect all subsequent decisions with regard to study design, QC procedures and protocols, and study implementation. Therefore, it is important to establish this up front, closely followed by detailing the operational specifications, which serve to help control scope and costs. Clearly defining study goals and specifications facilitates resolution of inevitable challenges that will be encountered in the various stages of implementation, especially given the operational complexities of H2S populations. The specifications should detail the study timeline, interdependencies (i.e., what processes must be completed before another can begin), responsibilities, quality indicators and thresholds, milestones, and deliverables, all within the framework of the agreed-upon goals of the study and using a planning criterion that states that the total survey error should be minimized given agreed-upon constraints. If the study is to be conducted in a regional area unfamiliar to the designers, a complete evaluation of locally available technical and human resources, research infrastructure, and traditions, as well as the review of the context of the research location, must be undertaken. Such an evaluation needs to take into account locally available substantive, methodological, technical, and possibly legal expertise. Some H2S studies have made attempts in that direction. In H2S research, this kind of predesign work is sometimes called formative research. If the study is to be conducted in more than one area (or country), the study goals and specifications will need to take into account what is achievable in an area (or country) and specifications adjusted as needed (Pennell, Levenstein, & Lee, 2011).

Clearly, when the study involves contractual relationships (often for data collection services), developing study specifications that adequately address such dynamic conditions will be a challenge in itself. Contingency planning becomes an important aspect of request for proposal (RFP) development, costing strategies, and negotiations in these situations. The RFP needs to outline the study requirements, the QC and monitoring protocols, and the operational challenges in enough detail to ensure the bidding survey organizations understand that the typical approaches used in the survey implementation and costing may not be sufficient. The RFP should clearly define expectations, deliverables, and lines of authority (especially important in multiple stakeholder situations). A well-developed bidding process should facilitate the development of study documentation with the goal of identifying study procedures and processes and tying these to outcomes. Such documentation is often lacking (Pennell *et al.*, 2011).

As the study is implemented, the evaluation of cost and error tradeoffs will need to be examined frequently. For example, the research context may be continually changing, as is the case with disaster research or research in areas of military conflict, or little may be known about the size and distribution of the target population, so the costs of the data collection are uncertain and will need to be evaluated once the study actually begins. Even defining the population may be a challenge in these situations. Correa-Velez and Gifford (2007) found in their study targeting asylum seekers that the technical definition of the target population changed as refugees crossed country borders and needed to be adjusted accordingly.

5.4.3 Sampling

The ideal QA situation is to select a probability sample of the H2S population. This is often not possible. The sampling techniques specifically developed for H2S populations can, however, be improved in various ways. One problem with respondent-driven sampling is that recruiters tend to recruit similar others, which can affect "representativity." This can be avoided by starting with a small number of seeds, deciding an upper limit of the number of recruits allowed per seed, thereby allowing for a specific number of recruitment waves, say, six. The seeds themselves should be a diverse group and it is important for recruiters to avoid coaching people so that they learn the eligibility criteria. When participation is compensated with incentives, persons often try to participate more than once. This can be avoided by collecting biomarkers. Sampling probabilities can be approximated by collecting information about who recruited whom, how new participants are related to the recruiter, and the approximate size of the participants' networks (Lansky *et al.*, 2007). A common problem is that people with large networks have a higher probability of being included on the frame than less "popular" people. By combining various forms of network sampling with Internet recruitment, we get a better chance to include more isolated population members. Another method that has been suggested is to ask recruiters to identify a person, who is least similar to themselves, for instance a gay person who is least "out" (Martin, Wiley, & Osmond, 2003). The QC activities are those that make sure that the QA approaches have actually worked as intended.

When using capture–recapture methods to estimate population sizes, it is possible to use loglinear modeling to evaluate and control for the degree of dependency among samples (Laporte, 1994). The formative research can be used as a QA approach. In venue sampling, the formative research can help determine which venues are feasible from a logistic point of view and reasonably safe (MacKellar, Gallagher, Finlayson, Sanchez, Lansky, & Sullivan, 2007).

Many of the studies of H2S populations are qualitative, and sampling errors cannot be estimated for them. Statistical adjustments also assume a probability sample. Still, some authors claim that inference can be well founded with nonprobability designs (Spreen & Zwaagstra, 1994) and that the term "representativity" is misleading in H2S research. The abundance of convenience samples in H2S research is an indication of a cultural clash between survey methodologists and some H2S researchers.

Perhaps the most immediate QA/QC action would be the development of standardized and documented sampling procedures that are adhered to by all involved in H2S research.

5.4.4   Questionnaire design

In H2S studies, the risk of measuring the wrong construct is great since the concepts studied are often nontraditional, sensitive, or complex. In addition, there may be language or cultural barriers. We suspect that H2S studies are more prone to measurement errors than many other surveys. This problem is made worse by the lack of collaboration with funders and users during the conceptualization process in most of the studies we examined. There is hardly any mention of how questions should be developed given the characteristics of H2S populations. There are exceptions, though. In Canales *et al.* (1995), for example, the authors used an appropriate acculturation scale and wrote simple questions that could be reasonably well understood by all levels of respondents. Respondents' literacy levels were tested before giving them the survey and assistance was provided to those who needed it. In this self-administered survey, bilingual subjects completed both English and Spanish versions of the questionnaire in a counterbalanced design, in which half of the respondents received the original language version first and the other half received the translated version first. But the risk of measurement error due to potential assistance effects was acknowledged. This is an example of a study where lots of work went into the questionnaire design. The translation process is described in detail.

The format, layout, and other visual aspects of the presentation or context of survey questions are also important. For instance, a sensitive study topic may require a self-administered mode to reduce measurement error. In surveys that need face-to-face interviews but contain sensitive topics, which is the case in many studies that target H2S populations (Bertrand, Seiber, & Escudero, 2001; Canvin, Bartlett, & Pinfold, 2005; Pauw & Brener, 2003), the design may need to employ both interviewer-administered and self-administered data collection. The H2S literature does not mention this problem.

Only a few studies in our review mention the need for pretesting the questions. One such study was done by O'Hegarty, Pederson, Thome, Caraballo, Evans, Athey *et al.* (2010). It is not clear whether pretesting sometimes is part of the focus group activities. In any case, pretesting is important and could pose challenges not experienced in other surveys, such as organizing focus groups and conducting cognitive interviews with members of the H2S population.

The literature on questionnaire design is very rich and implications for question development based on what is known about the response process (Tourangeau, Rips, & Rasinski, 2000) would be a valuable resource for H2S researchers. But here, we can identify a research gap. For populations that have little trust in researchers and support systems, that are isolated due to barriers of different kinds, or have social problems, there is need for research on alternative response processes with associated implications for question and questionnaire development. For instance, many H2S questionnaires lack cultural relevance.

The basic QA effort would be to pretest questions and questionnaires using standard methods such as expert reviews and cognitive interviewing, followed by QC activities such as interviewer monitoring and reinterviews (Biemer & Lyberg, 2003; Groves *et al.*, 2009; Pennell *et al.*, 2011).

5.4.5 Adaptation

The content, format, response options, or visual presentation of any part of a question, questionnaire, or instrument can be adapted. The purpose of such adaptation is to fit the needs of a new population, location, language, or mode, or any combination of these. The need for such adaptations is great in many H2S studies. There are only a few examples of adaptations in a mixed-mode situation or when a source questionnaire is used to study, say, different minorities. For an overview of some of these issues, see Harkness *et al.* (2010). Lack of adaptation can generate various kinds of errors, mostly measurement errors. The QA activities are to find areas of potential adaptations and implement necessary ones followed by the same QA and QC activities that were described earlier.

5.4.6 Translation

Translation, when needed, is dealt with very differently in the H2S literature from other survey literatures. Some studies do not translate survey materials. They either let the interviewers decide whether data can be collected from people who have problems with the source language or they define the target population to include only people who are, say, English speaking. These are problematic scenarios that probably stem from both lack of resources and lack of knowledge. Other studies put in lots of resources for translation. In Henning, Pollack, and Friedman (1992), the questionnaire was provided in five languages and Canales *et al.* (1995) describe the translation process in detail. Very little information is provided about QC of the translation process.

A couple of studies use back translation but do not seem to be aware of preferred procedures, such as team translation. Elliott and Fuller (1991) discuss interpretation and translation and show that they generate different error structures, which is important, since some other studies seem to take this issue lightly ("a bilingual research fellow helped us with the language issues"). We believe that translation and interpretation issues are very important in H2S research. Translation and adaptation techniques used in survey research more generally (Harkness, 2003; Harkness *et al.*, 2010) are relevant for research involving H2S populations that face cultural and linguistic barriers. When more than one cultural or linguistic group is involved, techniques for developing comparable questions are useful (Harkness *et al.*, 2010; Smith, 2003).

5.4.7   Interviewer recruitment, selection, and training

Our literature review shows that interviewers play an important role in implementing surveys of H2S populations. Interviewers do not merely ask questions and record respondent reports; interviewers sometimes identify and recruit respondents, persuade and motivate them to participate, teach the respondent their role in the survey process, collect biomarker data, and edit and transmit data (Lessler, Eyerman, & Wang, 2008; Loosveldt, 2008). Throughout all of these tasks, interviewers can affect data quality. This makes interviewer recruitment, selection, and training imperative for collecting quality data.

In surveys, interviewers can contribute to various error sources. Coverage and sampling errors can be influenced by interviewers; interviewers may fail to identify sample units, for example, by incorrectly following sampling procedures (Lessler *et al.*, 2008). This can be particularly of concern if complex sampling procedures are needed to sample H2S populations.

Interviewers contribute to unit nonresponse when they do not gain cooperation of sampled members of the target population and to item nonresponse when respondents fail to answer items on the questionnaire. The H2S literature indicates that nonresponse error is possible when lack of trust leads potential respondents to refuse to participate in the study. For example, Coe *et al.* (2008) reported that parents' mistrust (resulting from their lack of information about a UK government children's program) contributed to the parents not participating. Characteristics of H2S populations that lead to social desirability are relevant as well. Members of some populations may simply be too embarrassed to take part in a survey, as in the case of sex workers (Shaver, 2005). Gatekeepers can also lead to nonresponse by prohibiting interviewers from accessing members of the target population (Callan, 1971).

Interviewers influence measurement error in various ways, for example, by deviating from standardized question wording (Fowler & Mangione, 1990; Groves *et al.*, 2009). The concept of interviewer variance is mentioned very rarely in the H2S literature that we have studied. That is not really surprising, since it is a relatively ignored topic in most surveys. However, interviewer variance is probably a very serious addition to the total survey error in H2S studies, since they are often conducted under difficult circumstances, ask sensitive questions, and have few interviewers, who are generally not professionally trained.

Interviewers can also contribute to data processing error. This can occur if interviewers fail to follow data editing and transmission protocols and the data respondents provided are changed or if no protocol is in place (Lessler *et al.*, 2008).

Interviewer recruitment and selection

Our review of the H2S literature indicates that researchers sometimes recognize that interviewers influence the quality of the data collected and offer methods to ensure data quality. These researchers often suggest recruiting and selecting interviewers with characteristics that may help overcome mistrust of researchers or cultural barriers. For example, Geringer, Marks, Allen, and Armstrong (1993) recruited African-American interviewers from the target geographic area to survey respondents. They argue that this strategy helped to overcome trust and access barriers to the target population of low socioeconomic status African-Americans. Other researchers, though, do not recruit and select interviewers based on such characteristics. Which method is best for reducing interviewer effects on data among H2S surveys remains open for research. Some researchers complain that nurses and doctors are not good interviewers and that they sometimes do not adhere to instructions concerning the study. Sometimes, professional interviewers lack "cultural competence" (e.g., Dowrick *et al.*, 2009). Other H2S researchers argue that all interviewers should be professional.

Interviewer training

Interviewer training is necessary to provide interviewers with the skills to carry out their tasks in a survey. Interviewers require training to follow protocols for asking questions, probing inadequate responses, recording answers, and managing the interaction of the survey interview (Fowler & Mangione, 1990). In addition, interviewers may require training unique to the study and the study's population. To reduce the influence interviewers have on coverage and sampling errors, interviewers should be trained on the sampling procedures, such as venue-based designs or street-by-street canvassing (e.g., McMahon, Tortu, Torres, Pouget, & Hamid, 2003). Draus, Siegal, Carlson, Falck, and Wang (2005) suggest that in the respondent-driven sampling design, "the most important characteristic for interviewers to possess was a professional, nonjudgmental, and empathetic disposition" (p. 168). Interviewers who possessed these were able to recruit participants for the study.

Interviewers may also require training to overcome challenges of mistrust and cultural and linguistic barriers that make some populations H2S. For example, Greenfields (2009) describes using cultural sensitive training from a Gypsy community group to assist in creating a culturally sensitive health assessment among Travellers in the UK. Other studies (e.g., Kumar, Mudaliar, & Daniels, 1998) suggest community-based research techniques that allow for overcoming access and trust barriers that contribute to measurement and nonresponse error.

Finally, interviewers may require special training related to what data are being collected. For example, biomarker data collection is important in HIV surveillance studies. Interviewing psychiatric patients and people who are very sick demands a lot of training (e.g., Feild, Pruchno, Bewley, Lemay, & Levinsky, 2006).

Interviewer selection and training are important QA approaches. Interviewers must have characteristics and skills that make them fit to conduct interviews under difficult circumstances. There are few documented criteria for interviewer selection and few studies on the content of training programs. It is likely that H2S interviewers will need more training than most other survey interviewers. A general research effort directed towards developing training programs for H2S interviewers would fill an important research gap. It is especially important to simulate situations where interviewers approach respondents according to a specific sampling scheme and motivate them to participate. The QC approach would be to make sure that the intended respondents have been approached and motivated in a correct fashion.

5.4.8 Data collection

Choosing whether to use a self-administered or interviewer-administered mode of data collection (or a mix of the two) is always important in designing surveys.

Data collection modes also differ in coverage and sampling error (de Leeuw, 2008), and these can vary by the H2S target population. Certain data collection modes may provide inadequate coverage of the target population. Some populations, such as American Indians, are difficult to reach by mail and telephone. Using the Internet can also lead to sampling and coverage error if convenience sampling methods are used. Johnston *et al.* (2009) used the Internet to sample and survey Estonian men who have sex with men (MSM) because of greater anonymity, faster recruitment and data collection, lower costs, and ability to access the hidden population. The surveys were posted to Estonian and Russian gay-related websites. The web mode allowed lower costs, timely data collection, and access to the population, but it did not allow for sampling the target population using probability methods.

Measurement and nonresponse errors are also related to data collection. Interviews are in general not good for asking sensitive questions. For example, Gertler, Shah, and Bertozzi (2005) suspected that the number of sexually transmitted infections (STIs) they estimated among Mexican sex workers was an underestimate because of social desirability bias. Self-administered modes lead to less social desirability bias than to when an interviewer is present (de Leeuw, 2008; Tourangeau & Smith, 1996; Tourangeau & Yan, 2007). Measurement error and nonresponse error are also possible if the data collection mode does not fit the needs of the target population. For example, paper self-administered modes may be unsuitable for low literate populations.

Most H2S studies use face-to-face interviews. When the population consists of people who are vulnerable, afraid, stigmatized, or not interested in being researched, face-to-face interviewing is probably the only feasible mode, despite the concerns mentioned. There are, however, a number of studies that have used self-administered modes thereby showing that it can sometimes be an option. For instance, besides a web application, Chavez *et al.* (1989) used ACASI for illiterate respondents and Cherry and Rost (2009) used it for studying alcohol consumption. There are also examples of unusual combinations of modes such as observation, focus groups, and interviews (e.g., Pauw & Brener, 2003).

Nonresponse rates are in general difficult to assess since standard disposition codes are often not used in studies of H2S populations. Often, data collection is terminated when enough respondents are obtained. Unwillingness to participate in research is a problem in H2S groups. Freimuth (1995) states that we should call these populations hard to engage.

The survey methodology literature provides some techniques that are useful for the challenges faced in H2S populations research. The tailored design method (TDM) is a QA approach that encourages response and includes developing trust as a main component (Dillman, Smyth, & Christian, 2009). The tailored design method could be considered for research with populations that are H2S because of lack of trust.

The legal status of some H2S groups will influence their decision on whether to participate or not. We can suspect that the type of topics covered in H2S studies (e.g., health issues) are correlated with legal status and living conditions and therefore the risk of nonresponse bias is high.

The QA activities during data collection include choosing a cost-effective mode of data collection (de Leeuw, 2008), having a well-trained group of interviewers (Groves & McGonagle, 2001), minimizing any measurement errors using tested questionnaires (Groves *et al.*, 2009) and keeping nonresponse rates or at least nonresponse biases at reasonable levels (Bethlehem, Cobben & Schouten, 2011). Corresponding QC activities mainly comprise the collection and analysis of paradata together with nonresponse adjustment. The H2S literature is very sparse on these subjects.

5.4.9 Data processing and dissemination

Very little is mentioned about these process steps in the H2S literature. There is hardly any mention of QA and QC procedures regarding coding and data capture and there is very little discussion about the long-term use of study results. For instance, QA of coding means that we have a system for coder training and coding control since error rates can be very large for variables such as education and occupation. QC activities entail various verification processes (Biemer & Lyberg, 2003).

5.5   Identifying research gaps and training needs

It is clear that a vast majority of the studies reviewed represent a research culture that is different from that of mainstream survey research. Concepts such as data quality and total survey error are not really discussed. At the same time, attempts are made to make population inferences. It seems as if there is a need for a cross-fertilization between H2S researchers, who often are very good at getting information about their populations through formative research (e.g., Higgins, O'Reilly, Tashima, Crain, Beeker, Goldbaum *et al.*, 1996; and who know what factors make a population H2S (Flanagan & Hancock, 2010; Vlahov, Coady, Galea, Ompad, & Barondess, 2007), and survey researchers who know about error structures and how to control them. There are excellent literature reviews done by H2S researchers on topics and concepts such as the social demography of drug use (e.g., Kandel, 1991), culture (e.g., Fredriksen-Goldsen & Hooyman, 2005), the use of media in cancer screening (e.g., Freimuth, 1995), violence, shame, and poverty (e.g., Errante, 1997), ethical standards (e.g., Pettifor, 1979), and methods for epidemiologic surveys of minority groups (e.g., Chaturvedi & McKeigue, 1994). Survey researchers could help improve the actual conduct of surveys in these fields by conveying information about best methods and standard procedures for the survey processes (QA) and how to make sure that they work as intended (QC). There is a general lack of process documentation in the literature studied. Concepts such as interviewer variance, paradata, and statistical disclosure are seldom, if ever, mentioned. Occasionally, methodological problems are downplayed. One study stated that social desirability bias was no problem since "they got enough critical responses" and that interviewing could continue "until responses became redundant." There are exceptions, of course. Faugier & Sargeant (1997) argues that the researcher must actively control the entire sample selection and provides a checklist to facilitate such control. There is a literature on assessing respondent-driven sampling and other sampling methods used (e.g., Goel & Salganik, 2010; Heckathorn, 2007) and how to adjust for the fact that individuals with many contacts are more likely to be recruited. These authors also show that design effects are large and they have conducted simulation studies that indicate that the variance of respondent-driven sampling can be five to ten times higher than the simple random sampling variance. By and large, though, collaboration between the two research cultures could be beneficial to both.

We have identified a number of specific research and training needs based on what we have found during our review.

- Many studies are small and confined to just one or a few sites. There is a general need for replicating studies using other sites and sometimes other methods. That would provide information on the degree of stability in findings and it would provide an opportunity to accumulate information on larger geographical areas and larger populations, eventually on a national basis (Bowen & Boehmer, 2007).
- There is probably a need for an ethical standard specifically developed for studying H2S populations. Existing ethical standards might not be sufficient.

- There is need for a concerted effort on how to combine survey data on H2S populations with data from other sources, such as medical records, official statistics, focus groups, and medical tests.

- The training needs for H2S studies are extensive. Training strategies involving population members as recruiters and interviewers, subject-matter professionals, and users should be developed. The training should be culturally appropriate.

- The total survey error perspective is important for the design of H2S studies (and for other surveys as well!). Knowledge about error sources and their relative importance, how to implement best practices, and control their performance is a necessary next step. Such training should be offered.

- The ideas from the H2S literature on alternative ways of engaging population members and making them less defensive by using tactics such as blaming society rather than population members (Freimuth, 1995) and using themes such as strength-building rather than defect-repairing (Hogue, Johnson-Leckrone, & Liddle, 1999) should be explored more fully.

- We do not really know how to study groups that have totally different views from the mainstream on, say, health issues and who do not believe in the health care procedures used in the country where they currently live (Han *et al.*, 2007).

- Mixed-mode data collection seems to be increasing in H2S research. The web is advantageous for reaching more isolated population members and it would be good to build a platform for H2S mixed-mode options.

- Lack of funding is a recurring theme in the H2S literature. There are lots of small studies with no long-term funding. Some of these resources should be pooled and used by consortia to make larger studies possible.

- A modified model of the survey response process adjusted for H2S situations needs to be developed.

References

Agustín, L. M. (2007). Questioning solidarity: outreach with migrants who sell sex. *Sexualities*, 10(4), 519–34.

Andresen, E. M., Diehr, P. H., & Luke, D. A. (2004). Public health surveillance of low-frequency populations. *Annual Review of Public Health*, 25(1), 25–52.

Armstrong, B. (2003). The young men's clinic: addressing men's reproductive health and responsibilities. *Perspectives on Sexual and Reproductive Health*, 35(5), 220–25.

Barkan, S. E., Melnick, S. L., Preston-Martin, S., Weber, K., Kalish, L. A., Miotti, P., *et al.* (1998). The women's interagency HIV study. *Epidemiology*, 9(2), 117–25.

Bertrand, J. T., Seiber, E., & Escudero, G. (2001). Contraceptive dynamics in Guatemala: 1978–1998. *International Family Planning Perspectives*, 27(3), 112–18,136.

Bethlehem, J., Cobben, F., & Schouten, B. (2011). *Handbook of Nonresponse in Household Surveys*. Hoboken, NJ: John Wiley & Sons.

Biemer, P., & Lyberg, L. (2003). *Introduction to Survey Quality*. Hoboken, NJ: John Wiley & Sons.

Blair, J., & Czaja, R. (1982). Locating a special population using random digit dialing. *Public Opinion Quarterly*, 46(4), 585.

Boccia, D., Guthmann, J.-P., Klovstad, H., Hamid, N., Tatay, M., Ciglenecki, I., *et al.* (2006). High mortality associated with an outbreak of Hepatitis E among displaced persons in Darfur, Sudan. *Clinical Infectious Diseases*, 42(12), 1679–84.

Bodenmann, P., Vaucher, P., Wolff, H., Favrat, B., de Tribolet, F., Masserey, E., *et al.* (2009). Screening for latent tuberculosis infection among undocumented immigrants in Swiss healthcare centres: a descriptive exploratory study. *BMC Infectious Diseases*, 9, 1–8.

Bouchard, F. (2007). A capture–recapture model to estimate the size of criminal populations and the risks of detection in a marijuana cultivation industry. *Journal of Quantitative Criminology*, 23(3), 221–41.

Bowen, D. J., & Boehmer, U. (2007). The lack of cancer surveillance data on sexual minorities and strategies for change. *Cancer Causes & Control*, 18(4), 343–49.

Cáceres, C. F., & Rosasco, A. M. (1999). The margin has many sides: diversity among gay and homosexually active men in Lima. *Culture, Health & Sexuality*, 1(3), 261–75.

Callan, L. B. (1971). Adapting the windshield survey model to community health education. *HSMHA Health Reports*, 86(3), 202–03.

Canales, S., Ganz, P. A., & Coscarelli, C. A. (1995). Translation and validation of a quality of life instrument for Hispanic American cancer patients: methodological consider- ations. *Quality of Life Research*, 4(1), 3–11.

Canvin, K., Bartlett, A., & Pinfold, V. (2005). Acceptability of compulsory powers in the community: the ethical considerations of mental health service users on supervised discharge and guardianship. *Journal of Medical Ethics*, 31(8), 457–62.

Chaturvedi, N., & McKeigue, P. M. (1994). Methods for epidemiological surveys of ethnic minority groups. *Journal of Epidemiological & Community Health*, 48, 107–11.

Chavez, E. L., Edwards, R., & Oetting, E. R. (1989). Mexican American and white American school dropouts' drug use, health status, and involvement in violence. *Public Health Reports*, 104(6), 594–604.

Chavez, L. R., Hubbell, F. A., Mishra, S. I., & Valdez, R. B. (1997). Undocumented Latina immigrants in Orange County, California: a comparative analysis. *International Migration Review*, 31(1), 88–107.

Cherry, D. J., & Rost, K. (2009). Alcohol use, comorbidities, and receptivity to treatment in Hispanic farmworkers in primary care. *Journal of Health Care for the Poor and Underserved*, 20(4), 1095–110.

Coady, M. H., Weiss, L., Galea, S., Ompad, D. C., Glidden, K., & Vlahov, D. (2007). Rapid vaccine distribution in nontraditional settings: lessons learned from project VIVA. *Journal of Community Health Nursing*, 24(2), 79–85.

Coe, C., Gibson, A., Spencer, N., & Stuttaford, M. (2008). Sure start: voices of the hard-to- reach. *Child: Care, Health and Development*, 34(4), 447–53.

Coleman, S. M., Rajabiun, S., Cabral, H. J., Bradford, J. B., & Tobias, C. R. (2009). Sexual risk behavior and behavior change among persons newly diagnosed with HIV: the impact of targeted outreach interventions among hard-to-reach populations. *AIDS Patient Care & STDs*, 23(8), 639–45.

Correa-Velez, I., & Gifford, S. M. (2007). When the right to be counted doesn't count: the politics and challenges of researching the health of asylum seekers. *Critical Public Health*, 17(3), 273–81.

Creswell, J. W. (2007). *Qualitative inquiry & research design: choosing among five approaches*. Thousand Oaks, CA: Sage Publications.

Davis, R. E., Couper, M. P., Janz, N. K., Caldwell, C. H., & Resnicow, K. (2010). Interviewer effects in public health surveys. *Health Education Research*, 25(1), 14–26.

de Leeuw, E. D. (2008). Choosing the method of data collection. In E. D. de Leeuw, J. J. Hox, & D. A. Dillman (eds.), *International Handbook of Survey Methodology* (pp. 113–35). Hillsdale, NJ: Lawrence Erlbaum Associates.

de Leeuw, E., Hox, J., & Kef, S. (2003). Computer-assisted self-interviewing tailored for special populations and topics. *Field Methods*, 15(3), 223–51.

Dillman, D. A., Smyth, J. D., & Christian, L. M. (2009). *Internet, Mail and Mixed Mode Surveys: The Tailored Design Method* (3rd edn.). Hoboken, NJ: John Wiley & Sons.

Dowrick, C., Gask, L., Edwards, S., Aseem, S., Bower, P., Burroughs, H., *et al.* (2009). Researching the mental health needs of hard-to-reach groups: managing multiple sources of evidence. *BMC Health Services Research*, 9, 226.

Draus, P. J., Siegal, H. A., Carlson, R. G., Falck, R. S., & Wang, J. (2005). Cracking the cornfields: recruiting illicit stimulant drug users in rural Ohio. *Sociological Quarterly*, 46(1), 165–89.

Dunlap, E., Golub, A., & Johnson, B. D. (2003). Transient male–female relationships and the violence they bring to girls in the inner city. *Journal of African American Studies*, 7(2), 19–36.

Elliott, K., & Fuller, J. (1991). Health education and ethnic minorities: needs may differ, the techniques don't. *BMJ*, 302(6780), 802–03.

Ennett, S. T., Bailey, S. L., & Federman, E. B. (1999). Social network characteristics associated with risky behaviors among runaway and homeless youth. *Journal of Health and Social Behavior*, 40(1), 63–78.

Errante, A. (1997). Close to home: comparative perspectives on childhood and community violence. *American Journal of Education*, 105(4), 355–400.

Faugier, J., & Sargeant, M. (1997). Sampling hard to reach populations. *Journal of Advanced Nursing*, 26(4), 790–97.

Feild, L., Pruchno, R. A., Bewley, J., Lemay Jr., E. P., & Levinsky, N. G. (2006). Using probability vs. nonprobability sampling to identify hard-to-access participants for health-related research: costs and contrasts. *Journal of Aging and Health*, 18(4), 565–83.

Flanagan, S. M., & Hancock, B. (2010). "Reaching the hard to reach" – lessons learned from the VCS (voluntary and community sector). A qualitative study. *BMC Health Services Research*, 10, 92–100.

Ford, W. L., Weiss, G., Kipke, M. D., Ritt-Olson, A., Iverson, E., & Lopez, D. (2009). The Healthy Young Men's Study: sampling methods to recruit a random cohort of young men who have sex with men. *Journal of Gay & Lesbian Social Services*, 21(4), 357–73.

Fowler Jr., F. J., & Mangione, T. W. (1990). *Standardized Survey Interviewing: Minimizing Interviewer-related Error*. Newbury Park, CA: Sage.

Fredriksen-Goldsen, K., & Hooyman, N. R. (2005). Caregiving research, services, and policies in historically marginalized communities: where do we go from here? *Journal of Gay & Lesbian Social Services*, 18(3), 129–45.

Freimuth, V. S. (1995). Mass media strategies and channels: a review of the use of media in breast and cervical cancers. *Wellness Perspectives*, 11(2), 79.

Garland, J., Spalek, B., & Chakraborti, N. (2006). Hearing lost voices. *British Journal of Criminology*, 46(3), 423–37.

Geringer, W., Marks, S., Allen, W., & Armstrong, K. (1993). Knowledge, attitudes, and behavior related to condom use and STDs in a high risk population. *Journal of Sex Research*, 30(1), 75–83.

Gertler, P., Shah, M., & Bertozzi, S. (2005). Risky business: the market for unprotected commercial sex. *Journal of Political Economy*, 113(3), 518–50.

Goel, S., & Salganik, M. J. (2010). Assessing respondent-driven sampling. *Proceedings of the National Academy of Sciences of the United States of America*, 107(15), 6743–47.

Greenfields, M. (2009). Reaching Gypsies and Travellers. *Primary Health Care*, 19(8), 26–27.

Greenhalgh, T., Collard, A., & Begum, N. (2005). Sharing stories: complex intervention for diabetes education in minority ethnic groups who do not speak English. *BMJ*, 330(7492), 628–31.

Groves, R. M., Fowler Jr., F. J., Couper, M. P., Lepkowski, J. M., Singer, E., & Tourangeau, R. (2009). *Survey Methodology*. Hoboken, NJ: John Wiley & Sons.

Groves, R., & Lyberg, L. (2010). Total survey error: past, present, and future. *Public Opinion Quarterly*, 74(5), 849–79.

Groves, R., & McGonagle, K. (2001). A theory-guided interviewer training protocol regarding survey participation. *Journal of Official Statistics*, 17(2), 249–65.

Han, H.-R., Kang, J., Kim, K. B., Ryu, J., & Kim, M. (2007). Barriers to and strategies for recruiting Korean Americans for community-partnered health promotion research. *Journal of Immigrant and Minority Health*, 9(2), 137–46.

Harkness, J. (2003). Questionnaire translation. In J. A. Harkness, F. J. R. van de Vijver, & P. Ph. Mohler (eds.), *Cross-Cultural Survey Methods* (pp. 35–56). Hoboken, NJ: John Wiley & Sons.

Harkness, J. A., Villar, A., & Edwards, B. (2010). Translation, adaptation, and design. In J. A. Harkness, M. Braun, B. Edwards, T. P. Johnson, L. Lyberg, P. Ph. Mohler, B-E. Pennell, & T. W. Smith (eds.), *Survey Methods in Multinational, Multiregional, and Multicultural Contexts* (pp. 117–40). Hoboken, NJ: John Wiley & Sons.

Heckathorn, D. (2007). Extensions of respondent-driven sampling: analyzing continuous variables and controlling for differential recruitment. *Sociological Methodology*, 37(1), 151–208.

Henning, K. J., Pollack, D. M., & Friedman, S. M. (1992). A neonatal hepatitis B surveillance and vaccination program: New York City, 1987 to 1988. *American Journal of Public Health*, 82(6), 885–88.

Hidaka, Y., & Operario, D. (2006). Attempted suicide, psychological health and exposure to harassment among Japanese homosexual, bisexual or other men questioning their sexual orientation recruited via the internet. *Journal of Epidemiology and Community Health*, 60(11), 962–67.

Higgins, D. L., O'Reilly, K., Tashima, N., Crain, C., Beeker, C., Goldbaum, G., *et al.* (1996). Using formative research to lay the foundation for community level HIV prevention efforts: an example from the AIDS community demonstration projects. *Public Health Reports*, 111(Suppl. 1), 28–35.

Hogue, A., Johnson-Leckrone, J., & Liddle, H. A. (1999). Recruiting high-risk families into family-based prevention and prevention research. *Journal of Mental Health Counseling*, 21(4), 337.

Horwitz, R. H., Roberts, L. W., & Warner, T. D. (2008). Mexican immigrant women's perceptions of health care access for stigmatizing illnesses: a focus group study in Albuquerque, New Mexico. *Journal of Health Care for the Poor and Underserved*, 19(3), 857–73.

Hossain, Z. (2001). Division of household labor and family functioning in off-reservation Navajo Indian families. *Family Relations*, 50(3), 255–61.

Icard, L. D. (2008). Reaching African-American men on the "down-low": sampling hidden populations: Implication for HIV prevention. *Journal of Homosexuality*, 55(3), 437–49.

Johnston, L. G., Trummal, A., Lohmus, L., & Ravalepik, A. (2009). Efficacy of convenience sampling through the internet versus respondent driven sampling among males who have sex with males in Tallinn and Harju County, Estonia: challenges reaching a hidden population. *AIDS Care*, 21(9), 1195–202.

Jones, L., & Allebone, B. (1999). Researching "hard-to-reach" groups: the crucial role of the research associate. *International Journal of Inclusive Education*, 3(4), 353–62.

Kalton, G. (2003). Practical methods for sampling rare and mobile populations. *Statistics in Transition*, 6(4), 491–501.

(2009). Methods for oversampling rare subpopulations in social surveys. *Survey Methodology*, 35(2), 125–41.

Kalton, G., & Anderson, D. W. (1986). Sampling rare populations. *Journal of the Royal Statistical Society: Series A (General)*, 149(1), 65–82.

Kandel, D. B. (1991). The social demography of drug use. *Milbank Quarterly*, 69(3), 365–414.

Kish, L. (1965). *Survey Sampling*. New York: John Wiley & Sons.

Koné, A., Sullivan, M., Senturia, K. D., Chrisman, N. J., Ciske, S. J., & Krieger, J. W. (2000). Improving collaboration between researchers and communities. *Public Health Reports*, 115(2/3), 243–48.

Kumar, M. S., Mudaliar, S., & Daniels, D. (1998). Community-based outreach HIV intervention for street-recruited drug-users in Madras, India. In R. H. Needle,

S. Coyle, & H. Cesari (eds.), HIV prevention with drug-using populations – current status and future prospects. *Public Health Reports*, 113(Suppl. 1), 58–66.

Landry, P. F., & Shen, M. (2005). Reaching migrants in survey research: the use of the global positioning system to reduce coverage bias in China. *Political Analysis*, 13(1), 1–22.

Lansky, A., Abdul-Quader, A. S., Cribbin, M., Hall, T., Finlayson, T. J., Garfein, R. S., *et al.* (2007). Developing an HIV behavioral surveillance system for injecting drug users: the national HIV behavioral surveillance system. *Public Health Reports*, 122(Suppl. 1), 48–55.

Laporte, R. E. (1994). Assessing the human condition: capture–recapture techniques: allows accurate counts of those difficult to reach populations. *BMJ*, 308(6920), 5–6.

Lavelle, B., Larsen, M. D., & Gundersen, C. (2009). Strategies for surveys of American Indians. *Public Opinion Quarterly*, 73(2), 385–403.

Lessler, J. T., Eyerman, J., & Wang, K. (2008). Interviewer training. In E. D. de Leeuw, J. J. Hox, & D. A. Dillman (eds.), *International Handbook of Survey Methodology* (pp. 442–60). New York: Lawrence Erlbaum Associates.

Loosveldt, G. (2008). Face-to-face interviews. In E. D. de Leeuw, J. J. Hox, & D. A. Dillman (eds.), *International handbook of survey methodology* (pp. 201–20). New York: Lawrence Erlbaum Associates.

Lyberg, L., & Biemer, P. (2008). Quality assurance and quality control in surveys. In E. D. de Leeuw, J. J. Hox, & D. A. Dillman (eds.), *International Handbook of Survey Methodology* (pp. 421–441). New York: Lawrence Erlbaum Associates.

Lyberg, L., & Couper, M. (2005). *The use of paradata in survey research*. Invited paper presented at the ISI Meeting, Sydney, April.

MacKellar, D. A., Gallagher, K. M., Finlayson, T., Sanchez, T., Lansky, A., & Sullivan, P. S. (2007). Surveillance of HIV risk and prevention behaviors of men who have sex with men: a national application of venue-based, time-space sampling. *Public Health Reports*, 122(Suppl. 1), 39–47.

McMahon, J. M., Tortu, S., Torres, L., Pouget, E. R., & Hamid, R. (2003). Recruitment of heterosexual couples in public health research: a study protocol. *BMC Medical Research Methodology*, 3, 24.

Martin, J. L., Wiley, J., & Osmond, D. (2003). Social networks and unobserved heterogeneity in risk for AIDS. *Population Research and Policy Review*, 22(1), 65–90.

Merriam, S. B. (2009). *Qualitative research: a guide to design and implementation*. San Francisco: John Wiley & Sons.

O'Hegarty, M., Pederson, L. L., Thome, S. L., Caraballo, R. S., Evans, B., Athey, L., *et al.* (2010). Customizing survey instruments and data collection to reach Hispanic/Latino adults in border communities in Texas. *American Journal of Public Health*, 100(S1), S159–S164.

Pauw, I., & Brener, L. (2003). "You are just whores: you can't be raped": barriers to safer sex practices among women street sex workers in Cape Town. *Culture, Health & Sexuality*, 5(6), 465–81.

Pennell, B-E., Levenstein, R., & Lee, H. J. (2011). *Cross-Cultural Survey Guidelines*. Ann Arbor, MI: University of Michigan. Retrieved from http://ccsg.isr.umich.edu/.

Pettifor, J. L. (1979). Ethical issues with special populations. *Canadian Psychological Review/Psychologie Canadienne*, 20(3), 148–50.

Salganik, M. J., & Heckathorn, D. D. (2004). Sampling and estimation in hidden populations using respondent-driven sampling. *Sociological Methodology*, 34(1), 193–239.

Schroepfer, T., Matloub, J., Creswell, P., Strickland, R., & Anderson, D. (2009). A community-specific approach to cancer research in Indian Country. *Progress in Community Health Partnerships: Research, Education, and Action*, 3(4), 317–25.

Shaver, F. M. (2005). Sex work research: methodological and ethical challenges. *Journal of Interpersonal Violence*, 20(3), 296–319.

Smith, T. W. (2003). Developing comparable questions in cross-national surveys. In J. A. Harkness, F. J. R. van de Vijver, & P. Ph. Mohler (eds.), *Cross-Cultural Survey Methods* (pp. 69–92). Hoboken, NJ: John Wiley & Sons.

Spreen, M., & Zwaagstra, R. (1994). Personal network sampling, outdegree analysis and multilevel analysis: introducing the network concept in studies of hidden populations. *International Sociology*, 9(4), 475–91.

Stueve, A., O'Donnell, L. N., Duran, R., San Doval, A., & Blome, J. (2001). Time-space sampling in minority communities: results with young Latino men who have sex with men. *American Journal of Public Health*, 91(6), 922–26.

Sudman, S., Sirken, M., & Cowan, C. (1988). Sampling rare and elusive populations. *Science*, 240, 991–95.

Toktaş, Ş. (2006). The conduct of citizenship in the case of Turkey's Jewish minority: legal status, identity, and civic virtue aspects. *Comparative Studies of South Asia, Africa and the Middle East*, 26(1), 121–33.

Tourangeau, R., Rips, L. J., & Rasinski, K. A. (2000). *The Psychology of Survey Response*. Cambridge: Cambridge University Press.

Tourangeau, R., & Smith, T. W. (1996). Asking sensitive questions: the impact of data collection mode, question format, and question context. *Public Opinion Quarterly*, 60(2), 275–304.

Tourangeau, R., & Yan, T. (2007). Sensitive questions in surveys. *Psychological Bulletin*, 133(5), 859–83.

Vlahov, D., Coady, M. N., Galea, S., Ompad, D. C., & Barondess, J. A. (2007). Pandemic preparedness and hard to reach populations. *American Journal of Disaster Medicine*, 2(6), 281–83.

Vyavaharkar, M. V., Moneyham, L., & Corwin, S. (2008). Health care utilization: the experiences of rural HIV-positive African American women. *Journal of Health Care for the Poor and Underserved*, 19(1), 294–306.

PART II

Conducting surveys in difficult settings

6

Disaster research: surveying displaced populations

BETH-ELLEN PENNELL, YASHWANT DESHMUKH,
JENNIFER KELLEY, PATTY MAHER, JAMES WAGNER,
AND DAN TOMLIN

6.1 Introduction and background

Worldwide, natural disasters have increased over 200 percent in the past decade, affecting over two billion people (Guha-Sapir, Vos, Below, & Ponserre, 2011). In 2010 alone, natural disasters affected more than 200 million people and cost more than $100 billion USD worldwide (Yonetani, 2011). The rise in natural disasters highlights the ever increasing demand to understand the physical, mental, social, and economic needs of these populations. Researchers who study this hard-to-survey population, often in regions of the world with already limited research infrastructure, face many challenges and have few methodological resources to guide their efforts. This chapter discusses the difficulties in designing and conducting research in areas affected by disasters, provides practical recommendations for conducting such research, and makes recommendations for future research and development.

6.1.1 Defining disasters

The Center for Research on the Epidemiology of Disasters (CRED) defines a disaster as meeting one of the four following criteria: (1) ten or more people reported killed; (2) 100 or more people affected; (3) declaration of a state of emergency; or (4) call for international assistance (www.emdat.be/criteria-and-definition). Areas of war and conflict are also covered under this broad definition. These latter topics are covered in Chapter 7 and will not be discussed here. CRED further classifies disasters into five distinct natural disasters groups: geophysical (e.g., earthquakes, volcano), meteorological (e.g., storm, blizzard), hydrological (e.g., flood, storm surge), climatological (e.g., extreme temperature, drought), and biological (e.g., epidemic). In addition to natural disasters, CRED includes technical disasters in its classification framework (e.g., industrial accidents, transportation accidents) and complex or multiple disasters such as the 2011 event in Japan (i.e., earthquake, tsunami, and nuclear accident).

Categorizing natural disasters on these dimensions is useful in understanding the unique aspects of each disaster and how these will differentially affect the design and implementation of a study. For example, floods can pose different challenges from a hurricane or cyclone. In floods, structures have water damage, but a higher portion of structures may be intact, enabling sampling activities. In contrast, in a high impact hurricane or cyclone, entire coastal areas may be destroyed, making traditional sampling activities difficult, if not impossible. Such was the case in parts of the Gulf Coast in the United States after Hurricane Ike. The Bolivar Peninsula off Galveston was completely closed by local authorities. The main road through the area was impassable and nearly all coastal homes were destroyed. The ferry to the peninsula did not run for eight weeks after the hurricane (Paschenko, 2008).

As implied, the severity of the event will also have an impact on design and implementation. Events that are more severe in terms of the number of people affected and damage to structures will pose greater design and implementation difficulties than less severe events. Complex (multiple) events like the 2011 Japan earthquake, tsunami, and nuclear accident will pose greater challenges. The severity of the event will also have an impact on the timing of the study, that is, how soon after the event it will be feasible to undertake field work.

Disasters fall into three distinct phases: (1) rescue and relief; (2) recovery; and (3) development. In the rescue and relief phase of a disaster, saving lives and mitigating human suffering is the main goal. This phase may last from a couple of weeks to several months. In phase 2, the recovery phase, the main focus is to restore social and political stability and this phase can last from several months to several years. Phase 3 of a disaster, the development phase, focuses on improving long-term conditions. Each phase poses different challenges for researchers. For example, when a study is attempting to conduct operations in the rescue and relief phase, researchers may have limited access to respondents because travel to the site is impossible or dangerous. In the worst case, researchers may actually impede or divert rescue efforts. In contrast, in the development stage, although local conditions may be more stable, locating respondents may be more difficult as more time has passed between the event and field work.

The location of the event will also have an impact on survey design and implementation. If the infrastructure pre-event was already limited, conducting research post-event will be even more challenging. For example, field work in Haiti after the 2010 earthquake posed different challenges (many that continue today) than conducting field work in Japan after the complex triple event of 2011. Japan had a highly evolved disaster preparedness system in place whereas Haiti had a compromised infrastructure before the earthquake, with no country-wide disaster program. Even in transitional economies such as Thailand, where disaster preparedness was in place, the scope of the 2004 Indian Ocean tsunami completely overwhelmed available resources. The political context of the location is also important. In Indonesia and Sri Lanka, the Indian Ocean tsunami recovery was further affected by ongoing internal political conflicts that resulted in official governmental agencies selectively aiding groups depending on political affiliations and restricting researcher access to areas occupied by "rebel" groups. Here, the government instructed research agencies conducting evaluation studies to limit these efforts to "natural disaster victims" thus effectively leaving out "conflict victims struck by natural disaster" or the "multi-victims" (Deshmukh, 2006; Deshmukh & Prasad, 2009).

Finally, the goal of the research will dictate design. If the goal of the study is to acquire information to assess what aid is needed immediately, then the study will need to be done in phase 1 of the disaster. Under such conditions, researchers will face severe design and implementation constraints. However, if the goal is to assess the long-term impact of the event on mental health, the survey might best be conducted in phase 2 or 3 of the disaster recovery. With time, more rigorous designs can be implemented. Often, there will be multiple goals and the design will be adapted accordingly. For example, after Hurricane Ike, investigators conducted surveys two months, six months and fourteen months after the event. Both design and implementation strategies mirrored the evolving phases of the disaster and recovery (Freeland, 2010).

Table 6.1 provides a brief description of the events that will be discussed throughout the chapter.

Table 6.1 *Characteristics of referenced events*

Japan, Earthquake and Tsunami, March 11, 2011 (National Police Agency of Japan)
• 15,870 deaths, 6,114 injured, 2,814 missing, 341,411 displaced
• 1,075,195 buildings, 4,200 roads, 116 bridges, 29 railways destroyed or $122 to 235 billion estimated cost (World Bank)
Haiti, Earthquake, January 12, 2010 (US Geological Survey)
• 316,000 deaths, 300,000 injured, 1.3 million displaced
• 97,294 houses destroyed, 188,383 damaged
• $7.8 billion estimated cost (World Bank)
Hurricane Ike, Hispaniola, Cuba, and United States, September 1–14, 2008 (National Hurricane Center)
• 103 deaths
• $24.9 billion estimated cost (US), $50–200 million (Bahamas), $3–4 billion (Cuba)
Hurricane Katrina, Gulf Coast, United States, August 23–30, 2005 (NOAA's National Weather Service)
• 1,353 deaths, 1 million+ displaced
• 275,000 homes damaged or destroyed
• $81.2 billion estimated cost
Indian Ocean, Earthquake and Tsunami, December 26, 2004 (US Geological Survey)
• 11 countries affected
• 227,898 deaths
• 1.7 million displaced
• $6.9 billion estimated cost (World Bank)
Chernobyl, Russia, Nuclear Power Plant Explosion, April 26, 1986 (www.chernobyl-inter national.org)
• 7 million affected, 400,000 displaced, 5.5 million live in contaminated territories 20 years later
• Estimate of 6,000+ direct deaths (Bulletin of the Atomic Scientists)
• 5,722 deaths of cleanup workers (National Committee for Radiation Protection of the Ukraine Population)
• 2,000+ towns and villages destroyed
• $235 billion estimated cost (over 30 years)

6.2   Challenges in the design and conduct of survey research

6.2.1   Study design

The first step in designing a survey of populations affected by a disaster is to define the target population with precision. The target population will largely be a function of the analytical purposes of the survey. Some surveys may include all persons who resided in a specific geographic area on the day immediately preceding a disaster. Such a definition would include persons who remained in their homes and those who were subsequently displaced. One goal of such a survey might be to estimate the proportion of the population that was displaced. Other surveys might specifically focus on populations who have been displaced. An analytical goal of such a survey might be estimating the impact of displacement on the mental and physical health of such persons.

Once analytical goals have been clarified, the target population should be defined. For instance, a survey of earthquake survivors may need to define the geographic area impacted by the earthquake. There may be demographic criteria as well, such as age (e.g., only adults). Another critical aspect of defining the target population is the dimension of time. Displaced populations are likely geographically defined by where they *were* at some point in the past. To continue with the earthquake example, such a survey may define its target population as persons living in the affected area on the day of the earthquake. Under this definition, a person who moved into the area a week after the earthquake would not be part of the target population. On the other hand, a person who fled the area immediately following the earthquake would be eligible even if they were no longer in the geographic area impacted by the earthquake. An obvious, yet important criterion is whether one has to be alive to be part of the target population. If estimating the proportion of the population that was killed during a disaster was a goal of the study, then deceased persons could be part of the target population.

The circumstances surrounding a disaster can pose unique challenges in defining the target population and the circumstances of the event will come into play. For example, the 2004 Indian Ocean tsunami completely destroyed coastal fishing villages in Aceh. Many of the fishermen of the villages were at sea when the tsunami hit, so although they were technically "away" from the village at the time of the event, in many cases they were the only survivors of these villages (Brusset, 2009). Likewise, defining who is a victim is not always straightforward. As in the above example, the definition of a victim may be driven by political pressures (Deshmukh, 2006; Deshmukh & Prasad, 2009). Galea and colleagues (2008b) provide detailed discussion of practical issues associated with defining the target population in disaster research. This definition also flows from the analytic goals of the survey and should include demographic, geographic, and time dimensions. Imprecise definitions can lead to mismatches between the analytical goals of the survey and the final set of interviewed persons.

The next task is to design a sampling strategy. There are several methods available for sampling hard-to-reach, rare, or mobile populations (Elliott, Finch, Klein, Ma, Do, Beckett *et al.*, 2008; Kalton, 2002, 2009; Kalton & Anderson, 1986; McKenzie & Mistiaen, 2009;

Sudman, Sirken, & Cowan, 1988; Chapter 19 in this volume). The choice of sampling method is often based on the relative costs associated with each method. In many situations, preexisting sampling frames (i.e., lists of all persons in the target population) do not exist. In such situations, sampling frames must be constructed. Area probability samples (Kish, 1965) may provide theoretically complete coverage of the population and allow for the selection of samples with known probabilities, but are very expensive to create, especially post-disaster. Convenience samples, on the other hand, are much less expensive, but often do not have complete coverage and do not have known probabilities of selection.

The sampling method must assess the costs and errors associated with each available frame. The errors can include coverage errors, but may also be associated with other types of errors. For instance, a sampling frame of addresses may be inexpensive to obtain, but difficult to contact, as it is unknown which persons were associated with the sampled addresses at the time of the disaster. Random digit dial (RDD) sampling is facing growing coverage problems in the developed world, as a larger and larger proportion of households do not have landline telephone service (Blumberg & Luke, 2012). This coverage problem may be worse in post-disaster situations where long disruptions of telephone service can occur (Henderson, Sirois, Chen, Airriess, Swanson, & Banks, 2009; Chapter 8 in this volume).

There may be a temptation to choose a sampling method that will conform to the available budget and then simply conclude that "some data is better than no data" and in some situations, where the data are needed to guide relief efforts, this may be the best approach. However, it is still incumbent upon the investigator to examine the potential impact of errors on key estimates. The consequences of coverage or other errors associated with the choice of sampling methods need to be considered during the analysis. Who might be missed? What difference is it likely to make in key estimates? Galea, Brewin, Gruber, Jones, King, King *et al.*, (2007) note that their estimates of mental health issues in post-Katrina New Orleans are likely to be underestimates due to coverage issues related to their sampling frames. In this case, the underestimates are likely to be conservative (i.e., the impact of Katrina may have been worse than their estimates indicated).

Study designers should also be aware that it is possible to combine several sampling frames together in an attempt to overcome the weaknesses of each when used separately. For example, an address sample may be supplemented with time-location samples of refugee camps. This may improve the coverage of mobile persons who will be more difficult to locate. Methods for sampling and estimation from multiple frames have been widely discussed in the sampling literature (Bankier, 1986; Haines & Pollock, 1998; Hartley, 1962; Kott, Amrhein, & Hicks, 1998; Lepkowski & Groves, 1986; Skinner, Holmes, & Holt, 1994; Chapter 8 in this volume). A recent example of a survey using multiple frames is a survey of survivors of Hurricane Katrina in southern Mississippi (Galea, Tracy, Norris, & Coffey, 2008b). The survey used area probability sampling in the most damaged areas along the coast supplemented with an RDD sample of the less damaged areas.

Another sample approach that has been used to reach dispersed populations is to sample school records. La Greca (2006) selected schools based on the proximity to the disaster as well as demographic makeup of the area population. Barron Ausbrooks, Barrett, and Martinez-Cosio (2009) similarly found that sampling school districts was an efficient method to reach families who had relocated to Dallas in the wake of Hurricane Katrina.

Linked to the choice of sampling method is the mode of contact and interview. The choice of a sampling frame does not completely determine the mode of contact or interview. For example, RDD surveys often send prenotification letters to sampled households for which they have addresses. In the United States, address-based samples, which are built upon commercially available address lists derived from the US Postal Service, can be contacted by telephone for those addresses for which a telephone number can be found. However, for many displaced populations, a landline telephone survey may be unsuccessful in establishing contact immediately following a disaster. In the case of Hurricane Ike, it was several months before telephone service was re-established (Freeland, 2010). If the survey needs to be conducted immediately following a disaster or while the population is displaced, then this mode is unlikely to be very useful and may not be successful in the long term either, depending on the circumstances. Henderson *et al.* (2009) found that following Hurricane Katrina many victims were not reachable by phone. Thus, it was necessary to wait up to a month and a half for landlines to be re-established. Even after waiting, response rates were dramatically higher for in-person interviews (77 percent) than for landline (39 percent) or cell-phone interviews (35 percent).

In some contexts, mobile telephones may be the best mode to reach victims. After the Indian Ocean tsunami, the mobile phone systems in the Maldives were still working because the communication towers were located on hilltops and on multistoried buildings, often with generator back-up systems. Here, Deshmukh (2006) found that sampling these phones was an efficient and effective means of reaching respondents.

Similar problems may be faced by mail or Internet surveys. The services that allow these kinds of surveys to be delivered – postal service, Internet access – may be disrupted after a disaster. Face-to-face contact may be the only way to reach sampled persons. Even this may be difficult, as areas with heavy damage may be closed and survivors may be focused on more immediate needs. Locating displaced populations may be a particularly difficult task. Many sampling frames only provide limited information about households and household members, and rarely the names of sampled persons. In Bangladesh, Gray and Mueller (2012) note that large-scale flooding created a mobile population where migrant rosters were the only feasible way to identify the target population.

If the displaced population is housed in temporary housing, then this natural clustering of the population might provide an important means for sampling and contacting the target population, but even here complications can arise. After the 2004 Indian Ocean tsunami, government officials in Indonesia and Sri Lanka provided government-sanctioned lists that appeared to exclude all rebel-held areas. Therefore, the government lists had to be supplemented with new listings in these areas (Deshmukh, 2006). It is unlikely that all displaced persons will be located in such temporary housing, however. Some may have gone to the homes of relatives or friends. Ideally, such persons will have some chance of being selected and, if selected, there will be attempts made to locate them. It seems reasonable to expect that their experience of the disaster might be quite different from that of those persons who are in temporary housing. Norris, Sherrieb, and Galea (2010) noted that because of the devastation in Galveston Island and the Bolivar Peninsula after Hurricane Ike, almost three-quarters of the selected households had to be tracked to new locations. In one segment which included public housing, individuals living in this housing pre-hurricane were unable to be reached at all since they had been evacuated *en masse* prior to the hurricane and government agencies would not release information on the evacuation location. Similarly, in the Indian Ocean tsunami, many survivors left their villages to stay with family and friends permanently or relocated to areas inland that would not be impacted by future tsunamis (Brusset, 2009).

When populations are widely dispersed, then methods such as time-location sampling or multiplicity sampling may be necessary to identify eligible persons. (See Chapter 19 in this volume, for a more complete discussion.) Time-location sampling involves using a specific location to conduct interviews at a specific point in time, thus populations with no permanent residence can be interviewed at convenient locations. Time-location sampling has been an effective method for conducting research on the homeless, who share many of the characteristics of displaced populations (Chapter 9 in this volume). Like disaster-stricken displaced populations, the homeless rarely have a fixed location or address where they can be interviewed. Time-location sampling takes this issue into account by basing the sampling procedure on the support facilities for the intended sample. For the homeless, these support systems may include soup kitchens or day centers, whereas government organizations such as the US Federal Emergency Management Agency (FEMA) or local shelters may be useful starting points for those displaced by a disaster (Quaglia & Vivier, 2010).

Even after best efforts to construct a sample and interview eligible persons, it is likely that there will be some or even many missing units. It is important to describe how the missing elements might be different from those that are observed. Face-to-face contact has the advantage of allowing surveys to collect additional data on all the units, including those that are not interviewed. Interviewers can add observational data that may be of use, particularly in imputing missing values for nonresponding cases (Kreuter, Olson, Wagner, Yan, Ezzati-Rice, Casas-Cordero *et al.*, 2010). In a survey conducted after Hurricane Ike, interviewers observed whether each sampled housing unit was partially damaged, heavily damaged, or completely destroyed (Norris *et al.*, 2010). These observations were correlated with both the probability that a household would respond and with key outcomes from the survey. Examples of other observations of this type include evidence of relief efforts, power outages, repair to existing structures, construction of new housing units, and descriptions of the damage to the entire neighborhood. The key to designing useful paradata of this sort is to create observations that are likely to be correlated with both response and the key survey outcomes (Kreuter *et al.*, 2010; Little & Vartivarian, 2005).

Face-to face interviews have other advantages. Biological measures can be collected and face-to-face interviews can facilitate narrative accounts. In some contexts, such as the Chernobyl disaster, biological and physical symptoms were critical to understanding the psychological effects of the disaster (Bromet & Havenaar, 2006).

6.2.2   Questionnaire development

Developing survey instruments

One of the first decisions an investigator will face is the selection of a data collection instrument. Questions will need to be relevant to both the type and phase of the disaster and may include hazard knowledge, attitudes to risk, prior experience and exposure, as well as demographic details (Bird, 2009). Furthermore, collecting information on the context of the disaster may be critical to understanding the survey data as well as allow for nonresponse adjustment. Contextual data may include details on the timing, severity, and region-specific issues and challenges. Time has a very real impact on questionnaire development; shorter development time may impact survey data quality, but longer development time may delay data collection and the usefulness of the resulting data. Depending on the goals of the research, investigators may feel pressured into using preexisting instruments as is, or haphazardly adapting the instrument to the situation.

Given sufficient time, the tradeoffs between using a preexisting instrument or developing a new instrument can be evaluated to ascertain the best approach. Disaster research often does not allow such time. Zissman, Holcomb, Jones *et al.* (2010) reported a number of the tradeoffs (e.g., unilateral design vs. "design-by-committee"; rapid questionnaire design vs. translated, tested questionnaire; fewer indicators/questions vs. more indicators/ questions) when developing an aid assessment tool shortly after the Haiti earthquake. The tradeoffs were driven by two competing interests: the urgent need for data to guide rescue and relief efforts and the need for a methodologically sound assessment tool. The decision was made to give more weight to producing a methodologically sound product. Here, a "design-by-committee" approach was used to draft, translate, and adapt existing, standardized post-disaster indicators and questions. However, this decision came at a cost, both in terms of time and resources. Adapting existing instruments (i.e., identifying indicators of interest, creating and translating the questions, and loading the instrument onto handheld computers) delayed data collection by six weeks.

Disasters are unique events and it is highly unlikely to find well-matched instruments for every disaster situation. Most likely, researchers will need to adapt existing instruments or create new measures specific to the context of the event and location. Even here, investigators need to be cautious that the instrument is appropriate for the population. Knack, Chen, Williams, and Jensen-Campbell (2006) observe that many well-being scales were developed and validated with college-educated populations and may not be well suited to disaster populations with more varied backgrounds. Pilot work is recommended to guide instrumentation selection to ensure that a broad range of respondents can comprehend the questions.

Given the many dimensions of a disaster (i.e., type, phase, and location), developing an assessment tool or questionnaire for every conceivable contingency may be unrealistic. A more practical approach may be to develop assessment tools and questionnaires for the areas that are prone to disasters, with different versions for the type of disaster and the phase of disaster.

Developing entirely new instruments takes considerable time and resources but may be necessary. A Sri Lankan study (Fernando, 2008) that assessed mental health with populations affected by the tsunami (and the 1983–2009 civil war) recognized the need to create a mental health measure from scratch, believing that the existing European and European-American measures would not be adequate for this population. The European and European-American mental health measures were adapted to create new culturally appropriate measures, the Sri Lankan Index of Psychosocial Status – Adult Version (SLIPPS-A). The questionnaire was developed by using qualitative data (local narratives) in conjunction with quantitative data (i.e., a pilot test).

In most survey settings, open-ended questions are kept to a minimum because the questions take longer to administer, have higher item nonresponse, higher processing error, and the added cost of coding which may delay analysis (Bradburn, Sudman, & Wansick, 2004). However, in a disaster survey, open-ended questions may prove useful and necessary to capture the varied experiences of disaster populations.

Anecdotal accounts from field workers and reports from respondents indicate that following a disaster, respondents generally want to talk about their experiences. In the early phases of the disaster, affected populations are still "in shock," thus a mixture of fear and excitement contribute to a willingness to talk to interviewers for an extended period of time (King, 2002). Newman and Kaloupek (2004) conducted a content analysis of open-ended questions across post-disaster studies, and observed that allowing respondents to talk freely about their experiences is both useful and cathartic for these respondents. After Hurricane Katrina, respondents not only allowed their stories to be recorded, but also to make them available on a public website (www.hurricanekatrina.med.harvard.edu/oralhistories.php) (Overview of Baseline Survey Results: Hurricane Katrina Advisory Group 2006). In a study conducted after the Chernobyl nuclear meltdown, even the respondents who were part of the control group wanted their stories heard. Although the control group was not directly affected by the meltdown because they lived outside the radius of contamination, they were affected by the influx of victims relocating to their communities (E. Bromet, 2012).

An open-ended approach called "free listing" may also be used to create a context-specific disaster questionnaire (Bolton, 2004). Elements of post-disaster trauma are often missed by standardized questionnaires due to their specificity; free listing broadens the form of the question and functions as a net which will encompass a broader range of post-disaster problems. The technique begins with a broad primary question followed by probing for further, more specific problems. Once a list is complete, the interviewer returns to the top and goes down the list one by one asking for a short description of each item. This method allows the interviewer to avoid leading questions or comments. A similar approach was used by Irwin, Deshmukh and colleagues (2009) in their study of regional aspirations in Kashmir, but they went a step further and elicited solutions as well as problems. Key informant interviews can be used in combination with free listing to expand upon the data collection domains. Using specific problems identified in the list, knowledgeable persons are identified and given unstructured, narrative interviews where the respondents are given free rein to express their ideas and opinions. Interviewers are instructed to probe outside of the initial question, but most of the interaction comes from the respondents' answers.

Translation and adaptation

There is little literature on translating and adapting surveys for use with populations affected by disasters. Even in the context of well-funded surveys with adequate time for question-naire development, translation is far too often an afterthought. In the context of having only days or weeks to prepare a study for fielding, it may be tempting to avoid translation and allow bilingual interviewers to translate from the source questionnaires as they conduct the interview (i.e., with no written translation) or to use interpreters to translate the interviewers' questions and respondents' answers. Although sparse, research on this "on-sight" trans-lation, "on-the-fly translation," or "oral translation" suggests that such an undertaking is fraught with problems and can severely impact data quality (Harkness, Schoebi, Joye, Mohler, Faass, & Behr, 2008; Harkness, Villar, Kruse, Branden, Edwards, Steele, *et al.*, 2009a; Harkness, Villar, Kruse, Steele, Wang, Branden *et al.*, 2009b). However, in a disaster situation, where time is critical, the decision may be taken to allow interviewers to translate "on-site" especially in contexts where there are multiple languages and dialects. Such a decision should not be taken lightly and interviewers must be adequately trained for such an undertaking. Job aids that provide translations for critical terms may be one compromise approach.

With an increasing awareness of the important role translation plays in survey research, large-scale organizations such as the US Census Bureau (de la Puente, Pan, & Rose, 2003; Pan & de la Puente, 2005) and large cross-national studies such as the European Social Survey (Harkness, 2002/2006) have developed best practices for the development and testing of survey translations. These practices include having a team comprised of individ-uals with questionnaire development expertise, substantive understanding of the subject matter, source and target language expertise and experience (including formal translation training), and local knowledge, to develop and assess the translations. This approach, called TRAPD (Translation, Review, Adjudication, Pretesting, and Documentation), is further detailed in the Cross-Cultural Survey Guidelines (http://ccsg.isr.umich.edu).

The TRAPD approach to translation assumes that there is time in the development process for translators to provide feedback to questionnaire developers about problematic questionnaire items, often through iterative reviews. In the context of a disaster, time for such iterations may not be practical. Therefore, if more than one language or multiple languages are needed for fielding a survey of populations affected by disaster, the translation process must be brought forward to the questionnaire development phase. Here, the ques-tionnaire development team would also include translators so problems potentially intro-duced by translation could be avoided or minimized. In the above referenced Haitian survey, a person fluent in Haitian Creole was on the team that developed the survey instruments (Zissman *et al.*, 2010). The goal of the team was to develop both culturally appropriate questions and undertake adaptation and translation. The authors give an example of questions about water usage. Questions were modified from quantifying water volume in liters to a culturally relevant volume measure, that is, referencing vessels often used to carry water, a "gwo bokit" or a "galon."

Pennell, Mneimneh, Bowers, Chardoul, Wells, Viana *et al.* (2008) outline a process where translation proceeds in tandem with questionnaire development. Here, the development and translation process are carried out in a modular approach. This approach adds a measure of complexity and greater need for quality control checks across modules, and also necessitates a robust version control system since subsequent translation of modules often indicates changes needed to previously translated modules. Despite the need for these additional quality control measures, the approach can speed up the overall development process.

Deciding to translate and in what languages to translate can be a political decision as well as a decision based on cost, measurement, or coverage error. In some countries, the local spoken language is not "officially" recognized for political reasons and/or use of the official language may alienate local populations. For example, in Indonesia, the "Acehnese" dialect is not officially recognized for political reasons. (Bahasa Indonesian is the official language.) After the Indian Ocean tsunami, Deshmukh (2007) reported that many of the Acehnese people could not be surveyed properly using Bahasa Indonesian, for issues of trust as much as for language comprehension reasons. In Bromet's study in Chernobyl, investigators encountered pressure from their Soviet collaborators regarding translation of a set of measures on alcohol consumption. Here, the collaborators did not want to highlight a potential social problem (Bromet, 2012). In the end, Bromet and her team had to compromise on which items could be used and how these items were translated.

6.2.3   Field operations

Recruiting and training interviewers

The first decision a researcher will face in deciding how to implement the field work is whether to hire local interviewers or use travelling teams of interviewers. This choice will depend on the severity of the event (e.g., whether local interviewers are available), the language skills needed, the need for gender or other interviewer-respondent matching criteria, and an assessment of how "outsiders" might be viewed by the displaced population (Chan & Kim, 2010; Herrmann, Brodie, Morin, Blendon, & Benson, 2006; Chapter 8 in this volume).

Once the interviewers are recruited, training also introduces new challenges. As with any study, interviewer training will include technical aspects of the questionnaire administration and interviewing techniques, but in the context of a disaster, special circumstances will also need to be addressed, including issues of both respondent and interviewer safety, and handling potential respondent distress, among others (Chou, Su, Ou-Yang, Chien, Lu, & Chou, 2003). Additional training may be needed to implement complex sampling protocols and rules.

Community engagement

A recurring theme in both the disaster research literature and the first-hand accounts of those working in disaster-affected areas is the importance of forming partnerships in the local community. Gaining cooperation from country, state, regional and/or local governments can be critical. Government authorities can facilitate travel throughout the disaster zone, grant access to temporary shelters or refugee camps, and/or assist in obtaining government records, such as census figures or registries. In developing countries, gaining cooperation from local village elders or leaders is also important, as they may act as gatekeepers to the target population. Such leaders can also give insight to the situation and cultural norms. King (2002) suggests that community surveys should be backed up by interviews with community leaders, key informants, and experts or officers in charge of response; providing context for the survivor interviews.

Developing and maintaining relationships and partnerships with other nongovernmental organizations can also be important. Zissman and his colleagues (2010) learned from their work in Haiti that in order for data collection to have an impact on real-time decision-making, coordination was needed across both governmental and nongovernmental relief organizations as each often had its own agenda and sources of data. Although building these relationships may delay aspects of the project implementation, without these collaborations, data collection may simply not be feasible in some contexts. Evans and colleagues discuss at length the importance of community engagement in Chapter 25 of this volume.

Environmental hazards and security concerns

One of the challenges affecting field operations in areas impacted by disasters is the potentially dangerous environmental hazards and security concerns. Here again, the type, severity, and location of the event (and the state of infrastructure before the event) will need to be taken into account. Henderson *et al.* (2009) encountered physical, chemical, and biological hazards in their work in New Orleans, post-Katrina. They suggest including trained responders in the research team, although this approach may not be realistic given that disaster-affected regions will often overwhelm emergency services and such trained individuals may not be available. Security in post-disaster areas may also be compromised due to damaged government buildings and injured or otherwise occupied government workers (i.e., police or military personnel) attending to more immediate needs. Victims of disasters may have to take desperate measures to obtain food, money, or other resources. In these situations, looting or other acts of violence may occur, endangering interviewers. Knack *et al.* (2006) cited an incident near a Tennessee shelter for Katrina victims, where a disaster survivor was shot to death over a debit card worth several hundred dollars. Incidents like these discourage the use of monetary incentives in contexts where interviewers may become targets if it becomes known they are carrying money. Herrmann *et al.* (2006) and Brodie *et al.* (Chapter 8 in this volume) also note that incentives may be inappropriate in situations where survivors are in resource-poor, crowded conditions (e.g., some shelters after Hurricane Katrina). Here, those not included in the sample were resentful. Finally, it may also be necessary to ensure that interviewers and research staff are adequately protected from disease outbreaks, have received appropriate training on precautions, and have all appropriate and up-to-date inoculations.

Logistical issues

Field work in disaster research poses more than the usual logistical challenges, and even more so in resource poor areas. After the 2010 Haiti earthquake, researchers found that maps pre-event were missing entire streets, Internet access was limited, and the government was releasing incomplete and conflicting reports (Kolbe & Muggah, 2010). In the 2004 Indonesia tsunami and earthquake, much of the displaced population was housed in temporary living centers or located in makeshift houses on hilltops that were only accessible by aircraft or boat (Gupta, Suantio, Gray, Widyastuti, Jain, Rolos *et al.*, 2007). Similarly, Chan & Kim (2010), working in Pakistan after the 2005 earthquake, reported difficulties conducting field work due to treacherous terrain, uncertain weather conditions, and continuous landslides. Even in the United States, finding suitable accommodations for interviewers after hurricanes can be difficult. One approach used by interviewers after Hurricane Katrina was to rent recreational vehicles to travel and stay in affected areas, since most hotels in the region were either closed or fully occupied by survivors.

Another logistical issue that can arise is in communication with field staff and the central office, both via landline and Internet. In the Galveston Bay study, Internet access was a challenge when attempting to send sample listing files to the main office (Freeland, 2012). The field staff was able to find one restaurant on the island with consistent service and with the help of restaurant staff, they were able to transmit files. Here, the field staff was also issued mobile phones to address safety concerns and to facilitate rapid communication.

Ethical issues

Although an important consideration in any survey, addressing ethical issues that arise in the conduct of research with victims of natural disasters is a much more complex undertaking. In a disaster situation, the target population may be experiencing catastrophic loss, mental distress, and/or physical injuries. Several concerns arise in this context. How does the risk–benefit paradigm typically used to evaluate human subjects research change? Should the concept of vulnerable populations expand? Is decisional impairment a concern in obtaining informed consent? Should the role of coercion be re-examined in this context? How should respondent burden be viewed? Finally, how should we address the concerns and experiences of interviewers who may also be exposed to all aspects of the disaster and its aftermath? These are discussed in turn below.

Ethics review committees, or in the US context, Institutional Review Boards (IRBs), are asked to weigh the risk–benefit of research with human subjects. Weighing such risks and benefits in trauma-focused research is more challenging. A few studies have focused on the evaluation of the risk side of this equation, particularly in research that asks respondents to recall traumatic events. The concern is that such questioning will cause emotional harm or distress for the respondent. Newman and Kaloupek (2004) reviewed twelve studies that examined this question. Generally, they conclude that respondents in these studies report an overall positive gain from participation. Boscarino, Figley, Adams, Galea, Resnick, Fleischman *et al.* (2004) and Griffin, Resick, Waldrop, and Mechanic (2003) draw similar conclusions in their work with trauma victims. Respondents who may be at a greater risk of distress are those who have "preexisting distress, younger and older age, a history of multiple trauma exposure, social vulnerability, and greater physical injury severity" (Newman & Kaloupek, 2004, p. 393). This suggests that having respondents recall their experiences is appropriate, but caution should be given when interviewing those who may be more vulnerable. Often, ethics boards will require the research team to develop a protocol for handling cases of severe respondent distress.

The definition of vulnerable populations may need to be expanded in the context of a disaster. Racial and ethnic minorities and socially disadvantaged groups can be particularly vulnerable as they may be less able to protect their interests as a result of insufficient social and political power, education, and resources (Levine, 2004). Examples of this can be seen in events such as Hurricane Katrina and the earthquake in Haiti. The purposes and auspices of the survey may also be confused with the provision of aid, particularly in areas with no research tradition. Sumathipala and Siribaddana (2005) maintain that victims of the Sri Lanka tsunami were particularly vulnerable to the misconception that participation in survey research was a prerequisite for obtaining clinical care. In a study conducted in Haiti after the 2010 earthquake, respondents refused to participate because they had already been interviewed several times and never received the aid or assistance they had expected from such participation (Andre & Lusk, 2011). Respondents may also worry that aid or assistance may be taken away or reduced if they participate in a survey. In a study to assess recovery efforts for individuals residing in FEMA trailers after the Gulf Coast hurricane season of 2005, the researchers reported a low response rate and speculated that respondents worried that participating might influence the duration the trailers would be available (Larrance, Anastario, & Lawry, 2007). The authors concluded that "respondents may have exaggerated or underestimated responses if they believed it would be in their interest to do so" (p. 594). In the context of a disaster, the goals of the research, the benefits from participation, along with auspices and affiliations, must be made clear to potential respondents. That is, any link (or lack thereof) between participating in research and receipt of aid or other benefits should be explicit, and all study materials should clearly state the purpose of the research and list all affiliations. All research staff should wear clearly visible photo identification that identifies their employer.

Emphasizing and adhering to best practices in protecting respondent confidentiality is also important. An exception to blurring the line between conducting research and providing aid is worth noting here. Often, post-disaster studies of mental health will have as part of their protocol a mechanism for referring respondents to a mental health specialist upon respondent request. This may be particularly useful if the respondent expresses suicidal ideation, or if the respondent appears to experience severe distress during the interview. Often these protocols involve an on-call clinical team that can assess the situation and make referrals as necessary. After the Japan 2011 earthquake and tsunami multidisaster, respondents were measured on an impact-of-event scale and if they scored high, they were immediately directed to seek assistance with the public health department (Kyutoku, Tada, Umeyama, Harada, Kikuchi, Watanabe *et al.*, 2012). However, Bromet in her post-disaster work notes that referral systems are not always adequate. Where clinical resources can be made available, she suggests having clinicians on site and did so while conducting interviews after the World Trade Center disaster (Bromet, 2012). Obviously, such resources may not always be available, particularly in medically underserved regions of the world.

Voluntary consent decisions are another ethical concern. There is little research on whether or not disaster victims have decreased decision capacity. Collogan, Tuma, Dolan-Sewell, Borja, and Fleischman (2004) point out that lessons can be learned from examining studies of patients suffering from acute and post-traumatic stress disorders. Evidence from these studies show that generally, decision capacity is not diminished in these circumstances. However, very extreme stress reactions can lead to symptoms which one could certainly consider a sign of decisional impairment (Rosenstein, 2004), although presumably in these cases, the respondent would also have diminished capacity to participate in a survey in any case. Special attention is needed in designing consent procedures and should be guided by the context of the study, location of the research, and local research tradition (e.g., in some contexts, written informed consent might be inappropriate because of low levels of literacy issues or a general fear of signing official documents), while adhering to widely accepted international standards guiding informed consent (Marshall, 2001; Dawson & Kass, 2005).

Respondent burden can also take on a new meaning in disaster research. High-profile events, which may attract wide media attention, may also attract multiple research teams who may unwittingly seek out the same respondents. In Fleischman and Wood's 2002 review of 177 studies conducted from 1981 to 2001, they report that respondents felt overburdened due to multiple survey requests from differing organizations. Similarly, Richardson, Plummer, Barthelemy, and Cain (2012) reported that survivors of Hurricanes Katrina and Rita were "bombarded with requests to be participants in research studies" (p. 8). Newman and Kaloupek (2004) observe that researchers do not take the time to coordinate operations either due to time constraints or other competing interests.

Finally, in considering ethical issues encountered in the conduct of disaster research, the welfare of the interviewers must also be considered. In order for the research not to put interviewers at risk or to not impede rescue or relief efforts, an evaluation and assessment of on-the-ground conditions must first take place. Obviously, research efforts must be secondary to rescue and relief efforts. Often local governmental agencies will impose limits on access to these affected areas and may be a good source of information with regard to safety assessment. If interviewers are recruited locally, they may have experienced the disaster event themselves and may have family members who have sustained mental or physical trauma or even died as a result of the disaster. Richardson *et al.* (2012) report that one of the primary challenges their research team faced after Hurricanes Katrina and Rita was that the researchers themselves were responding to the needs of their own families, friends, students, and communities. Drawing again from studies of mental health, often a protocol is implemented that allow interviewers to seek the help of mental health specialists should they encounter a distressing situation or interview or encounter a situation that reminds them of previous traumatic events.

6.3. Conclusions and recommendations

Surveying populations affected by natural disasters is a highly challenging undertaking. The disaster context will impact every phase of the survey life cycle and evaluation of the cost-error tradeoffs will take on additional complexity. Compromises in design and implementation are inevitable but must be undertaken with an understanding of the survey error and cost consequences. The literature guiding investigators in this research is often limited and found in disparate disciplinary domains. The result is that either because of limitations placed on authors by publishers on manuscript length and/or deliberately glossing over design details, there is little detail to be found in the literature to guide those undertaking this type of research. Clearly, there is a need for greater transparency in approach and methods. Without candid disclosure and assessment of methods, it will be difficult to move forward with innovative approaches and techniques, and advancing designs that have optimal methodological rigor.

Below, we outline five characteristics that have been found to influence every phase of disaster studies: event type, severity of event, phase of event, location of event, and the goal of the research. Although, as we note, every event is unique, there are some common themes and approaches. These are summarized in Table 6.2 below.

Table 6.2 *Detailed recommendations*

Study design	Challenge	Recommendations
	Defining the target population	Define the target population based on time, geographic, and demographic boundaries (Galea *et al.*, 2008b)
	Coverage	Area probability samples can provide complete coverage of the population (Kish, 1965) and allow for known probabilities but they are expensive post-disaster
		Convenience samples are cheaper but do not have full coverage or known probabilities
		Telephone, mail, Internet and cell-phone surveys face coverage problems because all are likely to be disrupted by the disaster, so multiple frames are recommended
	Damaged areas	Use area probability sampling in the most damaged areas and RDD in the less damaged areas (Galea *et al.*, 2008b)
	Locating respondents	Use school records and school districts as an efficient way to sample relocated families (La Greca, 2006; Barron Ausbrooks *et al.*, 2009)

Table 6.2 (*cont.*)

Study design	Challenge	Recommendations
	Dispersed populations	Time-location sampling can be effective for widely dispersed populations (e.g., conducting interviews in support facilities like local shelters) (Quaglia & Vivier, 2010)
	Response Rates	In-person interviews appear to be the most effective mode of contact, have higher response rates (Henderson *et al.*, 2009) and allow for the collection of additional, observational data (Kreuter *et al.*, 2010)
Questionnaire development	Time	Due to time constraints, investigators may need to use preexisting instruments or adapt the instrument to the situation
		Develop assessment tools and questionnaires for areas that are prone to disasters
	Selecting measures	Questions should be relevant to the type and phase of the disaster (Bird, 2009)
		Pilot work is suggested to guide the instrument development and to ensure respondents can comprehend the questions
		Open-ended questions can be useful because they elicit a richer variety of experiences and allow respondents to talk about their experiences (King, 2002; Newman & Kaloupek, 2004)
		Free listing may be an effective open-ended method as it can address a broad range of problems (Bolton, 2004)
	Translation	TRAPD method is best, but in some circumstances, it may be necessary to allow interviewers to translate "on-the-fly"; Job aids with translations for critical terms is one possible compromise
		Translation can proceed in tandem with development, which can ultimately speed up the overall development process (Pennell *et al.*, 2008)
Field operations	Interviewers	Choose interviewers (locals or traveling teams) based on severity of the event, language skills needed, and interviewer-respondent matching criteria
		Interviewers must be aware of the risks and be willing to work in the affected areas; their mental and physical well-being must be taken into account
		Because disasters pose many risks to interviewers, one approach is to consider including trained responders in disaster research teams (Henderson *et al.*, 2009)
	Community Engagement	Community surveys should be endorsed by community leaders, key informants, and experts; these individuals can also provide context and depth to the study (King, 2002)
		Coordination with both governmental and nongovernmental organizations is needed (Zissman *et al.*, 2010)

Table 6.2 (*cont.*)

Study design	Challenge	Recommendations
	Physical Environment	Researchers should recognize the constraints of trying to reach a highly mobile population
		Disaster research teams should be prepared for a loss of emergency services in the aftermath of the disaster
	Respondent Concerns/Ethics	Because respondents can be overburdened by the sheer number of competing surveys in a large-scale disaster (Fleischman & Wood, 2002; Richardson *et al.*, 2012), it is important for research teams to coordinate with one another where feasible (Newman & Kaloupek, 2004)
		The research team should be mindful of the burden the disaster has caused for potential respondents (Newman & Kaloupek, 2004)
		Racial and ethnic minorities as well as socially disadvantaged groups should be recognized as particularly vulnerable following a disaster (Levine, 2004)
	Consent	Consent procedures should be guided by context and local laws (Dawson & Kass, 2005; Marshall, 2001)

References

Andre, R., & Lusk, J. L. (2011). *What do Haitians Need after the Earthquake?* Paper presented at the Economics Southern Agricultural Association Annual Meeting, Corpus Christi, TX.

Bankier, M. D. (1986). Estimators based on several stratified samples with applications to multiple frame surveys. *Journal of the American Statistical Association*, 81(396), 1074–79.

Barron Ausbrooks, C. Y., Barrett, E. J., & Martinez-Cosio, M. (2009). Ethical issues in disaster research: lessons from Hurricane Katrina. *Population Research and Policy Review*, 28, 93–106. doi: 10.1007/s11113-008-9112-7.

Berg, R. (2008). National Oceanic and Atmospheric Administration, National Hurricane Center. *Tropical Cyclone Report Hurricane Ike*. Miami, FL: National Hurricane Center.

Bird, D. K. (2009). The use of questionnaires for acquiring information on public perception of natural hazards and risk mitigation – a review of current knowledge and practice. *Natural Hazards and Earth System Sciences*, 9, 1307–25. doi:10.5194/nhess-9-1307-2009.

Blumberg, S. J., & Luke, J. V. (2012). *Wireless Substitution: Early Release of Estimates from the National Health Interview Survey, July–December 2011*. Atlanta, GA: Centers for Disease Control and Prevention, National Center for Health Statistics.

Bolton, P. (2004). Using ethnographic methods in the selection of post-disaster, mental-health interventions. *Prehospital and Disaster Medicine*, 19(1), 97–101.

Boscarino, J. A., Figley, C. R., Adams, R. E., Galea, S., Resnick, H., Fleischman, A. R., *et al.* (2004). Adverse reactions associated with studying persons recently exposed to mass urban disaster. *Journal of Nervous and Mental Disease*, 192(8), 515–24.

Bradburn, N., Sudman, S., and Wansick, I. (2004). *Asking Questions: The Definitive Guide to Questionnaire Design – for Market Research, Political Polls, and Social And Health Questionnaires* (revised edn.). San Francisco: Jossey-Bass.

Bromet, E. (2012). Personal communication.

Bromet, E., & Havenaar, J. (2006). Basic epidemiological approaches to disaster research: value of face-to-face procedures. In F. Norris, S. Galea, & M. Friedman (eds.), *Methods for Disaster Mental Health Research* (pp. 95–110). New York: Guilford Press.

Brown, P. (2005, January 21). Tsunami cost Aceh a generation and $4.4bn. *Guardian*. Retrieved from: www.guardian.co.uk/world/2005/jan/22/tsunami2004.international aidanddevelopment.

Brusset, E. (2009). *A Ripple in Development? Long Term Perspectives on the Response to the Indian Ocean Tsunami 2004: A Joint Follow-up Evaluation of the Links between Relief, Rehabilitation and Development (LRRD)*. Stockholm: SIDA.

Chan, E. Y. Y., & Kim, J. J. (2010). Characteristics and health outcomes of internally displaced population in unofficial rural self-settled camps after the 2005 Kashmir, Pakistan earthquake. *European Journal of Emergency Medicine*, 17, 136–41.

Chou, F. H. C., Su, T. T. P., Ou-Yang, W. C., Chien, I. C., Lu, M. K., & Chou, P. (2003). Establishment of a disaster-related psychological screening test. *Australian and New Zealand Journal of Psychiatry*, 37, 97–103.

Collogan, L. K., Tuma, F., Dolan-Sewell, R., Borja, S., & Fleischman, A. R. (2004). Ethical issues pertaining to research in the aftermath of disaster. *Journal of Trauma Stress*, 7(5), 363–72.

Dawson, L., & Kass, N. E. (2005). View of U.S. researchers about informed consent in international collaborative research. *Social Science & Medicine*, 61, 1211–22.

de la Puente, M., Pan, Y., & Rose, D. (2003). *An Overview of a Proposed Census Bureau Guideline for the Translation of Data Collection Instruments and Supporting Materials*. Washington, DC: US Census Bureau.

Deshmukh, Y. (2006). *LRRD1 Methodology: Long Term Perspectives on the Response to the Indian Ocean Tsunami 2004: A Joint Evaluation of the Links between Relief, Rehabilitation and Development (LRRD)*. Stockholm: SIDA.

(2007). *The "Hikmah" of Peace Dividend: Disasters and the Public Opinion*. Paper presented at WAPOR annual conference, Berlin, May 2007.

Deshmukh, Y., & Prasad M. G. (2009). *Impact of Natural Disasters on the QOL in Conflict Prone Areas: A Study of the Tsunami Hit Transitional Societies of Aceh (Indonesia) & Jaffna (Sri Lanka)*. Paper presented at the IX ISQOLS Conference Florence, July, 2009

Elliott, M. N., Finch, B. K., Klein, D., Ma, S., Do, D. P., Beckett, M. K., *et al.* (2008). Sample designs for measuring the health of small racial/ethnic subgroups. *Statistics in Medicine*, 27(20), 4016–29.

Fernando, G. A. (2008). Assessing mental health and psychosocial status in communities exposed to traumatic events: Sri Lanka as an example. *American Journal of Orthopsychiatry*, 78(2), 229–39.

Fleischman, A. R., & Wood, E. B. (2002). Ethical issues in research involving victims of terror. *Journal of Urban Health*, 79, 315–21.

Freeland, S. (2010). *The Galveston Bay Recovery Project: A Study Conducted by the National Center for Disaster Mental Health Research*. Ann Arbor, MI: Survey Research Center/Institute for Social Research, University of Michigan.

Freeman, S. (2012). Personal communication.

Galea, S., Brewin, C. R., Gruber, M., Jones, R. T., King, D. W., King, L. A., *et al.* (2007). Exposure to hurricane-related stressors and mental illness after Hurricane Katrina. *Archives of General Psychiatry*, 64(12), 1427.

Galea, S., Maxwell, A. R., & Norris, F. (2008a). Sampling and design challenges in studying the mental health consequences of disasters. *International Journal of Methods in Psychiatric Research*, 17, S21–S28. doi:10.1002/mpr.267.

Galea, S., Tracy, M., Norris, F., & Coffey, S. F. (2008b). Financial and social circumstances and the incidence and course of PTSD in Mississippi during the first two years after Hurricane Katrina. *Journal of Traumatic Stress*, 21(4), 357–68.

Gray, C. L., & Mueller, V. (2012). Natural disasters and population mobility in Bangladesh. In *Proceedings of the National Academy of Sciences of the United States of America*, 109(16), 6000–05. Retrieved from http://ejournals.ebsco.com.ezproxy.gvsu.edu/direct.asp?ArticleID=43BEAECBBF5977B55822.

Griffin, M. G., Resick, P. A., Waldrop, A. E., & Mechanic, M. B. (2003). Participation in trauma research: is there evidence of harm? *Journal of Traumatic Stress*, 16(3), 221–27.

Guha-Sapir, D., Vos, F., Below, R., & Ponserre, S. (2011). Annual Disaster Statistical Review 2010: The numbers and trends. *Center for Research on the Epidemiology of Disasters (CRED)*.

Gupta, S. K., Suantio, A., Gray, A., Widyastuti, E., Jain, N., Rolos, R., *et al.* (2007). Factors associated with E. Coli contamination of household drinking water among tsunami and earthquake survivors, Indonesia. *American Journal of Tropical Medicine and Hygiene*, 76(6), 1158–62.

Haines, D. E., & Pollock, K. H. (1998). Combining multiple frames to estimate population size and totals, *Survey Methodology*, 24, 79–88.

Harkness, J. A. (2002/2006). Round 3 ESS Translation Strategies and Procedures.

Harkness, J. A., Schoebi, N., Joye, D., Mohler, P., Faass, T., & Behr, D. (2008). Oral translation in telephone surveys. In J. M. Lepkowski, C. Tucker, J. M. Brick, E. de Leeuw, L. Japec, & P. J. Lavrakas (eds.), *Advances in Telephone Survey Methodology* (pp. 231–49). Hoboken, NJ: John Wiley & Sons.

Harkness, J. A., Villar, A., Kruse, Y., Branden, L., Edwards, B., Steele, C., *et al.* (2009a). *Interpreted Telephone Survey Interviews*. Paper presented at the International Workshop on Comparative Survey Design and Implementation, Ann Arbor, MI.

Harkness, J. A, Villar, A., Kruse, Y., Steele, C., Wang, Y., Branden, L., *et al.* (2009b). *Using Interpreters in Telephone Surveys*. Paper presented at the annual conference of the American Association for Public Opinion Research, Hollywood, FL.

Hartley, H. O. (1962). Multiple frame surveys. In *Joint Statistical Meetings Proceedings, Social Statistics Section*. Alexander, VA: American Statistical Association.

(1974). Multiple frame methodology and selected applications. *Sankhya*, 36, 99–118.

Henderson, T. L., Sirois, M., Chen, A. C., Airriess, C., Swanson, D. A., & Banks, D. (2009). After a disaster: lessons in survey methodology from Hurricane Katrina. *Population Research and Policy Review*, 28, 67–92. doi: 10.1007/s11113-008-9114-5.

Herrmann, M. J., Brodie, M., Morin, R., Blendon, R., & Benson, J. (2006). Interviewing in the face of disaster: conducting a survey of Hurricane Katrina evacuees. *Public Opinion Pros*. Retrieved from www.publicopinionpros.norc.org/from_field/2006/oct/herrmann.asp.

Irwin, C. (2009). PaK v IaK: getting beyond a referendum. Retrieved from www.peacepolls.org/peacepolls/documents/000648.pdf.

Kalton, G. (2002). Sampling considerations in research on HIV risk and illness. In D. G. Ostrow & R. C. Kessler (eds.), *Methodological Issues in AIDS Behavioral Research* (pp. 53–74). New York: Plenum Press.

Kalton, G. (2009). Methods for oversampling rare subpopulations in social surveys. *Survey Methodology*, 35(2), 125–41.

Kalton, G., & Anderson, D. W. (1986). Sampling rare populations. *Journal of the Royal Statistical Society: Series A (General)*, 149(1), 65–82.

King, D. (2002). Post disaster surveys: experience and methodology. *Australian Journal of Emergency Management*, 17(3), 39–47.

Kish, L. (1965). *Survey Sampling*. New York, John Wiley & Sons.

Knack, J. M., Chen, Z., Williams, K. D., & Jensen-Campbell, L. A. (2006). Opportunities and challenges for studying disaster survivors. *Analyses of Social Issues and Public Policy*, 6(1), 175–89.

Kolbe, A., & Muggah, R. (2010). Surveying Haiti's post-quake needs: a quantitative approach. *Humanitarian Practice Network* (48). Retrieved from www.odihpn.org/humanitarian-exchange-magazine/issue-48/surveying-haitis-post-quake-needs-a-quantitative-approach.

Kott, P. S., Amrhein, J. F., & Hicks, S. D. (1998). Sampling and estimation from multiple list frames. *Survey Methodology*, 24, 3–10.

Kreuter, F., Olson, K., Wagner, J., Yan, T., Ezzati-Rice, T. M., Casas-Cordero, C., *et al.* (2010). Using proxy measures and other correlates of survey outcomes to adjust for non-response: examples from multiple surveys. *Journal of the Royal Statistical Society: Series A (Statistics in Society)*, 173(2), 389–407.

Kyutoku, Y., Tada, R., Umeyama, T., Harada, K., Kikuchi, S., Watanabe, E., *et al.* (2012). Cognitive and psychological reactions of the general population three months after the

2011 Tohoku earthquake and tsunami. *PLOS ONE*, 7(2): e31014. doi:10.1371/journal.pone.0031014.

La Greca, A. M. (2006). School based studies of children following disasters. In F. Norris, S. Galea, M. Friedman, & P. Watson (eds.), *Methods for Disaster Mental Health Research* (pp. 141–57). New York: The Guilford Press.

Larrance, R., Anastario, M., & Lawry, L. (2007). Health status among internally displaced persons in Louisiana and Mississippi travel trailer parks. *Annals of Emergency Medicine*, 49(5), 590–601.

Lepkowski, J. M., & Groves, R. M. (1986). A mean squared error model for dual frame, mixed mode survey design. *Journal of the American Statistical Association*, 81(396), 930–37.

Levine, C. (2004). The concept of vulnerability in disaster research. *Journal of Traumatic Stress*, 17(5), 395–402.

Little, R. J. A., & Vartivarian, S. (2005). Does weighting for nonresponse increase the variance of survey means? *Survey Methodology*, 31(2), 161–68.

McKenzie, D. J., & Mistiaen, J. (2009). Surveying migrant households: a comparison of census-based, snowball and intercept point surveys. *Journal of the Royal Statistical Society: Series A (Statistics in Society)*, 172(2), 339–60.

Marshall, P. A. (2001). The relevance of culture for informed consent in U.S.-funded international health research. In *Ethical and Policy Issues in International Research: Clinical Trials in Developing Countries,* vol. II: *Commissioned Papers and Staff Analysis* (Chapter C) (pp. C1–C38). Bethesda, MD: National Bioethics Advisory Commission.

Newman, E., & Kaloupek, D. G. (2004). The risks and benefits of participating in trauma-focused research studies. *Journal of Traumatic Stress*, 17(5), 383–94.

Norris, F. H., Sherrieb, K., & Galea, S. (2010). Prevalence and consequences of disaster-related illness and injury from Hurricane Ike. *Rehabilitation Psychology*, 55(3), 221–30.

Overview of Baseline Survey Results: Hurricane Katrina Advisory Group. (2006). Retrieved February 11, 2014 from www.hurricanekatrina.med.harvard.edu/2006.

Pan, Y. and de la Puente, M. (2005). *Census Bureau Guideline for the Translation of Data Collection Instruments and Supporting Materials: Documentation on how the Guideline Was Developed.* Survey Methodology Research Report #2005–06. Washington, DC: US Census Bureau.

Paschenko, C. (2008, November 11). "Galveston-Port Bolivar ferry opens today." *Galveston Daily News*, Retrieved from www.galvestondailynews.com/.

Pennell, B.-E., Mneimneh, Z., Bowers, A., Chardoul, S., Wells, J. E., Viana, M. C., *et al.* (2008). Implementation of the World Mental Health Survey initiative. In R. C. Kessler and T. B. Ustun (eds.), *Volume: Patterns of Mental Illness in the WMH Surveys.* New York: Cambridge University Press.

Quaglia, M., & Vivier, G. (2010). Construction and field application of an indirect sampling method (time-location sampling): an example of surveys carried out on homeless persons and drug users in France. *Methodological Innovations Online*, 5(2), 17–25. doi: 10.4256/mio.2010.0015.

Richardson, R. C., Plummer, C. A., Barthelemy, J. J., & Cain, D. S. (2012). Research after natural disasters: recommendations and lessons learned. *Journal of Community Engagement and Scholarship*, 2(1), 3–11.

Rosenstein, D. R. (2004). Decision-making capacity and disaster research. *Journal of Traumatic Stress*, 17(5), 373–81.

Skinner, C. J., Holmes, D. J., & Holt, D. (1994). Multiple frame sampling for multivariate stratification. *International Statistical Review/Revue Internationale de Statistique*, 62(3), 333–47.

Sudman, S., Sirken, M. G., & Cowan, C. D. (1988). Sampling rare and elusive populations. *Science*, 240(4855), 991–96.

Sumathipala, A., & Siribaddana, S. H. (2005). Research and clinical ethics after the tsunami: Sri Lanka. *Lancet*, 366, 1418–29.

World Bank, (2010). Haiti, in The World Bank Open Knowledge Repository. Retrieved from www.worldbank.org/en/country/haiti.

Yonetani, M. (2011). Displacement due to natural hazard-induced disasters: Global estimates for 2009 and 2010. *Internal Displacement Monitoring Centre*. Geneva: Internal Displacement Monitoring Centre.

Zissman, M. A., Holcomb, K. T., Jones, *et al.* (2010). *Development and Use of a Comprehensive Humanitarian Assessment Tool in Post-Earthquake Haiti.* Lexington, MA: MIT Lincoln Laboratory. Retrieved from http://oai.dtic.mil/oai/oai?verb=getRecord& metadataPrefix=html&identifier=ADA534969.

7

Conducting surveys in areas of armed conflict

ZEINA N. MNEIMNEH, WILLIAM G. AXINN, DIRGHA GHIMIRE,
KRISTEN L. CIBELLI, AND MOHAMMAD SALIH ALKAISY

7.1   Introduction

The humanitarian tragedy of large-scale armed conflict continues to be part of human experience leaving a tremendous demographic, social, economic, and health impact on societies. Investigating the impact of such conflicts, assessing the community's needs, and guiding and evaluating interventions require collecting reliable information on the affected population. Survey research provides tools for collecting such information, but the obstacles to successful survey data collection in these circumstances are substantial. We argue that conducting surveys in armed conflict settings is difficult, but can be done and done well by following a few design and implementation principles. We begin this chapter by summarizing these principles and discuss them further in the remaining sections of the chapter. These principles are derived from the authors' experiences conducting surveys in such settings and reports from the literature and are based on observational rather than experimental evidence, but reflect the forefront of research on these topics. The first principle is to maintain an adaptive (flexible) approach at all phases of the survey allowing researchers to adjust the study protocols to such volatile circumstances. Second, mixed method approaches can be used to maximize that flexibility and minimize the weaknesses in a survey data collection design by capitalizing on the strengths of supplementary methods. Third, recruitment and training of interviewers require unconventional approaches such as: maintaining political neutrality during recruitment and training, and adding training components on psychological preparation, the art of politically neutral interactions, and handling conversations with respondents about the conflict. The fourth principle is to tailor data collection methods to deal with specific armed conflict challenges. Examples include: tailoring approaches to minimize refusals and noncontact, special efforts to secure interview privacy, and unconventional monitoring. Fifth, data collection in armed conflict settings often raises major ethical considerations that need to be carefully addressed. Overall, most good survey practice in armed conflict settings is no different from good general survey practice. But the challenges associated with these settings demand new mixes of existing approaches and flexibility to address the specific local conditions.

A handful of papers focus on specific technical or methodological challenges encountered during armed conflict research and offer some potential solutions (Barakat, Chard,

Jacoby, & Lume, 2002; Checchi & Roberts, 2005, 2008; Haer & Becher, 2012; Lawry, 2007; Mneimneh, Karam, Karam, Tabet, Fayyad, Melhem *et al.*, 2008; Thoms & Ron, 2007; Yamout & Jabbour, 2010). However, the literature lacks systematic coverage of the wide array of issues encountered in surveys in armed conflict. To fill this gap, we begin by defining "surveys in armed conflict" and describe a number of contextual dimensions that characterize armed conflicts and are relevant to survey research. We discuss how each of the dimensions poses methodological challenges to survey design and implementation. We discuss potential strategies for addressing the challenges that revolve around the set of five principles described above. We conclude with some future research and practical directions in this area.

7.1.1   Definition of surveys in armed conflict areas

Legal debate surrounds the definition of an "armed conflict." For our purposes, we define it broadly as a situation in which governmental, local, or external groups resort to violent confrontation causing social disruption, political upheaval, and casualties. Examples of armed conflicts considered in this review are those due to rebel insurgency after the US invasion of Iraq; the separatist movement and armed conflict in Nepal; and civil wars in Lebanon, Liberia, and Sierra Leone. This broad coverage allows us to be comprehensive in our review of the literature.

Conflicts usually occur in different phases: political unrest (and the threat of violence), active armed conflict, and post-conflict reconstruction. Researchers have conducted surveys during each of these phases. In this chapter, we focus on situations of political unrest and "active armed conflict," which are likely to pose the greatest challenges for survey research.

7.1.2   Contextual dimensions of armed conflict settings

Most of the surveys we identify investigate armed conflict situations that are characterized by a set of contextual dimensions that pose challenges to conducting surveys.[1] These dimensions may affect one or more of the phases of the survey life cycle. The dimensions we distinguish are summarized in Table 7.1.

7.2   Design and implementation challenges and recommendations for surveys in conflict settings

In this section, we draw upon the literature and the authors' collective experiences conducting surveys in Lebanon, Iraq, Nepal, Sierra Leone, Liberia, and Bosnia and Herzogovina to highlight challenges and recommend steps to improve surveys under armed conflict conditions. These recommendations may not apply to all war conflict situations and readers are highly encouraged to assess the applicability of each recommendation to their specific

---

1 Armed conflicts vary greatly. Some of the dimensions we discuss may not apply to certain types of conflicts and some dimensions may be very specific to a type of conflict and thus are not discussed above.

Table 7.1 *Dimensions of armed conflict situations*

Dimensions	Description
Violence and insecurity	Insecurity encompasses acts of violence that are often unpredictable and are of varying types and levels of intensity, as well as the threat of violence.
Political dynamics	Legal authority is highly contested and can quickly change hands during times of armed conflict. Law and order conditions that typically apply during peacetime often break down. Parties to the conflict may exert psychological pressure or manipulate groups or individuals in their quest for control.
Urgency	A sense of urgency usually pervades an armed conflict setting. Timeliness of information to assess the impact of the conflict, raise awareness and target relief is of great importance. This makes quick decisions of the essence, compromising the ability to foresee potential problems and plan contingencies.
Emotional stress	Situations of armed conflict create a tense and emotionally charged atmosphere. People may be preoccupied with feelings of fear, protecting loved ones, meeting basic needs such as food and water, and staying alive. Some may be also psychologically compromised because of experiencing traumatic events. People's interest in helping the affected communities is also usually heightened.
Compromised infrastructure	Essential infrastructure may be compromised or completely destroyed in situations of armed conflict creating challenges for transportation, communication, and availability of goods and resources. Situations of armed conflict often arise in less developed countries where infrastructure may already be compromised

setting. Though challenges can touch every stage of the survey life cycle, we mainly focus on the following stages: sample design and selection, questionnaire development and pretesting, interviewer hiring and training, data collection, and data security. For each of these stages, we group the challenges and the potential recommendations to address them under the specific dimension(s) that is (are) related to them. We also focus on face-to-face interviewing as the main data collection mode as it is the most commonly used mode in active armed conflict due to the damage in communication networks and lack of electricity that hinders the use of other modes. Table 7.2 provides a summary of the main challenges discussed below and offers recommendations for each.

7.2.1   Sample design and selection

Violence and insecurity

Violent and insecure conditions affect sample design and implementation in a number of ways. Due to the increased mobility and causalities of war, frames and population data (if existent) often quickly become outdated (Barakat *et al.*, 2002; Daponte, 2007) and researchers are forced to find innovative ways to create frames with good coverage and estimate or adjust existing population data. Overcoming such challenges calls for combining multiple sampling frames, such as existing household sampling frames, humanitarian aid camp lists,

Table 7.2 *Summary of challenges encountered during active armed conflict survey research and recommendations for addressing them*

Challenge type	Conflict dimension	Challenge	Recommendation
Sample design and selection	Violence and insecurity, political dynamics	Lack of or out-dated frames	Use multiple frames; draw on UN agency or NGO lists; collaborate with local inhabitants to construct new lists or create maps; consider respondent-drive techniques; use GPS or satellite imagery.
		Exclusion of insecure areas	Consider adaptive sampling; supplement survey data with other available data on areas that were excluded; adjust sample size for possible exclusions and implement replicate sampling.
		Sensitive demographic distribution	Draw on international sources such as NGOs or the UN and adjust accordingly.
Questionnaire development and pretesting	Urgency, political dynamics	Researcher does not share the same language or culture of affected population; time may not allow for thorough understanding of the situation	Collaborate with local experts and those native to the area; employ adaptation and translation best practices; conduct at least a minimum amount of pretesting, possibly sequential smaller scale pretests.
		Respondents may misunderstand or mistrust survey aims resulting in measurement errors	Carefully designed questionnaire material that includes any information on study sponsor and purpose.
		Fluctuating political events may affect responses	Adopt a flexible approach allowing for the redefinition of terms or addition of probes based on changing conditions; remain up to date on political events and collect data on events that may explain shifts in responses; incorporate mixed method data collection approaches to supplement survey data.
Interviewer hiring and training	Violence and insecurity, political dynamics	Limited human resources	Seek interviewers who are willing and able to work in difficult and risky conditions, who have local knowledge and the trust of and access to the community, and who are impartial and seen as politically neutral.

Table 7.2 (cont.)

Challenge type	Conflict dimension	Challenge	Recommendation
		Interviewers may be inexperienced in conducting interviews and struggle to remain objective	Train interviewers in the standardized approach; emphasize the difference between interviewing and previous work interviewers may have done and the need for objectivity; provide specialized training for interviewers on how to handle conversations with respondents about the conflict, exposure to trauma, or other sensitive topics.
Data collection	Violence and insecurity, political dynamics, urgency, emotional stress and compromised infrastructure	Limited access to affected communities	Implement a team structure that increases contact during safe times and limits repeated visits during insecure times; seek clearance from faction leaders, peace-keeping troops, or aid agencies that control access.
		Noncontact might be higher	If safe, ask neighbors or other community members about respondent's whereabouts; establish good relationships with key community members to mitigate concerns; use GIS information to stratify based on mobility and sample within strata accordingly; adjust interviewing hours to increase likelihood of contact as the security situation allows.
		Nonresponse might be higher	Recruit interviewers who are nonthreatening, known to, and trusted by the community; use a neutral institution or media outlet to introduce the survey and encourage participation; limit collecting personally identifying information and limit questions about the identity of fighting factions; provide clear and easy to understand assurances of confidentiality and explain how data will be protected.
		Interview privacy may be jeopardized	Use self-administered modes such as audio computer-assisted self-interviewing (ACASI) or MP3 players with

Category	Challenge	Recommendation
Violence and insecurity, urgency	Standard interviewer monitoring and quality assurance methods may be difficult to implement	headphones; use neutral private sites such as a clinic or NGO office with a private space for interviews (if feasible); conduct multiple simultaneous interviews or conversations to occupy all present during an interview. If working in teams, have supervisors re-contact a sample of cases the next day while still in the same area; ask interviewers to record interviews or use GPS devices to verify they went to the right location; conduct routine mock interviews to verify adherence to standardized techniques; examine paradata; use PDAs or laptops when possible – and with satellite or Internet connection for regular data monitoring.
Data security and documentation	Conflict conditions put data security at risk	Develop procedures to protect and backup several copies of the data in different locations; seek software to encrypt and automatically back up data once digitized.
	Documentation is not seen as a priority	Provide transparent and detailed documentation of the methods used, any challenges faced during the design and implementation of the survey, and ways of addressing them.

Note: These recommendations are based on observational rather than experimental evidence. Please refer to the main text for references.

other existing local list frames, respondent-driven frames, and newly constructed household frames. Some of the local list frames that have been used include UNICEF immunization lists in Afghanistan (Scholte, Olff, Ventevogel, de Vries, Jansveld, Cardoza, & Crawford, 2004), food distribution lists in Kosovo (Salama, Spiegel, Van Dyke, Phelps, & Wilkinson, 2000), and other lists from United Nations agencies and NGOs (Grein, Checchi, Escribè, Tamrat, Karunakara, Stokes *et al.*, 2003; Husain, Anderson, Lopes Cardozo, Becknell, Blanton, Araki *et al.*, 2011). Respondent-driven sampling (RDS) techniques might also be useful in situations when conventional sampling frames are unavailable (see Thompson, Chapter 24 in this volume, and Haer & Becher, 2012). Constructing new household frames in armed conflict settings requires a range of innovative methods that usually include creating maps. It is possible to create maps by combining a variety of approaches such as interviewing local leaders (Lawry, 2007; Salama *et al.*, 2000; Scholte *et al.*, 2004) or using more technological tools, such as Geographic Information System (GIS) and satellite imagery. Satellite maps could be especially useful for previously unmapped areas, such as refugee camps and places where internally displaced people are living. Such maps have been used by Kim, Torbay, and Lawry (2007) in the Nyala District of Darfur, Sudan, and by Lawry (2007) to count dwellings and neighborhoods. When maps are difficult to create and when the location and size of communities are not known, Geographical Positioning System (GPS) coordinates could be used (Checchi & Roberts, 2008). However, security issues must be carefully assessed when such devices are used. In areas with tight security and under the control of certain militia groups, sending interviewers with such devices may jeopardize their safety.

Another sampling challenge in armed conflict surveys is the potential need to exclude or replace areas that are heavily affected by the conflict or that are under the heavy control of armed groups with more stable ones (e.g., see Moore, Marfin, Quenemoen, Gessner, Miller, Toole *et al.* (1993) in Somalia, and Mullany, Richards, Lee, Suwanvanichkij, Maung, Mahn *et al.* (2007) in eastern Burma). Such exclusions or replacement could lead to sampling bias (Beyrer, Terzian, Lowther, Zambrano, Galai, & Melchior, 2007). The possibility for bias is high when the topic of the survey is related to the conflict or its effects (as is commonly the case). One potential way to address this is to use GIS information to stratify geographical areas based on their exposure to the conflict and their population displacement, and over-sample in areas where these populations have moved. This, however, calls for a good predictive mobility model. Such a model would need to be evaluated during field work and revised as researchers learn more about the mobility of affected populations in the targeted areas and as new conflict events unfold. Such an approach relies on implementing an adaptive sampling strategy (Thompson & Seber, 1996).[2] It is important to keep in mind that this approach will not completely address the potential biases arising from

---

[2] Using a multiplicity sampling approach could also help in reducing biases caused by outdated frames or area exclusions. However, well-defined clarifications and probes need to be administered to respondents concerning who should be classified as an immediate family member under this approach to avoid possible misreporting (see Chapter 19 in this volume for a more detailed discussion).

exclusions or undersampling heavily affected areas. It is likely that people who decide to stay in such heavily affected areas or who did not survive differ from those who moved to safer areas.

To address this, researchers can supplement their survey data with other available data on the excluded areas from other data collection methods. When measuring mortality for example, Tapp, Burkle, Wilson, Takaro, Guyatt, Amad *et al.* (2008) and Woodruff (2006) encourage researchers to consider data sources that are less resource intensive than population-based surveys and that could provide supplementary figures on death tolls such as enumeration of reported deaths from media sources and hospitals, fresh graves, and an increased demand for funeral materials. However, records of deaths from institutions (hospitals or morgues), media reports, and government death registries are all likely to miss significant mortality under conditions of severe armed conflict and violence (Spagat, Mack, Cooper, & Kreutz, 2009) thus, relying solely on such sources is not recommended. A combination of approaches, however, could generate a more complete picture of mortality trends over time. An example comes from Guha-Sapir and Degomme (2005, 2007) who combined estimates from multiple surveys and from demographic data sources to come up with an overall mortality estimate in Darfur and Iraq. Silva and Ball (2008) also combined witness testimonies and graveyard census data with a retrospective mortality survey to estimate conflict-related mortality in Timor-Leste. Thus, in launching a survey, one might consider implementing other supplemental data collections in an overall mixed method design.

Finally, because of the high degree of uncertainty in armed conflicts, sample designs may need to allow for unforeseen exclusions after selection. For example, to maintain the desired sample in the number of primary stage selection units, Mullany *et al.* (2007) and Roberts, Lafta, Garfield, Khudhairi, and Burnham (2004) selected more clusters to account for any exclusions due to insecurity. Sample sizes also need to be adjusted for noncontact and refusal rates that could be difficult to estimate in armed conflict settings.

Political dynamics

The political dynamics of the conflict can also affect and impose limitations on sample design. For example, the demographic composition of the population may be at the root of the conflict, making it highly sensitive to inquire about the number and location of particular groups of people, as was the case for Salama and colleagues in Kosovo (2000).

7.2.2   *Questionnaire material development and pretesting*

Urgency

Many issues in constructing questionnaires for armed conflict settings are direct extensions of general questionnaire design principles, but pretesting and the design of flexible instruments in a conflict setting deserve special attention. Researchers must often prepare for a survey in a very limited period of time (Mneimneh *et al.*, 2008). The urgency to collect information may be a particular problem for organizations or researchers who are not native to the area or are unfamiliar with the study population. Time in the field may be insufficient to allow for a thorough understanding of the situation and to establish trust with local partners (Barakat *et al.*, 2002). Even in situations where the researchers are local to the context, there may not be enough time to consider research questions thoroughly, prepare the questionnaire, and pretest it sufficiently (Yamout & Jabbour, 2010). This could jeopardize measurement quality. Existing instruments may provide a good starting point, but may not be available in the target language or may exclude content about issues specific to the population or the conflict. Collaborating with local experts early in the survey process can help, especially when developing local instruments or adapting existing ones. A growing literature is available to assist researchers on best practices for translation and adaptation of instruments to fit the local survey conditions (Harkness, Villar, & Edwards, 2010). More information and resources can be found in the *Guidelines for Best Practices in Cross-Cultural Surveys* (Survey Research Center, 2011) at http://ccsg.isr.umich.edu/.

Pretesting also deserves special consideration in armed conflict settings. Although pretesting is standard practice in survey research, unfortunately in armed conflict, the urgency to start collecting data can lead researchers to view pretesting as an added burden on their timeline (Mneimneh *et al.*, 2008). Pretesting is particularly important in conflict settings where important constructs related to the conflict dynamics may be difficult to specify or may be too sensitive to use without careful testing (Lawry, 2007). Pretesting offers an opportunity to observe such dynamics and potential mediating factors before starting to collect data. Sequential pretesting such as sequential cognitive interviewing, in which an initial pretest is used to identify problems, the questionnaire is revised, and then pretested again, is a valuable approach for implementing a sound questionnaire (Ghimire, Chardoul, Kessler, Axinn, & Adhikari, 2013). If the timeline is a major constraint, sacrificing numbers of pretest interviews in order to maintain a sequential test is a good choice to make. For example, as an illustration, rather than taking two weeks to conduct a fifty-case pretest, one could choose to pretest fifteen cases, revise the instruments, and conduct a second fifteen-case pretest within one week. Even conducting a few in-depth interviews with people who are involved in the community or the conflict itself could uncover many aspects of the survey or the instrument that the researcher did not envision.

Political dynamics

People's perceptions and interpretations of ongoing events become highly politicized during armed conflicts (Yamout & Jabbour, 2010). Goodhand (2000) notes that research in a conflict setting is unlikely to be viewed as neutral by respondents. From a measurement perspective, affiliating the study with any political party or even an aid agency may influence respondents' answers affecting the validity of the data (Mneimneh *et al.*, 2008). Respondents may mistrust the aims and credibility of the process or they may seek to use it for their own purposes (Barakat *et al.*, 2002). For example, expectations in relation to humanitarian relief may also cause respondents to overreport family size in hopes of receiving more aid (Grandesso, Sanderson, Kruijt, Koene, & Brown, 2005). Many of the articles included in our review mentioned the possibility of underreporting or exaggeration of abuses, depending on the respondent's perception of the relevant costs and benefits (Amowitz, Reis, Lyons, Vann, Mansaray, Akinsulure-Smith, *et al.*, 2002; Iacopino, Frank, Bauer, Keller, Fink, Ford *et al.*, 2001; Mullany *et al.*, 2007). Thus, researchers need to give careful thought to how the study is introduced in any scripted material and how it is presented by interviewers.

The adaptive design recommended earlier for sampling carries forward to construction of the instrument. The content of the questionnaire may need to change based on the fluctuating events of the conflict. Changes in the conflict events may call for the redefinition of terms or the addition of new probes mid-survey to capture such changes. The political context of the conflict may change while the survey is in the field and new incidents and events might cause shifts in respondents' attitudes or behavior. For example, Pham, Vinck, Wierda, Stover, and di Giovanni note that answers related to peace and justice in their Northern Uganda survey may have been affected by the intensification of the Lord's Resistance Army's attacks during data collection (2005). In such instances, adding new questions for respondents or local key community members, or keeping track of the dates of such events and related media information to inform the interpretation of the results can be helpful.

Of course, deviations from a standardized approach and changing questionnaire mid-stream could cause context effects (Schwarz & Sudman, 1992). These could be mitigated by adding any new questions at the end of the existing instrument or designing a separate self-administered component to be completed at the end of the original interview.

7.2.3   Interviewer hiring and training

Violence and insecurity

The lack of security in conflict situations limits the availability of people willing to work under risky conditions. Conflict-related studies have drawn on people from a range of professional backgrounds to serve as interviewers including community health, NGO or relief workers, nurses, midwives, doctors, community and school counselors, and university students. Interviewers need to be willing and able to work effectively in difficult and risky conditions. They also need to have the local knowledge of, trust in, and access to the community (Mullany *et al.*, 2007). In a conflict setting, it is particularly important for interviewers and field staff to be objective, impartial and perceived as politically neutral (Axinn, Ghimire, & Williams, 2012). People with experience in the health field or in social work often have such attributes and may also be less vulnerable due to their respected position in the community (Swiss, Jennings, Aryee, Brown, Jappah-Samukai, Kamara *et al.*, 1998). Health-related fields also present a valuable pool of skilled female candidates in certain countries where being interviewed by a female is more accepted than being interviewed by a male (Axinn, 1991). A private survey research company we interviewed has found midwives to be particularly effective as interviewers in Afghanistan because they are accepted as part of the workforce in areas where women are generally not allowed to work.

However, due to the nature of their work, interviewers belonging to the professions mentioned above might find it difficult to follow standardized interviewing techniques where interviewers are required to read questions exactly as written and to use nondirective probes (Groves, Fowler, Couper, Lepkowski, Singer, & Tourangeau, 2009a).[3] Training such interviewers on standardized interviewing becomes critical. People accustomed to care-giving may also struggle to maintain the objectivity needed for a scientific study and, in some cases, seek out highly affected members of the population resulting in selection biases (Kuper & Gilbert, 2006). Training protocols can highlight how survey interviewing may be different from previous work interviewers may have done as community health or relief workers. Special training may also be needed to address the sensitivity of the conflict situation and how to conduct certain sensitive conversations with respondents about the conflict and their possible exposure to trauma. For example, to avoid possible retraumatization of respondents, Amowitz *et al.* (2002) provided interviewers in Sierra Leone with "extensive sensitization training" by experts in sexual violence.

Political dynamics

It is important for researchers to remain attuned to the political context when recruiting interviewers and to the possible effect of interviewer backgrounds and experiences on the data collection process and data quality (Checchi & Roberts, 2008, Mneimneh *et al.*, 2008). Respondents are likely to have heightened suspicions about the motives and allegiance of the interviewer (Elkins, 2010). Certain styles or colors of dress or accents may signal affiliation with a particular political party and could bias respondents' answers. It may also be unsafe for interviewers of particular religious, racial, or ethnic backgrounds to travel in areas hostile to their group, making extra security precautions necessary. For example, Salama *et al.* (2000) found it difficult to find suitably qualified Serbian survey staff available and willing to participate in a survey of Serbians living in Kosovo, due to the security risks for ethnic Serbs. Authorities may also interfere in the recruitment of interviewers. Lawry (2007, p. 260) reports being "given" several unqualified data collectors by the local authorities in Sudan; these were obvious "minders" and could not be fired.

7.2.4   Data collection

Data collection challenges during armed conflict are numerous and many of them are caused by the different dimensions that define such conflicts (violence and insecurity, political

---

3 Though conversational interviewing is preferred by some researchers over standardized interviewing, its usefulness depends on the topic, the complexity of the survey, and the target population's familiarity with surveys (Axinn & Pearce, 2006).

dynamics, urgency, emotional stress, and compromised infrastructure). Data collection challenges we discuss here include accessing the community, recruiting respondents, ensuring interview privacy, and monitoring the quality of the data. Below, we address the challenges and potential solutions in each of these areas.

Community access and field structure: violence, insecurity, political dynamics, and compromised infrastructure

Accessing sampled communities that are directly exposed to violence or under the tight security of armed groups is one of the biggest challenges in armed conflict research. Adapting the field operations to those conditions becomes essential. Field operations structure and times of contact may have to be adjusted based on security conditions. For security reasons, all interviewing teams for the Salama *et al.* (2000) survey had to be accompanied by an international staff member and interviews had to be completed before a 4pm curfew. Mneimneh *et al.* (2008) rotated interviewing teams in areas where there was the need to limit repeat visits. Tradeoffs must be made, not only between survey error and cost but also between survey error and the security of interviewers and respondents. In Lebanon, Mneimneh *et al.* (2008) assigned all sampled units in one of four areas to one interviewer who had relatives in the area. Assigning one interviewer to such a large cluster is not customarily viewed as good practice and could have increased interviewer effects, but it also eliminated the risk of sending additional interviewers who are strangers in the insecure area.

In armed conflict, access to certain areas may require clearance from faction leaders, peace-keeping troops, or aid agencies (Mneimneh *et al.*, 2008). Prior contact with armed groups or political parties controlling certain selected areas is crucial – it may literally be a life and death issue. When conducting a study in Afghanistan, Lawry (2007) gained permission and assurance for safe passage from a foreign minister in Taliban-controlled Afghanistan for a Physicians for Human Rights study. In a similar example, the Chitwan Valley Family Study (CVFS) in Nepal, researchers were able to continue field operations throughout the armed conflict there by maintaining ongoing relationships with local leaders on all sides of the conflict (Axinn *et al.*, 2012). The CVFS investigators made a special effort to build new relationships with warring leaders as their predecessors were killed in the conflict and replacements took over leadership positions.

The level of damage to the country's infrastructure varies greatly from one conflict to another. It may be widespread or relatively confined to certain areas. It is not unusual for armed conflict to occur in less-developed countries where infrastructure may already be compromised and where protracted conflict may have prevented the maintenance or modernization of infrastructure. Damaged roads can make remote areas difficult or prohibitively expensive to reach. Some areas may only be accessible on foot, limiting material accessible to interviewers and increasing their exposure to risks. For example, for Mullany *et al.*'s survey (2007) in eastern Burma, the survey questions were limited to what could fit on one sheet of paper (reducing the amount of data collected) because interviewers had to carry all survey materials when traveling on foot. Interviewers may also need to travel with their own food and water supply especially when accommodation is limited (see Chapter 6 in this volume).

Respondent recruitment and cooperation: political dynamics and emotional distress

Respondents may be difficult to contact or they may refuse to participate because of the heightened emotional atmosphere and the political tension prevailing at times of armed conflict. It is important to anticipate potential reasons for noncontact or refusal in a specific conflict situation and to adjust data collection operations and contact procedures accordingly.

People are especially fearful and wary of strangers during times of conflict. This might make it difficult for the interviewer to establish contact with sampled members, increasing the level of nonresponse. To establish access and rapport with survey respondents, researchers usually recruit local members of the community as interviewers or guides (Haer & Becher, 2012; Lawry, 2007). Researchers should be aware, however, that local community members may have their own views and positions in the conflict, possibly increasing interviewer errors (Haer & Becher, 2012; Mneimneh *et al.*, 2008). Noncontact during conflict is also driven by respondents fleeing their usual place of residence to more secure areas. Safe procedures should be established for interviewers to track respondents, for example by asking neighbors or other members of the community about the respondent's whereabouts. Community members, however, may be reluctant to give such information. Recruiting interviewers who are politically neutral, who are trusted by the community, and who can establish good relationships with key community members could reduce informants' concerns under such difficult circumstances.

The use of a neutral institution or neutral media outlet with no political party affiliation to introduce the benefits of the survey and encourage the target population to participate (e.g., the UN or peacekeeper radio station) may also instill more trust in respondents and increase their cooperation. It is common for people in conflict settings to follow news about the conflict. Broadcasting information about the survey could thus have a wide reach and establish credibility through a neutral media outlet.

Respondents may also refuse to participate due to anxiety about the possible consequences of survey participation. Possible solutions include limiting the collection of personally identifying information and questions about the identity of fighting factions, providing highly transparent and easy to understand assurances of confidentiality, and explaining the details of how the data will be protected. For example, in Nepal, leaders of groups in armed conflict were allowed to tour the research facilities and audit respondent confidentiality procedures, assuring all parties had knowledge of steps taken to provide confidentiality (Axinn *et al.*, 2012).

Surveys in conflict settings are likely to involve respondents who are living in difficult conditions and who may receive or wish to receive assistance from relief organizations. In this context, respondents may refuse to participate out of fear that they will lose aid (Swiss *et al.*, 1998). It is important for researchers to be aware of respondents' special concerns related to the conflict and train interviewers on how to address those concerns.

Table 7.2 provides different recommendations for improving respondent recruitment and cooperation in armed conflict settings. Many of these recommendations are guided by a set of operational principles developed by Axinn *et al.* (2012).

Interview privacy: violence and insecurity

Locating sampled people who have left their dwellings for security reasons might require interviewers to visit crowded shelters or camps. This jeopardizes the privacy of the interview, possibly leading to misreporting (Iacopino *et al.*, 2001; Mneimneh & Pennell, 2011). Iacopino *et al.* (2001) reported that interviews with Kosovar-Albanian respondents had to be conducted in cramped refugee centers. Concerns about privacy during the interview are widely noted in the conflict survey literature (Amowitz *et al.*, 2002; Iacopino *et al.*, 2001; Roberts *et al.*, 2004). Three basic approaches to increase privacy in general could be used and might be effective in conflict settings: (1) use of self-administered modes; (2) use of neutral private sites; and (3) conducting multiple interviews or conversations simultaneously to occupy all those present during an interview. First, if programing and technical resources are available and security issues are not a major concern, researchers may consider using audio computer-assisted self-interviewing (ACASI) for all or part of the interview. MP3 players could also be used to read questions through headphones to the respondent, who can mark answers in paper and pencil. Using such self-administered modes during a face-to-face interview would not only reduce possible interviewer effects but also allow the interviewer to distract other members present during the interview and engage them in conversations. Second, regarding interviewing in neutral sites, the literature reports the use of local health clinics where interviews could be conducted with more privacy (World Health Organization, 2001). However, in certain armed conflict situations, it may not be safe or ethical to ask respondents to leave their homes or to ask interviewers to return to the sampled unit. The third approach is multiple simultaneous interviews or conversations. A private survey research company we interviewed has found that an effective way of interviewing women in Afghanistan was to send a female interviewer accompanied by a male colleague. The male colleague occupied the man of the house in conversation leaving the woman of the house to be interviewed by the female interviewer. The CVFS used a similar strategy in Nepal, conducting multiple simultaneous interviews to promote privacy (Axinn *et al.*, 2012).

Monitoring: violence, insecurity, and urgency

Time and security constraints associated with conflict conditions may make standard interviewer monitoring and quality assurance methods, such as direct field supervision and reinterviewing, difficult to implement. Researchers will often need to use innovative approaches to address those challenges and still validate a reasonable percentage of interviews. If interviewers are sent in teams, supervisors can recontact respondents the next day while they are still in the area. If appropriate, researchers may ask interviewers to record interviews, or use GPS devices to confirm that interviewers are going to the right place. GPS devices that transmit location information directly to a central management location can also be effective for assuring interviewers that their locations are being tracked during insecure conditions. When telephone service is available, mock interviews with supervisors over the phone can be used to check that interviewers are consistently applying standardized interviewing techniques. In fact, this technique has been employed in surveys dealing with sensitive topics where recording might be problematic (Groves, Mosher, Lepkowski, & Kirgis, 2009b). A less engaging but equally rigorous approach is to analyze process data (paradata) such as time stamps and interviewer location data while data collection is underway (Kreuter, Couper, & Lyberg, 2010). This allows researchers to look for any inconsistencies as well as implausible interview lengths by the total sample, by geographic areas, by interviewers, or other subcategories. Local supervisory staff may need to work long hours or even overnight to review completed questionnaires and provide feedback to interviewers while they are still in the assigned areas (Axinn & Pearce, 2006; Mneimneh *et al.*, 2008). When it is possible for interviewers to use PDAs, laptops, tablets, or netbooks, these devices offer a number of quality assurance and monitoring benefits such as built-in verification to reduce skip errors and invalid values (Vinck, Pham, & Kreutzer, 2011). Using technology for data collection also eliminates the need for a separate data entry phase and allows for daily data transfer for quality control checks.

7.2.5 Data security

Violence, insecurity, and urgency

Conflict conditions such as heavy bombardments and looting may render useless normally reliable forms of security such as walls, locked doors, and steel deadbolt locks (Swiss *et al.*, 1998). It is therefore critical that researchers in conflict settings develop procedures to protect and backup several copies of the data in different locations. Mneimneh *et al.* (2008) recounts an anecdote from a principal investigator in Lebanon who kept an electronic copy of the data in a plastic bag and hung from the ceiling above the entrance to his house. In case of evacuation, the data would be handy to grab while escaping to a safer location. Software tools can also be used to encrypt sensitive information and automatically back up data to external hard drives or remote servers via the Internet (if available).

7.3 Ethical considerations

Though all data collection from human subjects requires careful consideration of ethical issues, settings of high violence and urgent need common during armed conflict raise special concerns. We address those in this section.

7.3.1   Ethical concerns and the decision to carry out a survey

The ethics and feasibility of collecting survey data during armed conflict need to be carefully considered on a setting by setting basis. Security concerns may pose considerable risk to researchers, respondents, and field staff, not to mention that they could undermine the accuracy of results as well. How much risk should be tolerated? The tradeoff between the potential value of the survey results and potential risk to those involved in the survey need be weighed carefully (Goodhand, 2000; Lawry, 2007). Physicians for Human Rights does not consider it ethically defensible to place investigators, field staff or potential respondents at risk without a clear policy objective or possible solution to the situation on the ground (Lawry, 2007). A couple of extreme examples reported in the literature illustrate the risks faced by research teams and field staff operating in conflict areas. In Elkins' (2010) study in Iraq, survey teams experienced confiscation of completed questionnaires, detention, beatings, and death threats. In Brownstein and Brownstein's (2008) study, also in Iraq, one of the authors of the Iraq Family Health Study was shot and killed on his way to work.

In addition to increasing the risk to all those involved in armed conflict research, an ethical consideration that is rarely discussed in the literature is the diversion of available human resources away from relief work, a priority during wartime, to data collection efforts.

7.3.2   Ethical concerns and survey preparation and implementation

The urgency of conflict does not eliminate the need for ethical review of a study from an appropriate body, such as an institutional review board or an ethics review committee. Ethics committees may not exist in some countries or may be controlled by parties that refuse to approve a study if the findings are politically sensitive (Lawry, 2007). In such situations, researchers might want to seek a review from other non-local ethics committees affiliated with the researchers or study collaborators rather than foregoing any ethics review (see Cross-Cultural Survey guidelines at http://ccsg.isr.umich.edu/ for a list of resources and references on ethical guidelines for human subject research). It is also extremely important to avoid raising false hopes among respondents suffering the consequences of conflict and to provide clear and specific information about the purpose of the survey. For example, respondents need to be informed that participating in the survey involves no material gain (assuming no incentives are offered) and will have no bearing on their eligibility to receive aid.

Interviewing respondents who may have been traumatized by the conflict raises ethical concerns, especially when the questions ask about the trauma itself (Goodhand, 2000). It is often helpful to establish a protocol for referring respondents for support services. If resources are not available locally, someone skilled in counseling could be included in the team. See Chapter 6 in this volume for further discussion. It is important to keep in mind that the stress of working during conflict and exposure to accounts of horror can also take an emotional toll on the researcher and interviewers who might also require counseling attention.

Another key issue is protecting the security of the data and confidentiality or anonymity of respondents. Limiting the collection of personally identifying information is a useful precaution when completed questionnaires might be confiscated or fall into the wrong hands.

7.3.3   Ethical considerations and post-data production and reporting

The needs for producing timely data, assuring interviewer safety, and minimizing respondent burden must be balanced in establishing an acceptable limit for missing data, beyond which interviews might be sent back to the field for corrections. The dimensions of conflict may create challenges that force researchers to accept relatively higher rates of nonresponse or item missing data than what is usually tolerated in nonconflict survey settings. Solutions include asking interviewers to collect observation data on the area, the neighborhood, the housing unit, or the respondent himself/herself that could improve any data imputation used by researchers to account for missing data.

Finally, the political dynamics of the conflict may increase risks to the security of the data and the confidentiality of respondents and interviewers after the data is collected. The study must clearly address how and to whom their findings will be disseminated and used. Making results publicly available could be misused by political or non-political parties involved in the conflict in order to serve their own goals, possibly harming the research team, field staff, or respondents. Reporting or interpreting the results may also be subject to manipulation and censorship. As Thoms and Ron note (2007, p. 8), "Policy-makers opposed to a given study's findings will dismiss them as imprecise, while advocates may fail to acknowledge that their numbers come with biases and substantial margins of error."

7.4   Future directions

Conducting surveys in armed conflict settings requires a careful balance between the demand for timely and accurate data, and the safety of the research team, field staff, and respondents. The design and implementation challenges discussed above make this balance difficult to achieve especially in light of the scant empirical evidence and lack of comprehensive resources available to guide researchers. More work is needed on (1) empirically testing some of the methodological strategies, and (2) increasing accessibility of the recommended practices and tools.

7.4.1   Methodological research directions

Key areas for further methodological research include empirically investigating the recommendations made in Table 7.2 in relation to sample design, mixed methods, and interviewer training.

Research on the proper use of multiple sampling frames and adaptive sampling approaches in surveys conducted during active armed conflict is needed. Above all, data adjustment and estimation under such approaches requires special attention.

Like other researchers (Barakat *et al.*, 2002), we have called for the use of mixed methods in armed conflict research, to draw on the advantages and mitigate the limitations of the various data collection approaches. The combination of approaches available for researchers could greatly differ from one conflict setting to another. More research is needed on how to measure the quality of the different data sources and statistically combine them for accurate estimation of key outcome measures in such conflict settings.

Training interviewers to collect data in armed conflict settings may require the addition of unconventional training components like desensitization to minimize interviewer effects caused by interviewers' own political views or psychological traumatization. Such effects might be introduced when respondents engage in conversations about the conflict with the interviewer or when the interviewer gets emotionally involved because of the respondent's exposure to conflict-related trauma. Methods for implementing such training protocols and testing their effectiveness in reducing interviewer effects still need further investigation.

In all of these domains, new research featuring experimental designs conducted under armed conflict conditions would be particularly useful for adjudicating among design options.

7.4.2   Practical directions

To increase the rapid accessibility of recommendations and data collection tools to researchers interested in investigating populations affected by armed conflict, we highlight three important initiatives: (1) transparent documentation, (2) a bank for tools, and (3) a task force.

First, we advocate increasing the availability of complete, transparent, and detailed documentation of the methods used, challenges faced, and ways of addressing the challenges that were found to be effective. This standard practice is greatly needed in armed conflict research to allow for better interpretation of the results and guide future researchers. If not published, such documentation could be made available in a report format and archived so that they are accessible to researchers around the globe, especially in conflict-affected areas. An example of such online documentation and dissemination is the Households in Conflict Network (www.hicn.org/), which provides a forum for white papers on the causes and effects of violent conflict at the household level.

Second, we advocate establishing a bank of tools that researchers could easily access during the design stage of their studies, which would be of great benefit to the practice and science of armed conflict research. Tools could include questionnaires and related instruments in different languages that are commonly used in armed conflict settings (such as instruments that measure exposure to war, violence, landmines, mental health, physical abuse, injuries, malnutrition, etc.), training material for social and relief workers and other professionals who are often recruited for collecting survey data in conflict settings, as well as material on providing psychological support to respondents, interviewers, and field staff. Researchers in epidemiology and public health have established similar initiatives that offer resources and guidelines for research on specific topics in conflict contexts such as humanitarian emergencies (Checchi & Roberts, 2005; Standardized Monitoring and Assessment of Relief and Transitions (SMART), 2006); and injury and violence (Sethi, Habibula, McGee,

Peden, Bennett, Hyder *et al.*, 2004). The International Emergency and Refugee Health Branch (IERHB) of the Centers for Disease Control (CDC) website hosts a selection of papers on surveys carried out in conflict areas on health-related topics.[4] The proposed bank of tools would also coordinate existing resources such as these across disciplines.

Third, we advocate establishing a task force to maintain the above mentioned tools for conflict research. Such a task force could also play a role in archiving and making available other material such as unpublished methodological reports, and creating an online forum or bulletin board to help connect researchers with questions to those who may have answers or advice. Most importantly, a task force could advise and help design initiatives that would establish more empirical evidence on ways to balance the demands of timely and accurate data and the safety of all individuals involved.

7.5   Conclusion

During armed conflicts, decision-makers and relief organizations seek information about the nature and magnitude of the violence, its impact on communities, and the need for humanitarian and recovery assistance. Such information is usually gathered by a variety of methods, including surveys. The conflict conditions that make collecting data so critical also make designing and implementing surveys more challenging. The unique contextual dimensions of conflict – violence and insecurity, political dynamics, urgency, emotional stress, and compromised infrastructure – present key challenges at different stages of the survey life cycle. Though it might be beyond the researcher's control to minimize the challenges caused by these contextual conditions, we argue that researchers could mitigate the effect of those challenges on the quality of survey data by following five principles at the different survey design and implementation stages: implementing an adaptive and flexible approach; using mixed methods; employing unconventional approaches to interviewer recruitment and training; tailoring data collection procedures to the specific conflict situation; and careful consideration of ethics throughout the survey process. Incorporating these principles allows survey researchers to remain responsive to the conflict conditions and to make reasoned tradeoffs regarding the timely collection of quality data while maintaining the security of all those involved.

References

Amowitz, L. L., Reis, C., Lyons, K. H., Vann, B., Mansaray, B., Akinsulure-Smith, A. M., & *et al.* (2002). Prevalence of war-related sexual violence and other human rights abuses among internally displaced persons in Sierra Leone. *JAMA: The Journal of the American Medical Association*, 287(4), 513–21.

Axinn, W. G. (1991). The influence of interviewer sex on responses to sensitive questions in Nepal. *Social Science Research*, 20(3), 303–18.

---

4 www.cdc.gov/globalhealth/gdder/ierh/Publications/warrelatedinjuries.htm.

Axinn, W. G., Ghimire, D., & Williams, N. (2012). Collecting survey data during armed conflict. *Journal of Official Statistics*, 28(2), 153–171.

Axinn, W. G., & Pearce, L. D. (2006). *Mixed Method Data Collection Strategies*. Cambridge: Cambridge University Press.

Barakat, S., Chard, M., Jacoby, T., & Lume, W. (2002). The composite approach: research design in the context of war and armed conflict. *Third World Quarterly*, 23(5), 991–1003.

Beyrer, C., Terzian, A., Lowther, S., Zambrano, J. A., Galai, N., & Melchior, M. K. (2007). Civil conflict and health information: the Democratic Republic of Congo. In C. Beyrer & H. F. Pizer (eds.), *Public Health & Human Rights: Evidence-Based Approaches* (pp. 268–88). Baltimore: Johns Hopkins University.

Brownstein, C. A., & Brownstein, J. S. (2008). Estimating excess mortality in post-invasion Iraq. *New England Journal of Medicine*, 358(5), 445–47.

Checchi, F., & Roberts, L. (2005). *Interpreting and Using Mortality data in Humanitarian Emergencies: A Primer for Non-Epidemiologists*. Humanitarian Practice Network Paper 52. London: Overseas Development Institute.

(2008). Documenting mortality in crises: what keeps us from doing better? *PLoS Medicine*, 5(7), e146.

Daponte, B. O. (2007). Wartime estimates of Iraqi civilian casualties. *International Review of the Red Cross*, 89(868), 943–57.

Elkins, C. (2010). Evaluating development interventions in peace-precarious situations. *Evaluation*, 16(3), 309–21.

Ghimire, D., Chardoul, S., Kessler, R. C., Axinn, W. G., & Adhikari, B. P. (2013). Modifying and validating the Composite International Diagnostic Interview (CIDI) for use in Nepal. *International Journal of Methods in Psychiatric Research*, 22(1), 71–81.

Goodhand, J. (2000). Research in conflict zones: ethics and accountability. *Forced Migration Review*, 8(4), 12–16.

Grandesso, F., Sanderson, F., Kruijt, J., Koene, T., & Brown, V. (2005). Mortality and malnutrition among populations living in South Darfur, Sudan: results of 3 surveys, September 2004. *JAMA: The Journal of the American Medical Association*, 293(12), 1490–94.

Grein, T., Checchi, F., Escribè, J. M., Tamrat, A., Karunakara, U., Stokes, C., *et al.* (2003). Mortality among displaced former UNITA members and their families in Angola: a retrospective cluster survey. *BMJ*, 327(7416), 650.

Groves, R. M., Fowler, F. J., Couper, M. P., Lepkowski, J. M., Singer, E., & Tourangeau, R. (2009a). *Survey Methodology*. New York: John Wiley & Sons.

Groves, R. M., Mosher, W. D., Lepkowski, J. M., & Kirgis, N. J. (2009b). Planning and development of the continuous National Survey of Family Growth. *Vital Health Statistics*, 1(48), 1–64.

Guha-Sapir, D., & Degomme, O. (2005). Darfur: counting the deaths. Brussels: Belgium: Centre for Research on the Epidemiology of Disasters.

(2007). *Estimating Mortality in Civil Conflicts: Lessons from Iraq: Triangulating Different Types of Mortality Data in Iraq*. Working Paper. Brussels, Belgium: Center for Research on the Epidemiology of Disasters.

Haer, R., & Becher, I. (2012). A methodological note on quantitative field research in conflict zones: get your hands dirty. *International Journal of Social Research Methodology*, 15(1), 1–13.

Harkness, J. A., Villar, A., & Edwards, B. (2010). Translation, adaptation, and design. In J. A. Harkness, M. Braun, B. Edwards, T. P. Johnson, L. E. Lyberg, P. Ph. Mohler, B.-E. Pennell, & T. W. Smith (eds.), *Survey Methods in Multinational, Multiregional, and Multicultural contexts* (pp. 115–40). Hoboken, NJ: John Wiley & Sons

Husain, F., Anderson, M., Lopes Cardozo, B., Becknell, K., Blanton, C., Araki, D., *et al.* (2011). Prevalence of war-related mental health conditions and association with displacement status in postwar Jaffna District, Sri Lanka. *JAMA: The Journal of the American Medical Association*, 306(5), 522–31.

Iacopino, V., Frank, M. W., Bauer, H. M., Keller, A. S., Fink, S. L., Ford, D., *et al.* (2001). A population-based assessment of human rights abuses committed against ethnic Albanian refugees from Kosovo. *American Journal of Public Health*, 91(12), 2013–18.

Kim, G., Torbay, R., & Lawry, L. (2007). Basic health, women's health, and mental health among internally displaced persons in Nyala Province, South Darfur, Sudan. *American Journal of Public Health*, 97(2), 353–61.

Kreuter, F., Couper, M. P., & Lyberg, L. E. (2010). The use of paradata to monitor and manage survey data collection. In *Joint Statistical Meetings Proceedings, Survey Research Methods Section* (pp. 282–94). Alexandria, VA: American Statistical Association.

Kuper, H., & Gilbert, C. (2006). Blindness in Sudan: is it time to scrutinize survey methods? *PLoS Medicine*, 3(12), e476.

Lawry, L. (2007). Maps in the sand. Investigating health and human rights in Afghanistan and Darfur. In C. Beyrer and H. Pizer (eds.), *Public Health and Human Rights: Evidence-based approaches* (pp. 243–67). Baltimore: John Hopkins University.

Mneimneh, Z., Karam, E. G., Karam, A. N., Tabet, C. C., Fayyad, J., Melhem, N., *et al.* (2008, June). *Survey Design and Operation in Areas of War Conflict: The Lebanon Wars Surveys Experience*. Paper presented at International Conference on Survey Methods in Multinational, Multiregional, and Multicultural Contexts, Berlin, Germany.

Mneimneh, Z., & Pennell, B. E. (2011, May). *Interview Privacy and Social Desirability Effects on Reporting Sensitive Outcomes Research*. Paper presented at the Annual Conference of the American Association for Public Opinion Research, Phoenix, AZ.

Moore, P. S., Marfin, A. A., Quenemoen, L. E., Gessner, B. D., Miller, D. S., Toole, M. J., *et al.* (1993). Mortality rates in displaced and resident populations of central Somalia during 1992 famine. *The Lancet*, 341(8850), 935–38.

Mullany, L. C., Richards, A. K., Lee, C. I., Suwanvanichkij, V., Maung, C., Mahn, M., *et al.* (2007). Population-based survey methods to quantify associations between human rights violations and health outcomes among internally displaced persons in eastern Burma. *Journal of Epidemiology and Community Health*, 61(10), 908–14.

Pham, P., Vinck, P., Wierda, M., Stover, E., & di Giovanni, A. (2005). *Forgotten voices: A population-based survey of attitudes about peace and justice in Northern Uganda.* New York: International Center for Transitional Justice; and Berkeley, CA: University of California, Berkeley, Human Rights Center.

Roberts, L., Lafta, R., Garfield, R., Khudhairi, J., & Burnham, G. (2004). Mortality before and after the 2003 invasion of Iraq: Cluster sample survey. *The Lancet*, 364(9448), 1857–64.

Salama, P., Spiegel, P., Van Dyke, M., Phelps, L., & Wilkinson, C. (2000). Mental health and nutritional status among the adult Serbian minority in Kosovo. *JAMA: The Journal of the American Medical Association*, 284(5), 578–84.

Scholte, W. F., Olff, M., Ventevogel, P., de Vries, G.-J., Jansveld, E., Cardozo, B. L., & Crawford, C. A. G. (2004). Mental health symptoms following war and repression in eastern Afghanistan. *JAMA: the Journal of the American Medical Association*, 292(5), 585–93.

Schwarz, N., and Sudman, S. (1992). *Context effects in social and psychological research.* New York: Springer-Verlag.

Sethi, D., Habibula, S., McGee, K., Peden, M., Bennett, S., Hyder, A. A., *et al.* (2004). *Guidelines for conducting community surveys on injuries and violence.* Geneva, Switzerland: World Health Organization. Retrieved from http://teach-vip.edc.org/documents/Injury_surveillance/Comm%20Surveys%20WHO.pdf.

Silva, R., & Ball, P. (2008). Reflections on empirical quantitative measurement of civilian killings, disappearances, and famine-related deaths. In J. Asher, D. L. Banks, & F. Scheuren (eds.), *Statistical Methods for Human Rights* (pp. 117–40). New York: Springer.

Spagat, M., Mack, A., Cooper, T., & Kreutz, J. (2009). Estimating war deaths. *Journal of Conflict Resolution*, 53(6), 934–50.

Standardized Monitoring and Assessment in Relief and Transitions (SMART) (2006). *Measuring Mortality, Nutritional Status, and Food Security in Crisis Situations: SMART Methodology, Version 1* [manual]. Retrieved from www.smartmethodology.org/.

Survey Research Center. (2011). *Guidelines for Best Practices in Cross-Cultural Surveys.* Ann Arbor: Survey Research Center, Institute for Social Research, University of Michigan. Retrieved from http://ccsg.isr.umich.edu/.

Swiss, S., Jennings, P. J., Aryee, G. V., Brown, G. H., Jappah-Samukai, R. M., Kamara, M. S., *et al.* (1998). Violence against women during the Liberian civil conflict. *JAMA: The Journal of the American Medical Association*, 279(8), 625–29.

Tapp, C., Burkle, F. M., Wilson, K., Takaro, T., Guyatt, G. H., Amad, H., *et al.* (2008). Iraq War mortality estimates: a systematic review. *Conflict and Health* [online journal], 2(1).

Thompson, S. K., & Seber, G. A. F. (1996). *Adaptive Sampling*. New York: John Wiley & Sons.

Thoms, O. N. T., & Ron, J. (2007). Public health, conflict and human rights: toward a collaborative research agenda. *Conflict and Health* [online journal], 1(11).

Vinck, P., Pham, P., & Kreutzer, T. (2011). Talking peace: a population-based survey on attitudes about security, dispute resolution, and post-conflict reconstruction in Liberia. Berkeley, CA: University of California at Berkeley, Human Rights Center.

Woodruff, B. A. (2006). Interpreting mortality data in humanitarian emergencies. *The Lancet*, 367(9504), 9–10.

World Health Organization, Department of Gender and Women's Health. (2001). *Putting Women First: Ethical and Safety Recommendations for Research on Domestic Violence against Women*. Retrieved from www.who.int/gender/documents/violence/who_fch_gwh_01.1/en/index.html.

Yamout, R., & Jabbour, S. (2010). Complexities of research during war: lessons from a survey conducted during the summer 2006 war in Lebanon. *Public Health Ethics*, 3(3), 293–300.

8

Interviewing in disaster-affected areas: lessons learned from post-Katrina surveys of New Orleans residents

MOLLYANN BRODIE, CLAUDIA DEANE, ELIZABETH C. HAMEL, MELISSA HERRMANN, AND ERAN BEN-PORATH

8.1 Introduction and background on New Orleans in the wake of Katrina

8.1.1 Introduction

Even before Hurricane Katrina began to form as a tropical depression over the southeastern Bahamas, New Orleans was a city facing a number of social challenges. The city's majority Black population was plagued by high poverty rates, high rates of violent crime and high rates of chronic diseases, AIDS and infant mortality, exacerbated by one of the nation's highest uninsurance rates (Ritea & Young, 2004; Rudowitz, Rowland, & Shartzer, 2006; Webster Jr., & Bishaw, 2006). When the historic port then became the focus of a combination of natural and man-made disaster, its residents became that much more burdened, many uprooted from their homes, some to other dwellings in the city, others gone from the state for good.

In the wake of this disaster, the Kaiser Family Foundation (KFF) determined that one way it could serve the New Orleans community with which it had a long history, as well as the policymakers tasked with leading its recovery, was to apply its survey research expertise to giving a voice and national visibility to residents by reporting what their lives were like in the aftermath of the storm, what they had experienced, what they had lost, and what they needed from recovery efforts. The project turned into a five-year effort which produced four different surveys of the local population, conducted during all three phases of disaster as described in Chapter 6 of this volume (rescue and relief, recovery, and development). The surveys were carried out in conjunction with a team of experts at Social Science Research Solutions, and each was fielded using a different survey methodology, which by default had to evolve along with the changing situation on the ground. This chapter will serve as a case study of this evolving methodology, and what these efforts suggest for interviewing post-disaster populations in the US and internationally.

8.1.2   Putting Katrina in context

Hurricane Katrina hit the Gulf coasts of Louisiana and Mississippi in August 2005 as a Category 4 storm, a classic natural disaster for residents of the American segment of Hurricane Alley. As the heavy rains and winds began to pound the city, however, residents had no way of knowing that they were only experiencing the first phase of a three-phase catastrophe. Compounding the natural disaster taking place was a man-made disaster in the making, as New Orleans' levee system was breached and storm water from the lake bordering the city surged into its residential neighborhoods, leaving up to 80 percent of the city underwater. The city then suffered through a disastrous official response. A bipartisan inquiry by the US Senate concluded that the human suffering caused by Katrina "continued longer than it should have because of – and was in some cases exacerbated by – the failure of government at all levels to plan, prepare for and respond aggressively to the storm" (p. 2) and added that "these failures were not just conspicuous; they were pervasive" (US Senate Committee on Homeland Security and Government Affairs, 2006, p. 2). The losses from the hurricane and the failure of the levees were significant. Overall, roughly 1,200 people in the region lost their lives, making Katrina the third deadliest hurricane on record in the United States (Blake, Landsea, & Gibney, 2011). The economic damage was even more widespread, with Katrina estimated to be the third costliest natural disaster in the world since 1965, and the most economically damaging disaster ever in the United States (The Economist Online, 2011; Center for Research on the Epidemiology of Disasters Database, 2012). The Greater New Orleans Community Data Center (GNOCDC) estimates that Katrina caused the loss of 22 percent of jobs from 2004 to 2006 in the seven-parish Metropolitan Statistical Area (MSA) that includes New Orleans (Plyer & Ortiz, 2011). And the city's own health care safety net was decimated: One year after the storm, only three of nine acute care hospitals in Orleans Parish were open for business, and even then their capacity was limited (Rudowitz, Rowland, & Shartzer, 2006). The famed Charity Hospital – a key link in the health care social safety net – had flooded and then closed its doors for good.

Most important in terms of the needs of traditional survey methodology, the storm and the ensuing flooding caused a tremendous amount of dislocation. Estimates are that more than 780,000 people throughout the affected states were displaced for some period of time by Katrina. Some, but not all, of this population shift was lasting. The Decennial Census conducted in 2000 pegged New Orleans' population at roughly 485,000. Ten years later, the population was at 344,000, roughly 70 percent of its prior size, but up substantially from the 209,000 the Census Bureau estimated were left in the city a year after Katrina's advent (Plyer, 2012). To this extent, Katrina was a substantially different category of disaster than many others studied in the developed world, where the presumption is that residential patterns quickly revert to normal (Bourque, Shoaf, & Nguyen, 1997).

While New Orleans was not the only city impacted by Katrina, that Parish stands out as being the hardest hit for a number of reasons, including: the density of the population affected and the preexisting social challenges facing that population; the failure of the man-made levee system that so dramatically exacerbated an already disastrous weather event; the particular failures in disaster planning, including the city's inability to evacuate its less mobile inhabitants before and immediately after the storm; and the length of the recovery process, which is ongoing even as we write this in 2013.

8.2   Literature review

Disaster research presents a significant challenge to survey researchers because each event is complex and unique. In order to reach a representative sample of individuals affected by a disaster, survey researchers must carefully define and sample their population of interest (see Chapter 6 in this volume). To date, the ability to develop a set of "best practices" for disaster research has been limited by the preponderance of qualitative reports that focus on surveys of specific events rather than quantitative reports that synthesize conclusions across multiple surveys.

While there does seem to be an evolving tradition of employing traditional survey research in the disaster studies field, literature searches reveal little modern writing in the way of post-disaster research in the public opinion field itself. Searching in *Public Opinion Quarterly* on the word "disaster," for example, we found only a handful of loosely related modern writings laying out guidelines for conducting surveys in this kind of setting. At the same time, we know that survey research grew rapidly in the wake of one of the globe's greatest disasters, World War II, an era when Rensis Likert "used survey techniques to inquire into the impact of bombing on the economies of [Germany and Japan] and on the morale of their populations" (Wilson, 1957, p. 175).

We therefore turned to the disaster research field to look for guidelines for our New Orleans work. Here, we did find research that had been carried out in the wake of previous hurricanes, but in most cases the project structure did not meet our own needs. Following Hurricane Andrew in 1992, for example, researchers used a variety of approaches to sampling those affected by the disaster. Garrison, Bryant, Addy, Spurrier, Freedy, and Kilpatrick (1995) used a random digit dialing sample to study post-traumatic stress disorder (PTSD) among adolescents in Dade County, Florida. However, this project, and similar surveys that took place six months to several years after the disaster, offered little guidance for conducting a survey focusing on the immediate aftermath of a disaster. Another effort following Hurricane Andrew assessed PTSD among residents in the areas most affected by the storm in the shorter term, one to four months immediately following the disaster, but did not utilize a representative methodology (Ironson, Wynings, Schneiderman, Baum, Rodriguez, Greenwood *et al.*, 1997). Researchers reached a convenience sample of respondents by recruiting at food stores and respondents' places of employment, or by knocking on doors in places where they had established ties with residents. Ironson *et al.* summed up the challenges they faced, writing: "Although there would be benefits from having a random sample, it was not feasible at the time. Many people were not living in their homes, phone service was out for months in many affected areas, and since looting was present we thought residents might be alarmed or irritated by unknown researchers knocking on doors" (Ironson *et al.*, 1997, p. 130).

In fact, according to Norris, Friedman, Watson, Byrne, Diaz, and Kaniasty (2002), convenience samples seem to have a firm footing in this area of research. Norris and colleagues first developed a database of 160 survey samples representing 102 distinct disaster events (Norris *et al.*, 2002), and then updated the work to include a total of 225 samples representing 132 distinct events that occurred between 1981 and 2004 (Norris, 2006). Norris' review included surveys following three types of disasters: natural disasters (e.g., floods), technological disasters (e.g., nuclear accidents), and mass violence (e.g., terrorist attacks). Norris found that just under a third of disaster studies used convenience sampling, whereas only 19 percent used random sampling.

While convenience samples tend to be practical for post-disaster situations in which those affected may be displaced and therefore difficult to sample systematically, they have many limitations – at the most basic level, those who complete the survey might differ in meaningful ways from those who do not – that make it difficult to apply lessons learned from one disaster to future survey efforts. Due largely to the limitations of convenience sampling, Kessler, Keane, Ursano, Mokdad, and Zaslavsky (2008) argued that the area probability household sampling is the most appropriate approach to selecting a representative sample of survivors of a natural disaster. We agreed – a convenience sample would not meet our goal of providing a representative view of the real life experiences of those coping with the storm's aftermath, and we continued to seek a more representative methodology.

We did find support in the field of disaster studies for our goal, in that several researchers have been advocating for the usefulness of traditional survey research as opposed to more qualitative studies as an assessment tool. For example, writing in the January–March 2000 edition of the journal *Prehospital and Disaster Medicine*, disaster research experts Kimberley I. Shoaf and Corrinne Peek-Asa, from the University of California Los Angeles' Center for Public Health and Disaster Relief and the Southern California Injury Prevention Research Center respectively, wrote "Survey research in disaster public health" to convince their colleagues that "surveys are useful tools for identifying and evaluating the health impacts of disasters" (Shoaf & Peek-Asa, 2000, p. 62). The literature also reveals that several disaster researchers have concluded that, despite doubts about whether researchers could find willing respondents in times of crisis, post-disaster surveys were more than possible, in that the average person was just as willing to participate in a survey in the wake of a disaster as otherwise, and that they could tolerate this participation without a great deal of additional stress – although a mental health backup system is recommended for research conducted immediately after large-scale traumatic events (Bourque, Shoaf, & Nguyen, 1997; Galea, Nandi, Stuber, Gold, Acierno, Best *et al.*, 2005).

8.3   First survey foray: poll of Katrina evacuees in Houston shelters, September 2005

We began our exploration of the experiences and needs of New Orleans' Katrina survivors with an unusual project: a face-to-face survey of city evacuees who had arrived in Red

Cross-operated facilities in Houston, Texas, a city which had taken steps to make itself available to refugees, some of whom arrived on buses organized by the federal government, others who reached the city by their own means. The population of evacuees arriving in Houston was certainly among those hardest hit by the hurricane and flooding, a group that, by definition, had not been able to, or had failed to, evacuate before the storm; had lost access to their New Orleans homes; needed government assistance to get out of the city; and now had no place else to take them in. The eventual survey results confirmed the dire needs of this group: six in ten had family incomes of less than $20,000 in the previous year, seven in ten did not have a savings or checking account, and the same proportion had no usable credit cards (*Washington Post*/Henry J. Kaiser Foundation/Harvard School of Public Health, 2005). This is in line with previous research which has found that lower-income households, minority households, and those with elderly or disabled residents are less likely to evacuate (Gladwin & Peacock, 1997).

This project – which was jointly conducted with our survey partners at the *Washington Post* and the Harvard School of Public Health – represented the ultimate in surveying during a fluid situation under extremely tight time constraints. Katrina evacuees began arriving in Houston three days after the storm, and the population at the Houston Reliant Park Complex and the George R. Brown Convention Center, as well as a satellite network of smaller shelters around the city, began to swell rapidly, and nearly as rapidly began dispersing to dwellings elsewhere in the community. Once the decision to survey this population was made, we immediately began by hiring twenty-eight Houston-based interviewers, primarily Black to conform to the demographics of the evacuee population, reasoning that it would be too difficult to transport and house non-local interviewers in the newly crowded city. We also obtained maps of the large shelter buildings to establish a geography-based probability sampling plan with an every nth respondent design that would give us a representative picture of the evacuees.

One particular challenge of this project, a challenge which is quite generalizable in this type of work, was the need to get permission to access the shelter facilities. In this case, we were able to get official access from the Red Cross with little difficulty. The challenge came on the ground: in a fast-changing, high-pressure situation such as a pop-up evacuation shelter, official permission granted by the top levels of an organization does not always trickle down to individuals in charge of running the shelter on a day-to-day basis. In fact, our project managers and interviewers faced real trouble getting into the facilities on the first scheduled day of interviewing. The solution – using everyone in our survey network to try to gain the promised access, from a *Washington Post* staff writer on the ground in Houston, who worked through the media center to get access to the Reliant Center, to the Harvard professor who put us in contact with a Harvard physician running the shelter's medical center. We also used our on-the-ground project staff to meet face to face with shelter and county officials to convince them of the legitimacy of the research and of our official clearance by the Washington-based Red Cross leadership. Another aspect of the solution – acquiescing to requests at one of the large shelters to allow Red Cross volunteers to accompany our interviewers on the first day of interviewing.

Sampling was another challenging aspect, in the sense that the conceptual sampling plan crafted to ensure representativeness required a good deal of adjusting when faced with real life on the ground. For example, our initial assumption was that much of our interviewing would come from a fairly straightforward every nth cot sample of the grid of cots covering the floors of these enormous facilities. What interviewers discovered, however, was that relatively few people were actually in the cot area during the day, given the number of affairs they were trying to settle and the nature of this disaster, and the ones that were there were disproportionately likely to be elderly or infirm. If interviewers and project directors had not been alert to this, or had been loath to change the sampling design, this would have resulted in a severely biased sample. Instead, interviewers were redistributed to reflect the actual location of the target population, including being based near the doors outside the facility, and used random selection to interview every nth person in these locations. In this case, it was fortuitous that shelter residents were required to wear a distinctive wristband for access, and this allowed for their easy identification by interviewers.

Interviewing a post-disaster population also raises a significant number of ethical considerations (see Chapter 6 in this volume for a general discussion of ethical considerations in post-disaster research). Harvard's Human Subjects Committee – which vetted the survey before its implementation – raised this early on, noting the recent stress that respondents had been through. We attempted to address this through several modifications to our survey procedures. First, we explicitly asked permission to begin the interview, making very clear that although the survey had the blessing of the Red Cross, a decision not to participate would have no effect on access to Red Cross benefits. We did not actively attempt refusal conversion, or apply any pressure to interviewees whatsoever. And though it was a difficult decision given the financial neediness of the evacuees, the team decided not to offer incentives for survey participation. As Herrmann, Brodie, Morin, Blendon, and Benson (2006) wrote, "We did not want to put respondents, who would receive something of value that other people in need might want, or interviewers, who would have such things to offer, in danger."

In fact, finding respondents willing to be interviewed turned out to be one of the easiest aspects of the process, and 90 percent of the evacuees selected for the survey agreed to participate. As Herrmann *et al.* (2006) reported, "interviewers reported that respondents felt almost relieved to be talking with someone, and telling us what had happened and was happening." This seems to confirm research in the area of disaster studies, which finds that "for many events, victims not only are available to be interviewed, but also are very interested in talking about their experiences" (Shoaf & Peek-Asa, 2000, p. 58).

The burden of the interview was also shared more than usual by the interviewers in this case, who may have been unprepared to listen to the more graphic accounts of the storm. Project directors responded to this by spending a good deal of time briefing interviewers about what they might encounter when meeting the evacuees, and then debriefing them as to what they *did* encounter. The main frustration expressed by the interviewers was the desire to help in some way. We made sure that they were armed with comprehensive information about places the respondent might seek help and resources if needed. For the most part, the interviewers said they felt as though they were contributing in some way to the relief efforts by giving people a chance to unburden themselves of their stories.

Ultimately, over a three-day period, we completed 680 interviews with adult shelter dwellers, representing a shelter population numbering over 8,000 at that time. The results provided invaluable information to policymakers, planning officials, and numerous community groups as they continued the cleanup and rebuilding process.

8.4   One year after Katrina: in-person survey of Greater New Orleans

One year after Katrina, New Orleans was in the second phase of disaster "recovery", having made a great deal of progress on some fronts but not on others. So it seemed critical to assess the needs and views of the city's population as policymakers continued to determine what the "new" New Orleans would look like. As we prepared to conduct our first survey of the Greater New Orleans area – including Orleans Parish itself as well as Jefferson, Plaquemines, and St. Bernard Parishes – we were looking at an area where a significant number of residents remained dislocated, where formerly populous neighborhoods remained deserted, and where parts of the city that prior to the storm were merely open land were now covered with Federal Emergency Management Agency (FEMA) trailers. In addition, the housing landscape was changing daily, as New Orleanians continued to return home. Data published later would show that a year after the storm, the city itself was at roughly 50 percent of its pre-Katrina population (Liu & Plyer, 2007).

Prior maps of where people lived in the city, based on high-quality surveys by the federal government and other institutions, could no longer be depended upon as accurate, as they had not yet been reliably updated. We also suspected that attempting to do a landline phone survey of this population – the methodology predominant at a time when the nation's cell-phone-only adult population was estimated to be only 7 percent – would prove biased, a suspicion borne out by the eventual finding that three in ten in Orleans Parish did not have a landline at the time of the survey (Blumberg & Luke, 2012). In other words, one could not say for certain who was living in New Orleans in the fall of 2006, and we decided that though we clearly did not have the funding to conduct a house-to-house census, we did in some way have to start from scratch, without preconceptions as to the residential layout of the city and its environs, and that the most prudent course would be to conduct the survey face to face. In retrospect, it is clear we were not the only ones at a bit of a loss. In their 2009 article "After a disaster: lessons in survey methodology from Hurricane Katrina" Henderson, Sirois, Chen, Airriess, and Banks (2009) conclude that "the post-disaster context meant that experience from traditional survey methods often did not apply" (p. 67).

In the end, the Kaiser Post-Katrina Baseline Survey of the New Orleans Area was conducted in person from September 12 to November 13, 2006, among 1,504 randomly selected adults interviewed in English and Spanish. In addition, interviewers observed nearly 17,000 housing units in order to document the level of physical devastation that remained in the metro area. We benefited greatly from local experts as we planned the sample, wrote the survey content and conducted the survey, and would caution against working in such a fast-moving situation *without* relying on local expert guidance. In particular, we were able to partner with Dr. Karen DeSalvo at the Tulane University School of Medicine, who had been particularly involved in health care-related aspects of the crisis and recovery. Not only did having a local expert on our team lend us credibility – our advance letter bore Tulane's logo as well as our own – but more importantly it served as a continuing course corrective. We also benefited from the endorsement of Dr. Fred Cerise, the Secretary of the Louisiana Department of Health and Hospitals, who provided us with a letter of endorsement and introduction that we were able to give to respondents.

Even with all this assistance, the 2006 survey proved to be among the most difficult we have ever fielded. We faced particular challenges in three phases of the survey process that others polling in post-disaster conditions might also expect: in staffing; in sampling; and in weighting.

The staffing issue was simple: despite the fact that jobs were at a premium in New Orleans at this time, we could not find enough skilled, local interviewers to conduct the survey. Given the fact that the population had been halved, and that many of the city's skilled workers had departed, this should perhaps have been anticipated. In any case, the result was that we imported roughly half of our forty-one interviewers from Houston, relying in some cases on interviewers from the project described above, who already had experience interviewing Katrina evacuees. Because we then had to cover not only travel costs but extended housing costs, this had a major impact on our budget for the project.

The sampling challenges were even more daunting. As noted, the New Orleans of 2006 looked radically, and unsystematically, different from the New Orleans of the previous summer. Obviously, the 2000 Census estimates of population by area were not operable. Similarly, at the time we were drawing the sample, the updated version of the US Postal Service's Delivery Sequence File (DSF) had not yet been released.[1] To meet our goal of representing the three parishes surrounding New Orleans, as well as being able to represent the diversity of experience across each of Orleans Parish's fourteen census tract defined neighborhoods, we designed a two-stage stratified area probability sample. The basic demographic stratification was thus comprised of seventeen distinct census defined areas, called major strata. Within the seventeen parishes/neighborhoods the design utilized census block defined substrata, called minor strata. This ultimately included 456 geographic sampling points – each of about fifty households – distributed proportionate to the expected population across the four parishes and then within the fourteen census defined neighborhoods in Orleans Parish. Of necessity, each area's expected population was an estimate drawn from a combination of pre-Katrina population counts and rough estimates of the

---

1 DSF is a comprehensive database from the United States Postal Service, at the ZIP+4 level. This database relates the delivery status of every postal deliverable address in the US and whether each individual address is active, vacant, seasonal, etc. Using daily feedback from letter carriers, the database is updated on a nearly continuous basis. This source has become a standard for defining and enumerating nontelephone sample frames, from face-to-face designs to multimode (e.g., mail-telephone-personal) and strictly mail.

proportion of housing stock that had been destroyed, garnered from Census Bureau interim surveys and from FEMA. The design incorporated entire area segments, so that all geographic points within the four parish area were eligible for inclusion in the sample, whether or not they had been designated as housing locations prior to the storm. In other words, we allowed what the census had designated as "zero blocks" into the sample – knowing that even if the selected sampling point was in the middle of a park or a parking lot, we could well find people living there, given press reports of tent enclaves and parking lots full of FEMA trailers. In this case, however, we did not find any housing units in the selected zero blocks.

In order better to establish appropriate population estimates, we built an additional check into the design: field workers were asked to observe and record the physical condition of all housing units in each of the 456 geographic areas selected for the sample. The goal was to increase the amount of information we would have available when we came to the weighting stage, as well as to provide authorities with an enhanced portrait of the level of physical devastation remaining in the city. As such, interviewers were instructed to visit each address listed in the pre-Katrina DSF for their segment and to document its physical condition as completely destroyed, seriously damaged, or not seriously damaged. They also took photographs of each structure to further document the status of housing units. At those addresses randomly chosen for the survey, interviewers also attempted to assess whether the housing unit was occupied or vacant. New households, new buildings, the appearance of tents or trailer parks or any other changes from the listed addresses of the block were also documented during this phase. If there were more than five differences from their original list, interviewers were instructed to check in with project directors to get further guidance as to how to select from the additional housing units or deal with the lack of housing units.

Besides obstacles to sampling, surveys done of a population in flux also face difficulties at the weighting stage, and our first New Orleans survey was no exception. We were keenly aware that given the extent to which the flooding had impacted neighborhoods of New Orleans differently, ensuring that we were representing each neighborhood's views proportionate to its actual size would be critical in ensuring that we painted an accurate picture of New Orleans as a whole. Weighting was accomplished in two stages, with the second phase – computing a population weight to adjust for the probability of selection given the number of adults in the household – being quite straightforward. Computing the first stage weight, however, was considerably less straightforward.[2]

In creating the household weight, we had two main data sources available to us. First, while the survey was in the field, the Postal Service had released an updated, post-Katrina DSF file. This provided us with an external data source for post-Katrina counts of occupied housing units at the census block level. We also had the results of our field operation cataloguing the state of the housing stock in each of our 456 segments. Each of these data sources had weaknesses, however. In the former case, we were concerned that the DSF file tends to overstate the actual number of occupied housing units. While we would expect this

---

2 Note, no poststratification weighting was performed as there were no reliable post-Katrina demographic estimates for the area.

overstatement to be relatively small in a typical survey project, we were concerned that this tendency might be exacerbated in New Orleans, where a large number of residents might be receiving mail at an address but not residing there (i.e., those in the process of rebuilding or selling their properties). We were also worried that the DSF overstatement might not be uniform across neighborhoods and parishes. In the case of our estimates of housing destruction, we needed to be cautious in relying on our estimates from a limited number of segments in the smaller neighborhoods to estimate occupancy rates for the entire neighborhood.

Given these sources, and these concerns, we decided on a hybrid approach. The combined three-step process began with estimating the number of occupied households according to the October 2006 DSF for each minor stratum of the sample. For those census blocks where we had observed housing data from our field work, we then compared the observed count to the DSF count, and aggregated this ratio to the major stratum level, using this to estimate the DSF overstatement or understatement in each neighborhood. We then applied this adjustment for each neighborhood to the original DSF counts in each minor stratum. While the final adjustments made to DSF counts varied somewhat by neighborhood, they were relatively small overall, with an adjustment factor of 0.91 for the total four-parish area. The weighting complete, we were able to begin analysis and present to city and national officials and the public at large a portrait of a still-struggling population one year after the storm.

Overall, this first area-wide survey had an AAPOR Response Rate 3 of 51 percent (American Association for Public Opinion Research, 2011). This relatively high response rate in part reflected New Orleanians' general willingness to talk to us about Hurricane Katrina and the rebuilding process. It is worth noting that we did have emergency procedures in place to handle the needs of any respondents who experienced psychological distress in the immediate wake of the interview, but no respondent requested this service, although many did ask for and appreciated the resource list provided by interviewers.

8.5   NOLA at three years and five years post-Katrina: allowing the methodology to return to "normal" along with the city

8.5.1   *2008: address based, mixed mode*

One of the key take home points of surveying in New Orleans, relevant to interviewing in all post-disaster landscapes, is that you have to be constantly alert to changes on the ground and the ways those might aid your methodology and rein in your survey costs. Three years after the storm, when we returned to field the second of our city-wide surveys, New Orleans was a much different city than it had been even two years earlier, more populous, more settled. In fact, in 2009 the Census Bureau estimated it to have been 2008's fastest-growing city (US Census Bureau, 2009).

Our first area of assessment was the state of landline penetration. One year after the storm, our conclusion had been that we could not count on reaching a large enough segment of the city by phone, and thus we resorted to the costly but more reliable in-person methodology. Three years after the storm in 2008, however, we were confident that landline penetration had stabilized to the point where at least some segment of the survey interviews could be conducted by phone. But we were wary of moving to a fully phone-based survey given that our 2006 survey found that 30 percent of Orleans Parish residents had no landline, with most of those reporting that they were cell phone only. This anxiety over cell phones was exacerbated by the anecdotal evidence suggesting that many residents who had evacuated the city had come home with cell phones purchased in other areas, leaving us without an easy area code target. We therefore decided to eschew reliance on phone only, and instead created an address-based sample with a mixed-mode design, with phone surveys the method of first choice, but allowing respondents also to answer via the Internet and adding door-to-door visits as a last resort for low response rate areas (de Leeuw, 2005).

We also assessed the status of other available data sources that might be useful, noting that the Greater New Orleans Community Data Center had found that while immediately after the storm household counts based on the DSF were unreliable, these counts had stabilized after late 2006. This gave us confidence that we would be able to use the DSF information to design our sample and to weight the data. We therefore had a design which incorporated the robustness of address-based sampling with the flexibility of a multimode design.

Our sample was selected using a multistage stratified area probability design that was in many ways similar to the 2006 survey. In the first stage, a sample of segments based on census block groups was selected as primary sampling units (PSUs) in each of the fourteen census tract defined neighborhoods of Orleans Parish.[3] We used the updated DSF to increase the efficiency of the resulting sample by selecting PSUs using probabilities proportional to the number of residences in each neighborhood. We again used the DSF at the second stage of selection to choose a systematic random sample of addresses as secondary sampling units.

Even in a city with a population still in flux, we were then able to match about 45 percent of our selected addresses with a landline phone number. These respondents were sent a pre-notification letter, and then contacted by phone by an interviewer. Those *without* a listed telephone number were sent a letter inviting them to call a toll-free number to complete the survey or to visit a website and take the survey there. This latter group was offered a $15 incentive as compensation for the additional effort of having to reach out to take the survey, and also to compensate them in case of cell-phone costs. Respondents could receive this incentive as a check or have us donate it to one of four local charities (the latter was the more popular choice). Those who did not respond to this first wave of outreach, and who were living in low response rate segments, were visited at their homes by a trained interviewer from the 2006 survey.

In the end, we completed 669 interviews by telephone, 447 in person, and 178 via the Internet. Not surprisingly, response rates differed by means of outreach. Using AAPOR's

---

3 Note that in 2008, we moved from sampling a four parish area to focusing exclusively on Orleans Parish, which is coincident with the city of New Orleans, the area we had found contained the majority of residents still affected by the storm's aftermath.

Response Rate 3, the response rate for outgoing telephone interviews was 50 percent, while for web and telephone call in interviews combined it was 39 percent. The response rate for the in-person interviews was 31 percent. While this may seem surprising on its face, since in-person interviews tend to get higher response rates in general, it makes sense once we consider that the targets of these interviews were the population that by definition was hardest to reach – either unlisted and in a low response area, or listed and an initial non-responder (Groves, Fowler, Couper, Lepkowski, Singer, & Tourangeau 2004).

Household level and population level weights were then calculated for the data. Unlike the 2006 survey, poststratification weighting was possible in 2008, as Claritas had demographic projections incorporating census estimates for Orleans Parish as of summer 2006. We did use poststratification weighting on the 2008 survey, but to increase our comfort level with comparisons to the 2006 data, we also computed a version of the weight without the poststratification data. Comparing demographic estimates based on the two weights, we found that the differences were relatively small.

Our next challenge was determining whether the data collected via this mixed-mode survey could be fairly compared to the data collected exclusively via face-to-face interviewing in 2006. Given that documenting change over time was one of the primary goals of this survey, this was a major issue for our team. As such, we did an extensive review of mode effects.

8.5.2   An extended consideration of the effects of changing modes in the Kaiser New Orleans surveys

The decision to rely on mixed modes in the address-based sampling design of the second New Orleans survey allowed us to sidestep the cost implications and methodological complications associated with in-person interviewing, but raised the issue of possible mode effects. From a total survey error perspective, this might have meant trading in one type of error for another. The literature on mixed-mode research suggests that this methodology can reduce the error stemming from undercoverage or nonresponse associated with a single mode, but at the same time could introduce "mode effect" error (Brick & Lepkowski, 2008; de Leeuw, 2005; Dillman, 2006; Tourangeau, Rips, & Rasinski, 2000). The literature on mode effects identifies several dimensions of interviewing that could explain these biases. The most pertinent to the changing methodologies of the New Orleans surveys are the *method of contact* (phone, mail, email) and the *method of interviewing* (through an interviewer or self-administered) (de Leeuw, 2005; Tourangeau *et al.*, 2000).

We begin by looking at potential effects caused by method of contact. The early New Orleans surveys initiated with interviewers contacting respondents in person, but with the transition to address-based sampling, written communication became the initial form of contact, thus removing the human element. Follow-up invitations brought back the interviewer as a point of contact, though for many this was by phone rather than in person. Tourangeau *et al.* (2000) maintain that telephone contact affords the survey administrator less opportunity to establish the legitimacy of the survey, which could diminish the efforts respondents may put into answering.

A larger body of research focuses on the effects of the method of interviewing, specifically the presence or absence of an interviewer either in person or on the phone. This presence can affect responses by impacting the way respondents understand questions (for example, through vocal inflection), distracting respondents, affecting respondents' motivation to participate (based on the interviewer's likability for example), and the way questions are answered in the presence of others compared to when respondents are by themselves (Dillman, Smyth, & Christian, 2009).

One line of research has looked at the manner in which interviewers prime social desirability, meaning the respondent's sense of what answer the other person would like to hear.[4] For example, some studies find that self-administered questionnaires lead to more candid responses than interviewer-administered surveys, especially when they pertain to undesirable behaviors (Heeren, Edwards, Dennis, Rodkin, Hingson, & Rosenbloom, 2008; Link & Mokdad, 2005; Smith & Dennis, 2008).

While the question of social desirability was not prominent in the context of the New Orleans surveys, it is possible that respondents may have wanted to present themselves in a more sympathetic light when others were present, either in person or on the phone. Were that the case, we would expect respondents interviewed in person to provide systematically different responses.

Beyond social desirability lies the possibility that other psychological mechanisms affect the types of responses depending on the setting or mode of response. For example, telephone respondents tend to offer more positive responses than web respondents, and are more likely to gravitate toward the most positive response option (Christian, 2007; Dennis, Chatt, Li, Motta-Stanko, & Pulliam, 2005; Tarnai & Dillman, 1992). This would lead one to expect that phone respondents in New Orleans would be more optimistic and express more support for the recovery efforts than web respondents. The literature also indicates (though there are conflicting accounts) the possibility of an acquiescence effect, where people are more likely to agree with statements when read by interviewers compared to their responses to the same statements in self-administered surveys (Dillman *et al.*, 2009).

Data quality concerns also center on how well respondents understand the questions, how likely they are to respond to questions (rather than refuse or report they do not know the answer), and how likely they are to answer truthfully. Mode differences in data quality may stem from various attributes of each mode, such as the visual clarity that mail or web surveys can provide, or the ability of tone or inflection to make a question clearer in an aural-based setting (Dillman & Christian, 2003). Research suggests that in-person interviews provide higher-quality data in this regard compared to telephone interviews (Holbrook, Green, & Krosnick, 2003). Using item nonresponse as one measure of quality, research finds that web surveys tend to produce more "don't know" (DK) responses than in-person interviews (Heerwegh, 2009).

---

4 Social desirability refers to the idea that in the face of another person (or even on the phone), respondents would tend to present themselves in a more positive light compared to when they are answering questions outside of another person's earshot or eyes (Aquilino, 1994; de Leeuw & van der Zouwen, 1988; Kreuter, Presser, & Tourangeau, 2008; Tourangeau, Rasinski, Jobe, Smith, & Pratt, 1997).

An underlying cause for this could be the cognitive burden involved with each mode, meaning the "different demands on such skills as reading, listening, following directions, recognizing numbers, and keying" (Tourangeau *et al.*, 2000, p. 308). The implications for mixed-mode studies, and for switching modes within the same series of studies, are apparent: interviewer-mediated surveys, such as those conducted in person (in the Houston study or in the first New Orleans survey), require less literacy skills than self-administered ones. When an interviewer is present, one can ask for clarification, which cannot be provided in a self-administered survey. Respondents opting for the web survey option would be more likely, therefore, to misinterpret a question or skim through it, compared with situations where an interviewer can be consulted for clarification. Conversely, when respondents are asked questions on the phone, they cannot typically re-read and consider the question. Interviewers read the question leaving only seconds for respondents to answer. The upshot, at times, is known as a recency effect, where respondents on a phone survey are more likely to select the last category read to them (Krosnick & Alwin, 1987).

One issue with identifying mode effects is that they could be confounded with non-response error (Voogt & Saris, 2005), or as Safir and Goldenberg (2008) observe: "mode itself matters less than does the respondent behavior typically associated with mode" (Section 4.4.1). When respondents can self-select into one mode or another, different modes can attract different types of people. In other words, our ability to consider the mode as a source of variance in survey response is limited by the fact that characteristics such as age, education, or technical proficiency may drive people toward one mode or the other, which would produce its own bias.

In deciding to pursue a multimode design with the second New Orleans study, we had to consider the real possibility that mode effects such as these could hamper our trends and our ability to draw conclusions over time. We therefore continually assessed the possible implications of switching modes and sample approaches as we collected data, and conducted a complete analysis of potential effects after data collection. Our analysis showed that each mode did in fact attract different respondents. Those in listed-number households were more likely to be homeowners, were older, and were better off financially. Meanwhile, those dialing in were more likely to be female, somewhat older, and more likely to be low income. Web respondents were by far the youngest (half of them were under 35), the most likely to be White, and the most educated (more than 70 percent had a college degree).[5] Therefore, observed differences in responses by mode could be attributed not only to the method of administration, but also to the differences in the populations drawn to each method of contact.

We explored the question of mode effects by conducting question-by-question comparisons. Overall, we found evidence for small effects that are "typical for unambiguous, factual items that are not sensitive or socially desirable" (Brick & Lepkowski, 2008, p. 156). For the most part, the differences between modes did not appear to be systematic.

---

5 Details of this internal analysis available from authors.

We did find evidence that web respondents were less likely to state their mental health had improved, possibly an indicator that they were more comfortable to express concerns with their mental health, a finding that would be consistent with the social desirability paradigm. However, overall, social desirability did not factor much into the findings.

We found more compelling evidence of mode differences where interviewer-administered modes corresponded with more positive outlooks on progress questions. Web respondents were significantly less likely to say progress had been made compared to in-person or by-phone respondents on a variety of issues, including fighting crime, the availability of health services, and the strengthening of schools. However, in other instances, differences were found between phone and in-person respondents (both interviewer-mediated), while phone and web respondents answered similarly, which suggested it was not necessarily the interviewer causing the effect.

Since the areas where mode effects were most evident were on questions of progress in New Orleans and the respondents' satisfaction with various facets of their lives, we created scales for these items (nine questions for progress and eight for satisfaction). Overall (and counter to expectations), web respondents scored similar to computer-assisted telephone interviewing (CATI) respondents on the satisfaction scale, and lower only than the computer-assisted personal interviewing (CAPI) respondents. Furthermore, this difference was no longer statistically significant when controlling for respondents' social-economic background. On the progress scale, respondents on the web averaged more than a point (out of 9) lower than either of the in-person modes, a finding that held even with statistical controls for socio-economic factors. Thus, this line of questioning was the one context where the method of administration could affect the outcomes (albeit to a small extent) in the expected direction. Where interviewers were present, respondents tended to answer more positively.

For the few other instances where mode differences were apparent, further analysis showed that there was no consistent pattern to these differences. In other words, mode may have affected the levels of DK responses, or produced some small inconsistent differences for a few questions, but we found no evidence of a systematic effect and we expected some of that to be minimized further with proper weighting to the demographics underlying these differences.

With these findings as the backdrop, we felt confident that as long as maximum coverage was maintained and the data were weighted to account for systematic differences between sample composition and the target population, switching from in-person to multimode interviewing would have minor impact on trended information. At the same time, these changes made the research more affordable and feasible, while addressing the changing reality on the ground.

8.5.3   New Orleans five years after the storm: return to standard telephone methodology

Our survey team returned to New Orleans two years later to prepare for the third city-wide survey in this series, wanting to employ the most accurate and cost-efficient survey design we could while still preserving the trendability of our data. One important reference point was that by 2008, we had found that only a very small proportion of the target population (2 percent or less) was without either landline or cell-phone service. We also noted that our response rate was quite strong among the outgoing phone interviews that year. And finally, our internal mode effects analysis had not shown any strong pattern of mode effects. In combination, these three factors, in addition to budgetary constraints, led us to move to a dual frame (landline and cell phone), telephone-centered methodology.

In order to assure the widest possible coverage, we dialed cell-phone exchanges affiliated with the general New Orleans area code rather than attempting to target specific New Orleans exchanges or cell-phone switch centers. Overall, we completed 926 interviews by landline and 602 by cell phone. The response rate for this survey (AAPOR RR3) was 32 percent.

8.6   Lessons learned

In general, our work in New Orleans supports the conclusions of disaster researchers that classic survey research can and should be conducted in post-disaster areas, and that all phases of the process – from sampling to data collection – can be carried out with adequate rigor even in these challenging circumstances. At the same time, we suggest that researchers be prepared to deal with a fair amount of complexity, that they remain open to adapting and combining methodologies, and that they keep a closer than usual eye on the human component – the needs of interviewees and interviewers – than they may tend to do in a standard national survey. We would summarize our lessons learned as follows.

8.6.1   *The importance, and limitations, of official permission*

A post-disaster survey project is unusual in that in many cases public or nonprofit officials have a heavy presence on the scene of the disaster and thus in some ways may serve as gatekeepers to respondents. Even if they are not official gatekeepers, their seal of approval may carry more weight than in a typical situation, given respondents' uncertainty and sense of vulnerability. In our work with Katrina evacuees arriving in Houston, we needed the approval of Red Cross officials to gain access to the evacuee shelters in Houston, as well as acquiescence from Houston public officials. In our later work with New Orleans residents, we knew the city was a small enough place that the research would be noticed and decided to alert local authorities – such as the head of the state's health and human services department – of our intent, our goals and our expected procedures. In the first case, the project would have been impossible without this clearance. In the second case, we believe it would have been much less successful.

It is important to understand, however, that even in everyday life, clearance from top public officials does not always trickle down in an efficient way to gatekeepers on the ground. This maxim is doubly true in a post-disaster scenario, when there is an enormous amount of information being exchanged at any one time and many normal modes of communication may be down entirely. This requires several things from researchers. First, it is important to ensure that you have some physical evidence of the official permission, either electronic or written. It is also important that you keep skilled project directors with good communication skills and adequate authority on site during the project, to go directly to lower-level officials as necessary and present your case. Finally, it is worth working every angle of your network, including less formal angles – as we did in the Houston case by using a journalist on the ground, as well as a contact with a local physician.

8.6.2   Survey design lessons

The survey design lessons for those hard-to-reach populations that are on site after a disaster is essentially "don't let the perfect be the enemy of the good." On many occasions during these four New Orleans projects, we found we did not have the kind of data we would normally rely on in carrying out a random sample survey. For example, in the first New Orleans study of residents of the four parish areas, we had no census data *or* DSF residence data that would reflect the residential patterns of the city post-hurricane. Instead, we went in using a combination of pre-Katrina data and FEMA disaster reports. This ended up being good enough to get us started.

Post-disaster researchers also need to be both creative and willing to put in extra effort. In the case of the 2006 survey, we decided that to supplement the existing data on residential patterns, we would add a full listing of the status of each dwelling to our random sample survey of the segments. This obviously required interviewers, as well as project managers and eventually analysts, to do a fair amount of extra work. But we were able to use this to aid in improving the accuracy of our household weights at the back end of the process.

Another survey design lesson from our post-Katrina work: hybrid approaches are useful. In the 2006 New Orleans survey, as just mentioned, we used a hybrid weighting method relying on both the updated DSF counts and our own observed data. In the 2008 survey, we used a mixed-mode method to reach respondents, finding them in multiple ways with an eye to efficiency, convenience, and methodological rigor. And though we learned that outcomes may differ at times by mode, we found these differences small, for the most part, and correlated with mode selection more than the mode itself.

8.6.3   About interviewers

Field workers conducting face-to-face interviews in post-disaster scenarios are, by definition, put under much more pressure than interviewers in regular settings. They are placed in areas where there are not only potential physical risks – downed wires, etc. – but where the population may be unstable. In New Orleans, lawlessness was still an issue even a year after the storm, and our interviewers did enter, and of course then leave, places where they saw guns brandished.

But these interviewers also bear a good deal more responsibility for being the eyes and ears of the project than in normal circumstances. In a landscape which is unknown in terms of official data, they can report on the situation on the ground. In our Houston project, for example, it was interviewers who were able to flag for us the potential problems with our sampling plan, which drew heavily on samples from the beds laid out on the stadium floors, and highlighted that only the elderly and infirm in fact were in those areas for most of the day. Interviewers also routinely suggested new locations for interviewing based on the flow of foot traffic in the shelters. The advent of easy cell-phone connection to interviewers has made it possible for project managers to react to this information in real time and adjust the sample on the go.

Researchers should anticipate difficulty in obtaining adequate numbers of trained interviewers locally in a post-disaster area. We had this problem in 2006 in New Orleans, and in the end had to import those interviewers that we had trained in Houston in 2005. While, ideally, in-community interviewers would seem to be best, researchers should be prepared to look to surrounding areas – particularly those with some connection to the disaster area – as a source of project staff.

Finally, we did see evidence of some interviewer strain, particularly in the survey of Houston evacuees. Becoming a second-hand witness to the human costs of Hurricane Katrina weighed heavily on the interviewers. Researchers should be prepared to offer needed help not just to the interview*ees* in post-disaster scenarios, but also possibly to the interview*ers*.

8.6.4   Interviewing lessons

As the disaster research community has concluded, we also found that respondents that had lived through a major trauma were quite willing to be interviewed on the topic. Our response rates for the surveys were respectable compared to similar studies, and in the case of the Houston survey could be considered quite high: nine in ten of those chosen for the sample agreed to take the survey. In some cases, respondents reported finding it therapeutic to recount what had happened to a listener. Nonetheless, we took prior research at face value and did inform respondents that if they needed any counseling assistance in dealing with their underlying experience, or the act of reliving it through the survey, that such counseling would be available immediately. We did not find any respondents that felt the need to take us up on this offer, although making available a list of local resources did seem to be worthwhile and was welcomed by many respondents.

We also grappled with the issue of providing incentives to interviewees, a population that could badly use financial assistance. Yet, in the case of the Houston survey we deemed that financial incentives could put both the interviewee and interviewer in an uncomfortable, and perhaps even dangerous, position, and therefore elected to forgo incentives.

8.6.5   The need for flexibility and good communication

All these lessons emphasize the need for continuing flexibility, as well as the need for clear and open channels of communication between all levels of the project staff. Researchers attempting to survey post-disaster populations need to begin with an assessment of which of the usual tools in their survey box are available, and a willingness to cobble together the best old data available with the best new data one can collect. And they need to be in constant communication with their staff on the ground to see how the expectations on which they based their sampling and interviewing plans are squaring with the daily reality.

8.6.6   Value of the research

The series of New Orleans projects have not only been some of the most methodologically challenging to field in our careers, they have also been some of the most satisfying data to be able to publish and provide, and we believe the themes of flexibility and quick adaptation to changing conditions on the ground could be useful to others in similar situations, both domestically and internationally. In this particular case, the survey work allowed us to measure the extent to which the lives of residents of a storm-challenged American city remained disrupted one, three, and five years after the hurricane had hit. We were able to catalogue health needs, challenges in accessing health care services, and a changing level of psychological stress. We presented the city's mayor and a raft of other public officials with residents' priority list in terms of the ongoing recovery, and their report card on how well leaders were doing across a wide swath of city services. We also reminded the broader national community of the disproportionate effect the storm had on a key racial minority group. We are hopeful that the lessons learned about the needs of interviewers and interviewees, and the need for project flexibility and adaptability, will be useful to others facing post-disaster scenarios in the United States and abroad.

References

The American Association for Public Opinion Research (AAPOR). (2011). *Standard Definitions: Final Dispositions of Case Codes and Outcome Rates for Surveys* (7th edn.). Deerfield, IL: AAPOR. Retrieved from www.aapor.org/AM/Template.cfm? Section=Standard_Definitions2&Template=/CM/ContentDisplay.cfm&ContentID= 3156.

Aquilino, W. (1994). Interview mode effects in surveys of drug and alcohol use: a field experiment. *Public Opinion Quarterly*, 58(2), 210–40.

Blake, E. S., Landsea, C. W., & Gibney, E. J. (2011). *The Deadliest, Costliest, and Most Intense United States Tropical Cyclones from 1851 to 2010 (and Other frequently Requested Hurricane Facts)*. (NOAA Technical Memorandum NWS NHC-6). Retrieved from www.nhc.noaa.gov/pdf/nws-nhc-6.pdf.

Blumberg, S. J., & Luke, J. V. (2012). *Wireless Substitution: Early Release of Estimates from the National Health Interview Survey*. Hyattsville, MD: US Centers for Disease Control and Prevention, National Center for Health Statistics. Retrieved from www. cdc.gov/nchs/nhis.htm.

Bourque, L. B., Shoaf, K. I., & Nguyen, L. H. (1997). Survey research. *International Journal of Mass Emergencies and Disasters*, 15(1), 71–101. Retrieved from http://ijmed.org/articles/405/download/.

Brick, J. M., & Lepkowski, J. M. (2008). Multiple mode and frame telephone surveys. In J. M. Lepkowski, C. Tucker, J. M. Brick, E. D. de Leeuw, L. Japec *et al.* (eds.), *Advances in Telephone Survey Methodology* (pp. 149–69). Hoboken, NJ: John Wiley & Sons.

Center for Research on the Epidemiology of Disasters Database. (2012). The International Disaster Database (EM-DAT). Retrieved from http://www.emdat.be/.

Christian, L. M. (2007). How mixed-mode surveys are transforming social research: The influence of survey mode on measurement in web and telephone surveys. Unpublished doctoral dissertation, Washington State University, Pullman. Retrieved from www.dissertations.wsu.edu/Dissertations/Summer2007/l_christian_070807.pdf.

de Leeuw, E. (2005). To mix or not to mix data collection modes in surveys. *Journal of Official Statistics*, 21(2), 233–55.

de Leeuw, E., & van der Zouwen, J. (1988). Data quality in telephone and face-to-face surveys: a comparative meta-analysis. In R. Groves, P. Biemer, L. Lyberg, J. Massey, W. Nicholss, II, & J. Waksberg (eds.), *Telephone Survey Methodology* (pp. 283–300). New York: John Wiley & Sons.

Dennis, J. M., Chatt, C., Li, R., Motta-Stanko, A., & Pulliam, P. (2005). *Data Collection Mode Effects Controlling for Sample Origins in a Panel Survey: Telephone Versus Internet.* Retrieved from http://marketing.gfkamerica.com/knowledgenetworks/ganp/docs/Research-0105.pdf.

Dillman, D. A. (2006). Why choice of survey mode makes a difference. *Public Health Reports*, 121, 11–13.

Dillman, D. A., & Christian, L. M. (2003). Survey mode as a source of instability in responses across surveys. *Field Methods*, 15(2), 1–22.

Dillman, D. A., Smyth, J. D., & Christian, L. M. (2009). *Internet, Mail, and Mixed-Mode Surveys: The Tailored Design Method.* Hoboken, NJ: John Wiley & Sons.

Galea, S., Nandi, A., Stuber, J., Gold, J., Acierno, R., Best, C., *et al.* (2005). Participant reactions to survey research in the general population after terrorist attacks. *Journal of Traumatic Stress*, 18(5), 461–65. Retrieved from http://onlinelibrary.wiley.com/doi/10.1002/jts.20053/abstract.

Garrison, C., Bryant, E., Addy, C., Spurrier, P., Freedy, J., & Kilpatrick, D. (1995). Post-traumatic stress disorder in adolescents after Hurricane Andrew. *Journal of the American Academy of Child and Adolescent Psychiatry*, 34, 193–201.

Gladwin, H., & Peacock, W. G. (1997). Warning and evacuation: a night for hard houses. In W. G. Peacock, B. H. Morrow, & H. Gladwin (eds.), *Hurricane Andrew: Ethnicity, Gender and the Sociology of Disasters* (pp. 52–74). London: Routledge.

Groves, R. M., Fowler Jr., F. J., Couper, M. P., Lepkowski, J. M., Singer, E., & Tourangeau, R. (2004). *Survey Methodology.* Hoboken, NJ: John Wiley & Sons.

Heeren, T., Edwards, E. M., Dennis, J. M., Rodkin, S., Hingson, R. W., & Rosenbloom, D. L. (2008). A comparison of results from an alcohol survey of a prerecruited internet panel and the National Epidemiologic Survey on Alcohol and Related Conditions. *Alcoholism: Clinical & Experimental Research*, 32(2), 222–29. doi:10.1111/j.1530-0277.2007.00571.x.

Heerwegh, D. (2009). Mode differences between face-to-face and web surveys: an experimental investigation of data quality and social desirability effects. *International Journal of Public Opinion Research*, 21(1), 111–21.

Henderson, T. L., Sirois, M., Chen, A. C., Airriess, C., & Banks, D. (2009). After a disaster: lessons in survey methodology from Hurricane Katrina. *Population Research and Policy Review*, 28, 67–92.

Herrmann, M. J., Brodie, M., Morin, R., Blendon, R., & Benson, J. (2006). *Interviewing in the Face of Disaster: Conducting a Survey of Hurricane Katrina evacuees*. Retrieved from Public Opinion Pros: www.publicopinionpros.norc.org/from_field/2006/oct/herrmann.asp.

Holbrook, A. L., Green, M. C., & Krosnick, J. A. (2003). Telephone versus face-to-face interviewing of national probability samples with long questionnaires: comparisons of respondent satisficing and social desirability response bias. *Public Opinion Quarterly*, 67(1), 79–125.

Ironson, G., Wynings, C., Schneiderman, N., Baum, A., Rodriguez, M., Greenwood, D., *et al.* (1997). Posttraumatic stress symptoms, intrusive thoughts, loss, and immune function after Hurricane Andrew. *Psychosomatic Medicine*, 59(2), 128–41.

Kessler, R. C., Keane, T. M., Ursano, R. J., Mokdad, A., Zaslavsky, A. M. (2008). Sample and design considerations in post-disaster mental health needs assessment tracking surveys. *International Journal of Methods in Psychiatric Research*, 17, S6–S20.

Kreuter, F., Presser, S., & Tourangeau, R. (2008). Social desirability bias in CATI, IVR, and web surveys: the effects of mode and question sensitivity. *Public Opinion Quarterly*, 72(5), 847–65.

Krosnick, J. A., & Alwin, D. F. (1987). An evaluation of a cognitive theory of response-order effects in survey measurement. *Public Opinion Quarterly*, 51(2), 201–19.

Link, M. W., & Mokdad, A. H. (2005). Effects of self-reports of adult alcohol consumption: a comparison of mail, web and telephone approaches. *Journal of Studies on Alcohol*, 65, 239–45.

Liu, A., & Plyer, A. (2007). *A Review of Key Indicators of Recovery Two Years after Katrina: The New Orleans Index Second Anniversary Special Edition*. New Orleans, LA: The Brookings Institution Metropolitan Policy Program and the Greater New Orleans Community Data Center. Retrieved from www.brookings.edu/~/media/research/files/reports/2011/8/29%20new%20orleans%20index/200708_katrinaes.pdf.

Norris, F. H. (2006). Disaster research methods: past progress and future directions. *Journal of Traumatic Stress*, 19, 173–84.

Norris, F., Friedman, M., Watson, P., Byrne, C., Diaz, E., & Kaniasty, K. (2002). 60,000 disaster victims speak, Part 1: an empirical review of the empirical literature, 1981–2001. *Psychiatry*, 65, 207–39.

Plyer, A. (2012). *Facts for Features: Hurricane Katrina Impact* [press release]. The Greater New Orleans Community Data Center. Retrieved from http://gnocdc.org/TheNewOrleansIndexAtSix/index.html.

Plyer, A., & Ortiz, E. (2011). *The New Orleans Index at Six: Measuring Greater New Orleans' Progress toward Prosperity*. The Greater New Orleans Community Data Center. Retrieved from https://gnocdc.s3.amazonaws.com/reports/GNOCDC_New OrleansIndexAtSix.pdf.

Ritea, S., & Young, T. (2004, February 8). Cycle of death: How N.O. became the nation's murder capital. *The Times-Picayune*, p. A1. Retrieved from www.nola.com/speced/cycleofdeath/pdf/02080401.pdf.

Rudowitz, R., Rowland, D., & Shartzer, A. (2006). Health care in New Orleans before and after Hurricane Katrina. *Health Affairs*, 25(5), 393–406.

Safir, A., & Goldenberg, K. (2008). Mode effects in a survery of consumer expenditures. In *Proceedings of the American Statistical Association, Section on Survey Research Methods* (pp. 4436–43). Alexandria, VA: American Statistical Association.

Shoaf, K. I., & Peek-Asa, C. (2000). Survey research in disaster public health. *Prehospital and Disaster Medicine*, 15(1), 65–71.

Smith, T. W., & Dennis, J. M. (2005). *Online vs. In-Person: Experiments with Mode, Format, and Question Wordings. Public Opinion Pros* [online magazine] @ www.publicopinionpros.norc.org/.

(2008). *Mode Effects on In-Person and Internet Surveys: A Comparison of the General Social Survey and Knowledge Network Surveys*. Paper presented at the Section on Survey Research Methods at the Joint Statistical Meeting of the American Statistical Association. Denver, CO. Retrieved from www.amstat.org/sections/srms/proceedings/y2008f.html.

Tarnai, J., & Dillman, D. A. (1992). Questionnaire context as a source of response differences in mail versus telephone surveys. In N. Schwarz & S. Sudman (eds.), *Context Effects in Social and Psychological Research* (pp. 115–29). New York: Springer.

The Economist Online. (2011, May 21). *Natural Disasters: Counting the Cost: The Japanese Earthquake could be the Costliest Ever {Blog Graphic Detail}*. Retrieved from www.economist.com/node/21017096.

Tourangeau, R., Rasinski, K., Jobe, J., Smith, T. W., & Pratt, W. (1997). Sources of error in a survey of sexual behavior. *Journal of Official Statistics*, 13, 341–65.

Tourangeau, R., Rips, L. J., & Rasinski, K. (2000). *The Psychology of Survey Response*. New York: Cambridge University Press.

US Census Bureau. (2009). New Orleans was nation's fastest-growing city in 2008: population getting closer to pre-Katrina levels [press release]. Retrieved from http://www.census.gov/newsroom/releases/archives/population/cb09–99.html.

US Senate Committee on Homeland Security and Government Affairs. (2006). *Hurricane Katrina: A Nation still Unprepared* (S. Rept. 109–322). Washington, DC: US Government Printing Office. Retrieved from http://www.gpo.gov/fdsys/pkg/CRPT-109srpt322/pdf/CRPT-109srpt322.pdf.

Voogt, R. J., & Saris, W. E. (2005). Mixed mode designs: finding the balance between nonresponse bias and mode effects. *Journal of Official Statistics*, 21, 367–87.

Washington Post/Henry J. Kaiser Foundation/Harvard School of Public Health (2005). *Survey of Hurricane Katrina Evacuees*. Retrieved from http://kff.org/disparities-policy/report/survey-of-hurricane-katrina-evacuees/.

Webster Jr., B. H., & Bishaw, A. (2006). *Income, earnings and poverty data from the 2005 American Community Survey* [ACS-02]. US Census Bureau, American Community Survey Reports. Washington, DC: US Government Printing Office. Retrieved from www.census.gov/prod/2006pubs/acs-02.pdf.

Wilson, E. C. (1957). World-wide development of opinion research. *Public Opinion Quarterly*, 21(1), 174–78.

9

Reaching and enumerating homeless populations

IRENE GLASSER, ERIC HIRSCH, AND ANNA CHAN

Whether called roofless (India), *sin techo* (Latin America), *itinérants* (Quebec), *furosha* (Japan), or *gamino* (street child of Columbia), homeless individuals and families confront us with a failure to provide safe and permanent dwellings to meet our most basic human needs. In the United States, by the 1980s the homeless had migrated out of the skid rows and the Bowery of cities to become a visible presence in many neighborhoods of cities and suburbs. A major reason for the increase in homelessness was the great reduction of affordable housing, including the loss of 2.3 million units of low-income housing between 1973 and 1992 (Wagner & Gilman, 2012). A second reason was the retreat from a policy of financial assistance to single unemployed individuals, General Assistance (in some places called the "rent money"), in the 1980s as we moved from cash assistance to providing housing and food through homeless shelters and soup kitchens (Glasser & Bridgman, 1999). In addition, the stagnant and falling income of low-wage workers put housing out of reach for many workers (National Coalition for the Homeless, 2009).

As the US was confronting the visible homeless, policymakers, and the public wanted to know how many homeless individuals and families existed and who they were. The answer to these questions proved to be difficult. The numbers varied depending whether the count came from a census, surveys based on sampling, or administrative records such as shelter rosters.

A major challenge in counting the homeless is choosing which of the many definitions of homelessness to use. Does one include only the literal homeless, usually meaning those who reside in homeless shelters or on the street? Does one include the precariously housed, such as "couch surfers" or the *doubled-up*, who are individuals or families staying with another person on a very temporary basis? The doubled-up are defined by the National Alliance to End Homelessness (NAEH) as "a low-income individual or member of a family, who is living with friends, extended family or other non-relatives due to economic hardship. Low-income here is defined as 125 percent of the federal poverty line" (NAEH, 2011). It is important to note that the US Census does not attempt to provide an official count of all homeless individuals in the US. Rather, it strives to include the homeless population in its decennial censuses just as it strives to include all other residents of the US.

Ground-breaking work on estimating the homeless population includes the work of Rossi, Wright, Fisher, and Willis (1987) who sampled various networks within the homeless milieu of Chicago, and the work of Metraux, Culhane, Raphael, White, Pearson, Hirsch *et al.* (2001) who used administrative records to establish the size and characteristics of homeless populations.

In France, the Institut National d'Études Démographiques (INED) conducted a series of studies between 1993 and 2008 that developed sampling strategies based on the probability of an individual using a particular service (e.g., soup kitchen, mobile food van) (Marpsat, 2008). A key to the development of their statistical methods was the good relationships the surveyors had with homeless service providers throughout France.

Marpsat and Razafindratsima (2010) reviewed some of the advantages and disadvantages of several sampling strategies that have been tried in France in homeless, drug-using, and sex worker populations. One method includes two stage filter surveys with a follow-up sampling of the universe in question and time-location sampling (see Chapter 19 in this volume), which weighs the unequal probability that an individual will visit certain locations that will be sampled (for example, more people visit soup kitchens than clothing closets, which are organizations offering free or greatly reduced-cost clothing). Another method is respondent-driven sampling, wherein individuals in the community of interest are asked to recruit others they know in the community (see Chapter 23 in this volume).

Our research sought to discover and describe challenges of enumerating homeless individuals and families during the 2010 US Census. In this chapter, we describe our ethnographic research on homeless persons and suggest strategies that may improve the coverage of this population.

9.1   An overview: enumerating homeless population in the 2010 US Census

The United States Census counts every resident in the US every ten years in order to determine the number of seats each state has in the US House of Representatives and in order to distribute billions of dollars in federal funds to local communities. The decennial census is mandated by the US Constitution and has occurred every ten years since 1790. Until the Census of 1960 when the census forms were mailed to households, census enumerators visited every household for the decennial enumeration (US Census Bureau, 2000).

There are many well-documented challenges to obtaining an accurate decennial count (Schwede 2010). Portions of the population that are undercounted include renters, young men, non-relatives, immigrants, and those whose residences are in flux. From the beginning of the US Census in 1790, the census has been address based. One group that presents a great challenge to the decennial census is the homeless, who by definition do not have a permanent address.

In order to include homeless people in the 2010 US Census, the US Census Bureau conducted a service-based enumeration (SBE) on March 29, 30, and 31, 2010, using a seven-question individual census report (ICR). The SBE was part of the group quarter enumeration (GQE) operation that sought to count individuals living in group quarters, such as college residence halls, prisons, nursing homes, and homeless shelters. The GQE was a separate operation during the 2010 Census; it included around 3 percent of US population in 2010.

The strategy of the SBE for homeless populations was that on the first night the census takers enumerated individuals and families in emergency shelters, transitional shelters (typically those shelters with a longer stay and more intensive services than an emergency shelter), and in hotels and motels used to house the homeless. On the second day, the enumerators visited individuals at regularly scheduled mobile food vans and soup kitchens. The third day the enumerators counted people at pre-identified targeted unsheltered outdoor locations, such as at bus stops, encampments, and cemeteries.

An individual could have been counted at all three types of settings in that they could have been enumerated at a shelter the first day, at a soup kitchen the second day, and at an outdoor encampment the third day. They could also have been counted within a household *and* at an SBE site since there are people who have a permanent residence who may also utilize soup kitchens.

In the attempt to count people once and only once and at the correct location in the census, the Census Bureau had a mechanism in place for unduplicating persons within the SBE universe. The Census Bureau conducted a computer and clerical person matching using demographic response data on the SBE questionnaires in order to identify duplicates within the SBE universe. Based on predetermined criteria, duplicates were removed from the census count. After the unduplication process, those persons who were enumerated at soup kitchens and/or regularly scheduled food vans and who provided a valid address for a usual home elsewhere were removed from the SBE group quarters location and were counted at their permanent residence (Barrett, 2012).

Individuals and families living with another household (often referred to as the doubled-up homeless) were to be included in the US Census form that all residences received before April 1, 2010, regarding the people staying at the residence on April 1, 2010. The first question asked the individual filling out the form how many people were living or staying in the house, apartment, or mobile home on April 1, 2010. The second question asked if there were "additional people" staying there on April 1, 2010. This second question could include homeless individuals and families staying with the householder.

If an individual believed that he/she had been missed in the census he/she could have filled out the five-question Be Counted form. The Be Counted forms were to be made available at many community sites as well as at the questionnaire assistance centers.

Finally, a homeless person could have been counted in the transitory location enumeration which was administered between March 22, 2012 and April 16, 2012. This enumeration was designed for people who are mobile and may be living in places such as motels, hotels, marinas, circuses, or carnivals. Our research indicated that a number of homeless individuals briefly stay in inexpensive motel or hotel rooms between stays in shelters, outdoor locations, and doubled-up.

Despite these strategies, counting people without a fixed address (*sans domicile fixe*, to use the UN generic term for homeless) is enormously challenging. Ethnographic work conducted by the Census Bureau on the homeless enumeration over the past twenty-five years has documented the difficulties of accurately enumerating the homeless population. The challenges include the following.

Mobility

Homeless people often cycle through various living arrangements and can be constantly on the move: they may have access to a bed at a family or friend's place, then sleep in a car, then be imprisoned, and then enter a shelter. These arrangements may also be interspersed with episodes of having their own housing (Fleisher & Brownrigg, 1990; Glasser & Salo, 1991).

Tenuous attachment

Many homeless people are temporarily staying at a residence where they are unlikely to be reported on a census form. These people are often not included on the census form because the householder does not think of them as permanent members of the household (Glasser & Salo, 1991; Martin, 1999; de la Puente & McKay, 1995; Schwede & Ellis, 1994). Using the Living Situation Survey, Martin (1999) uncovered significantly more people per household than the 1990 Census had included, since people staying in the household who were not members of the family (the doubled-up) were often not included in the householder's census form. Doubling up with family and friends is a frequent precursor to literal homelessness (National Alliance to End Homelessness, 2010).

Not wanting to be found

Some homeless people are hiding and do not want to be identified. Examples include individuals hiding from the courts and police, individuals who fear that they will end up in a nursing home or mental hospital if the "authorities" knew their true state of health, and families with children who are trying not to be conspicuous to the state's protective services unit (Glasser & Salo 1991). Some homeless people may be deeply involved in the underground economy (Bourgois & Brownrigg, 1990) and therefore do not want to be counted.

Pretending to be housed

Some people are pretending to be housed. For example, individuals who work or are seeking work may not want their employer or potential employer to know that they are homeless (Liebow, 1993). People sleeping out of doors may be vague about their sleeping arrangements because they do not want to be harassed and want to keep their sleeping locations private (Glasser & Salo, 1991).

Usual address as a limited concept

The concept of having a usual residence, or living or staying one place "most of the time" may not be a relevant concept in various populations, including nomadic populations, itinerant workers, and some members of the homeless population (Martin, 2007). In Quebec, one commonly used term for homeless people is *les itinérants* (Glasser, Fournier, & Costopoulos, 1999) which suggests movement embedded within the concept of homeless.

As a result of these challenges, homeless individuals and families can be missed during the decennial census.

9.2   Methodology for 2010 ethnographic homeless enumeration study

Previous research on homeless populations suggest that more foundational knowledge and exploratory research are needed to understand how best to count this population. This study used qualitative ethnographic methods to understand the complexity of the living situation of the homeless population and to generate strategies to improve census coverage of this group.

Ethnography is the written description of a culture after a period of intensive observation and participant observation by the anthropologist who has lived within the culture of study. In taking extensive field notes and analyzing them, one is attempting to understand not just the behaviors one can see but the *world view* of the culture that makes those behaviors possible. A description of the more subtle aspects of ethnography is provided by Charles Frake, who says that describing a culture

> is not to recount the events of a society but to specify what one must know to make those events maximally probable. The problem is not to state what someone did but to specify the conditions under which it is culturally appropriate to anticipate that he, or persons occupying his role, will render an equivalent performance.

(Frake 1964, p. 112)

We were guided by the above rules of ethnography in our work with homeless populations. It is important to understand the *emic* or insider's point of view of homeless populations as well as of service providers in order to discover the most efficacious way of ensuring that homeless populations are fully included in the decennial census. This work contributes to the increased coverage of homeless populations in future decennial censuses.

We conducted ethnographic research related to the 2010 Census during the three months leading up to the service-based enumeration and two months after the enumeration for the purpose of gaining the homeless individual's and family's points of view of the census operation. Our primary data collection methods were unobtrusive observation, participant observation, brief interviews, and focus groups. These methods contribute to an ethnography of homeless populations.

We met homeless individuals wherever they were: in shelters, soup kitchens, and on the streets. We used the state-wide homeless coalition's listing of all services for the homeless as our guide for where to find homeless individuals and families. We further supplemented this list with additional locations based on our increasing knowledge gained by being in the field. We did not attempt to employ a statistical sampling of sites such as venue sampling (discussed in Chapters 19 and 20 in this volume) but rather we tried to be in all of the locations utilized by homeless persons.

9.2.1   Location and description of study sites

We conducted our unobtrusive observation, participant observation, brief interviews, and focus groups in three cities in a New England state. The three cities are described below:

- City One has the only shelter for single men and women within approximately forty miles. The city is easily accessible by public bus, for which many people have free passes or reduced fares. It is the regional hub for health and social services. City One has a seaport, with fishing and tourism industries that attract many people in search of a job.
- City Two has one of the ten family shelters in the state. This family shelter serves women and their children from the capital city as well as the immediate region. City Two also has a day center for the chronically mentally ill, and a group home for the mentally ill. It is easily accessible by bus to and from the capital city.
- City Three is approximately twenty minutes by bus from the capital city. It has one of the few soup kitchens in the area that serves breakfast and lunch and is also open during the hours in between so it can serve as a day respite center for people on the street. City Three has a food pantry and thrift shop which are well utilized.

During our visits to shelters and soup kitchens we brought something to eat (usually small oranges that were in season and were not often present in homeless settings) for everyone at the site. In the soup kitchen in City Three, we brought free bus passes, since many of the people there did not have a bus pass or a reduced fare pass.

We conducted our observations at all of the homeless-serving facilities that were listed by the state Coalition for the Homeless as important day and nighttime resources for the homeless as well as a single room occupancy (SRO) building that we discovered also served as a nighttime residence for homeless individuals. The homeless-serving facilities included:

- Emergency homeless shelter for twenty single adults in City One, where we spent six evenings. In order to enter this shelter one has to be buzzed in, as the doors are locked at all times. During the months of the study, we observed the fluidity of homeless people as they moved between this shelter, to the street, to doubled-up housing and back to the shelter. We were able to observe two people as they were being barred from the shelter for the night. The shelter has a lounge for men and one for women, as well as separate dorm rooms. There are no prepared meals at the shelter, so people have to leave to get meals. They are not charged rent at this shelter.
- Family shelter that provides nineteen beds for households with children and nine beds for households without children in City Two, where we spent three afternoons and evenings. This family shelter houses women and their children and allows the household to stay until they are able to secure housing.
- An SRO building used by homeless individuals in City One, where we spent four mornings. This site was originally designed for boat crew members who were between

jobs. Although not technically listed as a shelter, this SRO provides inexpensive housing for ten single people, who stay until they can move on.

- We conducted multiple observations and brief interviews throughout the three cities at five soup kitchens, one daytime respite program for people returning from prison, one daytime respite for people with chronic mental illness, and one congregate living facility for people with mental illness. It was in the soup kitchens that we encountered the doubled-up and the out-of-doors homeless individuals.

9.2.2   Observation of Census Day at two soup kitchens

A very important strategy of our research was to unobtrusively observe the census workers in action in the Monday noontime soup kitchen in City One and in the daily soup kitchen in City Three. In both cases, the observer did not interact with the enumerators and was treated as a diner (However having run a restaurant even for a soup kitchen I would use the term "patron" – Russell Curtis of the soup kitchen.

9.2.3   Post-enumeration focus groups at shelter and soup kitchen

In order to discover the homeless individuals' experience with the 2010 Census and to learn about the barriers to census participation from portions of the homeless population from an emic point of view, we conducted two focus groups on April 8 and 16, 2010, soon after the service-based enumeration was completed. We conducted one focus group at the shelter for single men and women and another focus group at the large soup kitchen that also serves as a day respite for homeless people.

In both settings, we introduced ourselves and we reviewed the reason for the focus group. We explained that the census is very important in determining political representation and that we wanted to get suggestions about how to improve the count from a group of people who are often undercounted. We told the participants that we would not be asking for any personal identifying information and asked them to sign a consent form. We encouraged them to say anything they wished regarding the census and gave each participant a $10 grocery gift card to compensate them for their time.

The focus groups' questions were: What was your personal experience with the recent 2010 Census count? Can you think of any way that the census could improve the accuracy of their count of people who do not have their own place? In addition to those questions, we asked follow-up questions for clarification during the groups.

9.2.4   In-depth interviews with service providers

We conducted interviews with homeless service providers including the Housing Hotline director, who knew many of the homeless living in the shelter and out of doors in City One as well as the entire county; the Housing Authority Community Center director of City One, who was knowledgeable about local homelessness and who places homeless families in local low-cost motels; the Community Police Officer in City One, who knew the people living out of doors and in the shelters; the police officer in City Three, who knew the people living out of doors; and the Director of Social Services in City Three, who was knowledgeable about homelessness in that city.

9.3 Analysis

Through our observations, brief interviews, and focus groups with homeless people who were living in the singles shelter, the family shelter, out of doors, motels, mariner's single room occupancy residence/shelter, and those living doubled-up, we were able to observe various patterns that have implications for the census. We took extensive field notes after our visits to each site and used text analysis (Bernard, 2011) in order to discover the behavior and movement of homeless individuals and families that could present barriers to census inclusion. We were guided by the principles of *grounded* theory, wherein the researcher generates an overall theory of causal relationships based on the analysis of the data obtained from field work (Glaser & Strauss, 1967).

9.4 Findings

We analyzed our field notes and discovered characteristics of each setting and patterns of behavior that have implications for the enumeration of homeless populations. Below, we provide brief descriptions and summarize our findings from the observations, focus groups, and interviews.

9.4.1 Enumerating homeless individuals and families within homeless shelters will capture only a portion of the homeless population on a given night

The shelter for single individuals includes people who stay for short periods of time as they cycle through living out of doors, with other people or families (doubled-up), or can afford their own rents. Our ethnographic work in the shelter for singles took place in the lounge of the shelter, where people were watching TV and talking. Many people staying in the singles shelter see this as a temporary situation until they can find a job. Living in a shelter is a back-up plan if they have absolutely nowhere else to live. Some examples of people we found in the singles shelter were:

- A 41-year-old White man, a carpenter who had been in the shelter for two weeks after leaving a roommate situation that did not work out.
- A White man in his 50s who had been in the shelter for two days. He had most recently been looking after an elderly sick man but then the man became too sick for him to care for. He told us about his drug and alcohol history as well as unattended medical problems.

Family shelters house families until they find their own apartment, which means that these shelters are often full. In the family shelter, the staff appeared to engage the parents (mostly mothers) in activities that would assist them in leaving homelessness, such as job training, General Education Diploma (GED) classes, mental health treatment, and substance abuse treatment. Some of the people we met in the family shelter were:

- An African-American woman of 24 years with two young daughters. She had been associated with this shelter and its transitional program for over two years. She had just finished her Certified Nursing Assistant training and was waiting to take the test.
- A Hispanic woman of 28 with her three children. She had been in the shelter for seven months. Before this, she was living with a friend for two years, but then a neighbor "ratted" on her since her friend was living in subsidized housing and could have lost her apartment for keeping a guest with her for two years.
- A 24-year-old White woman with her five-year-old child and her 55-year-old mother. They had been in the shelter for four months. Before this they had been in a motel, before that with a friend, and before that in another motel.

The observations regarding the differential length of stays between singles and family shelters are corroborated by the 2011 State Homeless Information Management System (HMIS). The mean number of days of singles shelter residence was 32 days with a median of 3 days for those leaving singles shelters in the state in 2011. In contrast, the mean number of days of family shelter residence was 64 days with a median of 33 days for those leaving family shelters in the state in 2011. The relatively short median shelter stay for singles underlines how many more people pass through the shelter system than would be in the shelter on the night of the census. Our observations are that when not in the shelter system many of these shelter residents live with family or friends or stay out of doors.

9.4.2   People who are not following the shelter rules, or who have not followed them in the past, can be barred from entering or staying in a shelter

We were able to observe two people as they were being barred from the shelter during our observations.

- One evening we spoke with a 30-year-old African-American man who had been released from prison in 2007 and told us that he could not go back into public housing because of his felony conviction. Before staying at the shelter, he had been with his fiancée. The next week, we observed that he was very drunk. The shelter manager asked him to leave.
- We saw two large men in their 40s fighting over who was going to be able to sit in a specific chair in the shelter lounge. As they were verbally arguing, they took their fight to the dorm room behind the lounge. When one of the men hit the other one, the shelter worker asked the man who was hitting to leave.

In addition to actually observing people being barred, individuals we met in soup kitchens told us of being barred from the shelter as in the following examples:

- We met a 40-year-old White man who said that he had been barred from the shelter because of drinking (even though it was a "wet" shelter). He said that instead of sleeping outside, he walked around all night.
- A White man in his 40s told us that he was barred from the shelter because of a fight. He now lives doubled-up in a neighboring town and comes into town daily for services such as the soup kitchen.

There is also evidence that in addition to barring people, the shelter workers will control who enters the shelter. The following excerpt from our field notes illustrates this:

- As I (Glasser) was entering the shelter at 6 pm, a woman outside of the shelter, thinking that I was in need of a bed, told me that she had been told that the shelter was full. After I did get into the shelter, the shelter worker on duty told me that in fact they were not full.

Being barred from the shelter, or being asked to leave after being admitted, has important implications for the census, since being barred means that the person needs to find an alternative place to stay, such as out of doors or doubled-up.

9.4.3   Those living alone out of doors are difficult to find and enumerate

As we talked with people eating in soup kitchens, we met a number of individuals who shared their stories with us about currently living out of doors. These people are difficult to enumerate, as they were not living in an encampment as out-of-doors homeless do in some locales, but in separate, private places hidden from view. The out-of-doors homeless are variously called rough sleepers (England), *les sans abri* (France, Quebec), *los sin techo* (Latin America) (Glasser, 1994). Below are brief descriptions of some of the individuals we met who were living out of doors.

- It was a very cold afternoon and already almost dark outside as we entered the soup kitchen. A 59-year-old African-American man told us that he had been living in an unheated garage for the past three and a half years and he feared that the house was about to be sold.
- A 40-year-old white man told us that he had had cancer and could not do manual labor anymore. He had been living in his car for the past six months and said that he would not go to the shelter.
- A 50-year-old White man told us that he had just gotten out of prison and had been living with friends and in his van. He told us that he was barred from the shelter.
- A 61-year-old African-American man told us that he had been sleeping in his car for several years. He told us that he had bills to pay and was saving money by sleeping in his car.

One day at the noontime soup kitchen we saw rescue workers carry out a man who had been living on the street. Apparently, he had come to the soup kitchen, started to be served, had fallen asleep sitting up, and could not be awakened. His friends and the soup kitchen director became worried and called the rescue workers to take him to the hospital.

The next week, the man was back in the soup kitchen. He told us that he has been in and out of the shelter for eleven years. He complained that he needed oxygen but the shelter would not allow him to be there with oxygen because people smoke in the shelter, even though they are not supposed to, and the staff were worried about an explosion. When we asked him where he planned to sleep, he said that he sleeps outside a lot. The hospital social worker told us that he could always come back to the emergency room to sleep.

9.4.4   Potential undercount of homeless individuals through a service not recognized as a homeless serving shelter

A key to the census of homeless individuals is the accurate listing of group quarters so that the census workers can approach the correct sites. This takes much time and research as sheltering homeless individuals and families might be intentionally discrete. For example, in one city in our previous research we knew of a husband and wife who sheltered homeless individuals through religious auspices, but were not listed in state-wide homeless coalition lists.

We found an SRO building that was designed for mariners who were between ship jobs but is in fact used as a shelter by homeless people. This SRO was not included in the lists of resources of the Coalition for the Homeless although eventually it could have been included as a group quarters location, as the census Bureau was continually adding locations in the service-based enumeration (Durante, 2012). The shelter consists of ten rooms on the top floor of a historic building (this service has existed since 1919) on a wharf. Each person has a room and there is no cooking in the room. The rest of the building has a café that is open to the public, and rest rooms and showers that are open from 6 am to 6 pm. These daytime services are designed for people who work on boats and need a respite during the daytime.

People pay $135/week, or as they can. They can also barter for their rent by performing chores, which we observed. The following excerpts illustrate some of the situations of people staying at the mariner's residence.

- A White man in his 20s had been at the mariner's residence for three months after being released from prison. Before prison, he had been renting a room in a friend's house in a neighboring town. He also had stayed with his mother, but she lived in "housing" (i.e., the local way of referring to subsidized housing) and could not house him legally. He paid no rent but was doing maintenance chores for the residence.
- A 60-year-old White man had been living in the mariner's residence for six months. He had a good work history but his mental illness meant that he could only work part time. When the mariner's shelter closed for renovations, he planned to live in the RV he had just bought and put it on a friend's property until the campgrounds open for the summer.

9.4.5   Low-cost hotels and motels may house homeless individuals who are between shelter stays and need specific strategies for enumeration

A number of people told us about sleeping in motels as an alternative to staying in a shelter, on the streets, or with a friend. In our conversation with the Director of the Community Center of

City One Housing Authority, she told us that she places homeless families in motels as an alternative to the family shelter, especially if she believed that the stay would be short and not too expensive for the city. The single people appeared to be paying for the motel room themselves. The following are some examples of people who told us about motel living.

- At the mariner's shelter, we talked with a 67-year-old White man who was a disabled veteran. Before his one month stay at the mariner's shelter, he was sleeping in his car. Before that, he was staying at a local motel, and before that he was in an apartment.
- We talked with a man and woman at a noontime soup kitchen who were staying at a local motel for the winter. They had a camper and said they would leave the motel by April 15 in order to camp in the woods. They said that they got their mail at their post office box and that they would not talk with anyone who came to their door.

9.4.6   Living doubled-up with another household is a frequently utilized alternative for homeless individuals; enumeration in doubled-up situations is very difficult

It was very common for people to have stayed with family and friends before and between episodes of living in a shelter or living out of doors. Since most of the people who hosted the people were renters themselves, with leases that specified who was to be in the apartment, there was a deterrent to including the guest on the census form for the household. Further, the hosts themselves were sometimes living in hard-won subsidized housing. Despite the assurances of confidentiality of the US Census and despite the specific question on the householder form asking about *additional* people staying at the residence, people with whom we spoke believed that the householder would not want to risk jeopardizing their housing by admitting to additional people staying with them.

The following are examples of people whose housing was tenuous because they were not the lease holders of the apartment and they did not have the funds to rent their own place.

- We talked with a middle-aged White woman at the soup kitchen in City Three who was having trouble finding a job. She was living with her boyfriend, but he said if she could not contribute to the rent she would have to leave by the end of March. She had no idea where she would go or who she should talk with to get help finding housing.
- A middle-aged White man at the soup kitchen in City Three had spent his last night doubled-up with friends. He pointed out that there were no shelters available in the immediate area. He tried a shelter several towns away but they limit entry to people from his town to three nights in a row. When he can't double-up with a friend he sleeps outside.

9.4.7   Homeless individuals are often in flux in terms of where they sleep each night

In the first focus group at the shelter, which took place one week after the census takers had come to the shelter, five out of the ten people in the focus group (all currently staying at the shelter) believed that they had *not* been counted by the census because they were not at the shelter that night (March 29) but were doubled-up (four people), or because they did not want to cooperate with the census (one man who was at the shelter).

One of the participants said that he was at the shelter the night of the census, but he did not fill out the census form because he feels "insignificant" as a person. One of the women not in the shelter on March 29 said that she had been at the local soup kitchen on the day that census workers came to count people but said that she did not have the patience to fill out the census form. She said she was not asked by census workers on her way out of the soup kitchen to answer those questions.

In discussions with shelter workers who were on duty the night of the census we found out that if someone did not fill out the form for any reason, they (the workers) filled out the form for them, although the people staying at the shelter did not appear to be aware of this.

The second focus group took place on April 16, 2010, at the large soup kitchen which also functions as a day respite in a city close to the capital city, two weeks after the census takers had been to this soup kitchen. When we asked the fifteen participants if they believed they had been counted, there was much confusion. The three people who had stayed in a shelter the night of March 29 thought that the form had been filled out for them and that "they had no choice" about participating in the census. The six participants who were doubled-up with someone else thought that they would not be counted in that household, because the doubled-up situation was very temporary. They said that if they are staying in someone's apartment for one night, how could the person say that they were "living there"? In fact, the census uses the words "living" and "staying" in the householder form in order to avoid implying more of a relationship between people at the same address than is actually true.

Two participants who were living in a single room occupancy building in the capital city did not recall getting any forms. One man was in a substance abuse residential program and did not recall any census workers being there. One man who had just gotten out of detoxification, and who did receive a census form where he was staying, told us that he tore up the form because he did not want to be bothered.

Two participants did not seem to remember where they actually were on Monday, March 29, so they did not know if they were in the shelter or with a friend, the two possibilities they suggested.

Many of the participants spend their day in the community room of a large day program in the capital city. The day center, although not a shelter, allows homeless individuals to sleep on chairs there throughout the night. These participants did not recall seeing census workers in the community room during the week of March 29. We know that the day center was on the list of places that the enumerators were directed to visit in order to find homeless individuals.

We asked the members of both focus groups for suggestions of how to improve the homeless count in future decennial censuses to be sure that everyone, including themselves, is counted in the census. The following were their suggestions.

- Utilize word of mouth from peers. If a small group of homeless persons understand the importance of the count and where it is going to take place, they will communicate with others and the count will be more effective. People are suspicious about why the government is asking them these questions. It is important to allay their fears and that is easier to do through peer networks.

- Have a toll-free number available that people can call if they realize they were missed by the census.
- Send people to places where homeless people hang out during the day. Among the places mentioned in both groups were: bus stations, train stations, libraries, emergency rooms of hospitals, clothing banks throughout the state, tent cities, homeless drop-in centers, and parks. Research with homeless individuals before the enumeration would have identified these sites.
- Continue to send census workers to soup kitchens to count people who may have been missed at other locations. Soup kitchens are very heavily utilized by homeless people in this state. Have the census workers circulate more among the diners, explaining the importance of filling out the census. Ensure that the census workers are present for more than one day in each soup kitchen in order to reach the maximum number of people.
- Consider doing the census before the winter shelters (also called "no freeze" shelters) close. Many close at the beginning of April, and may be cleared out by March 29.
- Consider giving out incentives (money or grocery cards) for people who answer the census, especially those who have someone else staying with them (i.e., the hosts in the doubled-up households).

9.4.8   Enumeration at soup kitchens is a potentially effective method of including the out-of-doors homeless and the doubled-up in the census

We conducted unobtrusive observations of the census workers in two soup kitchens in order to make recommendations for subsequent censuses. The two soup kitchen observations were two days apart (March 29 and March 31, 2010). The soup kitchen enumerations were conducted by two different census teams with two different strategies. We were not sure how much each soup kitchen team of enumerators had collaborated with the soup kitchen directors or how much they had collaborated with each other.

The purpose of the soup kitchen enumeration is to count people who might not be included in other enumerations, such as people living out of doors or people doubled-up with another person. The soup kitchen enumeration can also count people who might have been at a shelter on March 29 but who did not participate in the census. In both soup kitchen enumerations, everyone was asked to fill out the ICR form even if they felt they had been counted somewhere else. As stated earlier, the Census Bureau has a mechanism in place for counting individuals at their usual address even if they fill out the ICR form at a soup kitchen.

The observation of the soup kitchen enumeration of March 29 took place in a weekly soup kitchen that serves approximately seventy-five people each Monday. The soup kitchen included single men and women (approximately 75 percent of the patrons were male) and English and Spanish speakers.

As lunch was being served, the director of the soup kitchen spoke about the fact that there were census forms at the tables. He said that the census count was very important for the local community and asked that people fill out the forms. He turned the microphone over to the person directing the census count who talked about the importance of counting everyone. He said that he knew that some people would have already filled out forms at their homes, but said that it was okay to fill out another form, since they would be cross-checked. He told people that they could drop the completed forms off as they exited the church basement.

There were four census employees at the front of the hall and two sitting at a side bench. Although there were a number of Spanish-speaking people who were patrons at this soup kitchen, no one made any announcements or gave any instructions in Spanish. All the forms that could be seen were in English.

We sat at a table of six people. One person said that she had already filled out a form at home and so she did not intend to fill out another form. Several other people agreed with this and did not touch the forms. One couple filled out a form, but they were not sure what to do with the completed form and wound up getting up and going over to one of the census workers at the side of the hall. They both gave their forms to the census workers.

A number of questions were being asked about the forms. However, the census workers stayed at their positions, not offering any help in filling out the forms. On only one occasion did the census workers move to answer a question. Once people exited, however, four more census workers asked them at the door whether they had filled out a form. If they said no, the census worker asked if the individual would mind answering a few questions. One of the workers said that it would help the soup kitchen get funding if people filled out the forms. The census workers appeared to be effective in getting people to cooperate and answer the census questions. They were very polite and friendly and most of the soup kitchen diners appeared to be happy to speak with them. We did not see the census workers speak Spanish with any of the patrons.

The second soup kitchen enumeration observation took place on March 31, 2010, at a soup kitchen located in a church basement in a city near the capital city, which was one of the field sites of this ethnography. There were fifteen people sitting at the tables waiting for lunch to begin. Six census workers set up at two large tables off to the side of the church hall. The person directing the census count made an announcement about the importance of the census and said that they would be asking people to fill out the census form even if they had filled one out in another location. She then asked people as they came into the soup kitchen to speak with one of the census workers behind the table. If the person agreed, the census worker assured each person that their answers were confidential. They also passed out a half-page form entitled "Your Answers Are Confidential" that explained the confidentiality rules. The form had the same information in Spanish on the reverse of the form. They then asked if the individual would like to fill out the form him or herself or if they needed any help.

By the time lunch began, there were thirty-five patrons in the basement, thirty White and five Black. Eight were women. Many people willingly sat down at the census table but some did not. The census workers talked with approximately twenty people. Several patrons turned around and walked out when approached by the census worker. They never came back in. Others just said that they were all set and did not wish to participate. At least three people were never approached and did not participate. No one was positioned at the door to ask people who were exiting if they had filled out the form.

Some people engaged in lengthy discussions about why they did not wish to fill out a form. One individual, a middle-aged white male, said that the census "stunk." He suggested that every time a census had been done in a country in any part of the world genocide soon followed. He also asked why the census found it necessary to take GPS images of every address. He seemed to mean that actual photos were taken of every address, not simply GPS coordinates. He said the census worker did not have to answer that question since he, the patron, already knew the answer. This person never did agree to fill out a form. The census workers were persistent in trying to get cooperation without pushing it too far. Once it became clear that someone was not going to cooperate, they turned to another person.

There were several Portuguese-speaking individuals who attended this soup kitchen. There was no evidence that any of the census workers spoke Portuguese and no announcements were made in any language other than English. We did not know how many monolingual Portuguese or Spanish speakers were present, but it is not uncommon in this state to provide Portuguese and Spanish speakers for governmental events.

9.4.9 There was a high level of cooperation between the homeless service providers such as shelter and day center administrators and the US Census

Based on our post-enumeration focus groups and our conversations with shelter staff after the night of the census, it appeared that if the individual or family had been in a shelter or group home on the evening of the census, there was a high probability that they would be included in the count. This was due to a high level of cooperation between the homeless individuals, the group quarters administrators, and the census workers. We learned from one of the post-enumeration focus groups that the shelter residents understood that cooperating with "the authorities" (participant's words) which includes the census, is the price one pays for entering a shelter and that the benefits of receiving shelter for the night outweighs the costs of anonymity.

We also learned from our conversations with the administrators of all of the group quarters that there was a positive attitude toward cooperating with the census. When the census workers came to the shelter, if someone was not available to fill out their own form (e.g., they were sleeping), the administrator did it for them. In these days of competitive funding, it is our observation that most service providers are eager to count the *maximum* number of people residing with them.

Since 2006, homeless service providers have participated in the Housing and Urban Development (HUD) Point-in-Time (PIT) count every January and have tracked data for the HMIS. These data are important for continuing funding for housing and services for the homeless. Documenting the maximum number of shelter residents can benefit the agency for many types of services and funding from local, state, federal, and private sources of funding.

The high level of cooperation between the homeless service providers and the Census Bureau contrasts to the situation Glasser observed twenty years ago (Glasser & Salo, 1991), when service providers were not accustomed to cooperating with outside agencies as they now do with the HUD in the PIT count and with HMIS. Additionally, some of the homeless service providers twenty years ago were political activists who openly doubted that any accurate homeless count could be obtained.

9.5   Recommendations for future homeless enumeration

Our research has led us to recommend strategies for the enumeration that we believe will improve the coverage of homeless individuals and families in future censuses in the US.

9.5.1   *Improve enumeration strategies on the doubled-up population*

We recommend the continued development of effective strategies for counting the homeless guest within a household. Throughout our study and many other studies of homelessness, a pervasive observation is that staying doubled-up with family and friends is a frequent precursor to living on the streets or a homeless shelter (Bolland & McCallum, 2002). The host is most often a member of a lower-income household. If the host is a renter with a lease that prohibits guests from staying longer than a specified period of time (such as thirty days), it is widely thought in the homeless community that hosting a doubled-up person could jeopardize the host's family's housing.

Using the American Community Survey microdata file information on income and household relationships, NAEH estimates that nationally there were 6,800,587 doubled-up individuals in 2010 (NAEH, 2010). It is clear from our research that cycling between doubling up, the shelters, and the streets (for the single person) is a common pattern of homelessness.

9.5.2   *Make extensive use of the Be Counted form*

The self-administered Be Counted forms could have been instrumental in reaching those homeless people who told us that they did not remember filling out the census form or who believed that the person they were staying with on April 1 did not include them in the household form. However, we saw little evidence of the Be Counted form. We saw the Be Counted form in a rack with other community information in City One in the lobby of a community center that also houses a food pantry and a daily breakfast program. However, without a person to distribute the forms and explain how to fill them out, it appeared unlikely that the Be Counted form would have been utilized by the homeless. The Be Counted form has been the subject of extensive cognitive testing (Childs, Gerber, & Norris, 2009) and is continually being developed for clarity and accuracy. In the 2010 Census, there could have been more visibility of the questionnaire assistance centers with a toll-free number to call in the case that the individual thought that they had been missed.

9.5.3   Develop consistent and effective strategies at soup kitchens

- Have the census workers be available at the tables where people are eating in order to answer questions as people are filling out the forms at the tables and check that everyone has filled out the form as they are leaving the soup kitchen.
- Do not confront people as they enter the soup kitchen as this may result in refusals to cooperate and may cause some people to leave without eating.
- Leave the census forms at each place setting at a table and have the soup kitchen director make an announcement about the importance of the census.
- Employ census workers who can speak the native languages of the local community.
- Make multiple visits to the same soup kitchen to ensure that everyone is counted.
- Make pre-visits to soup kitchens in order to discover which days have the greatest numbers of individuals in the dining room.

9.5.4   Develop a close collaboration with homeless networks

We recommend a closer collaboration with networks of homeless and formerly homeless individuals in order to be certain that all of the homeless serving agencies are included as sites to be visited for the enumeration. Some of the problems we encountered might have been due to the lack of knowledge of homeless networks on the part of the census workers. An interesting example of becoming acquainted with homeless individuals and families before the census is India, which has had a protocol for including the homeless in the national census since 1961 (Gandotra, 1977). In 1991, the Indian census takers were instructed to take a count of all of the "houseless" (their term for homeless) who were living on the pavement on the blocks that were assigned to the census taker in a three-week period of time (Glasser, 1994). Thus, on the night of the census, the workers already knew the population to be included.

9.5.5   Further collaboration between the Census Bureau and the HUD

As researchers who have long been involved in studies of homelessness, we recommend further collaboration between the Census Bureau and HUD for the development of homeless enumeration methodology, since both agencies have considerable knowledge and research regarding homeless enumeration. HUD's ability to enumerate the homeless became feasible once it was required that states and cities receiving HUD funding establish administrative databases called HMISs. Plagued early on by problems with accurate data entry and reporting issues, these systems are becoming increasingly reliable as a means of getting accurate counts as well as sources of important performance measures for programs designed to end homelessness.

The annual HUD PIT count usually occurs in late January in order to minimize the number of people staying outside. Homeless people are counted using a combination of the HMIS data, surveys of those shelters not participating in HMIS, street counts, and homeless outreach teams, who count the out-of-doors homeless. The doubled-up are not included in PIT counts.

Both the census service-based enumeration and the HUD PIT count attempts to count every homeless person, even if they are staying out of doors. Both use surveys at homeless serving sites. The primary difference is the census does not use administrative databases such as HMIS to conduct the count. Both methods underrepresent the doubled-up homeless in their counts. Based on our participation in PIT counts in two states, we also observe that the PIT is accomplished by the homeless service providers networks (called Continua of Care), which make the PIT coverage as complete as possible.

9.6   Conclusion

Understanding the patterns of behavior among homeless individuals and families in the US decennial censuses has important implications for the accurate and complete surveying of this hard-to-reach population, both in the US and around the world. Our ethnographic work during the 2010 Census enabled us to witness the difficulties of enumerating all homeless individuals and families. Our work led us to recommend more involvement from the networks of service providers and of homeless individuals themselves that will lead to a more complete coverage, both in terms of a complete listing of all service locations and in garnering more interest in the census by homeless individuals. Many states in the US have active homeless coalitions that include many homeless individuals who could be recruited to be helpful to the decennial census. We recommend ongoing research and efforts to improve the coverage of the large numbers of individuals and families who double-up with family friends because they have no other home.

References

Barrett, D. (2012). Enumerating persons experiencing homelessness in the 2010 Census: results from the service-based enumeration. In *H2R/2012 Proceedings*. Alexandria, VA: American Statistical Association.

Bernard, H. R. (2011). *Research Methods in Anthropology: Qualitative and Quantitative Approaches*. Lanham, MD: Alta Mira Press.

Bolland, J., & McCallum, D. (2002). Touched by homelessness: an examination of hospitality for the down and out. *American Journal of Public Health*, 92(1), 116–18.

Bourgois, P., & Brownrigg, L. (1990). *Hypotheses and ethnographic analysis of concealment in the underground economy*. Ethnographic Exploratory Research #6, Center for Survey Methods Research, Bureau of the Census, Washington, DC. www.census.gov/srd/www/byname.html.

Childs, J., Gerber, E., & Norris, D. (2009). *Be Counted Form: Respondent Problems in Cognitive Testing, Revised Final Report.* www.census.gov/srd/papers/pdf/rsm2009-06.pdf.

de la Puente, M., & McKay, R. (1995). *Developing and Testing Race and Ethnic Origin Questions for the Current Population Survey Supplement on Race and Ethnic Origin.* Washington, DC: Bureau of Census and Bureau of Labor Statistics.

Durante, D. (2012). Enumerating persons experiencing homelessness in the 2010 Census: identifying service-based and targeted non-sheltered outdoor locations. In *H2R/2012 Proceedings.* Alexandria, VA: American Statistical Association.

Fleisher, M., & Brownrigg, L. (1990). *An ethnographic evaluation of street-to-system cycling of Black, Hispanic, and American Indian males.* Ethnographic Exploratory Research #9, Center for Survey Methods Research, Bureau of the Census, Washington, DC. www.census.gov/srd/www/byname.html.

Frake, C. (1964). A structural description of Subanun "religious behavior." In Ward H. Goodenough (ed.), *Explorations in Cultural Anthropology: Essays in Honor of George Peter Murdock* (p. 112). New York: McGraw-Hill Book Company.

Gandotra, S. (1977). *Census of India: Special Study-Houseless of India.* New Delhi: Director of Census Operations.

Glaser, B., & Strauss, A. (1967). *The Discovery of Grounded Theory: Strategies for Qualitative Research.* New York: Aldine.

Glasser, I. (1994). *Homelessness in Global Perspective.* New York: G. K. Hall Reference, A Division of MacMillan, Inc.

  (1996). The 1990 decennial census and patterns of homelessness in a small New England city. In Anna Lou Dehavenon (ed.), *There's No Place Like Home: Anthropological Perspectives on Housing and Homelessness in the United States* (pp. 19–33). Westport, CT: Bergin & Garvey.

Glasser, I., & Bridgman, R. (1999). *Braving the Street: Anthropological Perspectives on Homelessness.* New York and Oxford: Berghahn Books.

Glasser, I., Fournier, L., & Costopoulos, A. (1999). Homelessness in Quebec City, Quebec and Hartford, Connecticut: a cross-national and cross-cultural analysis. *Urban Anthropology and Studies of Cultural Systems and World Economic Development,* 28(2), 141–64.

Glasser, I., & Salo, M. (1991). *An ethnographic study of homeless in Windham, Connecticut.* Ethnographic Exploratory Research Report #17, Center for Survey Methods Research, Bureau of the Census, Washington, DC. www.census.gov/srd/www/byname.html.

  (2012). *Ending Homelessness in Rhode Island.* Presented at McAuley Ministries Annual Board Meeting. Retrieved February 11, 2014 from www.youtube.com/watch?v=zveBZ0PtS2U.

Liebow, E. (1993). *Tell Them Who I Am: The Lives of Homeless Women.* New York: The Free Press.

Marpsat, M. (2008). Introduction: the INED research on homelessness (1993–2008). *The INED Research on Homelessness, 1993–2008* (vol. I), ed. M. Marpsat (pp. 3–6). Paris: Institut National d'Études Démographiques.

Marpsat, M., & Razafindratsima, N. (2010). Survey methods for hard-to-reach populations: introduction to the special issue. *Methodological Innovations*, 5(2), 3–16.

Martin, E. (1999). Who knows who lives here? Within-household disagreements as a source of survey coverage error. *Public Opinion Quarterly*, 63(2), 220–36.

— (2007). *Strength of attachment: survey coverage of people with tenuous ties to residences.* Survey Methodology #2007–26, Center for Survey Methods Research, Bureau of the Census, Washington, DC. www.census.gov/srd/www/byname.html.

Metraux, S., Culhane, D., Raphael, S., White, M., Pearson, C., Hirsch, E., *et al.* (2001). Assessing homeless population size through the use of emergency and transitional shelter services in 1998: results from the analysis of administrative data from nine U.S. jurisdictions. *Public Health Reports*, 116, 344–52.

National Alliance to End Homelessness. (2010). *Economy Bytes Doubled up in the United States Report of May 18, 2010.* www.endhomelessness.org/library/entry/economy-bytes-doubled-up-in-the-united-states.

National Alliance to End Homelessness. (2011). Doubled up people by state – state of homelessness. www.endhomelessness.org/content/article/detail/3664/.

National Coalition for the Homeless. (2009). *The Forgotten Victims of the Subprime Crisis.* Report from the National Coalition for the Homeless. Retrieved February 11, 2014 from www.nationalhomeless.org/advocacy/foreclosuretohomelessness.

Rossi, P., Wright, J., Fisher, G., & Willis, G. (1987). The urban homeless: estimating composition and size. *Science*, 235, 1336–41.

Schwede, L. (2010). Who is counted? Subpopulation coverage in the US census. *Anthropology News*, May 2010, 5–6.

Schwede, L., & Ellis, Y. (1994). Exploring associations between subjective and objective assessments of household membership. In *Joint Statistical Meetings Proceedings, Survey Research Methods Section* (pp. 325–30). Alexandria, VA: American Statistical Association.

US Census Bureau. (2000). Factfinder for the nation: history and organization. www.census.gov/prod/2000pubs/cff-4.pdf.

Wagner, D., & Gilman, J. (2012). *Confronting Homelessness: Poverty, Politics, and the Failure of Social Policy.* Boulder: Lynne Rienner Publishers.

10

"Where are *our* costumes?": the All Ireland Traveller Health Study – our Geels 2007–2011

CECILY C. KELLEHER AND BRIGID QUIRKE

10.1 Introduction

10.1.1 The Traveller community

In this chapter, we describe the methodology for the All Ireland Traveller Health Study (AITHS) from inception to completion. This population is hard to reach in that it is nomadic, has traditionally been closed to outsiders, and is highly disadvantaged in both material and psychosocial terms, including generally low literacy levels, so it fulfills the criteria for this volume in several key respects. In methodological terms, as we describe, it is highly novel in the solutions employed to overcome these challenges and it is also a very large-scale study by the standards of the literature on ethnic minorities.

In August 2012 at the Olympics Games in London, a young boxer named John Joe Nevin won a silver medal and indeed got within a few adjudication points of winning a gold one. A native of a middle-sized country town in the midlands of Ireland called Mullingar, in a games of outstanding human achievement by many athletes who are global household names, such as Michael Phelps and Usain Bolt, this young man Nevin had duly taken his place in this illustrious company amongst the nations of the world as an Irish Traveller. In this chapter, we describe how we undertook a census survey of his people in a landmark collaboration that was a research initiative for, with, and by Travellers themselves.

The UCD-led All Ireland Traveller Health Study team comprised, in addition to chapter authors Cecily Kelleher and Brigid Quirke (in alphabetical order), Safa Abdalla, Fran Cronin, Leslie Daly, Anne Drummond, Patricia Fitzpatrick, Kate Frazier, Noor Aman Hamid, Claire Kelly, Jean Kilroe, Juzer Lotya, Catherine McGorrian, Ronnie G. Moore, Roisin Nic Charthaigh, Deirdre O'Mahony (RIP September 2, 2010), Brid O'Shea, Anthony Staines, David Staines, MaryRose Sweeney, Jill Turner, Aileen Ward, and Jane Whelan.

All the many contributors to this project are listed additionally in the study technical reports, available online at the Department of Health and Children website in the Republic of Ireland.

The All Ireland Health Study was jointly funded by the Department of Health And Children (DOHC) in the Republic of Ireland, and Department of Health, Social Services and Public Safety in Northern Ireland (DHSSPSNI). Field work funding support was received from the Irish Health Service Executive (HSE). The views expressed in this study are the authors' own and do not necessarily reflect the views and opinions of either the DOHC or DHSSPSNI.

Irish Travellers are a small indigenous minority group, who have been part of Irish society for centuries (Breathnach, 2006; Gmelch & Gmelch, 1976). They have a value system, language, customs, and traditions which make them an identifiable group both to themselves and to others. Their distinctive lifestyle and culture, based on a nomadic tradition, sets them apart from the general population. Travellers live primarily on the island of Ireland but do migrate more widely across the United Kingdom of Great Britain and the European continent. Our census ultimately established that the total population numbers 40,129 in 10,618 families; 1,562 (15 percent) of these families reside in Northern Ireland.

Travellers are officially recognized as a minority ethnic group in the United Kingdom (UK Parliament Race Relations Order, 1997). The Equal Status Act, 2000 (Government Publications, 2000), in the Republic of Ireland defines the Traveller community as follows: "Traveller community means the community of people who are commonly called Travellers and who are identified (both by themselves and others) as people with a shared history, culture and traditions, including historically, a nomadic way of life on the island of Ireland." This is the same definition as the Race Relations Order in Northern Ireland.

Travellers have not always had that name. Originally, they were called Tinkers, a generic name which had more positive historical connotations than it does now. Derived from the practice of tin-smithing, it referred to roving groups who had wares to sell to farmers in return for some payment, food, or shelter. In a world of subsistence farming and rural barter and trade, there was a place for their culture that was not always divisive (Breathnach, 2006; Gmelch & Gmelch, 1976).

It is not known how long Travellers have been distinct from the general population. While it is commonly argued that they emerged following the upheaval and dispossession of the Irish famine period in the 1840s, it is more likely that they have a much earlier history. While Travellers' history is largely unrecorded in the historical archives, some research dates their origins to before the twelfth century when the Mediaeval Tinkaer act was legislated (Kenny & McNeela, 2005; MacGreil, 2011).

In any event, their customs have been documented more systematically from the beginning of the nineteenth century. One of their hallmarks is the use of a language called Cant or Gammon. This is one of a kind of Shelta languages, an argot derived from the predominant spoken language of the community with changes and substitutions to make it comprehensible only to fellow community members who are familiar with it. It is useful in situations such as trading, one of the traditional occupations engaged in by Travellers (Gmelch & Gmelch, 1976; Harper & Hudson, 1971).

10.1.2 *Public policy and Travellers*

No formal government policies on Travellers existed before the 1960s. By then, poverty and hardship had driven Travellers to the larger urban areas and the only real means of engagement was through the welfare system. Tinkers were first given the more clinical and functional term *Itinerants* and treated as a social problem whose best solution was integration. From this action arose reaction from the community and the long process of identification and pride in one's origins emerged. Many members of the general population were impatient with any concession that made a special (and potentially costly) case for the recognition of difference and took the pragmatic utilitarian view that such people should accept that their way of life was marginalized, a threat to their health and well-being, and the solution lay with integration into the mainstream. This deeply political debate culminated in an assertion of identity in the community now called Travellers and in the publication of the report of the Task Force on the Travelling Community 1995 (Task Force on the Travelling Community, 1995). That report accepted the community's inherent right to an identity and the need for multifaceted cross-sectorial action to effect change.

10.1.3 Health status of Travellers

In the mid-1980s, a National Survey in the Republic of Ireland (Barry & Daly, 1986; Barry, Herity, & Solan, 1989) completed a census count of all known Travellers at that time and prospectively followed up mortality in the community during the following year. The survey was carried out by the Medical Directors of Community Care and public health nurses (PHNs). The results were stark. The population pyramid resembled that of a third world developing country and the mortality ratios for both men and women were greatly higher than that of the general population. Over the next two decades, no such exercise was repeated, though smaller-scale studies continued to report differentially poor health experience across a range of health outcomes.

In classical public health terms, the gap in health expectancy is easily explicable (World Health Organization, 2007). Sanitation, housing, and living conditions are critical to health and well-being. Access to health services and the capacity to engage effectively in the treatment and care regimens will influence outcomes. Educational achievement is a cornerstone to skills attainment and employment brings needed material income. Travellers tick every box of inadequacy on that list. However, a more subtle approach to understanding relative and absolute poverty in modern society is also needed. It is now well understood across the globe that minority communities find themselves in very similar social circumstances, and there has been no sense of common cause until recently, now that research on ethnic and minority communities has achieved much greater prominence (Benoit, Jansson, Millar, & Phillips, 2005; Tumiel-Berhalter, McLaughlin-Diaz, Vena, & Crespo, 2007). Such groups find themselves negotiating on the terms of their majority neighbors, often literally speaking a different language.

Travellers indeed report that they are subjected to overt prejudice. This can further undermine their sense of control of their immediate lives and underscore their lack of power in the dominant social hierarchy (All Ireland Traveller Health Study Team, 2010). It is corrosive because it inhibits positive initiatives for change and development, and obvious means of empowerment such as educational attainment are not valued and prioritized. Even when some

Travellers gain qualifications, they still find it difficult to obtain employment. Because of their relatively small numbers (less than 1 percent of the national population) and their close-knit, strongly familial culture (which, like many such communities, features intermarriage), Travellers have a higher incidence of certain rare genetic conditions (Lynch, Foulds, Thuresson, Collins, Annerén, Hedberg *et al.*, 2011). Health professionals often see this as the primary health issue, but the community itself feels victimized and stereotyped by this association. Travellers face high and excessive mortality from much more common and prevalent conditions, such as cardiovascular and respiratory diseases, mental ill-health, and cancers. The main reports and attendant publications from the AITHS document that the general health status is poor (Abdalla, Quirke, Fitzpatrick, Drummond, Daly, & Kelleher, 2010; Kelleher, Whelan, Daly, & Fitzpatrick, 2012; McGorrian, Daly, Fitzpatrick, Hamid, Malone, & Kelleher, 2013; McGorrian, Daly, Fitzpatrick, Moore, Turner, & Kelleher, 2012a; McGorrian, Frazer, Daly, Moore, Turner, Sweeney *et al.*, 2012).

Commitment to Traveller health was part of a national strategy 2002–05 document (Department of Health and Children, 2002). The AITHS was a commissioned project advertised in open tender, and a stakeholder group assessed the applications. The University College Dublin (UCD) team was therefore working to an outline protocol that had been forged through a process of negotiation over several years previously.

Following the publication of the National Traveller Health Strategy, the cross-border Institute of Public Health was commissioned by the Department of Health and Children to undertake a comprehensive consultation process throughout Ireland to ascertain the views of Travellers, Traveller organizations, the Health Service Executive (which runs the public health service in the Republic of Ireland), and health personnel in relation to the scope and conduct of the AITHS. This consultation involved over 600 people engaging in workshops in nine regions across the island of Ireland. It was completed in December 2003 with a national workshop to finalize and prioritize key values, principles, key challenges, and health issues for inclusion in the AITHS (Institute of Public Health in Ireland, 2004).

Overall, the burden of health problems experienced by Travellers was broadly attributable to social conditions, according to that report by the Institute, yet health policies have been dominated by disease-focused solutions that effectively ignore these social determinants, as suggested by the list of key health issues identified during the consultation process. One of these issues was the lack of recognition of Traveller culture and appropriate service provision.

10.2 Methodology

10.2.1 Instigation

A crucial factor in any research project is who instigates it. The sizable literature across disciplines of top down or bottom up strategies, particularly in community development initiatives, covers the theoretical, ethical, and methodological issues at stake (Fraser, Dougill, Mabee, Reed, & MacAlpine, 2006; Laverack & Labonte, 2000). This is clearly thrown into sharp relief where the community is marginalized, disadvantaged, or hard to reach in physical, infrastructural, or psychosocial terms. The agendas of the researched community, the commissioners or policymakers, and the investigators are at no time the same. The challenge is to meet a point of triangulated consensus and to sustain it through the project from inception to completion. If, rarely, the project arises as an idea that germinates into a proposal from the community itself, then participation will be a predisposition from the outset. Conversely, if the policymakers or commissioners see the need for the work, then they will be predisposed to fund it adequately. If the proposal comes from the scientific investigator, then there are three potential hurdles to initiation: obtaining the funding through peer review or similar mechanisms, persuading the community collectively and individually that there is something to be gained from participation, and seeking engagement with policymakers to disseminate and implement the findings. An important part of the AITHS story is about how the project met challenges in reconciling the three agendas.

10.2.2 Framework for the study

The study adopted a holistic approach to health, using a social determinants model that acknowledges the broader impact of social, economic, environmental, and political policy on health (Dahlgren & Whitehead, 1991). It also acknowledges the considerable influence that psychosocial and social capital factors (such as lack of bridging to the wider community, experience of discrimination) and infrastructural factors (such as accommodation standards) can have on health outcomes.

The proposal included Traveller community participation at every stage from design to dissemination. The study team used methodologies that were culturally appropriate. The research team attended cultural awareness training and was aware of and respectful of Traveller values and beliefs. The intention was to deliver this project in the closest partnership with the community, with real community ownership, and real community control. Peer researchers were drawn from the Traveller community.

The execution of the protocol took four years (2007–11) but built on a process of engagement dating back four decades. The study was overseen by a technical steering group, chaired by the deputy chief medical officer for the Republic of Ireland. It is crucial in designing a study on the scale of AITHS to consult with all stakeholders and to understand their positions. Where a voice must be heard above any others, it is to the person with the problem one gives the strongest ear. In this case, the study was for the purpose of improving the health of Travellers, so theirs had to be the clearest voice in the planning process.

The classical scientific investigator stands on what is argued to be objective evidence. This principle of proving cause and effect and removing conjecture, bias, and subjectivism has a long tradition and is enshrined in the experimental method of modern science (Davey Smith, Ebrahim, & Eggar, 2000). However, when applied to community development it can present a false chimera (Tones, 2000). In a classical randomized controlled trial for instance, the use of a placebo is to eliminate a preference effect which confounds the measurable therapeutic impact of a drug. In a community intervention that preference effect is always in place and may indeed be in itself the desired outcome of the intervention and a critical rate limiting step to effecting change (Mc Pherson, 2000).

10.2.3 Protocol development

The activists and advocates for Travellers could see that having no systematic data on the health status of the community was a weakness to effective advocacy (MacDonagh, 2002). Having an identifier in health records would be a step forward but in general there is no unique identifier in the Republic of Ireland and linkage to health records remains a challenge. The Traveller advocates wanted both, hence they are both included as actions in the Traveller Health Strategy. While the Traveller groups believed that the health status of Travellers was declining, the numbers or locations of Travellers in Ireland were unknown. Travellers were not identified as such in the vital health statistics system or in provider records. Over time, a tipping point was reached such that the majority of the Traveller community believed a study was necessary.

10.2.4 The Primary Health Care for Travellers Project (PHCTP)

Traveller groups were more involved in health matters since the development of the Primary Health Care for Traveller Projects (PHCTPs) in 1994 and the development of the Traveller health infrastructure in 1998 (Quirke, 2006a, 2006b), including the National Traveller Health Advisory Committee and the Regional Traveller Health Units based on recommendations from the Task Force on the Traveller Community (1995).

   The first barrier, access to the community, was overcome by utilizing this network of projects, which already existed in the Republic of Ireland prior to the commissioning of this study. Pavee Point Travellers Centre ("Pavee Point") was established in 1985. It is a voluntary, or nongovernmental, organization committed to the attainment of human rights for Irish Travellers. "Pavee" is one of a number of Cant words used by Travellers to describe themselves.

   The organization is comprised of Travellers and members of the majority population working together in partnership to address the needs of Travellers as a minority ethnic group experiencing exclusion and marginalization. The aim of Pavee Point is to contribute to improvement in the quality of life and living circumstances of Irish Travellers, through working for social justice, solidarity, socioeconomic development, and human rights.

   The PHCTP have had a key role in the delivery of health services to Travellers. The projects were initiated in 1994 as a joint partnership initiative with Pavee Point and the former regional Eastern Health Board and have the following objectives:

- To establish a model of Traveller participation in the promotion of health.
- To develop the skills of Traveller women in providing community-based health services.
- To liaise and assist in creating dialogue between Travellers and health service providers.
- To highlight gaps in health service delivery to Travellers and work towards reducing inequalities that exist in established services.

The Health
Board Areas

Figure 10.1   Map with list of the location of Primary Health Care Projects in each of the eight Traveller Health Units (which are co-terminous with the former Health Board boundaries)

At the start of the study there were over forty PHCTPs established around the country. Each PHCTP ran a training program to develop the capacity of Travellers to become community health workers. These projects involved over 400 Traveller women who were at different stages of training or had graduated to become Traveller community health workers (TCHWs). As part of their role, they identify and develop an understanding of the factors influencing their health, and act as advocates for Travellers and liaison workers between their community and the health services. Pavee Point worked closely with the study team, acting as a link between them and the Travellers and the Traveller organizations, and then established the national Traveller reference group. The main aim of this reference group was to develop the capacity of Travellers and Traveller organizations to participate effectively in AITHS. It was an important matter as to who would be trusted to undertake this field work. It was never seriously considered feasible that the data would be

Table 10.1 *Primary Health Care Projects (PHCPs): by Traveller Health Unit (THU) regions*

Eastern region

Ref.	Project
1	St. Margaret's Traveller Action Group *(Ballymun)*
2	Blanchardstown Traveller Support Group
3	Pavee Point *(Dublin 1)*
4	STAG *(Southside Traveller Action Group, Sandyford)*
5	Kildare Traveller Network *(Newbridge)*
6	Co-operation Fingal *(Balbriggan)*
7	Wicklow *(Newcastle)*
8	TravAct *(Coolock)*
9	Tallaght Travellers PHCP
10	Clondalkin Travellers Development Group
11	Exchange House *(Dublin 1)*
12	Athy Travellers Club
13	Ballyfermot Traveller Action Project

Midlands region

Ref.	Project
14	Longford Traveller Development Group
15	Tullamore PHCP
16	Laois Traveller Action Group
17	Athlone

Mid-western region

Ref.	Project
18	Limerick Travellers Development Group
19	Clare Care PHCP
20	Roscrea 2000
21	Thurles
22	Nenagh Community Network

North-eastern region

Ref.	Project
23	Louth PHCP *(Dundalk)*
24	Drogheda PHCP
25	Meath PHCP *(Navan)*

North-western region

Ref.	Project
26	South Donegal Support Group *(Killybegs)*
27	Donegal Traveller's Project *(Letterkenny)*
28	Sligo Travellers Support Group *(Sligo Town)*
29	Leitrim Travellers Project
30	Tubbercurry PHCP

Table 10.1 *(cont.)*

Southern region

Ref.	Project
31	Le Cheile Family Resource Centre *(Mallow)*
32	Traveller Visibility Group *(Cork)*
33	Kerry Travellers Support Group
34	West Cork Traveller Association *(Clonakilty)*

South-eastern region

Ref.	Project
35	Co. Wexford PHCP
36	Carlow / Kilkenny PHCP
37	Bunclody Traveller Women's Project
38	Waterford Travellers PHCP
39	Clonmel Travellers PHCP
40	New Ross PHCP
41	Cashel Primary Health Care

Western region

Ref.	Project.
42	Galway Travellers Support Group *(City)*
43	Galway Travellers Support Group *(County)*
44	Tuam Travellers Edu./ Dev Group
45	Roscommon Traveller Development Group
46	Mayo Travellers Support Group *(Castlebar)*
47	Mayo Travellers Support Group *(Westport)*

collected by outsiders. Health professionals known to the community were a possibility but in practice these were already stretched by existing workloads and could not be expected to play this role.

The obvious strategy was to provide training to the women who worked with the PHCTPs and hence create a national network of peer researchers. The role of these regional and national networks was expanded to act as a key link between Travellers, Traveller organizations, and the study team at UCD. Mechanisms considered for effective inclusion of Travellers in the implementation of the AITHS included:

- Ensuring that Travellers and Traveller organizations understand the rationale and implications of the study.
- Ensuring that Travellers and Traveller organizations "buy in" and have a sense of "ownership" of the study.
- Ongoing development of the capacity of Travellers to engage in the study.
- Identification of key informants in each region to support the study.

- Support for the mapping and count in areas with a Traveller population.
- Identification and development of a database or contact system with hard-to-reach groups, e.g., those in institutions or homeless.
- Development of a local database/census of Travellers in each region to facilitate the sampling framework for the study.

This was in fact a relatively rapid process by the standards of past surveys. In the run-up to the task force report (Task Force on the Travelling Community, 1995), the principal investigator was involved in a previous small-scale needs assessment project that involved only a few hundred families and the chief and only respondents were women, usually the most senior mother figure in the household (O'Donovan, McCarthy, McKenna, McCarthy, & Kelleher, 1995).

A critical step was to instill confidence in these women to communicate and work with their own peers and with outsiders. This was already achieved to a large extent before the commencement of the commissioned study. They were well used to engaging and working with outsiders. Their challenge was to trust the service providers (due to their reported previous negative experiences) and particularly to trust the commissioned academic institution, UCD. Travellers reported from previous experience that research-ers tend to come and take their information, but they never feed it back adequately, and it never changes anything. This was a critical bridging exercise. In the Republic of Ireland, the forty projects already existed. In Northern Ireland, a network had to be established from the outset. That group was established in association with Traveller organizations, particularly Pavee Point and An Munia Tobar in Northern Ireland. This was achieved by the field work coordinator visiting there and providing training on five occasions before the study started.

10.2.5 Mapping and scoping

The mapping exercise had several objectives:

- To identify the number and location of Travellers/Traveller families by project and region.
- To develop and maintain a comprehensive database of Traveller and HSE study coordinators.
- To identify Traveller peer researchers for training.
- To assess level of coverage of Traveller families in the country by study coordinators and peer researchers, and to identify gaps at local and regional level.
- To estimate the number of computers required for each project/region based on the number of Traveller families, the number of peer researchers, the number of coordinators, and the size of the area to be covered.
- To determine the capacity and challenges locally and regionally to facilitate the imple-mentation of the study.

10.2.6 Rationale for the mapping and enumeration process

A crucial methodological issue for the UCD research team was the need for a census to establish an accurate denominator for the study reports. For the purposes of this study, only Travellers who self-identified were included. Therefore, individuals who did not wish to be identified as Travellers were not included in the main census count, but were documented by the enumerators as individuals who were identified "by others." These were not sent to UCD.

The technical steering group suspected that Travellers were significantly underreported in the national census, so another process was required to identify and enumerate all the Traveller families in Ireland. The organizations began the task of locating and mapping where Travellers resided. The main purpose of the mapping process was to identify all Irish Traveller families on the island, so they could be offered the opportunity to participate in the study. This was an iterative process, using conventional census data from the periodic national census, an amenities census conducted by the Department of the Environment, and local knowledge of projects and health care workers about where families lived. Travellers live in a spectrum of accommodations and it can be difficult to distinguish them by type. Some may live literally at the side of the road, some in relatively permanent halting sites with excellent amenities, and some in houses of every standard. Mobility is a constant factor. Relatively few will be permanently moving about, but many will travel for significant periods of the year for festivals and family occasions.

As part of the ongoing work and engagement of the Travellers/Traveller organizations and HSE staff, we had finally identified 10,618 Traveller families in the North and South of Ireland by the commencement of our own census survey in the Republic of Ireland. This population count allowed us to estimate the numbers of peer researchers and computers required at the project level and to estimate the duration of the survey, planned for a six-week period.

10.2.7 Instrument development

The next question for the research team was precisely what data should be collected. From the beginning, the project was informed by a cross-sectorial social determinants framework which recognized that individual health outcomes are based on proximal lifestyle choices and health care utilization patterns, but contextualized in a family and community network informed by wider social and environmental policy (Dahlgren & Whitehead, 1991). We needed to capture that complexity and operationalize it using standard survey instruments already developed and validated in the scientific literature. It was clear that standard inter-view methodology would not suffice. Travellers have an uncommonly strong oral tradition and highly expressive verbal skills. This is because literacy levels are low, but also arguably because the capacity to communicate effectively carries a clear survival advantage in a community beset by conflict and needing bartering skills. Traditionally, a Traveller inter-viewer would memorize a short list of questions, conduct the interview, and then report the answers verbatim to a transcriber. That limits what can be collected and introduces immediate transcription error, as well as being highly inefficient. One solution was to tape-record the interviews, but this again had limitations as it still required subsequent transcription and raised concerns about confidentiality.

Our solution might seem obvious: a computer-assisted interview, which combines audio computer-assisted self-interviewing (ACASI) and a more conventional computer-assisted approach. We could predesign the questionnaire and upload the completed interview directly to UCD. What was needed now was a means of overcoming the literacy barrier. This we did by creating an electronic interview that provided visual cues and a recorded voiceover for each question.

An ongoing process of consultation with Travellers was initiated to provide an opportunity to comment on the meaningfulness and relevance of questions and to develop a sense of ownership regarding the contents of the questionnaire/electronic instrument. This achieved a balance of eliciting standard comparable data and prioritizing what was relevant to the Traveller community. For instance, the initial intent was to utilize the semi-quantitative food frequency questionnaire from the National Health and Lifestyle Surveys (Friel, Kelleher, Nolan, & Harrington, 2003), but feedback from Travellers suggested it was too detailed and not particularly relevant, so a much abbreviated instrument was used. Similarly, it was not deemed feasible to ask respondents directly about illicit drug use in the family environment for confidentiality reasons, but it was regarded as a highly relevant topic, so a question as to whether drugs were a problem in the community was inserted instead.

The training for the study was delivered as a trainers training course to coordinators and assistant coordinators of the projects, who in turn provided that training to the CHWs in their teams. The PHCTP coordinators coordinated the work of their PHC teams locally and also acted as the key link and resource to the study team. In areas where there were no PHCTPs, the regional networks covered these areas with CHWs who had contacts there or with key informants i.e., other Traveller organizations/projects, visiting teachers, public health nurses and Traveller training centers.

All peer researchers were trained to a standardized level. This had many advantages over using enumerators from outside the Traveller community (e.g., local authority social workers or housing welfare officers) both in terms of their acceptability to Travellers and also their local knowledge of where Travellers were living in their region.

10.2.8 Training of study coordinators

The trainers were granted leave by their employers in the Health Service Executive, FAS (a national training program; FAS means growth in Gaelic), Traveller training centres, community development projects, and Traveller organizations to attend the training days. The training costs, travel, and accommodation were funded by UCD study team. Eighty-five coordinators and assistant coordinators were trained to act as study coordinators and trainers in the North and South of Ireland. They then trained 400 Travellers at the local level to act as peer researchers for the study. Six training days were held with study coordinators extending from March 12 to the September, 9 2008. The training was iterative and linked to the development of the study instruments and protocols. We evaluated each session and used the feedback to inform further training. The project distributed 180 computers to the 400 peer researchers. The sense of personal gratification and empowerment these women gained from using the system they helped design was manifest and received due recognition at the conclusion of the project.

10.2.9 Summary outline of the process used to design and pilot the study instrument

- All potential questions were extracted from national and international studies, previous local and national Traveller studies, and national study instruments, such as CSO, Survey of Lifestyles, Attitudes and Nutrition, the Lifeways Cohort Study, and Insight '07. The potential questions were collated into a draft questionnaire and circulated to the Study Stakeholders, HSE, and Travellers via the Traveller organizations to access suitability for inclusion in the survey (All Ireland Traveller Health Study Team, 2010).
- Copies of the draft consultation questionnaires were also posted on the study website to facilitate wide dissemination and feedback.
- Feedback was documented on potentially suitable and unsuitable questions and deleted or added as appropriate.
- Wording was literacy-proofed for plain English, by NALA, the National Adult Literacy Agency, and changed as required.
- Response time was down to forty-five minutes when the first "mocked up draft" was ready following three rounds of consultation and adaptation.
- The paper instrument was then piloted with Travellers at the local level and changes were incorporated as required.
- Following regional consultation workshops, the study questions were adapted to Travellers' terminology (using their language and understanding) and relevant images, pictures, and icons were selected or developed by Travellers in these workshops to "act as question or answer prompts" and to ensure that the instrument reflected Travellers' rich oral and visual culture.
- The questionnaire was then translated into an oral/visual electronic format on laptop computers.
- A Traveller provided a "voiceover" to capture the Traveller wording and intonation of each question. This was available as an option for peer researchers who could not read the questions.
- The computer-designed instrument was piloted with Travellers and peer researchers.
- The questionnaire was finalized following this consultation process and the laptop computers were loaded with the audio visual instrument and distributed to the Study Coordinators to complete their final "trainers training session."
- The study coordinators returned to their projects to train their local peer researchers on the use of the computerized questionnaire.
- Final dress rehearsal was successfully completed for quality assurance of data collection and data upload process using modems.

10.2.10 Dress rehearsal, pilot, and data collection

Would this work? A pilot and dress rehearsal preceded the main survey data collection phase. The study finally went live on the October 14, 2008. Over a six-week period, pairs of Traveller peer researchers visited every household on the scoping list to conduct the interviews. That process (pilot, dress rehearsal, data collection phase) was repeated again in Northern Ireland in February 2009.

Demographic details of the household were recorded, and an interview was conducted with the main respondent. In advance, there was considerable discussion as to whether men would participate directly in the interview process. They were not engaged previously as it was traditionally held that health matters were of concern to women only. It was judged important to engage men directly, particularly in rating their health and risk factors. Provision was made for proxy participation with a briefer set of details. Travellers are not unique in this; men are known in general to be less likely to participate in surveys (Jackson, Chambless, Yang, Byrne, Watson, Folsom *et al.*, 1996) and, in many minority populations, women are the traditional caregivers and responsible for health matters. As it happened, the male participation rate was respectable, with more than half of the men responding directly, and a further fifth of respondents responding by proxy (McGorrian *et al.*, 2013). To compensate for the risk of low participation by men, as part of the consultation process it was agreed to include Traveller men as a specific focus group to ensure that their voices and concerns were heard.

10.2.11 Study organization

The study was divided into the following substudies:

- Census of the Traveller population;
- Quantitative study of health status and utilization;
- Retrospective and prospective linkage studies;
- Qualitative studies; and
- Service Providers Study.

Figure 10.2 shows the substudies related to each other.

Census of Traveller population

This was a census of the Traveller population, which included information on accommodation, education, employment, and demographic family information. Only Travellers who self-identified as Travellers were included in the census. The census was based on enumerating members of a family. The final response rate was 80 percent of all households approached, 78 percent in the Republic of Ireland and 93 percent in Northern Ireland, calculated as numerator/denominator.

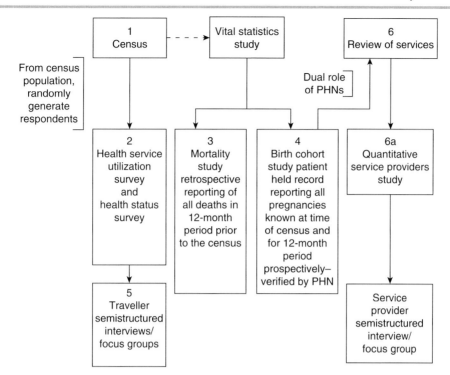

Figure 10.2   Summary of design and substudies in the All Ireland Traveller Health Study

Quantitative study of health status and health utilization

For efficiency purposes, the Travellers quantitative study was conducted at the same time as the census visit (see Figure 10.2) when subsamples based on age and gender were selected to answer questions on health status and utilization. The advantages of data collection at the same time as the census were that only one contact was made with each family and that all the relevant information was collected on a single visit. There were in effect five subgroup interviews. Based on the demographics of the household, if a child exactly aged 5, 9, or 14 was resident, the mother was interviewed about that child's health status. We picked these exact ages to ensure an adequate sample for those cohorts and to compare with other national children's surveys. If no such child was available, then another adult was randomly selected and interviewed, either about their health status or their health care utilization experience. This ensured an adequate random sample and equalized respondent burden for households.

Retrospective and prospective linkage studies

The survey also identified any deaths that had occurred in the previous twelve months in the immediate or wider family, and recorded name, age, address, and cause of death if known.

These were then cross-checked and traced for death certification through the General Registry Office and proved reasonably accurate. This approach replicated one taken with the US census in the period 1850–1930, when vital statistics and mortality was reported for the US population by this method during the main census data collection exercise (Kelleher, Lynch, Daly, Harper, Fitz-Simon, Bimpeh *et al.*, 2006; Kelleher, Lynch, Harper, Tay, & Nolan, 2004). It had the advantage of engaging the respondent families themselves in collecting this information and meant it was more likely we would get accurate names of Travellers and, because it was retrospective rather than prospective, no data capture exercise was necessary after the census.

Each death was verified as accurately as possible with public health nurses and a search made in the General Registry Office to verify date and cause of death. Due to a change in legislation the onus to register a death now lies with the families in Ireland, and, if there are no probate issues in relation to a last will and testament, such registration may not take place. This may be especially so with infant and young children's deaths and hence we were especially vigilant on this aspect. Although this was a census and mortality was expected to be excessive, we were still dealing with relatively small numbers, particularly in investigating cause-specific mortality. We explored the possibility of linkage of these deaths to the families surveyed in the census for the purposes of data analysis but this would have meant that the unique family identifier would not remain anonymous, so this did not prove possible. We did, however, record the death as a bereavement variable in the analysis and found that this was an independent predictor of poor mental health for the respondent who completed the health status interview (McGorrian *et al.*, 2013).

A second strategy was to establish a prospective birth cohort for all babies born within twelve months exactly from the census date. These were then to be followed for one calendar year from birth to establish infant mortality rates. All those women expecting a baby were asked to participate in the study at census stage, and over the next two years public health (or community) nurses were asked to assist with ascertainment and prospective informed consent. Mothers were asked to give consent for linkage to their hospital records rather than collecting any data directly. This meant that we could access their detailed perinatal record and compare the results across social classes in the general population (Hamid, Quirke, Turner, Daly, Kelleher, & Fitzpatrick, 2011). As mothers had to be identified and consent had to be obtained, the response rate to this component of the study was lower than for the main census, with just over half of the mothers agreeing. Even for mothers who gave consent, there was no possibility of linking to the census survey because that might compromise anonymity. The main report gives details of our estimates for the likely number of children born based on estimated fertility rates in the population, the previous findings in 1987, and the count in the main census. The ascertained number was in the event consistent with those estimates.

The qualitative studies

It was intended from the outset to conduct consultative focus groups with the Traveller community and with relevant service providers and policymakers. The objective was to complement the quantitative database and to explore issues that might not lend themselves easily to a closed quantitative instrument. A grounded theory approach was taken but there were agreed candidate topics that stakeholders felt were relevant, such as domestic violence and sexual orientation. It was also important to recruit a variety of participants (from different demographic groups and geographic areas) into the focus groups. Twenty-four focus groups were conducted on a range of topics including men's and women's health, mental health, suicide, and problems of addiction. Researchers also conducted 27 in-depth semi-structured interviews with key service providers in both jurisdictions. We also undertook a review of Travellers in prisons, though individual interviews were not possible, because the prisons had no systematic record of which prisoners were Travellers.

The service providers study

A sample of front-line service providers was selected for interviews about perceptions of Travellers' health status and health needs. Providers were asked to identify models of good practice through computer-assisted telephone interviews (CATI) and qualitative studies. Interviews were completed with 353 of 666 eligible health care providers (53 percent), representing front-line general practitioners, hospital consultants, and other senior service providers.

10.2.12 Confidentiality and consent

The Traveller population is a close-knit and closed community, suspicious of officialdom. As many cannot read and write, the challenge of obtaining informed consent was critical. In association again with the Traveller organizations, advance publicity of the Census Day was raised through projects, religious parish newsletters, and other means. Two DVDs were made to disseminate information to Travellers and Traveller organizations, the first at the outset explaining the purpose of the study and the second giving the results. The launch of the study, the field work commencement date, and the main report were all undertaken by the Minister for Health and Children. Speaking at the inception of the study in June 2007, she said:

> Traveller health is a priority area and considerable work has been undertaken, in consultation with the interest groups, in commissioning this Study. The purpose of the study is to examine the health status of Travellers, to assess the impact of the health services currently being provided and to identify the factors which influence health status. It will provide a framework for policy development and practice in relation to Traveller health.

A series of information leaflets was prepared and proofed for comprehensibility by the NALA. For the main census, a question was incorporated into the oral-visual questionnaire which asked the respondent to tick yes, if he or she understood and gave consent to participate. Names and addresses of Traveller families were never transmitted to UCD; only a study number was used. The only exceptions were for the mortality and birth cohort studies where names were needed for linkage and follow-up.

The study received ethical approval from two research ethics committees, that of UCD and the Office for Research Ethics Committee in Northern Ireland (ORECNI). The latter stipulated that field workers had an obligation to report any observed illegal activity, including evidence of child abuse, as is now common practice for health care providers. Again, respondents needed to be aware of this possibility as part of the informed consent and a helpline to report such events was put in place, though no reports were ever processed, apart from a solitary and obvious crank call.

10.2.13 Summary of data collection process in the main census survey

- UCD set up an outline matrix on coding for the study and asked coordinators to set up a code for each family (UCD only pre-set the regional codes). The team agreed on the broad content of the coding system, including peer researcher codes, family codes, site codes, area codes, etc., and used this to create the response categories in the interviewing system. The team asked the coordinators to update the information on these matrices on a daily basis, indicating the outcome of each contact family and the notes in the comments section.
- Data were collected from fifty-four study sites throughout Ireland.
- The census component of the study, highlighting the importance of the study and the use of the electronic instrument by Travellers, was launched by the Minister for Health and Children with a photo opportunity and press conference.
- Data were collected and uploaded from 180 computers located in the fifty-four study centres during the two data collection periods (Republic of Ireland in October and Northern Ireland in February).
- An average of 300 files were uploaded to the UCD server daily and monitored as part of quality control.
- A twelve-hour daily helpline was set up with information technology staff and program support to address issues and challenges as they arose.
- To facilitate completeness of the study, the census period was extended to allow inclusion of areas where there were issues in relation to staff turnover and problems with access to sites.
- At the end of the census, the team conducted an exit interview with each study coordinator and encouraged return of the completed matrix. In the matrix, the coordinator provided a final survey disposition for each family and indicated if new families had been added.

10.3 Recognition

Overall, very positive feedback was received from projects which participated in the study, with the benefits far outweighing the challenges. Most projects felt that the peer researchers gained several skills from this experience. It improved team work and gave them more confidence in their own abilities. Some peer researchers felt that their community now has

Figure 10.3   Certification ceremony for peer researchers

more respect for their professional role in Traveller health. Some comments noted during feedback included:

> It gave me a sense of pride as a Traveller, that we were able to carry out this research ourselves – it also was a good education and example to our children that Travellers are able to do this for themselves.

> It has been a fantastic learning experience, with Travellers building up their skills and knowledge.

> Hard work, long hours but worth it, I am proud I could do it.

Two recognition ceremonies were held, in Belfast in Northern Ireland and at the O'Reilly conferring hall in UCD, where the academic staff associated with the project gowned up in formal robes as for any university-conferring ceremony and awarded a certification of completion with accompanying photograph to every peer researcher who had taken part in the study (Figure 10.3). As we processed to the podium, the principal investigator overheard one woman in the audience exchange with another "Where are *our* costumes?" giving a wry laugh. So concluded aptly, on a witty note, a project that had been decades in the making.

References

Abdalla, S., Quirke, B., Fitzpatrick, P., Drummond, A., Daly, L., & Kelleher, C. C. (2010). *Vital Statistics Reports*. Department of Health and Children. Dublin: Stationery Office. Retrieved from www.dohc.ie/publications/aiths2010/TR2/AITHS2010_TechnicalReport2_LR_All.pdf.

All Ireland Traveller Health Study Team. (2010). *Summary and Technical Reports*. Department of Health and Children. Dublin: Stationery Office. Retrieved from www.dohc.ie/publications/traveller_health_study.html.

Barry, J., & Daly, L. (1986). *Travellers' Health Status Study Census of Travelling People*. Dublin: The Health Research Board.

Barry, J., Herity, B., & Solan, J. (1989). *The Travellers' Health Status Study – Vital Statistics of Travelling People, 1987*. Dublin: The Health Research Board.

Benoit, C., Jansson, M., Millar, A., & Phillips, R. (2005). Community-academic research on hard-to-reach populations: benefits and challenges. *Qualitative Health Research*, 15, 263–82.

Breathnach, A. (2006). *Becoming Conspicuous: Irish Travellers, Society and the State 1922–70*. Dublin: Dublin University Press.

Dahlgren, G., & Whitehead, M. (1991). *Policies and Strategies to Promote Social Equity in Health*. Background document to WHO: Strategy paper for Europe. Arbeitsrapport vol. 14. Stockholm: Institute for Futures Studies.

Davey Smith, G., Ebrahim, S., & Eggar, M. (2000). Should health promotion be exempt from rigorous evaluation? In R. Edmondson & C. Kelleher (eds.), *Health Promotion: new discipline or multidiscipline?* (pp. 18–28). Dublin: Irish Academic Press.

Department of Health and Children. (2002). *Traveller Health– A National Strategy 2002–2005*. Dublin: Department of Health and Children.

Fraser, D. G., Dougill, A. J., Mabee, W. E., Reed, M., & McAlpine, P. (2006). Bottom up and top down: analysis of participatory processes for sustainability indicator identification as a pathway to community empowerment and sustainable environmental management. *Journal of Environmental Management*, 78, 114–27.

Friel, S., Kelleher, C. C., Nolan, G., & Harrington, J. (2003). Social diversity of Irish adults' nutritional intake. *European Journal of Clinical Nutrition*, 57(7), 865–75.

Gmelch, G., & Gmelch, S. (1976). The emergence of an ethnic group: the Irish Tinkers. *Anthropological Quarterly*, 49(4), 225–38.

Government Publications. (2000). The Equal Status Act, 2000. Retrieved from www.irish statutebook.ie/2000/en/act/pub/0008/index.html.

Hamid, N. A., Quirke, B., Turner, J., Daly., L., Kelleher, C. C., & Fitzpatrick, P. (2011). *Report of Follow-Up of Birth Cohort Study*. Department of Health and Children. Dublin: Stationery Office. Retrieved from www.dohc.ie/publications/aiths_follow_ up.html.

Harper, J., & Hudson, C. (1971). Irish Traveller Cant. *Journal of English Linguistics*, 5, 78–86.

Institute of Public Health in Ireland. (2004). Design of the Travellers' All Ireland Health Study: Details. Dublin: Institute of Public Health of Ireland.

Jackson, R., Chambless, L. E., Yang, K., Byrne, T., Watson, R., Folsom, A., *et al.* (1996). Differences between respondents and non-respondents in a multicenter community-based study vary by gender and ethnicity. *Journal of Clinical Epidemiology*, 49, 1441–46.

Kelleher, C. C., Lynch, J. W., Daly, L., Harper, S., Fitz-Simon, N., Bimpeh, Y., *et al.* (2006). The "Americanisation" of migrants: evidence for the contribution of ethnicity, social deprivation, lifestyle and life-course processes to the mid-20th century Coronary Heart Disease epidemic in the US. *Social Science & Medicine*, 63(2), 465–84.

Kelleher, C. C., Lynch, J., Harper, S., Tay, J. B., & Nolan, G. (2004). Hurling alone? How social capital failed to save the Irish from cardiovascular disease in the United States. *American Journal of Public Health*, 94(12), 2162–69.

Kelleher, C. C., Whelan, J., Daly, L., & Fitzpatrick, P. (2012). Socio-demographic, environmental, lifestyle and psychosocial factors predict self-rated health in Irish Travellers, a minority nomadic population. *Health & Place*, 18, 330–38.

Kenny, M., & McNeela, E. (2005). *Assimilation Policies and Outcomes: Travellers' Experience. Report on a Research Project Commissioned by Pavee Point Travellers' Centre*. Dublin: Pavee Point.

Laverack, G., & Labonte, R. (2000). A planning framework for community empowerment goals within health promotion. *Health Policy and Planning*, 15(3), 255–62.

Lynch, S. A., Foulds, N., Thuresson, A. C., Collins, A. L., Annerén, G., Hedberg, B. O., *et al.* (2011). The 12q14 microdeletion syndrome; 6 new cases confirming the role of HMGA2 in growth. *European Journal of Human Genetics*, 19, 534–39.

MacDonagh, R. (2002). The web of self-identity: racism, sexism and disabilism. In R. Lentin & R. Mcveigh (eds.), *Racism and Anti-Racism in Ireland*. Belfast: Beyond the Pale Publications.

McGorrian, C., Daly, L., Fitzpatrick, P., Hamid, N. A., Malone, K. M., Kelleher, C. C. (2013). Frequent mental distress (FMD) in Irish Travellers: discrimination and bereavement negatively influence mental health in the All-Ireland Traveller Health Study. Transcultural Psychiatry, 50, 559–78.

McGorrian, C., Daly, L., Fitzpatrick, P., Moore, R. G., Turner, J., & Kelleher, C. C. (2011). Cardiovascular disease and risk factors in an indigenous minority population. The All-Ireland Traveller Health Study. *European Journal of Preventive Cardiology*, 19, 1444–53.

McGorrian, C., Frazer, K., Daly, L., Moore, R. G., Turner, J., Sweeney, *et al.* (2012). The health care experiences of Travellers compared to the general population: the All-Ireland Traveller Health Study. *Journal of Health Services Research and Policy*, 17(3), 173–80.

MacGreil, M. (2011). *Emancipation of Travellers*. Maynooth: National University College, Maynooth.

McPherson, K. (2000). Methodologies and evaluation in public health and health promotion. In R. Edmondson & C. Kelleher (eds.), *Health promotion: new discipline or multidiscipline?* (pp. 129–44). Dublin: Irish Academic Press.

O'Donovan, O., McCarthy, P., McKenna, V., McCarthy, D., & Kelleher, C. C. (1995). Health service provision for the Traveller community in Ireland. In *Appendix to Report of the Task Force on the Travelling Community*. Dublin: Stationery Office.

Quirke, B. (2006a). *A review of Travellers' health using primary care as a model of good practice*. Pavee Point Primary Healthcare for Travellers Project. Dublin: Pavee Point.

(2006b). Health inequalities in Ireland: the reality of Travellers' health. In T. O'Connor & M. Murphy (eds.), *Social Care in Ireland: Theory, Policy and Practice*. Cork: CIT Press.

Task Force on the Traveller Community. (1995). *Report of the Task Force on the Traveller Community*. Dublin: Stationery Office.

Tones, K. (2000). Evaluating health promotion: judicial review as a new gold standard. In R. Edmondson & C. Kelleher (eds.), *Health Promotion: New Discipline or Multidiscipline?* (pp. 29–45). Dublin: Irish Academic Press.

Tumiel-Berhalter, L. M., McLaughlin-Diaz, V., Vena, J., & Crespo, C. J. (2007). Building community research capacity: process evaluation of community training in a community-based participatory research program serving a predominantly Puerto-Rican community. *Programme for Community Health Partnership*, 1(1), 89–97.

UK Parliament Race Relations Order. (1997). Retrieved from www.legislation.gov.uk/nisi/1997/869/contents/made.

World Health Organization. (2007). A conceptual framework for action on the social determinants of health. Commission on Social Determinants of Health: World Health Organization, Geneva. www.who.int/social_determinants/thecommission/finalreport/en/index.html.

PART III

Conducting surveys with special populations

11

Representing the populations: what general social surveys can learn from surveys among specific groups

INEKE STOOP

11.1 The usual suspects: why don't they participate?

Some groups are unlikely candidates for survey participation. However, even groups deemed to be very difficult may turn out to be not so difficult in the end. People with learning disabilities – and their parents and carers – were much keener to answer questions about their own situation than expected (Stoop & Harrison, 2012a). Ethnic minorities may be hard to reach but, once reached by someone who speaks their language, may participate just as often as the majority population (Feskens, Hox, Lensvelt-Mulders, & Schmeets, 2007). Busy people may have little time to spare but are used to doing lots of things quickly and are thus generally not underrepresented in burdensome time use studies (Van Ingen, Stoop, & Breedveld, 2009).

When trying to identify hard-to-reach respondents, it rapidly becomes clear that being hard to reach may be related to sociodemographic and socioeconomic characteristics of individuals under study, but also depends greatly on the survey design. Survey mode, in particular, has been identified as an important factor in reaching different groups in the population. Geographically isolated groups may be easy to reach by telephone; mobile-only households may have no problem with a web-based survey; linguistic minorities may be quite happy to complete a questionnaire translated into their language; and the illiterate may enjoy a conversation with a face-to-face interviewer. Mixed-mode surveys aim to overcome the fact that different groups of people may be more or less easy to reach and more or less willing to respond in a particular mode (de Leeuw, 2008; de Leeuw, Dillman, & Hox, 2008; Dillman & Messer, 2010). More generally, securing participation by the hard to reach or hard to survey will depend on the design and topic of the survey and the efforts one is willing to make.

Section 11.3 of this book shows how hard-to-reach groups may be excluded, but can be included in surveys among the general public and specific populations. Preceding this, Section 11.2 explains why we should make sure that specific groups are included in general social surveys, why surveys among specific groups are special, and why the distinction between "us" and "them" plays a role in survey design and implementation. Section 11.4 describes how the European Social Survey (ESS), a biennial face-to-face survey held in more than thirty European countries, aims to include all members of the population, and why that is so difficult.

11.2 Specific groups and otherness

11.2.1 Specific groups in three types of survey

A first step in survey design is the identification of a target population. These could be all citizens, young people, unemployed men, residents of Chinese descent, people with learning disabilities, transgenders, etc. Specific or minority groups will play a different role in surveys among general populations, surveys that distinguish between groups in the population and surveys among these specific subgroups (see Figure 11.1).

In a *survey among the general population* (1), we would like minority groups, whether they are the mobile-only, gay people, unemployed, big city dwellers, immigrants, or transgenders or any other potentially difficult group, to be represented as well as mainstream groups in order to minimize error in survey outcomes. If members of one of these groups are underrepresented, and if they differ on survey target variables from nongroup members, the survey results will give an incorrect picture of the population. In this case, the membership of a minority group in itself is not important, and it is not even necessary to know whether a sample unit is gay or straight, or lives in a rural or urban area. If a specific group is underrepresented, what counts is the size of this group, the extent of underrepresentation, and the difference between the underrepresented minority group and the mainstream group.

In many surveys, outcomes are represented for *different subgroups in the population* (2). Based on a survey of unemployment, results can be published on unemployment among young and old, men and women, minority ethnic groups and majority groups. In this case, the representation of each group is important, members of these groups have to be identified as such, and subgroups have to be large enough to present accurate outcomes per subgroup. The underrepresentation of rare or hard-to-reach groups is more worrying than in the previous case because in an unemployment survey the aim is to identify those groups that suffer from unemployment.

A totally different case are *surveys among specific minority groups* (3). To conduct these surveys, a sampling frame must be available of these specific populations, or people have to be identified through screening questions in a general survey, or another sampling strategy

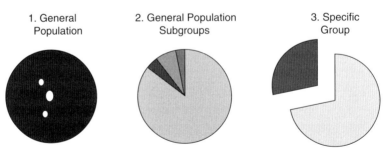

Figure 11.1   Representation of minority group – three scenarios
1) Minority groups (white spots) should be represented to cover full population
2) Minority groups (slices) should be represented, identified, and large enough to report on them
3) Separate survey among specific minority groups (slice).

(network sampling (see Chapter 23 in this volume), respondent-driven sampling (see Chapter 24 in this volume)) has to be used. Surveys among specific groups are usually set up to discover which problems these groups are confronted with, or how they cope, or which services and facilities they need. Conducting a survey among a specific group will be especially difficult when the group is specific because of a sensitive issue (e.g., people with HIV, sex workers; see Johnston & Sabin, 2010).

Examples of concerns in survey research are thus (1) how can I reach the mobile-only population; (2) how can I make sure that immigrants participate in my survey and how can I identify respondents belonging to these groups; and (3) how can I design and conduct a survey among transgenders?

The efforts the survey team is willing to deploy to reach the hard-to-reach groups and obtain their cooperation will depend on the type of survey. In a general survey, it might be possible to ignore small, specific groups that will probably have only a small effect on the final results whereas efforts to include them may take a fairly large slice of the survey budget. In the second case, when distinctions have to be made between specific subgroups, their representation is crucial. In this situation, one might want to consider adaptation of the survey design (different modes, different interviewers, different survey languages) to ensure the participation of specific subgroups. These adaptations will most likely result in design or mode effects that can make it more difficult to compare subgroups. Finally, for a survey among a specific group, efforts will have to be made to reach this group and to maximize their participation. This will mean that the survey design might have to be adapted from the start to children, the very elderly, minority language speakers, people with learning disabilities, etc.

11.2.2 Examples of "us" and "them" in survey design and implementation

A number of studies on nonresponse juxtapose "us" (the methodologists) and "them" (the sample "units" or target respondents). Social exchange theorists, on the other hand, argue that these parties should be equal. Dillman (2000) has consistently emphasized the importance of respect for respondents and he and Goyder (1987, p. 25) draw a sharp distinction between "heartless behaviourists, who seem bent on cajoling and coaxing all these stupid 'sample cases' who don't know what is good for them, into responding, and the believers in social exchange who feel that every citizen is perfectly able to make up his or her own mind on whether or not to cooperate" (Stoop, 2005, p. 101). Goyder, Boyer, and Martinelli (2006) and Singer (2011) have tried to integrate these two approaches.

The "us" and "them" issue plays a major role in surveys among minority groups. In some areas (the "us" areas), researchers largely belong to the same group as those they are studying. This holds, for instance, for African-American studies, studies of women, and studies of gay people. As an example of the latter, the entire editorial board of the Taylor and Francis Journal of Lesbian Studies is female.[1]

---

[1] www.tandfonline.com/action/aboutThisJournal?show=editorialBoard&journalCode=wjls20 (July 6, 2012).

In this type of research, the "them" group (Whites, men, straight people) are often seen as the oppressors:

> The race of an interviewer is often important for obtaining reliable responses to interview questions. Black respondents are often sceptical of the motives of White researchers because of the legacy of slavery, subsequent oppression and misuse of information by predominantly White institutions. Blacks often respond differently to questions asked by a White Researcher than by a Black interviewer.
>
> (Anderson & Stewart, 2007, p. 21)

In other areas, researchers ("us") do not belong to the group they are studying ("them"). Surveys among children, the elderly, or immigrants are examples. One could say that in these cases the in-group, the majority, collects information on the out-groups, the minorities. In most, though not all[2] cases, the specific groups have less power than the majority of the population. It is worthwhile considering here why information on "them" is sought: do they need help, do they have problems, do they cause problems, are they highly visible, do they lack capabilities, means, or networks, etc.? Put differently, why do sponsors fund surveys among specific minority (ethnic) groups? Is it because members of these groups need support, because they are a danger to our society or way of life, or because sponsors want to reduce immigration, or want immigrants to assimilate and integrate and become more like the majority?

To give an illustration, the website of the Dutch Ministry of the Interior and Kingdom Relations, which is responsible for the integration of immigrants into Dutch society, says the following (see also Box 11.1):

> The aim of Dutch integration policy is to have everyone in the Netherlands, including newcomers, feel a sense of community with each other and involvement with the Netherlands. The government wants people who settle in the Netherlands to take part in Dutch society regardless of where they come from or what they believe in. ...

Box 11.1 WESTERN AND NON-WESTERN MINORITIES IN THE NETHERLANDS

In the Netherlands, surveys among Dutch citizens of Turkish, Moroccan, Surinamese, and Caribbean descent are fairly frequent, much more so than surveys among people originating from Belgium, Japan, or the United States, for example. Interestingly enough, a distinction is drawn in the Netherlands between migrants from Western and from non-Western countries, where Western countries are countries in Europe (excluding Turkey), North America and Oceania, plus Indonesia and Japan, and non-Western countries are those in Africa, Latin America, Asia (excluding Indonesia and Japan), and Turkey (Feskens, 2009, p. 13). Clearly, the Western is "us" and the non-Western is "them," and the distinction Western/non-Western has very little to do with geography.

---

2 One exception are surveys among the wealthy. These have their own particular problems, including a low response rate (see the report on the Special Topic Contributed Paper Meeting 31 "Accounting for the very rich in household surveys of income and wealth" at the ISI 2007 [Irving Fisher Committee on Central Bank Statistics, 2008]).

Immigrants who settle in the Netherlands must speak the language and be familiar with Dutch society. Municipalities will actively approach them so that they can take a civic integration course that matches their abilities.[3]

The aim of immigrant surveys sponsored by this Ministry is to monitor the progress of integration.

The "us" and "them" issue is further reflected by the presence of survey questions directed at majority groups, and racial/ethnic incongruence between interviewers and respondents. A question intended to measure tolerance ("What would be your reaction when your daughter married a non-Western immigrant?") may not measure the same concept when answered by a non-Western immigrant. Research on translating questions (Harkness, 2003) and on cross-national research (Braun, 2003; Smith, 2003) has paid a lot of attention to measuring concepts in different cultural contexts. In national studies fielded in a single survey language, the effect of culture and context is easier to ignore.

In his book *Orientalism*, Edward Said (1979, p. 40) gives pertinent examples of the "we" and "them," or "Otherness":

> In Comer's and Balfour's language the Oriental is depicted as something one judges (as in a court of law), something one studies and depicts (as in a curriculum), something one disciplines (as in a school or prison), something one illustrates (as in a zoological manual).

Another "us/them" issue is the racial/ethnic congruence between interviewers and respondents. Schaeffer, Dykema, & Maynard (2010) give an overview of possible interviewers' effects on nonresponse error and measurement error. Whereas there is a fair amount of evidence that race or ethnicity has an impact on measurement error, and that congruence or incongruence of race and ethnicity can have an effect, they found very little evidence of an impact on nonresponse error. Davis, Caldwell, Couper, Janz, Alexander, Greene et al. (2013) found that African-Americans were more likely to prefer African-American interviewers, especially in a survey with substantial racial content, but they could not find an effect either on response rate or on survey outcomes.

The "us" and "them" issue is relevant in surveys among specific groups. Who is sponsoring the survey, what the aim of the survey is, and who does the interviewing, are all pertinent questions here. The issue is also relevant in general surveys, if only because of the type of questions and the possible bias towards mainstream culture in the design and implementation of the survey.

11.3 Hard-to-reach groups in general and specific surveys

11.3.1 From population of inference to response

Groves (1989, ch. 3) distinguishes the following populations.

- The *population of inference*, for instance the inhabitants of country A, or migrants living in city B, or gay people living in Europe.

---

3 www.government.nl/issues/integration (October 15, 2012).

- The *target population* is the finite set of persons that will be studied in a survey. From the target population, those persons are generally excluded who cannot be contacted or will not be able to participate, such as persons living abroad, and the nonresidential population (senior housing facilities, prisons).
- The *frame population* is the set of persons for whom some enumeration can be made prior to the selection of the survey sample.
- The *eligible sample* is the set of persons who are part of the sample that has been drawn from the frame population, excluding ineligible units such as incorrect addresses or persons who do not belong to the target population.
- The *survey population* is the set of people who, if they had been selected for the survey, would be respondents.

It will be clear that after every step, from population of inference to survey population, "difficult" people will drop out. When going from the *population of inference* to the *target population*, it is tempting to be restrictive and exclude difficult groups that may be hard to sample, hard to reach, or hard to interview. For example: same-sex couples instead of gay people, people living in residential households and not those living in senior housing facilities and prisons, people aged below 70 instead of no upper age limit, etc. Where difficult groups have been excluded in advance, survey costs are likely to be lower and response rates higher than with less restrictive definitions. The downside is, of course, that a part of the population is excluded from participation. How problematic that is will depend on the topic of the study, the size of the excluded groups, and the relationship between group membership and the core questions of the survey. In a study on health, excluding the very elderly will produce an overly optimistic picture of the health of the population; in a study on migration, excluding migrant workers living in hostels may provide an overly optimistic picture of integration; and in a study on criminal behavior, exclusion of people in prison will definitely underestimate participation in (serious) crime.

In the next step, from *target population* to *frame population*, more people will be lost depending on the sampling frames that are available. When the telephone directory is used, for instance, ex-directory and mobile-only households will be excluded. In a web-based survey where recruitment takes place via the Internet or emails, the non-Internet population is excluded. And even in an ideal case, when the sample is drawn from an up-to-date population register (as is the practice of a number of national statistical institutes in Europe) a number of people cannot participate, such as the homeless, seasonal migrants, and illegal aliens. After the sample has been drawn, *ineligibles* have to be excluded. Sometimes, these result from errors in the sampling frame (e.g., holiday addresses in an address file); in other cases, eligibility has to be assessed after the sample has been drawn (e.g., through a screening question). In practice, it may not always be easy to distinguish between ineligible sample units that are not part of the target population, noncontacts, and noncooperation (Groves, 1989).

Once the eligible sample has been defined, *nonresponse* is the next threat to full representation. It is not only the nonresponse rate that is important, but also the difference between respondents and nonrespondents, or rather the relationship between survey participation and core variables of the survey (Groves, 2006). Simply put, when a specific group does not respond to the survey (e.g., minority language speakers or the very elderly) and their nonparticipation is related to the topic of the survey (e.g., integration in society or health), the results of the survey will be biased.

One important factor in achieving high and representative response rates is the survey mode. In general, it can be said that interviewers in face-to-face surveys achieve the highest response rates (de Leeuw, 2008). Face-to-face surveys also make it possible to assess why people do not participate. When the interviewer visits the sample unit's address, the latter may be not at home, not able to participate, or not willing to participate. As in telephone surveys, noncontacts are followed up by additional (telephone or personal) calls. The timing of these calls is of great importance for establishing contact (D'Arrigo, Durrant, & Steele, 2009; Groves & Couper, 1998; Purdon, Campanelli, & Sturgis, 1999; Stoop, 2005). To allow contact with as many people as possible, not only the timing of calls is important, but also the duration of field work in order to reach people who have been away for extended periods. To increase the contact rate, interviewers can leave behind a card with a telephone number or call the target person if they have a telephone number. In both cases, there is a risk that the target person will refuse more easily than in a personal contact.

People may be unable to participate because they do not speak the fielding language of the survey or are mentally or physically unable to participate. The survey design greatly influences people's ability to participate. Translating questionnaires, adapting the questionnaire for the very elderly or those with limited mental capacities, rephrasing and simplifying questions, or coming back when an ill person has recovered, can substantially reduce the percentage of "not able."

Those who are able to participate still have to be willing to do so. Stoop (2012) gives a detailed overview of reasons for refusal and reasons for participation. In face-to-face surveys, well-trained interviewers can tailor their introduction to specific groups and emphasize those survey elements (an incentive, the topic, the sponsor, the scientific use) that might motivate that particular group to participate (see Groves & McGonagle, 2001; Groves, Presser, & Dipko, 2004; Groves, Singer, & Corning, 2000). Combined with the fact that samples for face-to-face surveys usually have good coverage (better than telephone or web-based surveys, for example), this makes face-to-face interviewing a good mode for optimizing survey representativeness (see also de Leeuw, 2008). Well-trained, professional interviewers conducting standardized interviews are thus a good – though costly – way of collecting data (Loosveldt, 2008).

A drawback of face-to-face interview surveys is that respondents may be less willing to answer sensitive questions or may provide more socially desirable answers (de Leeuw, 2008; Tourangeau & Smith, 1996). Also, less well-trained, less professional interviewers conducting interviews in a less standardized way may cause a substantial amount of measurement error. Other modes may also be more suited to particular groups (see also de Leeuw, 2005). In addition, some groups will be hard to reach (or only at great cost) in a face-to-face survey, for instance those living in distant or sparsely populated areas. Other modes could provide a solution for these groups. Face-to-face interviewing is therefore not a panacea.

11.3.2 Specific groups in general surveys

To be able to study specific groups in a general survey, a number of conditions have to be met. First, the sample size needs to be large enough to produce precise results on subgroups. Second, these subgroups must participate in the survey; and third, it must be possible to identify them as such. The three examples below illustrate some of the intricacies of identifying specific groups in general social surveys.

The first example is studying the health of the population and comparing age groups (including the very elderly). A large sample is required to ensure that the elderly population is sufficiently represented, or a stratified sample in which elderly people are overrepresented. The latter will be easily possible when the sample is drawn from a population register containing dates of birth. Identifying the elderly population in a survey should not be a problem, as age is a background variable that is almost always collected. A core problem here will be that the non-residential population (and thus elderly people living in senior residential facilities) are usually excluded from general surveys. To include this group, a special additional survey will have to be set up. A second problem could be that some survey modes may be less appropriate for elderly people and that, in order to include very elderly persons, questions may have to be rephrased, specific questions may have to be added, and specific interviewers may have to be deployed (West & Olson, 2010). Studying the health of the very elderly thus seems to be feasible provided additional efforts are made.

A second example is studying the quality of life of straight and lesbian, gay and bisexual people. One challenge here is to draft one or more questions that clearly identify this group. In a report on estimating the size and composition of the lesbian, gay, and bisexual population in Britain, Aspinall (2009, p. 25) discusses how sexual orientation can be measured and what its elements are: "how sexual orientation is constructed with respect to definitions in legislation and regulations; its function as an overarching or umbrella term that encompasses the dimensions of sexual identity, attraction/desire, and sexual behaviour; the overlap of these dimensions in individuals; and the dynamic nature of these dimensions, especially in young people." His report shows that many UK surveys contain a question on sexual orientation, though the questions differ across surveys. In other countries, asking questions on this topic may be much more controversial. One major concern is that including questions on sexual orientation will reduce the response rate. Tourangeau and Smith (1996) indicated that for these questions to be answered they have to be perceived as legitimate by the respondents. This could mean that questions on sexual orientation are more acceptable in a survey on health and well-being than in a survey on travel and public transport. Martin Mitchell concludes in his Sexual Orientation Research Review 2008[4] that: "Previous trends for 'bottom up' research, generated by lesbians, gays, and bisexuals (LGB)

---

4 www.natcen.ac.uk/study/sexual-orientation-research-review (July 13, 2012).

researchers themselves and a continuing hesitance to include sexual orientation in social policy research needed to be addressed."

A final example is identifying minority ethnic groups. De Voogd (2007) describes three. A priori targeting methods entail identifying a group before going into the field. One a priori method is the *onomastic* method, i.e., scanning telephone directories or population or address registers for names known to be typical of a certain ethnic group. Some groups may be easier to identify by name than others, and children from mixed marriages may not be found. Other a priori targeting approaches include concentrating interviews in areas known to have a high proportion of relevant minorities. This assumes a certain degree of ethnic or racial segregation. The final and most simple a priori targeting approach can be implemented when information on ethnic background is available from population registers.

The second and third approaches described by de Voogd (2007) involve identifying a group when in the field. In *facies* targeting, face-to-face interviewers recruit respondents based on their physical attributes, dress, or religious symbols. The third approach is based on *self-identification*, whereby potential respondents identify themselves as belonging to one or more of the target groups. This method is mainly used in the US.[5]

European law prohibits the processing of personal data on racial or ethnic origin.[6] The aim of combating racial discrimination and pursuing equal opportunities for all restricts the possibilities for collecting data on ethnic background. Simon (2007) gives an impressive overview of the variance of definitions of ethnic origin and the willingness in different countries to collect these data. He also presents a list of characteristics referring directly or indirectly to ethnic or national origin in the responses to the question: "According to your organisation, which variables make reference, directly or indirectly, to ethnic or national origin?" (see Box 11.2). Given the legal and practical problems it may not be easy – even when minority ethnic groups participate in surveys – to identify them and use them for further analysis.

11.3.3 Surveys among specific groups

The issue of conducting surveys among special populations will be covered extensively in the remainder of Part III of this book: "Conducting surveys with special populations." Nonresponse among specific groups has been discussed in previous sections of this chapter, and is a major topic of Part V: "Data collection strategies for the hard to survey." "Sampling strategies for the hard to survey" will be presented in Part IV. With regard to sampling, it

---

5 www.whitehouse.gov/omb/fedreg_1997standards/
www.whitehouse.gov/sites/default/files/omb/inforeg/statpolicy/standards_stat_surveys.pdf.
6 "Member States shall prohibit the processing of personal data revealing racial or ethnic origin, political opinions, religious or philosophical beliefs, trade-union membership, and the processing of data concerning health or sex life." Directive 95/46/EC of the European Parliament and of the Council of 24 October 1995 on the protection of individuals with regard to the processing of personal data and on the free movement of such data (article 8.1). Official Journal L 281, 23/11/1995 P. 0031 – 0050.

Box 11.2   ECRI/INED QUESTIONNAIRE (SIMON, 2007, P. 20)
VARIABLES ON ETHNIC OR NATIONAL ORIGIN

Ethnicity	Mother tongue	Continent and country of origin
Ethnicity of parents	Name and first name	(if outside Europe)
Appearance	Photo	Religious beliefs
Nationality	Race	Clothing
Citizenship	Skin colour	Traditions
Place of birth/ country of birth	Culture	Eating habits
Nationality or country of birth of parents	Customs	Sense of collective belonging
Language used	Religion	Tribe or ethnic group

---

should be noted that optimum sampling strategies depend very much on available national sampling frames and may therefore be hard to generalize.

Sampling problems

Some groups may be hard to sample but pose no additional problems. When a sampling frame is available, there is no particular problem at all. In countries like the Netherlands, the national statistical institute, Statistics Netherlands, can for example identify working women with young children from the population register, which is linked to administrative records. Organizations that cooperate with Statistics Netherlands can then invite these women to participate in a survey, which is no more difficult – and in fact probably easier – than a general survey. In other countries, it is only possible to identify and reach these women by asking screener questions in a general survey and asking them to participate in a follow-up survey. In countries with an up-to-date and accessible population register linked to administrative data – as in many Nordic countries and the Netherlands – conducting surveys among groups that are easily identifiable according to age, gender, labor market position, etc., is therefore not particularly difficult. Minority ethnic groups can be identified in a similar way, though this may be a little more difficult due to the factors given in Section 11.3.2. In other countries, host surveys with screener questions may have to be used.

Other surveys among specific groups do not have these sampling problems at all, because the group members are easily identifiable. One example is a survey among elderly people living in senior residential facilities. Once an accessible list is available (no minor feat), these people will be very easy to reach. Another example are surveys among students (such as the Programme for International Student Assessment or the Trends in International Mathematics and Science Study, where children answer questionnaires at school), among prisoners, and among members of the armed forces.

It becomes more difficult when the identifying characteristics of a specific group have not been recorded in registers, such as sexual orientation or physical disabilities. Especially where the incidence of a specific group is small, finding them through screening may become increasingly expensive. In such cases, commercial online panels are sometimes used that comprise many members of the specific group. Ellison and Gunstone (2009, p. 5), for example, base their study on the sexual orientation of LGBs on the British YouGov panel. This approach has some advantages, but also serious limitations:

> The chosen methodology has the benefit of allowing a large sample of people who have previously identified their sexual orientation as LGB to be included in the study. In addition, online self-completion surveys allow the respondent to experience some distance from the interviewer. An important caveat must be applied from the outset: even by weighting the results, it is impossible to know whether the composition of the sample by sexual orientation reflects that of the general population, or the LGB population. This applies equally to responses throughout the survey. The size and characteristics of the LGB population remain unknown.

11.4   Surveys of many different populations: example of European social survey

Cross-national surveys build on the lessons from general national surveys and surveys among specific groups in two ways. First, with regard to national populations, a cross-national survey should try to include and identify specific groups, such as the elderly and immigrants. This will ensure that the target population is fully represented in each country and also that these specific groups can be compared across countries. Secondly, when designing a cross-national survey, it needs to be recognized that each national population can be seen as a specific group in a comparative survey. This means that the concepts and questions should be relevant in every participating country, that the cross-national survey methodology can be adopted in every country, and that in some cases adaptations are required to accommodate national situations.

The ESS (see www.europeansocialsurvey.org) was conceived at the end of the last century to provide high-quality comparative data on social and political attitudes (ESF, 1999). It is an academic biennial face-to-face survey conducted in more than thirty European countries, which started in 2002. The ESS is similar in many ways to the American General Social Survey (GSS; see www3.norc.org/gss+website), except that it focuses specifically on comparing countries and on improving survey methodology. More information on the ESS may be found in Jowell, Kaase, Fitzgerald, and Eva (2007); Jowell, Roberts, Fitzgerald, and Eva (2007); Koch, Blom, Stoop, and Kappelhof (2009); Stoop, Billiet, Koch, and Fitzgerald (2010); and Stoop and Harrison (2012b). The survey data, including documentation and metadata, are publicly available at www.europeansocialsurvey.org.

One key asset of the ESS is that it allows the study of ethnic minorities across Europe because respondents in every country are asked about their citizenship and country of birth. One risk of the ESS is that it was developed in Western European countries, and that concepts and questions are therefore less relevant in Central European or Muslim countries. It is encouraging that since Round 1 many Central European countries have joined the ESS; recent additions are Kosovo and Albania. ESS questions have also been fielded in the Arab community in Israel, for example, in a special survey (Obeid & Baron-Epel, 2012).

Many components of the survey process, such as sampling designs and strategies for minimizing nonresponse, are aimed at ensuring that the data are representative of what could have been collected from the larger population. The questionnaire has a much more direct bearing on the nature of the data itself, however – not just the form in which it is captured, but also its quality. The quality of a questionnaire can also have an impact on the representation of the population, assuming that questions that are not relevant or not comprehensible for specific groups, languages, or countries can result in unit nonresponse, item nonresponse, or erroneous or biased answers.

11.4.1 Good questions and good translations

The ESS questionnaire comprises both core and rotating modules, taking about sixty minutes to complete in its source language English; in translation it may diverge from this length (European Social Survey, 2002). Academics compete for the chance to help design rotating modules that cover particular areas in more depth. In addition, there is a short supplementary questionnaire which fields the Schwartz scale of human values (twenty-one items) plus a number of alternative formulations of earlier questions for testing purposes (Saris & Gallhofer, 2007a, 2007b).

Stoop and Harrison (2012b) give a summary of the steps in questionnaire development in cross-national surveys. Data quality comes in two varieties: validity (the degree to which it has measured what it purports to measure) and reliability (the degree to which comparable results could be reproduced under similar conditions). Saris and Gallhofer (2007b) describe questionnaire design in the ESS. A comprehensive study on questionnaire design in general is given in Saris and Gallhofer (2007a). Harkness, Edwards, Hansen, Millar, and Villar (2010) and Harkness, Van de Vijver, and Johnson (2003) focus on questionnaire design from a comparative point of view.

An important step in making a questionnaire relevant for all potential respondents is to make sure that the concepts are relevant for every group. A core issue here is the choice between Ask the Same Question (ASQ) and Ask Different Questions (ADQ) (Harkness, 2007; Harkness *et al.*, 2010; Harkness *et al.*, 2003). Cross-cultural and cross-national surveys use a mix of ASQ and ADQ strategies (Harkness, 2011).

To facilitate comparability, it is crucial that the translation remains close to the content of the source questionnaire but is not a literal translation. In the ESS, annotations are added to the source questionnaire, which do not form part of the final questionnaire but serve as a guide to translators. Annotations can be used to explain specific concepts (government: "The people now governing, the present regime") or fairly general ("should" in the sense of "ought to"; not in the sense of "must") (ESS source questionnaire, Round 4). Translation is carried out in accordance with the TRAPD approach: Translation, Review, Adjudication, Pretesting, and Documentation (Harkness, 2003; 2007). These five steps are performed by three agents: translator, reviewer, and adjudicator. Two translators translate questions independently and then take part in one or more review sessions attended by an independent reviewer who has good translation skills and is familiar with the principles of questionnaire design and the particular study design and topics covered. The adjudicator takes the final decision on which translation options to adopt. Central to TRAPD is the team approach and the detailed documentation required. Additional procedures have been developed for countries with shared languages.

Countries go through these procedures for each of their main languages and for minority language groups constituting more than 5 percent of the population. Translation for minority language groups is costly, however, and very small minority language groups are still excluded. Some (telephone) surveys use trained interpreters to interview minority language speakers as a cost-effective solution. Positive results are achieved in this area, for instance in a health survey (Hu, Link, & Mokdad, 2010). However, given that the exact formulation can have large effects on the answers to attitude questions and the great care that is taken to translate the survey questionnaire into the main language, the use of interpreters is not allowed in the ESS. The consequence is, of course, that some sample units will not be able to respond due to language problems.

Questionnaires need to be tested before and after translation. A series of procedures has been implemented for this in the ESS. The Survey Quality Predictor program (SQP) looks at the form and structure of the question – its length, the number of complex words it contains, and so on – and then, based on what is known about the quality of items with similar features that have been fielded before, makes a prediction about how well the question will perform (Saris & Gallhofer, 2007a). SQP also helps to assess whether sources and target questions have the same formal structure. Cognitive interviewing tests what questions mean to respondents (Fitzgerald, Widdop, Gray, & Collins, 2011), and native speakers (Dept, Ferrari, & Wäyrynen, 2010) compare the source version and the translated version. In addition, pilot studies are conducted in which large numbers of items are tested on a sample large enough to include meaningful numbers of important subgroups.

In this way, serious efforts are made to obtain a questionnaire that is relevant for different groups and in different countries, where questions mean the same thing in each country, culture, and language and are easy to understand and answer.

11.4.2 Representing the populations

Contracting

In the ESS, national funders select their own field work organizations, so that the organization best able to conduct the survey in each country in accordance with the general specifications can be selected (Jowell, Roberts, Fitzgerald, & Eva, 2007). As a consequence, in some countries the survey is conducted by the national statistical institute or a university (an option that is not feasible in every country) and in other countries by a commercial survey agency or a not-for-profit organization.

Coverage

The target population of the ESS includes all persons aged 15 years and over (no upper age limit) resident within private households in each country, regardless of their nationality, citizenship, or language. Here, we see the first threat to the target of full representativeness: persons living in non-residential households are excluded from the target population. How many potential respondents are affected by this is not known, nor is the impact on the comparability of survey populations across countries, for example because of differences in the number of people in the armed forces or homeless people. A second threat is the exclusion of distant regions, for example inhabitants of Guadeloupe, French Guiana, Réunion, and Martinique (France), the Azores and Madeira (Portugal), Bonaire, Saint Eustace, and Saba (the Netherlands) and the Canary Islands, Ceuta, and Melilla (Spain).

Sampling

The sample must be selected using strict random probability methods at every stage and respondents must be interviewed face to face. Necessarily, different sampling frames, designs, and procedures have to be used across countries; an expert sampling panel helps each country to find the optimum solution in their case (see Häder & Lynn, 2007). Samples are drawn from population, household, or address registers or constructed in a controlled random walk procedure, depending on what is available in different countries.

Nonresponse

According to the ESS specifications, the proportion of noncontacts should not exceed 3 percent of all sampled units, and the minimum target response rate should be 70 percent. Detailed guidelines for response enhancement (Koch, Fitzgerald, Stoop, & Widdop, 2010) and feedback from previous rounds can help countries maximize their response rates. Field work progress is closely monitored. In addition, interviewers are provided with detailed contact forms (see Blom, Lynn, & Jäckle, 2008; Stoop *et al.*, 2010; Stoop, Devacht, Billiet, Loosveldt, & Philippens, 2003) to record information on respondent selection within households, the timing and outcomes of each visit, and interviewer observations with regard to each contact as well as characteristics of the household and the dwelling.

The contact form data are used to check adherence to the specifications, analyze non-response and provide feedback for the next round (see Stoop *et al.*, 2010). Based on these "paradata," response rates can be calculated in a harmonized way across countries, non-contacts and refusals can be distinguished, the effectiveness of field efforts and call schedules can be assessed, and nonresponse bias can be analyzed. One special feature of the ESS contact forms is that the resultant anonymized file is publicly available for secondary research. This means that researchers all over the world can – and do – use this information to analyze nonresponse (e.g., Blom, 2012; Kreuter & Kohler, 2009).

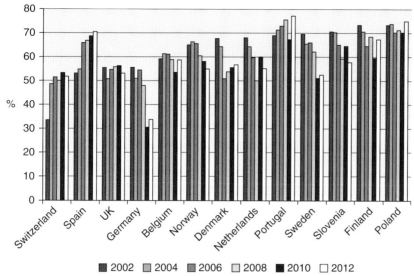

Figure 11.2   ESS response rates in countries participating in rounds 1–6
Note: This information is based partly on the contact forms (Matsuo, Billiet, Loosveldt, & Malnar, 2010) and partly on country reports (European Social Survey, 2012, 2014), as not all countries provided complete call records. Only countries for which the Round 6 data were released in 2013 are included.

The target response rate of 70 percent is exceeded in some countries, but is not reached in many (see Figure 11.2, which only includes those countries that have participated in each round – though some countries that did not participate in every round exceeded the 70 percent target). Some countries improve over time (e.g., Switzerland and Spain), whereas others (e.g., Germany, Sweden) perform worse.

Excluded and underrepresented groups

This short overview makes clear that even in a highly standardized survey such as the ESS, where great efforts are made to pursue high response rates and where improving survey methodology is an independent aim, some groups will remain underrepresented. These groups include people living in distant regions, minority language speakers, people who are mentally or physically unable to cooperate, and people who are unavailable during field work. Noncontact is a fairly limited problem in most countries, due to the large number of calls that have to be made.

Refusal is the main cause of nonresponse, in the ESS as in most surveys. Stoop *et al.* (2010) have shown that refusal is most likely related to participation in social activities, interest in politics, participation in voluntary or charity associations, watching television, and attitude towards surveys. This means that people who participate less in social activities, are less interested in politics, do less voluntary work, watch TV more, and do not like surveys are more likely to be underrepresented.

Even in a methodologically sound (and rather expensive) survey such as the European Social Survey, then, it is far from easy to obtain a high response rate from the general population. A higher response rate, especially among minority groups, might have been possible if, say, on-the-spot translation and interviewing by proxy had been allowed. A decrease in nonresponse error would then probably have resulted in an increase in measurement error. This shows that quality issues in studying hard-to-survey populations should never be viewed in isolation.

11.5 Conclusion

This chapter had three aims. The first was to show that being hard to reach or hard to survey can in many cases be ascribed to only a limited extent to characteristics of the survey population. The survey design in general and the survey mode in particular, the quality of interviewers, the care with which questions have been designed, the availability of a questionnaire in minority languages, the topic of the survey, and many other factors determine whether persons can be reached and whether they participate. The second aim was more philosophical, namely to show how surveys among minorities are often set up from an "us" (the researcher) versus "them" (the target population) perspective. As Singer (2011, p. 390) says: "we should improve the survey experience for respondents." This could imply that we have to convey the message that the survey is not for "us" but also for "them," as many survey methodologists will certainly agree.

The final aim of this chapter was to show how the European Social Survey strives for questionnaires that are relevant for all, and for a response representing all populations. Despite these efforts, specific groups are still underrepresented, though the ESS has now become a major source for studying and comparing immigrant populations in Europe.

References

Anderson, T., & Stewart, J. B. (2007). *Introduction to African American Studies: Transdisciplinary Approaches and Implications*. Baltimore: Inprint.

Aspinall, P. J. (2009). *Estimating the Size and Composition of the Lesbian, Gay, and Bisexual Population in Britain*. Equality and Human Rights Commission, Research Report 37.

Blom, A. G. (2012). Explaining cross-country differences in survey contact rates: application of decomposition methods. *Journal of the Royal Statistical Society: Series A (Statistics in Society)*, 175, Part 1, 217–42.

Blom, A., Lynn, P., & Jäckle, A. (2008). *Understanding Cross-National Differences in Unit Non-Response: The Role of Contact Data*. ISER Working Paper Series No. 2008–01, University of Essex.

Braun, M. (2003). Communication and social cognition. In J. A. Harkness, F. J. R. van de Vijver, & P. Ph. Mohler (eds.), *Cross-Cultural Survey Methods* (pp. 57–67). Hoboken, NJ: John Wiley & Sons.

D'Arrigo, J., Durrant, G. B., & Steele, F. (2009). *Using Field Process Data to Predict Best Times of Contact, Conditioning on Household and Interviewer Influences.* Working Paper M09–12. University of Southampton.

Davis, R. E., Caldwell, C. H., Couper, M. P., Janz, N. K., Alexander, G. L., Greene, S. M., *et al.* (2012). Ethnic identity, questionnaire content, and the dilemma of race matching in surveys of African Americans by African American interviewers. *Field Methods*, 25(2), 142–61.

de Leeuw, E. D. (2005). To mix or not to mix data collection modes in surveys. *Journal of Official Statistics*, 21(2), 233–55.

(2008). Choosing the method of data collection. In E. D. de Leeuw, J. J. Hox, & D. A. Dillman (eds.), *International Handbook of Survey Methodology* (pp. 299–316). New York: Taylor & Francis Group/Lawrence Erlbaum Associates.

de Leeuw, E. D., Dillman, D. A., & Hox, J. J. (2008). Mixed mode surveys: when and why. In E. D. de Leeuw, J. J. Hox, & D. A. Dillman (eds.), *International Handbook of Survey Methodology* (pp. 113–35). New York: Taylor & Francis Group/Lawrence Erlbaum Associates.

de Voogd, L. (2007). Ethnic and cultural surveys. What are the challenges in conducting surveys on ethnicity and religion. *Research World*, December 2007, 20–21.

Dept, S., Ferrari, A., & Wäyrynen, L. (2010). Developments in translation verification procedures in three multilingual assessments: a plea for an integrated translation and adaptation monitoring tool. In J. A. Harkness, M. Braun, B. Edwards, T. P. Johnson, L. E. Lyberg, P. Ph. Mohler, B. E. Pennell, & T. W. Smith (eds.), *Survey Methods in Multinational, Multiregional, and Multicultural Contexts* (pp. 157–73). Hoboken, NJ: John Wiley & Sons.

Dillman, D. A. (2000). *Mail and Internet Surveys: The Tailored Design Method* (2nd edn.). New York: John Wiley & Sons.

Dillman, D. A., & Messer, B. L. (2010). Mixed-mode surveys. In P. Marsden & J. Wright (eds.), *Handbook of Survey Research* (2nd edn.) (pp. 551–74). Bingley: Emerald Group Publishing Ltd.

Ellison, G., & Gunstone, B. (2009). *Sexual Orientation Explored: A Study of Identity, Attraction, Behaviour and Attitudes in 2009.* Equality and Human Rights Commission. Research Report 35.

ESF (1999). *The European Social Survey (ESS) – A Research Instrument for the Social Sciences in Europe.* Report prepared for the Standing Committee for the Social Sciences (SCSS) of the European Science Foundation. Strasbourg, European Science Foundation.

European Social Survey (2002). Core Questionnaire Development. www.europeansocial survey.org/index.php%3Foption=com_content%26view=article&id=62%26Itemid=404 (downloaded August 8, 2011).

European Social Survey. (2014). *ESS6–2012 Survey Documentation Report.* Edition 1.3. Bergen, European Social Survey Data Archive, Norwegian Social Science Data Services.

Feskens, R. C. W. (2009). Difficult groups in survey research and the development of tailor-made approach strategies. Dissertation: Universiteit Utrecht.

Feskens, R., Hox, J., Lensvelt-Mulders, G., & Schmeets, H. (2007). Nonresponse among ethnic minorities: a multivariate analysis. *Journal of Official Statistics*, 23(3), 387–408.

Fitzgerald, R., Widdop, S., Gray, M., & Collins, D. (2011). Identifying sources of error in cross-national questionnaires: application of an error source typology to cognitive interview data. *Journal of Official Statistics*, 7(4), 569–99.

Goyder, J. (1987). *The Silent Minority. Nonrespondents on Sample Surveys*. Cambridge: Polity Press.

Goyder, J., Boyer, L., & Martinelli, G. (2006). Integrating exchange and heuristic theories of survey nonresponse. *Bulletin de Méthodologie Sociologique*, 92, October 2006, 28–44.

Groves, R. M. (1989). *Survey Errors and Survey Costs*. New York: John Wiley & Sons.
   (2006). Nonresponse rates and nonresponse bias in household surveys. *Public Opinion Quarterly*, 70(5), 646–75.

Groves, R. M., & Couper, M. P. (1998). *Nonresponse in Household Interview Surveys*. New York: John Wiley & Sons.

Groves, R. M., & McGonagle, K. A. (2001). A theory-guided interview training protocol regarding survey participation. *Journal of Official Statistics*, 17(2), 249–66.

Groves, R. M., Presser, S., & Dipko, S. (2004). The role of topic interest in survey participation decisions. *Public Opinion Quarterly*, 68, 2–31.

Groves, R. M., Singer, E., & Corning, A. (2000). Leverage-saliency theory of survey participation. Description and an illustration. *Public Opinion Quarterly*, 64, 299–308.

Häder, S., & Lynn, P. (2007). How representative can a multi-nation survey be? In R. Jowell, C. Roberts, R. Fitzgerald & G. Eva (eds.), *Measuring Attitudes Cross-Nationally. Lessons from the European Social Survey* (pp. 33–52). London: Sage.

Harkness, J. A. (2003). Questionnaire translation. In J. A. Harkness, F. J. R. van de Vijver, & P. Ph. Mohler (eds.), *Cross-Cultural Survey Methods* (pp. 35–56). Hoboken, NJ: John Wiley & Sons.
   (2007). Improving the comparability of translations. In R. Jowell, C. Roberts, R. Fitzgerald, & G. Eva (eds.), *Measuring Attitudes Cross-Nationally. Lessons from the European Social Survey* (pp. 79–93). London: Sage.
   (2011). Questionnaire design. Cross-cultural survey guidelines. http://ccsg.isr.umich.%20edu/pdf/06QuestionnaireDesignFeb2012.pdf (downloaded October 15, 2012).

Harkness, J. A., Edwards, B., Hansen, S. E., Millar, D. R., & Villar, A. (2010). Designing questionnaires for multi-population research. In J. A. Harkness, M. Braun, B. Edwards, T. P. Johnson, L. E. Lyberg, P. Ph. Mohler, B.-E. Pennell, & T. W. Smith (eds.), *Survey Methods in Multinational, Multiregional, and Multicultural Contexts* (pp. 33–58). Hoboken, NJ: John Wiley & Sons.

Harkness, J. A., Van de Vijver, F. J. R., & Johnson, T. P. (2003). Questionnaire design in comparative research. In J. A. Harkness, F. J. R. van de Vijver, & P. Ph. Mohler (eds.), *Cross-Cultural Survey Methods* (pp. 19–34). Hoboken, NJ: John Wiley & Sons.

Hu, S. S., Link, M. W., & Mokdad, A. H. (2010). Reaching linguistically isolated people: findings from a telephone survey using real-time interpreters. *Field Methods*, 22(1), 39–56.

Irving Fisher Committee on Central Bank Statistics. (2008). STCPM31: Accounting for the very rich in household surveys of income and wealth. IFC Bulletin No 28. IFC's contribution to the 56th ISI Session, Lisbon, 2007, Switzerland, Basel: Bank for International Settlements, 399–431. www.bis.org/ifc/publ/ifcb28.pdf#page=409 (downloaded October 15, 2012).

Jäckle, A., Roberts, C., & Lynn, P. (2008). Assessing the effect of data collection mode on measurement. *International Statistical Review*, 78(1), 3–20.

Johnston, L. G., & Sabin, K. (2010). Sampling hard-to-reach populations with respondent-driven sampling. *Methodological Innovations Online*, 5(2), 38–48.

Jowell, R., Kaase, M., Fitzgerald, R., & Eva, G. (2007). The European Social Survey as a measurement model. In R. Jowell, C. Roberts, R. Fitzgerald, & G. Eva (eds.), *Measuring Attitudes Cross-Nationally. Lessons from the European Social Survey* (pp. 1–31). London: Sage.

Jowell, R., Roberts, C., Fitzgerald, R., & Eva, G. (eds.) (2007). *Measuring Attitudes Cross-Nationally. Lessons from the European Social Survey*. London: Sage.

Koch, A., Blom, A. G., Stoop, I., & Kappelhof, J. (2009). Data collection quality assurance in cross-national surveys: the example of the ESS. *Methoden Daten Analysen. Zeitschrift für Empirische Sozialforschung*, 3(2): 219–47.

Koch, A., Fitzgerald, R., Stoop, I., & Widdop, S. (2010). *Field Procedures in the European Social Survey Round 5: Enhancing Response Rates*. Mannheim, European Social Survey, GESIS.

Kreuter, F., & Kohler, U. (2009). Analyzing contact sequences in call record data: potential and limitations of sequence indicators for nonresponse adjustments in the European Social Survey. *Journal of Official Statistics*, 25(2), 203–26.

Loosveldt, G. (2008). Face-to-face interviews. In E. D. de Leeuw, J. J. Hox, D. A. Dillman (eds.), *International Handbook of Survey Methodology* (pp. 201–20). New York: Taylor & Francis Group/Lawrence Erlbaum Associates.

Matsuo, H., Billiet, J., Loosveldt, G., & Malnar, B. (2010). *Response-based Quality Assessment of ESS Round 4: Results for 30 Countries Based on Contact Files*. Onderzoeksverslag Centrum voor Sociologisch Onderzoek. CeSO/SM/2010-2.

Obeid, S., & Baron-Epel, O. (2012). *The Social Capital of the Arab Community in Israel*. Paper presented at the International Conference on European Social Survey, Nicosia, Cyprus, November 2012.

Purdon, S., Campanelli, P., & Sturgis, P. (1999). Interviewers calling strategies on face-to-face interview survey. *Journal of Official Statistics*, 15(2), 199–216.

Said, E. W. (1979). *Orientalism*. New York: Vintage books. 25th Anniversary Edition (2003).

Saris, W. E., & Gallhofer, I. N. (2007a). *Design, Evaluation, and Analysis of Questionnaires for Survey Research*. Wiley Series in Survey Methodology. New York: John Wiley & Sons.

(2007b). Can questions travel successfully? In R. Jowell, C. Roberts, R. Fitzgerald, & G. Eva (eds.), *Measuring Attitudes Cross-Nationally: Lessons from the European Social Survey* (pp. 53–77). London: Sage.

Schaeffer, N. C., Dykema, J., & Maynard, D. W. (2010). Interviewers and interviewing. In P. Marsden & J. Wright (eds.), *Handbook of Survey Research* (2nd edn.) (pp. 37–70). Bingley: Emerald Group Publishing Ltd.

Simon, P. (2007). *Ethnic Statistics and Data Protection in the Council of Europe Countries*. Study Report. Strasbourg: European Commission against Racism and Intolerance (ECRI).

Singer, E. (2011). Towards a cost-benefit theory of survey participation: evidence, further test, and implications. *Journal of Official Statistics*, 27(2), 379–92.

Smith, T. M. (2003). Developing comparable questions in cross-national surveys. In J. A. Harkness, F. J. R. van de Vijver, & P. Ph. Mohler (eds.), *Cross-Cultural Survey Methods* (pp. 69–91). Hoboken, NJ: John Wiley & Sons.

Stoop, I. (2005). *The Hunt for the Last Respondent*. The Hague, Social and Cultural Planning Office.

(2012). Unit non-response due to refusal. In L. Gideon (ed.), *Handbook of Survey Methodology for the Social Sciences* (pp. 121–47). Heidelberg: Springer.

Stoop, I., Billiet, J., Koch, A., & Fitzgerald, R. (2010). *Improving Survey Response: Lessons Learned from the European Social Survey*. Chichester: John Wiley & Sons.

Stoop, I., Devacht, S., Billiet, J., Loosveldt, G., & Philippens, M. (2003). *The Development of a Uniform Contact Description Form in the ESS*. Paper presented at the 14th International Workshop on Household Survey Nonresponse, Leuven, September 2003.

Stoop, I., & Harrison, E. (2012a). Classification of surveys. In L. Gideon (ed.), *Handbook of Survey Methodology for the Social Sciences* (pp. 7–21). Heidelberg: Springer.

(2012b). Repeated cross-sectional surveys using F2F. In L. Gideon (ed.), *Handbook of Survey Methodology for the Social Sciences* (pp. 249–76). Heidelberg: Springer.

Tourangeau, R., & Smith, T. W. (1996). Asking sensitive questions: the impact of data collection mode, question format, and question context. *Public Opinion Quarterly*, 60(2), 275–304.

Van Ingen, E., Stoop, I., & Breedveld, K. (2009). Nonresponse in the Dutch time use survey: strategies for response enhancement and bias reduction. *Field Methods*, 21(1), pp. 69–90.

West, B., & Olson, K. (2010). How much of interviewer variance is really nonresponse error variance. *Public Opinion Quarterly*, 74(5), 1004–26.

12

Surveying cultural and linguistic minorities

JANET HARKNESS, MATHEW STANGE, KRISTEN L. CIBELLI,
PETER MOHLER, AND BETH-ELLEN PENNELL

12.1 Introduction

Cultural and linguistic minorities can be hard to survey either as the target population of interest or as a subpopulation of a general population survey. The challenges associated with studying these minorities are important to understand in order to assess and address the survey error that can be introduced when designing and implementing studies that include these groups. This chapter begins with a description of what constitutes cultural and linguistic minorities, based on a systematic review of the literature (see Chapter 5 in this volume, for a complete description of the process). We note that the literature in this area is largely limited to research among cultural and linguistic minorities in the context of Western and industrialized countries. Therefore, we supplement this literature by drawing upon our own experience and discussions with colleagues who conduct research among cultural and linguistic minorities in other parts of the world. This review is followed by a discussion of the potential challenges faced by researchers interested in surveying cultural and linguistic minorities and approaches taken to address these challenges in the areas of sampling, questionnaire development, adaptation and translation, pretesting, and data collection. We then discuss additional approaches to studying these hard-to-survey populations including qualitative, mixed-methods, and community-based research methods and how these can complement survey methods. The concluding section addresses needed improvements in the documentation and development of research methods to expand solutions and increase the quality of hard-to-survey cultural and linguistic minority research.

12.2 Defining cultural and linguistic minorities

This section sets out the key features of cultural and linguistic minorities. Three core concepts are defined and discussed. First, we define minority populations followed by a discussion of linguistic and cultural minorities. The distinct concept of hard-to-survey is also relevant and discussed in this context (also see Chapter 1 in this volume). On the one hand, it is a relatively straightforward task to define these concepts; however, as we discuss below, applying these definitions in a survey context is far more complicated. Formal definitions serve as a good starting point for this discussion, however.

12.2.1 *Minority population*

The United Nations defines a minority population as

> a group of citizens of a State, constituting a numerical minority and in a non-dominant position in that State, endowed with ethnic, religious or linguistic characteristics which differ from those of the majority of the population, having a sense of solidarity with one another, motivated, if only implicitly, by a collective will to survive and whose aim it is to achieve equality with the majority in fact and in law.
>
> (United Nations, 1992)

For our purposes, this definition has several weaknesses, first among them that the definition of minority includes the concept itself. This definition acknowledges that some populations in nation states may be exploited and suppressed by the majority population. For the purpose of finding a workable definition for survey research, one could delete the political aspect of survival and equality and instead use the more commonly used term cohesion. In addition, one can subsume ethnic and religious characteristics under the term cultural. Thus, our definition of a minority population might read: *A minority group is a group of residents in a nation state, which is a distinct subgroup of that state's resident population. It is in a nondominant position, endowed with cultural or linguistic character-istics that differ from other groups. The subgroup has an internal cohesion based on its distinct characteristics.*

12.2.2 *Linguistic minority*

Linguistic minorities are groups using or preferring a language other than the majority or dominant language of a given society, community, or country. As defined by the European Charter for Regional or Minority Languages, "regional or minority languages" are: "traditionally used within a given territory of a State by nationals of that State who form a group numerically smaller than the rest of the State's population; and are different from the official language(s) of that State" (Council of Europe, 1992, Article 1). With 6,909 known living languages around the world (Lewis, 2009) and 193 internationally recognized sovereign states, the vast majority of languages are in fact minority languages.

Interestingly, there is no consensus in the literature as to the definition of a dialect or language variant. One simple test for language difference is mutual intelligibility (Childs, 2012). This definition explicitly acknowledges that some language differences are for political, religious, and other reasons. An example is the re-introduction of a Serb language after the dissolution of Yugoslavia in 1992 and the codification of Cyrillic as the official alphabet in Serbia versus Latin alphabets used in other parts of the former Yugoslavia (Neweklowsky, 2002).

It is also important to consider language proficiency and diversity within a particular linguistic minority even if the group's members share a common language or cultural ancestry, that is, members may speak only one language while others may be proficient in one or more languages. Members of a linguistic minority may also speak a number of different dialects.

Immigrant groups whose situation differs from that of indigenous national linguistic minorities present a special case. Indigenous linguistic minorities may have lived in a region for a long period. An example is Danish-speaking residents of northern Germany who became German nationals as a result of World War I.[1] Spanish-speaking immigrants in the United States are yet another example. The situation of immigrants is unique because they typically move into an existing majority language system. However, members of a cultural and linguistic immigrant group typically are at various stages of acculturation into the majority cultural frame and language. There is often political controversy with regard to use of the minority languages. For example, the German-speaking majority of the Alto Adige (Südtirol) became a minority after World War I, when the region became part of Italy. In an attempt to repress the linguistic minority, Mussolini relocated Italians from the south. After a long battle for autonomy, the Alto Adige became an autonomous region in 1972.[2] Another approach used to obstruct the survival of minority languages is to forbid the use of the language in schools. Historically, this happened in Scotland[3] and Wales[4] and is true today for the Tajiik's language Sarikol in China (Boehm, 2009)[5]. The list of such conflicts is long. The reason for the conflict often centers on the argument that retaining one's native language is seen as a refusal or failure to assimilate into the host or dominant country's language and culture; minority languages may also be associated with separatist movements or groups resisting the influence and control of the majority. The language a group prefers is in many instances one of the most obvious indicators of cultural identity, and in recognition of this, the United Nations and recent European Union legislation have attempted to ensure that languages spoken by minority groups receive official protection.

Finally, we turn to the notion of linguistic isolation. In the US context, people speaking English "less than well" have been termed "linguistically isolated" by the US Census Bureau. In response to advocacy groups, this terminology has been replaced in favor of less stigmatizing language.[6] However, the term "linguistic isolation" does provide a sense of the challenge faced by linguistic minorities who are not bilingual or do not speak the majority language proficiently. Linguistic minorities not proficient in the majority language are often marginalized in society, face higher unemployment, lower wages (Soifer, 2009), and tend to lack access to health and other social services (Lee, Nguyen, Jawad, & Kurata,

---

1 See www.schleswig-holstein.de/Portal/DE/LandLeute/Minderheiten/Daenisch/daenisch_node.html, last retrieved January 15, 2013.
2 See de.wikipedia.org/wiki/Geschichte_S%C3%BCdtirols, last retrieved September 21, 2012.
3 Reflected in the need for a Scottish Gaelic language act: www.legislation.gov.uk/ssi/2006/31/made, last retrieved January 15, 2013.
4 Similarly for Welsh: Welsh Language Act www.legislation.gov.uk/ukpga/1993/38/section/22/enacted, last retrieved January 15, 2013.
5 See www.ethnologue.com/show_language.asp?code=srh, last retrieved January 15, 2013.
6 See http://blog.aaanet.org/2011/05/04/elimination-of-linguistically-isolated-as-classification-by-the-u-s-census-bureau/, last retrieved January 23, 2014.

2008). They are also often excluded from surveys due to cost and other factors that are discussed further below.

12.2.3 Cultural minority

Johnson, O'Rourke, Chavez, Sudman, Warnecke, Lacey *et al.* (1997, p. 87) define culture from a cross-cultural psychology perspective as "a social group with a shared language and set of norms, values, beliefs, expectations, and life experiences." In social theory, culture is simply defined as the realm of values and value systems (Mohler, 1978; Parsons, 1991). The sociological definition avoids problems that may arise from linking culture directly with language. An example of a nonlinguistically defined cultural group is members of a religious denomination. Here, differences in values and norms may exist but often not in language use. Groups that are considered cultural minorities may or may not share the majority language of a society, community, or group as their first language. Cultural minority is defined by differences perceived by both the minority group itself and other groups. Therefore, there needs to be observable cultural differences between the target minority and other social groups in the society, including the dominant majority. The characteristics that constitute this difference are therefore ideas, i.e., values and beliefs including religion, customs such as specific dress codes, nutrition, and observance of holidays, as well as social behavior, which can encompass different communication styles, or gender-connected behavior.

12.2.4 Hard to survey

Most large societies have cultural and linguistic minorities, with considerable diversity among these groups throughout the world. Nonetheless, a defining feature of cultural and linguistic minorities in the context of hard-to-survey populations is the minority status of the group. To be considered a cultural and linguistic minority, the group must have a nondominant position in the cultural and/or linguistic fabric of the larger social unit. A nondominant position is often associated with lower social status, access to fewer resources associated with social capital, possible stigma, and exclusion. Groups who are numerically in the minority but whose culture and/or language plays a dominant role in a society would not be included in our definition. For example, linguistic groups in countries with several official languages of equal status, although numerical differences may be considerable (e.g., German, French, and Italian in Switzerland), the allocation of power makes the notion of minority as subordinate for the French- and Italian-speaking populations of Switzerland less appropriate.

Examples of cultural and linguistic minorities can include immigrant populations, native or indigenous populations, small culturally distinct peoples living within the borders of a state with a different majority culture and language, and tribal or ethnic groups in culturally and linguistically diverse countries. An immigrant group may be one of many immigrant groups in countries with high rates of immigration such as in the United States, the United

Kingdom, Canada, and Australia. In this context, people from different countries and backgrounds may be grouped together as "immigrants" or into relatively broad categories (e.g., "Asians" or "Latinos"). Immigrants may be from a particular country or region due to historical and economic ties, such as Turkish immigrants in Germany or Indonesians in the Netherlands. Indigenous or native populations include American Indians, First Nations people in Canada, or Aborigines in Australia. Groups that have been subsumed into states with a different majority culture include such examples as the Basques and Catalans in Spain. Many linguistic minorities can be found in highly linguistically diverse countries such as India and Indonesia and many African countries such as Nigeria, Liberia, and Sierra Leone, for example.

In the context of this chapter, the target population of interest should also be hard to survey, acknowledging that there are many cultural and/or linguistic minorities that are fairly easy to identify and interview. The Sorbish minority near Berlin, Germany, for example, are an acknowledged national minority in Germany, with their own language. They live in a well-defined area and are easily accessible and typically included in German national surveys. So, although the Sorbish minority is by definition both a cultural and linguistic minority, it is anything but hard to reach.

Some cultural and linguistic minorities are characterized by additional factors typically associated with hard-to-reach populations. For example, immigrant cultural or linguistic minorities may also be "undocumented" or in the host country illegally. Members of a cultural or linguistic minority may also be involved in activities that are illegal or stigmatized, for example sex workers (Agustín, 2007; Higgins, O'Reilly, Tashima, Crain, Beeker, Goldbaum *et al.*, 1996) and drug users (Johnson & Delgado, 1989; Kalunta-Crumpton, 2004), and sexual minorities (Stueve, O'Donnell, Duran, San Doval, & Blome, 2001). Fear and stigma associated with these situations or behaviors, added to the cultural and linguistic factors, make these subsets of cultural and linguistic minorities even more challenging to survey and therefore more prone to aspects of survey error.

In survey research, we seek a population that can be well defined. This definition must be able to be operationalized in the form of questions and procedures. We discuss this below.

12.3   Challenges and potential solutions

Researchers face various challenges when conducting studies of cultural and linguistic minorities whether these populations are the focus of the research or they are included in general population surveys. Challenges faced in defining, identifying, and gaining access to certain cultural and linguistic minorities contribute to researchers describing them as hard to survey. Further challenges arise in questionnaire development, adaptation, and translation. These issues are associated with potential sources of survey error that affect the quality of the collected data throughout the stages of the survey life cycle.

In this section, we draw upon the available literature on hard-to-survey cultural and linguistic minorities to discuss the challenges researchers face and present design and implementation solutions that can be effective in addressing these issues. We discuss sampling and coverage, questionnaire development, adaptation and translation, pretesting, aspects of data collection, and mixed-methods approaches. These approaches may not apply to all cultural and linguistic minority groups; researchers must judge each solution's appropriateness for the specific cultural and linguistic group under study.

12.3.1 Sampling and coverage

Identifying the target population in minority research is often problematic. Cultural and linguistic minorities may be hard to identify because the groups cannot be easily defined, they are small in number and/or widely dispersed among the general population, highly mobile, or they may resist contact from researchers. Language barriers or variation in languages can also present a barrier to survey participation, preventing coverage of cultural and linguistic groups. Often, researchers will face a combination of these factors. These challenges make constructing a sampling frame with adequate coverage of the population of interest and selecting a sample from that population difficult.

Defining the population

Defining the population of interest is the first task researchers must undertake. Frequently, no clear or agreed upon definition may exist for the minority group. For example, defining what constitutes the American Indian population in the United States is a challenge largely because of the diversity of approaches in considering American Indian identity. The population can include self-identified American Indians, the population residing on reservations, members listed on official tribal rolls, or individuals eligible for services by the Indian Health Service, among others (Lavelle, Larsen, & Gundersen, 2009)[7]. There can also be great diversity within a particular cultural and linguistic group. For example, while often lumped together under the umbrella term "Indian" or "Native American," the US Federal government recognizes 566 American Indian groups each with different language, cultural, economic, or social practices (US Bureau of Indian Affairs, 2012). In these cases, researchers must often establish their own operational definition. Indeed, this is true for the study of most cultural and linguistic minorities. For example, Latinos in the US are also a highly heterogeneous group, linked historically by a common language (Spanish) but from different countries with distinct cultures, varying rates of acculturation (Canales, Ganz, & Coscarelli, 1995), and diverse racial backgrounds (Lopez, 2008). Using broad cultural or ethnic categories can mask the specific concerns of diverse "hidden" communities when they are grouped into a general classification scheme. Too broad cultural and ethnic categories in general population surveys mean researchers are unable to make inferences to these populations. For example, a broad category of Asian masks the great cultural

---

7 The terminology used in Canada is "nation." The US terminology is rooted in legal conflicts of the past: nations can agree on treaties, tribes cannot, as stated in the US Indian Appropriation Act of March 3, 1871. See also www.bia.gov/FAQs/index.htm, last retrieved January 15, 2013.

diversity found in this group. The purposes of the research will likely determine how researchers define a target population, but researchers should consider collaboration with members of the cultural and linguistic minority in doing so. The goal is to develop a precise definition of the population that can be operationalized for data collection, particularly where household or other screening methods are needed to select a sample of the target population.

Researchers must also consider self-identification and the politics of cultural identity when conducting research among cultural and linguistic minorities. People may be motivated to identify with or to hide association with a particular cultural and linguistic group. For example, the US has seen increasing rates of self-identified American Indians and subsequent large increases in the census count of American Indians since 1960. This growth is too large to be attributed to demographic factors alone (Lavelle *et al.*, 2009; Passel, 1997). Increased self-identification as American Indian could be due to the concentration of American Indians in communities or perceived economic or other opportunities associated with the identity (Lavelle *et al.*, 2009). In contrast, some immigrants may not want to identify with their culture or language of origin in order to show that they have assimilated into their new country or for fear of deportation if they are "undocumented." How groups are classified can also be a contentious or sensitive issue. Out-of-date or inadequate terms for racial, ethnic, and linguistic groups may alienate some respondents causing them to refuse to respond altogether or skip offensive items (Garland, Spalek, & Chakraborti, 2006).

Developing the sampling frame

Another common issue in cultural and linguistic minority research is the lack of a reliable sampling frame (Faugier & Sargeant, 1997). Without a list, identifying members of a minority population may require extensive screening of households to identify the population of interest. Even where lists may exist, they can often be incomplete or out of date (Ngo-Metzger, Kaplan, Sorkin, Clarridge, & Phillips, 2004). Traditional methods of sampling, such as address-based sampling (ABS) and random digit dialing (RDD), may be ineffective when listings are inaccurate or unavailable, and when the population is highly mobile (Lavelle *et al.*, 2009). In these cases, sampling frames will have inadequate coverage of the population because of missing, duplicate, and erroneous elements. To overcome these challenges, other sampling techniques may be used, such as obtaining address lists from a service provider (e.g., Duffy, Goldberg, & Buchwald, 2006), using time-space sampling (e.g., Stueve *et al.*, 2001), or snowball, chain-referral, and respondent-driven sampling (RDS) techniques (Faugier & Sargeant, 1997; Heckathorn, 2007; see also Part IV of this volume). These sampling techniques allow researchers to recruit populations that are hard to identify and access, especially in contexts where cultural groups are distrustful or suspicious of outside researchers (e.g., Lavelle *et al.*, 2009; Shoultz, Oneha, Magnussen, Hla, Brees-Saunders, Cruz *et al.*, 2006). Another approach may be to use multiframe sampling or even aerial photography to compensate for inadequate coverage of other sampling frames (Behrens, Freedman, & McGuckin, 2009). Researchers should be cautious, though, about the assumptions of certain sampling techniques and understand the degree to which generalizability is limited by the sampling design (i.e., whether the design is a probability, quasi-probability, or nonprobability method of selection).

Other sampling considerations

Surveys may fail to provide adequate coverage of cultural and linguistic minorities because of the size of the subpopulation or the degree of dispersion of the subpopulation. Some cultural or linguistic minorities are clustered regionally, though many are not. When a cultural or linguistic minority is clustered, however, researchers may find that traditional approaches to sampling may be possible. Here, a frame can be constructed and targeted sampling or screening methods can be used to identify the target population. For example, Chavez, Hubbell, Misha, and Valdez (1997) used RDD to sample and survey Latinas living in Orange County, California. This approach worked because the target population was not geographically dispersed and had adequate phone coverage. Similarly, Sasao (1994) found that using Asian surname telephone listings was a successful method for sampling Asian Americans in five counties in California. This method was particularly beneficial for sampling from "ethnic enclaves" (e.g., Chinatown) which are often difficult for interviewers and researchers to access. However, given current rates of telephone and cell-phone-only coverage (Blumberg & Luke, 2011) and variation by demographics (e.g., 40.8 percent of Latinos reside in cell-phone-only households compared to lower rates among non-Latino Whites and African-Americans), the feasibility of telephone frames can be called into question depending on the goals of the survey. The increasing use of ABS, however, may provide new directions for sampling minority populations.

Even when the cultural and linguistic group is large and easily identifiable, such as the Latino population in parts of the southern United States, irregular housing creates an additional difficulty (O'Hegarty, Pederson, Thorne, Caraballo, Evans, Athey et al., 2010). If the minority is a subpopulation within a survey of the general population, it may be difficult to identify the sample member as a member of a cultural and linguistic minority if language or other barriers prevent contact (see Section 12.3.3 below). For example, a sample member who receives a mail survey in a language that they cannot read is not likely to respond to the request.

Mobility is yet another factor contributing to coverage problems of cultural and linguistic minority groups. This is particularly true of such US populations as Native Americans (Lavelle et al., 2009) and Latinos (Lindenberg, Solorzano, Vilaro, & Westbrook, 2001; O'Hegarty et al., 2010) and worldwide, asylum seekers and other displaced populations (Correa-Velez & Gifford, 2007). The nature of households and "fluid and complex" residence patterns of some cultural and linguistic minorities can present particular problems (Lindenberg et al., 2001; O'Hegarty et al., 2010). In these cases, traditional sampling techniques that sample households (e.g., ABS, RDD, and so on) may be inappropriate or inadequate.

Language barriers

Countries with sizable linguistic minority populations often exclude these groups from national surveys. As Lee and colleagues (2008) point out, most surveys conducted in the US are conducted in English only or English and Spanish (e.g., the Current Population Survey, the Behavioral Risk Factor Surveillance System, and the National Survey of Family Growth), excluding a sizable portion of the population that does not speak English or Spanish. On the other hand, the European Social Survey specifies that linguistic minority populations that comprise 5 percent or more of the participating countries' total population must be included with an appropriately translated instrument (European Science Foundation, 2001). Even when translation is provided for some languages, a translation may exclude speakers of less widely spoken dialects. For example, a 2010 government study interviewing Chinese immigrants to the US failed to take into account that many Chinese living in San Francisco spoke Cantonese rather than Mandarin (Zahnd, Holtby, & Grant, 2011). In China itself, it can be extremely difficult and costly to reach rural populations because there are so many local language variants and dialects. Interviewers working in rural China must be able to read and understand a Mandarin questionnaire but at the same time relay the questions to the respondents in a local dialect that can be understood.

12.3.2 Questionnaire development

A further set of challenges and opportunities for error arise in questionnaire development. The development of questionnaires for surveying hard-to-survey cultural and linguistic minorities must begin by following best practice recommendations for general questionnaire development (de Leeuw, Hox, & Dillman, 2007; Dillman, Smyth, & Christian, 2008; Groves, Fowler, Couper, Lepkowski, Singer, & Tourangeau, 2009). Researchers then must address language and questionnaire design issues pertinent to the specific hard-to-reach cultural and linguistic minority they are studying; notably, by providing survey instruments as well as other research materials such as consent forms (e.g., Carter-Pokras, Zambrana, Mora, & Aaby, 1999) in the appropriate languages through a careful process of adaptation and translation.

A small but growing literature demonstrates the effect cultural frame may have on survey response. When designing the questionnaire and other survey materials, it is important for researchers to attempt to identify and be informed by ways in which members of different cultures may differ systematically in how questions are understood and answered. Understanding of the population of interest and thorough pretesting are essential for the identification of potential problems with design considerations and instruments in order to avoid results plagued by measurement and nonresponse error. Often, such understanding comes through the use of qualitative research methods. We address these methods further in Section 12.4. Below, we discuss, in turn, adaptation and translation, current insights in the area of culture, cognition and response, and pretesting. In each of these areas we identify challenges that often arise, and, where possible, highlight current best practices or possible approaches to address these challenges.

Adaptation and translation

Adaptation is a process that changes aspects of a questionnaire to meet the need of the population of study. This process can involve changes to question content, format, response options, and the visual presentation of the instrument (Harkness, Villar, & Edwards, 2010). Researchers often employ adaptation to make questionnaires "culturally relevant." For example, a study of women of different ethnic backgrounds in the US found that some minorities defined and described physical activity in different ways than majority White women, requiring changes in question content (Eyler, Baker, Cromer, King, Brownson, & Donatelle, 1998). In a health survey of American Indians, Schroepfer, Matloub, Creswell, Strickland, and Anderson (2009) made changes to the response options to questions asking respondents about barriers to treatment. Lee and Schwarz (2014) has observed differences in how Latino Americans rate their health compared with English-speaking Americans, prompting her recommendation to order questions differently for Spanish-speaking respondents. Other factors frequently cited by researchers who study cultural and linguistic minorities are that lower educational and literacy levels encountered among these populations (Canales *et al.*, 1995; de la Puente & Stemper, 2003; Lavelle *et al.*, 2009; Lopez, 2008; O'Hegarty *et al.*, 2010) make self-administered surveys or heavily structured or complicated instruments such as diaries difficult to administer (Lopez, 2008). Others issues that have been found are a lack of familiarity using some types of response scales (particularly numeric scales) (Lopez, 2008) and comprehension problems with complex instructions which may result in errors or extensive missing data (Canales *et al.*, 1995). Other adaptations may need to be made to reflect differing cultural definitions of household, residence, and so on (Lavelle *et al.*, 2009).

Translation will often be required when surveying minority populations. When an official translation is not available, researchers sometimes ask bilingual interviewers to provide ad hoc translation of a written questionnaire – this practice is sometimes called "on sight" translation, "on the fly translation," or "oral translation." The use of interpreters is another technique sometimes employed in the absence of a translated questionnaire. In this case, the interviewer reads aloud the interview script in one language, which the interpreter is expected to translate into the language of the respondent. The interpreter also translates responses from the respondent into the interviewer's language. Some might argue that conducting an interview via translation "on the fly" is better than no interview at all. However, existing evidence suggests that these forms of ad hoc translation should be avoided due to the inevitable variance in translation performance.[8] In the cross-cultural survey research field, the current best practice recommendations are for team translations. This is described in the TRAPD team translation model: Translation, Review, Adjudication,

---

8 http://ccsg.isr.umich.edu/translation.cfm, last retrieved January 15, 2013.

Pretesting, and Documentation. This process is described in detail in Harkness *et al.* (2010); and in the online Cross-Cultural Survey Guidelines.[9]

Creating multiple language versions of an instrument can present many other operational issues including translation production which will impact the study timeline as well as interviewer recruitment, training, and matching interviewers to respondents, all contributing to increased costs (Harkness, Pennell, & Schoua-Glusberg, 2004). Since research goals and research tools are also culturally embedded, contact approaches, incentives, motivating material, and, most importantly, questions asked and response options offered may be culturally relevant to a group or be in some way inappropriate or offensive. Survey features, which may be motivating to one segment of the population, may have a discouraging effect to another segment.

Culture, cognition, and response

Below, we discuss the potential cultural and linguistic effects and sources of error that may arise at each of the four major stages of the survey response process – comprehension of the item (comprehension), retrieval of relevant information (retrieval), use of that information to make required judgments (judgment and estimation), and selection and reporting of an answer (reporting) (Tourangeau, Rips, & Rasinski, 2000). The effect of cultural frame has not been widely tested in the survey response context specifically. However, Uskul and Oyserman (2006) propose a process model for hypothesizing if members of different cultures will differ systematically in the following six areas (Uskul & Oyserman, 2006, p. 175):

(1) How the question is understood;
(2) What is identified as the relevant behavior, judgment, or attitude;
(3) What inferences are likely to be made from the research context, the questions being posed, or the question framework;
(4) How common or habitual the behavior to be identified is, how sensitive the subject matter is;
(5) The subjective theories used to reconstruct estimates to provide answers; and
(6) What is edited.

We address the questions posed in Uskul and Oyserman's model and cite examples in the literature in the context of the four components of the survey response process. The effect of Western European and North American (individualist) cultures and East Asian (collectivist) cultures[10] has received the most attention and is informed by a well-established conceptual

---

9 http://ccsg.isr.umich.edu/, last retrieved January 15, 2013.

10 Collectivist cultures are characterized by a focus on the embeddedness of individuals within social groups and interdependence among in-group members. One's self is defined by how one relates to others and is "malleable, context-dependent and socially sensitive" (Uskul & Oyserman, 2006, p. 183). By contrast, individualistic cultures emphasize the separation of individuals from social groups and the independence of the self from others. In individualistic cultures, the self is "permanent, separate from context, trait-like, and a causal nexus" (Uskul & Oyserman, 2006, p. 183).

framework and body of experimental evidence (Schwarz, Oyserman, & Peytcheva, 2010). Cultural psychologists identify another form of collectivism, honor-based collectivism – prevalent in the Middle East, Mediterranean, and Latin American countries – that has been the subject of relatively less empirical study (Uskul, Oyserman, & Schwarz, 2010). Research has found reliable differences between these cultural frames; however, other cultural frames may exist that have not yet been identified. While these frames serve as broad explanatory devices, individual differences and variations exist within all cultures and every individual has both individualist and collectivist aspects (Heine, 2008). It is also important to note that cultural differences can be overridden by contextual influences – i.e., a collectivist mindset can be evoked in a person from an individualist culture and an individualist mindset can be evoked in a person from a collectivist culture (Schwarz, Oyserman, & Peytcheva, 2010). In the survey context, this can be done consciously via "priming procedures." Language has been shown to prime the related cultural frame in people who are bilingual or multilingual. Below, we draw on examples to explore the likely effects of cultural frame on survey response and potential sources of error.

Comprehension

A number of problems can occur at the comprehension stage if a questionnaire is not available in a language that a sample member understands well or if the translation is of poor quality. As Harkness and colleagues have stated, "Good translations do not ensure a good survey but bad translations do guarantee a bad survey" (2010, p. 129). Comprehension errors can result from mistranslation, an ambiguous translation, or ambiguity carried through from the source questionnaire – for a review of translation challenges see Harkness *et al.* (2010) and Harkness *et al.*, Pennell, and Schoua-Glusberg (2004). Translation best practices should be followed and translated instruments thoroughly tested.

In addition to potential language-related comprehension challenges, cultural background has been shown to affect how respondents understand questions and constructs, as well as how they are influenced by the research context. Respondents must have a pragmatic understanding (meaning in context) of the question not simply a literal understanding (Uskul & Oyserman, 2006). A number of factors inform pragmatic understanding including conversational norms as well as aspects of the research context such as the survey title, sponsor, preceding questions, and response scales. The effect of these factors has been shown to differ systematically across cultures.

It is widely believed that respondents draw on conversational norms when answering a survey, as operationalized by Grice (1975) in the following maxims (Uskul & Oyserman, 2006, p. 176): (1) Maxim of relation: focus on what is relevant; (2) Maxim of quantity: provide new information; (3) Maxim of manner: be clear; (4) Maxim of quality: speak the truth. Uskul and Oyserman (2006) argue that these maxims are likely to be universal but that they will be applied within a cultural frame. That is, as Uskul and Oyserman (2006) explain, what it means "to be clear" will differ across cultures and respondents will expect their conversational partner (the interviewer in this case) to use culturally appropriate cues. A well-documented difference between collectivist and individualist cultures is greater sensitivity in collectivist cultures to the conversational context of the survey interview. This means that individuals from collectivist cultures are more likely to be attuned to and shift responses depending on features of the research such as the survey title, sponsor, etc. Further, differential sensitivity to the conversational context can give rise to systematically different interpretations of question meaning and result in differential question order effects (Schwarz *et al.*, 2010). For example, individuals from collectivist cultures are more likely to be affected by the content of previous questions and take more care to provide nonredundant answers to redundant questions (Haberstroh, Oyserman, Schwarz, Kühnen, & Ji, 2002). Cultural frames can be invoked or "primed," which is particularly important to consider with bilingual respondents whose cultural mindset may shift depending on the language of administration.

Retrieval

Survey questions often require respondents to draw on autobiographical memory to report various behaviors. Autobiographical memory can be influenced by cultural factors such as what is salient and therefore retrievable from memory and what is not memorable and therefore must be inferred (Schwarz *et al.*, 2010; Uskul & Oyserman, 2006). Research comparing autobiographical memory between collectivist and individualist respondents suggests that social relations and roles are more prominent for individuals from collectivist cultures whereas individual characteristics and experiences are more prominent for those from individualist cultures (Schwarz *et al.*, 2010). It is thought that culturally prominent characteristics may be represented in more detail and linked to a larger amount of other material making for differential recall unless less prominent characteristics are cued. However, more research is needed in this area to determine whether increased culturally prominent reports are due to higher accuracy or to higher recall and reporting bias. Again, language can serve as a prime and depending on the interview language, respondents may recall more or fewer memories. A further point is that the more difficult a retrieval task is, the more likely it is that respondents will rely on question content, response format, and other organizing frames (e.g., subjective theories) to infer their response (Uskul & Oyserman, 2006).

Judgment and estimation

Respondent judgment and estimation may be influenced by cultural differences and man- ifest in the need to estimate, by the design of response scales, or subjective theories used to arrive at estimates or answers.

   Different cultures require varying levels of attentiveness to aspects of life and the social context. Due to the emphasis on relationships and "fitting in," collectivist cultures require a higher degree of attention to and are likely to know more about others in the social context and one's observable or public behaviors (Schwarz *et al.*, 2010). Accordingly, individuals from collectivist cultures have been shown to be more attentive to their own public behaviors than individuals from individualist cultures and therefore rely less on estimation or cues from response scales (Ji, Schwarz, & Nisbett, 2000). Subjective theories are culturally sanctioned "rules of thumb" that respondents refer to when autobiographical memory is limited or the retrieval task is too burdensome (Uskul & Oyserman, 2006). These theories differ across cultures and may lead respondents from different cultures to vary systematically in their estimates. For example, a common rule of thumb is to estimate past behavior based on current behavior. Here, a respondent must ask himself or herself how the current situation is the same or different from the past. The extent to which the respondent believes that this is the same may be affected by culturally sanctioned theories about the stability or change in personality and behavior. For example, consistency in personality and behavior is valued in individualist cultures while change and adaptability are more valued, particularly in order to maintain harmony within the group, in collectivist cultures (Uskul & Oyserman, 2006).

Reporting

A range of potentially overlapping cultural, linguistic, and other factors may affect how and if cultural and linguistic minorities report an answer to a survey question. Language barriers may curtail responses to open-ended questions. Cultures differ in their views of the self and what is considered to be favorable, which may cause systematic variation in self-presentation. Individualist cultures encourage a positive image of the self while East Asian collectivist cultures focus on maintaining harmonious relationships, modesty, and "fitting in." Honor-based collectivist cultures promote enhancement of the self and close others and a less positive image of out-group members (Uskul *et al.*, 2010). Nonresponse and measurement error may both be increased by the perception of certain topics or questions as sensitive. For example, survey questions asking about residence and relationships are noted as being sensitive questions to American Indians (Lavelle *et al.*, 2009). Lindenberg *et al.* (2001) note the sensitivity of questions about substance abuse and sexual behaviors for Latinos because they are closely tied to traditional religious beliefs, gender roles and responsibilities, and nationalistic identification. Distrust or fear can also cause nonresponse or misreporting. If a cultural or linguistic minority is also "undocumented" or illegal in a given context, then a range of studies may be threatening.

Pretesting

Like all questionnaire design, pretesting is essential for identifying problems with an instrument that prevent or confound collection of the desired data. However, testing and assessment procedures typically required for monolingual survey instruments are rarely implemented for translated questionnaires. Instead, researchers commonly rely on "back translation" to detect translation errors. However, in the last decade, this method has been found to be inadequate on its own for detecting problems with translated questionnaires (Harkness *et al.*, 2010) and may provide limited or misleading insights (more details available at ccsg.isr.umich.edu/translation.cfm). Insufficient testing means that translation errors may be found when it is too late or may simply go undetected.

Pretesting techniques commonly used in the context of monolingual instruments can be applied to surveys of cultural and linguistic minorities, including pilot studies, cognitive interviews, focus groups, expert reviews, and behavior coding, among others (see Caspar & Peytcheva, 2011; Presser, Couper, Lessler, Martin, Rothgeb *et al.*, 2004). For instance, Canales and colleagues (1995) pretested their questionnaire with Spanish-speaking individuals and had it reviewed by Latinos with varying backgrounds. Pretesting can help evaluate whether questionnaire design, adaptation, and translation decisions were adequate for overcoming cultural and linguistic barriers and reducing survey error. However, different cultural and linguistic groups may respond differently to pretesting methods. For example, Pan, Landreth, Park, Hinsdale-Shouse, and Schoua-Glusberg (2010) found that Chinese, Russian, Korean, and Spanish subjects responded in remarkably different ways in cognitive interviews due to differences in communication styles and cultural norms. Their findings suggest that more appropriate ways of engaging non-English-speaking respondents and alternative probes are needed to collect high-quality and comparable data across different language groups in cognitive interviews. Pan *et al.* (2010) note that their results also have implications for behavioral coding. More research is clearly needed in this area.

12.3.3 Accessing the population and data collection

Data collection can be particularly challenging when groups are difficult to access and interview. Because research goals and research tools are culturally embedded, contact approaches, incentives, and motivating material need to be culturally relevant to the target population. Survey features, which may be motivating to one segment of the population, may have a discouraging effect to another segment in multipopulation surveys. Researchers must be cognizant of these challenges when designing and implementing data collection protocols.

Contacting the target population

Cultural and linguistic minority groups may be suspicious of outsiders or resist contact from strangers in general. They may also distrust researchers due to negative past experience or fear of exploitation. An example comes from Shoultz *et al.* (2006) who cite research in Hawaii that left some community members and organizations feeling exploited, resulting in a general skepticism of all research. Distrust and suspicion of researchers is also prevalent among some Native American Indians due to a history of mistreatment by the Federal government and previous exploitative experience with researchers (Lavelle *et al.*, 2009). Vulnerable groups such as undocumented immigrants typically avoid attention and may distrust researchers, particularly those associated with the government.

Researchers must plan for data collection protocols that overcome these access barriers. Cultural outreach through advertisements in local media and support from influential community members can help overcome challenges when groups prefer to conceal their identity or are distrustful of researchers. Han, Kang, Kim, Ryu, and Kim (2007) suggest using media – newspapers, radio, and television that target their content to specific cultural community – to recruit participants. To further overcome access barriers, Han *et al.* (2007) also suggest having a pool of bilingual community members help in developing recruitment materials; for example, seeking endorsement from community leaders.

Difficulties faced in contacting cultural and linguistic minorities may be further compli-cated by the mode of contact. The type of contact information available to members of the group and the sample frame available may limit or dictate the mode of contact, or at least the initial contact for the survey. For example, Latino Americans and American Indians are more likely to lack telephone service than other households in the US (Andresen, Diehr, & Luke, 2004; Lavelle *et al.*, 2009). Low literacy may also preclude mail or written ques-tionnaires. Indeed, in some cases, the local language may not have a written form (Pennell, Harkness, Levenstein, & Quaglia, 2010). For example, ethnographic research conducted in *colonias* (residential areas along the Texas–Mexico border) in preparation for the 2000 Census identified little or no knowledge of English along with limited formal education as key barriers to census enumeration (de la Puente & Stemper, 2003). Researchers may find employing interviewers to make initial contacts advantageous because interviewers can be useful in motivating participation, handling respondent inquiries, and assuaging concerns reluctant respondents may have (de Leeuw, 2008). Interviewers who are culturally and linguistically similar to participants are thought to help overcome trust barriers and facilitate rapport, which may help increase participation. For example, Garter (2003) hired native Africans and individuals of African origin to be interviewers in a study of HIV positive African immigrants living in the UK. Although employing interviewers to make initial contact in a study may help to reduce nonresponse, researchers must also be aware of potential interviewer effects that can introduce other sources of survey error (Groves *et al.*, 2009).

Interviewer recruitment and training

Just as interviewers who are ethnically and culturally similar to the target population may be recruited to contact the target population, they are also often employed as data collectors. Greenfields (2009) found in her study of Romany Gypsies and Irish Travellers in the UK that respondents are more likely to respond to members of their own community. Similarly, Han *et al.* (2007) report on strategies to overcoming barriers to researching Korean Americans. They note their success at hiring first generation Korean Americans as inter-viewers and members of their research staff. Other studies (e.g., Elebro, Rööst, Moussa,

Johnsdotter, & Essén, 2007; Lavelle *et al.*, 2009) also suggest that data collectors recruited from the target group can help overcome cultural barriers and alleviate issues of trust. Interviewers may also be necessary when a cultural or linguistic minority group is unfamiliar with completing self-administered questionnaires (Canales *et al.*, 1995). In all cases, interviewers will require training to administer screening and respondent selection protocols and translated and adapted questionnaires. Issues of cultural sensitivity may also be necessary to address in training.

Implementation

There are many factors to be considered in the operationalization of a study design. For example, the timing of data collection should be planned in accordance with aspects of the target population's culture. Data collection will need to be timed around specific cultural activities and events such as religious festivals and national holidays (Pennell *et al.*, 2010). Another consideration is the length of the data collection period. Behrens *et al.* (2009) suggest that longer data collection periods allow for multiple attempts to motivate respondents to respond and adequate time to reach geographically dispersed populations. The longer data collection period may reduce nonresponse, but often comes at an increased cost and extends the time before the data can be made available.

Incentives may be used by researchers to encourage study participation, but the appropriateness of incentives and the type of incentive to use will depend on the cultures under study (Pennell *et al.*, 2010). The types of data researchers aim to collect may also be considered culturally sensitive and researchers need to be aware of the cultural acceptance of collecting certain information. For example, the collection of biomarkers and other physical measures require interviewers to be trained on how to frame the request for this information as well as how to appropriately collect these data (Pennell *et al.*, 2010).

Ethical considerations

In the context of studies of cultural and linguistic minorities, researchers may need to gain special legal and cultural permissions from groups, such as tribal advisory boards (Lavelle, Larsen, & Gundersen, 2009) and other local authorities to gain access to members of the target population (Pennell *et al.*, 2010). Moreover, interviewers should strive to conduct interviews in private settings (Flanagan & Hancock, 2010). This is an important consideration given the effect the presence of other individuals can have on measurement error. Considerations of privacy vary by culture and may be difficult to achieve in some cultures (Mneimneh & Pennell, 2011). For example, in some contexts, interviews with women and children may not be able to be conducted in private. One solution in these instances is to conduct the interview in a location visible to others, but where the interview cannot be overheard (Pennell *et al.*, 2010).

12.4   Qualitative, mixed-methods, and community-based Research

In addition to surveys, researchers may find other methodologies useful when studying hard-to-survey cultural and linguistic minorities. These methods can be useful for exploratory research or when probability samples of the target population are too difficult or costly. Like all research methods, however, these approaches have both advantages and disadvantages.

Qualitative studies

Qualitative methodologies, particularly case studies, focus groups, in-depth interviews, and ethnographies are often used by researchers to explore and describe experiences of cultural and linguistic minorities (see Creswell, 2007; Denzin & Lincoln, 2005; Merriam, 2009 for a general discussion of qualitative research methods). Qualitative studies can be useful to gain insight into and about the population of interest at a relatively low cost. These methods are also very useful for exploring possible methodological and operational issues such as access barriers to stigmatized populations, e.g., migrants who are sex workers (e.g., Agustín, 2007) or HIV positive immigrants (Garter, 2003). In these instances, a qualitative study of a few members of the population can provide valuable insights.

The primary drawback of qualitative studies is that statistical generalizations to a wider population are not possible. Qualitative studies typically implement purposive sampling techniques in which study participants are selected because they are conveniently accessible, represent a wide and diverse variation of the population (i.e., maximum variation sampling), are considered a "typical case," are found using snowball or chain referral techniques, or for various other predetermined reasons (Creswell, 2007). Qualitative studies of cultural and linguistic minorities, however, are useful for understanding how researchers address the challenges of gaining access to groups, overcoming cultural and linguistic barriers, and identifying members of the target population. For example, Toktaş (2006) interviewed a convenience sample of thirty-one Jewish individuals living in Turkey to examine citizenship, legal issues, and identity of being Jewish in Turkey, a predominantly Muslim country. These interviews helped gain insight into this population's feelings of stigma, lack of work opportunities, and views of duties and responsibilities of being a citizen of Turkey, while also maintaining their cultural identity.

Mixed-methods research

Clark, Creswell, Green, and Shope (2008) recommend exploratory mixed-methods studies when researchers need to explore a topic before a quantitative study can be designed. Other types of mixed-methods design include triangulation designs in which both qualitative and quantitative approaches are used to develop a better understanding of the data and the context in which it is collected. An embedded design integrates a qualitative study as part of a quantitative study. A fourth type of mixed-method design is an explanatory design whereby a qualitative study follows a quantitative one to provide further explanation of the quantitative study's results. These four designs are all part of a mixed-methods research paradigm that combines methodological approaches to capitalize on the strength of each approach to provide a more thorough understanding of a research problem (Clark *et al.*, 2008; Creswell & Clark, 2010; Creswell, Klassen, Clark, & Smith, 2011).

Community-based methods

Community-based methods are sometimes used in minority research to address specific challenges when studying cultural and linguistic minorities. These methods (sometimes called participant-based research, community-based participatory research, and so on) involve researchers collaborating with groups that provide services to members of the target population or partnering with community groups comprised of the members of the target population (see Minkler & Wallerstein, 2011 for a general overview of community-based methodology). For example, researchers might work with governmental and non-governmental community organizations, such as American Indian tribal organizations (Lavelle *et al.*, 2009), health care providers (e.g., Gryczynski, Feldman, Carter-Pokras, Kanamori, Chen, & Roth, 2010; Schroepfer, Matloub, Creswell, Strickland, & Anderson, 2009), religious organizations (e.g., Wasserman, Bender, Kalsbeek, Suchindran, & Mouw, 2005), and so on.

Community-based methods help researchers gain access to members of the target population by obtaining legitimacy from association with the community group. Community-based methods may also assist in the identification of the population of interest who may be linked to the organization(s) with whom researchers collaborate. For example, Wasserman *et al.* (2005) used community-based methods when they collaborated with churches in North Carolina to reach their target population of recent Latin American and Caribbean immigrant women. Here, issues of trust and fear, particularly among undocumented immigrants, could also be examined and appropriately addressed. Collaborating with service providers and members of the target population is also beneficial for developing appropriate instrumentation and data collection implementation procedures. Such collaborative relationships can help determine ways to encourage participation and provide input on questionnaire design, translation, and adaptation. For example, Schroepfer *et al.* (2009) report that their mail survey designed to understand cancer treatment among American Indian communities benefited from changes suggested by community and health organizations.

Researchers can also discuss research findings with group members as a way to gauge the validity of these findings. Gryczynski *et al.* (2010) used community-based methods in this manner through the use of focus groups. Here, in their study of health care in the American Indian community living in Baltimore, Maryland, the researchers discussed their findings with representatives from an American Indian health service organization. Collaborating with community organizations may also have the added benefit of research findings influencing policy formation of the organizations affiliated with the cultural and linguistic groups studied.

However, bias can result if members of the target population reached through community-based methods are systematically different on key statistics compared to members of the target population who are not associated with these community groups. For example, cultural and linguistic minorities reached through health care providers are most likely different on key health measures compared to group members who lack health care. Measurement and nonresponse error can result if study participants are unwilling to disclose information that is critical of the organization or fear loss of service if certain information is provided to researchers. Participants may provide socially desirable responses or choose not to provide responses to certain questions in these cases.

12.5   Outlook: towards improving research practice

The future of research involving hard-to-survey cultural and linguistic minorities is one of much needed documentation and methodological studies. The published literature on these populations indicates that many aspects of the survey life cycle production process are either neglected or not discussed or revealed. The substantive focus of this research often takes priority and documentation of methodological challenges and solutions are given little to no consideration. For example, studies with linguistic minorities sometimes lack sufficient details about translation and adaptation procedures used and therefore make proper assessment of potential error from translation or adaptation impossible. Simply stating that instruments were translated or adapted is not sufficient to judge quality standards.

It is also very difficult to assess the quality of substantive results and methods used to study hard-to-reach cultural and linguistic minorities when documentation about survey design and procedures are neglected. Critical reviews and meta-analyses of the substantive results rely on comparability of studies, which can be established by comprehensive documentation. Thus, the field is in need of this knowledge in order to move forward with innovative and new methodological approaches (Mohler & Uher, 2003). In addition, collecting appropriate metadata and paradata will allow researchers to understand better the usefulness of methods applied and to assess survey process quality. Currently, researchers are developing standardized protocols for surveys among cultural and linguistic minorities, such as with Latinos in the US and Sorbs in Germany. If this trend continues, then many of these populations will no longer be considered hard to survey. Increased methodological research in these spheres will advance and enrich the research literature and allow for better understanding of how to design and conduct these challenging research studies.

References

Agustín, L. M. (2007). Questioning solidarity: outreach with migrants who sell sex. *Sexualities*, 10(4), 519–34.

Andresen, E. M., Diehr, P. H., & Luke, D. A. (2004). Public health surveillance of low-frequency populations. *Annual Review of Public Health*, 25(1), 25–52.

Behrens, R., Freedman, M., & McGuckin, N. (2009). The challenges of surveying "hard to reach" groups: synthesis of a workshop. In P. Bonnel, M. Lee-Gosselin, J. Zmud, & J. Madre (eds.), *Transport Survey Methods: Keeping up with a Changing World* (p. 145–52). Bingley: Emerald Group Publishing Ltd.

Blumberg, S. J., & Luke, J. V. (2011). Wireless substitution: early release of estimates from the National Health Interview Survey, January–June 2011. Retrieved from www.cdc.gov/nchs/data/nhis/earlyrelease/wireless201112.pdf.

Boehm, D. C. (2009). China's failed war on terror: fanning the flames of Uighur separatist violence. *Berkeley Journal of Middle Eastern & Islamic Law*, 2, 61.

Canales, S., Ganz, P. A., & Coscarelli, C. A. (1995). Translation and validation of a quality of life instrument for Hispanic American cancer patients: methodological considerations. *Quality of Life Research*, 4(1), 3–11.

Carter-Pokras, O., Zambrana, R. E., Mora, S. E., & Aaby, K. A. (1999). Emergency preparedness: knowledge and perceptions of Latin American immigrants. *Journal of Health Care for the Poor and Underserved*, 18(2), 455–81.

Caspar, R., & Peytcheva, E. (2011). Pretesting. In *Cross-Cultural Survey Guidelines*. Retrieved from http://ccsg.isr.umich.edu/pretesting.cfm.

Chavez, L. R., Hubbell, F. A., Mishra, S. I., & Valdez, R. B. (1997). Undocumented Latina immigrants in Orange County, California: a comparative analysis. *International Migration Review*, 31(1), 88–107.

Childs, G. T. (2012). What's the difference between dialects and languages? In E. M. Rickerson & B. Hilton (eds.), *The 5 Minute Linguist: Bite-Sized Essays on Language and Languages* (2nd edn.). Equinox Publishing.

Clark, V. L. P., Creswell, J. W., Green, D. O. N., & Shope, R. J. (2008). Mixing quantitative and qualitative approaches. An introduction to emergent mixed methods research. In S. Hesse-Biber & R. Leary (eds.), *Handbook of Emergent Methods*, (pp. 363–88). New York: Guilford Press.

Correa-Velez, I., & Gifford, S. M. (2007). When the right to be counted doesn't count: the politics and challenges of researching the health of asylum seekers. *Critical Public Health*, 17(3), 273–281.

Council of Europe. (1992). European Charter for Regional or Minority Languages (CETS 148).

Creswell, J. W. (2007). *Qualitative Inquiry & Research Design: Choosing among Five Approaches* (3rd edn.). CA: Sage Publications, Inc.

Creswell, J. W., & Clark, V. L. P. (2010). *Designing and conducting mixed methods research*. Los Angeles, CA: Sage Publications, Inc.

Creswell, J. W., Klassen, A. C., Clark, V. L. P., & Smith, K. C. (2011). *Best Practices for Mixed Methods Research in the Health Sciences*. National Institutes of Health. Retrieved from http://obssr.od.nih.gov/mixed_methods_research.

de la Puente, M., & Stemper, D. (2003). *The Enumeration of Colonias in Census 2000: Perspectives of Ethnographers and Census Enumerators* (Final report). Washington, DC: US Census Bureau.

de Leeuw, E. D. (2008). Choosing the method of data collection. In E. D. de Leeuw, J. J. Hox, & D. Dillman (eds.), *International Handbook of Survey Methodology* (pp. 113–35). New York: Psychology Press Taylor & Francis Group.

de Leeuw, E. D., Hox, J. J., & Dillman, D. A. (2008). International Handbook of Survey Methodology. NewYork: Psychology Press Taylor & Francis Group.

Denzin, N. K., & Lincoln, Y. S. (2005). *The SAGE Handbook of Qualitative Research* (3rd edn.). Thousand Oaks, CA: Sage Publications, Inc.

Dillman, D. A., Smyth, J. D., & Christian, L. M. (2008). *Internet, Mail, and Mixed-Mode Surveys: The Tailored Design Method*. New York: John Wiley & Sons.

Duffy, D., Goldberg, J., & Buchwald, D. (2006). Using mail to reach patients seen at an urban health care facility. *Journal of Health Care for the Poor and Underserved*, 17(3), 522–31.

Elebro, K., Rööst, M., Moussa, K., Johnsdotter, S., & Essén, B. (2007). Misclassified maternal deaths among East African immigrants in Sweden. *Reproductive Health Matters*, 15(30), 153–62.

European Science Foundation. (2001). *The European Social Survey (ESS) – A Research Instrument for the Social Sciences in Europe – Summary* (p. 59). Strasburg.

Eyler, A. A., Baker, E., Cromer, L. C., King, A. C., Brownson, R. C., & Donatelle, R. J. (1998). Physical activity and minority women: a qualitative study. *Health Education & Behavior*, 25(5), 640–52.

Faugier, J., & Sargeant, M. (1997). Sampling hard to reach populations. *Journal of Advanced Nursing*, 26(4), 790–97.

Flanagan, S., & Hancock, B. (2010). "Reaching the hard to reach"–lessons learned from the VCS (voluntary and community Sector). A qualitative study. *BMC Health Services Research*, 10(1), 92.

Garland, J., Spalek, B., & Chakraborti, N. (2006). Hearing lost voices. *British Journal of Criminology*, 46(3), 423–37.

Garter, P. (2003). Sexual health. *Research Matters*, 16, 55–62.

Greenfields, M. (2009). Reaching Gypsies and Travellers. *Primary Health Care*, 19(8), 26–27.

Grice, H. P. (1975). Logic and conversation. In P. Cole & J. Morgan (eds.), *Syntax and Semantics*. New York: Academic Press.

Groves, R. M., Fowler, F. J., Couper, M. P., Lepkowski, J. M., Singer, E., & Tourangeau, R. (2009). *Survey Methodology* (2nd edn.). New York: John Wiley & Sons.

Gryczynski, J., Feldman, R., Carter-Pokras, O., Kanamori, M., Chen, L., & Roth, S. (2010). Contexts of tobacco use and perspectives on smoking cessation among a sample of urban American Indians. *Journal of Health Care for the Poor and Underserved*, 21(2), 544–58.

Haberstroh, S., Oyserman, D., Schwarz, N., Kühnen, U., & Ji, L. J. (2002). Is the interdependent self more sensitive to question context than the independent self? Self-construal and the observation of conversational norms. *Journal of Experimental Social Psychology*, 38(3), 323–29.

Han, H. R., Kang, J., Kim, K. B., Ryu, J. P., & Kim, M. T. (2007). Barriers to and strategies for recruiting Korean Americans for community-partnered health promotion research. *Journal of Immigrant and Minority Health*, 9(2), 137–46.

Harkness, J. A., Pennell, B.-E. & Schoua-Glusberg, A. (2004). Survey questionnaire translation and assessment. In S. Presser, J. Rothgeb, M. Couper, J. Lessler, E. Martin, &
E. Singer (eds.), *Methods for Testing and Evaluating Survey Questionnaires*
(pp. 453–73). Hoboken, NJ: John Wiley & Sons.

Harkness, J. A., Villar, A., & Edwards, B. (2010). Translation, adaptation, and design.
In J. A. Harkness, M. Braun, B. Edwards, T. P. Johnson, L. E. Lyberg, P. Ph. Mohler,
B.-E. Pennell, & T. W. Smith (eds.), *Survey Methods in Multinational, Multiregional,
and Multicultural Contexts* (pp. 115–40). Hoboken, NJ: John Wiley & Sons.

Heckathorn, D. D. (2007). Extensions of respondent-driven sampling: analyzing continuous
variables and controlling for differential recruitment. *Sociological Methodology*,
37(1), 151–207.

Heine, S. J. (2008). *Cultural Psychology*. New York: W. W. Norton and Co.

Higgins, D. L., O'Reilly, K., Tashima, N., Crain, C., Beeker, C., Goldbaum, G., *et al.*
(1996). Using formative research to lay the foundation for community level HIV
prevention efforts: an example from the AIDS Community Demonstration Projects.
Public Health Reports, 111(Suppl. 1), 28–35.

Ji, L. J., Schwarz, N., & Nisbett, R. E. (2000). Culture, autobiographical memory, and
behavioral frequency reports: measurement issues in cross-cultural studies.
Personality and Social Psychology Bulletin, 26(5), 585–93.

Johnson, E. M., & Delgado, J. L. (1989). Reaching Hispanics with messages to prevent
alcohol and other drug abuse. *Public Health Reports*, 104(6), 588–94.

Johnson, T. P., O'Rourke, D., Chavez, N., Sudman, S., Warnecke, R., Lacey, L., *et al.*
(1997). Social cognition and responses to survey questions among culturally diverse
populations. In L. E. Lyberg, P. Biemer, M. Collins, E. D. de Leeuw, C. Dippo,
N. Schwarz, & D. Trewin (eds.), *Survey Measurement and Process Quality*
(pp. 87–113). New York: John Wiley & Sons.

Kalunta-Crumpton, A. (2004). A community without a drug problem? Black drug use in
Britain. *Social Justice*, 31(1–2), 200–16.

Lavelle, B., Larsen, M. D., & Gundersen, C. (2009). Strategies for surveys of American
Indians. *Public Opinion Quarterly*, 73(2), 385–403.

Lee, S., & Schwarz, N. (2014). Question context and priming meaning of health: effect of
differences in self-rated health between Hispanics and non-Hispanic whites.
American Journal of Public Health, 104(1), 179–85.

Lee, S., Nguyen, H. A., Jawad, M., & Kurata, J. (2008). Linguistic minorities in a health
survey. *Public Opinion Quarterly*, 72(3), 470–86.

Lewis, M. P. (ed.). (2009). *Ethnologue: Languages of the World* (16th edn.). Dallas: SIL
International.

Lindenberg, C. S., Solorzano, R. M., Vilaro, F. M., & Westbrook, L. O. (2001). Challenges
and strategies for conducting intervention research with culturally diverse populations. *Journal of Transcultural Nursing*, 12(2), 132–39.

Lopez, R. (2008). Por que? Questions of validity in Hispanic survey research. *MRA Alert!
Magazine*, 46(6), 24–25,32,34,39,42.

Merriam, S. B. (2009). *Qualitative Research: A Guide to Design and Implementation*. San Francisco: Jossey-Bass.

Minkler, M., & Wallerstein, N. (2011). *Community-Based Participatory Research for Health: From Process to Outcomes*. San Francisco: Jossey-Bass.

Mneimneh, Z., & Pennell, B.-E. (2011). *Interview Privacy and Social Desirability Effects on Reporting Sensitive Outcomes Research*. Paper presented at the Annual Conference of the American Association for Public Opinion Research, Phoenix, AZ.

Mohler, P. P. (1978). *Abitur 1917–1971: Reflektionen des Verhältnisses zwischen Individuum und kollektiver Macht in Abituraufsätzen*. Frankfurt: Lang.

Mohler, P. P., & Uher, R. (2003). Documenting comparative surveys for secondary analysis. In J. A. Harkness, F. J. R. van de Vijver, & P. Ph. Mohler (eds.), *Cross-Cultural Survey Methods* (pp. 311–27). Hoboken, NJ: John Wiley & Sons.

Neweklowsky, G. (2002). Serbisch. In M. Okuka (ed.), *Wieser Enzyklopädie des europäischen Ostens. Band 10. Lexikon der Sprachen des europäischen Ostens*. Klagenfurt and Celovec: Wieser. Retrieved from www.uni-klu.ac.at/eeo/Serbisch.pdf.

Ngo-Metzger, Q., Kaplan, S. H., Sorkin, D. H., Clarridge, B. R., & Phillips, R. S. (2004). Surveying minorities with limited-English proficiency: does data collection method affect data quality among Asian Americans? *Medical Care*, 42(9), 893–900.

O'Hegarty, M., Pederson, L. L., Thorne, S. L., Caraballo, R. S., Evans, B., Athey, L., *et al.* (2010). Customizing survey instruments and data collection to reach Hispanic/Latino adults in border communities in Texas. *American Journal of Public Health*, 100(S1), S159–64.

Pan, Y., Landreth, A., Park, H., Hinsdale-Shouse, M., & Schoua-Glusberg, A. (2010). Cognitive interviewing in non-English languages: a cross-cultural perspective. In J. A. Harkness, M. Braun, B. Edwards, T. P. Johnson, L. E. Lyber, P. Ph. Mohler, B.-E. Pennell, & T. W. Smith (eds.), *Survey Methods in Multinational, Multiregional, and Multicultural Contexts* (pp. 91–113). Hoboken, NJ: John Wiley & Sons.

Parsons, T. (1991). *The Social System*. London: Routledge.

Passel, J. S. (1997). The growing American Indian population, 1960–1990: beyond demography. *Population Research and Policy Review*, 16(1/2), 11–31.

Pennell, B.-E., Harkness, J. A., Levenstein, R., & Quaglia, M. (2010). Challenges in cross-national data collection. In J. A. Harkness, M. Braun, B. Edwards, T. P. Johnson, L. Lyberg, P. Ph. Mohler, and B.-E. Pennell (eds.), *Survey Methods in Multinational, Multiregional, and Multicultural Contexts* (pp. 269–98). Hoboken, NJ: John Wiley & Sons.

Presser, S., Couper, M. P., Lessler, J. T., Martin, E., Martin, J., Rothgeb, J. M., *et al.* (2004). Methods for testing and evaluating survey questions. *Public Opinion Quarterly*, 68(1), 109–30.

Sasao, T. (1994). Using surname-based telephone survey methodology in Asian-American communities: practical issues and caveats. *Journal of Community Psychology*, 22(4), 283–95.

Schroepfer, T. A., Matloub, J., Creswell, P., Strickland, R., & Anderson, D. M. (2009). A community-specific approach to cancer research in Indian country. *Progress in Community Health Partnerships: Research, Education, and Action*, 3(4), 317–25.

Schwarz, N., Oyserman, D., & Peytcheva, E. (2010). Cognition, communication, and culture: implications for the survey response process. In J. A. Harkness, M. Braun, B. Edwards, T. P. Johnson, L. E. Lyberg, P. Ph. Mohler, B.-E, Pennell, & T. W. Smith (eds.), *Survey Methods in Multinational, Multiregional, and Multicultural Contexts* (pp. 175–90). Hoboken, NJ: John Wiley & Sons.

Shoultz, J., Oneha, M. F., Magnussen, L., Hla, M. M., Brees-Saunders, Z., Cruz, M. D., *et al.* (2006). Finding solutions to challenges faced in community-based participatory research between academic and community organizations. *Journal of Interprofessional Care*, 20(2), 133–44.

Soifer, D. (2009). Linguistic isolation carries a heavy cost. *IMDiversity.com*. Retrieved from www.imdiversity.com/villages/hispanic/community_family/nam_linguistic_isolation_0409.asp.

Stueve, A., O'Donnell, L. N., Duran, R., San Doval, A., & Blome, J. (2001). Time-space sampling in minority communities: results with young Latino men who have sex with men. *American Journal of Public Health*, 91(6), 922–26.

Toktaş, S. (2006). The conduct of citizenship in the case of Turkey's Jewish minority: legal status, identity, and civic virtue aspects. *Comparative Studies of South Asia, Africa and the Middle East*, 26(1), 121–33.

Tourangeau, R., Rips, L. J., & Rasinski, K. A. (2000). *The Psychology of Survey Response*. Cambridge: Cambridge University Press.

United Nations. (1992). General Assembly Resolution 47/135. In *United Nations Forum on Minority Issues (2008): Compilation of Recommendations of the First Four Sessions 2008–2011*. Geneva.

US Bureau of Indian Affairs. (2012, September). Frequently Asked Questions. Retrieved from www.bia.gov/FAQs/index.htm.

Uskul, A. K., & Oyserman, D. (2006). Question comprehension and response: implications of individualism and collectivism, In B. Mannix, M. Neale, & Y. Chen (eds.), *Research on managing groups and teams: National culture & groups* (vol. 9, pp. 173–201). Oxford: Elsevier Science Press.

Uskul, A. K., Oyserman, D., & Schwarz, N. (2010). Cultural emphasis on honor, modesty, or self-enhancement: implications for the survey-response process. In J. A. Harkness, M. Braun, B. Edwards, T. P. Johnson, L. E. Lyberg, P. Ph. Mohler, B.-E. Pennell, & T. W. Smith (eds.), *Survey Methods in Multinational, Multiregional, and Multicultural contexts* (pp. 191–201). Hoboken, NJ: John Wiley & Sons.

Wasserman, M. R., Bender, D. E., Kalsbeek, W. D., Suchindran, C. M., & Mouw, T. (2005). A church-based sampling design for research with Latina immigrant women. *Population Research and Policy Review*, 24(6), 647–71.

Zahnd, E. G., Holtby, S., & Grant, D. (2011). *Increasing Cultural Sensitivity as a Means of Improving Cross-Cultural Surveys: Methods Utilized in the California Health Interview Survey (CHISS) 2001–2011*. Paper presented at the Annual Conference of the American Association for Public Opinion Research, Phoenix, AZ.

13

Challenges to surveying immigrants
DOUGLAS S. MASSEY

13.1 Introduction

In the last quarter of the twentieth century, virtually all developed nations became countries of immigration. International migration is inextricably bound to the globalization of the economy. As international trade and investment expand and markets penetrate more deeply into regions and sectors that were formerly outside or on the margins of global capitalism, the structural organization of society shifts in ways that accelerate geographic mobility (Massey, 1988). Since industrialization first permitted the global expansion of markets beginning in the early nineteenth century, two eras of globalization have prevailed (Hatton & Williamson, 2006; Massey, 2009; Williamson, 2004).

The first occurred during the nineteenth and early twentieth centuries and involved exchanges between the industrializing nations of Europe and their overseas extensions – settler societies in the Americas and Oceania and colonies in Africa and Asia. From 1846 to 1924, some 48 million migrants left Europe in response to the dislocations of industrialization, with more than 60 percent going to the United States and the rest proceeding mainly to Canada, Argentina, Brazil, and Australia (Massey, 1988). This first era was curtailed in 1914 by World War I, which squandered massive amounts of capital and labor in the trenches and destroyed the international order on which trade and commerce had rested (O'Rourke & Williamson, 1999).

The foundations for the second era were laid in the aftermath of World War II, when industrialized nations joined together to create a new set of transnational institutions to promote peace, prosperity, and more open trade across borders (Massey, 2009). The United Nations was formed to move disputes into mediation instead of war; the International Monetary Fund was created to ensure international liquidity in capital markets; the World Bank was founded to finance national growth and development; and the General Agreement on Tariffs and Trade and later the World Trade Organization were inaugurated to reduce barriers to trade and investment around the world (Kenwood & Lougheed, 1999).

The second era of globalization began slowly but accelerated rapidly during the final decades of the twentieth century. In the United States, for example, the fraction of GDP attributable to foreign trade rose from a nadir of 5 percent during the early 1930s to reach an average of 7 percent during the 1960s, 12 percent in the 1970s, 14 percent in the 1980s, and

18 percent in the 1990s (Massey & Taylor, 2004). Accompanying the revival of trade was a parallel expansion of international migration, with the number of legal immigrants to the US rising from just half a million persons in the 1930s to reach 3.3 million in the 1960s before rising to 4.5 million in the 1970s, 7.5 million in the 1980s, and 9.4 million in the 1990s (Massey, 1995). Similar trends were observed in other immigrant-receiving nations, such as Canada, Argentina, and Australia (Massey, Arango, Hugo, Kouaouci, Pellegrino, & Taylor, 1998).

In Europe, meanwhile, country after country shifted from the exportation to the importation of labor, with Britain, France, Germany, and the Benelux nations making the shift in the 1950s and 1960s and more peripheral nations, such as Sweden, Ireland, Italy, Spain, Portugal, and Greece doing so in the 1980s and 1990s (Massey *et al.*, 1998). By the end of the twentieth century, the transformation from emigration to immigration had spread to Japan, Korea, Taiwan, Hong Kong, Singapore, and Malaysia.

Immigration has thus emerged a characteristic feature of nearly all post-industrial societies and the percentage of immigrants is now rising in most developed nations. Among OECD nations, the average percentage of foreign born is currently 13.6 percent, ranging from 4.1 percent in Finland to 37 percent in Luxembourg (Organization for Economic Cooperation and Development, 2012). The presence of large populations of foreigners within nations presents a special challenge to survey researchers, for immigrants evince many of the characteristics typical of other hard-to-survey groups, such as high rates of geographic mobility, irregular housing arrangements, complex household structures, distrust of mainstream society, a stigmatized racial-ethnic status, and low levels of income and education. In addition, immigrants typically are not fluent in the host country language and in many nations display a wide diversity of tongues, thus rendering the translation of survey instruments difficult and costly.

13.2   Surveying immigrants in the United States

The United States has long been considered the premier "nation of immigrants," of course. Early in the nation's history, immigration was measured by counting foreign arrivals and tabulating their characteristics at ports of entry, but beginning in 1850 place of birth was asked as a regular part of the decennial census (Zolberg, 2006). After 1940, the birthplace question was no longer included in the complete census count, but as part of the "long form," a subsample of the census covering around a fifth of the US population. In 2010, the long form was replaced by the American Community Survey, which moving forward will be administered annually to around 2 million households and persons living in group quarters. Since 1970, foreign-born residents have also been asked to report their current citizenship, year of entry, and English language ability, in addition to all the other census questions posed to respondents (age, gender, education, occupation, etc.).

Using these data, the US Census Bureau regularly reports and produces detailed tabulations of the foreign-born population and an interactive online program allows users to construct their own tables to describe specific national origin groups and particular geographic regions. In addition, a Public Use Microdata Sample (PUMS) is released after the completion of each census, allowing anyone with programing skills to construct virtually any tabulation of immigrants they wish, subject to the stricture that they pertain to geographic entities containing at least 100,000 inhabitants. Using these data, analysts can also estimate statistical models to study immigrant adaptation and assimilation within various domains, such as language, education, employment, earnings, housing, marriage, family, and childbearing.

In addition to their own birthplace, from 1870 to 1970, the decennial census also asked respondents to report the birthplace of their parents, thereby enabling demographers to identify second generation immigrants separately from other members of the native-born population. In any immigrant-receiving society, a critical juncture in assessing the long-term prospects for assimilation and integration is what happens to members of the second generation. For this reason, studies of immigration to the United States historically have paid considerable attention to the children of immigrants. Given questions about parental birthplace, second generation immigrants can readily be identified and compared directly with first and third or higher generation immigrants on any characteristic measured in the census.

Unfortunately, after 1970, the question on parental birthplace was dropped from the decennial census, and despite vociferous protests from demographers was not reinstated on the 1980, 1990, or 2000 Censuses. As a result, during a period of mass immigration greater than any seen since the early twentieth century, in which record numbers of children were being born to immigrants, social scientists had no way to assess the progress of the second generation using nationally representative data. Unfortunately, the Census Bureau has decided not to include the parental birthplace question on the American Community Survey moving forward, so this deficit in the US statistical system persists (Massey, 2010).

This dearth of data was only partially mitigated by the private funding of specialized surveys launched at the end of the twentieth century, which sought to survey second generation immigrants in selected metropolitan areas. Although demographers were unable to get parental birthplace reinstated onto the census, however, beginning in 1996 they were successful in getting it placed on the demographic supplement to the Current Population Survey (CPS), which is administered by the Census Bureau on behalf of the US Bureau of Labor Statistics to produce monthly employment statistics. Every March it includes a detailed supplement with demographic questions that are used to generate intercensal population estimates. Unfortunately, the CPS is based on a rather small sample compared with the census long form or American Community Survey. As a result, CPS data only yield stable estimates for large immigrant groups (e.g., Mexicans) and geographic areas with large populations (e.g., Los Angeles).

Prior to 2002, the principal bureaucratic agency responsible for collecting and disseminating data on immigrant arrivals was the US Immigration and Naturalization Service, which was located in the Department of Justice. In that year, however, responsibility for immigration statistics was transferred to the Bureau of Citizenship and Immigration Services in the newly created Department of Homeland Security. Each year, the department's Office of Immigration Statistics extracts information from administrative encounters between foreigners and the US immigration bureaucracy to generate information on the number and characteristics of arriving foreigners.

Wherever an immigrant becomes a legal permanent resident of the United States, for example, he or she turns in a form whose information is then transferred to the Office of Immigration Statistics for processing. Unlike the census, however, the information available from the form is quite limited. Although it yields detailed information about visa category and sponsorship, it offers only basic data on demographic background (age, gender, marital status, place of birth, and place of intended residence) and very limited information on socioeconomic status (there is no information on education, for example) and nothing about an immigrant's circumstances before or after entry.

The arrival of temporary migrants is also tracked by the Office of Immigration Statistics, which publishes counts of people in various nonimmigrant visa categories (such as temporary workers, exchange visitors, students, diplomats, intra-company transferees, tourists, investors, and so on), but very little is known about the characteristics of the people in these classifications and nothing about them either before or after they enter the United States. The same office also keeps a running count of apprehensions along the Mexico–US border as well as deportations within the United States but records very few of their characteristics beyond nationality and gender.

Each year, the Office of Immigration Statistics publishes data from these sources in its *Yearbook of Immigration Statistics*, though typically at a lag of a year or more. Different sections pertain to legal immigrants, temporary immigrants, and apprehensions. Remarkably, the United States has no system in place to monitor the number and characteristics of people who leave the country; and in tabulating data on nonimmigrant entries and apprehensions, users should be aware that the numbers refer to events and not people. Those who enter on temporary visas or who are arrested by immigration authorities can and do encounter the statistical system multiple times in the course of a year, making counts in these categories problematic as indicators of international migration.

13.3   The rise of undocumented migration

A major difference between the current and the first era of globalization is that trading nations all now seek to impose limits on the number of migrants they accept, either temporarily or permanently. Whereas no nation imposed numerical limits on immigration prior to 1914, today authorities in all nations generally seek to control both the quantity and quality of foreigners crossing their borders. The globalizing forces that produce international migrants have not disappeared, however, and as a result a growing share of immigration today is unauthorized and most developed nations consequently have come to house significant populations of undocumented or illegal migrants (Cornelius, Martin, & Hollifield, 1994).

In the United States, undocumented migration did not exist as a practical category until 1924, when the Border Patrol was founded and the frontiers first enforced. At this time, however, the agency's mission was to prevent the entry of Europeans through Mexico and Canada rather than to block in-migration by Mexicans and Canadians themselves, who were not subject to numerical limitation under existing immigration laws. Although a mass deportation campaign against Mexicans forcibly removed some 450,000 migrants during the Great Depression, the large majority of these people were present legally and a good number were US citizens (Balderrama & Rodriguez, 2006; Hoffman, 1974).

Illegal migration did not really become a national issue until the early 1950s when visas from a temporary worker program created by Congress proved insufficient to accommodate the demand for Mexican farm workers, leading to a rise in unauthorized entries. In the context of an economic recession and rising antiforeign hysteria whipped up during the McCarthy Era, the US Immigration and Naturalization Service launched Operation Wetback to assuage public fears, deporting more than a million undocumented Mexicans working in border states during 1953–54. The crisis was quickly defused, however, not so much by the apprehensions as by the expansion of the guest worker program, which rose from around 68,000 visas annually in 1950 to nearly 450,000 in 1956 (Calavita, 1992). At the same time, legal immigration from Mexico was not subject to numerical limitation, and in response to labor shortages US employers began to sponsor workers for legal permanent residence in growing numbers. By the late 1950s, illegal migration had disappeared and the total legal inflow from Mexico averaged around half a million persons per year, about 50,000 legal permanent residents and 450,000 temporary workers (Massey, 2012).

The current era of undocumented migration dates to 1965, when Congress acted unilaterally to terminate Mexico's guest worker program and impose the first ever limits on legal immigration from the Western Hemisphere, which was initially capped at 120,000 visas per year with no country limitations. By 1976, however, each nation was subject to an annual quota of 20,000 residence visas, so that in twenty years Mexico went from access to 450,000 temporary work visas and a theoretically unlimited number of residence visas (in practice around 50,000 per year) to zero temporary work visas and just 20,000 residence visas (Massey & Pren, 2012a).

However, by 1965, the annual flow of migrants northward from Mexico to the United States was well established, sustained by strong migrant networks, and institutionalized in recruitment practices. As a result, when opportunities for legal entry were curtailed, the flows simply reestablished themselves under undocumented auspices. For example, when Massey and Pren (2012a) proxied undocumented entries as the number of apprehensions per Border Patrol officer (thereby controlling the enforcement effort), they found that apprehensions per officer rose from just 37 in 1965 to around 464 in 1977. Thereafter, growth in the volume of undocumented migration ceased and apprehensions per capita fluctuated around 400 per year through 1985. Annual entries of legal permanent residents expanded slowly from 38,000 to 61,000 (exceeding the cap of 20,000, because immediate relatives of US citizens are exempt).

In reality, therefore, the size of the inflow from Mexico changed very little after 1965. What changed was the legal status of those entering, which went from overwhelmingly legal to overwhelmingly illegal. From 1965 to 1985, the flow nonetheless remained circular and the undocumented population grew slowly. According to estimates by Massey and Singer (1985), between these dates 85 percent of undocumented entries were offset by departures, and in 1985 the total undocumented population stood at just 3 million. The increase in border apprehensions from 1965 through the late 1970s, however, is critically important to understanding the dynamics of international migration in the years that followed, for it was this development that transformed what had been an invisible circulation of innocuous workers into a yearly and highly visible violation of American sovereignty by aliens who were increasingly framed as invaders and criminals.

Chavez (2001, 2008) has documented the rise of what he calls the "Hispanic threat narrative" from 1970 to 2000, which Santa Ana (2002) and Massey, Durand, and Malone (2002) have pointed out was characterized by the deployment of marine and martial metaphors in anti-immigrant discourse, with the United States being "flooded" by a "rising tide" of illegal immigrants or "invaded" by dangerous "aliens" that posed a threat to American culture and society. Massey and Pren (2012a, 2012b) confirmed a strong empirical connection between the use of such metaphors in newspapers and the number of annual border apprehensions. The rise of this threat narrative was, in turn, associated with the passage of increasingly restrictive immigration legislation and the implementation of ever more stringent border policies (Massey & Pren, 2012a).

The sustained accumulation of anti-immigrant legislation and enforcement operations produced a massive increase in border apprehensions beginning in the late 1970s, even though the underlying flow of undocumented entries was leveling off. For any given number of people attempting to cross the border without authorization, more resources devoted to border enforcement (more Border Patrol agents and bigger enforcement budgets) generate more apprehensions, a statistic that politicians and bureaucrats can then use to inflame public opinion and argue for even more resources, stricter laws, and more enforcement operations, which generate still more apprehensions, thus creating a self-perpetuating cycle of escalating apprehensions and enforcement (Andreas, 2000; Massey & Pren, 2012a).

In sum, after 1977, anti-immigrant sentiment increasingly fed off itself to drive the bureaucratic machinery of enforcement forward to new heights, despite the lack of any real increase in illegal migration (Massey & Pren, 2012a). As a result, apprehensions paradoxically continued to rise even though undocumented entries had stopped growing. The end result of this feedback loop was the exponential growth in border enforcement in a way that was disconnected from the underlying traffic in unauthorized entries. From the point at which unauthorized entries stabilized in 1977 to 2010, the number of Border Patrol agents increased nearly five times and the agency's budget rose by a factor of sixteen (Massey & Pren, 2012a).

Numerous studies confirm that this increase in border enforcement did not have the desired effect in forestalling growth of the unauthorized population (Redburn, Reuter, & Majmundar, 2011). Indeed, from 1980 when Warren and Passel (1987) first estimated the number of undocumented Mexicans to be 1.13 million, the population grew to 2.04 million in 1990, reached 4.68 million in 2000, and peaked at 7.03 million in 2008 (Wasem, 2011). Other nationalities – overwhelmingly Latino – brought the total undocumented population to 11 million in that year. Not only did massive enforcement fail to prevent the entry of unauthorized migrants, however; it actually accelerated the *net* inflow, for while it had little effect on the inflow of illegal migrants it had a profound effect in reducing the outflow (Massey, 2007, 2011). As the costs and risks of unauthorized border crossing mounted, migrants minimized their exposure by shifting from a circular to a settled pattern of migration, essentially hunkering down and staying once they had successfully run the gauntlet at the border (Massey, Durand, & Malone, 2002).

Estimates reviewed by Wasem (2011) and analyzed by Massey and Pren (2012a) reveal that undocumented population growth accelerated after the Immigration Reform and Control Act (IRCA) began militarizing the border in 1986 and then accelerated again after the launching of Operation Blockade in El Paso and Operation Gatekeeper in San Diego accelerated in 1993 and 1994. Although the undocumented population declined in the immediate aftermath of IRCA's legalization programs, growth clearly resumed at a more rapid pace after 1988 and then accelerated in the latter half of the 1990s and continued up to 2008 when immigration was curtailed by the Great Recession. As already noted, by that date, the population of undocumented migrants by then stood at 11 million and constituted around 3.5 percent of the US population.

Although undocumented migrants may comprise a relatively small share of the US population, however, they constitute a much larger share of certain immigrant subgroups, representing 28 percent of all immigrants and more than half of all Hispanic immigrants present in the United States (Massey & Pren, 2012a, 2012b). In some populations, such as Mexicans, Guatemalans, and Hondurans, the percentage of unauthorized among immigrants is 60 percent or greater. Given that Hispanics now constitute 16 percent of the US population and are projected to reach 29 percent by 2050, the presence of so many unauthorized migrants constitutes a real barrier to the representative sampling and valid surveying of both immigrants and Hispanics, for if immigrants in general are hard to survey, undocumented migrants are doubly so, for they experience a source of marginalization not experienced by any other group in the United States – they are actively persecuted (Massey & Sánchez, 2010).

The massive increase in border enforcement over the past four decades has already been mentioned; but beginning in the 1990s, enforcement began to turn inward, focusing less on apprehending migrants at the border and more on locating, arresting, and deporting them within the interior of the United States. Whereas border apprehensions fell from 1.55 million in 1996 to 328,000 in 2011, internal arrests and deportations rose from 70,000 to 400,000 over the same period. In addition, between 2005 and 2010 some sixty-eight state and local agencies signed cooperative enforcement agreements with federal immigration authorities (US Immigration and Customs Enforcement, 2012) and state legislatures introduced some 6,140 immigration-related bills (National Council of State Legislatures, 2012).

The spread of enforcement efforts from the federal to the state and local levels has put great pressure not only on undocumented migrants, but all Hispanics. According to a 2010 survey conducted by the Pew Hispanic Center, 68 percent of foreign-born Hispanics worry about deportation some or a lot; but even among native-born citizens the figure was 32 percent (Lopez, Morin, & Taylor, 2010). Among native Hispanic respondents, 28 percent said they personally knew someone who had been deported, whereas among foreign-born Hispanics the figure was 35 percent – and among the undocumented it was 45 percent (Lopez, Morin, & Taylor, 2010).

Enforcement is often achieved through systematic ethnic profiling, in which Hispanics are singled out for requests to produce identification. As of 2010, 61 percent of Hispanics saw discrimination as a major problem holding them back in the United States, up from 47 percent in 2002; and another 24 percent saw it as a minor problem, bringing the total to 85 percent who viewed discrimination as problematic for Latinos. Among the foreign born, 70 percent saw discrimination as a major problem and among undocumented migrants 78 percent had this perception. When asked what the biggest cause of discrimination was, 36 percent spontaneously reported immigration status. Under these circumstances, it is hardly surprising that 52 percent of foreign-born Hispanics and 45 percent of natives said that people in the United States were less accepting of immigrants now than five years ago (Lopez *et al.*, 2010).

13.4   Undocumented migrants in government surveys

As undocumented migration began rising in the 1970s, demographers began to worry about its effects on measures of population growth and composition. To the extent that the undocumented are excluded from statistics on migration, of course, their absence obviously understates net migration into the country. In addition, to the extent that they are excluded from sources such as the decennial census, the CPS, and the American Community Survey, their absence also inflates mortality and fertility rates (Parrado, 2011). This inflation occurs because even though undocumented migrants are undercounted in censuses and surveys used to derive population estimates, the deaths and births they produce are included in the nation's registration system, given that live births and dead bodies are difficult to hide. In other words, whereas vital events associated with undocumented migrants are well captured in the numerators of fertility and mortality rates, therefore, person-years lived by undocumented migrants are undercounted in the denominators, leading to an upward bias that can be substantial in localities or groups containing large undocumented populations (Parrado, 2011).

In order to estimate the number of undocumented migrants present in the United States, demographers turned initially to census and CPS enumerations of the foreign born. After subtracting likely deaths, adjusting for legal in-migration and out-migration, and correcting for various forms of misreporting and census underenumeration, a residual always resulted that Warren and Passel (1987) interpreted to constitute an estimate of the undocumented population. Over time, this residual estimation method has been refined and perfected to affirm that, in the aggregate, undocumented migrants are indeed included in the census and federal surveys, though naturally subject to an undercount that researchers generally estimate to be in the range of 10 percent to 15 percent (Passel & Cohn, 2008; Wasem,

Card 1   **Card 2**

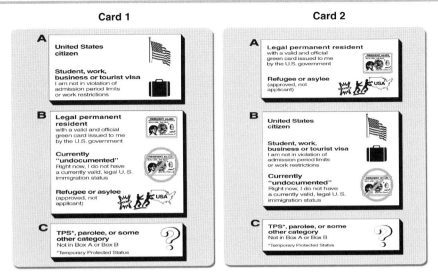

Figure 13.1   Example of cards used in two-card estimation of undocumented migration from social surveys

2011), though recent work comparing Mexican and US sources suggest it could be higher (Genoni, Rubalcava, Teruel, & Thomas, 2012).

In addition to the residual estimation method, demographers have also developed a "two card method," also known as the "grouped answers approach," to compute the number of undocumented migrants directly from survey data. In this approach, respondents are asked about their current immigration status and asked to reply using one of two different flash cards, each containing three boxes labeled A, B, and C (US Government General Accounting Office, 2006). As shown in Figure 13.1, on Card 1, Box A lists two categories: "United States citizen and student, work, business, or tourist visa"; Box B lists three categories "legal permanent resident, currently undocumented, and refugee or asylee"; and Box C includes the words "temporary protected status, parolee, or some other category." On Card 2, the boxes are defined differently: Category A is labeled "legal permanent resident and refugee or asylee"; Category B includes "United States citizen, student, work, business, or tourist visa, and currently undocumented"; and Category C is again "temporary protected status, parolee, or some other category."

Half the sample is randomly picked to receive Card 1 and the other half Card 2. Both sets of respondents are then asked to pick the box that includes their current immigration status. Since the category "currently undocumented" is included in Box B on both cards along with two other legal statuses, the threat of identifying oneself as undocumented is mitigated by the fact that in selecting "B" the respondent's actual status is unknown: it could be one of the two legal statuses or it could be undocumented, and there is no way for the interviewer or later researchers to know which one applies to that individual.

However, Box B on Card 1 includes "legal permanent resident, currently undocumented, and refugee or asylee" whereas Box A on Card 2 is simply labeled "legal permanent resident and refugee or asylee" (i.e., excluding "currently undocumented"). Since responding to Card 1 or Card 2 is randomly assigned, the two halves of the sample can each be used to generate independent, unbiased estimates of the categories covered in Box B of Card 1 and Box A of Card 2. When subtracted from one another they yield an unbiased estimate of the number of undocumented migrants while maintaining the anonymity about the legal status of individual migrants. Since the sample size is effectively halved, however, the efficiency of estimation is systematically reduced. As a result, although the method has been piloted successfully by the General Accounting Office, it has not been widely applied in actual surveys.

In contrast, aggregate estimates of the undocumented population using the residual method have now become routine and are regularly published by the Pew Hispanic Center (Passel & Cohen, 2011) and Homeland Security's Office of Immigration Statistics (Hoefer, Rytina, & Baker, 2011). However, because neither the residual nor the two-card method allows the identification of an individual's immigration status, it is impossible to study how illegal status affects behavior and outcomes. In order to assess outcomes and behaviors, researchers have applied the logic of the two-card method to the interview setting, asking foreign-born respondents successive questions about whether they fall into one of several broad categories, but not asking explicitly whether the person is undocumented.

On the Survey of Income and Program Participation (SIPP), for example, respondents are first asked whether they are US citizens; then whether they are legal permanent residents; followed by whether they have a tourist visa, student visa, work visa or permit, or other document permitting them to stay in the US for a limited time; and finally whether they have been granted asylum, refugee status, or temporary protected status. To end the series of questions, respondents are asked whether the visa or document they hold is currently valid, thus enabling researchers easily to classify respondents into four legal categories: citizens, legal immigrants, temporary visitors, and refugees/asylees.

If they do not fall into one of these rubrics they are by implication undocumented; but the question is not directly asked in order to mitigate the implicit threat. Although the SIPP is based on a representative national sample, the sample is not large and captures relatively few immigrants, especially since the undocumented do not qualify for receipt of public services and even legal immigrants are excluded from some programs. The same approach has been used with some success on localized surveys, such as the Los Angeles Family and Neighborhood Survey (Sastry, Ghosh-Dastidar, Adams, & Pebley, 2006).

13.5 Targeted surveys of immigrants

Given the importance of undocumented migration to US population dynamics and the limitations that standard surveys have in assessing the characteristics and behavior of those present without authorization, researchers have turned to alternative approaches that target immigrants specifically. One approach that has gained currency blends survey research with ethnographic methods to interview international migrants in communities of origin as well as the destination country. The other draws on official records of persons receiving legal permanent resident status to select representative samples of entering cohorts of legal immigrants, who are then queried about prior experiences as migrants in and out of legal status.

13.5.1 Ethnosurvey studies

The ethnosurvey is a multimethod data gathering technique that simultaneously applies ethnographic and survey methods within a single study. Developed initially by Massey, Alarcón, Durand, and González (1987) to study emigration from Mexico, the approach has since been applied in a variety of locales throughout Mexico and in other countries to generate reliable and valid data on international migration, both documented and undocumented. Unlike standard surveys based on national probability samples, ethnosurveys yield community level data that allow investigators to compare the characteristics and behavior of documented and undocumented migrants (Massey, 1987; Massey & Capoferro, 2004).

The basic idea underlying an ethnosurvey is that qualitative and quantitative data collection methods complement one another, and that when properly combined, one's weaknesses become the other's strengths, yielding a body of data with greater reliability and more internal validity than would be possible to achieve using either method alone (Massey, 1999). Whereas survey methods produce reliable quantitative data for statistical analysis, generalization, and replication, in guaranteeing quantitative rigor, they lose historical depth, richness of context, and the intuitive appeal of real life. Ethnographic studies, in contrast, capture the richness of the phenomenon under study, but the lack of quantitative data makes it difficult to prove the validity of conclusions to other scientists, and renders subjective elements of interpretation more difficult to detect and control. Qualitative field studies are also difficult to replicate.

The ethnosurvey was developed to capitalize on the strengths of both methods while minimizing their respective weaknesses and became the core data gathering approach of the Mexican Migration Project (MMP) (http://mmp.opr.princeton.edu/). Quantitative data are gathered using a semistructured interview schedule that lies midway between the highly structured instrument of the survey researcher and the guided conversation of the ethnographer. It represents a compromise instrument that balances the goal of unobtrusive measurement with the need for standardization and quantification. It yields an interview that is informal, nonthreatening, and natural, but one that allows the interviewer some discretion about how and when to ask sensitive questions. Ultimately, it produces a standard set of reliable information that carries greater validity than that obtained using normal survey methods.

The interview schedule is laid out in a series of tables with variables arranged in columns across the top and the rows referring variously to persons, events, years, or other meaningful categories. The interviewer holds a natural conversation with the subject and fills in the cells of the table by soliciting required information in ways that the situation seems to demand, using his or her judgment as to the timing and wording of specific questions or probes. Each table is organized around a particular topic, giving coherence and order to the "conversation," and certain specialized probes may be included to elaborate particular themes of interest.

Rather than fielding the instrument nationally, it is applied to a probability sample of specific communities selected according to a carefully designed sampling plan. During the implementation of the survey, qualitative field work continues and the flow of analysis is organized so that preliminary quantitative data from the survey are made available to ethnographic investigators before they leave the field. In this way, findings emerging from quantitative analysis are able to shape qualitative field work, just as insights from early ethnographies guide later statistical studies.

The semistructured questionnaire is readily adapted to compile event histories on various aspects of social and economic life, such as employment, migration, marriage, childbearing, and property ownership. Different facets of a respondent's life are covered by different tables in the event history questionnaire. Event histories gathered from randomly selected respondents yield a representative sample of a community's recent social history. When properly compiled and coded, the various event histories (employment, marriage, fertility, etc.) can be combined with the aid of a computer to construct a comprehensive life history for each respondent, summarizing key events for each person-year of life from birth (or some other relevant starting point) to the survey date.

Although individuals may be the ultimate units of analysis, their decisions are typically made within larger social and economic contexts. These contexts structure and constrain individual decisions so that analyses conducted only at the micro level are perforce incomplete. The ethnosurvey design is therefore explicitly multilevel, compiling data simultaneously for individuals, households, communities, and even the nations in which they reside. In the case of migration, although individuals ultimately make the decision to go or stay, it is typically reached within some larger family or household unit. Likewise, households exist within larger communities that influence family decision-making.

Information is thus solicited from all household members, which enables the estimation of contextual variables like dependency, family income, life cycle stage, and kinship connections to other migrants. At the same time, other modules gather information on variables that pertain directly to households themselves, such as property ownership, dwelling construction, home furnishings, length of residence, and tenure in the home. If communities themselves are sampling units, and quantitative information is gathered on multiple communities as part of a cluster sampling design, then field workers also complete community inventories that later enable researchers to construct aggregate-level data files.

A distinguishing feature of the ethnosurvey is the careful selection of sites and the use of representative sampling methods within them. The sites may be chosen according to specific criteria designed to enable comparative analysis between settings, or they may be chosen randomly from a universe of possible sites in order to represent a population of interest. The latter procedure yields a representative cluster sample that generates unbiased statistical estimates. Whether chosen randomly or according to a priori specifications, however, both internal and external validity are greatly enhanced by multiple field sites. A variety of sites also enhance the strength of inference in qualitative as well as quantitative analyses.

International migration is, by definition, a transnational social process and whenever a social process transcends geographic or cultural boundaries parallel sampling is recommended. Parallel sampling involves the gathering of contemporaneous samples in the different geographic locations that serve as loci for the social or economic process under study. In the case of migration, representative samples of respondents are surveyed in both sending and receiving areas. This strategy is necessary because migration, like most social and economic processes, is selective. Parallel sampling raises certain troubling technical issues, however. Whereas it is straightforward to design a representative sample of returned migrants who live in a particular sending community, it is more difficult to generate a representative sample of settled emigrants from that community who reside elsewhere. The main difficulty lies in constructing a sampling frame that includes all out-migrants from a community, since they are typically scattered across a variety of towns and cities, both domestic and foreign. New techniques of multiplicity sampling, however, solve the main problems of parallel sampling (Kalton, 2009; Kalton & Anderson, 1986).

In a multiplicity sample of out-migrants, respondents in sending communities provide information not only about themselves and others in the household, but also about some well-defined class of relatives – usually siblings – who live outside the community. When the survey of households in the sending community is complete, a sampling frame for settled out-migrant siblings will have been compiled and a random sample of emigrants may be chosen from it. Researchers then return to households containing relatives of the sampled siblings to obtain information necessary to locate them in destination areas. Then, they go to these destination areas to administer the interview schedule, yielding a representative sample of the out-migrant community.

As already noted, the ethnosurvey was originally applied as the central data gathering tool for the MMP, which undertook pilot surveys in four Mexican communities and their US branches in 1982–83 and since 1987 has continuously returned to the field each year to gather information in four to six new binational communities, steadily broadening the geographic coverage within both Mexico and the United States (Durand & Massey, 2004). At this writing, the dataset consists of random samples of 134 Mexican communities located in twenty states combined (in most cases) with network samples of settled out-migrants from those communities located in US destination areas. Although the combined sample cannot be considered representative of all Mexican migrants to the United States, systematic comparisons between the MMP and national samples done in Mexico have revealed a remarkably close correspondence with respect to social, economic, and demographic characteristics (Massey & Capoferro, 2004; Massey & Zenteno, 2000). The MMP database has become a standard source of information about the characteristics and behavior of undocumented Mexican migrants to the United States, with more than 2,000 registered data users.

A number of projects have sought to build on the success of the MMP by using ethnosurvey methods to study other migratory systems. In the early 1990s, for example, the

Economic Commission for Europe sponsored a round of 1,595 ethnosurveys in Poland, Lithuania, and Ukraine to study immigration to Western Europe in the wake of the break-up of the Soviet Union (Mullan & Frejka, 1994); and in 1998, the Latin American Migration Project (LAMP) was launched to study emigration from nations in the Americas other than Mexico (http://lamp.opr.princeton.edu/). By 2010, the LAMP had surveyed 8,557 house-holds located in fifty-two communities in ten Latin American and the Caribbean nations (Donato, Hiskey, Durand, & Massey, 2010).

More recently, the China International Migration Project (www.albany.edu/cimp/) has surveyed 3,120 households located in Fujian Province (Liang, Chunyu, Zhuang, & Ye, 2008) and between 2003 and 2005, scholars at the Universities of Leipzig and Mannheim fielded the Polish Migration Project (www.uni-leipzig.de/~lskalter/projekt1_en.php), which undertook 2,014 interviews in four Polish communities to study emi-gration to Germany and other Western European nations (Kalter, 2011). Even more recently, the African-European Migration Project (www.ined.fr/en/institut/partnerships/europe/mafe/) surveyed 4,010 households from Senegal, the Congo, and Senegal about emigration to various European destinations (Flahaux, Beauchemin, & Schoumaker, 2010).

13.5.2   The New Immigrant Survey (NIS)

The NIS (http://nis.princeton.edu/) was designed to be a longitudinal survey of an entering cohort of new legal immigrants to the United States, selected using probability methods from an administrative listing of legal permanent residents who entered the country during a specific period of time. Because such a design had not previously been attempted, the NIS began with a pilot survey of legal immigrants admitted to permanent residence in July and August of 1996. The overall response rate was 62 percent, yielding an interviewed sample of 1,224 persons, of whom 1,127 are adult immigrants. The pilot demonstrated the efficacy and cost-effectiveness of methods designed to locate immigrants, interview them, and follow them over time, and was shown to yield a representative sample of legal immigrants admitted during fiscal year 1996 (Jasso, 2011; Jasso, Massey, Rosenzweig, & Smith, 2005).

The first round of the NIS sampled new legal immigrants who received their residence documents during a twelve-month period from June 2003 to June 2004, yielding 8,573 adult immigrants interviewed with a response rate of 68.6 percent, as well as interviews with 4,336 spouses who were present in the household and detailed interviews with parents of about 1,062 children under 18 residing in the household. From adults, detailed information was obtained on characteristics and behaviors across a variety of social, demographic, and economic domains, including migration, marriage, childbearing, schooling, employment, and earnings, assets, transfers, language, religion, health, and insurance and cognitive assessments were carried out on children aged 3–12.

A key feature of the NIS was the compilation of migration histories that included visits and trips to the United States undertaken prior to receipt of permanent residence, thus enabling investigators to learn about migration in other legal statuses. According to Massey and Malone's (2003) analysis of pilot data, only one third of all "new" legal immigrants were in the United States for the first time when they received their residence documents, whereas 32 percent reported prior undocumented experience (21 percent entered without authorization and 11 percent overstayed a visa). In addition, 15 percent reported prior experience as temporary visitors, 11 percent as refugees, 6 percent as students or trainees, and 4 percent as temporary workers. Among some groups, the percentage of immigrants with prior undocumented experience was much greater. Among Mexicans, for example, 57 percent had at some point in time entered without authorization and another 9 percent had overstayed a visa. Using a different accounting method, Jasso, Massey, Rosenzweig, and Smith (2008) found very similar results. Immigration status is thus a fluid category that changes over time.

In the initial wave of the NIS, interviewers generally found that respondents were surprisingly open to talking about prior experiences as undocumented migrants and were not difficult to interview once located. As noted above, however, the social climate for immigrants in the United States had changed quite dramatically by the time of the second wave, which was fielded between June 2007 and December 2009. Despite the lengthy period in the field, the follow-rates were disappointingly low. Investigators were able to interview successfully only 3,902 of the original adult sample members for a response rate of 45.5 percent (46.1 percent once death and incapacitation were taken into account). Among spouses, 1,557 were re-interviewed for a response rate of 35.9 percent, whereas 53.3 percent of parents responded to questions about their minor children and another 28.1 percent of the now-adult children answered for themselves. The second round data are currently being processed and cleaned for public release early in 2013.

13.6 Second generation surveys

Given the lack of any data on second generation immigrants before 1996 and the absence of large nationally representative samples of the children of immigrants since that date, the Russell Sage Foundation and other funding agencies took the lead in funding specialized surveys of the children of immigrants in selected metropolitan areas. The first was the Children of Immigrants Longitudinal Study (www.icpsr.umich.edu/icpsrweb/ICPSR/studies/20520), which first went into the field in 1992 with a representative sample of 8th and 9th grade children attending public and private schools in the Miami and San Diego Metropolitan areas (with about 54 percent of respondents in the former Metropolitan Statistical Area and 46 percent in the latter). The total sample size was 5,262 and focused on children's demographic characteristics, language use, self-identities, and academic attainment in the United States. Although the survey included children of seventy-seven different national origins, the samples are most representative of the two dominant groups in each metropolitan area: Cubans in Miami and Mexicans in San Diego (Portes & Rumbaut, 2001, 2006).

The second wave occurred three years later, when most respondents were about to graduate from high school and sought to assess language knowledge and preference, ethnic identity, self-esteem, and academic attainment. This follow-up survey interviewed 4,288 of the original respondents for a response rate of 81.5 percent. In order to compile more accurate information about the children's families of origin, 2,442 parents constituting 46 percent of the original student sample were also interviewed. The third wave went into the field during 2001–03, when respondents were around 24 years of age. Most respondents by then were located at places of work or residence, not only in Miami and San Diego but in more than thirty states and military bases overseas. Respondents to this wave constituted 68.9 percent of the original wave and 84.3 percent of the second wave and provided updated information on their educational attainment, employment and occupational status, income, civil status, ethnicity of spouses, political attitudes and participation, ethnic and racial identities, delinquency and incarceration, attitudes and levels of identification with American society, as well as plans for the future (Portes & Rumbaut, 2001, 2006; Rumbaut & Portes, 2001).

The next second generation survey to enter the field was the Immigrant Second Generation Study in Metropolitan New York (www.icpsr.umich.edu/icpsrweb/RCMD/studies/30302?geography=New+York+City). The target population for this study was persons 18–32 who were born in the US to parents who immigrated after 1965 or who were born abroad but arrived in the US by age 12 and grew up in the United States. Following a pilot survey in July of 1996, formal interviewing took place during 1999 and 2000 and was based on a random telephone survey of 3,615 respondents from five second generation and three native-born groups living in New York City and the inner suburbs in New Jersey, Westchester, and Long Island, with a response rate of 53.2 percent. The data also include a supplemental survey of 557 respondents located in outer suburbs and in-person, plus in-depth interviews with 333 of original survey respondents (Kasinitz, Mollenkopf, Waters, & Holdaway, 2008; Kasinitz, Mollenkopf, & Waters 2004).

The last of the three specialized second generation surveys is the Immigration and Intergenerational Mobility in Metropolitan Los Angeles Study (www.icpsr.umich.edu/icpsrweb/ICPSR/studies/22627), which focused on young adults aged 20–39 from six foreign-born and foreign-parentage groups: Mexican, Vietnamese, Filipino, Korean, Chinese, and Central American (Guatemalan and Salvadoran), as well as native-born and native-parentage of Mexican-Americans, non-Hispanic Whites, and non-Hispanic Blacks, in the greater Los Angeles area (the counties of Los Angeles, Orange, Ventura, Riverside, and San Bernardino). A total 4,655 interviews were completed between the start of full-scale interviewing in April 2004 and its conclusion in October 2004. The survey was designed to provide basic demographic data as well as extensive information about language use, ethnic identity, religion, remittances, intermarriage, experiences of discrimination, parental background, respondent education, first and current job, wealth and income, encounters with the law, childhood and current neighborhoods of residence, political attitudes, voting behavior, naturalization, and transnational ties (Lee & Bean, 2012).

13.7 Immigrants and the future of surveys

Immigrants have become a fundamental component of post-industrial societies through-out the world, because international migration is intrinsic to broader processes of economic globalization and market expansion. Among OECD nations, the average percentage foreign born is currently 13.6 percent, and with a foreign-born percentage of 13.7 percent, the United States sits squarely in the middle of the pack. Countries exceeding the US foreign-born percentage now include Australia (25.4 percent), Austria (15.3 percent), Canada (20.2 percent), Switzerland (24.8 percent), Spain (14.1 percent), Ireland (16.7 percent), New Zealand (22.3 percent), Sweden (13.9 percent), and Luxembourg (36.9 percent). The percentage of foreigners is even higher, of course, in gateway cities, such as London, Frankfurt, Amsterdam, and Stockholm. The recruitment of immigrants into social surveys and their successful interviewing is no longer just an American issue.

Large immigrant populations have thus become a characteristic feature of developed societies throughout the world, creating problems for survey researchers. Immigrants historically have been difficult to survey because they have many of the characteristics common to other hard-to-survey groups: high rates of geographic mobility, irregular hous-ing arrangements, complex household structures, distrust of mainstream society, a stigma-tized racial-ethnic status, and low levels of income and education. In addition, immigrants in contemporary society evince two other traits that set them apart as especially problematic for survey researchers: they speak a diversity of foreign languages and significant shares are present without authorization.

The United States has long been a country of immigration, of course, but recent years have been characterized by two developments that have rendered the task of survey researchers more difficult: a remarkable rise in the size of the undocumented population and an associated increase in xenophobia and nativism, with particular animus directed at Hispanics, now the nation's largest minority group at more than 16 percent of the population (Massey & Sánchez, 2010). Illegal migrants constitute large fractions of certain national origins such as Mexicans and Central Americans, and all Hispanic origins report a rising fear of deportation, growing discrimination, and increasing feelings of ostracism and exclusion.

Given its status as a traditional immigrant-receiving nation, the United States has a long history of enumerating and surveying immigrants. Place of birth has been included as part of the US Census since 1850, was on the census long form from 1940 through 2000, and will be a part of the American Community Survey from 2010 onward, along with questions on citizenship, year of entry, and English language ability. Unfortunately, a question on the birthplace of parents, which had been a part of the census between 1870 and 1970, was eliminated in the latter year and has not been reinstated either on the long form or the American Community Survey, making it impossible to identify second generation immi-grants using a large, nationwide sample. The only source of national information on the second generation comes from the CPS, whose sample size is insufficient to support detailed work on most national origins and smaller geographic areas.

Undocumented migration began to rise in the United States after US authorities cut off Mexico's access to legal visas in 1965. In response to rising apprehensions at the border, immigration laws and enforcement operations became ever more restrictive, which had the counterproductive effect of reducing return migration back to Mexico rather than departures for the United States. As a result, the undocumented population grew at an unprecedented rate to stabilize at a current population of around 11 million persons. Work done between 1980 and 2000 indicated that most undocumented residents were captured in the decennial census and the March CPS, with an undercount estimated to be in the range of 10 percent to 15 percent, thus enabling demographers to use indirect methods to estimate the size and basic characteristics of the undocumented population.

There is growing evidence to suggest that these coverage rates may not persist into the future. A recent comparison of Mexican and US Surveys suggests that the undercount rate for recent arrivals may be as high as 30 percent (Genoni *et al.*, 2012). In addition the response rate on the NIS plummeted from 69 percent to 46 percent between the first and second waves (in 2003 and 2008), even though response rates on panel surveys are typically much higher than on cross-sectional surveys (Schoeni, Stafford, McGonagle, & Andreski, 2013) and all of the respondents were themselves legal (though many had prior illegal experience and were socially connected to current undocumented migrants).

These trends not only threaten response rates on government surveys such as the ACS and CPS, but also carry serious implications for targeted surveys of first and second generation immigrants. Given current public hostility toward immigrants and the draconian laws now in force, immigrants appear to be increasingly unwilling to come forward and speak frankly to strangers. Even using ethnosurvey methods, a recent pilot survey conducted in new immigrant destinations around Durham, NC, investigators were only able to achieve a response rate in the neighborhood of 50 percent. On the MMP, the network sampling methods traditionally used to undertake surveys among migrants settled in the United States are breaking down, as respondents in Mexico are increasingly unwilling to provide contact information on friends and relatives in the United States and those contacted are less willing to open their doors to project personnel. Even within Mexico, the rise of narco-violence has made interviewing in some sending regions dangerous, forcing investigators to abandon plans for surveying certain targeted communities in regions of pervasive narcotic trafficking.

The changing circumstances of field work in places of both origin and destination has prompted investigators to innovate and adopt new methods. Although ethnosurveys traditionally have not offered financial incentives to respondents, in some surveys done in urban areas of the Latin American Migration Project material incentives had to be offered and even then the response rate averaged just 65 percent compared to a project average of around 92 percent. In a recent survey done in Nepal, interviewers arrived at households with cell phones and instead of asking for contact information they simply arranged to speak by phone with out-migrant family members over the phone, either then or at a later time (Ghimire, Williams, Thornton, Young-DeMarco, & Bhandari, 2012). The prepaid cell phones or calling cards used for the interview may then be left for respondent households in recognition of their participation.

Whether these and other innovations yet to be developed are successful in overcoming the reluctance of immigrants to participate in surveys, whether the current anti-immigrant climate prevailing in the United States and other nations gives way to a renewed era of tolerance, or whether a political accommodation will be reached to legalize those migrants currently out of status remains to be seen. Whatever happens, immigrants have likely become a permanent structural feature of contemporary societies and methods will need to be developed and monitored to ensure their inclusion in surveys, now and in the future.

References

Andreas, P. (2000). *Border Games: Policing the US-Mexico Divide*. Ithaca: Cornell University Press.

Balderrama, F. E., & Rodriguez, R. (2006). *Decade of Betrayal: Mexican Repatriation in the 1930s* (2nd edn.). Albuquerque: University of New Mexico Press.

Calavita, K. (1992). Inside the state: the bracero program, immigration, and the I.N.S. New York: Routledge.

Chavez, L. R. (2001). *Covering Immigration: Population Images and the Politics of the Nation*. Berkeley: University of California Press.

    (2008). *The Latino Threat: constructing Immigrants, Citizens, and the Nation*. Stanford: Stanford University Press.

Cornelius, W. A., Martin, P. L., & Hollifield, J. F. (1994). Introduction: the ambivalent quest for immigration control. In W. A. Cornelius, P. L. Martin, & J. F. Hollifield (eds.), *Controlling Immigration: a Global Perspective* (pp. 3–41). Stanford: Stanford University Press.

Donato, K., Hiskey, J., Durand, J., & Massey, D. S. (eds.). (2010). *Continental Divides: International Migration in the Americas*. Thousand Oaks: Sage Publications.

Durand, J., & Massey, D. S. (2004). *Crossing the Border: Research from the Mexican Migration Project*. New York: Russell Sage Foundation.

Flahaux, M. L., Beauchemin, C., & Schoumaker, B. (2010). Partir, revenir: tendances et facteurs des migrations Africaines intra- et extra-continentales. *MAFE Working Paper* 7. www.ined.fr/fichier/t_telechargement/41828/telechargement_fichier_fr_wp7_flahaux_etal_2010.pdf.

Genoni, M., Rubalcava, L., Teruel, G., & Thomas, D. (2012). *Mexicans in America*. Paper presented at the annual meeting of the Population Association of America, San Francisco, May 5. http://paa2012.princeton.edu/download.aspx?submissionId=120862.

Ghimire, D. J., Williams, N., Thornton, A., Young-DeMarco, L., & Bhandari, P. (2012). *Innovation in the Study of International Migrants*. Working Paper, Population Studies Center, University of Michigan.

Hatton, T. J., & Williamson, G. G. (2006). *Global Migration and the World Economy: Two Centuries of Policy and Performance*. Cambridge, MA: MIT Press.

Hoefer, M., Rytina, N., & Baker, B.C. (2011). *Estimates of the Unauthorized Immigrant Population Residing in the United States: January 2007*. Washington, DC: Office of Immigration Statistics, US Department of Homeland Security.

Hoffman, A. (1974). *Unwanted Mexican Americans in the Great Depression: Repatriation Pressures*, 1929–1939. Tucson: University of Arizona Press.

Jasso, G. (2011). Migration and stratification. *Social Science Research*, 40, 1292–336.

Jasso, G., Massey, D.S., Rosenzweig, M.R., & Smith, J.P. (2005). Immigration, health, and New York City: early results based on the U.S. new immigrant cohort of 2003. *Federal Reserve Bank of New York Economic Policy Review*, 11(2), 127–52.

(2008). From illegal to legal: estimating previous illegal experience among new legal immigrants to the United States. *International Migration Review*, 42(4), 803–43.

Kalter, F. (2011). Social capital and the dynamics of temporary labour migration from Poland to Germany. *European Sociological Review*, 27(5), 555–69.

Kalton, G. (2009). Methods for sampling rare populations in social surveys. *Survey Methodology*, 35(2), 125–41.

Kalton, G., & Anderson, D.W. (1986). Sampling rare populations. *Journal of the Royal Statistical Society: Series A (General)*, 149(1), 65–82.

Kasinitz, P., Mollenkopf, J.H., & Waters, M.C. (2004). *Becoming New Yorkers: Ethnographies of the New Second Generation*. New York: Russell Sage Foundation.

Kasinitz, P., Mollenkopf, J.H., Waters, M.C., & Holdaway, J. (2008). *Inheriting the City: The Children of Immigrants Come of Age*. Cambridge, MA: Harvard University Press.

Kenwood, G., & Lougheed, A. (1999). *Growth of the International Economy 1820–2000: An Introductory Text* (4th edn.). New York: Routledge.

Lee, J., & Bean, F. (2012). *The Diversity Paradox: Immigration and the Color Line in Twenty-First Century America*. New York: Russell Sage Foundation.

Liang, Z., Chunyu, M.D., Zhuang, G., & Ye, W. (2008). Cumulative causation, market transition, and emigration from China. *American Journal of Sociology*, 114(3), 706–37.

Lopez, M.H., Morin, R., & Taylor, P. (2010). *Illegal Immigration Backlash Worries, Divides Latinos*. Washington, DC: Pew Hispanic Center. www.pewhispanic.org/files/reports/128.pdf.

Massey, D.S. (1987). The ethnosurvey in theory and practice. *International Migration Review*, 21(4), 1498–522.

(1988). International migration and economic development in comparative perspective. *Population and Development Review*, 14(3), 383–414.

(1995). The new immigration and the meaning of ethnicity in the United States. *Population and Development Review*, 21(3), 631–52.

(1999). When surveys fail: an alternative approach to studying illegal migration. In A.A. Stone, C.A. Bachrach, J.B. Jobe, H.S. Kurtzman, & V.S. Cain (eds), *The Science of the Self-Report: Implications for Research and Practice* (pp. 145–60). New York: Lawrence Erlbaum Associates.

(2007). Understanding America's immigration crisis. *American Philosophical Society Proceedings*, 151(3), 309–27.

(2009). The political economy of migration in an era of globalization. In S. Martinez (ed.), *International Migration and Human Rights: The Global Repercussions of US Policy* (pp. 25–43). Berkeley: University of California Press.

(2010). Immigration statistics for the 21st century. *ANNALS of the American Academy of Political and Social Science*, 631, 124–40.

(2011). Epilogue: the past and future of Mexico-U.S. migration. In M. Overmyer-Velázquez (ed.), *Beyond la frontera: The History of Mexico-U.S. Migration* (pp. 241–65). New York: Oxford University Press.

(2012). How Arizona became ground zero in the war on immigrants. In G. J. Chin & C. Hessick (eds.), *Illegals in the Backyard: State and Local Regulation of Immigration Policy*. New York: New York University Press.

Massey, D. S., Alarcón, R., Durand, J., & González, H. (1987). *Return to Aztlan: The Social Process of International Migration from Western Mexico*. Berkeley: University of California Press.

Massey, D. S., Arango, J., Hugo, G., Kouaouci, A., Pellegrino, A., & Taylor, J. E. (1998). *Worlds in Motion: International Migration at the End of the Millennium*. Oxford: Oxford University Press.

Massey, D. S., & Capoferro, C. (2004). Measuring undocumented migration. *International Migration Review*, 38(3), 1075–102.

Massey, D. S., Durand, J., & Malone, N. J. (2002). *Beyond Smoke and Mirrors: Mexican Immigration in an Age of Economic Integration*. New York: Russell Sage Foundation.

Massey, D. S., & Malone, N. J. (2003). Pathways to legalization. *Population Research and Policy Review*, 21(6), 473–504.

Massey, D. S., & Pren, K. A. (2012a). Unintended consequences of U.S. immigration policy: explaining the post-1965 surge from Latin America. *Population and Development Review*, 38(1), 1–29.

(2012b). Origins of the new Latino underclass. *Race and Social Problems*, 4(1), 5–17.

Massey, D. S., & Sánchez, M. (2010). *Brokered Boundaries: Creating Immigrant Identity in Anti-Immigrant Times*. New York: Russell Sage Foundation.

Massey, D. S., & Singer, A. (1985). New estimates of undocumented Mexican migration and the probability of apprehension. *Demography*, 32(2), 203–13.

Massey, D. S., & Taylor, J. E. (2004). *International Migration: Prospects and Policies in a Global Market*. Oxford: Oxford University Press.

Massey, D. S., & Zenteno, R. (2000). A validation of the ethnosurvey: the case of Mexico–U.S. migration. *International Migration Review*, 34(3), 765–92.

Mullan, B., & Frejka, T. (1994). The UN/ECE international migration surveys in Lithuania, Poland, and Ukraine: methodological issues. In R. van der Erf and L. Heering (eds.), *Causes of International Migration: Proceedings of a Workshop, Luxembourg, 14–16 December 1994* (pp. 223–54). Luxembourg: Office for Official Publications of the European Commission.

National Council of State Legislatures. (2012). *State Laws related to Immigrants and Immigration: 2012 Report*. Washington, DC: National Council of State

Legislatures. www.ncsl.org/issues-research/immig/state-laws-related-to-immigration-and-immigrants.aspx.

Organization for Economic Cooperation and Development. (2012). *International Migration Outlook 2010*. Paris: Organization for Economic Cooperation and Development. www.oecd.org/document/41/0,3343, en_2649_33931_45591593_1_1_1_1,00.html.

O'Rourke, K. H., & Williamson, G. G. (1999). *Globalization and History: The Evolution of a Nineteenth-Century Atlantic Economy*. Cambridge, MA: MIT Press.

Parrado, E. A. (2011). How high is Hispanic/Mexican fertility in the United States? Immigration and tempo considerations. *Demography*, 48(3), 1059–80.

Passel, J., & Cohn, D. (2008). *Trends in Unauthorized Immigration: Undocumented Inflow Now Trails Legal Inflow*. Washington, DC: Pew Hispanic Center. http://www.pewhispanic.org/2008/10/02/trends-in-unauthorized-immigration/.

(2011). *Unauthorized Immigrant Population: National and State Trends, 2010*. Washington, DC: Pew Hispanic Center. www.pewhispanic.org/2011/02/01/ unauthorized-immigrant-population-brnational-and-state-trends-2010/.

Portes, A., & Rumbaut, R. G. (2001). *Legacies: The Story of the Immigrant Second Generation*. Berkeley: University of California Press.

(2006). *Immigrant America: A Portrait* (3rd edn.). Berkeley: University of California Press.

Redburn, S., Reuter, P., & Majmundar, M. (2011). *Budgeting for Immigration Enforcement: A Path to Better Performance*. Washington, DC: National Academies Press.

Rumbaut, R. G., & Portes, A. (2001). *Ethnicities: Children of Immigrants in America*. Berkeley: University of California Press.

Santa Ana, O. (2002). *Brown Tide Rising: Metaphors of Latinos in Contemporary American Public Discourse*. Austin: University of Texas Press.

Sastry, N., Ghosh-Dastidar, B., Adams, J., & Pebley, A. R. (2006). The design of a multi-level survey of children, families, and communities: the Los Angeles Family and Neighborhood Survey. *Social Science Research*, 35(4), 1000–24.

Schoeni, R. F., Stafford, F., McGonagle, K., & Andreski, P. (2013). Response rates in national panel surveys. *ANNALS of the American Academy of Political and Social Science*, 645, 60–87.

US Government General Accounting Office. (2006). *Estimating the Undocumented Population: A "Grouped Answers" Approach to Surveying Foreign-Born Respondents*. Washington, DC: US Government General Accounting Office. www.gao.gov/new.items/d06775.pdf.

US Immigration and Customs Enforcement. (2012). *Fact Sheet: Delegation of Immigration Authority Section 287(g) Immigration and Nationality Act*. Washington, DC: US Immigration and Customs Enforcement. www.ice.gov/news/library/factsheets/287g.htm.

Warren, R. E., & Passel, J. S. (1987). A count of the uncountable: estimates of undocumented aliens counted in the 1980 United States Census. *Demography*, 24(3), 375–93.

Wasem, R. E. (2011). *Unauthorized Aliens Residing in the United States: Estimates since 1986*. Washington, DC: Congressional Research Service.

Williamson, G. G. (2004). *The Political Economy of World Mass Migration: Comparing Two Global Centuries*. Washington, DC: AEI Press.

Zolberg, A. R. (2006). *A Nation by Design: Immigration Policy in the Fashioning of America*. New York: Russell Sage Foundation.

14

Ethnographic evaluations on coverage of hard-to-count minorities in US decennial censuses

LAURIE SCHWEDE, RODNEY TERRY, AND JENNIFER HUNTER CHILDS

14.1 Introduction and background

The mission of decennial censuses in the United States is to count everyone living in the country once, only once, and in the right place. The counts are important for the following decade because census results are used for redistricting, allocating seats in the House of Representatives as well as providing information to distribute as much as $400 billion in federal funds annually. Fulfilling this mission is daunting in a country that is growing increasingly more diverse and complex.

14.1.1 The problem

Despite best efforts to count everyone, the US Census Bureau's own research shows persistent differential undercounts of some hard-to-count minority populations, such as African-Americans and Hispanics, across decennial censuses. Post-enumeration surveys and statistical studies have given estimates of the number of persons both missed and erroneously counted by the census and their characteristics. Ethnographic studies conducted during census data collections, but separate from those operations, have identified a range of factors affecting coverage and illuminated how and why they may affect enumeration in some racial and ethnic subpopulations. Though there is no reason to believe that race or ethnicity in and of itself leads to coverage error, it seems that some underlying variables associated in past studies with

The authors are very grateful for the substantial contributions of Mandi Martinez and Ryan King and the thoughtful reviews by Peter Miller, Yuling Pan, Terry DeMaio, Patricia Sanchez, and John Jones and a related review by Magda Ramos. We also thank Gia Donnalley and Kyra Linse for their many contributions, those who worked on coding/matching – Mandi Martinez, Tammy Gaich, Crystal Miller, Denise Gordon, John Jones, Kopen Henderson, Laura Becht, Eric Cheevers, Elda Robinson, Irvin Vann, and Julia Shaw – and Michelle Smirnova, for her contributions to the literature review. We are also very grateful to Timothy Johnson, our book section editor, for his continued support, encouragement, guidance, and reviews, and to Nancy Bates for very good comments that enabled us to clarify and strengthen parts of this chapter. We could not have accomplished this without your support. This report is released to inform interested parties and encourage discussion of work in progress. The views expressed on statistical, methodological, and operational issues are those of the authors and not necessarily those of the US Census Bureau.

undercounting may also be correlated with race (e.g., mobility, complex living situations, and language isolation). Other variables with hypothesized links to both undercoverage and race for possible future research include poverty, immigration, and legal status.

In this chapter, we present findings from comparative ethnographic and validation research on enumeration methods and coverage across sites targeted to specific race/ethnic groups during the 2010 Census Coverage Measurement (CCM) Survey. The CCM was the independent post-enumeration survey conducted after the 2010 Census for the purpose of estimating census coverage rates overall and for certain subpopulations (Mule, 2012).

Our purpose in this chapter is to identify types and sources of possible coverage error, the characteristics of persons and households that may be affected by them, and how they may be related to race/ethnic groups that are chronically undercounted. By having ethnographers observe live CCM interviews and debrief respondents immediately following the interview and validating these observations with a record check *post hoc*, we can examine types and sources of possible coverage errors and characteristics of persons and households affected by them by race/ethnic group. The record check study, along with data from the 2010 CCM, provides quantitative evidence of the groups that were undercounted and suggestions of why. The qualitative insights from ethnographers who actually observed the enumeration of these groups shed light on why some groups may be consistently undercounted. We conclude by discussing implications for the wider field of surveying hard-to-count populations.

14.1.2 Background

Historical undercount

In the 2010 Census, Black, Hispanic, and American Indian and Alaskan Native populations living on reservations were undercounted, while the non-Hispanic White population was overcounted (Mule, 2012). Since the 1940s, the Census Bureau has empirically documented that Blacks have consistently been undercounted relative to non-Blacks (US Census Bureau, 2010). Table 14.1 displays CCM results for the 1990, 2000, and 2010 Census years

Table 14.1 *Percentage net undercount by race and origin*

Race/ethnic group	1990	2000	2010
Non-Hispanic White	0.68*	−1.13	−0.84*
Non-Hispanic Black	4.57*	1.84*	2.07*
Non-Hispanic Asian	2.36*	−0.75	0.08
American Indian on Reservation	12.22*	−0.88	4.88*
American Indian off Reservation	0.68*	0.62	−1.95
Native Hawaiian/Other Pacific Islander	2.36*	2.12	1.34
Hispanic origin	4.99*	0.71	1.54*

*Statistically significantly different from zero.

Note: Undercounts are shown as positive numbers, overcounts as negative numbers.

Source: Excerpt from US Census Bureau, 2012 table.

(US Census Bureau, 2012), showing significant Black undercount rates from 1990 through 2010. In contrast, non-Hispanic Whites had an undercount in 1990 but a significant over-count in 2010. Significant undercounts for Hispanics and for American Indians on reservations were recorded in 1990 and 2010.

This follows decades of work at the Census Bureau to understand the conditions surrounding undercounts and to implement operations that will effectively enumerate hard-to-count groups in the census.

Ethnographic studies

Since the late 1960s, the Census Bureau has employed ethnographic methods to study living situations that could lead to differential undercount of minority populations in order to improve operations to count the hard to count in future censuses. The first ethnographic study was of low-income Blacks and Hispanics in Brooklyn (Valentine & Valentine, 1971). This qualitative study provided the first evidence of deliberate concealment as a reason for undercoverage. Other studies have added to the knowledge about motivational barriers to enumeration, which include providing "official" reports to the government, fear of prosecution, and doubts of the confidentiality of the data collection (for a summary, see Martin, Brownrigg, & Fay, 1990). In addition to motivated misrepresentation, misunderstanding of the census reporting rules also contributes to undercounting.

As part of the 1990 Census, several operations were implemented or improved to increase coverage and specifically reduce the differential undercount (US Census Bureau, 1993). The most notable with regard to differential coverage were attempts to distribute forms and/or enumerate known undercounted populations, including parolees and probationers and those staying in shelters and on the streets.

During the 1990 Census but separate from its data collection operations, ethnographic studies were conducted in twenty-nine sample areas throughout the continental US and Puerto Rico designed to understand living situations that led to differential undercounts by racial and ethnic groups (de la Puente, 1993). Mobility, complex households, concealment and distrust, difficult-to-access units, and language barriers were found across the groups. Mobility came in the form of children staying with other relatives, temporary household members due to recent immigration, homelessness, flexible household boundaries, and transient young men. Complex households were evidenced in forms of overcrowded apartments, which sometimes included temporary, unrelated new immigrants, and an unclear determination of who were visitors and who should be counted as usual residents.

The motivational factors for undercounting also persevered through ethnic and racial groups (de la Puente, 1993). Landlord and welfare regulations about how many people could reside in a unit and presence of illegal immigrants were related to how respondents reported to the census. Crime in unsafe neighborhoods also led to respondents being distrustful of strangers and unlikely to talk to anyone; this made gleaning accurate census information more difficult. Ethnographers also cited cultural resistance to government compliance as an enumeration problem.

Irregular housing was cited for the omission of people in these racial and ethnic groups (de la Puente, 1993). A common theme was structures (e.g., motels, units behind businesses, abandoned buildings) converted to accommodate more families or more people. The very rural nature of American Indian reservations posed additional difficulties locating housing units because of poor maps and people living in unconventional structures. The final "structural," in some senses, barrier to enumeration was a lack of knowledge of English, and in some cases illiteracy in the respondents' native language as well.

Census 2000 continued to improve operations aimed at reducing the historical undercount (Clark & Moul, 2004). In addition to operations that targeted transient populations, for the first time there was paid advertising as a part of outreach and promotions to inform the public about the census to increase response rates, both overall and in historically hard-to-reach communities. Though Census 2000 was the first to document a net overcount, there was still a differential undercount of Blacks (Robinson & Adlakha, 2002).

Building on past success with ethnographic methods, six independent ethnographic studies were mounted during Census 2000, again separate from census data collection operations (de la Puente, 2004). This series of studies found many of the same themes, including mobility, irregular housing, complex and fluid households, distrust and disinterest in the census process, and limited English proficiency. The complex households study showed the persistence of most of the enumeration barriers that the 1990 studies demonstrated and expanded our understanding of misenumeration due to mobility by demonstrating how differences in respondents' conceptual definitions of "household" and "usual residence" can result in enumeration errors (Schwede, Blumberg, & Chan, 2006).

For the 2010 Census, address-listing procedures were improved, procedures that resolve uncertain coverage situations were refined, and a new operation for people in transitory locations was implemented to reduce coverage problems. Yet, the net result was still differential undercoverage of the Black, Hispanic, and American Indian and Alaskan Native reservation populations.

While ethnographies throughout these decades have made the Census Bureau aware of barriers to enumeration and it has made operational improvements accordingly, the barriers persist.

14.2 Methodology

This chapter presents findings from a mixed-methods evaluation on enumeration methods and coverage conducted during data collection operations within the 2010 Census, focusing on household interviews observed during the CCM Survey.[1] For the first time in a census, ethnographers were able directly to observe and audiotape interviewer/respondent interactions during live interviews and debrief respondents on coverage-related issues. The CCM is a

---

1 The overall evaluation also included separate ethnographer observations of 2010 Census Nonresponse Follow-up and Update Enumerate Operations using the same methods in the same general site areas, but in different households; those findings are beyond this chapter's scope (see Schwede & Terry, 2013).

survey independent of the census that is conducted in a small sample of households after census data collection. The CCM household and person records are matched to their counterparts in the census dataset to estimate the accuracy of the census. Because the CCM interview is more complex regarding coverage than the initial census interview, observing this interview and debriefing afterwards provided a unique opportunity to examine the situations and identify factors that may lead to differential coverage of specific racial and ethnic groups.

During the CCM operations, a series of controlled small-scale ethnographic observation studies was targeted to study specific race/ethnic groups in seven sites with moderate or moderately high characteristics of specific hard-to-count groups (Bruce, Robinson, & Devine, 2013), one overcounted group site (non-Hispanic Whites), and a comparison site. The specific groups and sites included: African-Americans (Chicago, Illinois); Alaska Natives (Kodiak Borough, Alaska); American Indians (two southwest reservations); Asians, primarily Chinese (San Francisco, California area); Native Hawaiian and Other Pacific Islanders (Hawaii Island, Hawaii); Hispanics (Dallas/Fort Worth, Texas area); Middle Easterners (Detroit and Dearborn, Michigan); non-Hispanic Whites (Kansas City, Missouri area); and a generalized site (Broward County, Florida).

We developed standardized methods and trained ethnographers to conduct the field observation studies. One ethnographer was assigned to each of the nine sites according to past experience with that racial or ethnic group. The ethnographers accompanied interviewers to observe as many interviews and interviewers as possible in nine days. They requested the respondent's permission to tape, then remained unobtrusive as the interviewer conducted the interview, watching and listening for cues of possible coverage error, and taking notes. If any cue was detected, they were to conduct a short unstructured respondent debriefing to gather information on where the person lived or stayed the most time and on where they stayed specifically on Census Day to decide where each person should be counted, according to the census residence rule. Ethnographers transcribed and/or summarized the interviews. These summaries produced the ethnographer rosters we used as one data source. The ethnographers' reports identified factors that affected enumeration methods and coverage in their sites, enabling our cross-cutting analysis.

It is important to note that this was a qualitative study with convenience samples. As such, these samples are not random; the results cannot be viewed as representative of any larger or different population. The goals of the ethnographies were to identify and understand how factors within the interview as well as wider factors could affect differential coverage.

During August 2010, our ethnographers accompanied fifty-three interviewers, observing 318 CCM interviews. The distribution of interviews varied across sites. In addition, the proportion of the target race or ethnic group in the observed sample varied according to target population density in the site and in our observed households. Proportions of the observed target population households to all observed households per site ranged from 19 percent (Middle Eastern site) to 100 percent (Indian reservations).

Our analysis sample consists of persons who: (1) likely should have been counted at the observed housing unit on Census Day and appeared to have been correctly counted there in the final dataset; (2) likely should have been counted at the observed housing unit on Census

Day but appeared to have been omitted; or (3) likely should not have been counted at the observed housing unit on Census Day but appeared to have been incorrectly counted there.[2]

After the operations were complete, census staff matched the observed households and persons to the final localized census datasets to do a partial validation study of the census in the observed housing units. The purposes were to triangulate across data sources to identify consistencies and inconsistencies as to who should be counted at the observed housing units and to attempt to identify possible sources of error, using information from all sources. To determine if and where each person should be counted, our coding team compared rosters from four data sources: (1) the roster collected in the observed standard CCM interview; (2) the roster of persons the ethnographer assessed should be counted there and elsewhere; (3) the roster included in the final localized census unedited file; and (4) the final coverage measurement assessment of where each person should be counted. Possible coverage errors were identified by inconsistencies in the records of where a person was counted and where a person should have been counted according to the team who reviewed all sources. Because this assessment was made at a team level, no measure of reliability was possible. Coders came to consensus on how a person should be coded, based on training, standardized step-by-step instructions, practice cases done by all and discussed, the census residence rule guidelines, and by conferring with residence rules experts about difficult cases. Persons with insufficient information were coded as undetermined.

In addition to identifying where a person should have been counted, coders identified possible sources of coverage error, given all record sources. We identified persons and households as having possible coverage error by identifying inconsistencies between data sources. We offer the following limitation. In this study, all categories of the coverage error variable indicate *possible* coverage errors. We use caution when making statements about coverage error and note the possibility that neither the team assessment nor the ethnographer may be the most knowledgeable about where a person should be counted. Some persons' records may include updates from follow-up interviews after the ethnographer-observed interviews, which may result in a more informed determination for where the person should be counted (see Schwede & Terry, 2013, for more information).

14.3 Results

14.3.1 Record check of observed households

Our analysis sample consists of 289 housing units occupied on Census Day,[3] comprised of 956 persons. Of these, 11.2 percent were Hispanics of any race. People were distributed across non-Hispanic race groups as follows: Whites comprised 26.6 percent; American

---

2 We omitted from this analysis 210 persons identified in observed housing units who should have been counted elsewhere and appear to have been correctly not counted at the observed housing unit for two reasons: (1) a number of them had moved outside the geographical areas covered by our CCM record check dataset and this precluded our assessing these cases consistently; and (2) our ethnographers did not observe or debrief respondents in those other units. These types of persons are included in the CCM Survey estimates.

3 We omitted 29 sample housing units with no population on Census Day.

Indian and Alaska Natives, 21.3 percent; Blacks, 13.7 percent; Asians, 10.0 percent; Other, 1.8 percent; and Native Hawaiian and Other Pacific Islander, 1.7 percent. A larger-than-expected 5.1 percent reported multiple races, almost all of whom were in the Native Hawaiian and Alaska Native sites.[4]

Types of possible coverage error

Table 14.2 shows that 91.3 percent of persons had no indication of coverage error and appeared correctly enumerated. Of those remaining, 6.6 percent did have an indication of some type of possible coverage error, including people who were likely omitted or counted in the wrong place. Of the 289 occupied housing units, 42 had at least one person coded with a possible coverage error.

Table 14.2 also shows the specific types of possible coverage error identified through the record check. The most commonly identified problem is a possible omission at the observed housing unit; a person should have been counted there, but records indicate that the person was counted someplace else or not at all. The second most common problem was the inverse – a possible incorrect count at the observed housing unit per the census records, but the person should have been counted at another place. Four people were identified as possible overcounts, meaning that they were out of scope for the census (e.g., born/immigrated after Census Day, died/emigrated before Census Day), but counted in the census.

Characteristics of persons and households with possible coverage error

Of the 956 persons observed, 63 were judged to exhibit some form of coverage error. As shown in Table 14.3, the only race/ethnic group significantly more likely to have coverage error than the others was Native Hawaiian/Other Pacific Islander, of whom 25 percent had possible coverage error ($\chi^2 = 14.65$, df $= 1$, $p < .01$). Coverage error levels for the other race and ethnic groups were not significantly different from all others. These results should not be

Table 14.2 *Observed sample persons with possible coverage error by type of error*

Coverage error type	Frequency	Percent
No coverage error	873	91.3
Possible omission	32	3.4
Possible incorrect count	27	2.8
Possible overcount	4	0.4
Undetermined	20	2.1
Total	**956**	**100**

4 The remaining persons (8.5 percent) had missing data for race and ethnicity.

Table 14.3 *Frequency of persons with possible coverage error by race/ethnic group*

Race/ethnic group	Total in race/ethnic group	Persons with possible coverage error	Percent
Native Hawaiian/Other Pacific Islander	20	5	25.0[a]
Other race/ethnic group	42	4	9.5
Hispanics of any race	110	8	7.3
Multiple races	59	4	6.8
White	287	18	6.3
Black	134	7	5.2
Middle Eastern	26	1	3.9
American Indian/Alaska Native	213	7	3.3
Asian	97	3	3.1

[a] $p < .01$.

Note: 78 persons had incomplete race and Hispanic origin data. Of these persons, 14 had possible coverage error. To test significance, we conducted individual chi-square tests of independence comparing the proportion of people in a race/ethnic group with possible coverage error with all other groups. In these analyses, Hispanics of all races were in the Hispanic group, and all race groups included persons who were Hispanics and non-Hispanics of that race.

interpreted to suggest there is something inherent in being Native Hawaiian that causes coverage errors; rather, we presume there are factors associated with living situations more often observed among Native Hawaiians in this site that were associated with possible coverage errors.

As mentioned, 42 households had at least one person with possible coverage error. Half of these 42 households had five persons or more, even though these large households comprised just 30.5 percent of the sample. Households with five persons or more were significantly more likely to have possible coverage error ($\chi^2 = 8.9$, df = 1, $p < .01$). These findings are consistent with those from past censuses in finding large households to be at greater risk of coverage error. Past research has also documented that coverage errors are more likely to occur in complex than noncomplex households (e.g., de la Puente, 1993; Schwede *et al.*, 2006). We classified our households into the complex/noncomplex household typology, in which four types were grouped as noncomplex households – a nuclear family consisting of married parents with or without their joint biological children, a single parent and his/he biological children, or a person living alone – and all remaining types were classified as complex households. (Schwede, 2008). Of the 289 sample households, 106 were complex and 180 were noncomplex.[5] Of 42 households with any possible coverage errors, 18 were noncomplex and 23 were complex.[6] Possible coverage error was significantly associated with complex household type ($\chi^2 = 7.4$, df = 1, $p < .01$).

5 Three units lacked information to classify complexity.
6 One unit lacked information to classify complexity.

Sources of possible coverage errors

Using data from all sources, each person was coded with possible coverage error for each possible source. Up to three sources were coded for each person and are shown in Table 14.4. Mobility and tenuousness includes people who moved, people with more than one place to live, and people who were tenuously attached to the household. This was the largest source of possible error, and was often reported in connection with respondent confusion. Respondent confusion was coded when the respondent provided inconsistent responses or was observed answering a question different from the one that was asked; this could have led to a coverage error. For example, if an interviewer asked "Did you move here before or after April 1?" and the respondent answered, "After . . . we moved here about March 15th" – this would have been coded as "respondent confusion." Interviewer error included omitting or rewording questions, making assumptions (answering without waiting for the respondent to answer), not probing sufficiently, and not otherwise adhering to the interview protocol. Respondent concealment or refusal was identified when respondents refused to answer questions or otherwise indicated they were being untruthful when answering coverage-related questions. Hidden housing units were units identified in the CCM or by the ethnographer that had not been identified through previous census operations. Language barriers were identified when a lack of speaking the same language resulted in a possible coverage error. Five cases showed no evidence of why a possible coverage error should have occurred (other than that the records between operations were inconsistent), and sixteen cases showed other reasons for possible coverage errors, including omitting babies, computer glitches, and respondent frustration.

In order to understand better how these sources of possible error contributed to coverage error, we broke this down by type of possible coverage error. Table 14.5 shows sources of error for possible omissions. Table 14.6 shows the combined sources of error for people coded as possibly erroneously counted at the observed housing unit when they should have been counted elsewhere or not included in the census.

Table 14.4 *All sources of possible coverage error (multiple sources per person)*

	Frequency	Percent
Mobility/tenuousness	32	34.0
Respondent confusion	16	17.0
Interviewer error	10	10.6
Respondent concealment/refusal	9	9.6
Hidden housing unit	3	3.2
Language barrier	3	3.2
Unknown	5	5.3
Other	16	17.0
Total	**94**	**100**

Table 14.5 *Sources of possible omissions (multiple sources per person)*

	Frequency	Percent
Mobility/tenuousness	12	29.3
Respondent concealment/refusal	4	9.6
Respondent confusion	3	7.3
Hidden housing unit	3	7.3
Language barrier	3	7.3
Interviewer error	2	4.9
Unknown	5	12.2
Other	9	22.0
Total	**41**	**100**

Table 14.6 *Sources of possible overcounts/incorrect counts (multiple sources per person)*

	Frequency	Percent
Mobility/tenuousness	20	37.7
Respondent confusion	13	24.5
Interviewer error	8	15.1
Respondent concealment/refusal	5	9.4
Other	7	13.2
Total	**53**	**100**

In this small study, all instances of hidden housing units and language barriers are linked to possible omissions. Situations involving mobility or tenuousness, respondent confusion, concealment, and interviewer error are linked to both omissions and miscounts.

De la Puente (1993, 2004) cited language barriers and households with mobility, as well as irregular housing (including hidden housing units) as reasons for undercoverage in both the 1990 and 2000 studies. Respondent confusion and respondent concealment have been cited as reasons for undercoverage since the earliest ethnographic studies (Aschenbrenner, 1975; Valentine & Valentine, 1971). By having ethnographers actually observe the interviews in the current study, we were able to identify interviewer error as a direct contributor to both types of possible coverage error – omissions and miscounting.

Table 14.7 shows how these possible coverage errors were distributed among the racial and ethnic sites.

We saw sources of possible coverage error in mobility and tenuousness, respondent confusion, respondent concealment, interviewer error, hidden housing units, and language barriers. From the ethnographic reports, we can document the types of interviewer errors that occurred, how they were related to other sources of error, and identify how they may have contributed to possible coverage error. In order to understand how these chronically undercounted groups may be differentially impacted by cultural and other factors, we turn to

Table 14.7 *Sources of possible coverage error by race/ethnic site (multiple sources per person)*

	Interviewer error	Language barrier	Mobility/ tenuous	Concealment/ refusal	Confusion	Hidden housing	Other source	Unknown source	Total
African-American			3	2	1	3			9
Alaskan Native	4		3	4	7		1		19
American Indian	3		5		5		6		19
Asian				1					1
Hispanic			4		1		1		6
Native Hawaiian	2	3	8	2	1		1	4	21
Middle Eastern								1	1
White			8				5		13
Generalized	1		1		1		2		5
Total	10	3	32	9	16	3	16	5	94

Note: The site name indicates the group targeted for special attention in the site. Not all persons in the site were of the targeted race/ethnic group, so one should not assume that all of the sources of error in one row are attributed to the target group alone. For example, in the White site, more than half of the sources of error classified here applied to African-Americans, not Whites.

selected ethnographic reports for the groups documented empirically to be undercounted, as well as the Native Hawaiian group, which demonstrated potential coverage problems through our record check study.

14.3.2 Cross-cutting themes in the ethnographic studies

The ethnographic reports shed light on the possible sources for enumeration error separately from the record check study outlined above; we focus here on those sources of enumeration errors specifically associated with possible coverage error in Table 14.4. Comparing the results from the ethnographic observations and debriefings, we identified several cross-cutting themes paralleling the sources of error mentioned above: (1) interviewer error; (2) difficulty in gaining access to respondents; (3) language barriers; and (4) mobility.

Interviewer error

The first theme that goes to the heart of standardized interviewing methods is wide variation in interviewer behavior during their interviews, as documented by the ethnographers. To our knowledge, this is the first time that interviewer error has been empirically identified as a source of possible coverage error in a systematic decennial census evaluation of coverage. The ethnographers report a very wide range of interviewer behaviors, ranging from those who read questions exactly as worded all of the time as trained, to those who reworded or skipped most questions in the interview. Some interviewers routinely reworded questions to make them more conversational while a few interviewers deliberately shortened interviews to increase their productivity.

Ethnographers observed that some interviewers shortened questions to the extent that they confused respondents, especially the foreign born. They asked leading questions and seemed impatient when respondents did not reply immediately and sometimes continued without getting a respondent's answer. In addition to making major changes to wording or omitting questions, interviewers were also observed making errors by deciding on their own whether a person should or should not be listed, rather than adding the person to the roster, as instructed in training.

In most situations, interviewers seemed to react and modify their behavior to situations presented by respondents. In some situations, interviewers reworded or omitted questions to shorten the interview when they encountered respondents in the middle of doing something like eating dinner, perhaps to avoid break-offs. Interviewers also sometimes went off-script when attempting to interview angry or hostile respondents who may have been even more likely to break off or refuse. Ethnographers occasionally observed interviewers who were tired or rushing to finish at day's end. Ethnographers also observed nonstandardized behavior when a monolingual interviewer tried to conduct an interview with a respondent with little or no English fluency or with a hearing impairment. In these situations, interviewers may have felt the need to revise or reword questions to complete the interview. Leeman and Marsh (2013) elsewhere use the behavior coding method to document the extent of major rewording and omission of questions in the CCM.

In one Native Hawaiian site case, the respondent reported that the household was "in transition" around Census Day, but the interviewer recorded them as if they were living there. The ethnographer later learned during the debriefing that they had actually moved in after Census Day, and the owner could have been living there on Census Day. This interviewer error appeared to have resulted in misenumerating two households.

Rewording questions, an interviewer error, was also noted by ethnographers to be a source of respondent confusion, another independently identified source of possible coverage error. In these situations, it was because the interviewer deviated from the question script or procedures that the respondent provided conflicting or inconsistent responses (coded as confusion), creating a possible coverage error that might have been otherwise avoided.

Difficulty gaining access

Ethnographers observed difficulty in interviewers' gaining access to respondents which could contribute to missed addresses, hidden housing units, and could play a role in respondent refusal or concealment.

Hidden housing units were identified in the African-American site. These were observed to occur on the same property, but separate from the main unit. Persons in those units appeared to have been missed in the census.

The African-American site was in poor neighborhoods with a high incidence of crime. Many of the sample households were in multiunit structures behind locked main entry doors through which one needed to be buzzed in by a resident. The ethnographer observed many soft refusals through the buzzer system, which made gaining access to these multiunits very difficult.

In the Native Hawaiian site, some respondents lived in housing units with fenced proper-ties and locked gates in front of long driveways to maintain privacy. One interviewer went to an area labeled "dangerous" on the survey map and discovered a sign on one property giving a clear warning that trespassers were not allowed and threatening harm. The interviewer walked past the sign to the porch and fed treats to barking dogs. The owner appeared and yelled, "What are you looking for? That sign is out there. You should not come in here. Leave my property. Don't come back!"

On the American Indian reservations, in rural Alaska, and in the Native Hawaiian site, housing units were often isolated with no street names or numbers, making it difficult to find and verify sample housing units with descriptions such as white house with gray trim or house near a specifically numbered telephone pole. Respondents in these areas had difficulty providing addresses or locations for other people. Even if one might know how to get to a different address, it would be very difficult to describe the house in enough detail for an interviewer to locate it later. This factor made describing living situations for mobile or tenuously attached household persons difficult leading to possible cover-age error by the inability to provide complete information on mobile household members.

Language barriers

The language barriers tied specifically to possible coverage errors in the record check identified the Native Hawaiian/Other Pacific Islander site where Tongan and Marshallese respondents had difficulty understanding the English-language questions.

On both American Indian reservations, English is a second language for many respondents; most everyday discourse is in the indigenous language. Many interviews were conducted in a combination of English and the indigenous language because the observed interviewers were bilingual. During the interviews, it was often when topics of complex living situations arose that the discussions slipped into the respondents' native language. We note this here, not because it was tied to coverage error, but because it was observed as an adaptation to a potential barrier. There are two implications: (1) interviewers who speak the respondent's native language have an advantage; and (2) unless the instrument can be translated into other languages, data will be collected in on-the-fly translations, rather than through use of standardized translations, which is likely to introduce variation. Past ethnographies highlighted language as an enumeration barrier (de la Puente, 1993, 2004).

Mobility

Mobility takes many forms that may influence census coverage. Many persons move permanently from one place to another. When the move occurred very close to Census Day, these proved particularly difficult to count. Two persons in the White site coded as possible census omissions moved into the observed units just before Census Day, and one possibly omitted person in the Native Hawaiian site moved out right around Census Day. Respondent confusion about whether persons moved in or out before or after Census Day was a source of error in several cases. Because possible coverage error could be attributed to multiple sources, some errors due to mobility were also reflected as interviewer error when the interviewer contributed to the problem. Several cases illustrate that recording the situation accurately may be especially difficult for both respondents and interviewers when persons move just before or just after Census Day.

Other cases of mobility involve "cycling," which we define as going back and forth between two or more households on a regular or semiregular basis. These situations have been characterized as "boomerangs" or "floaters" in past research and have been associated with hard-to-count groups (Bates & Gerber, 1998). In the American Indian sites, there were several cases of cycling. In one, a man went between households and it seemed he should be counted at the observed unit because he spent more time there than anywhere else. In another instance, a grandmother traveled back and forth to a distant city to spend time with her grandchild, though the exact amount of time spent and the place she should be counted were unclear. In the generalized site, a young man went back and forth between a southern and a northern state; it was not clear where he should be counted. In the Alaska site, retired snowbirds moving among states were hard to count. (For information on snowbirds and other mobile populations, see Hunter Childs, de la Puente, & Salo, 2003.)

Again, ethnographers noted that respondents were sometimes confused as to whether they should mention persons with mobile or tenuous attachments to the household, and interviewers sometimes erred in deciding whether or not to include these persons on the roster. Past research has shown the connection with tenuousness and mobility and respondent uncertainty as to whether the person should be included as a household member (Bates & Gerber, 1998), but this study showed how interviewer error could exacerbate that problem by failing to roster someone that the respondent mentioned to a roster probe (as they were instructed to in interviewer training).

14.3.3 Ethnographic profiles

In addition to the cross-cutting themes, there were also characteristics specific to each ethnographic site that could contribute to the identified possible coverage errors.

Alaska Native site (Donkersloot, 2011)

Kodiak Island has one small maritime city with large warehouses, a marina, a fish processing plant, and a boatyard, with a Coast Guard base nearby. Inhabitants are traditionally mobile, moving among home bases in relation to subsistence and fishing cycles. The ethnographer for this site identified mobility for work as a factor in possible coverage error.

Several examples demonstrate the complexity found in this site. One person was cycling between his home and his job on the distant oil fields during the fall and winter: six weeks in the workers' dorm, then two weeks at home and back again. This man has a home where he and his family live, but he is away more of the time at the workers' dorm. This case shows the difficulties of applying a residence rule to complex living situations. By counting him at home, the nuclear family and the man's contributions to his family can be identified. However, according to the rule of counting persons where they live and sleep most of the time, he should be counted at the dorm, which would portray his household as a stem, not nuclear, family. In other cases, several men lived and slept on commercial fishing vessels for several months around Census Day. One of these men spends six to eight months a year aboard a vessel. It was not clear how to count these men correctly in the census. In the final example, interviewer error may have caused a respondent in the military to be miscounted because the interviewer inappropriately recorded a one-time overseas trip as a recurring monthly trip. In this site, primarily adult men were possibly affected by coverage error.

This profile shows how mobility for work in this particular geographic region could lead to omissions, as well as how interviewer error could exacerbate that problem. In addition, these situations were also shown to cause confusion for respondents, also leading to possible coverage error.

American Indian sites (Fortier, 2012)

The two observed southwest American Indian reservations are among 562 recognized tribal entities and 314 reservations in the US. On both reservations, American Indian people learn their respective native languages before learning English. The native language is used in most conversations and in tribal governance and is an essential part of spiritual and religious identity.

Several factors may affect coverage in these sites. Many observed households were very mobile. Some persons moved back and forth between households on and off the reservation for work, others were tenuous and cycled among places, children moved among households, and a number of persons moved around Census Day. Determining where each person in these situations should be counted can be very difficult – some of these were coded as possible coverage error and some as undetermined. Under these circumstances of lack of street names and numbers, remote and hard-to-reach residences, and frequent mobility, it is not surprising that respondents often had difficulty providing information for people who had moved out or were tenuously attached, making it harder to pinpoint where they should be counted and causing difficulty and confusion in the interviews.

A number of observed interviews went back and forth between English and the American Indian language. Because interviewers were recruited from the community, they sometimes were related to or acquainted with respondents and knew information relevant to the interview that was not always said aloud. Thus, this "insider knowledge" seemed very important in gaining respondent cooperation and clarifying situations where the respondents experienced mobility or had tenuously attached persons. The lack of city-style addresses in some areas and frequent mobility for work in distant locations or other reasons made it difficult for respondents to answer detailed questions on living situations for themselves or others causing them some difficulty and confusion in answering these questions. Because of these complexities and because of the limited English capability of some respondents, being able to speak the native language of respondents is a key to surveying these populations.

Another important cultural feature is the complexity of American Indian households and relationships, particularly those in tribal entities with patrilineal or matrilineal kinship systems. American Indian people in our reservation sites are related through matrilineal lines, reckoning descent from matrilineal clan affiliations. Generally, issues of family residence patterns and rules for clan exogamy and tribal endogamy constitute complex interrelationship patterns. These clans form the basic units of social cohesiveness and interchange, and are responsible for ceremonial obligations. These ritual obligations and the interrelationships between clan members can result in temporary household mobility. In a few cases, the ethnographer mentioned this mobility as a source of possible coverage error.

   In this profile, because of the complexities on reservations with the geography, language, and cultural differences, we observed the interrelation of mobility and respondent confusion and how they could lead to possible coverage error.

African-American site (Lacy, 2012)

Chicago, Illinois, has a large Black population with many characteristics previously associated with miscounts. The number of interviewers willing to go to the poor, economically distressed, high crime areas in this site after dark when residents tended to be home was small, particularly after a shooting occurred in the area a week earlier. Drugs were sold openly; in one case, an interviewer was advised by a respondent to stay away at a particular time due to a drug deal. Like in the 1990 ethnographic work in Harlem, this ethnographer witnessed "enumerator fear," a factor previously associated with differential undercounting (Hamid, 1992).

   This ethnographer identified several sources of possible coverage error: distrust leading to deliberate concealment of information; interviewer error; and mobility among the poor (Lacy, 2012). In two cases, female respondents appeared to conceal information about brothers living with them. In one, the woman identified her brother and said he had another address, but that she did not know it. She voiced concern that if she gave his other address, his status at college could be jeopardized. In the other case, the respondent's brother was present prior to the interview, but left as it was starting. The ethnographer suspected that he lived there, although he was not mentioned in the interview.

   There were several situations involving children moving between households. A grandmother said her grandchildren did not live with her, but "stayed" there because she babysits them while their mother, who lives elsewhere, works nights. The interviewer had passed this house often, saw the grandchildren there most times, and concluded the grandmother was concealing that they actually lived there. The census residence rule is based on usual residence, where one *lives and sleeps* most of the time. In this case, the children may live in one place and sleep in another. Other cases demonstrated mobility of children staying with fathers or grandparents on weekends only. Respondents seem to have trouble deciding on the proportions of time spent in each place and ethnographers noted the interviewer rewording questions to prompt respondents by asking if the child is "50/50" when they take a long time to ponder this. That is the most difficult situation to resolve because the question that follows requires knowing where the child was specifically on Census Day, which has been observed to be difficult for respondents to answer.

   Two other cases evidenced mobility in different forms – a man currently living in an apartment was homeless on Census Day, and another case of a man in jail continuously from before Census Day to the interview day who was nonetheless included on his fiancée's household roster when he should have been counted at the jail.

   This ethnographer concluded that grandchildren and adult men were at the most risk of possible coverage error in her site. Distrust and concealment were strong themes of possible coverage errors for this group, as has been found consistently since the Valentine and Valentine ethnographic study. Though the Census Bureau has worked on outreach and communications campaigns directly targeting these issues, as evidenced here, the problem has not been solved.

Native Hawaiian and other Pacific Islander site (Daniggelis, 2011)

The island of Hawai'i, or the "Big Island," has many sparsely populated rural areas where Native Hawaiians comprise a larger-than-average population share. Native Hawaiians are disproportionately affected by poverty, represented as victims and offenders and, thus, are more likely to be mobile and hard to enumerate (McMillen-Wolfe, 2011). They are also much more likely to live in large households than the general population, also a prevalent characteristic of hard-to-count populations.

The Native Hawaiian concept of *'ohana* is comprised of relatives by blood, marriage, or adoption and is the fundamental unit in Hawaiian social organization. It comprises a network of kin that can and often does include persons living in other housing units. This is the core economic unit that provides social and economic support for household members and other relatives. One instance of possible coverage error due to mobility was within an *'ohana*. This was a situation where three persons had moved just after Census Day, but had been living in an "'ohana unit" on Census Day. According to records, they seem to have been miscounted at the sampled unit.

In this site, not adhering to culturally appropriate behavior was also identified by the ethnographer as a barrier to enumeration. She identified two Hawaiian cultural values – *pono* (respectful in every way you can be) and *ha'aha'a* (humility) – as being important to follow while interviewing Native Hawaiians. Some interviewers did not routinely practice this. When interviewers rushed through interviews, shortened questions, or were impatient, problems occurred. The link between not following these cultural practices and "interviewer error" documented in Table 14.4 is shown in the following case. A possible omission occurred when the interviewer did not listen attentively and failed to roster a daughter-in-law that the respondent mentioned had lived there. During the debriefing, the ethnographer verified this and learned the daughter-in-law had since moved out, but should have been counted there. In another case, the ethnographer observed a Caucasian interviewer who was domineering, cut respondents off, and made jokes about Hawaiian names, thus "discouraging" a respondent from reporting that he was part Hawaiian. This type of behavior can lead to respondent concealment or refusal. Politeness and respect have also been noted to be valued by Koreans (Kang, 2006), Chinese (Pan & Lubkemann, 2012), and American Indians (Fortier, 2012).

Other instances of mobility involved determining where persons with multiple residences should be counted. Examples of persons splitting time between two residences included a grandchild going back and forth between grandparents' homes; a mother giving contradictory information about whether her children should be counted; a college student living away; and adults living away to get their high school diplomas, going back and forth to visit their parents on weekends.

In this site, nearly all possible sources of coverage error were observed to some degree. Mobility was the predominant factor, but interviewer error, language barriers, and respondent concealment and refusals were also seen. We suspect that the lack of cultural etiquette by the observed interviewers only compounded the difficulty enumerating this mobile group.

14.4   Summary and conclusions

Like de la Puente (1993, 2004), we found households with mobility, language barriers, and irregular housing (i.e., hidden housing units) as reasons for possible coverage error. We found specific evidence of these situations in the persistently undercounted groups. Like the first ethnographic studies cited earlier, we saw evidence of respondent confusion and concealment as reasons for possible coverage error. In the past census ethnographies, researchers have been present in the environment while the census was taking place and interviewed respondents about their census experience, but those researchers did not have the ability actually to observe the enumerations. In the current study, by having ethnographers observe the interviews, we also identified interviewer error as directly contributing to and exacerbating possible coverage error and we documented how these factors could be intermingled.

Looking at the ethnographic reports from specific groups that have experienced coverage problems, we saw four themes that could lead to coverage problems in these groups: (1) interviewer error; (2) difficulty in gaining access to respondents; (3) language barriers; and (4) mobility. We saw how these themes were sometimes closely intertwined with each other and with other previously identified factors. Interviewer error was observed in conjunction with respondent confusion as well as mobility. In situations where interviewers encountered hostile or nonnative English-speaking respondents, ethnographers noted that their standardized interviewing behavior sometimes became worse (Sando, 2012). Though this is an untestable hypothesis in the current study, these types of situations could lead to differential undercoverage. There could be an interaction between barriers to enumeration (e.g., mobility, language barriers, hidden housing units) and how the interviewer behaves toward the respondent that actually exacerbates the problem of differential coverage. This area requires further investigation.

Ethnographers also observed interviewers having difficulty gaining access to respondents. Sometimes, interviewers had difficultly accessing units because they were hidden. Sometimes, physical access barriers were accompanied with respondent hostility, acknowledging that they were difficult to access on purpose. Additionally, very rural and remote areas had the challenge of lacking street numbers or names, making it difficult both for interviewers and respondents when they needed to refer to an address by name – sometimes leading to respondent confusion or incomplete information.

Language barriers have also been a persistent problem for the Census Bureau despite efforts to improve non-English-language data collection tools. Most sites witnessed non-English-language interviews, but the language barrier seemed most notable in the site that also demonstrated the most mobility and complexity. The combination of not having a questionnaire in the respondents' native language and the need for the respondent to report complex living situations made the language factor particularly notable on the American Indian reservations. Fortunately, in this study, all observed cases on the American Indian reservations had native language speakers as interviewers.

Specific cultural variations were also observed within some chronically undercounted groups. In the Alaskan Native site, mobility for work was particularly notable and distinct from the other sites. Because of the remoteness, and the particular type of work that these respondents report, the living situations surrounding work life in rural Alaska pose specific challenges for surveying that make this site at risk for undercoverage.

In the American Indian group, the language use and the fluidity associated with the kinship network could make this a difficult group to survey. These challenges also highlight the importance of hiring people who know the language and customs to conduct interviews – thus being able to understand and translate the living situation into the survey report.

The African-American site demonstrated similar patterns to past ethnographic work, despite efforts to allay respondents' fears that the census was something that could be used against them. Respondents were observed concealing information about their household members' mobility, possibly for fear that the government would use it inappropriately.

Finally, in the Native Hawaiian site, our ethnographic study showed a disproportionate number of possible errors. The records check identified mobility as the source of most possible coverage errors in this site, but the ethnographer also noted that interviewer error contributed as well. Some interviewers' lack of cultural sensitivity in a culture with a history of distrust toward the government was shown by the ethnographer to lead to coverage mistakes.

This was one of three 2010 Census ethnographic evaluations to identify issues related to improving enumeration of hard-to-reach populations – undercounted race/ethnic groups, non-English speakers (Pan & Lubkemann, 2012), and persons in group quarters (Chan, 2012). Future research in preparation for the 2020 Census will be planned based on the findings of these and other studies on census processes and hard-to-reach populations.

References

Aschenbrenner, J. (1975). *Lifelines: Black Families in Chicago*. New York: Holt, Rinehart and Winston.

Bates, N. A., & Gerber, E. (1998). Temporary mobility and reporting of usual residence. *Survey Methodology*, 24(1), 89–98.

Bruce, A., Robinson, G. J., & Devine, J. (2013). A planning database to identify areas that are hard-to-enumerate and hard-to-survey in the United States. In *H2R/2012 Proceedings*. Alexandria, VA: American Statistical Association.

Chan, A. (2012). *Investigation of Methods to Evaluate the Coverage of Group Quarters Populations Report*. 2010 Census Program for Evaluations and Experiments. 2010 Census Planning Memoranda Series #240. US Census Bureau.

Clark, J., & Moul, D. (2004). Coverage improvement in the Census 2000 enumeration. *Census 2000 Testing, Experimentation, and Evaluation Program Topic Report No. 10, Tr-10*. Washington, DC: US Census Bureau.

Daniggelis, E. (2011). *A Comparative Ethnographic Study of Enumeration Methods and Coverage in a Native Hawaiian and Pacific Islander Site in the 2010 Census Coverage Measurement Survey Operation*. Report prepared under US Census Bureau contract.

de la Puente, M. (1993). Why are people missed or erroneously included in the census: a summary of findings from ethnographic coverage reports. In *Proceedings of the 1993 Research Conference on Undercounting Ethnic Populations of the U.S. Census Bureau* (pp. 29–66). Washington, DC: US Census Bureau.

(2004). Coverage improvement in the Census 2000 enumeration. *Census 2000 Testing, Experimentation, and Evaluation Program Report No. 15, Tr-15*. Washington, DC: US Census Bureau.

Donkersloot, R. (2011). *Comparative Ethnographic Studies of Enumeration Methods and Coverage in Race/ethnic Groups in the Census Coverage Measurement Person Interview Operation: Kodiak Island Borough, Alaska*. Report prepared under US Census Bureau contract.

Fortier, T. (2012). *Comparative Ethnographic Studies of Enumeration Methods and Coverage in Race/Ethnic Groups in the Census Coverage Measurement Person Interview Operation: American Indian Sites*. Report prepared under US Census Bureau contract.

Hamid, A. (1992). *Ethnographic Follow-up of a Predominately African American Population in a Sample Area in Central Harlem, New York City: Behavioral Causes of the Undercount of the 1990 Census. Ethnographic Evaluation of the 1990 Decennial Census Report #11*. Report prepared under US Census Bureau contract.

Hunter Childs, J., de la Puente, M., & Salo, M. (2003). Comparative ethnographic research on mobile populations. *Census 2000 Evaluation J.3: Ethnographic Studies. July 17, 2003*.

Kang, T. (2006). Household structure and its social and economic functions among Korean American immigrants in Queens, New York: an ethnographic study. In L. Schwede, R.L. Blumberg, & A.Y. Chan (eds.), *Complex Ethnic Households in America*. Lanham, MD: Rowman & Littlefield Publishers, Inc.

Lacy, K. (2012). *An Ethnographic Study of Enumeration Methods and Coverage in a 2010 Census Coverage Measurement Survey Operation Primarily among Blacks in a Chicago Field Site*. Report prepared under US Census Bureau contract.

Leeman, J., & Marsh, H. (2013). Behavior coding report of the 2010 Census coverage measurement person interviews. *2010 Census Program for Evaluations and*

Experiments. 2010 Census Planning Memoranda Series #251. Washington, DC: US Census Bureau.

McMillen-Wolfe, H. L. (2011). *Ethnographic Evaluation of Enumeration Methods and Coverage in the 2010 Non-Response Follow Up Operation on the Island of Hawaii, with Special Focus on Native Hawaiians and Other Pacific Islanders*. Report prepared under US Census Bureau contract.

Martin, E., Brownrigg, L., & Fay, R. (1990). *Results of 1988 Ethnographic Studies of Census Coverage and Plans for 1990*. Paper presented to the Census Advisory Committees of the American Statistical Association and on Population Statistics at the Joint Advisory Committee Meeting, Alexandria, VA.

Mule, T. (2012). Census coverage measurement estimation report: summary of estimates of coverage for persons in the United States. *DSSD 2010 Census Coverage Measurement Memorandum Series #2010-G_01*. Washington, DC: US Census Bureau.

Pan, Y., & Lubkemann, S. (2012). Observing census enumeration of non-English speaking households in the 2010 Census. *2010 Census Program for Evaluations and Experiments. 2010 Census Planning Memoranda Series #249*. Washington, DC: US Census Bureau.

Robinson, G., & Adlakha, A. (2002). Comparison of A.C.E. revision II results with demographic analysis, *A.C.E. Revision II Estimates Memorandum Series #PP-41*. Washington, DC: U.S. Census Bureau.

Sando, R. (2012). Exploring the Effects of Respondent Behavior on the Interview Process and Data Quality in a 2010 Census Case Study Evaluation. Presented at the International Conference on Methods for Surveying and Enumerating Hard-to-Reach Populations in New Orleans.

Schwede, L. (2008). Changes in the distribution of complex and noncomplex households in the United States: 1990 and 2000 Censuses. Unpublished research typology for classifying household types. Suitland, MD: US Census Bureau.

Schwede, L., Blumberg R. L., & Chan, A. Y. (2006). *Complex Ethnic Households in America*. Lanham, MD: Rowman & Littlefield Publishers, Inc.

Schwede, L., & Terry, R. (2013). Comparative ethnographic studies of enumeration methods and coverage across race/ethnic groups. *2010 Census Program for Evaluations and Experiments. 2010 CensusPlanning Memoranda Series #255*. Washington, DC: US Census Bureau. www.census.gov/2010census/pdf/comparative_ethographic_studies_of_enumeration_methods_and_coverage_across_race_and_ethnic_groups.pdf.

US Census Bureau. (1993). *Programs to Improve Coverage in the 1990 Census*. 1990 Census of the Population and Housing Evaluation and Research Reports, 1990 CPH-E-3, US Government Printing Office.

(2010). The *Development and Sensitivity Analysis of the 2010 Demographic Analysis Estimates by the Demographic Analysis Research Team* (December 16, 2010).

(2012). 2010 Census coverage measurement results news conference. May 22, 2012. http://2010.census.gov/news/press-kits/ccm/ccm.html.

Valentine, C. B., & Valentine B. L. (1971). *Missing Men: A Comparative Methodological Study of Underenumeration and Related Problems*. Report prepared under Joint Statistical Agreement with the Brookdale Hospital Center, Washington, DC: US Census Bureau.

15

Methodological and ethical issues arising in carrying out research with children and young people

SINÉAD HANAFIN, ANNE MARIE BROOKS, GILLIAN ROCHE, AND BAIRBRE MEANEY

15.1 Introduction and background

This chapter draws on key issues emerging from a National Children's Research Programme (NCRP) to identify methodological, practical, and ethical challenges when designing and implementing research studies with, and about, children and young people. The chapter commences with a brief overview of the NCRP with a summary of the key studies referred to in this chapter presented in the Appendix. More than sixty studies were carried out under the NCRP across areas of children's lives as diverse as their outcomes (including, for example, health, education, and safety), their relationships (for example, with their peers, families, and others), and services (for example, universal, targeted, and more intensive supports). Consequently, it is possible to draw out learning across multiple methodologies, methods, and analyses, and highlight challenges arising across several aspects of study design and implementation. The chapter is illustrative rather than comprehensive and focuses on those studies that best exemplify issues arising.

The overview is followed by issues in study design, including challenges in ensuring meaningful participation by children and young people, tensions arising between protection of children and their participation, issues arising in consent, assent and re-consent, and a consideration of confidentiality, anonymity, and privacy in the context of children's research. Challenges in study implementation are focused around areas such as sampling and recruitment, data collection, data analysis, and dissemination. The chapter concludes that while research with, and about, children raises challenges over and above that with adults, these can be overcome with appropriate consideration. The examples presented in this chapter can provide practical guidance in these areas.

The NCRP has been underway since the publication of the National Children's Strategy in 2000, which marked the commencement of a coordinated approach to policy and practice in relation to children's lives in Ireland (Department of Health and Children, 2000). The National Children's Strategy was framed by three goals, which focus on (1) giving children a voice in matters that affect them; (2) understanding children's lives better; and (3) providing high-quality services and supports for children.

Goal 2 states specifically that "Children's lives will be better understood and will benefit from evaluation, research and information on their needs, rights and the effectiveness of services" (p. 38). This goal was operationalized through four discrete, but interrelated, program areas, which operate in a complementary manner to achieve the objectives outlined, namely: a funded research program; a capacity-building program; a data and research infrastructure program; and a knowledge transfer program. The material presented in this chapter draws principally on studies from the funded research program.

15.2   Funded research studies

The funded research element of the NCRP was established in 2001. Up to 2012, more than thirty studies on different aspects of children's lives had been completed and this element continues to support policy and practice on relevant research on children's lives. A core focus of the funded research program, and a feature which sets it apart from other research on children's lives, is the centrality it gives to the voice of the child. This underlying principle is evident in all of the studies to a certain extent, but is demonstrable in the studies involving children directly, particularly those children and young people experiencing adverse conditions. The largest funded study under this program is *Growing up in Ireland: the National Longitudinal Study of Children* which has been underway since 2006. This study tracks the progress of almost 20,000 children and their families in two nationally representative cohorts: an infant cohort that includes approximately 11,100 children (data collected at age 9 months, at 3 years, and at 5 years) and a child cohort that includes 8,568 children (data collected at age 9 years and 13 years). The aim of *Growing up in Ireland* is to describe the lives of children in Ireland and to establish what is typical and normal, as well as what is atypical and problematic, for the purpose of providing evidence for the creation of effective and responsive policies and services for children and families. *Growing up in Ireland* also incorporates a nested qualitative component, with a sample of 120 families from each cohort for the first wave of data collection.

The breadth of research studies supported through this funded element of the NCRP presents an opportunity to highlight some of the challenges arising when undertaking research directly with children and young people. An overview of a small number of studies referred to in this chapter is provided in the Appendix, including examples with a focus on those living in atypical situations (e.g., children in foster care or children providing caring services to other family members), on those experiencing adversity (e.g., homelessness, domestic violence, illness, and hospitalization), and on those involved with certain services (e.g., the child protection services or the juvenile justice system). Other studies referred to in the Appendix were commissioned for the purpose of directly informing policy development (e.g., children and young people's attitudes to, and experiences of, parental corporal punishment child well-being; play and recreation; and the implementation and development of student councils in second-level schools).

15.3   Issues in study design

Planning research is a combination of technical and organizational skills. The final judgments about the population to be included, information to be collected, methods to be used and the processes of analysis are often a fine balance between what is appropriate, feasible, and ethically acceptable, and the resources available to the researcher. Sometimes, invalid assumptions about the homogeneity of adult populations can be made. But it is clear that when carrying out research with children, there is always a higher degree of difference to be taken into account since the status of the child will vary according to age, general cognitive ability, emotional status, and knowledge. These differences must be accommodated in study design and implementation. Issues of sampling and sample design are not considered in detail in this chapter, although details of sample design are provided for each study funded under the NCRP listed in the Appendix.

In respect of study design, there are a number of key areas to be considered when carrying out research with children. Among these are:

- Research designs that promote active and meaningful participation and reduce power differentials;
- The tension between protecting children and their right to participate;
- Informed consent and assent; and
- Confidentiality, anonymity, and privacy.

15.3.1   Challenges in using research designs that promote active and meaningful participation by children and young people

It has been argued that in the past, researchers habitually adopted methodologies that viewed children as objects (Christensen & Prout, 2002; Grover, 2004). Approaches chosen often ignored the child's perspective because of the assumption that children's thoughts and best interests could, and would, be reflected in the views of the adults in their lives (Balen, Blyth, Calabretto, Fraser, Horrocks, & Manby, 2006; Christensen & Prout, 2002). This rendered children "socially powerless and silenced in relation to adults" (Edwards & Alldred, 1999, p. 267). It is increasingly accepted, however, that adults cannot always be used as reliable proxies for children's views (Balen *et al.*, 2006; Murray, 2006) and since the early 1990s there has been a welcome shift in research approaches from those which view children as objects of the research to one which views children as knowing subjects (Cocks, 2006; Edwards & Alldred, 1999; Greene & Hogan, 2005). This new emphasis values the child's perspective and treats the child as an expert, with an active participatory role in the research encounter (Christensen & James, 2000; Greene & Hogan, 2005; Hill, 2006; Mason & Hood, 2011; Woodhead & Faulkner, 2000).

This view is congruent with the NCRP and also mirrors the sentiments of Article 12 of the UN Convention on the Rights of the Child, which affirms children's entitlement to express their views on matters affecting them (UN, 1989). Within this program, children and young people are increasingly involved in the design of the research, explicitly reflecting the commitment to active and meaningful participation in research. In *Growing up in Ireland*, for example, the establishment of a Children's Advisory Forum (CAF) was set out as a contractual requirement in the Request for Tender for the study. This was done to ensure that children are "provided with a direct platform to have their voices heard in the design, development and implementation of the study and, by doing so, to enhance the significance and relevance of the study" (Hanafin, Brooks, Roche, & Meaney, 2012). The CAF is currently made up of eighty-four children who sit on twelve committees in schools across Ireland.

Adopting this type of approach, however, raises many challenges. The promotion of active and meaningful participation by children and young people, and the reduction of power differentials between children and researchers, must be considered at every stage of the research process. It has been argued that disparities in power and status between adults and children are the greatest ethical challenge for researchers working with children and these challenges are especially evident where the social consequences of "opting out" are high. These include, for example, school contexts where the child's teacher may have a personal stake in ensuring student participation, or where young people are institutionalized. One study conducted with young people on remand from the courts and incarcerated in juvenile detention schools demonstrates the balance between conducting the research in an "objective" way and the need to ensure young people can meaningfully participate (Seymour & Butler, 2008). Following ethical approval (from the Irish Prison Service and the Dublin Institute of Technology, where the researchers were based), the researchers spent several days, prior to commencing the study, visiting each of the units in the children detention school system. The researchers noted that they "shared meals with the young people, chatted informally and engaged in activities such as football and computer games. The purpose was to allow potential participants an opportunity to decide if they wished to take part in the study and ask questions" (Seymour and Butler, 2008, p. 32).

A similar approach was adopted by Mayock and Vekić (2006), who conducted a study on young people who were homeless. The authors noted that the study began with a community assessment and a period of engagement with professionals working within services. This was followed by a long period of engagement with potential participants in settings such as hostels, night shelters, drop-in centres, places of detention, and street-based locations in order to ensure the young people had opportunities to discuss the research. The authors stated:

> It was imperative that young people did not feel under pressure to participate and, in all cases, prospective respondents received a detailed account of the research aims and their role in the study. Interviews were rarely conducted on the occasion of first meeting young people and, instead, prospective participants were asked to consider participating in the study at this juncture.

> (Mayock and Vekić, 2006, p. 11)

Although this type of approach has the potential to create some bias (including, for example, only interviewing the young people who returned to the original meeting setting and could therefore be approached again), it nevertheless highlights mechanisms used to minimize power differentials and particularly the importance of doing so where those taking part are vulnerable or in situations where opting out is, or may be, problematic.

Consideration of these issues needs to take place at each step of the research process, including in determining the types of studies to be conducted and funded, the population of children and young people to be included, methods to be used, settings for data collection, focus of analysis, and dissemination of findings from studies. These issues are considered in greater detail throughout this chapter and key challenges, as well as strategies to address them, are discussed.

15.3.2 Tension between protection and participation

While there is an increasing recognition that research with, and for, children is necessary because understanding their lives is critical to protecting, promoting, and supporting their health and well-being (DCYA, 2012), there continues to be some tension between protection and participation. This concern has arisen from an understanding of the importance of protecting children in all situations, but also from the recognition that research can harm children. Diekema (2006), for example, in an historical overview of pediatric research in the medical area highlights research conducted on children in the past that would not be considered nowadays. Examples include Jenner's use of his own one-year-old son to test the first smallpox vaccination and also the studies conducted by Krugman in the 1950s and 1960s, where newly arrived children at "an institution for mentally handicapped children" were infected with strains of the hepatitis vaccine in an attempt to study the natural history of the disease. Regulation in the area of children's research has increased and the primacy of protecting the child is often at its core. There is a growing unease, however, at the absence of research with children in some areas and this is particularly the case on the use of medication with this population. For example, in a recent study by Bourgeois, Murthy, Ioannidis, and Mandl (2012), the authors found a substantial discrepancy between the pediatric burden of disease and the amount of clinical trials research devoted to pediatric populations; they identified a particular problem in the paucity and quality of drug trials conducted with these children. An absence of research with children results in children being medicated with drugs that have been tested only on the adult population and that may not be suitable for use with children.

The breadth of the research funded under the NCRP means that it is possible to observe the extent to which concerns about protecting children in the research process differ according to context, nature of the area under investigation, and disciplinary position of the research team. It is very clear that concerns are not uniform across disciplinary areas, and practices considered acceptable by one group are often found to be unacceptable to another. Although in respect of most studies conducted under the program it was possible to negotiate an agreed approach, in some situations, even where ethics approval had been granted to carry out a study, permission to interact directly with children and young people was subsequently denied. One such study funded under the NCRP set out to examine the experiences of young people aged 13–14 in long-term foster care (Daly & Gilligan, 2005) and to answer the following research questions:

- What are the day-to-day experiences of education and schooling for young people aged 13–14 years in long-term foster care?
- What kind of social supports do these young people have available to them beyond their foster family?
- What relationship, if any, do placement conditions have with young people's education and schooling, as well as social supports?

The original intent was to carry out a national study covering all young people in the relevant age group (13–14 years) across the country who were in long-term foster care (defined as more than one year). However, multiple difficulties and delays in obtaining consent from all the relevant parties to speak to young people directly meant that all the data were collected from foster caregivers, and children and young people were not given a voice. While the DCYA's 2012 *Guidance for Developing Ethical Research Projects involving Children* rightly acknowledges the challenges in pursuing this type of research, a recent report by Shannon and Gibbons (2012) on the circumstances surrounding the lives of 196 children who died in the care of the state suggests that this was a lost opportunity to improve understandings of the challenges faced by these children and to identify potential mechanisms for overcoming these difficulties. There is, however, increasing awareness of the need to provide mechanisms to allow the voice of children to be heard in a more structured manner in care settings, as, for example, the publication of a report on a government consultation with children and young people in care (McEvoy & Smith, 2011). This consultation was carried out as part of the *Implementation Plan* of the Report of the Commission to Inquire into Child Abuse (OMCYA, 2009).

It could be argued that despite their vulnerability, young people themselves and their families should be the ultimate arbiters of decisions about whether to take part in research once appropriate ethical review has taken place. There is clear evidence emerging from the research program that potential participants in studies are competent to place clear boundaries around what they are willing to share with research teams, including withdrawal from the study. This was evident in a study conducted by Hogan and O'Reilly (2007) on the impact of witnessing domestic violence and the nature, scope, and adequacy of domestic violence services for children. One young person who had initially agreed to be interviewed for the study changed her mind; the authors wrote that "she explained to us that on further reflection 'while she was currently doing alright in her life,' opening up the story of her childhood of domestic violence with a researcher the day before she was leaving home to go back to college would not be the most sensible thing for her to do" (Hogan and O'Reilly, 2007, p. 14).

While a main concern in carrying out research is to minimize the risk of physical, psychological, or social harm to participants, it is also important to acknowledge that there are benefits for both the individual participant and for the broader community they represent. In terms of children's research, Edwards (2006) lists the benefits as including:

- Access to services, diagnosis, or treatment they may not otherwise be able to avail of;
- Gaining a novel experience and additional information through research participation and feedback; and

- Altruistic satisfaction in being part of a process that might contribute to improvements in therapies, services, or an increase in knowledge.

It is argued here that due consideration needs to be given to balancing appropriately the right of children or young people to take part in research about their lives and the need to protect them.

15.3.3 Consent, assent, and re-consent

Informed consent is based on three key components, namely: that potential participants gain knowledge through the provision of information they can understand; that the consent is voluntarily given; and that the potential participant has the capacity or competence to give their consent (Felzmann, Sixsmith, O'Higgins, Ni Chonnachtaigh, & Nic Gabhainn, 2010; Glasby & Beresford, 2007).

In practice, as well as ensuring informed consent, there are other issues to be addressed. These include seeking assent where children are not in a position to give consent; the requirement of additional parties to give consent; and in some circumstances, such as in longitudinal studies, the necessity for re-consent when the child reaches the legal age of consent. In a review of the literature on participation, Coyne, Hayes, Gallagher, and Regan (2006) differentiate between consent, assent, and permission as follows:

- **Consent** can be given by an autonomous person who is able to control their own lives by being in a position of self-determination.
- **Assent** is where a child over the age of 7 may give agreement based on evidence of knowledge and understanding, and a willingness to cooperate.
- **Permission**, the authors note, is where a parent or guardian gives consent on behalf of the child.

Coyne *et al.* (2006) propose that adolescents can consent, children in the middle childhood period can assent, and for babies and infants permission is required. It has been argued that age is a crude measure of competence and in the Irish context, there is little consensus about the age of maturity. In Ireland, children can legally join the workforce at 15 years of age at 16 they can give consent to medical treatments; at 17 they can consent to sexual activity; and at 18 they can vote in general elections and Constitutional referenda. Despite these discrepancies, age is often used as a criterion for capacity to consent and, in keeping with the UN Convention on the Rights of the Child (UN, 1989), the age of 18 years is used to differentiate between child and adulthood in many countries. One example of this in respect of research is the US Code of Federal Regulations, which governs research involving human subjects and also provides specifically for children as research subjects (US Department of Health and Human Services, 2009). This code defines children as "persons who have not attained the legal age for consent to treatments or procedures involved in the research under the applicable law of the jurisdiction in which the research will be conducted." In the UK, a nuanced approach, based on the Gillick principal and Fraser guidelines, is widely used to help assess whether a child has the maturity to make their own decisions and to understand the implications of those decisions. This approach draws attention to the developmental status of children by highlighting the role of cognition, reasoning, and competence.

Assessing competence to take part in research is a complex process. Hunfeld and Passchier (2012), for example, in a systematic review of the understanding and experience of children and adolescents in medical research, conclude that while they have a reasonable understanding of the purpose and risks of medical studies, they have much less understanding of the procedures involved. Felzmann *et al.* (2010) in a study commissioned to directly inform the development of *Guidance for Developing Ethical Research Projects Involving children* (DCYA, 2012) suggest that each of the following areas should be considered when carrying out research with children:

- The legal status of minors;
- The inclusion of additional parties in the consent process;
- Potentially, but not necessarily reduced psychological competence for consent in minors;
- Significant inter-individual differences in maturity, even within the same age group or study population; and
- Significant differences in knowledge and maturity between children of different ages and study population.

A study on understanding youth homelessness (Mayock & Vekić, 2006), carried out as part of the NCRP-funded research, provides some insight into the challenges of these processes with young people, particularly those in situations of risk. The aims of this study were:

- To identify young people's pathways or trajectories into, through, and out of homelessness;
- To examine the experience of homelessness from the perspective of young people;
- To identify facilitators and barriers to young people exiting homelessness; and
- To make policy recommendations related to service provision, early intervention, and the prevention of negative outcomes.

Given that these children were not living with their parents, gaining consent from guardians was particularly problematic, although the authors noted that this was achieved in all but a small number of cases where "the decision not to seek parental consent was taken only on the grounds that seeking such consent could potentially compromise the individual's safety … In those cases, consent was given instead by the young person's social worker" (Mayock & Vekić, 2006, p. 7).

Irrespective of how decisions about competence to take part in research are made, it is clear that in order for consent to be valid, the onus is on the researcher to ensure that he or she has taken all the necessary steps to ensure the person has been given an adequate amount of correct information and has been supported to develop an accurate understanding of the research (DCYA, 2012).

The issue of re-consent is emerging as an important issue in the area of children's research, particularly in respect of longitudinal and/or genetic research where seeking consent from adults for continued research on their data collected during childhood is slowly becoming standard practice. This approach recognizes that children's vulnerability is a temporary state that changes with cognitive development. Therefore, having an opportunity to confirm or reject a parental decision once the child reaches maturation is important (Goldenberg, Hull, Botkin, & Wilfond, 2009; Ries, LeGrandeur, & Caulfield, 2010).

15.3.4 Confidentiality, anonymity, and privacy

Confidentiality and anonymity are core to respecting and protecting participants in any study, and in many jurisdictions confidentiality issues are also governed by legislation relating to data protection. The main concerns about confidentiality in research relate to ensuring that information provided by the participant to the researcher or data that can be traced to the participant are not disclosed. The onus is on researchers to ensure safe data storage (physical and electronic), removal of identifying information through encryption, anonymization or modification, and/or receiving approval from participants for any disclosure of information to other parties (Felzmann *et al.*, 2010). As noted earlier, many methodologies used with children and young people to support their participation in the process can involve the use of focus groups and, in such situations, even where explicit ground rules have been set, it can be difficult to maintain confidentiality.

One area of particular concern arises in relation to child protection. In Ireland, child protection guidelines are in place, but mandatory reporting of child abuse is not yet legislated for. This is currently under development, but it is not yet clear which professionals or other stakeholders (including survey interviewers or other researchers) will be required by law to report child abuse and neglect (DCYA, 2012). In the interim, however, and in keeping with the requirements of *Children First: National Guidance for the Protection and Welfare of Children* (DCYA, 2011a), confidentiality and anonymity cannot be absolute in research with, and for, children, and guarantees of such cannot be given. In *Growing up in Ireland*, the Department of Children and Youth Affairs addressed issues of child protection and confidentiality through strict contractual conditions that require all field personnel to undergo vetting by An Garda Síochána (the national police service), which involves the disclosure of details of all convictions and prosecutions. Field staff were trained in the interpretation and implementation of the *Children First* national guidance, and in addition a detailed incident report system was put in place, with an emergency telephone number for contacting the study team on a 24-hour, 7-day basis.

It is important, however, that a balance is maintained between ensuring best practice in terms of child protection and allowing children the privacy they need to express their views. In the majority of research studies conducted under the NCRP a parent or guardian was present in the room at all times with the researcher and the child (albeit, if possible, out of earshot). While this offers greater protection to the child (and the researcher), it does, however, diminish the child's right to privacy. This issue was considered in a recent report on *Growing up in Ireland* where the authors noted that "interviewing the child with another adult in the room might place some constraints on the child's freedom of speech, in terms of their fear of being overheard by the adult or indeed the adult interfering with the child's responses" (Greene & Harris, 2011, p. 27). In an attempt to resolve this in the *Growing up in Ireland* study, the computer-aided personal interview (CAPI) included only those questions that were not considered to be of a "sensitive nature." A separate self-administered pencil and paper interview (PAPI) was used for the more sensitive questions (e.g., bullying and parental relationships) so that children could record their answers privately. Audio CD and headphones were also made available to help less-confident readers (Murray, McCrory, Thornton, Williams, & Quail, 2011).

15.3.5 Summary

This section has considered issues arising in the design of studies with and about children, and has provided examples, drawn from the NCRP, of challenges and solutions for ensuring meaningful participation in the research process, for balancing tensions between participation and protection, or between consent, assent, and re-consent, and finally issues relating to confidentiality, anonymity, and privacy. The findings show that, with a small number of exceptions, workable and practical solutions can be found to the complex and challenging issues that emerge in research with children.

15.4 Issues in study implementation

Many of the issues that arise in relation to study implementation have already been addressed in this chapter. However, three specific areas are now given further consideration:

- Recruitment, including access and gatekeeping;
- Data collection; and
- Data analysis and dissemination.

15.4.1 Recruitment, access, and gatekeeping

Gaining access to children to undertake research is acknowledged as problematic throughout the literature (Punch, 2002; Thomas & O'Kane, 1998; Young & Barrett, 2001) since children are almost never in a position to decide freely for themselves whether or not to take part. Access is almost always negotiated through what Hammersley and Atkinson (1983, p. 83) refer to as "gatekeepers" or those who control "avenues of opportunity" within certain settings.

Researchers from a variety of different disciplines and perspectives were involved in carrying out the studies in the NCRP and included, among others, researchers from health, educational, legal, sociological, and technological backgrounds. One of the overriding features associated with the implementation of the research is the extent to which multiple permissions have to be sought and achieved before a study can take place. There is, however, a notable lack of uniformity in terms of requirements and clear differences emerged in respect of recruitment, access, protection of children, and ethics requirements according to context and discipline. Researchers working in health settings are subject to many more restrictions than others, although it is expected that the recent publication of national ethics guidance on conducting research with children will help to streamline processes (DCYA, 2012).

Gatekeepers have a responsibility (which may be professional, parental, or other) to ensure that they make all the necessary decisions to protect the welfare of children. Understandably, there were many instances where much time, effort, and change in protocols were needed in order to meet gatekeepers' requirements before accessing children for the purposes of the studies funded under the NCRP. In one study on children's experiences of consultation and decision-making in Irish hospitals (Coyne *et al.*, 2006), the authors noted that permission to enlist the children as research participants was first sought from the ethics committees in the three hospital sites. When this was achieved, cooperation had to be sought from the health professionals directly involved with the sites, including senior nurse managers, ward sisters, and doctors. Meetings then had to be held with senior personnel from the three hospitals and follow-up discussions took place on an informal basis with healthcare providers. An information package was compiled and distributed to all units and the study team noted that "they spent time trying to identify key gatekeepers on the units in order to facilitate the data collection" (Coyne *et al.*, 2006, p. 24). All of this was achieved prior to seeking permission from a parent for their child to take part in the research and then finally assent was sought from the children. In contrast, a study of children's experiences of the healthcare system was carried out by researchers from a legal and human rights discipline (Kilkelly and Donnelly, 2006). Their chosen methodology included focus group interviews and the use of vignettes, and the data collection was carried out in community settings with children and parents, as well as individual interviews with healthcare professionals. However, the children (aged 5–14 years) and their parents were accessed through nongovernmental organizations working with children and/or in the healthcare setting, and ethics approval or other gatekeepers did not feature in this study.

Gatekeeping has a real and tangible effect on recruitment and response rates in respect of studies with children, and its impact can be quantitatively explored through an explication of the recruitment process used with the 9-year-old cohort of *Growing up in Ireland*. In the absence of a national population register, schools were used as the primary sampling units. Researchers did not have direct access to the names or contact details for children and this, coupled with issues relating to data protection and informed consent, meant that a significant burden in the generation and recruitment of the sample fell to the schools involved (see Murray *et al.*, 2011, for more detailed information). Despite this burden, there was a high level of cooperation from schools, with an overall response rate of 82.3 percent. However, this varied by the volume of the task, with schools having lower numbers of 9-year-olds (and consequently a lesser burden of work in sample selection) also having higher response rates. Response rates were about 88 percent for the schools with fewest 9-year-olds, compared with 75 percent of schools with the highest numbers of 9-year-olds.

Having worked through this first stage of access, with a fully acceptable response rate, secondary access issues arose regarding certain key informants. In particular, access to non-resident parents and nonparental caregivers were routed through the resident primary caregiver (usually the mother). The levels of response shown in Table 15.1 illustrate diminishing returns as the degrees of separation between researcher and respondent increased, and this impact is particularly noticeable for those instruments that were dependent on the supply of address information by the resident primary caregiver (see "Postal data collection" in Table 15.1).

For example, children in lone-parent families (in particular lone-father families) were more difficult to recruit, as were children in nonfamily units (e.g., children who were being fostered or in homes where their primary caregiver was not an immediate relative). In common with most surveys, children whose mothers were less educated, younger, or in lower social class categories were also less likely to participate. These differential participation rates, which were evident in the structure of the completed samples in this study, were addressed through re-weighting the data (Quail, Williams, McCrory, Murray, & Thornton, 2011; Thornton, Williams, McCrory, Murray, & Quail, 2011).

Table 15.1 *Response levels by study informant – Growing up in Ireland, 9-year-old cohort*

Study informant	Achieved sample size	Notes
School-based data collection		
Teacher of study child – on child	8,283	
Teacher of study child – on self	8,172	Target sample was 8,568 study children
Principal of study child – on child	8,396	
Home-based data collection		
Study child	8,518	Target sample was 8,568 study children
Primary caregiver of study child	8,568	
Secondary caregiver of study child	7,117	This questionnaire was relevant to 7,576 study children. The number of households with no secondary caregiver present was 992.
Postal data collection		
Nonresident parent	181	1,073 nonresident parents were identified. 343 were sent questionnaires.
Childcare provider – home-based	425	903 home-based carers were identified. 675 were sent questionnaires.
Childcare provider – centre-based	85	174 centre-based carers were identified. 126 were sent questionnaires.

Note: Study informant based on principal data collection instrument where multiple instruments were used with an informant. It is clear from the data presented that gatekeeping, while necessary, important, and providing protection, nevertheless can have a clear effect on the recruitment of children and young people to take part in research studies.

The time commitment involved was cited by parents as the main reason for refusing access to their child to participate in *Growing up in Ireland*. In this study, there was also evidence that the nature of questions being asked played a role. For example, some parents consented for their child to participate in parts, but not in all of the study. More specifically, questions of a more sensitive nature were not permitted during data collection (Williams & McCrory, 2011).

Similarly, the area of investigation and the target population was a key consideration for gatekeepers in a study by Hogan and O'Reilly (2007), which examined "the impact of witnessing domestic violence and the nature, scope and adequacy of domestic violence services for children." In this study, gatekeepers refused access to mothers and their children living in refuges on the basis that they were "too vulnerable." Others felt that "it was unethical to contact women and children who had left the refuge, either because they had returned to live with the violent man or because the professionals wanted to allow the women and children to bring some 'closure' to their experience" (Hogan and O'Reilly, 2007, p. 14).

15.4.2 Data collection

Earlier in this chapter, we discussed the importance of adopting an approach to research with children that views them as knowing subjects and it was noted that this often determines the methods and methodology used. Almost all studies funded under the NCRP adopted, or at least incorporated, some participative approaches to the collection of data. A multiplicity of methods was taken to the collection of data and favoured approaches included individual interviews (e.g., Buckley, Whelan, Carr, & Murphy, 2008), focus groups (e.g., Coyne *et al.*, 2006; De Róiste & Dinneen, 2005), systemic interviews with siblings (e.g., Hogan & O'Reilly, 2007), observation (e.g., Kehoe & Whyte, 2005), vignettes (e.g., Kilkelly & Donnelly, 2006), write and draw (e.g., Harris, Doyle, & Greene, 2011) and photovoice (e.g., Nic Gabhainn & Sixsmith, 2005). Other more traditional methods were also used, including questionnaire surveys (e.g., Downey, Hayes, & O'Neill, 2007; Kelly, Molcho, & Nic Gabhainn, 2009) and standardized testing (Murray *et al.*, 2011).

Many practical issues arise when collecting data from children and some of these have already been noted. Borgers, Sikkel, and Hox (2004), for example, have considered the question of the effects of negatively formulated questions, of the number of response options offered, and of offering a neutral mid-point as a response option to question the characteristics on the reliability of responses, and of using children and young adolescents as respondents. In considering all the findings, these authors concluded that offering about four response options is optimal with children as respondents. For a more detailed discussion on methods for improving data quality, see Scott (1997).

The importance of ensuring very clear, well-tested, and age-appropriate questions (which can be easily understood by children at different stages of development, cognition, maturity, and family circumstance) was evident throughout the development process of *Growing up in Ireland*. This process included pretesting, piloting, and full dress rehearsal prior to going into the field. Even something as apparently straightforward as asking the child questions about "mum" or "dad," as well as requiring great sensitivity, had the potential to result in confusion, particularly in situations where the study child's mother or father was in a new relationship. Where a resident partner was not the child's biological parent, it was important to be clear as to whether the child was referring to the biological or resident partner when referring to "mum" or "dad." These difficulties were even more intensified in situations where the study child resided with a biological parent and his or her partner, but also maintained contact with the nonresident biological parent. This issue was dealt with by dividing the core sensitive questionnaire for the child into four additional separable sections that explicitly identified to "mum," "dad," "mum's partner," and "dad's partner" (Murray *et al.*, 2011).

In all data collection with children and young people, it is important that the issues of literacy, learning difficulties, and sensitivity are taken into account and that materials are presented in a way that facilitates engagement by children and young people. Information sheets explaining the rationale for the study, processes that will take place, protections in place for participants and their data, and the agencies involved all need to be both explicit and presented in a child-friendly manner. In this context, the Children's Advisory Forum made a significant contribution in advising on matters affecting accessibility of information sheets, elements of the questionnaire for the child participants in the *Growing up in Ireland* study and in presenting findings to children and their families.

15.4.3 Data analysis and dissemination

There are many potential issues for children's research in data analysis and dissemination of findings, not least the question of how adult researchers can accurately and authentically give voice to children's views. Arising from the recent phenomenon of involving children in the overall research process, there is an emerging trend of including them in the analysis of data. One study commissioned for the purpose of informing the development of the National Set of Child Well-Being Indicators focused on children's well-being as portrayed through photographs they had taken themselves (Nic Gabhainn & Sixsmith, 2005). The researchers, in a novel approach, facilitated 266 children and young people, aged 12–18, to carry out the analysis of individual-level data themselves, followed by group-level data analysis and feedback. While this type of approach to analysis is unusual, there is a growing literature and practice of "children as researchers" (Kellett, Forrest, Dent, & Ward, 2004).

More commonly, issues arise from the multiplicity of stakeholders from whom data are collected. Across the breadth of the research, many studies collected data from multiple stakeholders in addition to children and young people. It is not clear why this should be the case and it is possible that such approaches arise because of perceptions that children's views need to be confirmed by adults, or that children themselves may not be capable of giving the depth of insight into their own lives that may be sought. It may also arise because such an approach is beneficial in giving a comprehensive understanding of children and young people's lives and facilitates the emergence of important insights and directions for policy and practice developments. Irrespective of the rationale for collecting data from multiple stakeholders, it is clear that such approaches give rise to both benefits and challenges in the analysis of data and the identification of key issues.

Similar to other studies elsewhere, the findings from *Growing up in Ireland* show that many children in Ireland have problems with being overweight and obese, and by 3 years of age, some 25 percent are already overweight or obese. In addition to the data collected on children in the study, weight and height measurements were also collected from the primary and secondary caregiver, as well as attitudinal data on whether they perceived their child to be overweight or obese. The findings also highlighted that parents are poor at recognizing when their child is overweight – more than half of mothers (54 percent) of overweight children and 20 percent of mothers of obese children reported them as being of normal weight (Layte & McCrory, 2011). This type of information, which has significant policy implications, was only possible because multiple types of data were collected from multiple stakeholders. These findings were replicated in those relating to education, where important mismatches were identified between the views of parents and teachers about the same child (McCoy, Quail, & Smyth, 2012). Some examples include:

- 60 percent of parents say their child is above average at reading, but only 39 percent of teachers say this;
- 52 percent of parents say their child is above average in maths, but only 33 percent of teachers say this; and
- 20 percent of parents say their child spends between 1 and 1.5 hours on homework, but only 1 percent of teachers say they give this amount of homework.

In some situations, however, where there are multiple stakeholder views, decisions must be made about privileging the voice of the child since, in the absence of a strong commitment to doing so, adult views can prevail. This was highlighted in one study where the findings from the analysis of photographs carried out by Nic Gabhainn and Sixsmith (2005) (described above) were integrated into the second round of a Delphi study employed to achieve consensus on a National Set of Child Well-Being Indicators (Hanafin *et al.*, 2007). While there was much overlap between children's views about things that made them feel well (e.g., family, friends, good communities) and adults' views of the same phenomenon, one issue identified by children had not emerged previously, either through an analysis of indicator sets elsewhere or through the panel of expertise convened to take part in the Delphi study. This issue was the importance of pets and animals to children in helping them to feel well. When, in a subsequent round of the Delphi study, this area was presented to the panel of expertise, it was rejected as an indicator area of children's well-being. In this situation, the commitment to privileging the voice of children prevailed and an indicator on "pets and animals" was subsequently included in the National Set of Child Well-being Indicators.

As with all research, dissemination of information and transfer of knowledge arising from studies is an important step and in this regard, insights and guidance from children and young people about content and presentation of findings can be invaluable. *Growing up in*

Ireland, for example, is guided in this area by the Children's Advisory Forum and relevant findings from the study have been provided for each child and their family in a child-friendly format. In terms of setting an overall research agenda, the Children and Young People's Forum at the Department of Children and Youth Affairs made specific contributions to the development of the recently published *National Strategy for Research and Data on Children's Lives 2011–2016* (DCYA, 2011b; for a fuller description of the consultation processes informing the strategy, see Roche, Hanafin, & Sharek, 2011).

15.5 Conclusions

This chapter has presented key issues arising from the design and implementation of research funded under the NCRP and has drawn attention to benefits and challenges when carrying out research with children and young people. Underpinning the NCRP, and operationalized in more than thirty research studies, is a commitment to listening to children's voices and to the meaningful participation by children and young people in research about their own lives. Some discussion has been presented on the tensions arising between protecting children in the research process while at the same time respecting and promoting their right to participate. Informed consent, assent, and re-consent have been considered, along with issues of confidentiality, anonymity, and privacy. While these issues occur with all populations, there are additional challenges to reflect on when carrying out research with children, especially those in vulnerable situations.

The complexities of gaining access and recruiting children into the research process are discussed and the crucial role played by gatekeepers is presented, including a quantification of their impact at different stages of the process. Some reflections on the multiplicity of data collection methods are presented, as well as challenges in analysis, perception, and generalizability, together with solutions and strategies employed by researchers under the NCRP. Throughout the chapter, studies carried out under the NCRP have been used as exemplars to explicate and provide evidence of the complexities involved, the challenges to be addressed, and also the benefits accruing from including children and young people at every stage of the research process.

On the basis of the evidence presented here, it is concluded that although research with and about children raises challenges over and above that with adults, these can be overcome with appropriate consideration and the examples presented in this chapter can provide practical guidance in these areas.

Appendix

Examples of research studies funded under the National Children's Research Programme, indicating the research purpose, sampling techniques, research methods and population accessed in each study.

Title of research project	Purpose of research	Sampling technique	Methods and population accessed
The child's right to be heard in the healthcare setting: perspectives of children, parents and health professionals (Kilkelly & Donnelly, 2006)	To present an overview of the extent to which children are listened to in the healthcare setting from the perspectives of children, parents, and health professionals.	Convenience sampling was used to identify participants. Children and parents were accessed through nongovernmental organizations (NGOs) working with children and/or in the healthcare setting, and included children who had experienced standard or typical levels of contact with the healthcare setting, as well as those who had experienced higher levels of contact due to serious illness. Health professionals were also identified using the convenience method and the snowball technique was also used. The inclusion of a range of ages and genders among the children, as well as some diversity in background and geographical location in all categories, reduces the limitations of this sampling technique, but does not address the issue of the representativeness of the sample.	Individual and group interviews with children, parents and service providers. Vignettes, picture cards, and story boards were developed for children aged 5–8 and 9–11. Children (aged 5–14) and parents were accessed through NGOs working with children and/or in the healthcare setting. Health professionals were also identified using the convenience method and the snowball technique.
Giving children a voice: investigation of children's experiences of participation in consultation and decision-making in Irish hospitals (Coyne *et al.*, 2006)	To examine children's experiences of participation in consultations and decisions about their healthcare within the hospital setting.	The samples in this study were drawn from three different care settings (two children's hospitals and one large district hospital) based on three specific criteria (participants had to be between the ages of 7 and 18, attending one of the three settings and have been hospitalized with an acute or chronic illness). The size of the sample (n=55) was sufficient to permit valid conclusions to be drawn (Carey, 1994).	Focus groups and individual interviews. Inclusion criteria: Children aged 7–18 attending one of three different care settings – two children's hospitals and one large district hospital. Children who could be interviewed without parents or health providers present. All focus groups and individual interviews were tape-recorded and field notes were used to keep a systematic record of observations made during each interview.

| Young people's views about opportunities, barriers and supports to recreation and leisure (De Róiste & Dinneen, 2005) | In the context of policy development around young people's recreation and leisure, to determine what young people in Ireland do in their free time; what barriers and supports do they experience; and what are their aspirations with regard to recreation and leisure. | A survey was undertaken with over 2,260 young people, aged 12–18 years, via a random sample of fifty-one schools across the Irish Republic. Most counties had two schools in the sample, with additional schools from the more populated counties. A further 100 young people participated in focus groups and interviews, designed to gain insight into the additional needs of young people with disabilities and those at a socioeconomic disadvantage. Subsamples of young people from minority groups were also accessed, but are not presented as representative in the way that the main sample is. The research undertaken in these substudies was designed to broaden the sample so that minority groups were assured a voice. The findings from these smaller studies may serve as signposts for future research. | Survey: 2,260 young people, aged 12–18, through a national random sample of fifty-one schools. Researchers visited 90 percent of the schools selected to administer the questionnaire, with a trained research assistant administrating the remaining questionnaires. Focus groups and interviews with minority groups, including young people with sensory impairments (visual and auditory), intellectual disabilities, physical disabilities, members of the Traveller community, and those attending early school-leaver training centres. |
| Young people on remand (Seymour & Butler, 2008) | To examine the services and supports required by young people to promote greater compliance with the conditions of bail and thereby to reduce the use of detention on remand. | The research sought to recruit a sample of young people currently in detention, who had been remanded on bail or who had been detained on remand in the previous two years. Purposive sampling was used to recruit the cohort through the children detention school system. | Semistructured interviews with young people, their parents, and professionals, courtroom observation and a survey with key service providers. |

Title of research project	Purpose of research	Sampling technique	Methods and population accessed
Ethical review and children's research in Ireland (Felzmann et al., 2010)	To provide an overview of the current mechanisms for applying for and achieving ethics approval for studies being undertaken with children in Ireland.	The survey sample frame was developed from a listing of operational research ethics committees (RECs) provided by the Irish Council of Bioethics and was expanded to include additional committees identified through a literature/documentary review process. Researchers of children in Ireland were identified through the literature/documentary review process, with web-based searches of organizations and institutions expressing an interest in research with children or on children's issues. Children and young people were accessed through schools. The principals of primary schools who had participated in a children's survey were contacted. A list of 113 schools known to have participated in research was identified from the Department of Education and Science data file of schools and twenty primary schools were randomly selected from the list compiled. Fifteen of the twenty Principals from each of the twenty schools identified recruited a parent, thirteen of whom participated in the study.	A postal questionnaire administered to fifty research ethics committees. Semistructured telephone interviews with twenty-six chairpersons of research ethics committees. Focus groups carried out with children's researchers. Participative workshops with children and young people accessed through schools. Semistructured telephone interviews undertaken with parents of children who had taken part in previous research projects.

Study	Aim	Sampling	Methods
Children's perspectives on parenting styles and discipline: a developmental approach (Nixon & Halpenny, 2010)	To explore children's perspectives on parenting styles and discipline.	The approach to sampling did not specifically strive to recruit a nationally representative sample of children and adolescents. Rather, the aim was to recruit a sample of children from different backgrounds to facilitate exploration and representation of a range of experiences. The sample was accessed through primary and secondary schools in three counties in Ireland.	Thirty focus group interviews with 132 children and adolescents, ranging in age from 6 to 17, from primary and secondary schools in three counties in Ireland (Dublin, Westmeath, and Monaghan). A sociodemographic questionnaire accompanied parental consent forms and was returned for each child who participated in the research.
Play and technology for children aged 4–12 (Downey et al., 2007)	To examine how technology impacts on the play of children in Ireland and what children say about the role of technology in their lives.	The sample was a purposive one and is not nationally representative. The sample obtained was intended to reflect urban, rural, gender and socioeconomic variations, and the means of achieving this was through ensuring a balance of school types.	The research involved a survey and focus groups with 292 children aged 4–12 in ten primary schools all over Ireland. Teachers and parents were also interviewed.
Young people and public libraries in Ireland: issues and opportunities (McGrath, Rogens, & Gilligan, 2010)	To examine public library provision for young people aged 13–17 in Ireland; to investigate their opinions and perceptions of current library services; and to obtain their ideas for creating a public library service that would appeal to their age group.	Two sets of key informants were identified in the study: young people aged 13–17 (both library users and nonusers) and staff from all thirty-two city and county public library services.	Focus group discussion with 154 young people. Short individual questionnaires completed by focus group participants. Survey of staff at thirty-two city and county public libraries to ascertain current service provision. Meetings with library personnel.

Title of research project	Purpose of research	Sampling technique	Methods and population accessed
Service users' perceptions of the Irish child protection system (Buckley *et al.*, 2008)	To explore the views of young people and adults who used the child protection services.	Purposive sampling was used to select which key stakeholders should be approached and, in turn, the service providers also employed purposive sampling in the selection of the service users they invited to participate in the study. It has been established that such nonprobability sampling is particularly suitable for exploratory research (Burton, 2000).	In-depth interviews conducted in sixteen counties in Ireland with sixty-seven services users, including fifty-four adults and thirteen young people. Links were made with participants via a range of organizations, including family support services, refuge and treatment services, community and youth projects, and redress bodies. Thirteen of the service users interviewed were young people who had been the subject of child protection concerns.
Study of young carers in the Irish population (Fives, Kennan, Canavan, Brady, & Cairns, 2010)	To examine a mechanism through which young carers (aged 5–18) in the Irish population can be identified; to investigate the impact of caring on their lives; and to examine ways in which they can be assisted.	The aim was to access a sample of young carers in the Irish population reflective of a range of caring scenarios and a range of ages between 5 and 17 years. There was no "sampling frame" from which to draw a random sample of young carers in the Irish population. Young carers are, for the most part, not on the databases of HSE carer professionals or those of the nonstatutory carers' organizations. In the absence of a sampling frame, the research team employed three closely related sampling methods – purposive, convenience and snowballing.	Interviews with young carers and agency staff. Recruitment took place over two phases: Phase 1 involved contact with statutory and nonstatutory agencies thought likely to have knowledge of young carers, and a national information campaign which invited young carers to participate in the research. Neither of these methods yielded many contacts, thus the sampling methods were reviewed, broadened, and re-launched. In Phase 2, additional potential service contacts were identified, snowball and convenience sampling was employed, and a direct media campaign was launched to boost recruitment. The final sample included twenty-six young carers, aged 5–18 years.

Study	Aim	Sampling	Data collection
health behaviour in school-aged children (HBSC) Ireland 2006. Middle childhood study: socio-demographic patterns in the health behaviours, risk behaviours, health outcomes, and social contexts of young people's health (Kelly *et al.*, 2009)	To increase understanding of the health and well-being of 9-year-olds in Ireland and to use the findings to inform and influence health promotion policy and practice at national level.	Sampling for the HBSC survey is conducted in accordance with the structure of the national educational system within countries, which in Ireland is stratified by region, but the primary sampling unit is always the school classroom. Thus, the nonindependence of students within classrooms is considered in the procedures for sample size calculation and these are based on the deft values identified in previous survey rounds (Roberts, Francois, Batista-Foguet, & King, 2000; Roberts, Tynjala, Curie, & King, 2004). Based on self-reported data from school children, a nationally representative sample of 9-year-old children was identified using the sampling frame provided in a national list of primary schools supplied by the relevant government department.	Age-appropriate classes (3rd and 4th years) were selected and a modified HBSC questionnaire was piloted, amended accordingly, and administered in each of the randomly selected schools.
Understanding youth homelessness in Dublin city: key findings from the first phase of a longitudinal cohort study (Mayock & Vekić, 2006)	To generate an in-depth understanding of the process of youth homelessness, with a focus on trajectories into, through, and out of homelessness.	Research did not aim to generate a representative sample of young people whose experiences are generalizable to the entire homeless youth population, but rather to recruit a cohort of young people with a varied range of experiences of homelessness, via the use of purposive sampling combined with targeted sampling techniques to assist the achievement of diversity in relation to age and gender, and variability of living arrangements, present and past.	A community assessment was undertaken, which involved a period of engagement with professionals working directly with young homeless people. Life history interviews were conducted with young homeless people recruited through service settings.

Title of research project	Purpose of research	Sampling technique	Methods and population accessed
Children's understandings of well-being (Nic Gabhainn & Sixsmith, 2005)	Through an exploration of children's perspectives and understandings of well-being, to contribute to the development of a National Set of Child Well-being Indicators.	For the first three phases of this research, children were accessed through schools. School lists were downloaded from the Department of Education and Science website. The rationale was to ensure that the schools in both urban and rural locations were sampled. Within each geographical area and school type (primary/postprimary), those schools selected first were allocated to the initial photographs stage (Phase 1). If a single sex school was selected, a second school of the same type but with pupils of the other sex was selected. The next set of schools selected was allocated to the categorization stage (Phase 2) and the last selected schools were allocated to the schema development stage (Phase 3). All schools in Phases 2 and 3 were required to be co-educational. A number of extra schools were selected in order to obviate the need to return to the sampling frame should any school be unwilling to participate; thus sampling with replacement was undertaken.	A participatory research design, with individual and group-level data collection and analysis. Children were given a disposable camera and asked to photograph things, people, or places that made them well or kept them well.

| Lives in foster care: the educational and social support experiences of young people aged 13–14 years in long-term foster care (Daly & Gilligan, 2005) | To consider the educational experiences and social supports available in the daily lives of young people, aged 13–14 years, in long-term foster care. | This was a national study covering all young people in the 13–14 age group who were in long-term foster care. Due to multiple difficulties and delays, only the adult foster carers of these children were interviewed. | Foster carers were the main informants for the study due to the potential difficulties of obtaining consent to speak to the young people directly. Telephone interviews were carried out using a semistructured questionnaire template. |
| Listening to children: children's stories of domestic violence (Hogan & O'Reilly, 2007) | To identify the impact on children of witnessing domestic violence and to identify the nature, scope and adequacy of domestic violence services for children. | The sampling framework utilized purposive sampling, which is designed to enhance understandings of selected individuals' or groups' experience(s), or for developing theories and concepts. Researchers seek to accomplish this goal by selecting "information-rich" cases, i.e., individuals, groups, organizations, or behaviors that provide the greatest insight into the research question (Devers & Frankel, 2000, p. 264). Thus, the first phase of recruitment was purposefully to target children, through their mothers, via the professionals working with victims of domestic violence. | In-depth interviews were conducted with a sample of key professionals, mothers, and children. This study used creative and child-centred methods of engagement, including systemic interviews with siblings and draw-and-write techniques. |

Title of research project	Purpose of research	Sampling technique	Methods and population accessed
Second-level student councils in Ireland: a study of enablers, barriers and supports (Kehoe & Whyte, 2005)	To describe the operation of student councils in second-level schools in Ireland; to identify enablers and barriers to good practice in the establishment, development and operation of student councils; and to identify ways in which student councils can play a meaningful role in schools.	Schools were identified using data (compiled by the Statistics Office in the Department of Education and Science) that cataloged all second-level schools in the Republic of Ireland by type, size, and gender. Schools were selected using the following criteria: school type and size; location; gender; fee-paying and boarding schools; schools with and without student councils. Eighteen schools were selected under the criteria of school type and size, and invited to participate. Each of the four school types was proportionately represented in the achieved sample. Schools with and without student councils were approached, but only schools that had functioning student councils or were in the process of establishing a council agreed to participate. The organization of the focus groups was left to each school. They were asked to select a random sample of students and not solely students they thought would be able to express themselves well. In total, 251 students were consulted in the ten schools.	Focus groups were conducted in the participating schools. Members of student councils were interviewed in pairs or in a group as appropriate. School principals, teachers, and liaison teachers were consulted through semistructured interviews and focus groups. Members of the schools' boards of management were consulted during their meetings or through a survey questionnaire. The researchers also attended one student council election and two student council meetings during the course of the study. In three schools selected as profiling "models of good practice," one focus group was conducted with student council members and a group of students from mixed-year groups. Semistructured interviews were also conducted with each of the three schools' principals, teachers, and liaison teachers.

| Growing up in Ireland: national longitudinal study of children | To examine the factors that contribute to or undermine the well-being of children in contemporary families in Ireland and through this, to contribute to the setting of effective and responsive policies relating to children and to the design of services for children and their families. | A nationally representative sample of 900 schools was selected from all over Ireland, including mainstream national schools, private schools, and special schools. Over 2,300 individual teachers cooperated in the schools, as well as principals and support staff. The sample of 8,500 9-year-old children was then randomly selected from within these schools.

The infant cohort is made of 11,000 children selected randomly from the Child Benefit Register. | A series of home- and school-based questionnaires were administered to primary and secondary caregivers, nonresident parents, teachers, school principals, and children themselves (where appropriate) in an infant cohort (i.e., 11,100 children recruited at age 9 months) and a child cohort (i.e., 8,568 children recruited at age 9). The mode of administration is a combination of computer-assisted personal interviews (CAPI), computer-assisted self-interviews (CASI) and pencil and paper interviews (PAPI). Direct measures are also used (e.g., Maths and Reading Assessments, Height and Weight). |

References

Balen, R., Blyth, E., Calabretto, H., Fraser, C., Horrocks, C., & Manby, M. (2006). Involving children in health and social research: "human becomings" or "active beings." *Childhood*, 13(1), 29–48.

Borgers, N., Sikkel, D., & Hox, J. (2004). Response effects in surveys on children and adolescents: the effect of number of response options, negative wording and neutral mid-point. *Quality and Quantity*, 38(1), 17–33.

Bourgeois, F. T., Murthy, S., Ioannidis, J. P. A., & Mandl, K. D. (2012). *Clinical Drug Trials: A Paucity of Pediatric Representation Mismatched to Global Disease Burden*, Pediatric Academic Societies 2012, Annual Meeting.

Buckley, H., Whelan, S., Carr, N., & Murphy, C. (2006). *Service Users' Perceptions of the Child Protection System*. Office of the Minister for Children and Youth Affairs. Dublin: Government Publications.

Burton, D. (2000). *Research Training for Social Scientists: A Handbook for Postgraduate research*. London: Sage.

Carey, M. A. (1994). The group effect in focus groups: planning, implementing and interpreting focus group research. In J. M. Morse (ed.), *Critical Issues in Qualitative Research Methods*. Thousand Oaks, CA: Sage Publications.

Christensen, P., & James, A. (2000). Childhood diversity and commonality: some methodological insight. In P. Christensen and A. James (eds.), *Research with Children: Perspectives and Practices* (pp. 160–78). London: Falmer Press.

Christensen, P., & Prout, A. (2002). Working with ethical symmetry in social research with children. *Childhood*, 9(4), 477–97.

Cocks, A. (2006). The ethical maze: finding an inclusive path towards gaining children's agreement to research participation. *Childhood*, 13(2), 247–66.

Coyne, I., Hayes, E., Gallagher, P., & Regan, G. (2006). *Giving Children a Voice: Investigation of children's experiences of participation in consultation and decision-making in Irish hospitals*. Office of the Minister for Children. Dublin: Government Publications.

Daly, F., & Gilligan, R. (2005). *Lives in Foster Care: The Educational and Social Support Experiences of Young People Aged 13 to 14 Years in Long-Term Foster Care*. Dublin: Children's Research Centre, Trinity College, Dublin.

DCYA. (2011a). *Children First: National Guidance for the Protection and Welfare of Children*. Department of Children and Youth Affairs. Dublin: Government Publications.

(2011b). *National Strategy for Research and Data on Children's Lives 2011–2016*. Department of Children and Youth Affairs. Dublin: Government Publications.

(2012). *Guidance for Developing Ethical Research Projects involving Children*. Department of Children and Youth Affairs. Dublin: Government Publications.

De Róiste, A., & Dinneen, J. (2005). *Young People's Views about Opportunities, Barriers and Supports to Recreation and Leisure*. National Children's Office. Dublin: Government Publications.

Department of Health and Children. (2000). *The National Children's Strategy: Our Children – Their Lives*. Dublin: Government Publications.

Devers, R., & Frankel, R. (2000). Study design in qualitative research. 2: Sampling and data collection strategies. *Education for Health*, 13(2), 264.

Diekema, D. S. (2006). Conducting ethical research in pediatrics: a brief historical overview and review of pediatric regulations. *Journal of Pediatrics*, 149(1), S3–S11.

Downey, S., Hayes, N., & O'Neill, B. (2007). *Play and Technology for Children Aged 4–12*. Office of the Minister for Children. Dublin: Government Publications.

Edwards, P., & Alldred, P. (1999). Children and young people's views of social research: the case of research on home-school relations. *Childhood*, 6(2), 261–81.

Edwards, S. J. L. (2006). Restricted treatments, inducement and research participation. *Bioethics*, 20(2), 77–91.

Felzmann, H., Sixsmith, J., O'Higgins, S., Ni Chonnachtaigh, S., & Nic Gabhainn, S. (2010). *Ethical Review and Children's Research in Ireland*. Office of the Minister for Children and Youth Affairs. Dublin: Government Publications.

Fives, A., Kennan, D., Canavan, J., Brady, B., & Cairns, D. (2010). *Study of Young Careers in the Irish Population*. Office of the Minister for Children and Youth Affairs. Dublin: Government Publications.

Glasby, J., & Beresford, P. (2007). In whose interests? local research ethics committees and service user research. *Ethics and Social Welfare*, 1(3), 282–92.

Goldenberg, A. J., Hull, S. C., Botkin, J. R., & Wilfond, B. S. (2009). Pediatric biobanks: approaching informed consent for continuing research after children grow up. *Journal of Pediatrics*, 155(4), 578–83.

Greene, S., & Harris, E. (2011). *Qualitative Research Methodology: A Review of the Current Literature and its Application to the Qualitative Component of Growing up in Ireland*. Department of Children and Youth Affairs. Dublin: Government Publications.

Greene, S., & Hogan, D. (2005). *Researching Children's Experience: Approaches and Methods*. London: Sage.

Grover, S. (2004). Why won't they listen to us? On giving power and voice to children participating in social research, *Childhood*, 11(1), 81–94.

Hammersley, M., & Atkinson, P. (1983). *Ethnography: Principles in Practice*. London: Tavistock.

Hanafin, S., Brooks, A. M., Carroll, E., Fitzgerald, E., Nic Gabhainn, S., & Sixsmith, J. (2007). Achieving consensus in developing a national set of child well-being indicators. *Social Indicators Research*, 80(1), 79–104.

Hanafin, S., Brooks, A. M., Roche, G., & Meaney, B. (2012). Advancing understandings of child well-being through the strategic development of a National Children's Research Programme. *Child Indicators Research*, published online (pp. 1–20). doi:10.1007/s12187-012-9147-5.

Harris, E., Doyle, E., & Greene, S. (2011). *Growing up in Ireland: The Findings of the Qualitative Study with the 9-Year-Olds and their Parents*. Department of Children and Youth Affairs. Dublin: Government Publications.

Hill, M. (2006). Children's voices on ways of having a voice: children's and young people's perspectives on methods used in research and consultation. *Childhood*, 13(1), 69–89.

Hogan, F., & O'Reilly, M. (2007). *Listening to Children: Children's Stories of Domestic Violence*. Office of the Minister for Children. Dublin: Government Publications.

Hunfeld, J. A., & Passchier, J. (2012). Participation in medical research: a systematic review of the understanding and experience of children and adolescents. *Patient Education and Counselling*, 87(3), 268–76.

Irish Council for Bioethics. (2004). *Operational Procedures for Research Ethics Committees*. Dublin: Irish Council for Bioethics.

Kehoe, A., & Whyte, J. (2005). *Second-Level Student Councils in Ireland: A Study of Enablers, Barriers and Supports*. National Children's Office. Dublin: Government Publications.

Kellett, M., Forrest, R., Dent, N., & Ward, S. (2004). Just teach us the skills please, we'll do the rest: empowering ten-year-olds as active researchers. *Children and Society*, 18(5), 329–43.

Kelly, C., Molcho, M., & Nic Gabhainn, S. (2009). *Health Behaviour in School-Aged Children HBSC Ireland 2006. Middle Childhood Study: Socio-Demographic Patterns in the Health behaviours, Risk Behaviours, Health Outcomes and Social Contexts of Young People's Health*. Office of the Minister for Children and Youth Affairs. Dublin: Government Publications.

Kilkelly, U., & Donnelly, M. (2006). *The Child's Right to be Heard in the Healthcare Setting: Perspectives of Children, Parents and Health Professionals*. Office of the Minister for Children. Dublin: Government Publications.

Layte, R., & McCrory, C. (2011). *Growing up in Ireland: Overweight and Obesity among 9-Year-Olds*. Department of Children and Youth Affairs. Dublin: Government Publications.

Mason, J., & Hood, S. (2011). Exploring issues of children as actors in social research. *Children and Youth Services Review*, 33(4), 490–95.

McCoy, S., Quail, A., & Smyth, E. (2012). *Influences on 9-Year-Olds' Learning: Home, School and Community. Growing up in Ireland: National Longitudinal Study of Children in Ireland: Child Cohort*. Department of Children and Youth Affairs. Dublin: Government Publications.

McEvoy, O., & Smith, M. (2011). *Listen to our Voices! Hearing Children and Young People Living in the Care of the State – Report of a Consultation Process*. Department of Children and Youth Affairs. Dublin: Government Publications.

McGrath, B., Rogers, M., & Gilligan, R. (2010). *Young People and Public Libraries in Ireland: Issues and Opportunities*. Office of the Minister for Children and Youth Affairs. Dublin: Government Publications.

Mayock, P., & Vekić, K. (2006). *Understanding Youth Homelessness in Dublin City: Key Findings from the First Phase of a Longitudinal Cohort Study*. Office of the Minister for Children. Dublin: Government Publications.

Murray, A., McCrory, C., Thornton, M., Williams, J., & Quail, A. (2011). *Growing up in Ireland: Design, Instrumentation and Procedures for the Child Cohort*. Department of Children and Youth Affairs. Dublin: Government Publications.

Murray, C. (2006). Peer-led focus groups and young people. *Children and Society*, 20(4), 272–86.

Nic Gabhainn, S., & Sixsmith, J. (2005). *Children's Understandings of Well-Being*. Office of the Minister for Children. Dublin: Government Publications.

Nixon, E., & Halpenny, A. M. (2010). *Children's Perspectives on Parenting Styles and Discipline: a Developmental Approach*. Office of the Minister for Children and Youth Affairs. Dublin: Government Publications.

OMCYA. (2009). *Report of the Commission to Inquire into Child Abuse, 2009: Implementation Plan*. Office of the Minister for Children and Youth Affairs. Dublin: Government Publications.

Punch, S. (2002). Research with children: the same or different from research with adults. *Childhood*, 9(3), 321–41.

Quail, A., Williams, J., McCrory, C., Murray, A., & Thornton, M. (2011). *Sample Design and Response in Wave 1 of the Infant Cohort (at 9 Months) of Growing up in Ireland*. Department of Children and Youth Affairs. Dublin: Government Publications. Available at: www.ucd.ie/issda/static/documentation/esri/GUI-SampleDesignRespo nseInfants.pdf (accessed November 2012).

Ries, N. M., LeGrandeur, J., & Caulfield, T. (2010). Handling ethical, legal and social issues in birth cohort studies involving genetic research: responses from studies in six countries. *BMC Medical Ethics*, 11(4). doi:10.1186/1472-6939-11-4.

Roberts, C., Francois, Y., Batista-Foguet, J., & King, A. (2000). Methods. In C. Currie, K. Hurrelman, W. Settertobulte, B. Smith, & J. Todd (eds.), *Health and Health Behaviour among Adolescents*. WHO Health Policy for Children and Adolescents Series. Copenhagen: WHO Regional Office for Europe.

Roberts, C., Tynjala, J., Curie, D., & King, M. (2004). Methods. In C. Currie *et al.* (eds.), *Young People's Health in Context: International Report from the HBSC 2001/2002 Survey*. WHO Health Policy for Children and Adolescents Series, Issue 4. Copenhagen: WHO Regional Office for Europe.

Roche, G., Hanafin, S., & Sharek, D. (2011). *Report on Public Consultation Processes for National Strategy for Research and Data on Children's Lives 2011–2016*. Dublin: Department of Children and Youth Affairs. Available at: www.dcya.ie.

Scott, J. (1997). Children as respondents: methods for improving data quality. In L. E. Lyberg, P. Biemer, M. Collins, E. D. de Leeuw, C. Dippo, N. Schwarz, & D. Trewin (eds.), *Survey Measurement and Process Quality* (pp. 331–50). New York: John Wiley & Sons.

Seymour, M., & Butler, M. (2008). *Young People on Remand*. Office of the Minister for Children. Dublin: Government Publications.

Shannon, G., & Gibbons, N. (2012). *Report of the Independent Child Death Review*. Department of Children and Youth Affairs. Dublin: Government Publications.

Thomas, N., & O'Kane, C. (1998). The ethics of participatory research with children. *Children and Society*, 12(5), 336–48.

Thornton, M., Williams, J., McCrory, C., Murray, A., & Quail, A. (2011). *Sample Design and Response in Wave 1 of the Nine-Year Cohort of Growing up in Ireland*. Department of Children and Youth Affairs. Dublin: Government Publications. Available at: www.ucd.ie/issda/data/growingupinireland/ (accessed November 2012).

UN. (1989). *Convention on the Rights of the Child*. Geneva: United Nations. Available at: www2.ohchr.org/english/law/crc.htm.

US Department of Health and Human Services. (2009). *HHS Regulatory Requirements for Research involving Children (Federal Regulations on Protection on Human Subjects)*. Available at: www.hhs.gov/ohrp/humansubjects/guidance/45cfr46.html#46.404 (accessed November 2012).

Williams, J., & McCrory, C. (2011). *Report on Pre-Piloting, Piloting and Dress Rehearsal Phases of the Child Cohort of Growing up in Ireland*, Technical Series No. 2. Department of Children and Youth Affairs. Dublin: Government Publications. Available at: www.growingup.ie/fileadmin/user_upload/documents/Technical_Reports/Growing_Up_in_Ireland_-_Report_on_Pre-Piloting__Piloting_and_Dress_Rehearsal_Phases_of_the_Child_Cohort.pdf (accessed November 2012).

Woodhead, M., & Faulkner, D. (2000). Subjects, objects or participants? Dilemmas of psychological research with children. In P. Christensen & A. James (eds.), *Research with Children: Perspectives and Practices* (pp. 9–35). London: Falmer Press.

Young, L., & Barrett, H. (2001). Issues of Access and identity: Adapting Research Methods with Kampala Street children. *Childhood*, 8(3), 383–95.

16

Challenges in the first ever national survey of people with intellectual disabilities

SALLY MALAM, ERIC EMERSON, AND IAN DAVIES

16.1 Introduction and background

The population of adults with intellectual disabilities[1] has been largely neglected in survey research, as the significant impairments in communication and understanding that are common among this population were considered too great a barrier to their participation in large-scale surveys. While there had been qualitative research, prior to 2002 there had never been a nationally representative survey conducted with this population. In surveys concerning this population, data was largely collected from proxy respondents, such as parents or caregivers. In the absence of a sampling frame for the whole population, surveys generally used convenience samples of those in touch with services.

In March 2001, the UK government White Paper[2] *Valuing People: A New Strategy for Learning Disability for the 21st Century* (Department of Health, 2001) was published, setting out the Government's commitment to improving the life chances of people with intellectual disabilities in England. This was the first White Paper in thirty years concerning this population, and there had been a significant amount of change in service provision in that time. One important issue highlighted in the White Paper was the lack of national information available for England about people with intellectual disabilities, with much information based on estimates from administrative data, in the absence of survey research.

A consultation exercise reported in the White Paper identified severe prejudice and discrimination, resulting in marginalization for this population. It highlighted huge inequalities and difficulties in accessing services. Cross-cutting these problems, it found that people with intellectual disabilities often felt excluded or unheard. They wanted to be fully part of society and to gain greater independence and control. This understandable desire for social inclusion, often articulated as "nothing about us without us," was identified as a key issue to address when considering how to overcome the problems facing this group.

---

1 In the UK, intellectual disabilities are usually referred to as "learning disabilities," although the preferred term of many within this population is "learning difficulties." The UK term "specific learning disabilities" is equivalent to the North American term "learning disabilities." The term "mental retardation" was previously used in many countries to refer to intellectual disabilities.

2 White papers are documents produced by the UK government setting out details of future policy on a particular subject. A White Paper will often be the basis for a Bill to be put before Parliament. The White Paper allows the government an opportunity to gather feedback before it formally presents the policies as a Bill.

This social exclusion, coupled with the lack of accurate information about this population, and the need for much broader consultation to feed into policy decisions, gave rise to a commitment by the Department of Health in England to fund a four-year national research program focusing on the well-being of people with intellectual disabilities. In May 2002, as part of this program, the UK Department of Health commissioned a team to explore the feasibility of a national survey of adults with intellectual disabilities in England. This feasibility stage led to a full English national survey being conducted over the next two years, with results published in 2005 (Emerson, Malam, Davies, & Spencer, 2005).

The primary aims of the survey were to:

- Establish from people with intellectual disabilities themselves what their lives are like;
- Describe the use of services by people with intellectual disabilities, their views on these services, and identify any gaps in provision.

The research faced three key challenges, all feeding into an overarching challenge of inclusion. These involved:

- Bringing together an inclusive research team, to be involved at all stages of the project from design through to dissemination of results;
- Defining, mapping, and accessing an inclusive sample, covering a diverse group estimated to make up only 2–3 percent of the adult population, only some of whom were in receipt of services, with others effectively "off the map";
- Designing a data collection method and tools that would maximize inclusion of the population as survey respondents, in order to avoid yet another survey of proxy respondents. Related to this challenge was the need to ensure that the target group for this research would be able to access and understand the results of the research.

A further challenge, following on from the survey, was to build on this success and ensure greater inclusion in research in future. This challenge, it could be argued, has been less successfully addressed over the last ten years.

16.2   The challenge of putting together an inclusive research team

The first challenge of putting together an inclusive research team had to be addressed before the research was commissioned by the Department of Health. Teams conducting public sector policy research usually include a partnership between a specialist research agency and an academic with specific policy knowledge. In the team put together to tender for this project, the social research agency, TNS BMRB (at that point BMRB[3]), provided vast experience of large-scale robust qualitative and quantitative research, often among hard-to-survey populations and researching sensitive issues. For example, research has been carried out with young offenders, the homeless, gay men, the visually impaired, people with mental

---

3 BMRB: formerly the British Market Research Bureau. TNS: Taylor Nelson Sofres.

health problems, and victims of child abuse. Eric Emerson, Professor of Disability and Health Research at the University of Lancaster, provided policy knowledge (his research had fed into the White Paper), and many years of research experience among people with intellectual disabilities, bringing academic rigor to the project.

The team differed, however, from previous collaborations in the inclusion of Central England People First (CEPF), a self-advocacy group run for and crucially *by* people with intellectual disabilities, with experience of carrying out their own research. This organization differs from others representing people with intellectual disabilities, many of which are run by supporters, carers, and parents. This inclusion of this partner ensured that the voice of people with intellectual disabilities would be heard throughout the project. It proved a key factor in being awarded the contract to test the feasibility of the study.

There were some real challenges to making this partnership work, but also huge advantages. Throughout the life of the project, and beyond, this team proved that an inclusive research partnership was both possible and valuable.

16.2.1 The challenges of inclusion

It would have been easy to involve CEPF as consultants and thus avoid many of the challenges of working in partnership. This would, however, have run counter to the ethos of full inclusion. The client team at the Department of Health included people with intellectual disabilities, involved at all stages of the project and present at all key meetings, and the research team was designed along the same lines.

This inclusive approach introduced three main challenges:

- Extending timescales at all stages of the project;
- The need to learn and implement accessible communication skills;
- Overcoming preconceptions and learning to trust CEPF as true partners.

The first learning was that this research project could not adhere to the usual tight deadlines and breakneck pace. More time needed to be built in to prepare for meetings and to read and comment on documentation. Longer meetings were needed, to allow enough time for explanations and discussions, and to include regular breaks. The inclusion of people with intellectual disabilities on both the client and research team meant that it was relatively easy to persuade all involved of the need for a slower pace on this project.

Aligned to this was the need for all communication to be accessible. This meant a substantial change to the way researchers work and a need for team members to learn new skills. It is standard practice to provide documents in two formats where people with intellectual disabilities need to access information: the "regular" document and a second document, written accessibly. For this project, the ideal was just to produce one accessible document, wherever possible. CEPF trained the wider team in how to write in simpler and more concise English, use larger and clearer fonts, and to use pictures to help explain meaning. This approach was taken for all written communications, for regular progress reports, and for all research outputs. The final report (Emerson *et al.*, 2005) was produced and published solely as an accessible document (albeit with a longer and shorter version). This was, to our knowledge, the first and so far only time that such an approach has been used to disseminate the results of a major national survey commissioned by a government department.

Even the contract for CEPF was produced as an accessible document, although this still needed to be accompanied by the full legal document, illustrating that, in some situations, the need to be inclusive must be balanced against other legal or technical requirements. This also applied to the need to discuss highly technical aspects of the project. It is not always possible to keep such discussions inclusive and, at the same time, discuss technical issues in sufficient detail. This is, of course, a common issue in all forms of partnership working where some specific technical issues are only likely to be understood by a subset of participants. In such situations, however, a simple summary of final decisions and rationale can and should always be produced, to ensure all partners at least understand the outcome. As long as issues such as these (and the need to resource them) are taken into account at the planning stage, there is no reason why people with intellectual disabilities cannot be fully included in a research team.

Perhaps the biggest barrier for researchers is overcoming preconceptions about the ability of people with intellectual disabilities to play a valuable role in a research team. The research team first met when preparing for the tender pitch. For a commercial company, a considerable leap of faith was required to rely on CEPF to prepare for and deliver their part of the presentation with a large contract at stake. Having taken this first step, and committed to learning the new skills needed to make the partnership role, the benefits that this would bring rapidly became clear.

While, in the experience of the team, previous partnerships between professional researchers and organizations such as CEPF were often partnerships in name only, this team learned to trust each other and work together. This opportunity was strongly appreciated by CEPF as a new experience:

> One of the most important things … one of the things I picked up at an early stage is about how far you were letting us do what we had to do … then that's what it's all about, trusting a partner, is letting the people get on with it. And that had never been done before. No one gave us the opportunity, to say well, 'look you've got what you need there. Do it.' And you gave a lot of time … to actually let us do the work and then we would all also meet up maybe later on and say 'look, this is what we've done. How does that look to you?' And that was quite an important factor of it I think.

> (Ian Davies, CEPF, May 2011).

The whole team has appreciated the value of this partnership in the ten years since it began, and lessons learned have helped to inform approaches to research more generally.

16.2.2 The benefits of inclusion

The team at CEPF offered combined experience of over thirty years as self-advocates. They were part of an extensive network of organizations and contacts with intellectual disabilities around the UK. They had experience of winning funding to conduct their own research projects and speaking at conferences. Previous experience had included, for example, conducting qualitative research among patients with intellectual disabilities at a secure psychiatric hospital.

They played a role at all stages of the project, from winning the contract, throughout the design and feasibility stage, and setting up the survey, through to exploring the results and co-writing the report. At all stages, they passed on skills, such as accessible reporting, to the rest of the team, along with their knowledge and opinions.

There were some areas where CEPF took a lead role, including early consultation exercises to develop best practice research methods and questionnaire design, along with interviewer training and accessible reporting.

CEPF organized a two-day conference at University College Northampton in August, 2002, to feed into the survey design. They gathered together thirty-five delegates with intellectual disabilities from across England. Thirteen support persons, plus researchers from BMRB and CEPF, also attended. The findings from this conference were reported back by CEPF in late August and were used to inform both research method and questionnaire design.

Over the two days, the delegates talked about what they thought should go into the national survey and how the research team should run the survey. They did this by breaking into five workshop groups on wide-ranging topics, each of which lasted an hour. There were also large open sessions where people reported back from the workshops and discussed the ideas that had been shared. Each workshop used a list of questions that CEPF had prepared to help to get people talking.

CEPF made significant contributions to what questions should be asked and how. It is particularly important within such surveys to include some measure of the severity of impairment and need for support. While a number of well-validated scales existed, CEPF advised that participants with intellectual disabilities would find these intrusive and demeaning. As a result, the team devised a more acceptable way of measuring severity of impairment and need for support. While this created additional work, the new scales worked extremely well and have since been incorporated in the recommended data set for measuring the health (and health inequalities) of people with intellectual disabilities across the European Union.

Once the survey was underway, CEPF played a vital role in training interviewers. Obviously in a survey of this nature, it is important that interviewers are fully briefed in the technicalities of their task. In addition, it is essential that they understand the particular challenges of interviewing people with intellectual disabilities. CEPF ran three interactive sessions during each full day's briefing, each of which they designed themselves based on their previous experience.

In the first session, they asked interviewers to think about the importance and mechanics of speaking up in their own lives and how they thought this would differ for people with intellectual disabilities. The second session looked more generally at the lives of people with intellectual disabilities, with interviewers encouraged to ask questions to raise their awareness of the issues facing this group of people. The final session looked more specifically at the issues that they might encounter during the interviews. This session concerned how best interviewers could hear the voice of people with intellectual disabilities, focusing particularly on issues of accessibility of questions, giving respondents space and time to answer questions, and avoiding the interview being dominated by supporters and carers, along with the importance of building rapport to ensure respondents felt comfortable enough to give honest answers. Interviewer feedback on these sessions was immensely positive, and they reported that it helped ensure that they conducted interviews, wherever possible, with the person with intellectual disabilities and not a support person as a proxy respondent.

CEPF also played a key role in the final report. While the data analysis was led by Professor Emerson, he worked closely with CEPF to decide what the chapters of the report should cover and ensure that the final report was fully accessible. They also provided a short commentary on each chapter for inclusion within the report, thus ensuring that the perspective of people with intellectual disabilities was represented.

16.3　The challenge of designing an inclusive sample

The second challenge of inclusion was to define, map, and access a diverse population that is estimated to be around 2–3 percent of English adults (Emerson, Hatton, Robertson, Roberts, Baines, Evison, *et al.*, 2012). The White Paper defined the population as all adults with an intellectual disability starting in childhood which reduces their ability to cope independently. It excluded people with a specific difficulty in learning, such as dyslexia (Department of Health, 2001). Fairly accurate national prevalence figures are available for children with intellectual disabilities, but known administrative prevalence drops from 4.2 percent of children in education to 0.6 percent of adults (Emerson, 2011). This reflects a lack of contact with publicly available services for many adults with intellectual disabilities in England and offers evidence of the scale of the challenge of accessing this population.

The White Paper suggested conducting a national survey of people with intellectual disabilities who were in contact with Social Services. This was problematic, since Social Services do not deal with all adults with intellectual disabilities. People with less severe intellectual disabilities are unlikely to be in touch with Social Services, as are those suffering most from social exclusion, particularly from minority ethnic communities, and those living in private households. Use of this sample source alone would have led to serious sample bias; even if it were to be used, it would need to be supplemented with other sources.

There was also concern over whether this approach would be replicable. The stated intent of the White Paper was to improve access to, and the quality of, service provision to this group. If successful, this would mean changes to the extent and nature of the population known to Social Services over time. Repeating the sampling approach in ten years time would be likely to provide a sample that was not directly comparable to that used for the original survey. This concern made it even more important to ensure that the sample source(s) used reflected the full population, in order to ensure to maximize the chances of replicability.

Furthermore, there were doubts over the consistency of Social Services records. The experience of a recent Australian survey was that "contact with providers provided one of

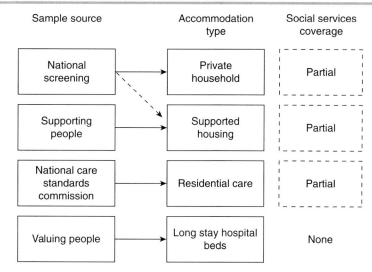

Figure 16.1   Map of population by accommodation type

the most problematic elements of the survey, largely due to the large numbers of providers involved and the extent to which they operate under different models (thus the difficulties of imposing a standard sampling procedure)" (EQual and Donovan Research, 2000). The Department of Health had also expressed concern over the accuracy, consistency, quality, and comprehensiveness of the information available to Local Authorities (Department of Health, 1999).

16.3.1 Mapping and accessing the population

In order to identify the gaps in coverage of the population by Social Services, adults with intellectual disabilities were mapped according to where they lived. As illustrated in Figure 16.1, on this basis the population can be split into four groups: private households, supported housing, residential care, and long stay hospital beds; Social Services would only provide partial coverage of three of these four types, and no coverage at all of people in long stay hospital beds.

Potential alternative (and comprehensive) sample sources were identified for people with intellectual disabilities living in each of these four contexts, to test out alongside the option of using Social Services lists. Approaches to using each of these sources were developed and partially tested at the feasibility stage and then fully tested at a dress rehearsal stage, before the final sampling decisions were taken.[4]

---

4 Fuller details of the sampling approach and testing can be found on the Department of Health website at www. dh.gov.uk/en/Publicationsandstatistics/PublishedSurvey/ListOfSurveySince1990/Generalsurveys/DH_4081207.

National screening of private households

The only way to identify and access a representative sample of adults with intellectual disabilities living in private households who are not in receipt of services was through screening the national population. A postal screening survey was considered and rejected as inappropriate for a group with intellectual disabilities, particularly those living alone. The BMRB omnibus survey, which interviewed 1,700 adults in England face to face, in home each week, was identified as the most cost-effective source. This survey uses random locale sampling, a sophisticated form of quota sampling, to provide a nationally representative sample. Sampling from all British households occurs at the census sample unit level (after stratification by known geographic and demographic variables), and interviewing quotas are set only in terms of characteristics which are known to have a bearing on individuals' probabilities of being at home and so available for interview. Rules are given which govern the distribution, spacing, and timing of interviews. This gives interviewers very little choice in the selection of respondents.

An ad hoc random probability survey would have offered a slightly more robust sample but would have proved prohibitively expensive. A screening questionnaire was tested at the feasibility stage, including re-contacting those identified to take part in a pilot survey to give an indication of the likely success of this approach, and to fine tune the screening questions.

Any screening approach requires a set of questions that can clearly identify an adult within the household as having intellectual disabilities, while excluding those who only have specific learning difficulties such as dyslexia. While tests exist for identifying eligibility for the receipt of statutory services, they are time consuming to administer and were judged too personally intrusive for use on a survey. Instead, a set of questions was developed based on the definition in the White Paper, and these were tested and validated.

The initial set of questions identified:

- If there was anyone in the household (or for whom someone in the household had responsibility, living in another private household) aged 16 or over with a "learning disability";
- If this person had a general difficulty in learning things;
- If they had had this difficulty from childhood;
- If it still made life difficult for them now.

An explanation was included of what we meant by a "learning disability" as follows:

> Anyone who, when they were a child, had a real difficulty in learning many things. They may well have attended a special school or would have had special help in an ordinary school. They may also have other disabilities. Adults with these types of learning difficulties usually need some help to go about their lives; for example help with money and budgeting, understanding things or help with getting dressed. This does NOT include people who just have a very specific difficulty in learning, for example, people who only have difficulty with reading, which is sometimes called dyslexia.

Following the feasibility stage, the term "learning disability" was replaced with the term "learning difficulty" to ensure people did not self-exclude based on the choice of words. We also removed the question on whether their disability still made life difficult for them, as people with an intellectual disability may be able to adjust to the demands of their lifestyle, but this does not mean they no longer have a disability. These changes introduced a risk of over-inclusiveness, but screening at the main survey was used to ensure only those with an intellectual disability were included.

The revised questions were placed on the omnibus survey for twelve weeks, and the resulting sample was evaluated against three criteria:

- Were rates of identification in line with best estimates of true prevalence in England?
- Did prevalence rates vary systematically in a way consistent with knowledge of the epidemiology of intellectual disabilities?
- Were people being wrongly identified as having intellectual disabilities?

Analysis concluded that prevalence was around 50–100 percent higher than administrative population estimates would have suggested (i.e., based on people known to services), with respondents identified in around 0.55 percent of households. In recruitment for the main survey, this fell slightly, more in line with administrative estimates. Crucially, the prevalence rates were higher than would have been obtained through just contacting people known to Social Services, meaning the survey should be accessing those not in receipt of services.

Prevalence rates were higher in more deprived areas, for households with lower socioeconomic status, and among men and younger people, all in line with expectations. Based on questions in the dress rehearsal survey about level of independence, and education, it was estimated that between 1 percent and 4 percent might have been wrongly identified as having an intellectual disability. A decision was made to screen further at the main survey for educational attainment to minimize this risk.

A major disadvantage of this approach was the time taken to build up a sample, given the need to identify a very small population, and then to ask them to agree to take part in a later survey. Enough sample was recruited each week to deliver an average of eight achieved interviews in the final survey. Since our best estimate was that around two in three adults with intellectual disabilities live in private households, this would make it very difficult to build a sufficiently large sample. In order to build sample more quickly, questions were also placed on the weekly telephone omnibus survey (using a random digit dialing quota sampling approach), increasing achieved interviews to thirteen per week of recruitment. After fifty-seven weeks of recruitment, this delivered 750 interviews in the final survey.

The dress rehearsal also made it clear that there would be few respondents from this source aged 55 or over. Evidence suggested that the older population would largely be in receipt of services, or not living in private households, so would be accessed through other sample sources. Across the population, there would also be few respondents from minority ethnic groups, reflecting the population profile. It would not be practical to boost this population through national screening.

Some way was, therefore, needed to boost the number of interviews in private households and to boost the number of respondents from minority ethnic groups to enable sufficient analysis.

Private households known to Social Services

Despite reservations, the decision was taken to boost the sample of private households using Social Services databases. There was no national database, so sample could only be obtained via each Social Services Department at a local level. This approach was tested with five local departments at the dress rehearsal stage. To minimize the total burden, for the main survey, twenty-eight departments were selected to ensure coverage by region, affluence, and prevalence of minority ethnic population. The use of this sample source also afforded the opportunity of boosting the numbers of interviews with minority ethnic respondents by oversampling areas with higher minority ethnic populations. Each selected department was asked to select fifty adults with intellectual disabilities at random from their lists and to contact them to request permission to pass on their details for the research. As expected, this approach was extremely time consuming and only nineteen of the selected departments provided lists of sample. A total of 480 interviews were achieved.

Supported housing and residential care

The UK Office of the Deputy Prime Minister's "Supporting People" initiative had produced local databases of supported accommodation providers, and these were in the process of being collated into a national database for a national survey. The National Care Standards Commission (NCSC) had similarly compiled a list of all registered residential care homes in England offering services to adults with intellectual disabilities. Both sample sources were made available to the Department of Health for the survey.

Using the same approach designed for Social Services, providers were selected at random from both databases, and were invited to make a random selection of ten of their customers with intellectual disabilities, and to ask them to take part in the survey. This approach ultimately delivered 1,481 interviews.

NHS long-stay hospitals

At the time of the survey, despite a move away from the use of long stay beds, there were still an estimated 1,000 people with intellectual disabilities living in long stay NHS hospitals.[5] The Valuing People team at the Department of Health commissioned the compilation of a list of local NHS trusts providing any such beds. Forty trusts were selected with probability proportionate to size and each was asked to select up to ten residents for the survey. The inclusion of this sample source required ethical approval to be attained, both nationally and

---

5 Hospitals run by the National Health Service, the publicly funded healthcare system in England.

at a local level for each trust. This was very time consuming and extremely difficult to achieve. From the seventeen trusts where approval was attained in time (they were given six months to provide approval), 263 interviews were achieved for the final survey. If the survey were to be repeated, it is unlikely that the remaining population size in this type of accommodation would justify inclusion within the survey.

16.3.2 Interviews achieved and population estimates for corrective weighting

In total, 2,974 interviews were achieved, with a response rate[6] of 71 percent out of the individuals identified as eligible for the survey, across the range of sample sources. Success rates in provider recruitment and achieving interviews varied by sample type as shown in Table 16.1.

Given the complex sampling approach taken to ensure total coverage, there were two major sources of potential sample bias:

- The probability of selection of respondents within each of the Social Services, Supporting People, and NCSC samples, given the relative size of different providers;
- The achieved samples sizes within private households and the various forms of supported accommodation, relative to the estimated population profile.

The first of these sources of bias was corrected by weighting back to information from the original samples and local authority data. Respondents identified through Social Services were weighted to account for the different size of each local authority. Respondents identified through the Supporting People and NCSC databases were weighted to account for the size of each provider.

The second source of bias was more challenging, in the absence of national population data. A wide variety of administrative data was used to provide best estimates of the

Table 16.1 *Response rates and interviews by sample type*

Sample source	Response rate at provider level/initial screening stage	Response rate among selected/ issued individuals	Number of achieved interviews
National screening	74%	70%	750
Social Services	68%	71%	480
Supporting people providers	65%	68%	562
NCSC providers	54%	70%	919
NHS hospitals	35%	83%	263
TOTAL	N/A	71%	2,974

6 Response rate calculated as RR= I/(S-N) where I = number of interviews, S = number of sample records issued and N = number of records identified as ineligible for the survey.

population size within each source and likely overlap between sources, with a particular challenge in identifying which of the respondents identified through national screening would also be known to statutory services (and therefore who could equally have been sampled through Social Services). Ultimately, those identified within the questionnaire as having a higher level of support needs, and whose support was not arranged by a friend or family member, were assumed to fall within this population for the purposes of weighting. The final data were then weighted back to the estimated profile.

16.4   The challenge of designing an inclusive data collection approach

The third challenge was to ensure that as many people with intellectual disabilities as possible would be able to take part in responding to the survey. The danger with a conventional survey research approach was that response would be restricted to the most "able" among this group and that most would have to be represented by support people acting as proxies. This would run counter to the spirit of the project. Related to this challenge was the need to ensure that the target group for this research would be able to access and understand the results of the research.

Face-to-face interviewing was the only approach considered for this research, but this still left a number of challenges. Key challenges and possible solutions were identified and explored though sixty qualitative in-depth interviews at the exploratory stage of the research: thirty with people with intellectual disabilities and thirty with parents, carers, and support workers. Insights from this research were used along with information and advice from CEPF and their consultation exercise (see Section 16.2.2) to develop the best design.

The exploratory stage uncovered a number of insights into how best to administer the survey, with the key learning that the wide-ranging nature of this population means there can be no "one size fits all" solution; the research would need to be tailored to the needs of every respondent. In particular, it was essential to:

- Take the time to chat and build rapport with the respondent before starting the interview, to ensure they feel confident enough to answer honestly;
- Take a flexible and informal approach to the interview, so that it feels like a friendly chat, and not a test or interview;
- Provide comprehensive and accessible information to reassure people;
- Use multiple methods of communication, including written, verbal, and visual;
- Tailor the interview to the attention span and concentration levels of the respondent – take enough time and plenty of breaks. Do not push the respondent to finish the interview or move on before they are ready;
- Talk to the respondent, not the support person, and do not be patronizing.

This was fed into the interviewer training and briefing (see Section 16.2.2). In addition, a number of key design decisions were made and fully tested at the dress rehearsal stage, before starting field work on the main survey, in terms of questionnaire coverage, obtaining consent, tailoring the interview according to ability to respond, and maximizing the possibility that the person with intellectual disabilities can answer at least some questions for themselves.

16.4.1 Questionnaire coverage

Based on experience from the qualitative research, the decision was taken to keep interview length to a maximum of ninety minutes, including breaks, with interviewers briefed to look out for tiredness and check whether a break is needed at regular intervals, stopping the interview if the respondent appeared distressed in any way.

Prioritization of questionnaire coverage was based on the developmental work described above, along with desk research to explore coverage of key issues in other key national statistics surveys in England. It also drew on two other key disability research projects including the Australian National Satisfaction Survey of Disability Services (EQual and Donovan Research, 2000), and the US National Core Indicators Survey of People with Developmental Difficulties,[7] both of which focused on service users. There was little scope to use harmonized questions from national statistics surveys as the wording tended to be too complex, but the other disability surveys proved a useful source of potential questions. A questionnaire was drafted, tested, and refined through a small-scale pilot and larger dress rehearsal.

The final questionnaire topics covered were:

- Demographics;
- Housing;
- Support needs;
- Privacy;
- Caring for others;
- Income;
- Employment;
- Education and training;
- Health;
- Leisure activities;
- Relationships and social networks;
- Access and involvement, including transport; and
- Support services.

16.4.2 Consent process

Before any interview could take place, it was vital to obtain informed consent from the person taking part in the interview. The approach was based on that developed for the Department of Health evaluation of Person Centered Planning (Robertson, Emerson,

---

7 www.nationalcoreindicators.org/.

Hatton, Elliott, McIntosh, Swift *et al.*, 2006). This involved taking time to explain the survey and the interview process to the respondent, using an illustrated information card, and then checking (using a series of simple questions) that the individual had understood this explanation.

The four main points that needed to be understood were: the topics to be covered, the aims of the survey, what they may not like about taking part, and how they could let the interviewer know if they want to stop the interview at any point. The questions and the wording of the card were refined at the pilot stage of the project.

If respondents were deemed to have understood all of the main points, they were asked to give consent. If they were not deemed to have understood fully, then proxy consent was obtained from a close relative or independent support person for the interview to continue. Ethical considerations meant that a paid support worker could not give consent.

16.4.3 Flexibility of question wording

The accepted wisdom in quantitative research is that question wording is fixed. Interviewers are trained never to rephrase questions, to ensure that all data collected is comparable. Even with questions worded in the simplest way possible, this approach would still exclude the majority of respondents in a survey of people with intellectual disabilities. The initial exploratory work found that only those respondents who were most able would cope with such an inflexible approach. This survey needed the flexibility to rephrase and explain questions to respondents, to make them as relevant as possible. There is no point asking a question using words the respondent does not recognize. The decision was taken on this survey to break the rules. It was deemed better to get information from as many people as possible within this group than to get more conventionally acceptable information from their support workers or a family member.

Interviewers were trained to rephrase questions on this survey, and to use friends, family, and support people to help them in this task. While it was important for respondents to answer the questions for themselves wherever possible, this could involve using any help available in making the questions clear to them. People who live with or who support a respondent are likely to know how to rephrase a question to make it more relevant to them. It was, of course, essential that the interviewer remain in control and to ensure that the reworded question being asked was broadly the same one.

The interviewer was also provided with a book of picture show cards to help them explain the questions. For most show cards, pictures were used from existing sources including the Change Picture Bank[8] and the Valuing People clip art collection[9]. Both are sources of pictures created by and tested with people with intellectual disabilities. An example of a show card to help ask questions on complex topics is given in Figure 16.2. The pilot exercise demonstrated the importance of printing these on card, rather than paper, and binding them into a book format, to make them easier to handle.

---

8 www.changepeople.co.uk.   **9** www.valuingpeopleclipart.org.uk/.

This year, have you been ...?

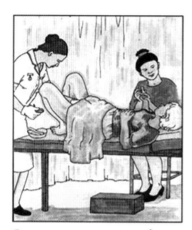

For a cervical smear test

To have your breasts checked for lumps

SHOWCARD 56

Figure 16.2   Example picture show card

In addition, interviewers were asked to draw pictures, mime, point at things, and so on to help make the questions more accessible. One of the functions of the interviewer briefing was to help them develop these skills.

16.4.4 Assessment procedure and questionnaire tailoring

A core tenet of the approach was to maximize the ability of people with intellectual disabilities to answer at least some questions for themselves. The prevailing attitude towards the feasibility of this approach was typified in this response from a caregiver interviewed at the qualitative stage of the research:

> If you're going to talk to the learning disabled, you're only going to get the views of the top echelon 'cause people who are disabled like [name] won't talk to you ... It's very difficult. I don't mean to be rude to anybody, but there are those who are more able, the ones that can hold down a job, who are quite verbal and do have opinions ... There are those like [name] who are quite able in a physical sense, but are not able to communicate.
>
> (carer, London)

Our finding at the pilot stage was that there were varying levels of ability to cope with different questions, but that many people could answer at least some questions for themselves, albeit with help. It was clearly not necessary to restrict direct questioning to a minority.

In order to maximize participation wherever possible, the structure of the questionnaire was designed to include questions at three levels:

- Level 1: simple "yes/no" questions for all to answer and should be answered by individuals in many cases;
- Level 2: slightly more complex questions, e.g., scale questions, three or more pre-codes, etc., and may be answered by the individual or the support person depending on the circumstances;
- Level 3: complex questions intended for a support person.

An assessment procedure was developed to help the interviewer determine which level of question an individual was likely to be answer for themselves, which they would need help with, and which they would not be able to respond to at all. Figure 16.3 illustrates this process.

The assessment procedure involved determining:

- Whether a support person is present at the interview;
- Whether the learning difficulty is so severe that the individual is unable to communicate and the support person will have to take the lead in responding;
- Whether the individual is happy for the support person to answer some of the questions or wishes only to answer questions for themselves. It is important that the individual has the right to choose who is present (if anyone) and to what extent they should be involved in the interview; and
- Finally, for those able to communicate, a series of questions to assess the comprehension of questions and reliability of individual's responses, i.e., their ability to respond.

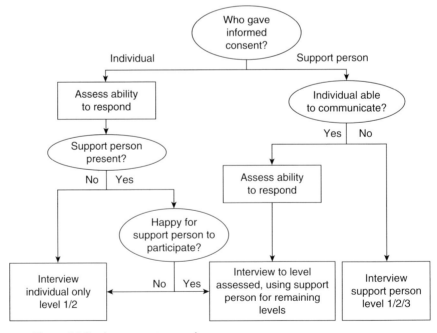

Figure 16.3   Assessment procedure

The main risk is that some people who have difficulty understanding questions will take shortcuts, such as saying yes to everything (satisficing or acquiescence) or selecting either the first or the last item from a list (primacy and recency effects). The assessment questionnaire repeated questions with answer lists in different orders and included check questions to find out if consistent answers were being given to level 1 and level 2 questions. Picture show cards were used to aid understanding.

By entering the outcome at each stage of the assessment into the on-screen questionnaire, the interviewers were prompted with the outcome. They were reminded before each set of level 1 and level 2 questions throughout the questionnaire whether the individual was likely to be answering the question alone or with help or if someone would be answering the question on their behalf. In addition, the interviewer was asked to record at regular intervals who was answering the questions to measure the level of success of this approach and to use for analysis purposes.

One important lesson learned at the pilot was that, if the individual was at all able to contribute (even if deemed not able to answer even level 1 questions consistently at the assessment stage), then all questions (except level 3 questions) should be addressed to the individual themselves. In this way, the response usually became a team effort between the individual and the support person, rather than the support person responding on their behalf. Even if the individual was totally unable to communicate, and the support person was answering all of the questions, the questions were addressed towards both the individual and support person to ensure the individual did not feel they are being talked about as though they were not present.

16.4.5 Success of the inclusive interviewing approach

The approach and tools were tested out in an initial pilot with twenty respondents identified through personal contacts and national screening, and then in a full dress rehearsal of 176 interviews, testing out all sample sources other than NHS hospitals (Malam, 2002, 2003). As a measure of success of the final design, in the survey of almost 3,000 adults with intellectual disabilities, the respondents answered most of the questions for themselves in 46 percent of interviews and answered jointly with a support person in a further 23 percent. The support person answered most questions on the respondent's behalf in only 31 percent of interviews.

A fully accessible report was published (Emerson *et al.*, 2005), meaning more people with intellectual disabilities could access the results for themselves. This revealed a general picture of isolation for people with intellectual disabilities. Nine in ten were single and always had been, and only one in four had friends without intellectual disabilities outside of their family. Half still lived with their parents, and those who did not live with family were much less likely to see them than is the case for the other adults in England. While this group had clear support needs, some had their own caring responsibilities, with 7 percent having a child, and one in ten caring for another adult.

The majority did not have unmet support needs, and most declared themselves happy with the support they received. This is not, however, the same as experiencing inclusion and independence. For example, only one in six of those of working age had a paid job, compared with six in ten in the general population. Half of respondents said someone else controlled how much money they could spend. People with intellectual disabilities were less likely than the general population to have enough money to buy what they wanted and other barriers included high levels of ill-health, and experiences of bullying for a significant minority.

The data were also made available for secondary analysis and policy development and have been the basis of a number of published papers since then (e.g., Emerson, 2010, 2011; Emerson & Hatton, 2008a, 2008b; Robertson and Emerson, 2010).

16.5   The challenge of building on this success

To the best of our knowledge, this remains the only survey of the whole population of adults with intellectual disabilities conducted at a national level. It has not been repeated in England. Research in most countries tends to focus either on broader surveys of adults with disabilities or on surveys of people in receipt of services.

For example, in Ireland, census respondents who self-identified as having a disability were followed up in 2006 to take part in the National Disability Survey. In Kenya, national household screening has been used to identify and interview people with disabilities. In the UK, the longitudinal Life Opportunities Survey has been initiated to follow-up on an annual basis a cohort of 40,000 people to understand better the experience of disability in the UK. While such surveys include people with intellectual disabilities, they tend to use a standard questionnaire for all and do not tailor the survey to enable the inclusion of people with intellectual disabilities as respondents.

An ongoing research program conducted by Mathematica[10] in the US is one example of a survey of adults with disabilities (in this case, on the Ticket to Work program) that has taken some steps to accommodate people with intellectual disabilities. The research offers the option of telephone and face-to-face interviews, uses a cognitive testing tool at the start of the interview to assess whether a proxy will need to do the interview on the respondent's behalf, and offers the option of assisted interviews using a support person or friend, to avoid the need for proxy interviews whereever possible.

Nonetheless, figures from the technical appendices from the 2005 and 2006 surveys suggest that around eight in ten interviews with respondents with intellectual disabilities were conducted with proxies.

For example, in 2006 while around 515 interviews were conducted with this group (9 percent of the total number of interviews), they made up over a third of proxy interviews, equating to around 420 of these interviews being conducted with proxies (Livermore, Wright, Roche, & Grau, 2009). This illustrates the scale of the challenge of accommodating the needs of this population, within a survey of a broader group of people with disabilities. As part of the fourth round of research on this program, several additional methodological experiments have been built in, to compare methods for determining the need for a proxy and to evaluate potential mode effects. It will be of interest to assess the results of these

---

10 www.mathematica-mpr.com/disability/tickettowork.asp.

experiments, in terms of implications for research with people with intellectual disabilities as part of a broader survey of people with disabilities.

Surveys that do take a more inclusive approach to researching this population still do not tend to cover the entire population, by including nonservice users. Fifteen US states currently participate in the National Core Indicators project.[11] This gathers data from services users in participating states, including tailored questions for both individuals and support people. This was a valuable resource for questionnaire design when designing the English survey and is still ongoing annually. It does not, however, include people who are not in receipt of services. The work in Australia in 1999, used to inform the English survey, was also conducted solely among users of disability services (EQual and Donovan Research, 2000).

Given the time and expense involved in running a fully inclusive national survey, it is perhaps unsurprising that it has not been repeated. The usual driver for collecting information is to evaluate existing services, so it is logical to restrict such research to service users, who are much easier to access. However, in order to evaluate the broader-ranging aim of providing a better quality of life for all, as set out in the English Valuing People White Paper (Department of Health, 2001), research is also needed among people with intellectual disabilities who are not in touch with services. A review of available sources of information in England concluded that a regularly repeated national survey about the life experiences of people with intellectual disabilities is needed to supplement other available data, in order truly to evaluate the success of a national policy initiative such as Valuing People (Hatton, Emerson, & Lobb, 2006). The authors also concluded that the methods and technology for conducting such research exists, but that the challenge is to produce a *feasible* method for regular national surveys.

This would require adaptation of the approach taken for the previous survey to become less time consuming and costly, without unacceptable impact on data quality and inclusivity. Primarily, this would mean designing a more efficient (i.e., quicker and cheaper) way of recruiting respondents in private households who are not in receipt of services. There is no obvious solution that provides a nationally representative sample, using a data collection method that will be accessible to this group. It seems inevitable that some compromise would have to be made in the quality of the original screener, perhaps revisiting the use of a postal survey, which is likely to exclude some people with intellectual disabilities living alone. While identifying nonservice users is the key sample area to review, lessons could also be learned from the National Core Indicators project and similar research to identify more streamlined ways to recruit service users.

The inclusive nature of the interview is also costly, given the time it takes fully to train interviewers, and the time spent at interview to ensure that respondents can answer for themselves. Within a limited budget, a decision may have to be made over whether it is more important to deliver an inclusive sample of the population or to maximize inclusivity at the interview itself.

---

11 www.nationalcoreindicators.org/.

The methods used in the survey are publicly and fully documented on the English Department of Health website,[12] offering the opportunity for researchers to explore the potential to streamline the design or to adapt it for use in other countries. At a more fundamental level, they offer evidence of the benefits of an inclusive approach to research that can and should be applied more broadly to research projects.

References

Department of Health. (1999). *Facing the Facts: Services for People with Learning Disabilities – A Policy Impact Study of Social Care and Health Services*. London: Department of Health.

(2001). *Valuing People: A New Strategy for Learning Disability for the 21st Century: A White Paper*. London: Stationery Office.

Emerson, E. (2010). Self-reported exposure to disablism is associated with poorer self-reported health and well-being among adults with intellectual disabilities in England: cross sectional survey. *Public Health*, 124, 682–89.

(2011). Health status and health risks of the "hidden majority" of adults with intellectual disability. *Intellectual and Developmental Disabilities*, 49, 155–65.

Emerson, E., & Hatton, C. (2008a). Socioeconomic disadvantage, social participation and networks and the self-rated health of English men and women with mild and moderate intellectual disabilities: cross sectional survey. *European Journal of Public Health*, 18, 31–37.

(2008b). The self-reported well-being of women and men with intellectual disabilities in England. *American Journal on Mental Retardation*, 113(2), 143–55.

Emerson, E., Hatton, C., Robertson, J., Roberts, H., Baines, S., Evison, F., *et al.* (2012). *People with Learning Disabilities in England 2011*. Durham: Improving Health & Lives: Learning Disability Observatory.

Emerson, E., Malam, S., Davies, I., & Spencer, K. (2005). *Adults with Learning Difficulties in England 2003/04*. London: NHS Health and Social Care Information Centre.

EQual and Donovan Research. (2000). *National Satisfaction Survey of Disability Services. A Report Prepared for the Steering Committee for the Review of Commonwealth/State Service Provision and the National Disability Administrators*. Canberra: AusInfo.

Hatton, C., Emerson, E., & Lobb, C. (2006). *Evaluating the Impact of Valuing People: Report of Phase 3: Moving towards Evaluating Valuing People in Practice*. Lancaster: Lancaster University.

Livermore, G., Wright, D., Roche, A., & Grau, E. (2009). *2006 Work Activity and Use of Employment Supports under the Original Ticket to Work Regulations. National Beneficiary Survey: Methodology and Descriptive Statistics*. Washington, DC: Mathematica.

12 www.dh.gov.uk/en/Publicationsandstatistics/PublishedSurvey/ListOfSurveySince1990/Generalsurveys/DH_4081207.

Malam, S. (2002). *Learning Difficulties Feasibility Study Report*. London: NHS Health and Social Care Information Centre.

—— (2003). *Learning Difficulties Survey Dress Rehearsal Report and Proposals for Main Stage*. London: NHS Health and Social Care Information Centre.

Robertson, J., & Emerson, E. (2010). Participation in sports by people with intellectual disabilities in England. *Journal of Applied Research in Intellectual Disabilities*, 23, 616–22.

Robertson, J., Emerson, E., Hatton, C., Elliott, J., McIntosh, B., Swift, P., *et al.* (2006). A longitudinal analysis of the impact and cost of person centred planning for people with intellectual disabilities in England. *American Journal of Mental Retardation*, 111(6), 400–16.

17

Conducting research on vulnerable and stigmatized populations

SANDRA H. BERRY AND PATRICK P. GUNN

17.1 Introduction

Researchers are often interested in studying vulnerable and stigmatized groups using survey research methods. This may arise from purely academic interest in human behavior and its motivations, from a concern about the safety and well-being of these groups, or from a concern about the risks these groups may pose for others. Interest in these groups may take several forms. One is the estimation of the size of the group – how many are there? A second is from an interest in how policies affect them, such as whether the public health system addressees their needs. A third is how policies might be enacted to change their behavior, in particular, to discourage behaviors that are dangerous to themselves or others, such as sexual risk behaviors. For example, there was longstanding interest in sex workers among academics that took on new significance with the onset of the AIDS epidemic. Suddenly, they were viewed not only as an interesting subculture, but also as a group that was vulnerable for HIV infection and a potential route of transmission for HIV from drug users to the general population. This resulted in a burst of interest in studying them systematically that posed new methodological challenges (Kanouse, Berry, Duan, Lever, Carson, Perlman *et al.*, 1999).

For the purposes of this chapter, we consider vulnerable and stigmatized populations to be groups that if publicly identified might (May-Chahal & Cawson, 2005) be subjected to shame, scorn, ridicule, or discrimination in their interactions with others (Amstadter, McCauley, Ruggiero, Resnick, & Kilpatrick, 2008), suffer damage to financial standing, employability, or reputation within the community (Kanouse, Berry, Gorman, Yano, & Carson, 1991), be subject to legal sanctions including criminal penalties, civil liability, or administrative actions (Ross, Timpson, Williams, Amos, McCurdy, Bowen *et al.*, 2007), or be subject to persecution, threats, or reprisals as a result of research participation. These groups might include, for example, drug users and dealers; sex workers, pimps and sex traffickers; victims of sexual assault, sexual harassment or domestic violence and the perpetrators of these acts; sexual minorities, such as "swingers" or child molesters; people with stigmatizing medical conditions or who have had socially sanctioned medical procedures, such as abortions; and people who have committed crimes, such as driving under the influence or failing to pay child support. It may also include people who are in debt and being sought by debt collectors, people who are being stalked or harassed, and people who are living "under the radar" and do not want to be singled out, such as undocumented immigrants. People who are part of a group that discourages contact with outsiders or has a strong code of privacy may also be vulnerable if they are known to be research participants. Vulnerability may be defined socially, legally, or organizationally. For example, students who cheat on exams or plagiarize term papers may not be subject to criminal or civil penalties but may nevertheless be a vulnerable and stigmatized population in the context of a college community or military academy with a strict code of conduct.

A key issue in relation to vulnerable and stigmatized groups is identification of the individuals who are part of them and, in particular, whether they are identified by their behavior or by labels that they would endorse themselves. For example, some people who trade sex for money self-identify as sex workers while others may see themselves as the sexual partners of people who are willing to help with living expenses. Some people who might objectively be classified as abusive parents see themselves as concerned about the moral development of their children (May-Chahal & Cawson, 2005). The particular status of individuals may be known or unknown to their families, friends, employers, neighbors, and others.

17.2   Group identification and sampling

There are two approaches to identifying and sampling these groups. We may seek to identify them within larger groups or we may attempt to identify and sample them as members of the group of interest. When seeking vulnerable groups within a larger survey population, we might identify them directly or indirectly. Within a large population survey, we might simply ask whether respondents have a particular characteristic of interest, such as being a victim of rape (Amstadter *et al.*, 2008; Raghavan, Bogart, Elliott, Vestal, & Schuster, 2004) or having terminated a pregnancy. Alternatively, we may do this indirectly, such as by asking how many times a woman has ever been pregnant even for a short period of time, how many live births she has had, and how many miscarriages or still births and carry out subtraction to identify women with unaccounted for pregnancies that may have been ended by elective termination. Similarly, we may ask directly whether a person is living in the US without citizenship or legal status or we might seek this information indirectly by asking country of birth and if not born in the US questions about visa type, date of entry, etc., and use that information to infer the probability of illegal status. People who are receiving transfer payments despite having domestic arrangements or sources of income that would disqualify them may be identified through asking questions about household composition and sources of income. Alternatively, in a situation of trust, a respondent may be willing to admit that they conceal income or a partner to qualify for medication programs or obtain support for their families. Clearly, identifying vulnerable groups by inference raises ethical issues. Is someone who is caught up in the flow of a questionnaire aware that they are disclosing something they may prefer to conceal? Would they disclose the information if they were aware of the implications of the questions, even under a guarantee of confidentiality? These issues need to be addressed as part of the informed consent process, which is considered below.

The other approach is to seek out the vulnerable group as a specific focus of the study. This usually requires knowledge about the particular group and ingenuity on the part of the researcher (Magnani, Sabin, Saidel, & Heckathorn, 2005). Some groups may be accessed using standard probability sampling procedures. For example, sex workers who solicit clients in the street are considered a vulnerable and stigmatized population, but they are nevertheless observable when they are working and can be approached by researchers to engage them in interviews. Using time/location sampling procedures researchers can develop a probability sample of sex workers who solicit in public (Kanouse *et al.*, 1999). Similar procedures may be used to develop samples of street drug dealers. However, although it may be possible to identify and approach the group members there may be issues with gatekeepers who manage access, such as pimps in the case of sex workers. In some cases, even when access is public the influence of gatekeepers is so powerful that probability sampling is impossible. In addition, although individuals who conduct illegal activities in public might be approachable, being seen to interact with researchers may put them at risk. While it is relatively easy to identify and enumerate massage parlors where sexual services are performed, it is very difficult to get past the operators to interview the masseuses. Similarly, even when brothels are identifiable, it may be impossible to get past the operators to sample the sex workers systematically.

Other groups may be sampled at locations where they gather for some specific purpose. They may be identifiable within these locations, even though their status may be generally hidden (Ross & Timpson, 2007). Street sex workers in some cities are frequently arrested so they may be sampled through jails, though their stay there may be brief (Berry, Duan, & Kanouse, 1996). People who seek care for stigmatizing medical conditions may be sampled through their medical providers using multistage probability sampling to build lists that are used for selecting a sample for follow up interviewing or for "real-time" sampling at the treatment locations. People who seek treatment for HIV, sexually transmitted illnesses (STIs), drug addiction, or because they are victims of violent assaults and seek treatment at STI clinics or hospital emergency rooms may be sampled in this way. People who have been convicted of drunk driving may be attending court ordered treatment programs where they can be reached for sampling. People within a stigmatized group may also have locations where they go to meet each other. Traditionally, gay men and women have had specific bars where they go to meet each other and these have served as locations for sampling and, recently, party hotel locations have been used for this purpose (Ramchand, Becker, Ruder, & Fisher, 2011). However, as gay sexual orientation has become more accepted, this approach is less necessary. For the most part, being gay has become redefined as a relatively rare but not highly stigmatized characteristic, except in particular social situations, such as while engaging in high-risk sexual activities. While probability sampling procedures may be used in connection with these locations, the study results can only be generalized to the subset of the group that is accessible. This may be nearly all the street sex workers or low-level drug dealers, but only a fraction of the HIV+ or people with STI, since many are unaware of their condition or do not seek treatment. Most people who drive while under the influence of drugs or alcohol are not arrested, convicted, and sent to treatment.

Where standard probability sampling methods are perceived to be impossible or too costly, researchers often use various kinds of convenience sampling methods, such as "snowball" or chain-referral sampling (Wharton, 2007). This requires that at least some members of the group be accessible to researchers and that most members of the group be identifiable to the other members. For example, call girls and escorts sometimes work together and are in contact with each other, so they can recruit each other to be interviewed. However, a woman who works alone or only through a madam and has no contact with other escorts would not be accessible in this way. When members of the group are in contact with each other, it may even be possible to use more systematic approaches that combine chain-referral techniques with weighting based on network characteristics, such as respondent-driven sampling (RDS) (Ramirez-Valles, Garcia, Campbell, Diaz, & Heckathorn, 2008). Where the members of the group have strong incentives to participate, are known to each other, and are willing to acknowledge their status recruiting in this way seems to work effectively and large samples of drug users have been successfully recruited in using RDS (Iguchi, Ober, Berry, Fain, Heckathorn, Gorbach *et al.*, 2009). In contrast, it would be difficult to recruit a sample of women who have a serious bladder condition resulting in incontinence using RDS, since they are rarely known to each other, are not in direct contact, and would generally be unwilling to risk exposure in order to recruit others.

While traditionally recruitment of vulnerable populations was done face to face in locations where they were meeting, it is now the case that they are meeting on the Internet through interest groups and chat rooms. In some cases, they might be identified and approached through social media. However, highly vulnerable groups are aware of the risks of identification and sometimes take steps to "vet" people who try to enter their sites. For example, prior to repeal of Don't Ask, Don't Tell, a popular social networking site for gay members of the military had specific procedures requiring referral from a known source and checking the status of new entrants. A researcher would only be able to enter the site as someone who qualified as a member of the group and then would face issues of disclosure of the purpose of participation. Even when researchers can access the site openly, the ability to recruit participation is often limited to soliciting volunteers and it is unknown how the characteristics of the portion of the group that is on the website and willing to volunteer relates to the characteristics of the group overall.

For extremely hidden groups that can only be accessed through self-identification, research participation is limited to the members of the group who reveal themselves or are discovered and then become available to researchers. Women who have been trafficked for sex work and are held by force in undisclosed locations are not accessible for sampling, unless they escape and seek help or are discovered by law enforcement. Victims of domestic violence who are not injured severely enough to require medical treatment can remain hidden for years until and unless they decide to come forward and seek help from the police or shelters. Some groups are available for such a short time and are so risk averse that they are not approachable. For example, the clients of street sex workers typically conduct negotiations in a matter of minutes and disappear. Even when they are arrested in police sweeps, they spend very little time in custody and are unwilling to cooperate in research.

17.3   Motivating participation

Why would someone who is part of a vulnerable and/or stigmatized group want to be identified by researchers and take part in a research study? Although the literature on the design features influencing survey response and nonresponse among vulnerable and stigmatized populations is not well developed, it seems that the same factors survey researchers have found to be important for general populations also apply to these special groups – in slightly different ways. Using the Groves *et al.* description of tools for reducing unit nonresponse, the first factor is "contactability," whether interviewers can find and communicate with the group members. If this can be done directly and repeatedly, preferably face to face, the probability of cooperation improves. Where the researcher has only one opportunity to interact with the group member, must rely on others to elicit cooperation, or must solicit volunteers the probability of success is lower (Groves, Fowler, Couper, Lepkowski, Singer, & Tourangeau, 2009).

Once contact is made, a number of factors influence the participation decision. One is clearly burden. Normally, we think of burden as interview length and the cognitive effort of answering questions, but for vulnerable populations it includes other factors, including the psychological cost through possible negative appraisals of self and the costs of disclosing identity to others, such as the risk of social or legal sanctions. Respondents need to be convinced that they are safe from external threats in order to participate and they need to feel they are psychologically safe as well. All respondents need to feel that they will be respected and not judged when they participate in surveys and this is particularly true for respondents who are in stigmatized groups. The tone of contact materials and interviews needs to be carefully crafted so this is clear and the demeanor of interviewers has to be appropriate. On the plus side, everyone has a story to tell and being vulnerable and stigmatized may make it much more difficult to tell that story so the prospect of safe, nonjudgmental survey participation may be appealing. Like most respondents, vulnerable and stigmatized groups are influenced by other incentives including the desire to help others through survey participation, the desire to further their own interests through promoting understanding and acceptance, and financial incentives (although from a human subject's concern these should not be so large as to be coercive).

17.4   Involving the group of interest in research design

Before designing a survey, researchers need to understand the group being studied and this may be accomplished through use of publicly available information sources and key informants (Lever, Kanouse, & Berry, 2005). In some cases, there is an academic literature and even highly stigmatized groups often have some kind of advocacy group representing their legal interests, if not their social position, and it is useful to contact them. However, the degree to which they represent the larger group or are knowledgeable about its characteristics is questionable. In a recent study of a vulnerable population, we identified nine groups that represented various aspects of the group and that offered to put us in contact with their affiliates and members to conduct surveys. However, only a few actually were able to provide contacts that resulted in interviews (Berry, Brown, & Schell, 2010).

The researcher should be aware that just as the researcher attempts to engage advocacy groups to further the interests of research, the advocacy group is seeking to further its aims through interaction with the researchers. Advocacy groups have a well-founded suspicion of researchers who they perceive to be using access to the population to further the researchers' own professional interests or a potentially threatening policy and not being sincerely interested in the well-being of the group. While it is usually inappropriate and sometimes unwise for a researcher to become closely affiliated with the interests of an advocacy group, it is often possible to convince them of the value of an unbiased researcher perspective to seek and present the full story for the group. Despite best efforts, advocacy groups are sometimes hostile and unwilling to cooperate, but their influence over the larger group and control of access may actually be limited so research may proceed even without endorsement.

In formulating the research, it is very helpful to use informal contacts and networking to identify and engage members of the group that are not involved in formal advocacy roles to improve the formulation of research as well as data collection methods. Assistance organizations can provide access and even regulatory or enforcement agencies may be helpful. Sometimes the researcher can reach out through trusted providers of services, goods, or supplies that the population needs. It may be possible to form an advisory committee of group members to review materials and procedures from the perspective of the group. Once they become familiar with the research goals and the researchers, having a formal role in the study design is often appreciated and is a source of valuable advice. The terms that researchers, medical personnel, and policy makers use can often be poorly understood or even offensive to the research participants. Advisors can also comment on consent materials and how the description of privacy protections is communicated in relation to specific concerns.

17.5 Collecting data

It is frequently suggested that only people who would qualify as research participants are effective data collectors. In part, this comes from a genuine belief that only they can distinguish accurate from inaccurate responses, but it also seems related to an understandable desire to obtain the benefit of employment opportunities and direct access to the data collection process. While involving the affected group in design of data collection is valuable, having them actually determine whether responses are valid or not introduces a serious form of bias. Moreover, respondents may answer differently to someone they perceive to be part of their network than they would to a trained, neutral interviewer, for example, endorsing the group's public position instead of providing their own opinions. In addition, having group members collecting data poses confidentiality problems since they may be part of dense social networks. Finally, within any group, there are bound to be varying perspectives and characteristics that can affect relationships between interviewers and respondents, so a trained, neutral, uninvolved interviewer can minimize response effects (Holbrook, Farrar, & Popkin, 2006). Where possible, it is best to use computerized audio computer-assisted self-administration for data collection, with the interviewer's role limited to enlisting participation, obtaining informed consent, and assisting with technical problems.

Because of the sensitivity of the research data, particular care needs to be taken to maintain confidentiality during the data collection and data management process. Participants need to be protected from inadvertent disclosures as well as other breaches of confidentiality. For example, disclosure to a family member about the topic of the study may be catastrophic to the participant's most intimate relationships. Disclosure to neighbors or employers as part of tracking procedures may harm community standing or employability. Interviewers and staff need to understand that they may not discuss the study or take any actions on their own to disclose identities beyond the study team even in the face of subpoena or ethical concerns they might have (see Traynor, 1996). Supervisors and managers need to be familiar with the issues that might arise and the procedures for dealing with them, including allowing staff opportunities to discuss experiences and concerns in a safe atmosphere. All study staff should sign nondisclosure agreements that clearly spell out their responsibilities for data protection. Studies of very sensitive populations may require legal advice in the design of data collection and data safeguarding and management procedures. Maintaining confidentiality may also require the development of a Data Safeguarding Plan for approval as part of human subjects protection approval.

17.6   Risks and protections for research subjects

The risks to vulnerable and stigmatized groups are greater than for general research participants. Therefore, the protections need to be stronger. One class of risk is legal, including risk of subpoena of research data as part of a civil, criminal, or administrative proceeding. For example, if the research is known to include questions that might identify welfare fraud, a keen prosecutor might want to gain access to identifiable data to develop cases against study participants. A study of drug dealers might be subpoenaed in relation to a narcotics investigation. Undocumented US residents may be the targets of immigration proceedings. Colleges may wish to identify and expel cheaters.

Despite some promising developments, legislatures and courts have so far declined to articulate a clear "researcher's privilege" that would enable researchers to protect all data from disclosure. However, Congress has effectively granted researchers engaged in certain qualifying research collecting sensitive data protection from legally compelled disclosures under certain more limited circumstances. Congress authorized issuance of a Certificate of Confidentiality pursuant to the Public Health Service Act § 301 (d), 42 U.S.C § 241(d):

> The Secretary may authorize persons engaged in biomedical, behavioral, clinical, or other research (including research on mental health, including research on the use and effect of alcohol and other psychoactive drugs) to protect the privacy of individuals who are the subject of such research by withholding from all persons not connected with the conduct

of such research the names or other identifying characteristics of such individuals. Persons so authorized to protect the privacy of such individuals may not be compelled in any Federal, State, or local civil, criminal, administrative, legislative, or other proceedings to identify such individuals.

Certificates of Confidentiality allow the investigator and others who have access to research records to refuse to disclose identifying information on research participants in any civil, criminal, administrative, legislative, or other proceeding, whether at the federal, state, or local level. Certificates of Confidentiality may only be granted for studies collecting information that if disclosed could have adverse consequences for subjects or damage their financial standing, employability, insurability, or reputation (such as drug use, sexual behavior, HIV status, mental illness) and have typically been issued quickly for studies that qualify.

Research need not be federally supported to be eligible for this privacy protection, but it must be within a mission area of the National Institutes of Health and must be approved by an Institutional Review Board (IRB). The Public Health Service component agencies, the Food and Drug Administration, the Health Resources and Services Administration, and the National Institutes of Health issue Certificates of Confidentiality. There is very little legal precedent considering the scope of the protections afforded by Certificates of Confidentiality. However, in at least one case from 1973 (*People* v. *Newman*), a New York state court of appeals found that a certificate provided a substance abuse program with a proper basis for refusing to turn over the names of program participants. Researchers are expected to inform subjects in the consent form about the Certificate of Confidentiality protections and any circumstances under which disclosures would be made. Typically, these would include disclosures to protect the subject and others from harm (such as suicidal intention, child abuse, elder abuse, intention to harm others) and certain types of federal audits.

There are other types of legal protection available for some federally funded research. The privacy of research subjects in Department of Justice-funded research is protected by statute – 42 USC Section 3789g. Similarly, the privacy of research subjects in Agency for Health Care Quality and Research-funded research is protected by a statute, 42 USC Section 299a-1(c), titled "limitation on use of certain information." For these studies, Confidentiality Certificates are not appropriate because other protections are available which are arguably broader than the protections afforded by the Certificate of Confidentiality (Traynor, 1996). Where research is done in partnership with the court system or law enforcement, the use of confidentiality, data safeguarding, and/or non-prosecution agreements pursuant to which legal authorities undertake not to identify subjects or target them for individual action should be considered.

Researchers collecting data on vulnerable and stigmatized groups should also seriously consider the risks for participants and researchers of obtaining data that might be subject to subpoena and should be prepared to undertake a sophisticated legal defense to protect the data. This should include an advance plan for dealing with an effort by a third party to compel legal disclosure of identifiable data. Part of that plan may include initially securing a Certificate of Confidentiality or identifying a clear basis for statutory protection. The next step is to assert that protection in the face of a subpoena, first informally to the subpoenaing party in an attempt to cause that party voluntarily to withdraw the subpoena or limit it in a manner that omits the request for the sensitive data. Failing that, the plan should set forth measures formally to seek protection from the court by motion. If that motion fails, the researcher may appeal to a higher court. If all appeals are exhausted, the researcher has the option of refusing court order to provide the data. In such instance, the court would have the discretion to hold the researcher in contempt. Contempt sanctions are decided at the discretion of the court, but may include money fines or, in extraordinary circumstances, jail until compliance with the order (Scarce, 1994).

Some researchers have asserted that storing research data in another country will enhance protection. However, under federal (and, generally, state) law, a person served with a subpoena generally is obligated to produce responsive documents under his or her "custody or control."[1] What "control" means is an issue that may be litigated. "Control" under the federal rules means "the legal right, authority, or practical ability to obtain the materials sought upon demand" (*Bank of New York v. Meridien BIAO Bank Tanzania*, 1997). Under this broad standard, the fact that documents are located in a foreign county does not necessarily immunize them from subpoena (*Sangyong Corp. v. Vida Shoes Int'l Inc.*, 2004). Once ordered to produce the overseas data, the researcher has the option of producing them, being held in contempt of court, or appealing to the court of last resort. Of course, if the US researcher has given up all ability to obtain the data, that might be sufficient to break the chain of control and thus immunize the data from US subpoena. But this would be of limited value to the researcher who wishes to analyze the data.

17.7 Human subjects protections and obtaining consent

Informed consent is a vital part of conducting studies of vulnerable and stigmatized groups. Normally, this is considered as part of IRB review and these studies may raise some special issues. For example, Subpart C of the Common Rule affords protections to some vulnerable populations, including incarcerated individuals. The extent to which these protections should be applied to participants who are not physically detained, but who nonetheless are living under conditions of decreased autonomy, including individuals who under strict conditions of parole or probation, is unclear. Studies that involve prisoners will need to be approved by an IRB that includes a prisoner representative.

Where studies are identifying vulnerable or stigmatized populations by inference, or are obtaining access to groups without disclosing the research purpose, obtaining IRB approval may require formally waiving some elements of informed consent. Deception or incomplete disclosure of all elements of informed consent is allowed under special circumstances as spelled out in the Common Rule, but can present some thorny issues (Barrera & Simpson, 2012; Christensen, 1988). Professional organizations may also have standards addressing this point that apply to researchers.

---

1 See Federal Rule Civ. Proc. 26.

17.8 Conclusions

There are often compelling reasons to study vulnerable and stigmatized groups. Their experiences illuminate often hidden parts of our culture and highlight social, economic, and health problems that we need to address. We can successfully engage them as research participants with careful advance investigation of their circumstances and concerns, thoughtful consideration of risks and protections, and a willingness to put the time, effort, and resources into conducting research respectfully, responsibly, and safely.

References

Amstadter, A. B., McCauley, J. L., Ruggiero, K. J., Resnick, H. S., & Kilpatrick, D. G. (2008). Service utilization and help seeking in a national sample of female rape victims. *Psychiatric Services*, 59(12), 1450–57.

Bank of New York v. Meridian BIAO Bank Tanzania, Ltd., 171 F.R.D. 135 (S.D.NY. 1997).

Barrera, D., & Simpson, B. (2012). Much ado about deception: consequences of deceiving research participants in the social sciences. *Sociological Methods & Research*, 41(3), 383–413.

Berry, S. H., Brown, R. A., & Schell, T. L. (2010). RAND Survey of Gay, Lesbian, and Bisexual Military Personnel. In *Sexual Orientation and US Military Personnel Policy: An Update of RAND's 1993 Study* (pp. 255–73). Santa Monica, CA: RAND Corporation.

Berry, S. H., Duan, N., & Kanouse, D. E. (1996). Use of probability versus convenience samples of street prostitutes for research on sexually transmitted disease and HIV risk behaviors: How much does it matter? In R. Warnecke (ed.), *Health Survey Research Methods Conference Proceedings* [Sixth Conference] (pp. 93–97). Hyattsville, MD: US Department of Health and Human Services, Centers for Disease Control and Prevention.

Christensen, L. (1988). Deception in psychological research. When is its use justified? *Personality and Social Psychology Bulletin*, 14(4), 664–75.

Groves, R. M., Fowler, F. J., Couper, M. P., Lepkowski, J., Singer, E., & Tourangeau, R. (2009). *Survey Methodology* (2nd edn.). Hoboken, NJ: John Wiley & Sons.

Holbrook, A. L., Farrar, I. C., & Popkin, S. J. (2006). Surveying a Chicago public housing development: methodological challenges and lessons learned. *Evaluation Review*, 30(6), 779–802.

Iguchi, M. Y, Ober, A. J, Berry, S. H., Fain, T., Heckathorn, D. D., Gorbach, P. M., *et al.* (2009). Simultaneous recruitment of drug users and men who have sex with men in the United States and Russia using respondent-driven sampling: sampling methods and implications. *Journal of Urban Health*, 86(1), S5–S31.

Kanouse, D. E., Berry, S. H., Duan, N., Lever, J., Carson, S., Perlman, J. F., *et al.* (1999). Drawing a probability sample of female street prostitutes in Los Angeles County. *Journal of Sex Research*, 36(1), 45–51.

Kanouse, D. E., Berry, S. H., Gorman, E. M., Yano, E. M., & Carson, S. (1991). Response to the AIDS epidemic: a survey of homosexual and bisexual men in Los Angeles County. RAND Report R-4031-LACH. Santa Monica, CA: RAND.

Lever, J., Kanouse, D. E., & Berry, S. H. (2005). Racial and ethnic segmentation of female prostitution in Los Angeles County. *Journal of Psychology and Human Sexuality*, 17(1/2), 107–29.

Magnani, R., Sabin, K., Saidel, T., & Heckathorn, D. (2005). Review of sampling hard-to-reach and hidden populations for HIV surveillance. *AIDS*, 19(2), S67–S72.

May-Chahal, C., & Cawson, P. (2005). Measuring child maltreatment in the United Kingdom: a study of the prevalence of child abuse and neglect. *Child Abuse & Neglect*, 29(9), 969–84.

People v. *Newman* (1973). 32 N.Y.2d 379, 298 N.E.2d 651, 345 N.Y.S.2d 502 (1973), *cert. denied*, 414 U.S. 1163.

Raghavan, R., Bogart, L. M., Elliott, M. N., Vestal, K. D., & Schuster, M. A. (2004). Sexual victimization among a national probability sample of adolescent women. *Perspectives on Sexual and Reproductive Health*, 36(6), 225–32.

Ramchand, R., Becker, K., Ruder, T., & Fisher, M. P. (2011). Party intents: a portal survey to assess gay and bisexual men's risk behaviors at weekend parties. *Evaluation Review*, 35(4), 428–51.

Ramirez-Valles, J., Garcia, D., Campbell, R. T., Diaz, R. M., & Heckathorn, D. D. (2008). HIV infection, sexual risk behavior, and substance use among Latino gay and bisexual men and transgender persons. *American Journal of Public Health*, 98(6), 1036–42.

Ross, M. W., & Timpson, S. C. (2007). Stigma consciousness concerns related to drug use and sexuality in a sample of street-based male sex workers. *International Journal of Sexual Health*, 19(2), 57–67.

Ross, M. W., Timpson, S. C., Williams, M. L., Amos, C., McCurdy, S., Bowen, A. M., *et al.* (2007). Responsibility as a dimension of HIV prevention normative beliefs: measurement in three drug-using samples. *AIDS Care*, 19(3), 403–09.

Sangyong Corp. v. *Vida Shoes Int'l Inc.*, 2004 WL 1125659, at *4 (S.D.N.Y. May 20, 2004).

Scarce, R. (1994). (No) trial (but) tribulations: when courts and ethnography conflict. *Journal of Contemporary Ethnography*, 24(2), 123–49.

Traynor, M. (1996). Countering the excessive subpoena for scholarly research. *Law and Contemporary Problems*, 59(3), 119–48.

Wharton, V. W. (2007). Gender variance and mental health: a national survey of transgender trauma history, posttraumatic stress, and disclosure in therapy. Unpublished master's thesis. Smith College School for Social Work, Northampton, Massachusetts.

18

Surveying political extremists

TIMOTHY P. JOHNSON, ALLYSON L. HOLBROOK,
AND KEITH ATTERBERRY

18.1 Introduction

Collecting survey data from political extremists (or persons affiliated with extremist political groups) presents a set of unique challenges. Many of these challenges are faced by researchers investigating other hard-to-survey populations (e.g., political extremists are rare, difficult to identify, and under some circumstances may be reluctant to participate in research), but not in combination as they are with this particular group of potential respondents. In this chapter, we first develop a working definition of political extremism. We next provide an overview of the challenges faced by researchers who want to study political extremism and examine some of the strategies employed by investigators when attempting to study political extremists. Finally, we examine some of the ethical issues involved in conducting survey research with persons who espouse extremist political ideologies.

18.1.1 Defining "political extremism"

"Political extremists" have multiple self-identities and it is a challenge to develop an operational definition that adequately covers this diversity. In practice, political extremism at the individual level has been defined in two primary ways. First, it is often viewed in terms of the behaviors associated with it. For example, van Es and Koenig (1976) see political extremism as the use of coercion to force change in political institutions and authority. Political extremists, then, have sometimes been defined as those who engage in these behaviors or who advocate them. Secondly, others have defined political extremists in terms of the attitudes or beliefs that they hold. In his *Dictionary of Political Thought*, Scruton (1982) suggests that political extremism involves pushing ideas to their limits, intolerance of competing viewpoints, confronting and eliminating opposition, and demonstrating a disregard for the rights of others. Similarly, Midlarsky (2011, p. 7) provides a definition of political extremism that integrates both beliefs and behaviors, which he suggests is:

> the will power by a social movement in the service of a political program typically at variance with that supported by existing state authorities, and for which individual liberties are to be curtailed in the name of collective goals, including the mass murder of those who would actually or potentially disagree with that program.

This definition is problematic, however, in that it does not leave room for the all-too-common scenario in which governments behave in an extremist manner. In addition, defining extremism in terms of behaviors alone is potentially problematic because factors other than extreme beliefs may predict behavior (e.g., opportunity). However, advocating action to advance politically extreme positions does seem like an important component of the definition. We here conceptualize *political extremists* as individuals who have social, economic, religious, and/or political goals that they believe require the transformation of an existing social order in order to achieve.

As an alternative to studying political extremists at the individual level, researchers have sometimes focused instead on politically extreme groups and their members (in part because identifying political extremism at the individual level is quite difficult). Paralleling the individual definition above, *politically extremist groups* can be viewed as those formal and informal organizations that advocate transformation of an existing social order in order to achieve their social, economic, religious, and/or political goals.

When defining a group or an individual as extremist, it is important to incorporate a definition independent of political orientation or where an individual or group falls on the political spectrum of beliefs. There are political extremists and extremist groups represented on both the right and left ends of the political spectrum. In addition, a definition of a group or individual as politically extreme should not include normative evaluations of right or wrong. The US has a long history of political extremists who have enormously affected the course of our history (many would argue for the better) and whose points of view have ultimately triumphed and are now considered mainstream. For example, both the Founding Fathers and Martin Luther King, Jr., would be considered political extremists relative to the existing political orders of their day by our definition.

18.1.2 Typology of Extremist Groups

Political extremism is not a new phenomenon. There is, in fact, a history of both left- and right-wing extremism, in the United States (cf., George, 1970) and throughout the world (Atkins, 2004; Midlarsky, 2011). In Table 18.1, we provide a basic typology of known domestic extremist political groups that have recently or are currently operating in the US. Because the landscape of politically extreme groups is constantly changing, we acknowledge that it is likely incomplete at any given point in time but suspect that it nonetheless covers many of the currently active and generally recognized right- and left-wing extremist groups. Many of these groups focus on a single issue, such as abortion or animal rights. It is noteworthy that at present, there appear to be more right-wing groups in existence, although this was not always the case. During the 1960s and 1970s, now largely defunct left-wing liberation groups, such as the Weather Underground and the Black Panthers, were far more active. However, left-wing extremist movements remain common today in many other nations where "Green" parties and communist parties are more prevalent (Seger, 2001).

Today, left-wing extremist groups in the US are largely focused on animal rights and environmental issues. The US Department of Homeland Security (2009a, p. 7) has recently defined left-wing extremists as "groups or individuals who embrace radical elements of the anarchist, animal rights, or environmental movements and are often willing to violate law to achieve their objectives." They have been described as practicing a no-harm doctrine that emphasizes the safety of humans, animals, and the environment, while inflicting economic damage on businesses and other institutions. Some, however, do actively threaten and harass scientists and others (Miller, 2007; Ringach & Jentsch, 2009). Research conducted by Smith (1994) suggests that left-wing extremists are younger, better educated, more likely to be from minority race/ethnic groups, and more likely to reside in urban areas, compared to right-wing extremists in the US.

In contrast, right-wing extremist groups are more diverse in their emphasis. Blee and Creasap (2010) have suggested that these movements are typically recognized more for the things they oppose than for what they support. Indeed, among the extremist groups listed in Table 18.1 are those known for their anti-abortion, anti-immigrant, anti-gay, anti-government, anti-Muslim and anti-minority agendas. The US Department of Homeland Security (2009b, p. 2) has classified these as:

> groups, movements and adherents that are primarily hate-oriented (based on hatred of particular religions, racial or ethnic groups), and those that are mainly antigovernment, rejecting federal authority in favor of state or local authority, or rejecting government authority entirely. It may include groups and individuals that are dedicated to a single issue, such as opposition to abortion or immigration.

18.1.3 Overview of existing research

Political extremism has been the subject of research across multiple academic disciplines. Some of the specific topics of interest examined in the English language literature in recent years have included: the development of social movements and collective action (Postmes & Brunsting, 2002; Sageman, 2004; Thomas, Smith, McGarty, & Postmes, 2010; Wojcieszak, 2009); collective identity formation (Baray, Postmes, & Jetton, 2009; Futrell, Simi, & Gottschalk, 2006; Futrell & Simi, 2004); the development of extremist beliefs (Adams & Roscigno, 2005; Ezekiel, 2002); extremist communication strategies (de Koster & Houtman, 2008; Gersenfeld, Grant, & Chiang, 2003; Glaser, Dixit, & Green, 2002; Levin, 2002; Schafer, 2002; Stromer-Galley, 2003; Weatherby & Scoggins, 2005/06); and the correlates of extremist beliefs (Green, Abelson, & Garnett, 1999; Janowitz & Marvick, 1953; McClosky & Chong, 1985; Pinderhughes, 1993; Schuman & Krysan, 1996; Sidanius, 1984, 1988; Van Hiel, 2012; Van Hiel, Duriez, & Kossowska, 2006). This research has been published in the communications, criminal justice, political science, psychology, public opinion, public policy, and sociology literature. Much of this research has employed qualitative research methodologies, such as participant observation, semi-structured interviews, and reviews of documents and websites. Although less common, use of standardized survey methodologies also have been reported throughout this literature. It is to these survey methodologies that we now turn our attention.

Table 18.1 *Types of domestic political extremist groups in the United States, 2012*

Right-wing groups
(a) Neo-Nazi or White separatist groups (e.g., American Front, Aryan Nations, Creativity
     Movement, Council of Conservative Citizens, the Hammerskin Nation, White Revolution, Nazi
     Low-Riders, National Socialist Movement, National Alliance, Ku Klux Klan)
(b) Black separatists (New Black Panther Party for Self Defense)
(c) Anti-Semitic groups (e.g., Institute for Historical Review, League of American Patriots
     [LOAP])
(d) Militia, extreme survivalist, or anti-government groups (e.g., Elohim City, Militia of Montana,
     Little Shell Pembina Band)
(e) Minutemen and other similar groups (related to militia groups)
(f) John Birch Society

Left-wing groups
(a) Communists
(b) Weather underground
(c) Extreme left parties and groups much more common in Europe than in US (communists,
     democratic socialists, populist socialists, social populists)
(d) Anarchists
(e) Black liberation movements active in US in the 1970s (e.g., Black Liberation Army and
     Republic of New Africa, Black Panthers)

Single-issue groups
(a) Gun control
(b) Abortion
(c) Environmentalism
(d) Genetic engineering
(e) Animal rights (PETA)
(f) LGBT rights
(g) Capital punishment

Other groups
(a) Extreme libertarians
(b) Extreme religious groups – Islamic extremism, Branch Davidians Greater Ministries
     International – have been associated with both right- and left-wing

18.2   Some challenges in surveying political extremists

There are multiple potential difficulties that should be addressed when designing surveys of
political extremists. Developing adequate operational definitions of who is and who is not a
political extremist is itself a challenge and, almost irrespective of the definition employed, it
is likely to represent a rare and difficult-to-find population. Once identified and located,
these individuals may be highly suspicious, distrustful, and reluctant to participate. They
may also express open hostility towards researchers. In addition, it is important to recognize

that the term "political extremist" is not a self-definition, but one externally imposed by researchers and as such may have little, no, or a different meaning to the persons being studied.

18.2.1 Identifying political extremists

As discussed earlier, two of the most common strategies for identifying political extremists are based on their (1) membership in organizations deemed to espouse extreme political beliefs or philosophies, or (2) personal behaviors or activities considered to represent extremist political beliefs. In practice, researchers have tended to study members (Barrett-Fox, 2011; Blee, 1999; 2003; Ezekiel, 2002; Simi & Futrell, 2006; Van Hiel, Duriez, & Kossowska, 2006) or former members (Almond, 1954; Ernst & Loth, 1952; Kimmel, 2007) of political groups more frequently, perhaps because of the common assumption that organizational membership is a strong reflection of personal values and beliefs and also because of convenience. Of course, being a member of a formal organization is neither a necessary nor sufficient condition for being a political extremist. Not all members of politically extreme groups are necessarily themselves political extremists, although research often makes this tacit assumption. Likewise, not all political extremists choose to associate with formal organizations. With little supporting evidence available, many researchers nonetheless tend to make the assumption that few individuals who do not harbor extremist views would elect to join one of these organizations. One might further speculate that strength of extremist views is correlated with likelihood of seeking to participate in organized extremist groups, although there is now again little evidence with which to support this assumption.

Identifying individuals as extremists via one or more specific types of behaviors also makes the (invalid) assumption that these behaviors are evidence of political extremism. Some examples include participation in certain types of protests or rallies (Postmes & Brunsting, 2002), participating in online chat rooms or forums dedicated to particular groups or topics (Madison, 2010; Wojcieszak, 2009), or contributing money to particular political candidates (Schuman & Krysan, 1996). In most cases, of course, these behaviors are not illegal and are even constitutionally protected. Specific forms of political expression, such as attendance at a flag burning ceremony, spending time online in a discussion forum sponsored by a radical environmentalist group, or sending money to the campaign of a fringe political candidate who openly advocates secession from the United States might be reasonably defined as evidence of having extremist political views. Of course, participation in some illegal activities, such as burning a cross with the intent to intimidate an individual or group, can also be used to identify political extremists (Green *et al.*, 1999). Depending on the behaviors examined, one might expect to identify persons with varying levels of commitment to extremist political beliefs. Persons willing to break laws might reasonably be viewed as having stronger commitments to their beliefs, on average, than do individuals who express their extreme views via less risky methods such as communicating with like-minded others via online forums.

In general, these operational definitions of political extremism, while intuitive and often creative, are heterogeneous. This makes comparisons across studies an additional challenge to accumulating knowledge on this topic.

18.2.2 Distrust of researchers

Like many other externally stigmatized communities, it is commonly reported that political extremists, both on the left and the right, are suspicious of researchers and their intentions (Blee & Creasap, 2010; Futrell, Simi, & Gottschalk, 2006; Jipson & Litton, 2000; McClosky & Chong, 1985; Van Hiel, 2012). Moreover, researchers sometimes are suspected of being informants for law enforcement agencies (Blee, 1999; Speckhard, 2009). Members of extremist groups often encounter broad social disapproval and condemnation of their beliefs (Simi & Futrell, 2009). Hence, they may be understandably concerned about how they will be portrayed in the academic literature and fear that they and/or their beliefs will be misrepresented (Blee, 1999; Jipson & Litton, 2000; Speckhard, 2009).

Conversely, researchers have expressed fears regarding their physical safety when entering the social environments of political extremists (Blee, 2003; Blee & Creasap, 2010; Hamm, 1993; Speckhard, 2009). As Jipson and Litton (2000, p. 154) have observed, many political extremists exist in "high-tension environments" that often lead them to make quick judgments regarding whether a researcher represents a threat. Consequently, considerable effort may be necessary to convince persons who have reasons to be suspicious of researchers and their motivations. Qualitative researchers conducting in-person interviews and engaging in participant observation report that time is necessary to gain the trust of extremists (Jipson & Litton, 2000; Speckhard, 2009). Quantitative surveys, by their very nature, do not often have this luxury.

18.3   Ways in which political extremists have been surveyed

Multiple strategies have been employed for selecting samples of political extremists and for collecting survey data from them. Most of these are approaches commonly employed by survey methodologists. Their application, however, can become more difficult and challenging when employed to conduct research with political extremists. In this section, we turn our attention to some of the particular challenges involved in doing so.

18.3.1 Sampling and coverage issues

Van Hiel (2012, p. 168) has observed that "hardly any data have been collected on true extremists." Perhaps one of the reasons for this is because they are both a hard-to-identify *and* a hard-to-reach population. They are also unlikely to be geographically clustered. Indeed, the challenges associated with constructing sampling frames of political extremists are very difficult to address adequately. In this section, we review the types of sampling and sampling frame construction methods that have been reported and consider the advantages and limitations of each.

Group membership frames

Many studies of political extremists construct their sampling frames based upon membership in formal organizations (Blee, 1999; Simi & Futrell, 2006; Speckhard, 2009). As part of her qualitative research into women who belong to White supremacist groups, Blee (1999) describes the process by which she first developed a sampling frame of White supremacist groups in the United States. This involved (1) identifying groups that were included in lists maintained by several national organizations that monitor these types of extremist activities, (2) taking out subscriptions to materials published by all organizations she could identify that emphasized these beliefs (e.g., flyers, magazines, newsletters, web pages and postings), and (3) accessing other available materials produced by these organizations (e.g., music, radio, television, and other recordings). These materials were reviewed to identify those groups with women in leadership roles and/or that appeared to have "significant" female membership. Interestingly, Blee reports that referral, or snowball, sampling could not be used in her study, as interpersonal, interorganizational, and financial conflicts within this movement made using referrals impractical, as they would likely be truncated and exclusionary of rivals, both within and across groups. Rather, she obtained referrals from numerous other sources, such as family and friends of group members, journalists, law enforcement personnel, other researchers, and activists within the movement.

Postmes and Brunsting (2002) reported the process by which they employed an email list sample frame made available from a single Dutch environmental organization. They were fortunate enough to have access not only to this frame but to additional information that enabled them to distinguish among "hardcore activists" (i.e., those subscribing to a mailing list that provided information regarding demonstrations, blockades, and sabotage actions), those belonging to an "environmental pressure group" (i.e., those subscribing to a mailing list regarding relevant letter writing, petitioning, and lobbying activities), and persons considered to be "sympathizers" (i.e., nonmembers who subscribed to a list that provided information about relevant environmental issues) within the frame. Having access to such a list frame saves investigators the effort of having to construct one from scratch. Compared to Blee's much more labor-intensive frame, however, that employed by Postmes and Brunsting is limited to a single organization and likely provides less coverage of the target group of interest in the Netherlands.

Other researchers have also employed frames of members of extremist political parties and organizations that they were able to access. There are several examples in which lists of political party members in the US and European nations were employed to survey members of extremist organizations. Early studies focused on samples of former members of the Communist party in the US and European nations (Almond, 1954; Ernst & Loth, 1952). Knutson (1974) constructed a sample frame of members of the governing bodies of a number of political parties in Los Angeles County, including the Communist and Nazi parties. Sherwood (1966, p. 18) developed a frame of "present officers in [conservative] Midwestern male voluntary organizations which have publicly expressed concern with questions of 'Americanism.'" Van Hiel, Duriez and Kossowska (2006) successfully collected questionnaires from members of Communist, anarchist, right-wing extremist organizations in Belgium, and Billig and Cochrane (1979) sampled individuals affiliated with, among others, the Communist and National Front parties in Birmingham and Bristol, England. DiRenzo (1967) reported a survey of members of the Italian Parliament, including neo-Fascists and Communists, and Roccato and Ricolfi (2005) reported surveys of "political militants" who were recruited in their party offices in two Italian cities. Baray, Postmes, and Jetten (2009) accessed a list frame of college student members of the Turkish Nationalist Action Party, at the University of Ankara, as part of their study of the relationship between the social and personal identities of right-wing political party members. Other surveys of members of extreme right political parties have been reported in France (Ivaldi, 1996), the Netherlands (Esser & van Holsteyn, 1997) and Italy (Ignazi & Ysmal, 1992).

Crime perpetrator frames

A different process is described by Green *et al.* (1999) by which they constructed a sample frame of suspected hate crime perpetrators in North Carolina. An initial list of names was developed from the archives of an advocacy group, North Carolinians against Racial and Religious Violence, that included clippings from newspapers in that state, as well as victim reports made to that organization and affiliated groups. Using the names identified in these materials, the researchers were able to identify a sample of suspected perpetrators (a sample of other White supremacists also were identified using this method). The researchers suggest that their approach to frame construction resulted in a frame that represented the two ends of the spectrum in terms of level of violence. Specifically, those responsible for physical actions, such as assaults and cross burnings, at one extreme, and those who send harassing letters or make harassing phone calls, at the other extreme, were most likely to become known to law enforcement officials and, hence, make their way into the perpetrator frame developed by Green and associates. The perpetrators of many other types of hate crimes (e.g., damaging property, graffiti, shouting epithets) were much less likely to be identified and enter the sampling frame. Ironically, these activities might account for the majority of the hate-related crimes of interest. Hamm (1993) also reports having worked with corrections administrators, educators, and guards to conduct qualitative interviews with imprisoned skinheads in several states.

Somewhat similarly, to study racially motivated violence, Pinderhughes (1993) developed a frame of youth in Brooklyn, New York, who were participating in a program that worked with delinquents in an educational setting. After navigating access to this population, he was able to survey them regarding their attitudes towards other groups. Of course, this frame was restricted to perpetrators residing within a small geographic area.

Political contributor frames

Sample frames have also been constructed from publicly available lists of individual donors to political campaigns. In several instances, this has proved to be a useful strategy for constructing frames of individuals who, presumably, harbor extremist political views. One example is the study reported by Schuman and Krysan (1996), who surveyed persons in the greater metropolitan Detroit area having made contributions to the 1991 Louisiana gubernatorial campaign of David Duke, former Grand Wizard of the Knights of the Ku Klux Klan. They compared this sample with neighbors living on the same streets as the contributors, and with a probability sample of persons in the White segments of the Detroit metro area. Although this is a useful strategy to identify persons with views strong enough to warrant financial contributions, it is dependent on the quality of the information on the contributor list reported by the political campaign. Schuman and Krysan reported that the lists provided by the Duke campaign were generally accurate. Groves, Presser, and Dipko (2002) used a similar approach, obtaining a sample of contributors to the campaigns of several nonmainstream US presidential candidates, including Lyndon Larouche. In Europe, Ivaldi's (1996) survey of supporters of the far right French National Front included nonmember sympathizers who had given money to the party. Of course, this approach to frame construction can only be employed in those instances when a person with an extreme ideology elects to participate in the democratic process. Furthermore, although potential respondents identified using this process were known to support a candidate who is a political extremist, researchers can only indirectly infer that they themselves are also political extremists.

Constructing frames online

Another strategy for constructing sampling frames of political extremists is via the Internet. Indeed, some extremist groups were early adopters of computer technology and the Internet (Stern, 2001/02). As Levin (2002) has observed, extremists easily recognize the Internet's key advantages, including its global reach, economy, message control, and US First Amendment protections for the communication of ideas. The fact that the Internet is largely unsupervised and unregulated may also make it attractive to extremists (Gerstenfeld, Grant, & Chiang, 2003). This medium is used by extremists to engage in recruitment and allows them to maintain communications with geographically widespread group members as well as other extremist groups (Zhou, Reid, Qin, Chen, & Lai, 2005). Stern (2001/02), for example, has reported on the growth of the use of computers for communication by members of right-wing extremist groups, suggesting that the free and rapid flow of information was an important reason for the growth of the militia movement in the 1990s. Blee and Creasap (2010, p. 277) observe that the Internet also offers anonymity to individuals and movements that champion extremist propaganda and encourage violence. They note that online forums can permit individuals to engage in extremist dialogues "with little risk to their reputations, jobs or family relationships." De Koster's (2010) research suggests that users of a popular extremist website who report offline stigmatization for their beliefs find freedom of expression, "solidarity and comradeship" online. Homogeneous online communities also may offer members of extremist movements social support, a sense of belonging (Simi & Futrell, 2006), and increased self-efficacy (Wojcieszak, 2009).

Given the attractiveness of the web to extremists, some researchers have sought to construct sampling frames via this medium. Wojcieszak (2008) reports an online survey in which she constructed sampling frames by systematically sampling the email addresses of participants in online discussion forums concerned with neo-Nazi and radical environmentalist topics. Internet chat rooms affiliated with extremist groups also have been employed to experimentally manipulate scenarios, or vignettes, to determine what social factors are associated with bias-related motivations to resort to violence (Glaser, Dixit, & Green, 2002). Madison (2010) reported on a survey conducted with persons recruited through fourteen anti-illegal immigration-related online forums, including some hosted by Yahoo and Facebook. Other investigators have recruited respondents to take part in online interviews by posting invitations on discussion forums with moderator permission (de Koster & Houtman, 2008). There are also a number of examples of the construction of samples of extremist groups, rather than individuals, on the web via algorithms and data mining techniques (e.g., Chau & Xu, 2007; Du Plessis, 2008; Freiburger & Crane, 2008; Perry & Olsson, 2009; Qin, Zhou, & Chen, 2011; Zhou *et al.*, 2005).

While an efficient tool for recruiting persons with extremist political views and/or sympathies, it is important to acknowledge that, as with other populations of interest, it is not currently possible to construct a representative sample frame of political extremists or extremist organizations via the web, as those who are non-Internet users will not be covered. Given that utilizing the Internet as an information source is known to be a correlate of political activity (Moy, Manosevitch, Stamm, & Dunsmore, 2005), one might speculate that web-based sample frames such as those employed in the studies reported here might be overrepresentative of persons more willing to act on their beliefs. Evidence consistent with this comes from Madison (2010) and Wojcieszak (2009), who both find increased political action and/or participation among members of both left-wing and right-wing groups who also report greater participation in online discussion groups.

Screening the general population

Another strategy that can potentially be used to construct a representative frame of political extremists is to generate a random sample of a general population and conduct a screening to locate persons who self-identify as either being members of extremist groups or as having opinions and attitudes consistent with extremist beliefs and ideologies. Although we are unaware of any studies that have screened random samples for the primary purpose of identifying political extremists, there are numerous examples (c.f., Roccato & Ricolfi, 2005) of survey data being employed to compare the attitudes, beliefs, and behaviors of extremists with nonextremists in the general population (Adorno, Frenkel-Brunswik, Levinson, & Sanford, 1950; van Es & Koenig, 1976; Van Hiel, 2012), as well as within samples of students (Altemeyer, 1996; Franklin, 2000; Sidanius, 1984; Tarr & Lorr, 1991) and union members (Fichter, 2008). Van Hiel (2012), for example, reports a study that employed data from multiple waves of the European Social Survey (ESS), which employs random sampling within all participating nations, to make comparisons among persons with extreme left-wing, extreme right-wing, and moderate ideologies. Van Es and Koenig (1976) employed data from a survey of male household heads in west central Illinois to study associations between social participation, social status, and measures of extremist attitudes. In Sweden, Sidanius (1984) found greater interest in politics among high school students identified as being "left" and "right extremists," compared to those classified as moderates. Altemeyer (1996) has reported extensive research into right-wing authoritarian ideologies in samples of Canadian college students. It should be noted that the sample frames employed in most of these studies (other than Van Hiel, 2012) were convenience in nature. Most certainly, the main reason that there have been no attempts to build sample frames via random screening of the general population is the excessive cost that would be involved in doing so.

Snowball sampling

Although snowball sampling does not appear to be a common method for identifying and approaching potential respondents as part of surveys of political extremists, we wish to acknowledge that it is an important methodology employed by ethnographers and other qualitative researchers when conducting research with these populations (Futrell, Simi, & Gottschalk, 2006; Speckhard, 2009). Also, to our knowledge, there are no examples of the use of respondent-driven sampling (RDS) (Heckathorn, 1997) methods to conduct surveys of political extremists. Because RDS requires a high degree of trust between researchers and respondents, its use to recruit samples of political extremists may not be possible (D. D. Heckathorn, personal communication, October 20, 2012).

18.3.2 Field issues

Data collection modalities and the challenges involved in contacting and obtaining the cooperation of respondents will also require careful consideration when conducting survey research with persons identified as political extremists.

Mode of data collection

Over the past sixty years, surveys of political extremists have employed each of the commonly available data collection modalities. As Table 18.2 indicates, these include mail, paper-and-pencil questionnaires, web, face-to-face, and telephone modes. And, as with other populations, these various modes bring different strengths and limitations to the study of this subgroup. For example, self-administered questionnaires will afford respondents greater levels of privacy, potentially leading to more candid reporting of non-normative beliefs, opinions, and behaviors. Interviewer-assisted interviews, face-to-face interactions in particular, will provide greater opportunities for mutual self-revelation and in many cases

Table 18.2 *Data collection modes, by type of sample frame used*

Mode	Group membership frame	General population frame	Political contributor frame	Crime perpetrator frame	Online frame
Mail surveys					
Knutson (1974)	X				
McCloskey & Chong (1985)		X			
Schuman & Krysan (1996)			X		
Sherwood (1966)	X				
Van Hiel *et al.* (2006)	X				
Paper-and-Pencil questionnaires					
Adorno *et al.* (1950)		X			
Altemeyer (1996)		X			
Baray *et al.* (2009)	X				
Billig & Cochrane (1979)	X				
Pinderhughes (1993)				X	
Roccato & Ricolfi (2005)	X				
Sidanius (1984)		X			
Tarr & Lorr (1991)		X			
Web					
Postmes & Brunsting (2002)	X				
Madison (2010)					X
Wojcieszak (2008)					X
Face-to-face Interviews					
Almond (1954)	X				
DiRenzo (1967)	X				
Ernst & Loth (1952)	X				
Van Es & Koenig (1976)		X			
Van Hiel (2012)		X			
Telephone interviews					
Fichter (2008)	X				
Green *et al.* (1999)				X	
Groves *et al.* (2004)			X		

may be successful in achieving higher response rates. To our knowledge, however, there have been no formal comparisons of alternative modes for the collection of survey data from political extremists.

Obtaining cooperation

As discussed earlier, persons with extreme political beliefs will have reasons to be suspicious and even hostile towards perceived outsiders, including those seeking to conduct survey research with them. This problem may not always be hopeless, however. As several experts have advised us, many persons with extreme political views are very interested in communicating their opinions and beliefs, and it would not be correct to assume immediately that all would be hostile towards or reluctant to participate in a survey. William Ayers (personal communication, February 13, 2012), for example, suggests that many extremists "want people to come in." They want to tell their story and are typically excited when someone expresses a nonjudgmental interest in listening to them. Providing assurances of accurate and fair presentation of the views expressed, however, is essential. To quote Ayers' recommended approach, the key message to communicate to perspective respondents is that "I'm interested in how you see the world and I want to represent it honestly and fairly." Willem de Koster (personal communication, March 2, 2012) echoes these points, advising that when extremists react in a hostile manner towards social scientists and other perceived "outsiders," it is because "they are used to being portrayed negatively, both in the media and in scholarly publications." He advises stressing that "no normative judgment of participants will be made" in the research. Because "extremists are not used to being able to speak about themselves to a non-hostile interested outsider," if they can be assured of a researcher's interest in speaking *with* them, rather than *about* them, there is a greater likelihood of obtaining their cooperation. Speckhard (2009, p. 209), commenting on her research with terrorists in the Middle East, makes similar observations: "they do want their words and concerns put in front of policymakers and those they might never be able to otherwise influence, except by acts of terrorism. They want their voices to be heard and their unique points of view to be presented to those who have the power to possibly address them fairly." Surveys may be one approach to facilitating such communication and it is essential for survey researchers who want to study political extremists to convey an absence of judgment and a genuine interest in their positions and beliefs.

Interestingly, those surveys that report response rates of extremist group members vs. those of control groups in fact report that extremists are at least as likely as others to agree to participate, if not more so. Green *et al.*'s (1999) telephone surveys of the general public and hate crime perpetrators in North Carolina found essentially no differences in response rates between these two groups (15.3 percent among perpetrators vs. 14.8 percent among the general public). The general public, though, had a higher refusal rate (19.7 percent vs. 12.6 percent of hate crime perpetrators). Postmes and Brunsting's (2002) online survey of environmental activists, sympathizers, and controls in the Netherlands obtained the highest response rate among activists, followed by sympathizers, with control group participants having the lowest response rate (note: the overall response rate was 20 percent; the exact response rates for each subgroup were not reported). Schuman and Krysan's (1996) survey of contributors to the political campaign of David Duke, as well as two control groups, found the highest response rates among Duke contributors (86 percent), compared to neighbors of Duke contributors (78 percent) and the general population in the same city (74 percent). Groves *et al.*'s (2004) telephone survey of contributors to the campaigns of nonmainstream US presidential candidates reported higher response rates (73.6 percent vs. 48.3 percent) and cooperation rates

(54.8 percent vs. 34.1 percent) in comparison to a random digit dialed control sample of the general population. Indeed, these findings indicate that, if anything, the atypical levels of activism and social engagement often displayed by political extremists may translate into above average levels of curiosity and/or willingness to consider participating in surveys, presumably in particular those concerned with salient topics. Of course, in some of these cases, political extremists were identified by their political activism (e.g., Schuman & Krysan 1996) whereas members of the two control groups were not, so willingness to express one's opinion actively, be it through survey participation or contributing to the campaign of a political candidate, may be confounded with political extremism in this research. These findings further suggest that political extremists, by virtue of their interest in public affairs and greater willingness to participate in surveys, may be overrepresented in social surveys more generally.

18.4 Ethical considerations when surveying political extremists

Conducting surveys of persons with extremist political beliefs and behaviors can, perhaps not surprisingly, also introduce ethical issues beyond those commonly considered when conducting research with other populations. It is of course most important that researchers avoid inadvertently setting up conditions which increase the risk that respondents will be harmed as a consequence of their participation in a survey.

18.4.1 Informed consent

While informed consent must be an absolute requirement in all survey research, its specific form will vary depending on the specifics of the study being conducted. Written consent, for example, is commonly viewed as the standard approach to informing respondents about the benefits, if any, and risks of participation. This will be impracticable, though, when conducting telephone interviews, although all of the key elements of consent (e.g., the identity of the researchers and their contact information, the general purpose of study, the procedures involved, etc.) can nonetheless be presented orally by an interviewer in advance of requesting verbal consent. In some instances, collecting information regarding a respondent's identity may also place that person at risk. For example, respondents who answer questions regarding illegal and/or violent activities are at increased risk of criminal prosecution should their self-reports be made public. For this reason, respondents are sometimes not asked to sign a consent form, as doing so may provide the only information regarding the respondent's identity that is collected during the survey. Given these risks to respondent confidentiality, it is critical that researchers studying political extremism work carefully with Institutional Review Boards (IRBs) to clarify both their responsibilities and procedures for minimizing the risk of confidentiality breach.

18.4.2 Data security

There may be reasons why governmental agencies, news media, and/or political opponents sometimes wish to gain access to information collected as part of surveys of political extremists. It is thus important that consent procedures also inform potential respondents regarding the procedures that will be employed to ensure both their confidentiality and the security of the data being collected. Of course, immediately separating any information that could be potentially used to identify respondents from their answers is conventional practice in survey research. Given the greater risks to respondents of confidentiality breach, however, we would urge researchers to consider carefully their plans for ensuring data security and avoid maintaining identifying information any longer than is necessary to ensure that data collection has been successfully accomplished. Protection of respondent confidentiality can also have serious consequences for researchers that need to be recognized. Approximately twenty years ago, an ethnographer in Washington State was jailed for more than five months for refusing to reveal information from interviews he had conducted with a member of an animal rights group (Scarce, 1994). As in this example, researchers need to have a clear understanding of their professional responsibilities to protect data and the personal costs of doing so.

18.4.3 Avoiding research deception

Given the suspicions with which persons with extremist political opinions will often view researchers, it is also imperative that research deception be avoided. Glaser, Dixit, and Green (2002) report a study in which they negotiated an IRB waiver of informed consent as part of an online experiment designed to investigate the social factors most likely to be associated with interracial violence advocacy among participants in a White racist Internet chat room. Without their knowledge, respondents were interviewed by researchers who did not self-identify as such, and asked how they would respond to various scenarios (e.g., interracial marriage, job competition, minority in-migration). The investigators understood the ethical ramifications of their study design and argued that, as often the case with social psychological experiments, deception was necessary in order to obtain participation and avoid biased answers. Their IRB agreed because the interviews took place in a public environment, the topics of study were commonly discussed there, and respondents participated without coercion. We recommend that researchers carefully consider the tradeoffs between the ethical costs of conducting deceptive research and the professional rewards of obtaining experimental data. One important consideration, not discussed by these researchers, is the likelihood that published examples of deceptive research might be cited by members of extremist political groups as a rationale for dismissing all researchers as untrustworthy. At a minimum, we believe it is important to debrief adequately any respondents who were involved in research that included deception of any kind.

18.4.4 Research self-disclosure

A related point is the importance that researchers fully disclose their identity to survey respondents. We believe that researcher self-identification is a necessary condition to achieving informed consent and avoiding research deception. Self-disclosure also contributes directly to addressing respondent suspicions about the nature of the research in which they are being asked to participate. In this regard, de Koster (2010) has recommended that researchers create a website to describe their research and to provide relevant professional and contact information to potential research subjects. He comments that

> because you will be asking people about an issue that is commonly thought of as "sensitive," it helps if you provide as much information as possible about yourself. If you are not perceived as simply a faceless name connected to some abstract institution, but a real flesh-and-blood human being who is open about his goals and motives, your recruitment might be more effective.

18.5 Conclusions

Extremist political ideologies have inflicted enormous damage worldwide over the past century. Yet, as this chapter demonstrates, there has been only a relatively modest amount of survey research concerned with various forms of political extremism. This dearth of research is perhaps at least in part a consequence of the methodological and ethical challenges associated with identifying, locating, and reaching out to these hard-to-survey populations. Our hope is that, in reviewing the approaches previously used in conducting surveys of political extremists, the research community can begin to understand better the advantages and limitations of alternative research strategies for understanding these important, albeit small and difficult-to-reach populations.

References

Adams, J., & Roscigno, V. J. (2005). White supremacists, oppositional culture and the World Wide Web. *Social Forces*, 84, 759–78. doi:10.1353/sof.2006.0001.

Adorno, T. W., Frenkel-Brunswik, E., Levinson, D., & Sanford, R. N. (1950). *The Authoritarian Personality*. New York: Harper & Row.

Almond, G. A. (1954). *The Appeals of Communism*. Princeton: Princeton University Press.

Altemeyer, B. (1996). *The Authoritarian Specter*. Cambridge, MA: Harvard University Press.

Atkins, S. E. (2004). *Encyclopedia of Modern Worldwide Political Extremists and Extremist Groups*. Westport, CT: Greenwood Press.

Baray, G., Postmes, T., & Jetten, J. (2009). When "I" equals "we": exploring the relation between social and personal identity of extreme right-wing political party members. *British Journal of Social Psychology*, 48, 625–47.

Barrett-Fox, R. (2011). Anger and compassion on the picket line: ethnography and emotion in the study of Westboro Baptist Church. *Journal of Hate Studies*, 9, 11–33.

Billig, M., & Cochrane, R. (1979). Values of British political extremists and potential extremists: a discriminant analysis. *European Journal of Social Psychology*, 9, 205–22.

Blee, K. M. (1999). White on white: interviewing women in U.S. white supremacist groups. In F. W Twine & J. Warren (eds.), *Racing Research, Researching Race: Methodological Dilemmas in Critical Race Studies* (pp. 93–109). New York: NYU Press.

(2003). Studying the enemy. In B. Glassner & R Hertz (eds.), *Our Studies, Ourselves: Sociologists' Lives and Work* (pp. 13–23). Cary, NC: Oxford University Press.

Blee, K. M., & Creasap, K. A. (2010). Conservative and right-wing movements. *Annual Review of Sociology*, 36, 269–86.

Chau, M., & Xu, J. (2007). Mining communities and their relationships in blogs: a study of online hate groups. *International Journal of Human-Computer Studies*, 65, 57–70.

de Koster, W. (2010). "Nowhere I could talk like that": togetherness and identity on online forums. Unpublished doctoral dissertation, Erasmus Universiteit, Rotterdam, The Netherlands.

de Koster, W., & Houtman, D. (2008). "Stormfront is like a second home to me": on virtual community formation by right-wing extremists. *Information, Communication & Society*, 11, 1155–76.

DiRenzo, G. J. (1967). Professional politicians and personality structures. *American Journal of Sociology*, 73, 217–25.

Du Plessis, M. (2008). A Content Analysis of Extremist Web Sites Based on Internet User Activities. Unpublished master's thesis, University of Pretoria, South Africa.

Ernst, M. L, & Loth, D. (1952). *Report on the American Communist*. New York: Henry Holt and Company.

Esser, M., & van Holsteyn, J. (1997). Kleur bekennen: Over leden van de Centrumdemocraten. In J. van Holsteyn & C. Mudde (eds.), *Extreem-rechts in Nederland* (pp. 75–92). Den Haag: Sdu.

Ezekiel, R. S (2002). An ethnographer looks at neo-Nazi and Klan groups. *American Behavioral Scientist*, 46, 51–71.

Fichter, M. (2008). German trade unions and right extremism: understanding membership attitudes. *European Journal of Industrial Relations*, 14, 65–84.

Franklin, K. (2000). Antigay behaviors among young adults: prevalence, patterns, and motivators in a noncriminal population. *Journal of Interpersonal Violence*, 15, 339–62.

Freiburger, T., & Crane, J. S. (2008). A systematic examination of terrorist use of the internet. *International Journal of Cyber Criminology*, 2, 309–19.

Futrell, R., & Simi, P. (2004). Free spaces, collective identity, and the persistence of U.S. white power activism. *Social Problems*, 51, 16–42.

Futrell, T., Simi, P., & Gottschalk, S. (2006). Understanding music in movements: the white power music scene. *Sociological Quarterly*, 47, 275–304.

George, J. H. (1970). A brief survey of American political extremism from post World War I to 1970. *Proceedings of the Oklahoma Academy of Science*, 50, 191–94. Retrieved from http://digital.library.okstate.edu/oas/oas_pdf/v50/p191_194.pdf.

Gerstenfeld, P. B., Grant, D. R., & Chiang, C. P. (2003). Hate online: a content analysis of extremist Internet sites. *Analyses of Social Issues and Public Policy*, 3, 29–44.

Glaser, J., Dixit, J., & Green, D. P. (2002). Studying hate crime with the internet: what makes racists advocate racial violence? *Journal of Social Issues*, 58, 177–93.

Green, D. P., Abelson, R. P., & Garnett, M. (1999). The distinctive political views of hate-crime perpetrators and white supremacists. In D. A. Prentice & D. T. Miller (eds.), *Cultural divides: understanding and overcoming group conflict* (pp. 429–64). New York: Russell Sage Foundation.

Groves, R. M., Presser, S., & Dipko, S. (2004). The role of topic interest in survey participation decisions. *Public Opinion Quarterly*, 68, 2–31.

Hamm, M. S. (1993). *American skinheads: the criminology and control of hate crime.* Westport, CT: Praeger.

Heckathorn, D. D. (1997). Respondent-driven sampling: a new approach to the study of hidden populations. *Social Problems*, 44, 174–99.

Ignazi, P., & Ysmal, C. (1992). New and old extreme right parties: the French Front National and the Italian Movimento Sociale. *European Journal of Political Research*, 22, 101–21.

Ivaldi, G. (1996). Conservation, revolution and protest: a case study in the political cultures of the French National Front's members and sympathizers. *Electoral Studies*, 15, 339–62.

Janowitz, M., & Marvick, D. (1953). Authoritarianism and political behavior. *Public Opinion Quarterly*, 17, 185–201.

Jipson, J. J., & Litton, C. E. (2000). Body, career and community: the implications of researching dangerous groups. In G. Lee-Treweek & S. Linkogle (eds.), *Danger in the Field: Risk and Ethics in Social Research* (pp. 147–67). London: Routledge.

Kimmel, M. (2007). Racism as adolescent male rite of passage: ex-Nazis in Scandinavia. *Journal of Contemporary Ethnography*, 36, 202–18.

Knutson, J. N. (1974). *Psychological Variables in Political Recruitment: An Analysis of Party Activists.* Berkeley: The Wright Institute.

Levin, B. (2002). Cyberhate: a legal and historical analysis of extremists' use of computer networks in America. *American Behavioral Scientist*, 45, 958–88.

McClosky, H., & Chong, D. (1985). Similarities and differences between left-wing and right-wing radicals. *British Journal of Political Science*, 15, 329–63.

Madison, P. (2010). *Anti-Illegal Immigration Movement: An Exploration of Civic Engagement, Political Engagement, Internet Use, Activism, and Radicalism.* Paper presented at the Annual Meeting of the Midwest Association for Public Opinion Research, Chicago, IL.

Midlarsky, M. I. (2011). *Origins of Political Extremism.* Cambridge: Cambridge University Press.

Miller, G. (2007). Science and the public: animal extremists get personal. *Science*, 318, 1856–58.

Moy, P., Manosevitch, E., Stamm, K., & Dunsmore, K. (2005). Linking dimensions of internet use and civic engagement. *Journalism and Mass Communication Quarterly*, 82, 571–86.

Perry, B., & Olsson, P. (2009). Cyberhate: the globalization of hate. *Information & Communications Technology Law*, 18, 185–99.

Pinderhughes, H. (1993). The anatomy of racially motivated violence in New York City: a case study of youth in Southern Brooklyn. *Social Problems*, 40, 478–92.

Postmes, T., & Brunsting, S. (2002). Collective action in the age of the internet: mass communication and online mobilization. *Social Science Computer Review*, 20, 290–301.

Qin, J., Zhou, Y., & Chen, H. (2011). A multi-region empirical study on the internet presence of global extremist organizations. *Information Systems Frontiers*, 13, 75–88.

Ringach, D. L., & Jentsch, J. D. (2009). We must face the threats. *Journal of Neuroscience*, 29, 11417–18.

Roccato M., & Ricolfi, L. (2005). On the correlation between right-wing authoritarianism and social dominance orientation. *Basic and Applied Social Psychology*, 27, 187–200.

Sageman, M. (2004). *Understanding Terror Networks*. Philadelphia: University of Pennsylvania Press.

Scarce, R. (1994). (No) trial (but) tribulations: when courts and ethnography conflict. *Journal of Contemporary Ethnography*, 23, 123–49.

Schafer, J. A. (2002). Spinning the web of hate: web-based hate propagation by extremist organizations. *Journal of Criminal Justice and Popular Culture*, 9, 69–88.

Schuman, H., & Krysan, M. (1996). A study of far right resentment in America. *International Journal of Public Opinion Research*, 8, 10–30.

Scruton, R. (1982). *A Dictionary of Political Thought*. New York: MacMillan.

Seger, K. A. (2001). *Left-Wing Extremism: The Current Threat*. Oak Ridge, TN: Center for Human Reliability Studies, Oak Ridge Institute for Science and Education. Retrieved from www.fas.org/irp/world/para/left.pdf.

Sherwood, J. J. (1966). Authoritarianism and moral realism. *Journal of Clinical Psychology*, 22, 17–21.

Sidanius, J. (1984). Political unrest, political information search, and ideological homogeneity as a function of sociopolitical theory: a tale of three theories. *Human Relations*, 37, 811–28.

(1988). Political sophistication and political deviance: a structural equation examination of context theory. *Journal of Personality and Social Psychology*, 55, 37–51.

Simi, P., & Futrell, R. (2006). Cyberculture and endurance of white power activism. *Journal of Political and Military Sociology*, 34, 115–42.

(2009). Negotiating white power activist stigma. *Social Problems*, 56, 89–110.

Smith, B. L. (1994). *Terrorism in America*. Albany: State University of New York Press.

Speckhard, A. (2009). Research challenges involved in field research and interviews regarding the militant jihad, extremism, and suicide terrorism. *Democracy and Security*, 5, 199–222.

Stern, K. S. (2001/02). Hate and the internet. *Journal of Hate Studies*, 1, 57–107.

Stromer-Galley, J. (2003). Diversity of political conversation on the internet: users' perspectives. *Journal of Computer-Mediated Communication*, 8(3), April.

Tarr, H., & Lorr, M. (1991). A comparison of right-wing authoritarianism, conformity and conservatism. *Personality and Individual Differences*, 12, 307–11.

Thomas, E., Smith, L., McGarty, C., & Postmes, T. (2010). Nice and nasty: the formation of prosocial and hostile social movements. *Revue Internationale de Psychologie Sociale*, 23(2/3), 17–55.

US Department of Homeland Security. (2009a). (U//FOUO) *Leftwing Extremists likely to Increase Use of Cyber Attacks over the Coming Decade.* Washington, DC: Strategic Analysis Group, Homeland Environment and Threat Analysis Division. Retrieved from www.foxnews.com/projects/pdf/Leftwing_Extremist_Threat.pdf.

(2009b). (U//FOUO) *Rightwing Extremism: Current Economic and Political Climate Fueling Resurgence in Radicalization and Recruitment.* Washington, DC: Extremism and Radicalization Branch, Homeland Environment Threat Analysis Division. Retrieved from www.fas.org/irp/eprint/rightwing.pdf.

van Es, J.C., & Koenig, D.J. (1976). Social participation, social status and extremist political attitudes. *Sociological Quarterly*, 17, 16–26.

Van Hiel, A. (2012). A psycho-political profile of party activists and left-wing and right-wing extremists. *European Journal of Political Research*, 51, 166–203.

Van Hiel, A., Duriez, B., & Kossowska, M. (2006). The presence of left-wing authoritarianism in Western Europe and its relationship with conservative ideology. *Political Psychology*, 27, 769–93.

Weatherby, G.A., & Scoggins, B. (2005/06). A content analysis of persuasion techniques used on white supremacist websites. *Journal of Hate Studies*, 5, 9–31.

Wojcieszak, M. (2008). False consensus goes online: impact of ideologically homogeneous groups on false consensus. *Public Opinion Quarterly*, 72, 781–91.

(2009). "Carrying online participation offline" – mobilization by radical online groups and politically dissimilar offline ties. *Journal of Communication*, 59, 564–86.

Zhou, Y., Reid, E., Qin, J., Chen, H., & Lai, G. (2005). U.S. domestic extremist groups on the web: link and content analysis. *IEEE Intelligent Systems, September/October*, 44–51.

PART IV

Sampling strategies for the hard to survey

19

Probability sampling methods for hard-to-sample populations
GRAHAM KALTON

19.1 Introduction

There are no universally accepted definitions of such terms as "hard-to-reach," "elusive," and even "mobile" populations, although all are well recognized as populations that are difficult to sample (see Kish, 1991, for a taxonomy of elusive populations). A common but not universal characteristic of these populations is that they are rare populations for which no separate sampling frames exist. The prime focus of this chapter is on sampling these types of populations using probability sampling methods. Rather than attempt a formal classification, I will present a range of illustrative examples:

- Blacks, Hispanics, American Indians/Alaska Natives, Vietnamese immigrants;
- Religious groups;
- Abused children, abused adults;
- Persons with AIDS, rare forms of cancer, dementia;
- Street prostitutes;
- Men who have sex with men (MSM), lesbians;
- Users of illicit drugs;
- Disabled scientists;
- Pregnant women;
- Children in poverty, the very rich;
- Homeless persons, nomads;
- International travelers, visitors to museums or shopping malls; and
- Drivers and passengers of cars in transit.

These examples are mostly drawn from other reviews such as Christman (2009), Kalton (1991, 2009), Kalton and Anderson (1986), Kish (1965a, 1991), Sudman and Freeman (1988), and Sudman and Kalton (1986). Flores Cervantes and Kalton (2008) present a review of the sampling methods for such populations in the context of telephone surveys and

This chapter draws heavily on the author's paper "Methods for oversampling rare subpopulations in social surveys" published in December 2009 by Statistics Canada in *Survey Methodology*, 35(2), 125–41, catalogue number 12–001-X. Readers are referred to that paper for more details on some of the methods discussed. The author is grateful to the editor of *Survey Methodology* for permission to use material from that paper.

Elliott, Finch, Klein, Ma, Do, Beckett *et al.* (2008) review sampling methods for the widely encountered need to sample rare race/ethnic populations.

There are different analytic objectives for surveys of this diverse set of populations. With static populations, a main distinction is between surveys aiming to estimate the size of the population and its prevalence in the general population and surveys aiming to study the characteristics of the population. For example, is the main survey objective to estimate the proportion of children in poverty or the health, education, and housing conditions of poor children? With mobile populations, a key issue is whether the population of inference is the "visit" or the "visitor." For example, is the population of inference the trips made by international travelers or the persons who engage in international travel?

This chapter presents a general overview of probability sampling designs for selecting samples of hard-to-sample populations. The focus on probability sampling methods is based on the belief that well-executed probability sampling is necessary to provide the security of valid statistical inference for the survey findings. From the perspective of survey design-based inference, the conditions that need to be met for such a sample design are:

(1) *Known selection probabilities.* The selection probabilities of sample members must be known directly from the sample selection process without the need to depend on model assumptions.
(2) *High coverage.* The sample design and its implementation should cover a high proportion of the target population.
(3) *High response rate.* A high proportion of the sampled members of the target population should respond to the survey.
(4) *Weighting.* Weights should be used in the analysis to compensate for unequal selection probabilities (and also for differential nonresponse and noncoverage).
(5) *Operationally feasible.* The implementation of the survey design, that is, the combination of sample design and data collection procedures, must be feasible within the constraint of the overall survey budget and lead to survey estimates that satisfy precision requirements.

Section 19.2 of this chapter reviews a range of the standard probability sampling techniques that are used for sampling what Tourangeau (Chapter 1 in this volume) calls hard-to-sample populations, with a focus on examples rather than theoretical properties. These techniques include large-scale screening, the use of a large host survey for screening, disproportionate stratification, the use of multiple frames, and network sampling. In practice, a combination of these techniques is generally used. Since the technique of location sampling is widely used in sampling mobile and other hard-to-sample populations, it is discussed separately, in Section 19.3.

Despite the range of standard probability sampling methods that has been developed for sampling hard-to-sample populations, it is often not possible to satisfy all five conditions listed above. Some compromises are therefore often needed. For example, in cases where full coverage of the ideal target population is not practicable, the survey's objectives may sometimes be adequately served by restricting the target population to those who can be sampled at acceptable cost. Early examples include studies that restricted the coverage of American Indians and Alaska Natives to those living on or near reservations (Cohen, DiGaetano, & Waksberg, 1988) and the coverage of Hispanics to those living in counties where the prevalence and numbers were sufficiently high (Gonzalez, Ezzati, White, Massey, Lago, & Waksberg, 1985). The ongoing National HIV Behavioral Surveillance (NHBS) system, which studies persons at high risk for HIV infection, restricts its coverage to 20 jurisdictions with high AIDS prevalence (US Centers for Disease Control and Prevention, 2012). Another example arises with the use of location sampling, discussed in Section 19.3; in this case, the restriction limits the coverage to members of the target population who visit the locations from which the sample is selected. In general, when sampling less than the full target population, the extent of coverage loss and the possible effects on the survey results should be carefully assessed. If the loss is sizable, the survey results should be presented as relating to the population surveyed, not the ideal target population. The practice of attempting to extend the survey inferences to the full target population by making post-stratification adjustments to target population totals is generally highly problematic since it depends on the dubious assumption that the uncovered portion of the target population has similar characteristics to the covered portion.

Another common type of compromise involves the choice of the mode of data collection used to identify and collect data from a sample of a hard-to-sample population. Cost considerations may lead to opting for a less expensive mode, but that choice may result in greater rates of noncoverage and nonresponse. In particular, mail questionnaires and telephone interviewing can be cost-effective ways to screen for some populations, but problems with screener misclassification, nonresponse, and noncoverage need to be carefully assessed.

Finally, when a cost-effective probability sample design that can provide an adequate sample size for the target population cannot be devised, it may prove necessary to resort to nonprobability methods and accept the inherent uncertainty about the validity of the survey findings. In fact, social science and epidemiological journals contain many examples of results from surveys of hard-to-sample populations that employed some form of nonprobability sampling. Some discussion of the use of nonprobability sampling methods is included in Section 19.4.

19.2 Standard probability sampling techniques for sampling hard-to-sample populations

Given the diversity of types of hard-to-sample populations, no single approach to sample design can fit all cases. The following are some of the questions to be answered in narrowing down the range of design choices:

- How rare is the population? The challenges of sampling a target population that comprises one hundredth of the general population are far greater than those for a target population that comprises one tenth of the general population.

- How readily can members of the target population be identified? Is the target population a "hidden" population, with many of its members reluctant to admit to that membership in a survey setting? Can a few simple questions be asked to identify members of the population, or is a more complex approach needed? If the identification is expensive, a two-phase sampling approach may be appropriate.
- Is there a large-scale survey that can serve as a screener sample for identifying members of the target population?
- Is the target population more concentrated in some parts of the sampling frame? If so, using disproportionate stratification to oversample those parts may be effective.
- Are there one or more partial sampling frames (generally list frames) of the hard-to-sample population that are available for use in sampling? If so, selecting the sample from more than one frame may be effective.
- Is the target population accessible by sampling households? Special techniques are needed to sample the homeless and nomads, frequently involving some form of location sampling.

19.2.1 Screening

A central component of most probability sample designs for hard-to-sample populations is some form of screening – that is, selecting a sample from a larger population to identify members of the target population. Household screening is widely used. Sometimes screening is used alone; at other times it is used in combination with the techniques described later in this section that aim to make the screening more efficient.

Two types of misclassification can occur with screening: false positives (i.e., persons incorrectly identified as members of the target population) and false negatives (persons incorrectly classified as not members of the target population). False positives cause some loss of efficiency because they would be included initially in the follow-up interview, although they can be simply dropped from the survey once it is established they are not in the target population. False negatives are of much greater concern because they are a source of noncoverage. A number of surveys have found sizable noncoverage from false negatives (see, for example, Camburn & Wright, 1996; Horrigan, Moore, Pedlow, & Wolter, 1999; and Judkins, DiGaetano, Chu, & Shapiro, 1999). Tourangeau, Kreuter, and Eckman (2012) describe the results of some experiments on possible causes for what they term "motivated underreporting"; see also Chapter 1 in this volume.

The survey screening instrument and procedures should be designed to minimize false negatives. For example, in a survey of a racial minority, it may be preferable to ask in the screener for the person's race rather than ask whether the person is a member of the race under study. If an age range is used for defining the hard-to-sample population, it may be better to ask about a wider age range in the screener, creating some false positives that can then be dropped in the main survey.

A large screening sample size is needed when a hard-to-sample population is very rare, is almost evenly distributed in the overall population, and when there are no partial lists of appreciable coverage. In such circumstances, the cost of screening is likely to be a major component of overall survey costs, pointing to the need for economical sample designs and data collection procedures for the screening.

Where practical, using an inexpensive mode of data collection for screening, such as a mail questionnaire or telephone interviewing, can result in major economies. When the main data collection is also conducted by mail or telephone, the sample can be geographically unclustered, thus avoiding the reduction in the effective sample size resulting from such clustering; however, if the main data collection involves in-person contact with members of the hard-to-sample population, then geographical clustering will likely be needed for the screening sample. An important distinction between these two modes is that with telephone screening, the interviewer may be able to proceed immediately to the main interview when a member of the target population is identified, but as a rule a mail screener will require a separate follow-up data collection.

While screening by mail or telephone can be economical, the suitability of these modes needs to be assessed for the target population under study, in particular with regard to noncoverage, nonresponse, and response errors. What is the coverage of the general sampling frame specifically for the target population? For example, coverage of landline telephone screening may be acceptable for older adults but unacceptably low for young adults, many of whom live in cell-phone-only households. How well will members of the target population respond to the screener? Screening by mail may yield an acceptable response rate for scientists and engineers but an unacceptable rate for recent immigrants. It is generally not possible to determine the screening response rate just for the target population. It should not be uncritically assumed to be the same as that for the general population since it often will be lower than the overall rate (although sometimes it may be higher). How well will members of the target population report their membership of that population when one of these modes is used? It is generally more difficult to overcome a reluctance to report membership of a hidden or sensitive population when these modes are used than with in-person screening.

There are several ways to economize on the screening costs for face-to-face interviewing. Although geographical cluster sampling increases the variances of survey estimates, it is generally used with face-to-face interviewing for efficiency of data collection. The cluster sample sizes are constrained to limit the loss of precision from clustering. In the case of a rare population, the cluster sample size for members of the rare population is the relevant quantity to consider. Although screening costs have the effect of reducing the optimum cluster sample size for the target population, the overall screening sample size in a cluster is still much larger than what is traditionally used for a general population survey (Kalton, 2003).

A common practice in household screening is to collect the screening data for all household members from a single "knowledgeable" household informant. This approach needs to be carefully assessed in each particular case because its use may lead to significant undercoverage for some populations. When it is adopted, there can be a considerable efficiency gain for the main survey in retaining all eligible members of the target population in the sampled households. This procedure also needs careful consideration since in some cases it may lead to contamination effects and/or lower response rates. The loss of precision resulting from the within-household intraclass correlation is another factor to consider; however, that loss is generally negligible for estimates for subclasses defined, for example, by sex and age. Recognizing these issues, the savings in screening costs arising from selecting all those eligible in a sampled household can nevertheless be attractive when surveying a hard-to-sample population, particularly when that population is highly clustered by household (e.g., a target population defined by race/ethnicity).

In general, the larger the number of individuals for whom a single informant can provide screening data, the more economical is the screening. One way to expand on the number of individuals for whom screening data are collected is known as *focused enumeration*. With focused enumeration, a sample of index addresses is selected and members of the target population at each index address and the *n* neighboring addresses on either side (e.g., $n = 2$) are identified from a respondent at the index address initially, and from the neighboring addresses if the index respondent cannot provide the necessary identification. See Bolling, Grant, and Sinclair (2008) for an application of focused enumeration for oversampling ethnic minorities in the British Crime Survey. A significant disadvantage of focused enumeration is that it may well produce sizable undercoverage of the target population.

Network, or multiplicity, sampling is another way to expand on the screening net. With network sampling, the informant is asked not only to provide screening data for all household members but also to provide these data for other persons linked to the informant in a clearly defined way who are living elsewhere, such as siblings, parents, and children (Sirken, 2004, 2005; Sudman, Sirken, & Cowan, 1988). A key requirement is that every member of the linkage must know and be willing to report on the target population membership of all those linked to them, a factor that influences the choice of linkages (see, for example, Rothbart, Fine, & Sudman, 1982).

Sometimes with network sampling, the original informant is able to provide the survey data for each of the members of the target population that he or she has identified. However, the informant must know and be willing to report the data, which can be problematic in terms of accuracy and/or sensitivity (see, for example, Sudman & Freeman, 1988). In most cases, the survey data must be obtained from the target population members themselves, in which case the informant must be able and willing to provide accurate contact information for the target population members. That also can be problematic.

The multiple routes of selection with network sampling need to be taken into account in determining the selection probabilities. Conceptually, one can consider member j of the target population divided into, say, l_j parts corresponding to the l_j potential informants for that member; these parts then are sampled for the survey. See Chapter 23 in this volume for some theory behind this technique. Weights are then needed in the analysis to compensate for the variable network sizes.

Although there are a number of reported applications of network sampling (see Kalton, 2009, for some other examples), it has not been widely used. An important limitation is the risk that the sampled informant may not accurately report the target population status of other members of the linkage, either deliberately or through lack of knowledge. Nonresponse for the main survey data collection is another concern. In addition, ethical issues arise when sampled persons are asked about the target population membership of those in their linkage, particularly when that membership is a sensitive matter. The benefits of network sampling are partially offset by the increased sampling errors arising from the variable weights that the method entails, and by the costs of locating the linked target population members.

Underlying all these screening approaches is the assumption that the target population members can be identified relatively easily. When accurate identification is expensive, a *two-phase design* can be useful, starting with an imperfect screening classification in the first phase, to be followed up with accurate identification for a disproportionate stratified subsample at the second phase. Whether the two-phase approach is cost-effective depends in part on the relative costs of the imperfect classification and the accurate identification: since the imperfect classifications use up some of the study's resources, they must be much less expensive than the accurate identification (Deming, 1977). Also, the imperfect classification must be reasonably effective to gain major benefits from a second-phase disproportionate stratification.

Two- or even three-phase screening can be useful in surveys of persons with specific health conditions. The first-phase screening often consists of a questionnaire administered by survey interviewers, and the second phase is generally conducted by clinicians, often in a medical center. See, for example, the surveys by Haerer, Anderson, and Schoenberg (1986) studying epilepsy and Langa, Plassman, Wallace, Herzog, Heeringa, Ofstedal *et al.* (2005) studying cognitive impairments in the elderly (Kalton, 2009, provides some further details).

A common practice with two-phase designs is to take no second-phase sample from the stratum of those classified as nonmembers of the target population at the first phase. The proportion of the population in that stratum is usually very high, and the prevalence of the target population in it is very low. As a result, a moderate-sized sample from this stratum will yield almost no members of the target population. However, the cut-off strategy of taking no sample from this stratum is risky. If the prevalence of the target population in this stratum is more than minimal, a substantial proportion of the population may go unrepresented in the final sample. The risk of missing a sizable proportion of the target population can be reduced by adopting a broader definition of the stratum of those classified as members of the target population at the first phase, as was done by Haerer *et al.* (1986). This approach reduces the number of false negatives at the second phase at the cost of generating more false positives.

A special type of hard-to-sample population is one whose members are defined by the experience of some recent event, such as a divorce or death of a spouse. A *panel survey design* may be needed for this type of target population, following a large screening sample over time to identify those who experience the event. An example is the initial sample design tested for the National Children's Study (NCS), which aims to sample women early in pregnancy and follow them and then their children until the children reach age 21. That design involved screening a large sample of households for eligible women and then keeping in touch with them over a period of four years, recruiting those who became pregnant into the study (Montaquila, Brick, & Curtin, 2010). (See Section 19.3.2 for an alternative sampling approach being tested for the NCS.)

Finally, it should be noted that panel designs can be useful in repeated surveys of a hard-to-sample population defined in terms of static characteristics (such as race/ethnicity). If a sample of such a population is developed at one point in time, that sample can be retained in a panel to study that population's characteristics at later points, possibly with supplementary samples added to represent those who entered the target population after the original sample was selected. Fecso, Baskin, Chu, Gray, Kalton, and Phelps (2007) describe how this approach has been applied in sampling US scientists and engineers over a decade. For the decade of the 1990s, the National Survey of College Graduates (NSCG) was conducted in 1993 with a stratified sample of college graduates selected from the 1990 Census of Population long-form sample records. Those found to be scientists or engineers were then resurveyed in the NSCG in 1995, 1997, and 1999. To represent new entrants to the target population, another survey – the Survey of Recent College Graduates – was conducted in the same years as the NSCG. A subsample of the recent college graduates was added in to the next round of the NSCG panel on each occasion.

A variant of this approach that is sometimes used in panel surveys is to identify future members of the target population in an initial survey, to keep track of them, and then to include them in the panel survey when they become eligible. In particular, for surveys of a specific age group, those younger than the minimum age can be identified in the initial round and added into the panel when they enter the eligible age range.

19.2.2 Use of existing surveys for screening

When considering how to sample members of a hard-to-sample population, it is natural to want to take advantage of an existing large-scale survey as a host survey for screening. There are indeed some good examples of this approach, including the NSCG described in Section 19.2.1. Using disproportionate stratification (see Section 19.2.3) based on the responses to the census long-form education question reduced the amount of screening needed for the survey, but many of those sampled in the 1993 NSCG still turned out not to be scientists or engineers. The American Community Survey (ACS) has replaced the census long form, and it now serves as the sampling frame for the sample of scientists and engineers. With the recent inclusion of a question on field of degree in the ACS, the screening has become more efficient.

This example highlights some important issues with using an existing large-scale survey for screening. First, the host survey may not collect the exact data needed for the screening. For the NSCG, this problem was largely resolved by adding the field of degree question to the ACS, but adding questions to surveys is often unacceptable to those responsible for the potential host survey, particularly when these questions do not mesh well with that survey's objectives. Also, the host survey would need to add a question asking permission for the sample members to be contacted for the follow-up survey. Second, there is often a significant delay between the data collection for the host survey and the follow-up, and during that period members of the target population may move and thus be difficult to trace. When the target population is defined by transient characteristics (e.g., children in poverty), some of those identified in the host survey may no longer be in the target population at the time of follow-up and, of much greater concern, some of those not so identified will have become members of that population.

Of course, the initial consideration is whether or not the host survey is large enough to produce the sample yield required for the target population. With very rare target populations, this rules out most potential host surveys. Another consideration is the quality of the host survey. What are its coverage and response rates, in particular for the target population? What is the likely extent of response errors in the answers to the screening questions? Yet another consideration is whether the large-scale survey can yield a sample of the target population that can be fielded efficiently. If, say, the survey of the target population is to be conducted by face-to-face interviewing, is it possible to develop a geographically clustered sample from the host survey? Thus, for a variety of reasons, with a reluctance of those conducting the host survey to allow their survey to be used for screening often being the key one, using a large-scale survey to screen for a hard-to-sample population is not as frequent as might be expected.

When a single round of a repeated survey is not large enough to serve as the host survey, the sample of the target population can be accumulated over several rounds (Kish, 1999). For example, a sample of a rare target population can be accumulated over one or more years from the US National Health Interview Survey until a sufficient sample size is achieved (US National Center for Health Statistics, 2009a). However, with accumulation over time, the estimates produced are period, rather than point-in-time, estimates that can be difficult to interpret when the characteristics of analytic interest vary markedly over time (Citro & Kalton, 2007). For example, how is a three-year period poverty rate for a target population of immigrants to be interpreted when the poverty rate has varied a great deal over the period?

Another way to use a large-scale survey for screening is when several surveys of different rare populations share resources to conduct the host survey. This approach is particularly appropriate when the various target populations are fairly disjoint sets since the problems raised by some sample members being eligible for more than one follow-up survey will then rarely occur. It does lead to a longer screening questionnaire, and for this reason is less attractive for mail screening. A good example of this approach is the US National Immunization Survey (NIS), which initially focused on the vaccination coverage of children aged 19 to 35 months (US National Center for Health Statistics, 2009b). The survey is conducted by a very large-scale telephone screening since few households have children in that age range. The NIS screening is now also used to identify other rare populations of interest in the State and Local Area Integrated Telephone (SLAITS) program (US National Center for Health Statistics, 2009c).

Panel surveys are sometimes considered for screening for a hard-to-sample population. Since their members remain the same across waves of data collection, panel surveys are generally not large enough for sampling hard-to-sample populations defined in terms of static characteristics, such as race/ethnicity, but they can be used for sampling persons experiencing new events, as described in Section 19.2.1 for the NCS.

Finally, a large sample can be recruited into a panel and provide data that will identify members of a variety of rare populations that may be of future interest. They are then followed in the panel and, based on their rare population memberships, included in the samples for the surveys for which they qualify. Körner and Nimmergut (2004) describe a German "access panel" that could be used in this way. There are now several web panels that recruit large samples of households for surveys on different topics over time (Callegaro & DiSogra, 2008). Some of them oversample rare populations of particular current interest, such as the Dutch immigrant panel associated with the Longitudinal Internet Studies for the Social Sciences (LISS) panel conducted by CentERdata (2013) and the US KnowledgePanel Latino, a panel of Hispanics conducted by Knowledge Networks (2013). These panels are based on probability samples and provide computers and Internet access for sampled households without them. They do, however, face severe problems with low response rates.

19.2.3 Disproportionate stratification

The efficiency of screening can be increased by concentrating the sample in segments of the population where the rare population is more prevalent. This approach is often adopted for sampling Blacks or Hispanics by oversampling geographic areas where these minorities are more concentrated. The method requires that segments of the population with greater concentrations can be identified on the survey's sampling frame so that they can be treated as strata for oversampling. The method can sometimes be readily applied, as with geographical stratification; in other cases, its application requires a good deal of ingenuity to construct the strata; and, in many cases, it is not applicable.

When applied appropriately, disproportionate stratification can improve the efficiency of the sample design for a hard-to-sample population, although the gains in efficiency are often only modest. The most common misapplication is to focus on the sample size achieved, without accounting for the unequal selection probabilities associated with the disproportionate stratification. Rather, the focus should be on the effective sample size that takes into account the loss of precision in the survey estimates arising from the unequal weights needed to compensate for the unequal selection probabilities. The focus on sample size rather than effective sample size can, for example, lead to a heavy oversampling of a stratum with high prevalence of the rare population, even though the stratum covers only a small proportion of that population. The argument is sometimes advanced that this oversampling is acceptable because the analyses will not use the weights. However, ignoring the weights for point estimates effectively turns the sample into a nonprobability sample with all the risk of bias associated with that approach.

As has been noted by many authors, if element variances and data collection costs are roughly equal across the strata and simple random samples are drawn within each stratum, disproportionate allocation significantly improves the precision of the survey estimates only when three conditions are satisfied: (1) the prevalence of the target population needs to be much higher in the oversampled strata; (2) the proportion of the target population that falls in the oversampled strata needs to be high; and (3) the per-unit cost of the survey data collection needs to be high relative to the screening cost (e.g., Kalton, 2009; Kalton & Anderson, 1986; Waksberg, 1973). Clark (2009) has extended this general approach for use with two-stage sampling and for sample designs that aim to produce estimates for the overall population and for subpopulations.

In many cases, not all of the three conditions listed above are met, and consequently the gains in precision under the optimal allocation of the sample across the strata are not large. Also, the variation in the optimal sampling fractions across the strata is not great. Moreover, the optimal allocation requires knowledge of the proportions of the members in each stratum who are in the target population, as well as the relative cost of identifying and collecting the survey data from a member of the target population to the cost of screening out a non-member. Using inaccurate estimates of these quantities reduces the precision gains, and it can even lead to a loss in precision. There are two lessons from these results. First, in most cases researchers should be disabused of any expectation that disproportionate stratification is a magic bullet. Second, if compiling the data needed to allocate the population members to the strata is costly, this approach may not be cost-effective. If the stratification costs are minimal, however, a well-designed disproportionate allocation can still be useful.

Disproportionate stratification requires that the stratification variable or variables are included on the sampling frame being used, either as part of the frame itself or appended to the frame from another source. As has been noted already, geographical stratification is often used when sampling minority populations that tend to cluster geographically. With face-to-face interviewing and area sampling, for example, census blocks or block groups can be used in forming area segments, assigning the segments to strata based on their prevalence of the target population (Waksberg, Judkins, & Massey, 1997).

Another approach for applying disproportionate stratification in sampling certain minorities is to form the strata based on last names and sometimes also first names and geographical location. With a sample drawn from a list of names, such as the Medicare beneficiaries listed on the Medicare Enrollment Database, the method involves identifying names that are likely to be from the minority under study. Based on population census data, the Census Bureau has produced lists of names that are associated with particular racial/ethnic groups that can be used for this purpose (Word & Perkins, 1996). A number of studies have used this approach (e.g., Elliott, Morrison, Fremont, McCaffrey, Pantoja, & Lurie, 2009a, and Fiscella & Fremont, 2006). Flores Cervantes and Kalton (2008) describe the use of the approach in the California Health Interview Survey, conducted by telephone, oversampling likely Korean and Vietnamese names from telephone directories. With address-based sampling, there is an initial step of adding names to the addresses using data from some other source. In this case, the accuracy of the information in that data source and its overall quality are important factors to be considered.

Another possibility with address-based sampling is to make use of ancillary data that can be added to the addresses from commercial databases. These data have the potential to then be used for disproportionate stratification, although there are serious issues about the quality of these data and the extent of missing data. DiSogra, Dennis, and Fahimi (2010) report some success with this approach, but the findings of Brock-Roth, Han, and Montaquila (2012) are less encouraging.

As Kish (1965b) has noted, units can be stratified according to ratings provided by field staff. His example involved having interviewers classify dwellings by personal judgment into high-, medium-, and low-income categories based on the buildings' exteriors; the ratings were used for oversampling the higher income strata. The subjectivity of this approach presents no threat to the validity of the sample; all that matters is how well the interviewers' judgments worked. As another example, Elliott, McCaffrey, Perlman, Marshall, and Hambarsoomians (2009b) describe a subjective stratification based on the external assessment of dwellings for sampling Cambodian immigrants in Long Beach, California.

Sometimes, the researcher has access to a partial list of the members of the rare population (see Chapter 22 for an example). If so, the list can be used in either a single or dual frame approach. With a single frame approach, the population is divided into two mutually exclusive strata, a list stratum and a residual stratum of those on the general frame who are not on the list frame. This division can be achieved by merging the list frame onto the general frame and creating a separate stratum of the list frame members for oversampling. If it is not feasible to remove all the members of the list frame from the general frame, the duplication can be removed on a sample basis by unique identification, i.e., by checking if each member sampled from the residual frame is also on the list frame and, if so, dropping the member from the sample.

When there are multiple frames and all the frames are list frames, as sometimes occurs in health studies, it may be possible to combine the frames into a single unduplicated list (Anderson & Kalton, 1990); however, this can often create difficult record linkage problems. Alternatively, the unique identification procedure can be extended to multiple partial lists by placing the lists in priority order for stratum identification: all sample members selected from the first list stratum are retained, those sampled from the second list are retained only if they were not on the first list, and so on. This approach works best when searches can be made for each sampled unit on the other frames. If a sample member has to be contacted to establish whether the sampled listing was the one that uniquely identified that person, it is often – but not always – more economical to collect the survey data regardless. In this case, the analysis must make allowance for the multiple routes of selection.

There are two general approaches for taking multiple routes of selection into account in the analysis (Kalton, 2009). One method calculates each sampled unit's overall selection probability across all the frames and uses the inverse of that probability as the base weight for the analysis (leading to the Horvitz–Thompson estimator) or the inverse of the expected number of selections (leading to the Hansen–Hurwitz estimator). In general, the application of this approach requires knowledge of each sampled unit's selection probabilities for all of the frames – information that is not always available. When selection probabilities are not known for frames other than the frame(s) from which the unit is sampled (but presence/absence on the frames is known), the weight share method can be used (see Chapter 21 in this volume).

The second general approach for dealing with multiple routes of selection uses the multiple frame methodology introduced by Hartley (1974). The sample is partitioned into subsets according to which combination of frames could have led to the sample members' selection. Then, for each subset, estimates are produced for the samples obtained from each frame, and a weighted sum of these estimates is used for the subset. The overall estimate is then the sum of the subset estimates. The multiple frame methodology has been the subject of much recent research, which is beyond the scope of this chapter. See Lohr (2009) for a review.

19.3   Location sampling

There are many hard-to-sample populations for which the probability sampling procedures described in Section 19.2 are, for one reason or another, not suitable. Location sampling, also known as venue-based sampling, time-space sampling, center sampling, and intercept sampling, is an important additional technique for some of these populations. Many applications of location sampling use nonprobability designs, but the technique can be structured in an attempt to satisfy the requirements of probability sampling.

In essence, location sampling is sampling visitors to specified locations. The technique is widely used for two different purposes. One is to sample the population of *visits* and the other is to sample the population of *visitors* to the locations (Kalton, 1991). In many applications, sampling visits is relatively straightforward. Sampling visitors is an extension of sampling visits that is far more challenging: it requires assessing the extent of coverage of the target population provided by visitors and also accounting for the multiple routes of selection for visitors who visit the locations more than once during the period of data collection.

19.3.1 Sampling visits

There are several applications where the visit can be viewed as the appropriate unit of analysis: mall intercept surveys where samples of shoppers are selected to find out about their purchases; visits to museums; visits to national parks; and international travelers (Kalton, 1991). Other examples include the two ambulatory health care surveys conducted by the US National Center for Health Statistics (2012). In all these cases, visitors making multiple visits have greater chances of selection for the sample but, with the visit as the unit of analysis, no weighting adjustment is made for multiple visits.

The first step in developing a probability sample of visits is to define the target population. This definition requires the determination of the locations (e.g., all international airports, border points, and seaports; all entrances to, or exits from, the museum) and the overall time period. Then, within the overall time period, the time intervals during which each of the locations is operating are determined. In general, the basic sampling frame can then be set out in a two-way table of locations × time intervals. A cell of this table is inapplicable when a location is not in operation in that time interval.

Given this structure, the sampling design involves selecting a sample of clusters (the location × time interval combinations) and then selecting visits within each sampled cluster. In many applications of location sampling, at least one of these two stages of sampling is treated rather loosely, and even with nonprobability selections. However, the selection of a statistically valid and efficient sample requires that careful attention be paid to each stage of this design. In general, a location probability sample design for visits can simply draw on the methods developed for other two-stage sample designs. For example, as is commonly done in other types of two-stage sampling, the location × time interval clusters can be sampled with probabilities proportional to their estimated numbers of visits (PPES), and visits can be sampled with equal probability within each selected cluster. Similarly, the clusters can be stratified before selection. In this case, in addition to the usual types of stratification factors, stratification by time is generally important for providing balance across the time period that defines the target population. Kalton (1991) provides more details.

The choice of a probability sample design for the visits within selected clusters is heavily dependent on the circumstances relating to the mode and other aspects of data collection. Sometimes, the visitors are a captive population for a period of time, as when they are international passengers to be surveyed on planes or ships. In such cases, the sample can be selected from the passenger roster, and those selected can be asked to complete the data collection during their flight or voyage. The main challenge here is to achieve a high response rate from those sampled.

In most other cases, the sample design involves sampling visitors as they flow into or out of the location. Sometimes, this design may not be difficult to implement, as, for example, with hospital discharges with data obtained from medical records. However, when the survey data are to be collected from the sampled visitors at the time of sampling, difficulties often arise in gaining cooperation because of the reluctance of persons in transit to be delayed in order to respond to the survey. Sampling entrants is often preferable to sampling leavers in this respect. However, for surveys of visits (as distinct from visitors), the data sought generally include reports of experiences from the visit. These experiences could be collected later by mail or telephone, but costs increase and response rates are affected.

Systematic sampling is commonly used for sampling entrants or leavers. If the clusters are sampled using PPES, and the estimated numbers of visits are predicted well, the numbers of visits sampled will be roughly equal in all of the sampled clusters, which produces an equal probability sample overall and is often helpful for the field work operations. A field work team may then comprise a counter, who applies the systematic sampling to the flow and identifies the sampled visitors, and a number of interviewers who conduct the interviews. This structure can work well if the measures of size are reasonably accurate and the flow is an even one. However, problems can arise in failing to have enough interviewers available when the visitors arrive or depart in large groups.

Instead of sampling visitors on entry or departure from the sampled locations, sometimes the samples are drawn from visitors present at the sampled locations at various points of time, for example, in sampled hospitals on sampled days. The resultant sample of those present overrepresents the visits of visitors who spend longer times at the location, termed length biased sampling (e.g., Cox, 1969). Fluss, Mandel, Freedman, Weiss, Zohar, Haklai *et al.*, 2013), provide an example of this issue in a national survey of postsurgical complications in Israel where the sample of patients was drawn from those present in the general surgery units of all major hospitals on particular days. They describe the weights they used to adjust for the length biased sampling. Without an adjustment, the estimates produced would overstate the extent of complications, because those with complications have longer hospital stays and hence greater selection probabilities.

19.3.2 Sampling visitors

Location sampling has been used to sample a variety of hard-to-sample populations. The general requirement is that a set of locations can be identified such that a high proportion of the target population will visit one or more of these locations during the data collection period. While the general designs for sampling visitors are based on designs for sampling visits, there are two important differences. One is that whereas the population of locations for sampling visits can be reasonably easily identified, the construction of a population of locations for sampling visitors often requires a good deal of creativity.

The second difference is that with the visitor as the unit of analysis, the fact that visitors may make multiple visits during the given time period must be taken into account (Kalsbeek, 2003; Kalton, 1991; Sudman & Kalton, 1986). The multiple visits may be any combination of repeat visits to the same location and visits to any other locations on the sampling frame during the survey period. The concern here is not that members of the target population are actually sampled more than once but rather that they have multiple chances of selection. At the design stage, the objective is to create a combination of the most parsimonious list and the shortest time interval that has high coverage since that will help to control the multiple chances of selection. Thus, in constructing the list of locations, it is preferable to drop from the list locations that do not improve the coverage provided by other locations on the list.

One approach for handling the multiplicity problem is to treat visits as eligible only if they are the first visits to any of the locations on the frame during the survey period. All subsequent visits are treated as ineligible. This clean solution to the problem is being used, for example, in a feasibility study for the National Children's Study, sampling pregnant women at their first visit to any of the prenatal care providers on the sampling frame. To provide almost universal coverage, women who have not had prenatal care and women whose prenatal care provider was not on the provider sampling frame are sampled at birthing hospitals (Hubble & Brenner, 2012).

While this approach of uniquely identifying visitors by their first visits can sometimes work well, in many cases it leads to uneconomic data collection later in the survey period when only a small proportion of the visitors are making their first visits. If all sampled visitors are treated as eligible for data collection at any visit, multiplicity adjustments need to be made to the weights in the analysis using, for example, the weight share method (see

Chapter 21). However, determining the number of visits made can be difficult for two main reasons: first, some visits will occur after the sampled visit, and, second, respondents have to be asked about all visits to any location on the frame. In many cases, it is not practical to present all these locations to the respondents and instead some general description of the frame has to be used. That general description, along with memory errors, can lead to significant response errors. In this situation, the best that can be hoped for is that respondents can provide some general indications of their visit frequencies. The resultant multiplicity weights may serve adequately for estimating means and proportions of the target population with certain characteristics but are problematic for estimating target population totals and subtotals.

Location sampling is widely used to sample populations that have no fixed abode for both censuses and surveys: homeless persons may be sampled at shelters and at soup kitchens when they go for food (e.g., Ardilly & Le Blanc, 2001; Kalton, 1993a). One way for sampling nomads is to sample them at watering points when they take their animals for water (e.g., Kalsbeek & Cross, 1982; Kalton, 1993a). Conducting the survey during the dry season minimizes the number of active watering points, and the time period can be chosen to account for the watering needs of the nomads' animals (e.g., camels need watering much less often than cattle).

Location sampling has also been used for sampling a variety of rare – often very rare – populations that tend to congregate in certain places. In Italy, location sampling has been used to sample legal and illegal immigrants (Meccati, 2004). For a 2002 survey of the immigrant population of Milan, 13 types of centers were identified, ranging from centers that provide partial lists from administrative sources (e.g., legal and work centers, language courses), centers that have counts of those attending (e.g., welfare service centers, cultural associations), to centers with no frame information (e.g., malls, ethnic shops).

Location sampling has often been used to sample men who have sex with men, with the locations being such venues as gay bars, bath houses, and bookstores (Kalton, 1993b; MacKellar, Valleroy, Karon, Lemp, & Janssen, 1996; US Centers for Disease Control and Prevention, 2012). Based on a cross-sectional telephone survey, Xia, Tholandi, Osmond, Pollack, Zhou, Ruiz, and Catania (2006) found that men who visited gay venues more frequently had higher rates of high-risk sexual behaviors and also that the rates of high-risk behaviors varied by venue. These findings draw attention to the need to adjust for the multiple routes of selection in the analysis and, more generally, the difficulty of producing a representative sample of the target population by location sampling.

McKenzie and Mistiaen (2009) carried out an experiment to compare location (intercept) sampling with both area sampling and snowball techniques for sampling Brazilians of Japanese descent (Nikkei) in São Paulo and Paraná. The locations included places where the Nikkei often went (e.g., a sports club, a metro station, grocery stores, and a Japanese cultural club) and events (e.g., a Japanese film and a Japanese food festival). Based on this experiment, they conclude that location sampling (and snowball sampling) oversampled persons more closely connected with the Nikkei community and thus did not produce representative samples. This not-unexpected finding highlights the concern about using location sampling for sampling rare populations in general, although not for sampling visits to specified sites.

19.4 Concluding remarks

Noncoverage and nonresponse make virtually all probability samples of human populations imperfect to some degree. This observation applies particularly forcibly to samples of hard-to-sample populations. When screening is required, some false negatives will occur and add to other sources of noncoverage. Location samples fail to cover members of the hard-to-sample population who do not visit one of the locations in the given time period. In both cases, these sources of noncoverage may well lead to biased survey estimates for the ideal population of interest. Nonresponse is equally of special concern for hard-to-sample populations for several reasons. One is that some of these populations are "hidden" populations, many of whose members will not want to participate in surveys about their populations. Also, as noted earlier, screening adds an extra opportunity for nonresponse, and conducting interviews in a location where the sample person is engaged in other activities is challenging. These concerns need to be addressed in constructing the survey design.

Given the extremely high cost of obtaining a probability sample of many hard-to-sample populations, it is not surprising that many studies of these populations use nonrandom, or not strictly random, sampling methods. Using such methods leads to questions about the validity of the survey's findings for the target population of inference. Underpinning each of the findings is an implicit model about the selection process, and assessing the validity of the findings requires an evaluation of the applicability of that model for each finding. For example, consider the analysis of responses obtained to a request to respond to a web survey, posted at various websites. A model that assumes that the respondents represent an equal probability sample of the US population is clearly false. However, how should one assess the findings when the sample is post-stratified to account for known differences between web respondents and the general population (for example by age, race, and education)? For a given finding, is it reasonable to regard the estimate from the respondents within each post-stratum as approximately unbiased for the population value in that post-stratum? This would be the case if the respondents were an equal probability sample within each post-stratum, but it could also hold under a less stringent model.

Snowball sampling (also known as chain-referral sampling) has a long history for sampling hard-to-sample populations whose members know each other. It has, for example often been used for compiling samples of hidden populations such as injection drug users and sex workers. The model assumptions underlying any attempt to generalize the results of a study using this nonprobability sampling method are highly questionable, and much has been written about the limitations of the standard snowballing approach. A number of years ago, Heckathorn (1997) introduced a modified form of snowball sampling known as respondent-driven sampling (RDS), and he and his colleagues have explicated a set of assumptions under which RDS produces unbiased estimates (e.g., Salganik & Heckathorn, 2004; see also Gile & Handcock, 2010). Since RDS depends on these model assumptions, it does not fit within the design-based mode of inference. A number of researchers have examined how failures in these assumptions can affect the study estimates and have developed approaches for testing the validity of these assumptions. The results from an RDS study should be critically assessed with regard to the likely magnitude of the departures from the assumptions and on how these departures might affect the study findings.

There is one application of snowballing that does fit within the design-based inferential framework. With this application, the snowballing process is continued until no new members of the target population are discovered. If the frame constructed in this manner can be confidently judged to have high coverage, then a probability sample of those on the frame can be selected and design-based inference can be applied. However, if the frame coverage is questionable, then it becomes necessary to consider methods based on social network analyses (see, for example, Silva, Klinger, & Weikart, 2010).

Another form of sampling that is sometimes used for hard-to-sample populations is fashioned on probability sampling but avoids some of the requirements of a full probability sample design. The World Health Organization's Expanded Program on Immunization (EPI) rapid assessment surveys, which have been conducted thousands of times in developing countries around the world, aim to estimate the immunization coverage of children in a given area. The standard design involves a probability sample of 30 clusters and 7 children in each selected cluster. The clusters are selected with probabilities proportional to estimated sizes, not actual sizes, but no weighting adjustment is made to account for the difference between the two. Within the cluster (e.g., a village), the interviewer selects a "random" household to start the process, and then proceeds to take the next closest household, and so on until 7 eligible children have been selected. This design avoids the costs of the listing process that would otherwise be used to select a probability sample of households and children, but it can lead to biased estimates, as noted by a number of reviewers, with various modifications being proposed (see, for example, Bennett, 1993, and Turner, Magnani, & Shuaib, 1996).

As noted at the outset, the use of probability sampling provides the security of the design-based mode of inference (subject to the important limitations arising from imperfect implementation). Nonprobability sampling lacks this property. Instead, researchers have to make subjective judgments about the possible biases in the study estimates. One nonprobability design may appear superior to others in a particular case, but there is unfortunately no objective metric for making the choice of a nonprobability design, or indeed for making the choice between a nonprobability sample and a probability sample with serious imperfections, such as one with an extremely low response rate (thus itself depending heavily on model assumptions). Of course, costs need to be taken into account. Also, the uses of the survey data need to be considered: are the results obtained from the survey fit for the purpose for which they are to be used? These are challenging questions with no easy answers.

References

Anderson, D. W., & Kalton, G. (1990). Case-finding strategies for studying rare chronic diseases. *Statistica Applicata*, 2, 309–21.

Ardilly, P., & Le Blanc, D. (2001). Sampling and weighting a survey of homeless persons: a French example. *Survey Methodology*, 27, 109–18.

Bennett, S. (1993). Cluster sampling to assess immunization: a critical appraisal. *Bulletin of the International Statistical Institute, 49th Session*, 55(2), 21–35.

Bolling, K., Grant, C., & Sinclair, P. (2008). *2006–07 British Crime Survey (England and Wales). Technical Report. Volume 1*. London: TNS BMRB. Retrieved from www. homeoffice.gov.uk/rds/pdfs07/bcs0607tech1.pdf.

Brock-Roth, S., Han, D., & Montaquila, J. M. (2012). The ABS frame: quality and considerations. In *Joint Statistical Meetings Proceedings, Survey Research Methods Section* [pp. 3779–93]. Alexandria, VA: American Statistical Association.

Callegaro, M., & DiSogra, C. (2008). Computing response metrics for online panels. *Public Opinion Quarterly*, 72, 1008–32.

Camburn, D. P., & Wright, R. A. (1996). *Predicting Eligibility Rates for Rare Populations in RDD Screening Surveys*. Paper presented at the American Association for Public Opinion Research Conference, Salt Lake City, UT. Retrieved from www.cdc.gov/nis/pdfs/sample_design/camburn1996.pdf.

CentERdata (2013). Longitudinal Internet Studies for the Social Sciences (LISS) panel. Retrieved from www.lissdata.nl/lissdata/About_the_Panel/General.

Christman, M. C. (2009). Sampling of rare populations. In D. Pfeffermann & C. R. Rao (eds.), *Handbook of Statistics (Vol. 29A). Sample Surveys: Design, Methods and Applications* (pp. 109–24). Amsterdam: Elsevier.

Citro, C. F., & Kalton, G. (eds.) (2007). *Using the American Community Survey: Benefits and Challenges*. Washington, DC: National Academies Press.

Clark, R. G. (2009). Sampling of subpopulations in two-stage surveys. *Statistics in Medicine*, 28, 3697–717.

Cohen, S. B., DiGaetano, R., & Waksberg, J. (1988). Sample design of the NMES Survey of American Indians and Alaska Natives. In *Joint Statistical Meetings Proceedings, Survey Research Methods Section* (pp. 740–45). Alexandria, VA: American Statistical Association.

Cox, D. R. (1969). Some sampling problems in technology. In N. L. Johnson & H. Smith Jr. (eds.), *New Developments in Survey Sampling* (pp. 506–27). New York: John Wiley & Sons.

Deming, W. E. (1977). An essay on screening, or on two-phase sampling, applied to surveys of a community. *International Statistical Review*, 45, 29–37.

DiSogra, C., Dennis, J. M., & Fahimi, M. (2010). On the quality of ancilliary data available for address-based sampling. In *Joint Statistical Meetings Proceedings, Survey Research Methods Section* (pp. 4174–83). Alexandria, VA: American Statistical Association.

Elliott, M. N., Finch, B. K., Klein, D., Ma, S., Do, D. P., Beckett, M. K., *et al.* (2008). Sample designs for measuring the health of small racial/ethnic subgroups. *Statistics in Medicine*, 27, 4016–29.

Elliott, M. N., McCaffrey, D., Perlman, J., Marshall, G. N., & Hambarsoomians, K. (2009b). Use of expert ratings as sampling strata for a more cost-effective probability sample of a rare population. *Public Opinion Quarterly*, 73, 56–73.

Elliott, M. N., Morrison, P. A., Fremont, A., McCaffrey, D. F., Pantoja, P., & Lurie, N. (2009a). Using the Census Bureau's surname list to improve estimates of race/ethnicity and associated disparities. *Health Services Outcomes Research Methods*, 9, 69–83.

Fecso, R. S., Baskin, R., Chu, A., Gray, C., Kalton, G., & Phelps, R. (2007). *Design Options for SESTAT for the Current Decade: Statistical Issues.* Working Paper SRS 07–201. Arlington, VA: National Science Foundation, Division of Science Resources Statistics.

Fiscella, K., & Fremont, A. M. (2006). Use of geocoding and surname analysis to estimate race and ethnicity. *Health Services Research*, 41, 1482–500.

Flores Cervantes, I., & Kalton, G. (2008). Methods for sampling rare populations in telephone surveys. In J. M. Lepkowski, C. Tucker, J. M. Brick, E. D. de Leeuw, L. Japec, P. Lavrakas *et al.* (eds.), *Advances in Telephone Survey Methodology* (pp. 113–32). Hoboken, NJ: John Wiley & Sons.

Fluss, R., Mandel, M., Freedman, L. S., Weiss, I. S., Zohar, A. E., Haklai, Z., *et al.* (2013). Correcting of sampling bias in a cross-sectional study of post-surgical complications. [Published online September 4, 2012]. *Statistics in Medicine*, 32, 2467–78.

Gile, K. J., & Handcock, M. S. (2010). Respondent-driven sampling: an assessment of current methodology. *Sociological Methodology*, 40, 285–327.

Gonzalez, J. F., Ezzati, T. M., White, A. A., Massey, J. T., Lago, J., & Waksberg, J. (1985). Sample design and estimation procedures. In K. R. Maurer (ed.), *Plan and Operation of the Hispanic Health and Nutrition Examination Survey, 1982–84* (pp. 23–32). Vital and Health Statistics 1(19). Washington, DC: US Government Printing Office.

Haerer, A. F., Anderson, D. W., & Schoenberg, B. S. (1986). Prevalence and clinical features of epilepsy in a biracial United States population. *Epilepsia*, 27, 66–75.

Hartley, H. O. (1974). Multiple frame methodology and selected applications. *Sankhyā*, 36, 99–118.

Heckathorn, D. D. (1997). Respondent driven sampling: a new approach to the study of hidden populations. *Social Problems*, 44, 174–99.

Horrigan, M., Moore, W., Pedlow, S., & Wolter, K. (1999). Undercoverage in a large national screening survey for youths. In *Joint Statistical Meetings Proceedings, Survey Research Methods Section* (pp. 570–75). Alexandria, VA: American Statistical Association.

Hubble, D. L. & Brenner, R. A. (2012). Sample design issues in the National Children's Study. In *Joint Statistical Meetings Proceedings, Survey Research Methods Section* [CD-ROM]. Alexandria, VA: American Statistical Association.

Judkins, D., DiGaetano, R., Chu, A., & Shapiro, G. (1999). Coverage in screening surveys at Westat. In *Joint Statistical Meetings Proceedings, Survey Research Methods Section* (pp. 581–86). Alexandria, VA: American Statistical Association.

Kalsbeek, W. D. (2003). Sampling minority groups in health surveys. *Statistics in Medicine*, 22, 1527–49.

Kalsbeek, W. D., & Cross, A. R. (1982). Problems in sampling nomadic populations. In *Joint Statistical Meetings Proceedings, Survey Research Methods Section* (pp. 398–402). Alexandria, VA: American Statistical Association.

Kalton, G. (1991). Sampling flows of mobile populations. *Survey Methodology*, 17, 183–94.

(1993a). *Sampling Rare and Elusive Populations*. New York: Department for Economic and Social Information and Policy Analysis, United Nations.

(1993b). Sampling considerations in research on HIV risk and illness. In D. G. Ostrow & R. C. Kessler (eds.), *Methodological Issues in AIDS Behavioral Research* (pp. 53–74). New York: Plenum Press.

(2003). Practical methods for sampling rare and mobile populations. *Statistics in Transition*, 6, 491–501.

(2009). Methods for oversampling rare subpopulations in social surveys. *Survey Methodology*, 35, 125–41.

Kalton, G., & Anderson, D. W. (1986). Sampling rare populations. *Journal of the Royal Statistical Society: Series A (General)*, 149, 65–82.

Kish, L. (1965a). Selection techniques for rare traits. In J. V. Neel, M. W. Shaw, & W. J. Schull (eds.), *Genetics and the Epidemiology of Chronic Diseases*. Public Health Service Publication No. 1163. Washington, DC: US Government Printing Office.

(1965b). *Survey sampling*. New York: John Wiley & Sons.

(1991). Taxonomy of elusive populations. *Journal of Official Statistics*, 7, 339–47.

(1999). Cumulating/combining population surveys. *Survey Methodology*, 25, 129–38.

Knowledge Networks. (2013). KnowledgePanel Latino. Retrieved from www.knowledge-networks.com/resources/kp-latino.html.

Körner, T., & Nimmergut, A. (2004). Using an access panel as a sampling frame for voluntary household surveys. *Statistical Journal of the United Nations Economic Commission for Europe*, 21, 33–52.

Langa, K. M., Plassman, B. L., Wallace, R. B., Herzog, A. R., Heeringa, S. G., Ofstedal, M. B., *et al.* (2005). The Aging, Demographics, and Memory Study: study design and methods. *Neuroepidemiology*, 25, 181–91.

Lohr, S. L. (2009). Multiple-frame surveys. In D. Pfeffermann & C. R. Rao (eds.), *Handbook of Statistics (Vol. 29A). Sample Surveys: Design, Methods, and Applications* (pp. 71–88). Amsterdam: Elsevier.

MacKellar, D., Valleroy, L., Karon, J., Lemp, G., & Janssen, R. (1996). The Young Men's Survey: methods for estimating HIV seroprevalence and risk factors among young men who have sex with men. *Public Health Reports*, 111(Suppl. 1), 138–44.

McKenzie, D. J., & Mistiaen, J. (2009). Surveying migrant households: a comparison of census-based, snowball and intercept point surveys. *Journal of the Royal Statistical Society: Series A (Statistics in Society)*, 172, 339–60.

Meccati, F. (2004). Center sampling: a strategy for sampling difficult-to-sample populations. In *Proceedings of Statistics Canada Symposium: Innovative Methods for Surveying Difficult-to Reach Populations*. Retrieved from http://www.statcan.gc.ca/pub/11–522-x/2004001/8740-eng.pdf.

Montaquila, J. M., Brick, J. M., & Curtin, L. R. (2010). Statistical and practical issues in the design of a national probability sample of births for the Vanguard Study of the National Children's Study. *Statistics in Medicine*, 29, 1368–76.

Rothbart, G. S., Fine, M., & Sudman, S. (1982). On finding and interviewing the needles in the haystack: the use of multiplicity sampling. *Public Opinion Quarterly*, 46, 408–21.

Salganik, M. J., & Heckathorn, D. D. (2004). Sampling and estimation in hidden populations using respondent-driven sampling. *Sociological Methodology*, 34, 193–239.

Silva, R., Klinger, J., & Weikart, S. (2010). Measuring lethal counterinsurgency violence in Amritsar District, India using a referral-based sampling technique. In *Joint Statistical Meetings Proceedings, Survey Research Methods Section* (pp. 552–80). Alexandria, VA: American Statistical Association.

Sirken, M. G. (2004). Network sample surveys of rare and elusive populations: a historical review. In *Proceedings of Statistics Canada Symposium: Innovative Methods for Surveying Difficult-to Reach Populations*. Available from www5.statcan.gc.ca/bsolc/olc-cel/olc-cel?catno=11–522-X20040018614&lang=eng.

(2005). Network sampling developments in survey research during the past 40+ years. *Survey Research*, 36 (1), 1–5. Retrieved from www.srl.uic.edu/Publist/Newsletter/pastissues.htm.

Sudman, S., & Freeman, H. E. (1988). The use of network sampling for locating the seriously ill. *Medical Care*, 26, 992–99.

Sudman, S., & Kalton, G. (1986). New developments in the sampling of special populations. *Annual Review of Sociology*, 12, 401–29.

Sudman, S., Sirken, M. G., & Cowan, C. D. (1988). Sampling rare and elusive populations. *Science*, 240, 991–96.

Tourangeau, R., Kreuter, F., & Eckman, S. (2012). Motivated underreporting in screening interviews. *Public Opinion Quarterly*, 76, 453–69.

Turner, A. G., Magnani, R. J., & Shuaib, M. (1996). A not quite as quick but much cleaner alternative to the Expanded Programme on Immunization (EPI) cluster survey design. *International Journal of Epidemiology*, 25, 198–203.

US Centers for Disease Control and Prevention. (2012). *National HIV Behavioral Surveillance (NHBS)*. Retrieved from www.cdc.gov/hiv/bcsb/nhbs/index.htm.

US National Center for Health Statistics. (2009a). *National Health Interview Survey (NHIS)*. Retrieved from www.cdc.gov/nchs/nhis/methods.htm.

(2009b). *The National Immunization Survey (NIS)*. Retrieved from www.cdc.gov/nis/about_eng.htm.

(2009c). *State and Local Area Integrated Telephone Survey (SLAITS)*. Retrieved from www.cdc.gov/nchs/about/major/slaits/nsch.htm.

(2012). *About the Ambulatory Health Care Surveys*. Retrieved from www.cdc.gov/nchs/ahcd/about_ahcd.htm.

Waksberg, J. (1973). The effect of stratification with differential sampling rates on attributes of subsets of the population. In *Joint Statistical Meetings Proceedings, Social Statistics Section* (pp. 429–34). Alexandria, VA: American Statistical Association.

Waksberg, J., Judkins, D., & Massey, J. T. (1997). Geographic-based oversampling in demographic surveys of the United States. *Survey Methodology*, 23, 61–71.

Word, D. L., & Perkins, R. C. (1996). *Building a Spanish Surname List for the 1990s – A New Approach to an Old Problem*. Population Division Technical Working Paper No. 13. Washington, DC: US Census Bureau.

Xia, Q., Tholandi, M., Osmond, D. H., Pollack, L. M., Zhou, W., Ruiz, J. D., & Catania, J. A. (2006). The effect of venue sampling on estimates of HIV prevalence and sexual risk behaviors in men who have sex with men. *Sexually Transmitted Diseases*, 33, 545–50.

20

Recent developments of sampling hard-to-survey populations: an assessment

SUNGHEE LEE, JAMES WAGNER, RICHARD VALLIANT, AND STEVE HEERINGA

20.1 Introduction

While there are difficulties in precisely defining hard-to-survey (H2S), hard-to-find, rare, hidden, or elusive populations (see Chapter 1 for a discussion of definitions), there is general agreement that it is very difficult to locate certain population subgroups. Studying such groups using cross-sectional surveys of the general population is challenging, because sample sizes are often too small to provide reasonable precision for point estimates and statistical power for comparisons. If the H2S groups are the target population of a study, sampling of their members becomes an issue.

Sampling for scientific data collection with these H2S populations is one of the most notable challenges discussed in the sampling literature (e.g., Kalton, 2009; Sudman, Sirken, & Cowan, 1988). Some studies mistakenly argue that frames do not exist for these populations (e.g., Paquette & de Wit, 2010). It is true that there are no readily available sampling frames exclusively of these population members. However, it is technically possible to sample from the general population and screen for the target population members. This type of screening presents two challenges. First, building a sampling frame for such H2S populations is costly. Assume that a study has HIV positive cigarette smokers as its target population, as in Humfleet, Delucchi, Kelley, Hall, Dilley, and Harrison (2009). A large number of households sampled from the general population need to be screened to find enough people who meet the criteria of both being HIV positive and smoking cigarettes. Second, depending on the level of social stigma and discrimination associated with the H2S population of interest, some population members may misreport their eligibility intentionally in the screening interviews in order not to reveal their identity. HIV positive cigarette smokers are associated with socially stigmatized HIV status as well as the socially undesirable status of being a smoker. For these reasons, traditional probability sampling approaches, although ideal, are often regarded as being infeasible and impractical. Although expensive to conduct, there are many studies of H2S populations using probability samples (see Table 15.1 of Binson, Blair, Huebner, & Woods, 2007). Examples include the use of multistage area probability samples and random digit dialed (RDD) telephone samples (e.g., Catania, Osmond, Stall, Pollack, Paul, Blower et al., 2001; Cochran & Mays, 2000).

Sampling statistics as a field has yet to provide practical solutions that yield samples with desirable properties of unbiasedness and efficiency for targeting H2S populations. Meanwhile, the demands for data on these populations outgrew what sampling statistics had offered and have stimulated methodological developments. It appears that academic fields other than sampling statistics have led these developments. Public health, in particular, has used various sampling methods for H2S populations including, but not limited to, venue-based sampling, time-location sampling, web-based sampling, and respondent-driven sampling.

This chapter attempts to complement the other chapters in this volume by providing an overview of venue-based, time-location, and web-based sampling methods. In Section 20.2, we discuss a conceptual mismatch between the sampling and nonsampling literature on the nature of sampling. Section 20.2.1 discusses the importance of understanding sampling methods from the total survey error framework. We introduce venue-based, time-location, and web-based sampling methods with their background and assumptions in Section 20.3. We also examine implementation issues in several published studies. Section 20.4 summarizes the benefits and limitations of these methods from the total survey error perspective.

20.2   Conceptual mismatch between sampling and nonsampling literatures

The discussion of probability versus nonprobability sampling is important for understanding the bias and variance properties of sample survey estimators. Sampling theory contains two general approaches to making inference from samples selected from a finite population. One is the design-based approach, in which a probability sample must be selected from the population and properties of estimators are calculated with respect to the distribution generated by repeated sampling. This is the approach taken in texts like Cochran (1977), Hansen, Hurwitz, and Madow (1953), and Särndal, Swensson, and Wretman (1992). The other approach is model based, in which a superpopulation model that approximately describes the distribution of an analysis variable is used for inference (Valliant, Dorfman, & Royall, 2000). Both of these approaches provide theoretical conditions for the consistency or unbiasedness of estimators made from samples and for inference to a target population from these samples. In the design-based approach, a probability sample is required; in the model-based approach, a probability sample may be selected but inference can also be made from nonprobability samples if a realistic superpopulation model can be identified.

Probability samples are preferred by most practitioners – in part because the survey designer cannot be accused of consciously or unconsciously injecting his/her biases into the way that the sample is selected, and, in part, because inferences can be made without resorting to models. Of course, selecting a probability sample does not guarantee that any particular sample will yield good estimates for a rare subgroup. When a separate frame is not available for the rare population, and a sample from the general population must be selected, the sample may contain few, if any, rare cases. The long-run property of design-unbiasedness is of little comfort in that case. On the other hand, a probability sample that is large enough to identify an adequate number of H2S cases for analysis may be so expensive that it is not feasible. The methods described in Part IV of this collection attempt to work around these inefficiencies.

Once we move to the nonsampling literature, the classification of sampling methods appears to be misunderstood. Central to this confusion is the term "representative sampling" or "representative sample." This term is not new to the sampling literature and it caused some controversy a few decades ago in statistics. As Kruskal and Mosteller have noted (1979a; 1979b; 1979c), there had been no clear definition of "representative" universally accepted in the scientific literature, reflecting Neyman (1934) and Stephan and McCarthy (1958). Kish (2003) also added that representative sampling had been used to indicate random sampling at one time, proportionate sampling at another time, and purposive sampling yet at other times. In some articles, the conceptually vague term, "representative sample," means one that permits good estimation but only for specific analyses for a specified set of variables and cannot be equated with either unbiasedness or good inference properties for all variables and all analyses (Binson *et al.*, 2007, and Stoop, 2005). Kish (2003) stated, "In my view, representative sampling is a term that can be avoided and it is disappearing from the technical vocabulary."

While the sampling literature moved away from using "representative" to categorize sampling methods, it is frequently found outside of the sampling literature, where it is used as though "representative" meant providing results representing the target population across all variables and analyses (e.g., Remafedi, 2002). Some even classify sampling into three categories: probability, nonprobability, and representative sampling (Semaan, Lauby, & Liebman, 2002). This type of categorization can be misleading because these categories are not mutually exclusive. All types of probability samples are "representative" in the sense of permitting estimators to be constructed that are unbiased in repeated sampling. Some nonprobability samples may allow model-unbiased estimators to be formed for some quantities, and, in that sense, can also be considered as representative samples. Given the vague nature of the term, "representative sample," it may be advisable to stay away from using it or to define it clearly if it must be used. A probability sample, on the other hand, satisfies the following four, specific conditions (Särndal *et al.*, 1992):

(1) A set of samples can be defined that are possible to obtain with the sampling procedure.
(2) Each possible sample has a known probability of selection.
(3) Every element in the target population has a non-zero probability of selection.
(4) One set of sample elements is selected with the probability associated with the set. Weights for sample units can be computed that are intended to project the sample to the target population.

In this chapter, sampling methods that violate one or more of these conditions are considered as nonprobability samples.

20.2.1 Sampling and total survey error

Sampling literature often discusses error properties using terms such as sampling error and nonsampling error. Sampling error for probability samples concerns sampling variance (not sampling bias) because they are to produce unbiased or approximately unbiased estimators. Nonprobability samples, on the other hand, are subject to both sampling bias and variance. Under the total survey error framework, nonsampling error is further classified into coverage, nonresponse, and measurement errors (Groves, 1989). Recently, there has been an increasing amount of criticism of probability sampling. RDD sampling has been a frequent target of this criticism due to its decreasing response rates and a sharp drop in landline telephone coverage. These threats to probability samples come from nonsampling errors. Similarly, nonprobability samples are not free from these nonsampling errors.

A prerequisite for sampling is a clear definition of the target population. As Meyer and Wilson (2009) pointed out, it is even more important for H2S population studies, because the definitions can be elusive. For instance, sexual minorities can be defined differently when based on sexual identity rather than sexual behavior or attraction (Sell, 2007). The overlap among these three definitions is estimated to be only around 20 percent, and these traits change over time (Laumann, Gagnon, Michael, & Michaels, 1994).

While the target population needs be defined precisely in relation to the research interest, it is not uncommon to see various definitions for the same type of H2S populations. For instance, Table 1 of Paquette and de Wit (2010) shows a range of definitions for "men who have sex with men" (MSM) used in surveillance systems around the world. It can be as vague as "men having sex with another man" for the German surveillance system and as specific as "men having oral, anal or petting with another man in the previous 6 months, between ages of 15 to 49 years old and residents of target towns for the previous 6 months or more" for the Serbian system. Injection drug user (IDU) studies reviewed in Table 2 of Malekinejad, Johnston, Kendall, Kerr, Rifkin, and Rutherford (2008) also show various definitions of IDUs. In some extreme cases, the definition of the target population is entirely left up to study participants (e.g., Heckathorn & Jeffri, 2003). The specificity of the target population definition may affect the level of coverage error.

Nonresponse is also an issue. For nonprobability samples, it is often the case that even calculating response rates is a difficult, if not impossible, task. While the set of respondents is known, counts of nonrespondents may not be known. More importantly, nonresponse may follow systematic patterns because of the sensitive nature of some of the H2S populations and the study content. This means that nonresponse in these studies is unlikely to occur at random. There are at least two ways in which nonresponse in H2S population studies may be nonignorable. First, some members of the rare group may be unwilling to admit their identity during screening. Second, among those that do cooperate, some persons may refuse to answer specific questions about their characteristics. For example, some IDUs may admit to being IDUs but refuse to respond to HIV-related questions. For probability samples of the general population, there have been numerous studies to evaluate nonresponse error. A common set of characteristics associated with nonresponse in many surveys (e.g., gender, age, race/ethnicity, education) is often used to correct for potential nonresponse biases. Unfortunately, this is not true for recently developed sampling methods. Without information about nonrespondents, it is impossible to estimate the extent of any nonresponse bias and to make any corrections for it.

Many of the new sampling approaches for H2S populations rely on formative research conducted during the development of the actual sampling plan. The data for formative research usually comes from informants knowledgeable about the target H2S population. The selection of informants and the validity of information given by them opens the door for measurement error. Because the formative research data are used to design practical sampling procedures, this measurement error directly influences sampling error.

20.2.2 Recent developments for H2S population sampling

Recently, a series of new sampling methods has been proposed. Chapters 23 and Chapter 24 in this volume review network-based sampling, including respondent-driven sampling. In this chapter, we introduce venue-based, time-location, and web-based sampling methods. We include their background, common usage, and error properties. For each method, we also examine published actual applications.

20.3   Venue-based, time-location, and web-based sampling

20.3.1 Venue-based sampling

When H2S populations gather at certain identifiable venues, one may consider using venue-based sampling. As the term suggests, venue-based sampling involves sampling sites where the H2S group is likely to be found. Other terms that are sometimes used interchangeably with venue-based sampling include facility-based sampling (e.g., Magnani, Sabin, Saidel, & Heckathorn, 2005), location sampling (Chapter 19 in this volume) and site-based sampling (e.g., Binson *et al.*, 2007). Other studies distinguish venue-based from facility-based approaches (e.g., Speizer, Beauvais, Gomez, Outlaw, & Roussel, 2009). Although some studies treat venue-based sampling as equivalent to time-location sampling (e.g., Semaan *et al.*, 2002), we differentiate the two by specifying that venue-based sampling does not involve the time element. Instead, venue-based sampling, as described here, assumes that all times are equivalent, i.e., the entire target population will visit a venue during the time when data are collected. When a sample of both venues and times is selected, this is time-location sampling, which we discuss in Section 20.3.2. Some studies also use the term, "community-based sampling" (e.g., Nieto, Young, Lind, Shahar, Samet, Redline *et al.*, 2000) or "community venue sampling" (e.g., Meyer & Wilson, 2009) as methods encompassing venue-based sampling. Yet other studies referred to "community-based sampling" within small geographic areas, sometimes using probability methods (e.g., Jason, Jornal, Richman, Rademaker, Huang, McCready *et al.*, 1999) and other times using nonprobability methods (e.g., Cabral, Napoles-Springer, Miike, McMillan, Sison *et al.*, 2003). In enumerating the homeless, the method has been called the "public place method" (US Department of Housing and Urban Development, 2008). We use the term "venue" in this chapter, because this is broader than facility or site and is not geographically confined as community is.

The method

Venue-based sampling is neither new to the sampling literature nor specific to H2S populations. Exit polls are a classic example (Kalton, 1991). Because the majority of voters go to voting precincts to cast their votes, exit polls use precincts, a type of venue, as a sampling unit. Voters leaving the precincts are sampled for the poll. This essentially follows a two-stage cluster sample design, where precincts are primary sampling units (PSUs). Often, precincts are selected in the first stage using stratified probability proportionate to size (PPS) or probability proportionate to estimated size (PPeS) sampling (Kish, 1965). The size measure is the number of voters in the precinct, usually estimated, since the voting occurs after designing the sample. In the second stage, a systematic sample of voters leaving the polling place is selected following the equal probability selection method within each state. This yields a probability sample of the population of persons who vote at polling places, because non-zero selection probabilities can be assigned to each precinct and each voter prior to the poll. In this example, the time dimension can safely be ignored since all times that the polls are open are selected for the sample.

The critical elements for exit polls are the estimation of a size measure in the first stage and the use of systematic sampling in the second stage. If the size measure is not valid, the PPS or PPeS portion of the first-stage sampling is subject to error. This does not introduce bias directly but can increase variances of estimates. However, if an inadequate number of field data collectors are assigned to a precinct because of a poor measure of size, it may not be possible to execute the subsampling of voters in the way planned, leading to undercoverage bias.

There are various examples of venue-based sampling for H2S populations: correctional facilities for those engaged in illegal activities (e.g., Thaisri, Lewitworapong, Vongsheree, Sawanpanyalert, Chadbanchachai, Rojanawiwat *et al.*, 2003), drug treatment centers for IDUs (e.g., Razak, Jittiwutikarn, Suriyanon, Vongchak, Srirak, Beyer *et al.*, 2003), and STD clinics for MSM and commercial sex workers (CSWs) (e.g., Ghys, Diallo, Ettiegne-Traore, Kale, Tawil, Carael *et al.*, 2002; Sarkar, Bal, Mukherjee, Chakraborty, Saha, Ghosh, & Parsons, 2008; Valleroy, MacKellar, Karon, Rosen, McFarland, *et al.*, 2000). According to Paquette and de Wit (2010), venue-based sampling is a popular approach for sampling MSM for HIV surveillance systems. Out of twenty-six systems in twenty-three developed countries around the world, sixteen used venue-based sampling. The venues considered in these systems included social venues (e.g., clubs, gyms), events (e.g., gay parades, LGBT film festivals), venues offering sex on premise (e.g., bath houses), public cruising (e.g., parks), and social organizations and groups that MSM are likely to frequent. These venues are not necessarily geographic points and may be mobile.

Venue-based sampling for H2S populations starts with formative research that collects information for frame development. Often, the information about popular venues and their sizes is obtained through ethnographic methods (e.g., Meyer, Schwartz, & Frost, 2008) from informants who are familiar with the target population. Formative research data are mostly qualitative in nature and are used to build a sampling frame of venues. Sometimes, the data are enhanced by field workers' visits to the venues in order to confirm their existence and gather detailed size information. Formative research is analogous to locating precincts and esti-mating their size measures in exit polls. Upon building the frame, venues are sampled as PSUs following PPeS in the first stage. Venue types, locations, or characteristics can be considered for stratification. In the second stage, visits to the selected venues are sampled using various methods. If the rate of selection at the second stage is inversely proportional to that of the first-stage selection, then all visits will have an equal probability of selection. In practice, the second-stage sampling rate can be altered if there are many more or fewer visits than anticipated. These changes will require the use of weights to account for differential probabilities of selection.

Overall, venue-based sampling resembles the two-stage cluster sampling of exit polls. There are three key differences between exit poll sampling and venue-based sampling. First, there is no standard procedure for venue-based sampling. The steps mentioned above are some common elements found in studies using venue-based sampling but by no means are universal. Second, visit patterns are different in the two settings. Because voters will show up at the precincts only once in exit polling, sampling exits and inferences about them are equivalent to those about the voters. On the other hand, in venue-based sampling, visits are not necessarily the same as visitors because some may make multiple visits to the venues and some may not visit at all. Because inferences are made about the visitors not visits, this can incur biases. The third difference is that polls have a defined and limited time duration. The time frame of the universe of possible times is usually short enough (e.g., 8 am to 8 pm) that sampling from these is not needed. For most studies of H2S populations, the time frame of the target population is not of limited duration. If sampling of times is not used, then this implies either (1) an assumption that all times are equivalent in terms of counts and distribution of characteristics of the target population, or (2) that inferences are to be made only for the set of persons who visit the venues during the time periods when data are collected.

Assumptions

Venue-based sampling (without time sampling) provides probability sampling when (1) the list of venues from the formative research covers all potential venues, (2) all population members visit the identified venues in the same pattern across venues insensitive to time, (3) all the venues are accessible, and (4) the sampling of visits follows a probability principle. This method's potential to provide unbiased estimates is hampered by inappropriate proce-dures or operational limitations. For example, some venue-based sample studies omit formative research altogether by using researcher's judgments to construct the frame and to select samples. Even when formative research is conducted, completeness, credibility, and validity of the information from the informants will determine the quality of the sampling frame. The accessibility and permanency of the venues also influence the first-stage sampling bias. Some venues may not be safe enough for data collection activities; and some venues may be demolished, closed, or moved. In the second stage, the selected sampling approach will determine the error properties. The literature includes systematic sampling with pre-specified intervals and samples drawn up to predetermined sizes without further details. If too many people visit the venue at one time, field staff may not be able to track them at the prespecified intervals or approach those sampled for interviews.

As noted above, venue-based sampling selects visits but makes inferences about the visitors, assuming that all members of the target population visit the venues on the frame during the period of data collection. If this assumption does not hold (e.g., Chutuape, Ziff, Auerswald, Castillo, McFadden, & Ellen, 2009), the inference population becomes restricted, sometimes severely so, to those who visit the sampled venues. Overall selection probabilities depend on how often individual population members visit the frame venues. If this is not incorporated into the estimation procedure, those who visit the venues more frequently will be overrepresented. Duplicates at the same venue or across venues are problematic, but there is no clear consensus on how to identify and handle them. Moreover, if the characteristics associated with frequency of going to the frame venues are related to the study variables, this will introduce sampling bias.

For example, assume that gay community activities are used as venues in a study of MSM. It is clear that MSM who are actively involved in gay communities have higher chances to be found not only at multiple venues but also more frequently across all venues than those who are not involved as much. These two types of MSM are likely to differ systematically with respect to substantive characteristics. While venue-based sampling has the potential to produce probability samples, violating these assumptions will quickly convert the probability design into convenience sampling. As a result, the replicability of venue-based sample estimates across different geographies, times, and studies is uncertain.

The maternal mortality study

Danel, Graham, Stupp, and Castillo (1996) presented an interesting approach to estimate maternal mortality rates in a region in Nicaragua using two types of samples. The first type used a two-stage cluster sample, where communities in the region were selected with probability proportional to number of households in the first stage and households were sampled randomly in the second stage. The second type used a three-stage venue-based sample. Health care facilities operated by the Ministry of Health including large health centers and smaller urban and rural health posts were defined as the venues. In the first stage, municipalities in the region were selected with PPS, where the measure of size was the number of health care facilities. In the second stage, health care facilities were selected with PPS, where the measure of size was the number of adults in the catchment area of the facility. A systematic sample of adults seeking care at the selected facilities was drawn in the third stage. In both sample types, maternal mortality information was collected about respondents' adult sisters. The estimated mortality rates were very comparable.

The authors attributed the comparability to the high usage rate of outpatient health care due to their low cost. In other words, the health care facilities cover the target population reasonably well because they are widely used by the target population. One's health facility usage is not likely to be systematically related to his or her sisters' maternal mortality status. Additionally, the study targeted the general adult population. Unlike most H2S populations, correct calculation of size measures in the first and second stages of sampling is unlikely to be error prone. These satisfy the key assumptions for venue-based sampling to be able to provide a probability sample.

The HIV positive cigarette smokers study

Two outpatient clinics in the San Francisco Area that served HIV positive persons were selected as venues in Humfleet *et al.* (2009) to study HIV positive cigarette smokers. The selection of these clinics appears to be based on researchers' judgments. The participant recruitment was done through doctor referrals, distributing posters/flyers at the clinics, and sending recruitment letters to the clinic patients' home addresses. The sample was clearly not a probability sample. The two venues differed in terms of location and clientele. The first clinic was located near San Francisco's Castro area and provided HIV testing and counseling services as well as substance abuse treatment and mental health services. The other clinic was located in the Mission District and served HIV positive persons exclusively. The former venue had more gays (75.0 percent vs. 57.3 percent), more males (94.9 percent vs. 72.4 percent), and fewer unemployed clients (56.5 percent vs. 73.5 percent) than the latter.

The study was conducted to examine the effectiveness of different intervention programs. The intervention outcomes were not compared across sites, but it is possible that the outcomes differed given the differences in the clinics and their clientele. The authors indicated that the sample size (n=184) limited generalizability. However, it is not clear what the intended scope of generalization is (e.g., HIV positive cigarette smokers at the two clinics, HIV positive cigarette smokers in San Francisco or overall HIV positive cigarette smokers) and whether the generalizability is limited due to the sample size or the sampling bias.

20.3.2 Time-location sampling

Background

Time-location sampling is an extension of venue-based sampling that explicitly accounts for the time dimension involved with the sampling. It is a method for sampling flows of human populations, recently used to sample H2S populations who congregate in specific locations (e.g., Kanouse, Berry, Duan, Lever, Carson, Perlman, & Levitan, 1999; MacKellar Gallagher, Finlayson, Sanchez, Lansky, & Sullivan, 2007; Stueve, O'Donnell, Duran, Doval, & Blome, 2001). Time-location samples are meant to sample visits to a specified universe of locations, just like venue-based samples, but at times selected from a specified range of times.

The method

The sample frame development and selection of time-location sampling generally follow those of venue-based sampling. The only difference is that the time element is considered in the time-location sampling as the flow of the population may vary over time. Through formative research, the times are broken into reasonable intervals for each location. Operational considerations often play a key role in creating intervals. These intervals need to be big enough that study staff will be able to select reasonably large samples of visits but not so large that study staff will be expected to work unreasonably long shifts. The combination of location and time interval forms a frame of PSUs. In order to create a sample in which all visits have an equal probability of selection, the first-stage units are selected with PPeS. A sample of the PSUs can be selected using controlled selection techniques (Ernst, 1981; Ernst, Guciardo, Izsak, Lisic, & Ponikowski, 2008; Goodman & Kish, 1950) or balanced sampling (Deville and Tillé, 2004; Valliant *et al.*, 2000) to ensure adequate control of both the location and time dimensions. In the second stage, a systematic selection of visits is usually made.

Assumptions

As time-location sampling is similar to venue-based sampling, the same type of assumptions are made. Mainly, if the goal is to find H2S populations, then time-location sampling is prone to errors of undercoverage and overcoverage. First, there may be undercoverage if not all target population members visit the locations on the sampling frame. In a study of MSM (Xia, Tholandi, Osmond, Pollack, Zhou, Ruiz, & Catania, 2006), for example, about 83.5 percent of all MSM in California are found to visit venues on the study frame, but those who do not are substantially different from those who do. A second difficulty is overcoverage of persons who make frequent visits.

Converting a sample of visits to a sample of persons requires knowledge of the number of times that a person visits any of the time-locations on the frame. This is very difficult for two reasons. First, it may be difficult for a person to report the number of visits, particularly if these visits are frequent. Second, given that the sampling involves a time dimension, we also need to know any future visits that may occur for each person during the data collection period. This can be very difficult for eligible persons to estimate. Although the number of estimated visits can be used to weight each person, reasonable assumptions are required to use such weights (Kanouse *et al.*, 1999) and inaccurately estimated numbers can lead to biases.

National HIV behavior surveillance – men who have sex with men (NHBS-MSM)

Perhaps the largest example of time-location sampling is the NHBS-MSM (MacKellar *et al.*, 2007). This study began in 2003–05. It has a repeated cross-sectional design where the first wave was conducted in 17 metropolitan areas and the second wave in 2008 with 21 cities (US Centers for Disease Control and Prevention, 2010). Formative research was conducted by local teams under the direction of a centralized study staff for the frame construction. Local groups submitted periodic reports on their work and were subject to audit. Frame construction involved developing a list of locations attended by MSM. Interviews with knowledgeable persons were conducted to determine a complete list of locations or venues, typically including bars, dance clubs, businesses, social and religious organizations, parks, beaches, and special events, and continued until no new venues were discovered. Staff observed each venue to estimate flow patterns at the listed venues. The sampling frame was updated on a monthly basis to account for changes in the population of eligible locations.

Venues where less than 75 percent of the visits were by MSM were considered ineligible. Such a rule might lead to undercoverage, if some part of the MSM population only visits locations where less than 75 percent of the visits were by MSM. Time-location combinations were defined such that at least eight eligible MSM were expected in each. These requirements were set for cost reasons. Places with very few MSM would be expensive to sample on a per interview basis. The time slots were defined by day of week and time of day. For example, a time slot could be Wednesday from 6pm to 10pm.

The sampling was completed in two stages. In the first stage, locations were randomly selected without PPeS. In the second stage, one time slot was selected from all eligible time slots. Alternative time-locations were sampled as potential substitutes if a sampled time-location produced an insufficient number of eligible persons. Some public events, such as Gay Pride parades, were selected with certainty. Once the time-location and the date were selected, a team of interviewers conducted the field work. All men who appeared to be over the age of 18 years were counted and asked to complete a short screening interview to determine eligibility. All eligible men were asked to complete a twenty-five-minute interview on the spot. The questionnaire included questions about the venue visit patterns. While these could be used to produce inferences about visitors rather than visits through weighting, the authors note that no method for developing weights for person-level analysis had been developed or validated.

The street prostitute study

Kanouse and colleagues (1999) describe a study of female street prostitutes in Los Angeles County conducted from May 1990 to February 1991. A decision was made to limit the study to "street prostitutes," as other types of prostitutes would be too difficult to sample. As the first step of the frame construction, formative research was conducted with knowledgeable experts to identify locations where street prostitutes could be found to be working. Nearly 200 such interviews were completed. Time-location sizes (the expected number of eligible persons) were estimated in the second step based on two or more on-site visits to each location and expert interviews. Time-locations were sampled with PPeS. Time-locations with an estimate of fewer than two women were treated as ineligible.

In the second stage, only one woman was selected per area. Interviewers went to the selected location at the selected time. They started from a random point within the area and randomly selected a direction to walk either clockwise or counter-clockwise circling around the area. They then selected the first woman they saw. If the first woman was not eligible or not interviewed, then they continued in the same direction until they either obtained an interview or returned to the starting point. Once an interview was obtained, the interviewer continued walking around the location, counting the women present, until the time period was over.

Comparison of time-location sampling with respondent-driven sampling

Very few studies have experimentally compared sampling methods for H2S populations. An exception is a recent study that compared respondent-driven sampling to time-location sampling for MSM in Brazil (Kendall, Kerr, Gondim, Werneck, Macena, Pontes *et al.*, 2008). The two samples produced significantly different social class statuses of MSM. It is difficult to assess whether these differences are due to sampling, nonresponse, or measurement error issues associated with each sampling method. More needs to be known about the errors, other than sampling error, associated with each method before firm conclusions can be drawn.

20.3.3 Web-based sampling

Background

Web-based sampling, although labeled as sampling in the literature outside of statistics and survey methodology, is not a new sampling method but a data collection mode that makes contacts to the potential target population members over the web. This yields sampling procedures unique to the web environment.

   Web-based sampling can take a form of traditional probability sampling, but only under some restrictive circumstances. If all population members use the web and their web contact information is available, then a probability sample can be drawn. However, this occurs only for special situations. See Couper (2000, 2007) for a general overview of web surveys.

   For some H2S populations that are avid web users for sexual purposes, such as MSM, the web is considered to be a desirable medium (Bull, McFarlane, & Reitmeijer, 2001; McFarlane, Bull, & Rietmeijer, 2000; Mettey, Crosby, DiClemente, & Holtgrave, 2003; Ross, Tikkanen, & Mansson, 2000). Perceived anonymity, sexual partner availability, and a lower level of discrimination against sexual minorities have accelerated their web usage. The web has emerged as a new HIV risk venue (McFarlane *et al.*, 2000; Rosser, Oakes, Bockting, & Miner, 2007). Web surveys have well-recognized benefits, regardless of the target population, such as administrative convenience, lower costs, fast turnaround time, and lower social desirability resulting from absence of interviewers and respondent anonymity. These benefits, coupled with its being a popular venue for some H2S populations, make the web appear to be promising for studying those populations and building HIV/ AIDS behavioral surveillance systems (Chiasson, Parsons, Tesoriero, Carballo-Dieguez, Hirshfield, & Remien, 2006).

The methods

Sampling for web-based surveys in the nonstatistical literature takes various forms, which, in turn, yield numerous sampling mechanisms. First, participant recruitment strategies listed in Chiasson *et al.* (2006) include email blasts, chat rooms, instant messengers, and banner advertisements. The majority of HIV surveillance systems in developed countries reported in Paquette and de Wit (2010) use these types of web-based sampling for recruiting participants. While the number of completed interviews may be impressive, this approach produces convenience samples. Coverage properties are unclear, because it requires access to the web and access to these recruitments is unrestricted and open to any web users. Moreover, the sampling mechanism is determined by respondents' self-selection. For instance, MSM web users are a subset of the MSM population, and those who participate in these studies are a distinctive subset of the MSM web users. Self-selection plays a role in both steps, and researchers do not have any control over selection or information about the breakdown of the target population into web users and study participants. Undoubtedly, generalizability is a concern. A number of studies reported biases of using web-based convenience samples of sexual minorities (e.g., Liau, Millett, & Marks, 2006; McFarlane *et al.*, 2000; Ross *et al.*, 2000).

Inferences are sometimes possible from volunteer web samples but strong modeling assumptions are needed (see Lee & Valliant, 2009; Valliant & Dever, 2011). If a model that describes the analysis variables collected in the survey holds for both the sample and non-sample cases, then inference to the full target population can, in principle, be made. However, appropriate models may require the use of many covariates (e.g., age, race, gender, education, and income). To apply the standard modeling techniques used in finite population estimation (like raking, post-stratification, or general regression estimation), the population totals of covariates for the H2S population must be available. Neither these population totals nor precise estimates of them are usually available for H2S populations.

Alternatives to convenience samples are pre-recruited web panels from which H2S population samples are drawn. Unlike the open-access web surveys, this approach starts with a list of panel members whose background information is known. If information relevant for the H2S population of interest is available, it can be used as a screening tool to identify the eligible panel members and build a frame. Another benefit of pre-recruited panel web sampling is the possibility of examining response patterns with auxiliary data available for all panel members. For instance, if the list includes basic demographic characteristics (e.g., age) and sexual orientation information, the latter information can be used to draw samples of sexual minorities. The former can be used to evaluate the character-istics associated not only with sampling of sexual minorities but also with nonresponse within the sample.

However, not all panels are the same. Some panels are restricted only to web users who self-select into the panel. As web nonusers will have zero selection probabilities and panel members' self-selection determines the sampling mechanism, it produces nonprobability samples. This approach may not be suitable when generalizations beyond web users are desired and at best may be able to represent web users within the target population. The other type of pre-recruited web panels starts with a probability approach (e.g., RDD telephone surveys) to sample those who then are invited to join the panels and extends beyond web users by providing web access to web nonusers. These panels may legitimately represent the general population. The initial recruitment of a panel, however, is subject to nonresponse, which may lead to subsequent inadequate coverage. The initial recruitment can also be quite expensive, which makes this approach impractical for many researchers. If the panel does not suffer from coverage problems, true probability samples can be drawn.

Unrestricted open-access web-based sample

For a study of Latino men who use the Internet to have sex with men, Rosser, Miner, Bockting, Konstan, Gurak, Stanton *et al.* (2009) used the unrestricted open-access web method. Banner advertisements prepared in English and Spanish were placed on www.gay.com, the largest gay-themed website in the US. This website, at the time of data collection, reported to have 2.56 million unique visitors, including some 157,000 visitors on their Latino subsite. The ads were viewed over 47 million times in three weeks between November and December, 2002. The ads linked to the survey website were clicked over 33,000 times. Among these, 1,742 enrolled in the survey. After excluding 196 ineligible enrollees, the survey was completed by 1,026 eligible persons. The remaining 520 dropped out during the survey. The survey takers were compensated with $20 for their participation. As noted earlier, the final sample is essentially a set of volunteers. The authors compared those who completed and those who dropped out and found that dropouts were more likely to be Puerto Rican, Black, to identify as bisexual or heterosexual than homosexual, to be in a seroconcordant and monogamous relationship, to use the Internet for contact, and not to have met men for sex on the web. Given this, the basis of their conclusion that dropouts did not seriously skew the data is dubious. Generalizations may not be possible for variables highly related to the dropout patterns.

How the response rate should be calculated is unclear, because the level of eligibility and the number of duplicates among some 47 million ad viewers or some 33,000 clicks cannot be determined. The response rate may be as low as 0.002 percent if all the ad viewers were eligible without duplicates. It may be 3 percent when assuming only those who clicked the ads were eligible for the study and clicked only once. Moreover, there is no information about those who did not participate in the study. These uncertainties limit understanding of nonresponse bias.

Web as a venue

Raymond, Rebchook, Curotto, Vaudrey, Amsden, Levino *et al.* (2010) implemented three nontraditional sampling methods for MSM in the San Francisco Bay Area for building an HIV surveillance system. The first two methods were based on the web. The first method was the unrestricted open-access approach using a banner advertisement on a total of twenty-four websites. Similar to Rosser *et al.* (2009), the ad directed those who clicked on it to the screening survey page. After eligibility was determined, the survey was conducted. The second web-based approach was novel; it considered websites to which the Bay Area MSM frequented as venues and used those websites as PSUs in time-location sampling. Formative research combined qualitative and quantitative approaches, such as focus groups, in-depth interviews with informants, and analysis of MSM web use data from the NHBS. A total of fifteen venues were identified. With an integration of time elements, forty-one sampling events were created. On a randomly selected day and time, the study staff logged on to the selected web venues and enumerated men who were online. A systematic sample was selected, and either instant messages or emails with the survey request were sent. Those who responded to the request were screened for eligibility and invited to the survey. The third method followed the NHBS type of time-location sampling.

The comparison results were striking not only for the survey variables but also for sampling productivity. The open-access approach elicited 17,000 clicks and produced 666 completes. Among over 15,000 men enumerated in the web venue sample, 57 MSM completed the surveys. The time-location sampling yielded 1,574 completes from 44,000 enumerated (although it is unclear how many of these were selected for the eligibility screener interview). Eligibility rates among those who completed the screener interview varied widely: 16 percent in the open-access web sample; 100 percent in the web venue sample; and 70 percent in the time-location sample. These three methods showed large differences in characteristics, such as age and substance use. Additionally, the item missing rate for the HIV status was higher in the unrestricted web sample at 13 percent, compared to 2–3 percent in the other two approaches. The statistical significance of these differences was not tested in the paper, and we could not conduct the tests because standard errors were not reported. Overall, there were no clear patterns to describe the comparability among these samples. What is clear is that estimated characteristics of MSM in the Bay Area may appear vastly different depending on the sampling approach.

20.4 Conclusion

We have examined three sampling methods recently suggested for H2S populations: venue-based, time-location, and web-based sampling. These methods do not easily map onto the traditional classification of probability versus nonprobability sampling. Depending on the actual sampling procedures, they do have the potential of providing probability samples allowing generalizations. For instance, depending on the target population and the frame availability, web-based sampling can produce a sample with nonzero known selection probabilities. Both venue-based and time-location sampling can provide samples equivalent to what stratified multistage cluster sampling provides. When the selection probabilities can be calculated, the design weights can also be calculated and further adjusted if the frame information about the target population and/or auxiliary information about nonrespondents is available. If such auxiliary information is available, standard model-related estimation techniques can be used. However, the ability to use methods like generalized regression estimation is often severely limited by absence of H2S population information on covariates needed to construct the estimators. Even when auxiliary data are available, the main issue with the methods of sampling summarized in this chapter is that they are subject to coverage error, nonresponse error, and inappropriate application. Even when a probability design is planned, these problems can easily lead to biased estimators.

For venue-based and time-location sampling, formative research is the basis of sampling. The quality of formative research directly influences the overall quality of sampling and, hence, inferences. Data collected during formative research are subject to all aspects of total survey error: coverage, sampling, nonresponse, and measurement errors. These errors, in turn, affect sampling properties of the actual study. When formative research is omitted and researchers' judgments are used, the estimates apply only to those included in the sample. Much of the formative research is based on qualitative data obtained from informants. Who these individuals are, how these individuals are selected, who agrees to respond, how valid their information is, and how the information is incorporated in the frame development determine sampling error.

The labels put on the sampling methods examined in this chapter do not necessarily convey information about their error properties. For the traditional sampling and data collection methods, nonsampling error properties have been examined extensively in the literature and some common characteristics associated with these errors have been well documented. For instance, young males are often associated with nonresponse and undercoverage in probability samples of households. These characteristics are used not only to understand the errors but also to make post-survey adjustments. However, this is not true for the sampling methods examined in this chapter. As seen in Raymond *et al.* (2010), it is difficult to summarize the pattern of these errors. Therefore, it is not surprising to see the lack, if not the absence, of statistical adjustments applied in studies using these methods. As noted above, auxiliary information needed for the adjustments may also be lacking for H2S populations.

Arguing whether or not to use these new methods to sample H2S populations is not productive. Rather, it is important to understand their strengths and weaknesses and to discuss ways to ameliorate or eliminate the weaknesses. The current literature on these sampling methods does not provide standard procedures or clear guidance on their implementation. It is entirely possible that the estimates are plagued by multiple layers of errors beyond sampling error.

Studies using these new sampling methods should provide detailed descriptions about sampling procedures. This will allow readers and data users to understand the error properties and the extent to which the estimates may be generalized. In defense of a venue-based sample study of the HIV risk population, Ellen and Fichtenberg (2007) argued that the interpretation of such studies should be at the community level rather than the individual level, because factors beyond individuals play important roles in transmitting diseases. This type of argument, however, needs further clarification on the intended scope of the community. If it is beyond the selected venues, generalization becomes problematic whether it is sought for communities or individuals. Additionally, it is sensible to collect auxiliary information about those potentially omitted in the formative research and those who do not respond. This information can be used not only to understand the errors but also to compensate for them.

We have emphasized the importance of selecting probability samples for making sound generalizations to the population. Inferences using nonprobability samples are sometimes possible (e.g., Copas & Li, 1997; Valliant & Dever, 2011), but models are the basis for inference, not repeated sampling. In many applications of venue-based, time-location, and web-based sampling, neither repeated sampling nor model-based inferences to the full target populations may be justified.

References

Binson, D., Blair, J., Huebner, D. M., & Woods, W. J. (2007). Sampling in surveys of lesbian, gay, and bisexual people. In I. H. Meyer & M. E. Northridge (eds.), *The Health of Sexual Minorities: Public Health Perspectives on Lesbian, Gay, Bisexual, and Transgender Populations* (pp. 375–418). New York: Springer.

Bull, S., McFarlane, M., & Reitmeijer, C. (2001). HIV and sexually transmitted infection risk behaviors among men seeking sex with men on-line. *American Journal of Public Health*, 91(6), 988–89.

Cabral, D. N., Napoles-Springer, A. N., Miike, R., McMillan, A., Sison, J. D., Wrensch, M. R., *et al.* (2003). Population- and community-based recruitment of African Americans and Latinos. The San Francisco Bay Area Lung Cancer Study. *American Journal of Epidemiology*, 158(3), 272–79.

Catania, J. A., Osmond, D., Stall, R. D., Pollack, L., Paul, J. P., Blower, S., *et al.* (2001). The continuing HIV epidemic among men who have sex with men. *American Journal of Public Health*, 91, 907–14.

Chiasson, M. A., Parsons, J. T., Tesoriero, J. M., Carballo-Dieguez, A., Hirshfield, S., & Remien, R. H. (2006). HIV behavioral research online. *Journal of Urban Health*, 83(1), 73–85.

Chutuape, K. S., Ziff, M., Auerswald, G., Castillo, M., McFadden, A., & Ellen, J. (2009). Examining differences in types and location of recruitment venues for young males and females from urban neighborhoods: findings from a multi-site HIV preventions study. *Journal of Urban Health*, 86(1), 31–42.

Cochran, W. G. (1977). *Sampling Techniques*. New York: John Wiley & Sons.

Cochran, S. D., & Mays, V. M. (2000). Relation between psychiatric syndromes and behaviorally defined sexual orientation in a sample of the U.S. population. *American Journal of Epidemiology*, 151, 516–23.

Copas, J. B., & Li, H. G. (1997). Inference for non-random samples (and discussion). *Journal of the Royal Statistical Society: Series B (Statistical Methodology)*, 59, 55–95.

Couper, M. P. (2000). Web surveys: a review of issues and approaches. *Public Opinion Quarterly*, 64(4), 464–94.

(2007). Issues of representation in eHealth research (with a focus on Web surveys). *American Journal of Preventive Medicine*, 32(5), S83–89.

Danel, I., Graham, W., Stupp, P., & Castillo, P. (1996). Applying sisterhood method for estimating maternal mortality to a health facility-based sample: a comparison with results from a household-based sample. *International Journal of Epidemiology*, 25(5), 1017–22.

Deville, J.-C., & Tillé, Y. (2004). Efficient balanced sampling: the cube method. *Biometrika*, 91, 893–912.

Ellen, J. M., & Fichtenberg, C. M. (2007). Venue-based sampling in STD research: generalizable to and independent of whom? *Sexually Transmitted Diseases*, 34(8), 532–33.

Ernst, L. R. (1981). A constructive solution for two-dimensional controlled selection problems. In *Joint Statistical Meetings Proceedings, Section on Survey Research Methods* (pp. 61–64). Alexandria, VA: American Statistical Association.

Ernst, L. R., Guciardo, C. J., Izsak, Y., Lisic, J. J., & Ponikowski, C. H. (2008). Implementation of controlled selection in the National Compensation Survey redesign. In *Joint Statistical Meetings Proceedings* (pp. 977–84). Alexandria, VA: American Statistical Association.

Ghys, P. D., Diallo, M. O., Ettiegne-Traore, V., Kale, K., Tawil, O., Carael M., *et al.* (2002). Increase in condom use and decline in HIV and sexually transmitted diseases among female sex workers in Abidjan, Côte d'Ivoire, 1991–1998. *AIDS*, 16, 251–58.

Goodman, R., & Kish, L. (1950). Controlled selection – a technique in probability sampling. *Journal of the American Statistical Association*, 45(251), 350–72.

Groves, R. M. (1989). *Survey Errors and Survey Costs*. New York: John Wiley & Sons.

Hansen, M. H., Hurwitz, W. N., & Madow, W. G. (1953). *Sample Survey Methods and Theory* (vols. I–II). New York: John Wiley & Sons.

Heckathorn, D. D., & Jeffri, J. (2003). Social networks of jazz musicians. In *Changing the Beat: A Study of the Worklife of Jazz Musicians, vol. III: Respondent-Driven Sampling* (pp. 48–61). Survey Results by the Research Center for Arts and Culture, National Endowment for the Arts Research Division Report #43. Washington, DC: National Endowment for the Arts.

Humfleet, G. L., Delucchi, K., Kelley, K., Hall, S. M., Dilley, J., & Harrison, G. (2009). Characteristics of HIV-positive cigarette smokers: a sample of smokers facing multiple challenges. *AIDS Education and Prevention*, 21(Suppl. 3), 54–64.

Jason, L. A., Jornal, K. M., Richman, J. A., Rademaker, A. W., Huang, C.-F., McCready, W., *et al.* (1999). A community-based study of prolonged fatigue and chronic fatigue. *Journal of Health Psychology*, 4(1), 9–26.

Kalton, G. (1991). Sampling flows of mobile human populations. *Survey Methodology*, 17(2), 183–94.

    (2009). Methods for oversampling rare subpopulations in social surveys. *Survey Methodology*, 35(2), 125–41.

Kanouse, D. E., Berry, S. H., Duan, N., Lever, J., Carson, S., Perlman, J. F., & Levitan, B. (1999). Drawing a probability sample of female street prostitutes in Los Angeles County. *Journal of Sex Research*, 36(1), 45–51.

Kendall, C., Kerr, L., Gondim, R., Werneck, G., Macena, R., Pontes, M., et al. (2008). An empirical comparison of respondent-driven sampling, time location sampling, and snowball sampling for behavioral surveillance in men who have sex with men, Fortaleza, Brazil. *AIDS and Behavior*, 12(Suppl. 4), 97–104.

Kish, L. (1965). *Survey Sampling*. New York: John Wiley & Sons.

(2003). The hundred years' war of survey sampling (reprinted from *Statistics in Transition*, 1995). In G. Kalton & S. Heeringa (eds.), *Leslie Kish, Selected Papers* (pp. 5–19). New York: John Wiley & Sons.

Kruskal, W. H., & Mosteller, F. (1979a). Representative sampling. I. The current statistical literature. *International Statistical Review*, 47, 13–24.

(1979b). Representative sampling. II. The current statistical literature. *International Statistical Review*, 47, 111–27.

(1979c). Representative sampling. III. The current statistical literature. *International Statistical Review*, 47, 245–65.

Laumann, E. O., Gagnon, J. H., Michael, R. T., & Michaels, S. (1994). *The Social Organization of Sexuality: Sexual Practices in the United States*. Chicago: University of Chicago Press.

Lee, S., & Valliant, R. (2009). Estimation for volunteer panel web surveys using propensity score adjustment and calibration adjustment. *Sociological Methods & Research*, 37(3), 319–43.

Liau, A., Millet, G., & Marks, G. (2006). Meta-analytic examination of online sex-seeking and sexual risk behavior among men who have sex with men. *Sexually Transmitted Diseases*, 33, 576–84.

McFarlane, M., Bull, S. S., & Rietmeijer, C. A. (2000). The internet as a newly emerging risk environment for sexually transmitted diseases. *Journal of the American Medical Association*, 284, 443–46.

MacKellar, D. A., Gallagher, K. M., Flnlayson, T., Lansky, A., & Sullivan, P. S. (2007). Surveillance of HIV risk and prevention behaviors of men who have sex with men – a national application of venue-based, time-space sampling. *Public Health Reports*, 122 (Suppl. 1), 39–47.

Magnani, R., Sabin, K., Saidel, T., & Heckathorn, D. (2005). Review of sampling hard-to-reach and hidden populations for HIV surveillance. *AIDS*, 19(Suppl. 2), S67–S72.

Malekinejad, M., Johnston, L. G., Kendall, C., Kerr, L. R. F. S., Rifkin, M. R., & Rutherford, G. (2008). Using respondent-driven sampling methodology for HIV biological and behavioral surveillance in international settings: a systematic review. *AIDS and Behavior*, 12, S105–S130.

Mettey, A., Crosby, R., DiClemente, R., & Holtgrave, D. (2003). Associations between internet sex seeking and STI associated risk behaviours among men who have sex with men. *Sexually Transmitted Infections*, 79, 466–68.

Meyer, I. H., Schwartz, S., & Frost, D. M. (2008). Social patterning of stress and coping: does disadvantaged status confer excess exposure and fewer coping resources? *Social Science & Medicine*, 67, 368–79.

Meyer, I. H., & Wilson, P. A. (2009). Sampling lesbian, gay, and bisexual populations. *Journal of Counseling Psychology*, 56(1), 23–31.

Neyman, J. (1934). On the two different aspects of the representative method: the method of stratified sampling and the method of purposive selection. *Journal of the Royal Statistical Society*, 97(4), 558–625.

Nieto, F. J., Young, T. B., Lind, B. J., Shahar, E., Samet, J. M., Redline, S., *et al.* (2000). Association of sleep-disordered breathing, sleep apnea, and hypertension in a large community-based study. *Journal of the American Medical Association*, 283(14), 1829–36.

Paquette, D., & de Wit, J. (2010). Sampling methods used in developed countries for behavioural surveillance among men who have sex with men. *AIDS and Behavior*, 14, 1252–64.

Raymond, H. F., Rebchook, G., Curotto, A., Vaudrey, J., Amsden, M., Levine, D., *et al.* (2010). Comparing internet-based and venue-based methods to sampling MSM in the San Francisco Bay Area. *AIDS and Behavior*, 14, 218–24.

Razak, M. H., Jittiwutikarn, J., Suriyanon, V., Vongchak, T., Srirak, N., Beyer, C., *et al.* (2003). HIV prevalence and risks among injection and noninjection drug users in northern Thailand: need for comprehensive HIV prevention programs. *Journal of Acquired Immune Deficiency Syndromes*, 33, 259–66.

Remafedi, G. (2002). Suicidality in a venue-based sample of young men who have sex with men. *Journal of Adolescent Health*, 31, 305–10.

Ross, M., Tikkanen, R., & Mansson, D. (2000). Differences between internet sample and conventional samples of men who have sex with men: implications for research and HIV interventions. *Social Science & Medicine*, 51, 749–58.

Rosser, B. R. S., Miner, M. H., Bockting, W. O., Konstan, J., Gurak, L., Stanton, J., *et al.* (2009). HIV risk and the internet: results of the Men's INTernet Sex (MINTS) Study. *AIDS and Behavior*, 13(4), 746–56.

Rosser, B. R. S., Oakes, J. M., Bockting, W. O., & Miner, M. (2007). Capturing the social demographics of hidden sexual minorities: an internet study of the transgender population in the United States. *Sexuality Research and Social Policy*, 4, 50–64.

Sarkar, K., Bal, B., Mukherjee, R., Chakraborty, S., Saha, S., Ghosh, A., & Parsons, S. (2008). Sex-trafficking, violence, negotiating skill, and HIV infection in brothel-based sex workers of Eastern India, adjoining Nepal, Bhutan, and Bangladesh. *Journal of Health Population and Nutrition*, 26(2), 223–31.

Särndal, C.-E., Swensson, B., & Wretman, J. (1992). *Model Assisted Survey Sampling*. New York: Springer-Verlag.

Sell, R. (2007). Defining and measuring sexual orientation for research. In I. H. Meyer & M. E. Northridge (eds.), *The Health of Sexual Minorities: Public Health Perspectives on Lesbian, Gay, Bisexual and Transgender Population* (pp. 355–74). New York: Springer.

Semaan, S., Lauby, J., & Liebman, J. (2002). Street and network sampling in evaluation studies of HIV risk-reduction interventions. *AIDS Review*, 4, 213–23.

Speizer, I. S., Beauvais, H., Gomez, A. M., Outlaw, T. F., & Roussel, B. (2009). Using multiple sampling approaches to measure sexual risk-taking among young people in Haiti: programmatic implications. *Studies in Family Planning*, 40(4), 277–88.

Stephan, F. F., & McCarthy, P. J. (1958). *Sampling Opinions: An Analysis of Survey Procedure*. New York: John Wiley & Sons.

Stoop, I. A. L. (2005). *The Hunt for the Last Respondent: Nonresponse in Sample Surveys*. Social & Cultural Planning Office: The Hague, Netherlands.

Stueve, A., O'Donnell, L., Duran, R., Doval, A., & Blome, J. (2001). Methodological issues in time-space sampling in minority communities: results with Latino young men who have sex with men. *American Journal of Public Health*, 91, 922–26.

Sudman, S., Sirken, M. G., & Cowan, C. D. (1988). Sampling rare and elusive populations. *Science*, 240, 991–96.

Thaisri, H., Lewitworapong, J., Vongsheree, S., Sawanpanyalert, P., Chadbanchachai, C., Rojanawiwat, A., *et al.* (2003). HIV infection and risk factors among Bangkok prisoners, Thailand: a prospective cohort study. *BMC Infectious Diseases* [online journal], 3, 25. doi: 10.1186/1471–2334–3–25.

US Centers for Disease Control and Prevention. (2010, September 24). Prevalence and awareness of HIV infection among men who have sex with men – 21 cities, United States, 2008. *Morbidity and Mortality Weekly Report*, 59, 1201–07. Retrieved from www.cdc.gov/mmwr/preview/mmwrhtml/mm5937a2.htm.

US Department of Housing and Urban Development, Office of Community Planning and Development. (2008). *A Guide to Counting Unsheltered Homeless People* (2nd rev. edn.). Washington, DC: Author. Retrieved from www.hudhre.info/documents/counting_unsheltered.pdf.

Valleroy, L., MacKellar, D., Karon, J., Rosen, D. H., McFarland, W., Shehan, D. A., *et al.*, (2000). HIV prevalence and associated risks in young men who have sex with men. *Journal of the American Medical Association*, 284, 198–204.

Valliant, R., & Dever, J. (2011). Estimating propensity adjustments for volunteer Web surveys. *Sociological Methods & Research*, 40, 105–37.

Valliant, R., Dorfman, A. H., & Royall, R. M. (2000). *Finite Population Sampling and Inference: A Prediction Approach*. New York: John Wiley & Sons.

Xia, Q., Tholandi, M., Osmond, D. H., Pollack, L. M., Zhou, W., Ruiz, J. D., & Catania, J. A. (2006). The effect of venue sampling on estimates of HIV prevalence and sexual risk behaviors in men who have sex with men. *Sexually Transmitted Diseases*, 33(9), 545–50.

21

Indirect sampling for hard-to-reach populations

PIERRE LAVALLÉE

21.1   Introduction

In survey sampling, some populations are hard to reach because they happen to be hard to survey. Their relative rareness and the absence of a suitable sampling frame are two main reasons for this. As mentioned by Kalton and Anderson (1986): "The initial consideration in designing a sample for a rare population is whether there exists a separate frame for that population. If a separate frame exists, is available for sample selection and is deemed adequate, the sample may be selected from it using standard methods and no problems arise." When no sampling frame is available for the desired target population, one might then choose a sampling frame that is indirectly related to the targeted rare population. We can then speak of two populations U^A and U^B that are related to one another. We wish to produce an estimate for the population U^B by selecting a sample from the population U^A for which a sampling frame is available and using the existing links between the two populations. This sampling process is referred to as indirect sampling (Lavallée, 2002, 2007). Producing estimates in the context of indirect sampling can be difficult to achieve if the links between U^A and U^B are not one-to-one. A solution for this is to use the *generalized weight share method* (GWSM).

The population U^B can be the hard-to-survey population itself or it can be a population that contains it as a subpopulation. Fortunately for the statistician, it turns out that hard-to-reach populations can often be found by surveying clusters. This is the case, for example, with infectious diseases (Thompson, 1992). In this chapter then, we will assume that the population U^B is partitioned into clusters. Selection of clusters will then be performed through the indirect sampling process. Since sampling clusters rather than individual units might allow easier tracking of units that are part of the hard-to-reach populations, we can foresee considerable reductions in costs since a large part of the costs are related to the identification of the hard-to-reach populations. As well, cluster sampling allows for the production of results at the cluster level itself, in addition to the units.

Sampling hard-to-reach populations through selection of clusters can be illustrated by the following three examples that we will develop further in Section 21.3.

Example 1:   *Surveying a rare ethnic group.* Suppose that we want to survey a rare ethnic group within a city. The members of this ethnic group might be living in small communities that can be viewed as clusters. By surveying clusters, entire communities get surveyed. Therefore, the yield of the sample in terms of people from the targeted ethnic group is likely to be larger than by surveying individuals directly, i.e., ignoring the clustered aspect of the target population.

Example 2: *Surveying smokers.* Suppose that we want to measure the health issues of smokers in a given country. Smokers can be viewed as a hard-to-reach population because there is no list available of smokers. Sometimes such a list is available (for example, from local health centers because of cancer diagnostics) but it offers only a partial coverage of smokers. If no list is available, sample selection of smokers can then be done through families (including, for example, aunts, cousins, etc.), which can be viewed as clusters. By sampling entire families, rather than individuals, we are more likely to find some smokers.

Example 3: *Surveying homeless people.* Suppose that we want to measure health and living conditions of homeless people in a big city. Ardilly and Le Blanc (2001) proceeded by reaching the homeless persons through services that are provided to them – overnight accommodation and meals. These two types of services can be seen as being part of two different sampling frames. During a certain period of time, one can assume that each homeless person will receive a given set of services. By sampling services, we get indirectly a sample of homeless persons to be surveyed.

Using indirect sampling as briefly described above is one way for surveying hard-to-reach populations. Other approaches exist, such as network sampling, adaptive cluster sampling, snowball sampling, respondent-driven sampling, and the use of multiple frames. With appropriate modifications, these approaches can all be put into the context of indirect sampling. For example, in the case of adaptive cluster sampling, the population of interest U^B is made of clusters, while the sampling frame U^A contains the elements of these clusters from U^B. One can use the theory and developments surrounding indirect sampling and the GWSM to obtain a unified mathematical framework for the above approaches.

After an overview of indirect sampling and its ready application to hard-to-reach populations, the chapter will describe briefly indirect sampling and the GWSM in the context of network sampling, adaptive cluster sampling, snowball sampling, respondent-driven sampling, and the use of multiple frames.

21.2 Indirect sampling

With indirect sampling, we wish to produce an estimate for a population U^B using a sample selected from the sampling frame U^A and the existing links between the two populations. We proceed by selecting a sample s^A containing m^A units from the population U^A containing M^A units according to some sample design chosen by the survey statistician. Let π_j^A represent the selection probability of unit j in U^A. We assume that $\pi_j^A > 0$ for all $j \in U^A$. On the other hand, the population U^B contains M^B units. It is divided into N^B clusters, where cluster i contains M_i^B units.

We assume there exists a relationship between a unit j of population U^A and some unit k of cluster i in U^B, the latter noted as unit ik. This relationship is described by an indicator variable $l_{j,ik}$, where $l_{j,ik} = 1$ if there is a link between unit $j \in U^A$ and unit $ik \in U^B$, and 0 otherwise. Note that there might be some cases where no link exists between a unit j of population U^A and any unit k from cluster i of population U^B, which amounts to $L_j^A = \sum_{i=1}^{N^B} \sum_{k=1}^{M_i^B} l_{j,ik} = 0$. In such a case, unit j is of no use to help find units of U^B, which compromises the efficiency of the sampling strategy but does not introduce any bias.

To produce unbiased estimates, each unit k of the population U^B must have a non-zero probability of being surveyed through U^A. This translates into the following constraint: Each cluster i of U^B must have at least one link with a unit j of U^A, i.e., $L_i^B = \sum_{k=1}^{M_i^B} \sum_{j=1}^{M^A} l_{j,ik} > 0$.

The indirect sampling process is as follows:

- We select a sample s^A of m^A units from the frame U^A.
- For each unit j selected in s^A, we identify the units ik of U^B that are linked to j, i.e., $l_{j,ik} = 1$.
- For each unit ik identified, we assume that we can set up the list of M_i^B units of cluster i containing this unit. Each cluster i then represents, within itself, a population U_i^B where $U^B = \cup_{i=1}^{N^B} U_i^B$. Let s^B be the set of n^B clusters identified by the units $j \in s^A$, i.e., $s^B = \{i \in U^B \mid \exists j \in s^A \text{ and } L_{j,i} > 0\}$ where $L_{j,i} = \sum_{k=1}^{M_i^B} l_{j,ik}$.
- We survey **all** units k of the cluster $i \in s^B$ and measure a variable of interest y_{ik} as well as the number of links $L_{ik}^B = \sum_{j=1}^{M^A} l_{j,ik}$ between unit ik of U^B and the frame U^A.

The last step is an important aspect to which the survey process (or measurement) is subjected. If a unit is selected in the sample, then every unit of the cluster containing the selected unit will be surveyed.

For the population U^B, we seek to estimate the total $Y^B = \sum_{i=1}^{N^B} \sum_{k=1}^{M_i^B} y_{ik}$. The estimation of the total Y^B indirectly through the sample s^A selected from the frame U^A can be a major challenge, in particular if the links between the units of U^A and U^B are not one-to-one. Indeed, with multiple ways to reach a given unit of U^B comes an issue of double counting, which goes unaddressed if inferences are made using the inclusion probabilities or weights arising from U^A. A correct procedure must somehow factor in the multiple entry points into U^B. A solution to this estimation problem is the use of the GWSM (Lavallée, 1995, 2002, 2007).

21.2.1 The generalized weight share method

The GWSM produces an estimation weight for each surveyed unit from the population U^B by transforming the sampling weights inherited from U^A. This estimation weight is basically an average of the sampling weights of the selected units from population U^A. Lavallée (1995) presented for the first time the GWSM within the context of the problem of cross-sectional weighting for longitudinal household surveys. The GWSM is a generalization of the weight share method described by Ernst (1989).

By using the GWSM, we want to assign an *estimation weight* w_{ik} to each unit k of a surveyed cluster i. To estimate the total Y^B belonging to the population U^B, we can then use the estimator

$$\hat{Y}^B = \sum_{i=1}^{n^B} \sum_{k=1}^{M_i^B} w_{ik} y_{ik} \qquad (21.1)$$

where n^B is the number of surveyed clusters and w_{ik}, the weight assigned to unit k of cluster i. With the GWSM, the estimation method is based on the sample s^A, together with the existing links between U^A and U^B. The links are in fact used as a bridge to go between the populations U^A and U^B.

The steps of the GWSM are as follows:

(1) For each unit k of cluster i of s^B, we calculate an initial weight w'_{ik}, as follows:

$$w'_{ik} = \sum_{j=1}^{M^A} l_{j,ik} \frac{t_j}{\pi_j^A} \qquad (21.2)$$

where $t_j = 1$ if $j \in s^A$, and 0 otherwise. In this step, we assess the amount of over-representation for ik in the sample drawn s^B due to the multiple links leading to it from U^A. Note that a unit ik having no link with any unit j of U^A automatically has an initial weight of zero. Observe also that a unit ik exhibiting just one link with units in U^A gets an initial weight equal to its design weight.

(2) For each unit k of cluster i of s^B, we get the total number of links L_{ik}^B:

$$L_{ik}^B = \sum_{j=1}^{M^A} l_{j,ik} \qquad (21.3)$$

We assess here the maximum possible number of contributors to the overrepresentation of ik.

(3) We calculate the final weight w_i:

$$w_i = \frac{1}{L_i^B} \sum_{k=1}^{M_i^B} w'_{ik} \qquad (21.4)$$

where $L_i^B = \sum_{k=1}^{M_i^B} L_{ik}^B$.

(4) We assign $w_{ik} = w_i$ for all $k \in U_i^B$.

Putting all together, we have for a unit ik of the population U^B that

$$w_{ik} = \sum_{j=1}^{M^A} \frac{t_j}{\pi_j^A} \frac{L_{j,i}}{L_i^B} \qquad (21.5)$$

To estimate the total Y^B, we use Equation 21.1. Because the estimation weights coming from the GWSM are the same for the set of M_i^B units of each cluster i, the estimator Equation 21.1 can be written as a function of clusters only. Thus, we have

$$\hat{Y}^B = \sum_{i=1}^{n^B} \sum_{k=1}^{M_i^B} w_{ik} y_{ik} = \sum_{i=1}^{n^B} w_i \sum_{k=1}^{M_i^B} y_{ik} = \sum_{i=1}^{n^B} w_i Y_i \qquad (21.6)$$

The estimator $\hat{Y}^B$, given by Equation 21.1, can then also be written as

$$\hat{Y}^B = \sum_{j=1}^{M^A} \frac{t_j}{\pi_j^A} Z_j \qquad (21.7)$$

where

$$Z_j = \sum_{i=1}^{N^B} \frac{Y_i}{L_i^B} L_{j,i} \qquad (21.8)$$

Equations 21.6 and 21.7 reveal the advantage there is in addressing duplication through the weights rather than inclusion probabilities: the linearity of the transformation used in the GWSM results in an estimator which can just as easily be interpreted under U^A than under U^B. We can switch from one form to the other as we see fit. It turns out that form Equation 21.6 is natural for point estimation and Equation 21.7 better suited for variance estimation.

As we can see from Equation 21.7, the estimator $\hat{Y}^B$ is in fact only a Horvitz–Thompson estimator where the variable of interest is the peculiar variable Z_j (Horvitz & Thompson, 1952). As shown in Lavallée (1995, 2002, 2007), the estimator $\hat{Y}^B$ is unbiased for estimating Y^B. Also, the variance of the estimator $\hat{Y}^B$ is given by:

$$Var(\hat{Y}^B) = \sum_{j=1}^{M^A} \sum_{j'=1}^{M^A} \frac{(\pi_{jj'}^A - \pi_j^A \pi_{j'}^A)}{\pi_j^A \pi_{j'}^A} Z_j Z_{j'} \qquad (21.9)$$

where $\pi_{jj'}^A$ is the joint probability of the selection of units j and j'. The variance $Var(\hat{Y}^B)$ can be estimated unbiasedly using the following equation:

$$\widehat{Var}(\hat{Y}^B) = \sum_{j=1}^{m^A} \sum_{j'=1}^{m^A} \frac{(\pi_{jj'}^A - \pi_j^A \pi_{j'}^A)}{\pi_{jj'}^A \pi_j^A \pi_{j'}^A} Z_j Z_{j'} \qquad (21.10)$$

(Särndal, Swensson, & Wretman, 1992). Other variance estimators are proposed in the scientific literature, such as Jackknife and Bootstrap estimators. For more information, one can consult Wolter (2007) and Särndal *et al.* (1992).

The GWSM offers some clear advantages over other estimation methods. First, the GWSM exploits selection probabilities π_j^A only for the selected units j in the sample s^A. This is a major simplification compared to other weighting methods such as the one based on the exact calculation of selection probabilities of surveyed units. Second, in a given context, the links between the population U^A from which the sample is selected and the population U^B can be very complex and yet, the GWSM can be applied relatively easily. Third, since we are surveying the full set of units from the selected clusters, it can happen that we must calculate an estimation weight for a unit of U^B that is surveyed, but that has no link with population U^A from which the sample is selected. The problem is then to get an estimation weight for these units so that we can produce unbiased estimates. The GWSM allows for the calculation of estimation weights for these units. Finally, in simple problems related to classical sampling (or direct sampling) theory where no duplication exists, the GWSM gives generally the same results as the classical theory.

21.3   Indirect sampling for hard-to-survey populations

Suppose that it is desired to produce estimates for a hard-to-survey population U_d^B that is contained in a larger population U^B, i.e., $U_d^B \subseteq U^B$. This target population can be, for example, a rare ethnic group (Example 1 above), smokers (Example 2), or homeless people (Example 3). Let this target population U_d^B contain M_d^B units. Note that the quantity M_d^B is often unknown itself or it can even be a parameter of interest to be estimated. As above, the population U^B is divided into N^B clusters, where cluster i contains M_i^B units.

Although, by definition, we do not have a sampling frame for the hard-to-survey population U_d^B, we might have access to a frame U^A that is at least related to population U^B. Contrary to populations U_d^B and U^B, we assume that we have some information on each of the M^A units of U^A. Considering Example 1, we might decide to survey the desired ethnic group by simply using an area frame. The frame U^A is then simply a set of addresses (cities, streets, etc.) from which we can select a sample s^A of m^A units with some sample design. Looking at Example 2, because no list of smokers is available, sample selection of smokers can then be done through the individuals from families, which can be viewed as clusters. In this case, the frame U^A is one of individuals where, unfortunately, we are not able to know, without surveying, whether a given person is a smoker or not. Lastly, considering Example 3, by constructing a sampling frame U^A from the set of services (overnight accommodation and meals) provided to homeless people, this target group can then be reached.

An appropriate sampling frame U^A for the hard-to-survey population U_d^B should have well-defined links $l_{j,ik}$ between the units j of population U^A and the units k of clusters i of the population U^B, if not U_d^B itself. If $L_j^A = \sum_{i=1}^{N^B} \sum_{k=1}^{M_i^B} l_{j,ik} = 0$ for a unit j of s^A, then there are simply no units of U^B identified with this unit j. In Example, 3, this would mean that a given service (e.g., a meal) has not been delivered to any homeless person.

As a result of the selection process, if a unit is selected in the sample, then all units of the cluster containing the selected unit will be surveyed. For hard-to-reach populations, this turns out to be beneficial because it helps the identification of units of the hard-to-reach population. In Example 2, surveying all units in selected clusters means that every family member of the selected person would be submitted to the search for smokers.

We now describe in detail the three examples given in the Introduction in the context of indirect sampling with the application of the GWSM.

21.3.1 Example 1: surveying a rare ethnic group

Recall that we want to survey a rare ethnic group within a city. The members of this ethnic group are assumed to be living in households that are part of small communities, which can be viewed as clusters. Typical examples of small communities in cities are Chinatown and Little Italy, which can be viewed as clusters of their respective ethnic groups. For some other ethnic groups, the communities can be the "family" in the broad sense, which can be defined as grandparents with their children, grandchildren and spouses.

We are interested in households containing at least one member of the ethnic group of interest. For this survey, it is desirable to use an area frame. The frame U^A is then a set of addresses from which we can select a sample s^A of m^A addresses according to some sample design. This is illustrated in Figure 21.1.

In Figure 21.1, the population U^B corresponds to the complete population of the city, which is living in households that are represented by the dots. Each box represents a small community, which is seen as a cluster of households. The hard-to-reach population U_d^B (i.e., the ethnic group of interest) can be viewed as a domain of interest d of U^B. The communities belonging to the ethnic group of interest are represented by the dark boxes. The pale boxes represent communities that do not belong to the ethnic group of interest.

We seek to estimate the total $Y_d^B = \sum_{i=1}^{N^B} \sum_{k=1}^{M_i^B} y_{d,ik}$, where $y_{d,ik} = y_{ik}$ if unit (household) k of cluster (community) i belongs to the domain d, and 0 otherwise. Y_d^B corresponds to the total of the variable y for the ethnic group of interest (domain d). We can also write $Y_d^B = \sum_{i=1}^{N^B} Y_{d,i}$ where $Y_{d,i} = \sum_{k=1}^{M_i^B} y_{d,ik}$. Note that because each community of domain d

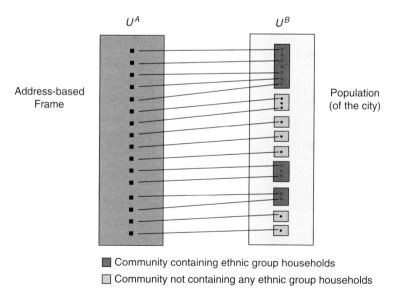

Community containing ethnic group households
Community not containing any ethnic group households

Figure 21.1   Surveying a rare ethnic group

contains only households of the ethnic group of interest, we can write $Y_d^B = \sum_{i=1}^{N_d^B} Y_i$ where N_d^B is the total number of communities of the ethnic group in the population.

Using indirect sampling, we proceed as follows. We select a sample s^A of addresses from the frame U^A. For each address j selected in s^A, we identify the households ik of U^B that have $l_{j,ik} = 1$, i.e., that are living at address j. For each household ik belonging to the ethnic group of interest, we survey all the M_i^B households of the related community i. We then measure the variable of interest y_{ik} and the number of links $L_{ik}^B = \sum_{j=1}^{M^A} l_{j,ik}$ between each surveyed household ik of U^B and the frame of addresses U^A. Note that in general, a household belongs to a single address, which implies that $L_{ik}^B = 1$. We have $L_{ik}^B = 0$ whenever the address is not part of the frame U^A. If the household ik identified by some address j in s^A does not belong to the ethnic group of interest, we stop surveying the cluster i to which this household belongs. Because this cluster i is not part of the ethnic group of interest U_d^B, there is no point in measuring the variable of interest y_{ik} and we then set $y_{ik} = 0$ for all $k \in i$.

To estimate Y_d^B, we use the estimator

$$\hat{Y}_d^B = \sum_{i=1}^{n^B} \sum_{k=1}^{M_i^B} w_{ik} y_{d,ik} = \sum_{i=1}^{n^B} w_i Y_{d,i} \tag{21.11}$$

where the weights w_{ik} (or w_i) obtained using the GWSM are given by Equation 21.5. Using Equation 21.11, we can then easily estimate totals for the ethnic group of interest.

21.3.2 Example 2: surveying smokers

We want to measure the health issues of smokers in a country. As mentioned earlier, smokers can be viewed as a hard-to-reach population because no list of smokers is available. However, sample selection of smokers can be done through families, which can be viewed as clusters.

The frame U^A can be a list of the persons living in the country. This list could be obtained, for example, from the last census or from administrative records. We select a sample s^A containing m^A persons from U^A containing M^A persons according to some sample design. The population U^B contains the same persons as in U^A, and thus, $M^B = M^A$. It is divided into N^B families (clusters), where family i contains M_i^B persons. Since populations U^A and U^B are the same, there is a one-to-one relationship between person j of population U^A and person k of clusters i of the population U^B, which is reflected into the indicator variable $l_{j,ik}$, where $l_{j,ik} = 1$ if j and k refers to the same person, and 0 otherwise. This implies that the indices j and k are exchangeable and, because of this, only the index j will thereafter be used to identify the persons of U^A or U^B. This is illustrated in Figure 21.2.

Since the population U^B is the list of persons living in the country, the hard-to-reach population U_d^B (i.e., the smokers) can be viewed as a domain of interest d, where $U_d^B \subseteq U^B$.

To survey the population of smokers using indirect sampling, we can proceed as follows: We select a sample s^A of m^A persons (smoker or not) from the frame U^A. For each person j

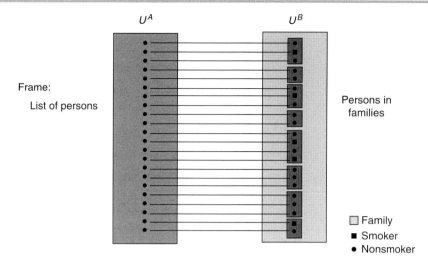

Figure 21.2   Surveying smokers

selected in s^A, we set up the list of the M_i^B members of its family (cluster) i, and identify all smokers in the family by interviewing them, for example. Let s^B be the set of n^B families identified by the persons of s^A. We survey all the smokers contained in each family $i \in s^B$ and measure a variable of interest y_{ik}.

We want to estimate the total $Y_d^B = \sum_{i=1}^{N^B} \sum_{j=1}^{M_i^B} y_{d,ij}$, where $y_{d,ij} = y_{ij}$ if person j of family i is a smoker, and 0 otherwise. We can also write $Y_d^B = \sum_{i=1}^{N^B} Y_{d,i}$ where $Y_{d,i} = \sum_{j=1}^{M_i^B} y_{d,ij}$. To estimate Y_d^B, we use the estimator

$$\hat{Y}_d^B = \sum_{i=1}^{n^B} \sum_{j=1}^{M_i^B} w_{ij} y_{d,ij} \tag{21.12}$$

where the weights w_{ij} (or w_i since $w_{ij} = w_i$ for $j \in i$) obtained using the GWSM are given by Equation 21.5. Now, because of the one-to-one relationship between U^A and U^B, we have $L_{j,i} = 1$ (i.e., each person belongs to only one family) and $L_i^B = M_i^B$. Therefore, Equation 21.5 reduces to

$$w_i = \sum_{j=1}^{M^A} \frac{t_j}{\pi_j^A} \frac{1}{M_i^B} \tag{21.13}$$

for $j \in i$. Using Equations 21.12 and 21.13, we can then easily estimate totals for smokers.

21.3.3 Example 3: surveying homeless people

We want to measure the health and living conditions of homeless people in a big city. Following Ardilly and Le Blanc (2001), we proceed by reaching homeless persons though services provided to them – that is, overnight accommodations and meals. During a certain period of

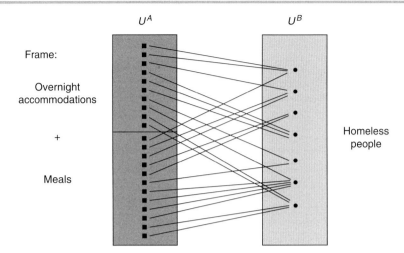

Figure 21.3   Surveying homeless people

time, one can assume that each homeless person will receive a given set of services. By sampling services, we get ultimately a sample of homeless persons to be surveyed. This is illustrated in Figure 21.3.

The frame U^A of M^A services (overnight accommodations and meals) is built by considering a given reference period, e.g., a particular week of the year. For the meals, we can consider all individual plates served at breakfast, lunch, and dinner during the full week. For overnight accommodations, we can consider all beds offered in the social centers of the city during the same week. With indirect sampling, we then select a sample s^A of m^A services from U^A. The population U^B (which is the same as the target population) contains M^B homeless people. Contrary to Examples 1 and 2, U^B is not divided here into clusters, which is the same as saying that each cluster i contains $M_i^B = 1$ homeless person. We can then omit index i for the rest of the section.

There is a relationship between the homeless person k of U^B and service j of U^A if this homeless person used this service (overnight accommodation or meal). That is, $l_{j,k} = 1$ if the service $j \in U^A$ has been used by the homeless person $k \in U^B$, and 0 otherwise. To produce unbiased estimates, each homeless person k of U^B must have used at least one service. This means that we must have $L_k^B = \sum_{j=1}^{M^A} l_{j,k} > 0$. In practice, this might not be achieved if some homeless people happen not to use any services provided by the city during the reference week chosen for sampling.

For homeless people, the indirect sampling process is as follows. We first select a sample s^A of m^A services from the frame U^A. For each service j selected in s^A, we identify the homeless person k of U^B that has used this service, i.e., with $l_{j,k} = 1$. For each homeless person k identified, we assume that we can set up the list of all services used by this person. In practice, this can be done by asking the social centers if the surveyed homeless person k has used other services during the reference week. Let s^B be the set of m^B homeless people identified by the units $j \in s^A$.

For the (target) population U^B, we seek to estimate the total $Y^B = \sum_{k=1}^{M^B} y_k$ using

$$\hat{Y}^B = \sum_{k=1}^{m^B} w_k y_k \tag{21.14}$$

From Equation 21.5, we have

$$w_k = \sum_{j=1}^{M^A} \frac{t_j \, l_{j,k}}{\pi_j^A \, L_k^B} \tag{21.15}$$

where $L_k^B = \sum_{j=1}^{M^A} l_{j,k}$ is the total number of services used by homeless person k during the reference week. As we can see from Equation 21.15, estimator Equation 21.14 takes into account duplicate selections of homeless persons by dividing the weights w_k by the total number of services L_k^B used by the homeless persons k. That is, even if a given homeless person has been selected in s^B through more than one service, no overestimation occurs because the weights Equation 21.15 take into account this multiplicity. Note that this holds in general with the weights Equation 21.5 obtained from the GWSM. Using Equations 21.14 and 21.15, we can then easily estimate totals for homeless people.

21.4 Network sampling

Network sampling is a survey method often used in social surveys. It proves to be particularly useful in delimiting populations that are hard to sample because they are rare or difficult to identify (Sirken, 1970b, 2004). In this type of sampling, the notion of a *network* often corresponds to a circle or set of contacts. We select units called *enumeration units* and we ask them to mention persons that they know corresponding to the desired criteria that are referred to as *target units*. Surveying smokers as in Example 2 is a typical example of the use of network sampling. Sanders and Kalsbeek (1990) used network sampling in a similar fashion to survey pregnant women.

Network sampling seems to emerge under several forms in the literature. The form of network sampling that appears most commonly in the literature is that coming from Birnbaum and Sirken (1965) and Sirken (1970a). They gave a formal statistical framework for network sampling by developing *multiplicity estimation*. This form of estimation takes into account the number of times a target person can be mentioned by the enumeration units. Levy (1977), Sirken (1970a, 1972), and Sirken and Levy (1974) used multiplicity estimation to evaluate the number (or the proportion) of persons in the population meeting a given criteria. Note that multiplicity estimation was used by these authors to estimate population counts rather than totals of quantitative variables. Multiplicity estimation certainly contributed to inspire the multiplicity approach described by Huang (1984).

Referring to Example 2 (surveying smokers), we can represent network sampling by Figure 21.4.

As seen in Figure 21.4, the enumeration units form the population U^A whereas the target units (those which have the desired characteristics) form the population U_d^B. According to

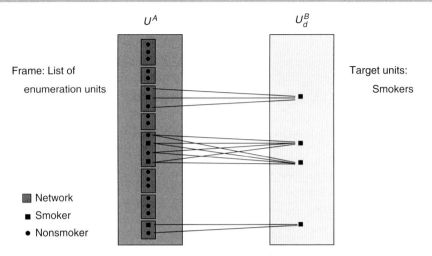

Figure 21.4   Surveying smokers in the context of network sampling

Sirken (1970a), a simple random sample s^A of m^A enumeration units is selected from the population U^A containing M^A units. Each enumeration unit j therefore has the same selection probability $\pi_j^A = m^A/M^A$. The population U_d^B has M_d^B target units.

As for the GWSM, Sirken (1970a) used an indicator variable l to denote the link between the enumeration units of U^A and the target units of U_d^B. Therefore, we have $l_{j,k} = 1$ if enumeration unit $j \in U^A$ identifies target unit $k \in U^B$, and 0 otherwise. We see here that the links are often many-to-one between U^A and U_d^B.

Sirken (1970a) was interested in the estimation of the population count M_d^B of the target population U_d^B. He calculated the following *multiplicity weight* ω_j, associated to each unit j selected in s^A:

$$\omega_j = \sum_{k=1}^{M_d^B} \frac{l_{j,k}}{L_k^B} \tag{21.16}$$

where $L_k^B = \sum_{j=1}^{M^A} l_{j,k}$. The multiplicity weight ω_j is so named because it keeps count of the number of times L_k^B that target unit k can be mentioned by the different enumeration units of U^A. The multiplicity estimator $\hat{M}_d^{Net,B}$ of M_d^B is given by:

$$\hat{M}_d^{Net,B} = \sum_{j=1}^{m^A} \frac{\omega_j}{\pi_j^A} \tag{21.17}$$

It is relatively simple to show that multiplicity estimation (and network sampling) is a particular case of the GWSM (and indirect sampling). Actually, comparing Figure 21.2 and Figure 21.4, both lead to the exact same mathematical results. First, since $U_d^B \subseteq U^B$, we can expand the population U_d^B of smokers (Figure 21.4) to the complete population U^B (Figure 21.2) by adding the nonsmokers that are part of U^B, but not U_d^B. Second, because both populations U^A and U^B contain the same people, we can identify the families (that correspond, in fact, to the networks) either in population U^B as in Figure 21.2, or in population U^A as in Figure 21.4. This means that the small rectangles representing networks in population U^A in Figure 21.4 can also be put as clusters (or families) in population U^B in Figure 21.2.

Let us consider the results obtained in Section 21.3.2. If we want to estimate the total number M_d^B of smokers, we simply set, in Equation 21.12, $y_{d,ik} = 1$ if person k of family (or network, or cluster) i is a smoker, and 0 otherwise. Using Equation 21.7, Equation 21.12 can then be written as

$$\hat{M}_d^B = \sum_{j=1}^{M^A} \frac{t_j}{\pi_j^A} Z_{d,j} \qquad (21.18)$$

where

$$Z_{d,j} = \sum_{i=1}^{N^B} \frac{L_{j,i}}{L_i^B} \sum_{k=1}^{M_i^B} y_{d,ik} \qquad (21.19)$$

In Equation 21.19, all target units (smokers) k of a given cluster i have the same proportion of links $L_{j,i}/L_i^B$ from $j \in U^A$. Now, because the populations U^A and U^B in Figure 21.2 have one-to-one links, we must have $L_{j,i} = 1$ and $L_i^B = M_i^B$ if unit j of U^A identifies a unit k that belongs to cluster i of U^B, and 0 otherwise. Therefore, for each unit k that belongs to cluster i, we have $L_{j,i}/L_i^B = 1/M_i^B$. But, for a target unit k belonging to cluster i, M_i^B is precisely the number of persons of U^A that can identify this target unit, which corresponds to L_k^B in Figure 21.4. Therefore, for any target unit k belonging to a cluster i, we must have $L_{j,i}/L_i^B$ of Figure 21.2 equal to $\omega_{j,ik} = l_{j,k}/L_k^B$ of Figure 21.4. Thus, Equation 21.19 can then be rewritten as

$$Z_{d,j} = \sum_{i=1}^{N^B} \sum_{k=1}^{M_i^B} \omega_{j,ik} y_{d,ik} = \sum_{k=1}^{M^B} \omega_{j,k} y_{d,k} = \sum_{k=1}^{M_d^B} \omega_{j,k} = \omega_j \qquad (21.20)$$

since $y_{d,k} = 1$ if person k is a target unit (smoker), and 0 otherwise. As a result, we get that $\hat{M}_d^B$ given by Equation 21.18 is equivalent to $\hat{M}_d^{Net,B}$ given by Equation 21.17. This implies that network sampling can be expressed mathematically in the context of indirect sampling. Note that a similar result has been obtained by Lavallée (2002, 2007), but using a different graphical representation.

Sirken (1972) extended multiplicity estimation to the case where the sample s^A is no longer a simple random sample but rather a stratified sample. Owing to the generality of the GWSM, it is simple to show again that multiplicity estimation is an application of the GWSM.

Sirken (1970a, 1972) showed that multiplicity estimation is unbiased. With respect to the precision of estimates, network sampling seems to have an advantage compared to conventional sampling, where each enumeration unit only reports for itself. Indeed, under certain conditions, Sirken (1970a) showed that multiplicity estimation, and thus network sampling, can give lower variances than those associated to conventional estimators. Based on the preceding results, this speaks as well in favour of indirect sampling (and the GWSM).

21.5 Adaptive cluster sampling

Thompson (1992, 2002) discussed sampling methods to use for populations that are difficult to sample whether because there is no sampling frame or these populations are migratory or elusive. There are, for example, problems such as enumerating populations of fish in a lake, assessing the number of trees in a forest, or estimating the number of people belonging to certain target groups (a particular ethnic origin or a socioprofessional category) in a city. To solve this last class of problem, Thompson (1990) proposed adaptive cluster sampling (ACS).

ACS is similar to network sampling and is particularly useful to produce estimates for populations that are difficult to reach. To illustrate how ACS works, we refer to Example 1 on surveying a rare ethnic group within a city. As mentioned earlier, the members of this ethnic group are assumed to be living in households that are part of small communities, which can be viewed as clusters. We use an area frame U^A from which we first select a sample s^A of m^A addresses according to some sample design. For each selected address, we ask whether some members of the households of this address are part of the ethnic group of interest and we retain the households containing these members. This is illustrated in the left portion of Figure 21.5 where each square represents an address and each dot an address with members of the ethnic group of interest. If an address leads to households with the desired members, we then go to see the contiguous neighbors of this address and to see whether we can find other members of the desired ethnic group. For the new addresses where we found members of the desired ethnic group, we go to see their neighbors, and so on until we find no more neighbors containing members of the ethnic group of interest. See Figure 21.5 for the

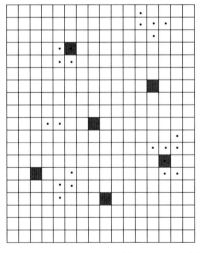 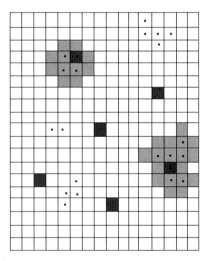

  • Address with members of the ethnic group
  ■ Address selected in the initial sample
  ▨ Address selected through ACS

Figure 21.5 Surveying a rare ethnic group using adaptive cluster sampling

resulting pattern. The set of surveyed units form clusters. At the end, we can obtain a considerable sample with, a priori, very little information about the units of the hard-to-reach population that we are interested in. Note that the sample is modified (or adapted) as the interviews progress.

With ACS, the final clusters containing the target units (e.g., the members of the ethnic group) are not distinct. This is due to the *edge units*, which are units adjacent to the clusters of target units but are not part of them. Let us come back to the previous example and consider two contiguous addresses **a** and **b**. Let address **a** contain no members of the ethnic group of interest, and address **b** contain some members of this ethnic group. If address **a** is selected but not **b**, the interviewing process of ACS will stop there because unit **a** does not belong to the target group of interest. On the other hand, if address **b** is selected, the survey process will continue and address **a** will be surveyed because it is contiguous to **b**. The edge unit **a** can thus be surveyed through two clusters. Note, however, that it will not contribute to the estimates because it is not part of the target group of interest. Thompson (1990) bypassed this problem by defining *networks* that are the final clusters, excluding the edge units. The networks of the edge units are of size 1.

The networks are mutually exclusive and exhaustive. Whichever units are selected in the starting sample, we will have the same composition of networks at the end of the survey process. This comes from the fact that the established procedure to identify the "neighbors" of the selected units is independent from the selection process. ACS is therefore only a form of cluster sampling where the clusters here are networks selected from their component units. This type of sampling is often employed in practice. Actually, both Examples 1 and 2 follow this sampling process.

Adaptive cluster sampling was described in detail by Thompson (1990, 1991a, 1991b, 1992, 2002) and Thompson and Seber (1996). Following Thompson (1990), a sample s^A is selected containing m^A units in the population U^A containing M^A units using some sample design. Assume that π_j^A represents the selection probability of unit j and that $\pi_j^A > 0$ for all $j \in U^A$. The population U^B contains M^B units. Thompson (1990) assumed that the populations U^A and U^B are the same, and thus, $M^A = M^B$. This constraint is, however, not mandatory for the use of ACS. The population U^B is divided into N^B networks, where network i contains M_i^B units. Note that the networks are themselves contained in overlapping clusters that include the edge units.

Once the sample s^A is selected, the units j of s^A are surveyed. This corresponds to surveying the units k of U^B that are contained in the cluster to which the unit j is linked. The process of ACS then requires going to survey the "neighbors" of the selected units, until no more target units are found. At the end of the survey process, for each unit j of s^A, the corresponding cluster is partitioned into networks: one network of size M_i^B linked to this unit j and containing the desired target units, and some networks of size $M_i^B = 1$ containing the edge units, the units k of U^B that are not target units.

Thompson (1990) was interested in the estimation of the mean $\overline{Y}_d^B = (1/M_d^B) \sum_{i=1}^{N^B} \sum_{k=1}^{M_i^B} y_{d,ik}$ of the population U_d^B of target units, where $y_{d,ik} = y_{ik}$ if $ik \in d$, and 0 otherwise.

Referring to Example 1, the ethnic group of interest is viewed as a domain of interest d and we have $U_d^B \subseteq U^B$ where the population U^B is the complete population of the city. In Figure 21.1, each box represents a small community, which is in fact a network, using ACS terminology. The ethnic group is living into communities that are represented by the dark boxes. The pale boxes represent communities that do not belong to the ethnic group of interest. Note that some of these last boxes can be edge units.

To estimate Y_d^B, Thompson (1990) calculated, for each selected unit j of s^A and linked to network i, the variable $\mu_{d,j}$ defined by

$$\mu_{d,j} = \frac{1}{M_i^B} \sum_{k=1}^{M_i^B} y_{d,ik} = \frac{Y_{d,i}}{M_i^B} \qquad (21.21)$$

The estimation of the total Y_d^B was then given by

$$\hat{Y}_d^{ACS,B} = \sum_{j=1}^{m^A} \frac{\mu_{d,j}}{\pi_j^A} \qquad (21.22)$$

In Section 21.3.1, we described the indirect sampling process for surveying an ethnic group of interest. We mentioned that "for each household ik belonging to the ethnic group of interest, we survey all the M_i^B households of the related community i", without specifying how the M_i^B households of the related community i would be surveyed. ACS is actually one clever way to proceed, and it can be shown that ACS can be put in the context of indirect sampling. Actually, Lavallée (2002, 2007) showed that Equation 21.22 is a particular case of the GWSM. This proof closely follows the one given in Section 21.4 about network sampling.

Thompson (1990) proved that ACS is unbiased. For the precision of estimates, this type of sampling seems to be worthwhile in comparison to conventional sampling when the hard-to-reach population forms clusters. The collection process of ACS associated with the mathematical framework of indirect sampling (and the GWSM) is certainly an approach to consider for hard-to-reach populations.

21.6 Snowball sampling and respondent-driven sampling

21.6.1 Snowball sampling

As seen before for surveying some hard-to-reach populations, we may want to survey clusters of individuals by first selecting one or many elements of the clusters. This is the case, for instance, in Examples 1 (surveying a rare ethnic group) and 2 (surveying smokers).

To survey "a man's immediate social environment," Coleman (1958) mentioned the use of *snowball sampling*. This type of sampling is similar to the ones that we mentioned earlier, i.e., indirect sampling, network sampling, and ACS. However, with snowball sampling, the sizes of the sampled clusters are not fixed, but rather decided by the selection parameters.

Goodman (1961) discussed snowball sampling with τ phases[1] and κ names, which can be described in the following way: A random sample s of n individuals is selected from a population of size N, where each individual k is selected with a probability $\pi_k > 0$. The precise sample design used to select the sample is not important in the whole snowball survey process. At the first phase, each of the n individuals selected in s is asked to provide κ names of individuals belonging to the same population. It should be noted that the individuals that are a part of s, or named at each selection phase, do not need to be part of the population of interest. However, the networks (or sets of acquaintances) from which the names of the individuals are chosen must be specified in the survey process. For example, we can ask an individual to name κ people from his or her immediate family, or κ people of the same nationality. The individuals named by the individuals selected in s, and who are not part of s, form the first phase of the survey. Note that we create here clusters of size κ, which may however be overlapping. At the second phase, we ask in turn each individual from the first phase to provide κ individuals. In a similar way, the new individuals named by the individuals from the first phase, and who are neither part of the first phase nor of s, form the second phase of the survey. This process continues until we have completed τ phases. For further details on snowball sampling, one can consult Coleman (1958), Frank (1977, 1978), Frank and Snijders (1994), and Goodman (1961).

Snowball sampling can also be viewed as similar to the survey process underlying indirect sampling. Recall that the survey constraint associated with indirect sampling is that all units of the selected clusters from the population U^B must be surveyed. This in fact corresponds to snowball sampling with $\tau = 1$ phase and $\kappa = \infty$ names. Indeed, by selecting the sample s^A and by surveying the corresponding units in U^B, we have, so to speak, the selection of units in U^B. Now, the process of surveying the rest of the individuals of the cluster corresponds to the survey process where we ask each individual k from cluster i to name all the M_i^B individuals contained in this cluster, whatever that number may be. This can be illustrated by Example 2 where we select a sample s^A (smoker or not) from the frame U^A. For each person j selected in s^A, we set up the list of all the M_i^B members of its family i and identify the smokers in the family.

Snowball sampling can also be seen as similar to the ACS. If we refer to Figure 21.5, we then have snowball sampling with $\tau = \infty$ phases and four "names." With snowball sampling, we are looking to survey households belonging to the population of interest (e.g., containing members of a rare ethnic group). We then randomly choose a sample of addresses (i.e., small squares) of households and identify the addresses where we found individuals belonging to the population of interest. In the identified addresses, we are then going to see the four adjacent addresses (north, south, east, and west) to identify other individuals belonging to the population of interest. Note that in practice the "four adjacent addresses" are likely to be simply "adjacent neighbors," however many there are. We proceed in this manner until we

---

1 The sense of the term "phase" used here by Goodman (1961) differs from that commonly used in sampling theory, namely a design where each phase represents a level of sampling where the second-phase units are selected within the units selected at the first phase, and so on.

find no more adjacent addresses belonging to the population of interest. The process of naming individuals in snowball sampling corresponds here to identifying adjacent addresses. We thus "name" all the addresses during a sufficient number of phases (not specified in advance), until all the "named" addresses systematically bring us back to addresses already named.

21.6.2 Respondent-driven sampling

Heckathorn (1997) proposed the use of *respondent-driven sampling* (RDS), which can be seen as an advanced version of snowball sampling. RDS surveys clusters (networks) of individuals by initially selecting one or many members of the clusters called "seeds." See, for instance, Goel and Salganik (2010), Heckathorn (2002, 2007), Salganik (2006), Salganik and Heckathorn (2004), and Thompson (2006, 2011).

   RDS with κ names for selecting n individuals works as follows. We first select a sample, not necessarily random, of target individuals, which makes wave 0. These individuals form the seeds. We then give κ coupons to each seed and ask them to give the coupons to other target persons among their acquaintances. Because each coupon is uniquely marked, we can monitor the recruitment patterns within the population. The persons recruited by persons composing wave 0 make wave 1. To constitute wave 2, we give κ coupons to each person of wave 1 and ask them to distribute the coupons to other target persons among their acquaintances. The persons recruited by persons from wave 1 are part of wave 2. We then repeat the process until we achieve a sample of size n. Note that each person of the RDS sample receives a monetary incentive to participate in the survey, together with another monetary incentive for recruiting persons for the next wave. At the end of the RDS process, the sample contains n target individuals (including the seeds) belonging to the hard-to-survey population of interest. A classical example of the use of RDS comes from surveying jazz musicians in a city (Heckathorn & Jeffri, 2001).

   RDS is often considered to be a nonprobabilistic method because the sample of seeds is usually nonrandom and the recruitment depends on the number of acquaintances of each recruited (selected) person. However, Salganik and Heckathorn (2004) have shown, under some assumptions, that RDS can produce unbiased estimates, irrespective of the way the sample of seeds was obtained. Chapter 24 in this volume and Lu, Bengtsson, Britton, Camitz, Kim, Thorson *et al.* (2012) discussed the effects of violating assumptions underlying RDS. Volz and Heckathorn (2008) developed a probabilistic approach to support estimation. Because of its similarities with snowball sampling, RDS may be put in the context of indirect sampling, but this still needs to be worked out in future work.

21.7   The use of multiple frames

As mentioned before, a population is often hard to sample because of the lack of an appropriate sampling frame for it. Now, even when a frame is available, it might not be enough to cover it all. Therefore, the use of multiple frames may be required. This is illustrated by Example 3 where homeless people in a city are surveyed through the use of two frames of services (Ardilly & Le Blanc, 2001). The first frame U^{A1} contains the list of all M^{A1} overnight accommodations provided to homeless persons through a given period of time. The second frame U^{A2} contains the list of all M^{A2} individual plates served at breakfast, lunch, and dinner meals to homeless persons during that same period of time. The overall frame U^A from which the sample is selected is constructed by simply merging together the two frames, i.e., $U^A = U^{A1} \cup U^{A2}$ and thus $M^A = M^{A1} + M^{A2}$. In addition to the application of Ardilly and Le Blanc (2001) to survey homeless people, another application of indirect sampling is the one from Deville and Maumy-Bertrand (2006), where they measure tourism in the region of Brittany in France. Mecatti (2004) used a similar approach for studying immigration (legal and illegal) in Italy.

Estimation in the context of multiple frames has first been formalized by Hartley (1962). Hartley (1962, 1974) considered the case where the target population is covered by two different sampling frames, but where the overlap of the two frames is completely known. Casady and Sirken (1980) suggested using the multiplicity estimator developed for network sampling in the context of two frames. With their approach, the number of frames where a target unit appears (defined as the multiplicity) is taken into account in the estimation process. More recently, Mecatti (2007) used a similar approach for more than two frames. Note that both approaches of Casady and Sirken (1980) and Mecatti (2007) can be put in the context of indirect sampling. This is not surprising since we saw in Section 21.4 that the multiplicity estimator of network sampling is a special case of the estimator obtained through the GWSM of indirect sampling.

In Section 21.3.3, we described the use of the GWSM to solve the estimation problem related to surveying homeless people through the use of multiple frames. In the present section, we will provide more details on the specific aspects of indirect sampling and the GWSM in the context of multiple frames. GWSM offers a different way to attack the estimation problem in this context. For more details on multiple frame estimation, one can read Lohr (2011), Lohr and Rao (2000, 2006), and Skinner and Rao (1996).

In the general context of multiple frames, the frame U^A where the sample is selected is constructed from frames U^{A1}, U^{A2}, ..., U^{AP}. We have $\cup_{p=1}^{P} U^{Ap} = U^A$ and $\sum_{p=1}^{P} M^{Ap} = M^A$. For simplicity, we assume here that $P = 2$, but the generalization to $P > 2$ is straightforward. Samples s^{A1} and s^{A2} of m^{A1} and m^{A2} units are selected from the frames U^{A1} and U^{A2}, respectively. We have $s^A = s^{A1} \cup s^{A2}$. Note that this can be seen as using a stratified design for the selection of sample s^A. Indeed, we can see each frame U^{Ap} as one "stratum" from which we select a sample s^{Ap}.

As before, the population U^B still contains M^B units. This population is divided into N^B clusters where cluster i contains M_i^B units. Again, we are interested in estimating the total $Y^B = \sum_{i=1}^{N^B} \sum_{k=1}^{M_i^B} y_{ik}$ for some characteristic y of U^B. We assume that there exists a link between each unit j of population $U^A = U^{A1} \cup U^{A2}$ and at least one unit k of cluster i of population U^B, i.e., $L_j^A = \sum_{i=1}^{N^B} \sum_{k=1}^{M_i^B} l_{j,ik} \geq 1$ for all $j \in U^A$. It is also assumed that each cluster i of U^B has at least one link with a unit j of U^A.

In the context of multiple frames, the links usually reflect the possibility of selecting a particular unit ik of U^B from U^{A1}, from U^{A2}, or both. If unit ik can be selected through the population U^{A1}, there must be at least one link, i.e., $l_{j,ik} = 1$, with some unit j of U^{A1}. The same holds for U^{A2}. If the unit ik can be selected from both populations, then we must have $l_{j,ik} = 1$ for some unit j of U^{A1}, and $l_{j,ik} = 1$ for some unit j of U^{A2}, and therefore $L_{ik}^B = \sum_{j=1}^{M^{A1}} l_{j,ik} + \sum_{j=1}^{M^{A2}} l_{j,ik} \geq 2$.

To estimate the total Y^B, we use the Equation 21.1 or 21.7. With the GWSM, the estimation process uses the samples s^{A1} and s^{A2} together with the links existing between the populations U^{A1} and U^{A2}, and the target population U^B. The initial weight given by Equation 21.2 can be expressed as follows

$$w'_{ik} = \sum_{j=1}^{M^{A1}} l_{j,ik} \frac{t_j^{A1}}{\pi_j^{A1}} + \sum_{j=1}^{M^{A2}} l_{j,ik} \frac{t_j^{A2}}{\pi_j^{A2}} \tag{21.23}$$

where $t_j^{A1} = 1$ if $j \in s^{A1}$, and 0 otherwise, and similarly for t_j^{A2}. The final weight w_i is given by Equation 21.4.

The estimator $\hat{Y}^B$ given by Equation 21.7 can then be written as

$$\hat{Y}^B = \sum_{p=1}^{2} \sum_{j=1}^{M^{Ap}} \frac{t_j^{Ap}}{\pi_j^{Ap}} Z_j^{Ap} \tag{21.24}$$

where

$$Z_j^{Ap} = \sum_{i=1}^{N^B} \frac{Y_i}{L_i^B} L_{j,i}^{Ap} \tag{21.25}$$

with $L_{j,i}^{Ap} = \sum_{k=1}^{M_i^B} l_{j,ik}$ for $j \in U^{Ap}$. Using Equation 21.24 and because of the "stratified" aspect of the use of multiple frames, the variance of $\hat{Y}^B$ is directly given by

$$Var(\hat{Y}^B) = \sum_{j=1}^{M^{A1}} \sum_{j'=1}^{M^{A1}} \frac{(\pi_{jj'}^{A1} - \pi_j^{A1} \pi_{j'}^{A1})}{\pi_j^{A1} \pi_{j'}^{A1}} Z_j^{A1} Z_{j'}^{A1}$$
$$+ \sum_{j=1}^{M^{A2}} \sum_{j'=1}^{M^{A2}} \frac{(\pi_{jj'}^{A2} - \pi_j^{A2} \pi_{j'}^{A2})}{\pi_j^{A2} \pi_{j'}^{A2}} Z_j^{A2} Z_{j'}^{A2} \tag{21.26}$$

21.8 Conclusion

In this chapter, we looked at the possibility of using indirect sampling for hard-to-survey populations. We exploited the fact that hard-to-survey populations are often found in clusters. The selection of clusters is then performed through the indirect sampling process, and the estimates are produced by using the GWSM. By sampling clusters rather than individual units, we can more easily track units that are part of the hard-to-reach populations.

Approaches other than indirect sampling exist for surveying such populations. Network sampling, adaptive cluster sampling, snowball sampling, respondent-driven sampling, and the use of multiple frames are a subset of such methods. With some modifications, we saw that these approaches can be put into the context of indirect sampling. One can then use the theory and developments surrounding indirect sampling and the GWSM to obtain a unified mathematical framework for the above approaches. For instance, calibration, nonresponse adjustment, and the use of weighted links (in particular, the ones that minimize the variance of estimates) can all be used for improving the efficiency of the above methods, as described in Lavallée (2002, 2007).

Indirect sampling is in constant evolution and all developments made to the method can be directly applied to the sampling methods described in this chapter. It is hoped that this will help in the difficult task of sampling members of hard-to-survey populations.

References

Ardilly, P., & Le Blanc, D. (2001). Sampling and weighting a survey of homeless persons: a French example. *Survey methodology*, 27(1), 109–18.

Birnbaum, Z. W., & Sirken, M. G. (1965). Design of sample surveys to estimate the prevalence of rare diseases: three unbiased estimates. *Vital and Health Statistics*, 2(11), 1–8.

Casady, R. J., & Sirken, M. G. (1980). A multiplicity estimator for multiple frame sampling. In *Joint Statistical Meetings Proceedings, Survey Research Methods Section* (pp. 601–05). Alexandria, VA: American Statistical Association.

Coleman, J. S. (1958). Relational analysis: the study of social organization with survey methods. *Human Organization*, 17(4), 28–36.

Deville, J. C., & Maumy-Bertrand, M. (2006). Extension of the indirect sampling method and its application to tourism. *Survey Methodology*, 32(2), 177–86.

Ernst, L. (1989). Weighting issues for longitudinal household and family estimates. In D. Kasprzyk, G. Duncan, G. Kalton, & M. P. Singh (eds.), *Panel Surveys* (pp. 135–59). New York: John Wiley & Sons.

Frank, O. (1977). Survey sampling in graphs. *Journal of Statistical Planning and Inference*, 1(3), 235–64.

 (1978). Sampling and estimation in large social networks. *Social Networks*, 1, 91–101.

Frank, O., & Snijders, T. (1994). Estimating the size of hidden populations using snowball sampling. *Journal of Official Statistics*, 10, 53–67.

Goel, S., & Salganik, M. J. (2010). Assessing respondent-driven sampling. *Proceedings of the National Academy of Sciences*, 107(15), 6743–47.

Goodman, L. A. (1961). Snowball sampling. *Annals of Mathematical Statistics*, 32(1), 148–70.

Hartley, H. O. (1962). Multiple frame surveys. In *Joint Statistical Meetings Proceedings, Social Statistics Sections* (pp. 203–06). Alexandria, VA: American Statistical Association.

(1974). Multiple frame methodology and selected applications. *Sankhya*, Series C, 36, 99–118.

Heckathorn, D. D. (1997). Respondent driven sampling: a new approach to the study of hidden populations. *Social Problems*, 44(2), 174–99.

(2002). Respondent driven sampling II: deriving valid population estimates from chain-referral samples of hidden populations. *Social Problems*, 49(1), 11–34.

(2007). Extensions of respondent-driven sampling: analyzing continuous variables and controlling for differential recruitment. *Sociological Methodology*, 37, 151–208.

Heckathorn, D. D., & Jeffri, J. (2001). Finding the beat: using respondent-driven sampling to study jazz musicians. *Poetics*, 28, 307–29.

Horvitz, D. G., & Thompson, D. J. (1952). A generalization of sampling without replacement from a finite universe. In *Journal of the American Statistical Association*, 47, 663–85.

Huang, H. (1984). Obtaining cross-sectional estimates from a longitudinal survey: experiences of the income survey development program. In *Joint Statistical Meetings Proceedings, Survey Research Methods Section* (pp. 670–75). Alexandria, VA: American Statistical Association.

Kalton, G., & Anderson, D. W. (1986). Sampling rare populations. *Journal of the Royal Statistical Society: Series A (General)*, 149, Part 1, 65–82.

Lavallée, P. (1995). Cross-sectional weighting of longitudinal surveys of individuals and households using the weight share method. *Survey Methodology*, 21(1), 25–32.

(2002). *Le sondage indirect, ou la méthode généralisée du partage des poids*. Éditions de l'Université de Bruxelles (Belgique) et Éditions Ellipses (France), 215 pages.

(2007). *Indirect Sampling*. New York: Springer.

Levy, P. S. (1977). Optimum allocation in stratified random network sampling for estimating the prevalence of attributes in rare populations. *Journal of the American Statistical Association*, 72(360), 758–63.

Lohr, S. L. (2011). Alternative survey sample designs: sampling with multiple overlapping frames. *Survey Methodology*, 37(2), 197–213.

Lohr, S. L., & Rao, J. N. K. (2000). Inference from dual frame surveys. *Journal of the American Statistical Association*, 95, 271–80.

(2006). Estimation in multiple-frame surveys. *Journal of the American Statistical Association*, 101(475), 1019–30.

Lu, X., Bengtsson, L., Britton, T., Camitz, M., Kim, B. J., Thorson, A., *et al.* (2012). The sensitivity of respondent-driven sampling. *Journal of the Royal Statistical Society: Series A (Statistics in Society)*, 175, Part 1, 191–216.

Mecatti, F. (2004). Center sampling: a strategy for surveying difficult-to-sample populations. In *Proceedings of the Statistics Canada Symposium 2004* [online archive]. Ottawa, Ontario: Statistics Canada.

(2007). A single frame multiplicity estimator for multiple frame surveys. *Survey Methodology*, 33(2), 151–57.

Salganik, M. J. (2006). Variance estimation, design effects and sample size calculations for respondent driven sampling. *Journal of Urban Health*, 83(Suppl. 7), 98–112.

Salganik, M. J., & Heckathorn, D. D. (2004). Sampling and estimation in hidden populations using respondent-driven sampling. *Social Methodology*, 34, 193–239.

Sanders, L. L., & Kalsbeek, W. D. (1990). Network sampling as an approach to sampling
pregnant women. In *Joint Statistical Meetings Proceedings, Survey Research
Methods Section* (pp. 326–31). Alexandria, VA: American Statistical Association.

Särndal, C.-E., Swensson, B., & Wretman, J. (1992). *Model Assisted Survey Sampling*. New
York: Springer-Verlag.

Sirken, M. G. (1970a). Household surveys with multiplicity. *Journal of the American
Statistical Association*, 65(329), 257–66.

(1970b). Survey strategies for estimating rare health attributes. In *Proceedings of the
Sixth Berkeley Symposium on Mathematical Statistics and Probability* (pp. 135–44).
Berkeley: University of California Press.

(1972). Stratified sample surveys with multiplicity. *Journal of the American Statistical
Association*, 67(337), 224–27.

(2004). Network sample surveys of rare and elusive populations: a historical review. In
Proceedings of the Methodological Symposium 2004 [online archive]. Ottawa,
Ontario: Statistics Canada.

Sirken, M. G., & Levy, P. S. (1974). Multiplicity estimation of proportions based on ratio of
random variables. *Journal of the American Statistical Association*, 69(345), 68–73.

Skinner, C. J., & Rao, J. N. K. (1996). Estimation in dual frames surveys with complex
designs. *Journal of the American Statistical Association*, 91, 349–56.

Thompson, S. K. (1990). Adaptive cluster sampling. *Journal of the American Statistical
Association*, 85(412), 1050–59.

(1991a). Stratified adaptive cluster sampling. *Biometrika*, 78(2), 389–97.

(1991b). Adaptive cluster sampling: designs with primary and secondary units.
Biometrics, 47, 1103–15.

(1992). *Sampling*. New York: John Wiley & Sons.

(2002). *Sampling* (2nd edn.). New York: John Wiley & Sons.

(2006). Targeted random walk designs. *Survey Methodology*, 32(1), 11–24.

(2011). Adaptive network and spatial sampling. *Survey Methodology*, 37(2), 183–96.

Thompson, S. K., & Seber, G. A. (1996). *Adaptive Sampling*. New York: John Wiley & Sons.

Volz, E., & Heckathorn, D. D. (2008). Probability based estimation theory for respondent
driven sampling. *Journal of Official Statistics*, 24(1), 79–97.

Wolter, K. M. (2007). *Introduction to variance estimation* (2nd edn.). New York: Springer.

22

Sampling the Māori population using proxy screening, the Electoral Roll, and disproportionate sampling in the New Zealand Health Survey

ROBERT GRAHAM CLARK AND ROBERT TEMPLETON

22.1 Introduction

This chapter describes an instructive example of a hard-to-reach subpopulation: the indigenous Māori population of New Zealand (NZ). This population shares some characteristics with others described in earlier chapters: it is relatively rare, oversurveyed, and geographically dispersed, and there is no adequate population frame. There are some unique features as well: Māori are less rare than many indigenous populations and have a special status in the NZ electoral system, so that the Electoral Roll provides a useful partial frame. A combination of strategies to oversample Māori in the NZ Health Survey is found to work well. A novel approach to setting the large number of design parameters required by this design is described, based on numerical optimization using a training and validation dataset.

The Māori peoples are the indigenous population of New Zealand and as such are important for social, political, and historical reasons. They have higher rates of poverty and illness than the general population and so are a particular priority in public health planning. For all these reasons, many surveys in NZ aim to oversample Māori, to give more precise statistics than would be produced by an untargeted survey of the population.

Māori constitute 14 percent of NZ adults and achieving a higher sample proportion in a household survey requires a combination of imperfect strategies. There is no general population register that can be used as a sampling frame. The Electoral Roll gives a partial frame and electors may indicate Māori descent on the Roll. However, not all Māori choose to do so, and addresses on the Roll are out of date, particularly when an election is not imminent. There is a five-yearly census conducted by Statistics New Zealand, which can be used for area targeting, although Māori are reasonably dispersed across NZ (particularly across the North Island), and populations shift between censuses, particularly at fine area levels. Proxy screening of households is another option, but this tends to underidentify Māori.

All of these strategies have been used in the NZ Health Survey, a multistage household interview survey collecting information on health behaviors, use of health services, and current health status. Since May 2011, the survey is conducted continuously with an annual sample size of approximately 14,000 adults and 5,000 children. Prior to this it was run roughly three yearly. A major goal is to provide accurate and precise statistics on ethnic subpopulations, particularly the Māori and Pacific peoples. This chapter describes the strengths and weaknesses of three tools for sampling the Māori population in the NZ Health Survey.

Section 22.2 gives some background on the Māori population. Section 22.3 discusses proxy screening. This was used in the 2006/07 NZ Health Survey, including a subsample where the proxy information was collected but not used, enabling evaluation of the proxy data against more rigorously collected survey data. Section 22.4 outlines the use of disproportionate sampling by area, based on census data on Māori and other subpopulations. Section 22.5 discusses the Electoral Roll, which has been used since May 2011 to sample addresses apparently containing an enrollee with Māori descent, in conjunction with area sampling. Section 22.6 shows how these contrasting strategies can be combined to reflect the errors and uncertainties attached to each, by using separate training and validation datasets to develop the design. Section 22.7 is a summary.

22.2   The Māori population

Māori are the indigenous people of New Zealand. There were over 560,000 people who identified as belonging to the Māori ethnic group in the 2006 Census of the New Zealand population, representing 15 percent of the total population.

Māori are a population of particular interest in New Zealand because of the government's special obligations to them under the Treaty of Waitangi. The Treaty of Waitangi was an agreement entered into by representatives of the Crown and of Māori in 1840, which established British authority in New Zealand (later transferred to the New Zealand Parliament) and which guaranteed Māori full protection of their interests and status and full citizenship rights. Part of the obligation of the New Zealand Government stemming from this agreement is the need to collect good quality statistical information to inform Māori development and decision-making and to monitor the effects of government policies and programs on Māori.

In addition to treaty obligations, understanding the Māori population is important because they are a large group within the New Zealand population with a distinct demographic and social profile. The Māori population is a youthful and growing population. Although there will be more older Māori (as a proportion) in coming years, Māori will continue to have a relatively young population. Fertility rates for Māori women are higher than those for non-Māori and well above replacement level, contributing to the growing Māori population.

In addition to the youthful demographic profile, there exist substantial inequities in terms of outcomes for Māori across areas such as:

- *The social determinants of health*: e.g., education, employment, income, and housing;
- *Health risk behaviors*: e.g., tobacco use, nutrition, gambling problems, and patterns of alcohol use; and
- *Long-term health conditions*: e.g., diabetes, heart disease, and cancer.

Hence, monitoring Māori outcomes across a range of social measures is critical to most official social and health surveys undertaken in New Zealand because of historical obligations and also because Māori are a large distinct subpopulation of New Zealand, where substantial disparities exist across a range of social and health outcomes compared to non-Māori.

There is no comprehensive population register in NZ and consequently it has been standard to employ area sampling practices when conducting official social surveys. One reason behind this is the relatively high mobility of the NZ population; 55 percent for the total population (among those aged over 5 years) changed their place of residence between the 2001 and 2006 Censuses. This is even higher for Māori, with 60 percent having moved between those censuses. This mobility makes constructing and maintaining population registers a challenge.

The preeminence of area-based sampling means the geographic distribution of Māori is important in terms of understanding some of the special issues involved in collecting Māori social and health statistics. Although the majority of Māori live in the North Island of New Zealand (87 percent) and in urban areas, Māori are relatively well spread across all parts of the country. In fact, 82 percent of Māori live in areas (meshblocks) where they are a minority (a meshblock is a standard geographic unit used in the New Zealand Census and in household surveys). This makes surveying them directly in an area-based face-to-face approach more costly because dwellings without Māori living in them can only be excluded after a cost-incurring doorstep screening exercise.

There are, however, some population list resources that can be useful, including the Electoral Roll. As well as being eligible for the general Electoral Roll, Māori have the option of voting in one of seven Māori electorates. Hence, the electoral registering process includes a declaration of one's ethnic ancestry and this information is stored, regardless of whether the person opts to be on the Māori Roll or the General Roll. An electronic version of the Roll is available to those doing scientific and health related research. The Electoral Roll on its own covers about 80 percent of the Māori population. It is not always completely up-to-date, with more push for greater coverage and up-to-date information in the lead up to elections. For these reasons, the Roll on its own is not considered an ideal frame. An approach, described later, is to combine the roll information with an area frame approach, to create an effective sampling frame with good coverage properties.

22.3   Proxy screening for Māori and other subpopulations

The 2006/07 NZ Health Survey used a proxy screening tool to oversample Māori, Pacific, and Asian people. The first stage of selection was a sample of meshblocks (small areas containing on average about 100 people), stratified by District Health Board (twenty-one broad regions) and based on census data on ethnic and total population sizes. The second stage of selection was of dwellings within meshblocks. This was divided into two parts: a core and a booster sample. In the core sample, one adult and one child (if any) was selected from each household. In the booster sample, screening questions were first asked of any adult contact

Table 22.1 *Screener and survey classification of Māori status for adults in the core sample*

Unweighted count proportion within screener result proportion within survey result		Survey result (gold standard)	
		Non-Māori	Māori
Proxy screener result	Non-Māori	7,747	256
		96.8%	3.2%
		98.9%	20.5%
	Māori	84	992
		7.8%	92.2%
		1.1%	79.5%

in the household regarding the number of adults and children in the household and their ethnicities (Māori, Pacific, Asian, or other, with multiple identification possible). One eligible adult and one eligible child (if any) was then selected, with eligible meaning Māori, Pacific, or Asian according to the proxy screener. The final sample consisted of adults and children selected via either the core or booster avenues.

To enable probabilities of selection in the pooled sample to be calculated, the proxy screening questions were also asked of the core dwellings. For more information on this question of the use of a screening tool on a core and a booster sample, see also Wells (1998). The use of both a core and booster sample means that underidentification in the proxy screener does not result in bias, only in increased standard errors, because all people have a chance of selection in the core sample (and hence in the pooled sample), and the probability of selection in the pooled sample can be calculated for each respondent.

For respondents in the core sample, we have both the survey report of ethnicity and the proxy screener results. The survey report is based on self-identification by the respondent towards the end of a detailed interview, whereas screener results on all household members are collected from any adult on first contact. Thus, we can identify how many Māori, Pacific, and Asian people were missed by the screener. This is useful to assess the efficiency of the booster sample. It also allows us to evaluate the undercoverage that would result if we were to omit the core sample and rely wholly on the screening tool to survey Māori or other ethnicities.

Table 22.1 shows the number of adults cross-tabulated by their screener and their survey identification as Māori / non-Māori. The major discrepancy between the survey and screener is that 20.5 percent of Māori (according to the survey) fail to be identified in the screener. There is very little overidentification of Māori in the screener.

Table 22.2 shows the rates of underidentification of Māori, Pacific, and Asian adults, broken down by single adult vs. multiadult households. Weighted rates, reflecting the unequal probability nature of the sample design, are shown in brackets. It is clear that the screener does worse at identifying Māori than Pacific or Asian adults, with misclassification rates over 20 percent, as opposed to 10–13 percent. Surprisingly, the identification of Māori

Table 22.2 *Unweighted (weighted) underidentification rates (in percent) of proxy screener by type of household*

	Single adult households	Multiple adult households	All households
Māori[a]	17.8 (18.3)	21.5 (22.1)	20.5 (21.7)
Māori[b]	17.5 (18.0)	20.9 (21.5)	20.0 (21.1)
Pacific[c]	14.9 (15.4)	8.6 (7.6)	9.8 (0.0)
Asian[d]	17.5 (16.5)	11.7 (10.6)	12.5 (10.9)
Māori, Pacific, or Asian[e]	17.0 (17.2)	16.3 (15.3)	16.4 (15.4)

[a] Proportion of respondents where proxy screener indicates non-Māori, but survey indicates Māori.
[b] Proportion of respondents where proxy screener indicates noneligible (not Māori, Pacific, or Asian), but respondent reports as Māori in the survey.
[c] Proportion of respondents where proxy screener indicates noneligible (not Māori, Pacific, or Asian), but respondent reports as Pacific in the survey.
[d] Proportion of respondents where proxy screener indicates noneligible (not Māori, Pacific, or Asian), but respondent reports as Asian in the survey.
[e] Proportion of respondents where proxy screener indicates noneligible (not Māori, Pacific, or Asian), but survey shows otherwise.

is nearly as poor for single adult households as for multiadult households. Clearly, it is not proxy reporting of ethnicity that is the problem, given that 18 percent of Māori adults living alone do not identify as Māori in the screener. The situation is different for Pacific and Asian respondents, who are correctly identified much more often in single adult households.

No definite explanation of this underreporting of Māori in the screener has been identified. Perhaps some respondents correctly intuit that responding as Māori in the screener may increase their chances of being selected for the main survey, because of the fact that Māori are an oversurveyed group. Or the fact that the first contact involves a very brief ethnicity question may be off-putting to Māori respondents.

Suppose a survey is to be conducted of Māori only, using the screener to enhance the design. What are the consequences of about 20 percent of this population being missed in the screener?

First, if we were to apply the full survey only when the screener indicated a Māori respondent, we would undercover the full population by about 20 percent. The covered subpopulation of Māori are apparently slightly less healthy than the full Māori adult population, with obesity and smoking rates a few percentage points higher. They are also more concentrated in the most deprived quintile of meshblocks in NZ (42.6 percent vs. 38.9 percent).

Secondly, a two-phase design could be used, where some adults would be sampled even when the screener indicated they are non-Māori. To enable a simple rough evaluation, suppose that we can take a simple random sample of adults, rather than using a complex multistage design. Further, suppose the cost of applying the screener is 0.3 times of the cost of applying the subsequent full interview (this was confirmed as broadly reasonable by the survey company that conducted the 2006/07 survey). This abjectly fails Deming's (1977) rule, also quoted in Kalton and Anderson (1986), that the ratio of second-to first-phase costs needs to be at least 6:1 and preferably 40:1 or more. The approximate formula (1) on page 70 of Kalton and Anderson (1986) can be used to give a more precise indication of the usefulness of the screener:

$$R \approx \frac{[kP - (k-1)W_1P_1][(c-1)\{P + (k-1)W_1P_1\} + (k-1)W_1 + 1]}{kP[(c-1)P + 1]}$$

where R is the factor by which the variance is reduced by using a screener, P is the proportion of the population who belong to the subpopulation, W_1 is the proportion of adults who are identified as subpopulation members by the screener (positive screens), P_1 is the proportion of positive screens who really are in the subpopulation, and k is the ratio of the sampling fraction applied to positive screens to the sampling fraction for others. Formula (2), also on page 70 of Kalton and Anderson (1986), gives the optimal value of k:

$$k_0^2 = \frac{P_1[(c-1)(P - W_1P_1) + (1 - W_1)]}{(P - W_1P_1)[(c-1)P_1 + 1]}$$

Using the proportions from Table 22.1 and assuming that the cost of applying the full survey is the same for Māori and non-Māori, we obtain $P=0.14$, $P_1=0.92$, $W_1=0.12$, and $c=1$. The value of k_0 is then 5.2. Substituting $k=k_0$ into the formula for R gives the variance for estimating means for the Māori population relative to equal probability sampling: $R=0.55$. However, we really want to know the efficiency relative to equal probability sampling where the screener is not even applied. This means that the per-respondent cost becomes 1.3 times cheaper, so the relevant relative efficiency is 0.55*1.3 which equals 0.71. Thus, the use of the screening tool improves the cost-efficiency of the survey by 29 percent, which is not too bad.

In summary, household screening for Māori resulted in a substantial undercount (21 percent) and small overcount (1 percent), even for single adult households. This was less accurate than screening for other ethnicities, perhaps because Māori are oversurveyed. At least some fraction of adults not screening as Māori should still be surveyed, to avoid undercoverage bias. The use of the screener can improve the variances of estimated population means for Māori by a ballpark 30 percent, in surveys where Māori are the only priority.

22.4 Disproportionate sampling by area

Statistics New Zealand conducts a five-yearly census which includes an ethnicity question. Population sizes by Māori and other ethnicities are available for each meshblock. It makes sense to use this data to improve the sample size of Māori, by assigning higher selection probability to areas where more Māori live. Disproportionate sampling can increase the achieved sample size of Māori for fixed cost. However, the unequal selection probabilities need to be corrected for by appropriate use of survey weights, otherwise Māori statistics would overrepresent Māori living in higher-density areas (such as Auckland) at the expense of the substantial number of Māori living in other parts of New Zealand. The resultant increased variation in survey weights tends to lead to higher standard errors, partially undoing the benefit of disproportionate sampling.

Kalton and Anderson (1986) derived results on the best allocation of sample sizes to strata, to balance optimally the sample size of a subpopulation and the variability of the estimation weights. Assuming that the only aim is to estimate means for the subpopulation, and also assuming simple one-stage stratified sampling, as well as some simplifying assumptions, they found that the probability of selection in stratum h should be proportional to $\sqrt{\varphi_h/(R + \varphi_h)}$ where φ_h is density (i.e., the proportion of the population in stratum h who belong to the subpopulation), and R is the cost of identifying whether a sampled unit is in the subpopulation relative to the cost of fully surveying the unit.

Densities are available for all meshblocks in NZ, so it makes sense to use this information in sampling. However, there are too many meshblocks (approximately 40,000) for them to be feasible strata. Instead, the NZ Health Survey uses multistage sampling, with meshblock as the primary sampling unit, followed by households, followed by one adult and one child per selected household. Clark (2009) extended Kalton and Anderson's optimal allocation to multistage sampling. Under simplifying assumptions, the best design is to assign a final person probability of selection proportional to $\sqrt{\varphi_g/(R + \varphi_g)}$ where φ_g is the density for meshblock g. In single-stage stratified sampling, the probabilities of selection fully specify the design. In multistage sampling, these probabilities of selection could be implemented by assigning higher selection probabilities to high-density meshblocks, or by assigning higher sampling fractions within these meshblocks, or by a combination. Clark (2009) found that in most cases, an approximately optimal strategy is to

- Select meshblocks with probability proportional to $N_g\sqrt{\varphi_g/(R + \varphi_g)}$, where N_g is the total population for meshblock g; and to
- Use a fixed sample size (including both Māori and non-Māori) within each selected meshblock.

This is a modification of a standard self-weighting design. If the subpopulation is relatively rare, then $N_g\sqrt{\varphi_g/(R + \varphi_g)}$ may be replaced by $N_g\sqrt{\varphi_g}$.

The preceding strategies will only be of much use if Māori are geographically clustered. If the density varies little across meshblock, then the above design will be close to equal probability sampling. Figure 22.1 is a histogram showing the number of Māori living in meshblocks with various densities. The figure shows that there is some but not dramatic concentration of Māori people in meshblocks. Similar calculations show that the median value of the meshblock density across all Māori in NZ is 23 percent, and only 17 percent of Māori live in meshblocks where they are the majority.

The optimal designs of Clark (2009) and Kalton and Anderson (1986) also assume that design data is perfectly accurate. In reality, census data will be out of date to some extent. Changes between census dates are likely to be greater at the meshblock level than for

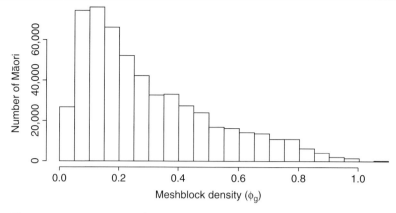

Figure 22.1   Histogram of Māori meshblock densities

broader regions. For this reason, the 2006/07 NZ Health Survey design calculated probabilities of selection using densities defined for each District Health Board, a broad region
containing on average about 200,000 people.

Table 22.3 shows the relative efficiency achieved by using a design based on Clark (2009),
with density defined at various geographic levels. The table was calculated using matched
meshblock data from the 2001 and 2006 NZ Censuses. The second column of data shows the
efficiency based on using 2001 NZ Census data calculated under the assumption that this data
is perfectly accurate at the time of surveying. The final column shows the efficiency of a
design based on 2001 data if the actual meshblock counts were as in the 2006 Census. The
best design when the 2001 Census data is perfectly accurate uses meshblock level data,
giving a reduction in variance of 23 percent (efficiency of 0.77) compared to equal probability sampling, for fixed cost. However, the final column shows that when the efficiency is
more realistically evaluated using 2006 Census data, the efficiency deteriorates to 0.88. In
fact, allocating probabilities of selection based on the area unit densities is slightly superior.

22.5   Using the Electoral Roll

Screening for Māori respondents on the doorstep is expensive and inefficient, as discussed
in Section 22.3. In many countries, there is little other choice, because there are no
adequate frames of ethnic and other subpopulations. However, New Zealand Māori
have the opportunity to indicate their descent and can choose whether to vote in a general
electorate or a Māori electorate. As a result, the Electoral Roll constitutes a partial frame of
Māori.

Figure 22.2 is an extract from the first page of the NZ voting enrollment form. A question
just before Section B of the form is "are you a NZ Māori or a descendant of a NZ Māori?"
The list of enrollees answering yes to this question has been used as a supplementary
sampling frame of Māori in the NZ Health Survey since May 2011. This frame is certainly
not perfect, in particular:

Table 22.3 *Approximate relative efficiency (compared to equal probability sampling) of various designs meshblock selection probability proportional to $N_g \sqrt{\hat{\varphi}_g}$ where φ_g estimated using 2001 Census data at various levels of aggregation*

Level of aggregation of 2001 Census data	Average total population (all ages) per area (2001 Census)	Efficiency estimated using 2001 Census data	Efficiency estimated using 2006 Census data
Meshblock[a]	110	0.766	0.876
Area unit	2,200	0.857	0.870
Territorial authority	53,000	0.921	0.923
District Health Board	180,000	0.937	0.937

[a] 0.01 added to φ_g to avoid assigning zero probability of selection to any meshblocks.

(1) Address and other information may be somewhat out of date, particularly when there has not been an election recently.
(2) Self-identification of Māori may be different on the Roll than in the survey, leading to over or undercoverage.
(3) The survey aims to cover the whole population, so non-Māori also need to be given appropriate chance of selection in the survey.

To deal with these issues, the 2011–14 Health Survey sample is selected as follows:

- A sample of meshblocks, called the "area component," is selected from the whole of New Zealand, with probabilities of selection based on 2006 Census total population and population by ethnicity. 215 meshblocks were selected in this way for every quarter of enumeration.
- Addresses where at least one person indicated Māori descent were selected from the Electoral Roll. These addresses were grouped into meshblocks. A sample of meshblocks, called the "roll component" was selected with probability proportional to the number of addresses. This sample was forced to be nonoverlapping with the area component. 100 meshblocks were selected in this way for every quarter.
- A sample of households was selected in the area component by taking a systematic sample from each selected meshblock in this component. One adult and one child was selected and surveyed from each selected household.
- A sample of addresses was selected from each meshblock in the roll component. One adult and one child was selected and surveyed from each selected address, without reference to their ethnicity. Electoral Roll data was not used at this stage – the selected adult was not necessarily the same as the Māori enrollee, and the Māori enrollee might even have moved. This was done to enable a probability of selection to be calculated for every respondent, to avoid (for example) underrepresentation of people who have moved without updating their electoral enrollment.
- Ethnicity (including Māori identification) was collected as part of the survey, and was used in calculating statistics for Māori and other subpopulations.

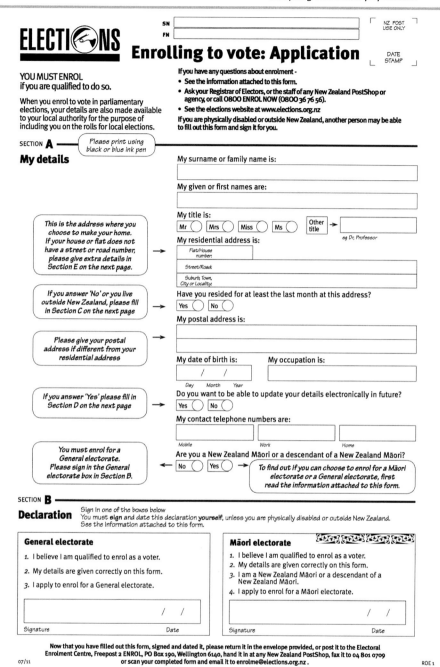

Figure 22.2   First page of NZ voting enrollment form

The sample contained 215 meshblocks in the area component and 100 in the roll component in each quarter of enumeration. Approximately 14 percent of approached households were selected via the roll component. The next section will discuss how the relative sizes of the area and roll components, as well as the method of disproportionate sampling, were chosen.

It turned out that 52 percent of adult respondents in the roll component were Māori, compared to only 14 percent of adults in the whole population (estimated using data from September quarter 2011). It is clear that the Roll is able to increase substantially the rate of Māori in sample, without incurring screening costs. The Roll as used here is far from perfect though, with nearly half of all selected adults being non-Māori. Weighted estimates showed that approximately 68 percent of the adult Māori population lives in Māori addresses (i.e., addressed where at least one enrollee has indicated Māori descent).

To clarify further the potential gain from the use of the Māori Roll, suppose that we were to stratify the population of all adults by Māori vs. non-Māori address, and then select an optimally allocated sample. The relative efficiency for Māori statistics would then be 0.73, compared to equal probability sampling, i.e., a 27 percent gain. While we might hope for greater gains in efficiency, this is a much greater gain than from either disproportionate sampling by area or from proxy screening.

22.6   Combining sampling strategies efficiently

22.6.1   Overview

The previous three sections cover three strategies for sampling the Māori population. It is not at all clear how to put these together in practice, in a way that reflects the out-of-datedness and different ethnicity definitions of the census area data, the undercoverage and overcoverage of the Electoral Roll, and the underidentification of Māori by the proxy screener. This section will describe a methodology for simultaneously making these and other design decisions while reflecting the imperfections of the design information. The approach was used to design the 2011–14 NZ Health Survey sample.

First, we will express the design in terms of twelve design parameters that need to be set. Then, we will discuss how to estimate the variances that will result from any given set of values for these parameters, using 2001 Census data and 2006/07 NZ Health Survey data. Finally, the design parameters are numerically optimized.

22.6.2   Expressing the design in terms of fifteen design parameters

Section 22.4 suggested that to optimize for a given subpopulation, meshblock probabilities of selection should be proportional to $N_g\sqrt{\varphi_g}$, with a fixed number of households to be selected from each selected meshblock. This means that household probabilities of selection are proportional to $\sqrt{\varphi_g}$. However, this design is approximately optimal when a single subpopulation is of interest and when the densities φ_g are known perfectly. In reality, in the NZ Health Survey, the Māori, Pacific, and Asian populations are all important, although Māori statistics are given the highest priority. National all-ethnicity estimates are also important. Moreover, the densities are not known perfectly. Table 22.3 showed that census densities at the broader area unit level appear to give better results than meshblock densities, when five-year-old census data is used. Even better results might be achievable by using an appropriate mix of meshblock, area unit, and district health board densities.

Such a mix can be given by making meshblock probabilities of selection in the area component of the sample proportional to the population size N_g multiplied by a targeting factor f_g:

$$f_g = w_1 \sqrt{\text{Maori MB density}} + w_2 \sqrt{\text{Maori AU density}} + w_3 \sqrt{\text{Maori DHB density}}$$
$$+ w_4 \sqrt{\text{Pacific MB density}} + w_5 \sqrt{\text{Pacific AU density}} + w_6 \sqrt{\text{Pacific DHB density}}$$
$$+ w_7 \sqrt{\text{Asian MB density}} + w_8 \sqrt{\text{Asian AU density}} + w_9 \sqrt{\text{Asian DHB density}}$$
$$+ w_{10} \times 1.$$

(22.1)

where the parameters $w_1, \ldots, w_{10}$ are nonnegative weights that sum to 1, and MB, AU, and DHB refer to meshblock, area unit, and district health board, respectively. The final parameter w_{10} is there to make sure that no probabilities of selection are too close to zero in meshblocks with few subpopulation members. A fixed sample size within meshblocks of twenty was assumed. (The within-meshblock sample size could have been treated as another design parameter to be optimized, but for simplicity was set independently. Intraclass correlations for many health variables are low, and the value of twenty was chosen mainly to be less than the meshblock size for the great majority of meshblocks.)

A further parameter, p_{screen}, is needed to define the use of the proxy screener for ethnicity. It is assumed that the proxy screener is applied to the twenty selected households in each meshblock in the area component. Of these households, $20 p_{\text{screen}}$ are defined to be the booster households, and one adult and one child of eligible ethnicity according to the screener (Māori, Pacific, or Asian, if any) is selected. The remaining $20(1-p_{\text{screen}})$ households are defined to be core households. One adult and one child is selected from each household regardless of their screening results.

Finally, a parameter p_{roll} defines the use of the Electoral Roll. The complete sample consists of a roll component and an area component. The roll component is selected as described in Section 22.5, such that a proportion p_{roll} of the combined sample is in the roll component, with the remainder coming from the area component.

22.6.3 Estimating the variance for any given set of values for the design parameters

To choose values for the twelve design parameters, we want to be able to estimate the variances that would be achieved for any given set of values. The estimation should reflect that the 2006 Census data is five years old when the continuous survey commences in 2011. It should also reflect the imperfections of the Electoral Roll and the proxy screening tool.

To achieve this, for any given set of design parameters, a hypothetical design is constructed using the Electoral Roll and the 2001 Census data. The probabilities of selection for this design are then calculated for every respondent in the 2006/07 NZ Health Survey. These sample data are then used to estimate the variance that will be achieved for estimates for the total population, and the Māori, Pacific, and Asian subpopulations. The discrepancy between ethnicity as recorded by the 2006/07 survey and the design data from the 2001 Census and other sources enables a realistic assessment of any set of design parameters.

We want an estimator for the variance that will be achieved from the hypothetical new design of an estimated prevalence for Māori and other subpopulations. A commonly used approximation is:

$$
\hat{\text{var}}(\hat{P}_{sub}) \approx P(1-P)n_{sub(hypothetical)}^{-1}\left(1 + c_{w(hypothetical)}^2\right)
$$

$$
= P(1-P)n_{sub(hypothetical)}^{-1}\frac{\displaystyle\sum_{s_{sub(hypothetical)}} \pi_i^{-2}/n_{sub(hypothetical)}}{\left(\displaystyle\sum_{s_{sub(hypothetical)}} \pi_i^{-1}/n_{sub(hypothetical)}\right)^2}
$$

$$
= P(1-P)\left(\sum_{s_{sub(hypothetical)}} \pi_i^{-2}\right)\left(\sum_{s_{sub(hypothetical)}} \pi_i^{-1}\right)^{-2}
$$

(22.2)

where P is the population prevalence, $\hat{P}_{sub}$ is the estimated prevalence for the subpopulation, π_i are the probabilities of selection for the hypothetical design, $s_{(hypothetical)}$ is a sample selected using the hypothetical design, $s_{sub(hypothetical)}$ is the subset of this sample who belong to the subpopulation, and $n_{(hypothetical)}$ and $n_{sub(hypothetical)}$ are the sizes of $s_{(hypothetical)}$ and $s_{sub(hypothetical)}$, respectively (see, for example, Gabler, Häder, & Lahiri, 1999, and Kish, 1992). We can't apply Equation 22.2 as is, because the hypothetical sample has not actually been selected. Instead, the 2006/07 survey data is used. We can calculate the probability of selection π_i under the hypothetical sample design for every unit in the 2006/07 sample, using the 2001 Census to obtain densities by ethnicity which lead to the meshblock selection probabilities via Equation 22.1, and also using an Electoral Roll extract from 2006. The 2006/07 survey data file contains a weight w_i which reflects the design used to select this sample. We can then estimate the right-hand side of Equation 22.2 by replacing sums over $s_{sub(hypothetical)}$ with sums over the subset of the 2006/07 sample who belong to the subpopulation, which will be denoted by $s_{sub(06/07)}$, weighted by $w_i\pi_i$ to reflect the difference between the 2006/07 design and the hypothetical design:

$$
\hat{\text{var}}(\hat{P}_{sub}) = P(1-P)\left(\sum_{s_{sub(06/07)}} w_i\pi_i^{-1}\right)\left(\sum_{s_{sub(06/07)}} w_i\right)^{-2}
$$

(22.3)

The variance estimator Equation 22.3 uses the 2006/07 sample data to estimate the variance that will be achieved by the hypothetical new design defined by any given set of design parameters.

The crucial feature of estimator Equation 22.3 is that the design data used to calculate π_i in Equation 22.3 is based on out-of-date census and roll information, as well as the somewhat error-prone proxy screening data from the 2006/07 survey. In contrast, the ethnicity used to define the subpopulation sample $s_{sub(06/07)}$ is based on the gold-standard survey-collected ethnicity. Hypothetical designs will be penalized to some extent when there are differences between the survey ethnicity and the design ethnicity.

22.6.4 Optimizing the design parameters

The objective criterion for the survey was defined to be

$$F = SE(\hat{P}_{Maori}) + SE(\hat{P}_{Pacific}) + SE(\hat{P}_{Asian}).$$

where $\hat{P}_{subpop}$ is an estimated prevalence for a given subpopulation, with the true prevalences assumed to equal 0.2. The standard errors were estimated as described in Section 22.6.3. This objective criterion was defined in consultation with the Ministry of Health, by tabulating estimates of the standard errors for designs which would result from various definitions of F. Ministry staff then chose a criterion reflecting their priorities for Māori, Pacific, Asian, and all-ethnicity statistics. Standard errors for all-ethnicity prevalences were given no weight in the final criteria, because national standard errors were considered to be low enough even without being explicitly reflected in F.

The estimated objective criterion F was then coded as a function of $w_1, \ldots, w_{10}$, p_{roll} and p_{screen} in the R statistical software environment (R Development Core Team, 2012). This function was then minimized using the *optim* function in R. Table 22.4 summarizes the optimal designs. Each option refers to an optimization with some or no design parameters constrained to equal 0. Option 1 is equal probability sampling and is included for comparison purposes. Option 2 is the unconstrained optimal design. Option 3 constrains p_{screen} to equal 0. The Ministry of Health felt that the screener could give a poor first impression to respondents, and the table shows that the objective criteria F is not too much worse when it is omitted. The final option, 4, sets various other parameters to zero for simplicity, based on those parameters which were close to 0 in Option 3. An option similar to this one was implemented for 2011–13.

Some notable features from the designs in Table 22.4 are:

- The optimal design gives almost no weight to Māori densities in the area targeting.
- Approximately 14 percent of the total sample should be selected using the Roll, with the remaining 86 percent coming from the area component.
- Omitting the screen increases the Māori standard error by 4 percent (from 0.97 percent to 1.01 percent) and increases F by 9 percent (0.77 to 0.84), while reducing the national standard error. This was considered to be an acceptable price to improve the initial contact process.
- Options 2, 3, and 4 give some weight to MB densities, but more to AU densities, and almost no weight to the DHB data.

Typical approaches to sample design would have based area targeting on meshblock densities only, since this would be optimal if the census design data was perfectly accurate and up to

Table 22.4 *Numerically optimized designs (all cost equivalent assuming 1 cost unit for each full interview and 0.3 for each household in sample)*

Design parameter	Interpretation	Option 1: equal probability sample	Option 2: unconstrained optimal design	Option 3: no screener	Option 4: simplified design with selected design parameters zeroed
w_1	Māori MB weight	0	0.00	0.01	0.00
w_2	Māori AU weight	0	0.05	0.03	0.00
w_3	Māori DHB weight	0	0.00	0.00	0.00
w_4	Pacific MB weight	0	0.33	0.29	0.31
w_5	Pacific AU weight	0	0.26	0.34	0.37
w_6	Pacific DHB weight	0	0.01	0.01	0.00
w_7	Asian MB weight	0	0.05	0.11	0.09
w_8	Asian AU weight	0	0.23	0.18	0.20
w_9	Asian DHB weight	0	0.03	0.00	0.00
w_{10}	Weight attached to "1"	1	0.05	0.02	0.03
p_{roll}	Proportion of total households selected via roll sample	0	0.09	0.14	0.14
p_{screen}	Proportion of area sample households where screen is applied	0	0.61	0.00	0.00
Properties of optimal design					
SE (%) Māori		1.18	0.97	1.01	1.01
SE (%) Pacific		1.90	1.32	1.46	1.46
SE (%) Asian		1.41	1.17	1.31	1.31
SE (%) National		0.41	0.55	0.47	0.47
F relative to option 1		1.00	0.77	0.84	0.84

date. The approach described in this section allows the limitations of the design data to be taken account of, so that broader level area data are used in combination with meshblock data for a more robust design. To borrow some terminology from the statistical learning literature (e.g., Hastie, Tibshirani, & Friedman, 2009), the objective criteria (3) makes use of separate training and validation datasets. The design probabilities π_i are optimal according to the 2001 Census data (the training dataset), but are instead evaluated in (3) using the 2006/07 survey data (the validation dataset). If these two datasets agreed on ethnicity, the numerically optimized design would have weight attached to meshblock densities but none attached to area unit and district health board densities. The discrepancies between the training and validation datasets enable a realistic evaluation of the strengths and weaknesses of the design data, and the numerically optimized design reflects this. The approach here is based on a general methodology for sample design using imprecise design data developed in Clark (2013).

22.7 Summary

Three main strategies have been identified for sampling the Māori population, as well as the Pacific and Asian populations which are also of interest:

- Proxy screening based on ethnicity reported by any adult contact from the household. This approach may give a poor impression of the survey and misses about 20 percent of the Māori population.
- Targeting the sample by area using census data. If Māori statistics were the only priority, this would give about a 23 percent reduction in variance for fixed cost if census data were perfect (based on Table 22.3). The gains are less when the census is some years out of date.
- Using the Electoral Roll as a frame, in conjunction with an area-based sample of the general population. The NZ Electoral Roll includes individuals' addresses as well as their identification as being Māori or of Māori descent. About 68 percent of Māori adults are covered by a sample of such addresses from the Roll.

All three methods are far from perfect, with the Electoral Roll being the most useful resource. A combination of the three strategies should work well, but requires many interrelated design parameters to be chosen. A statistical learning approach, using past census and survey data, is an effective means of choosing many design parameters, while reflecting the strengths and weaknesses of proxy screening, the Electoral Roll, and census areal counts.

References

Clark, R. G. (2009). Sampling of subpopulations in two-stage surveys. *Statistics in Medicine*, 28(29), 3697–717.

    (2013). Sample design using imperfect design data. *Journal of Survey Statistics and Methodology*, 1, 6–23.

Deming, W. E. (1977). An essay on screening, or on two-phase sampling, applied to surveys of a community. *International Statistical Review*, 45, 29–37.

Gabler, S., Häder, S., & Lahiri, P. (1999). A model based justification of Kish's formula for design effects for weighting and clustering. *Survey Methodology*, 25, 105–06.

Hastie, T., Tibshirani, R., & Friedman, J. (2009). The Elements of Statistical Learning: Data Mining, Inference and Prediction. New York: Springer. Retrieved from www-stat. stanford.edu/~tibs/ElemStatLearn/.

Kalton, G., & Anderson, D. W. (1986). Sampling rare populations. *Journal of the Royal Statistical Society: Series A (General)*, 149(1), 65–82.

Kish, L. (1992). Weighting for unequal pi. *Journal of Official Statistics*, 8(2), 183–200.

New Zealand Ministry of Health. (2011). *The New Zealand Health Survey Sample Design Years 1–3 (2011–2013)*. Wellington, New Zealand: author. Retrieved from www.health.govt.nz/publication/new-zealand-health-survey-sample-design-years-1–3–2011–2013.

R Development Core Team. (2012). *R: A Language and Environment for Statistical Computing* [computer software manual]. Vienna, Austria: author. Retrieved from www.R-project.org/.

Wells, J. E. (1998). Oversampling through households or other clusters: comparisons of methods for weighting the oversampled elements. *Australian & New Zealand Journal of Statistics*, 40, 269–77.

23

Network-based methods for accessing hard-to-survey populations using standard surveys

TYLER H. McCORMICK AND TIAN ZHENG

23.1 Introduction

Standard surveys often exclude members of certain groups, known as *hard-to-survey groups*. One reason these individuals are excluded is difficulty accessing group members. Persons who are homeless are very unlikely to be reached by a survey that uses random digit dialing, for example. Other individuals can be accessed using standard survey techniques, but are excluded because of issues in reporting. Members of these groups are often reluctant to self-identify because of social pressure or stigma (Shelley, Bernard, Killworth, Johnsen, & McCarty, 1995). Individuals who are homosexual, for example, may not be comfortable revealing their sexual preferences to an unfamiliar survey enumerator. A third group of individuals is difficult to reach because of issues with both access and reporting (commercial sex workers, for example). Even basic demographic information about these groups is typically unknown, especially in developing nations.

One approach to estimating demographic information about hard-to-reach groups is to reach members of these groups through their social network. Some network-based approaches, such as respondent-driven sampling (RDS), recruit respondents *directly* from other respondents' networks (Heckathorn, 1997, 2002), making the sampling mechanism similar to a stochastic process on the social network (Goel & Salganik, 2009). RDS (see Chapter 24 in this volume) affords researchers face-to-face contact with members of hard-to-reach groups, facilitating exhaustive interviews and even genetic or medical testing. The price for an entry to these groups is high, however, as RDS uses a specially designed link-tracing framework for sampling. Estimates from RDS are also biased because of the network structure captured during selection, with much statistical work surrounding RDS being intended to re-weigh observations from RDS to have properties resembling a simple random sample. Though methods such as RDS can be advantageous (researchers interview members of hard-to-survey groups directly, for example), financial and logistical challenges often prevent researchers from employing these methods, especially on a large scale.

In this chapter, we focus on methods that utilize social network structure, but collect data about networks and hard-to-survey groups *indirectly* via standard surveys. *Indirectly* in this context means that survey respondents provide information, through carefully crafted network-based questions, about a general population and members of hard-to-reach groups. These methods are easily implemented on standard surveys and require no specialized sampling methodology.

We focus specifically on *aggregated relational data* (ARD), or "How many X's do you know?" questions (Killworth, McCarty, Bernard, Shelley, & Johnsen, 1998). In these questions, "X" defines a population of interest (e.g., How many people who are homeless do you know?). A specific definition of "know" defines the network the respondent references when answering the question. In contrast to RDS, ARD do not require reaching members of the hard-to-survey groups directly. Instead, ARD access these groups indirectly through the social networks of respondents on standard surveys. ARD never afford direct access to members of hard-to-survey populations, making the level of detail achievable though RDS impossible with ARD. Unlike RDS, however, ARD require no special sampling techniques and are easily incorporated into standard surveys. ARD are, therefore, feasible for a broader range of researchers across the social sciences, public health, and epidemiology to implement with significantly lower cost than RDS. The work presented in this chapter draws heavily on related work in the statistics literature. Though we present statistical results, the focus of this chapter is on designing surveys that reduce common sources of bias found in estimates using ARD. In the following sections, we provide background on ARD (Section 23.2) and related methods for deriving network features using ARD questions in standard survey (Section 23.3), including discussions of potential sources of bias using ARD and methods we profile to address these challenges. More specifically, Section 23.3 provides recommendations for selecting populations that reduce bias in estimating degree, or respondent network size. These degree estimates are necessary for estimating hard-to-reach population sizes. Section 23.3.3 moves beyond estimating sizes of hard-to-count populations with these data and provides survey design recommendations for estimating demographic profiles of such groups. We end with a discussion (Section 23.4).

23.2   Network-related questions in standard surveys

In this section, we discuss methods for asking network-related questions using standard surveys. By standard surveys, we mean a design where respondents are sampled randomly without replacement from a sampling frame (including various types of stratified or cluster designs). Asking respondents on a survey about their social network serves to increase the sample size of the survey, including both respondents sampled directly and reports about individuals they are connected to through their social network. The data we discuss in this chapter attain this network information indirectly. They are considerably easier to obtain than complete network data and there are currently limited lines of research using this type of data. A dearth of methods for indirect network data remains, however, and the few existing methods estimate very specific characteristics of the network and do not address relationships between groups.

23.2.1 Coverage methods

Several methods to collect social context of survey respondents have been developed, mostly to estimate the respondent's network size, or *degree*. One of the earliest methods was the *reverse small-world* method in (Bernard, Johnsen, Killworth, McCarty, Shelley, & Robinson, 1990; Killworth & Bernard, 1978; Killworth, Bernard, & McCarty, 1984) which, motivated by the small-world experiments of Milgram (1967), asked respondents to name someone they would use if they were required to pass a message to a given *target*. By asking respondents about a large number of such targets, it is possible that a respondent will enumerate a large proportion of his acquaintance network. Unfortunately, however, this procedure required a large number of (as many as 500) targets and, thus, remained impractical for most surveys. In contrast, the *summation* method (McCarty, Killworth, Bernard, Johnsen, & Shelley, 2001) requires fewer categories. Respondents are asked how many people they know in a list of specific relationship types, for example, immediate family, neighbors, coworkers, etc., and these responses are then summed to yield an overall estimate. These relationship types often overlap, however, so degree estimates suffer from double-counting.

23.2.2 Sampling methods

Pool and Kochen (1978) developed the *phone book method* where a respondent was provided randomly selected pages from the phone book and based on the proportion of pages which contained the family name of someone known to the respondent, it was possible to estimate the respondent's social network size. The estimation was improved greatly in later work by Freeman and Thompson (1989) and Killworth, Johnsen, Bernard, Shelley, and McCarty (1990), which instead of providing respondents pages of phone books provided them with lists of last names. The general logic of the phone book procedure was then developed further as the *scale-up* procedure (Killworth *et al.*, 1998) using ARD. ARD questions ask respondents "How many X's do you know?"[1] and are easily integrated into standard surveys. Here, X, represents a subpopulation of interest.

Among methods to measure network information indirectly, we find the most promise in ARD. ARD are most often used to estimate the size of populations that are difficult to count directly. The scale-up method, an early method for ARD, uses ARD questions where the subpopulation size is known (people named Michael, for example) to estimate degree in a straightforward manner. Information about the size of some populations is often available through administrative records, such as the Social Security Administration in the United States. Suppose that you know two persons named Nicole, and that, at the time of the survey, there were 358,000 Nicoles out of 280 million Americans. Thus your two Nicoles represent a fraction (2/358,000) of all the Nicoles. Extrapolating to the entire country yields an

---

1 The definition of "know" defines the network of interest, though the methods presented here do not depend on the definition of "know."

estimate of $(2/358{,}000) \times (280 \text{ million}) = 1{,}560$ people known by you. Then, the size of unknown subpopulations is estimated by solving the given equation for the unknown subpopulation size with the estimated degree. Using this method, ARD has been used extensively to estimate the size of populations such as those with HIV/AIDS, injection drug users, or the homeless (for example, Killworth *et al.*, 1990; Killworth *et al.*, 1998).

Unlike the previously described methods, ARD allows researchers to choose specific subpopulations of interest without sampling or surveying members of these subpopulations directly. This feature holds potential to learn additional information about these subpopulations and their relationship to the overall network. Shelley, Killworth, Bernard, McCarty, Johnsen, and Rice (2006), for example, uses ARD to explore how the structure of the network of seropositive individuals affects the dissemination of information about their disease status.

Despite the potential value of ARD and the ease of obtaining these data through standard surveys, the literature on learning about network structure from ARD remains underdeveloped. The scale-up method, for example, is easy to implement but does not account for network structure. Consider, for example, asking a respondent how many people named "Rose" she/he knows. If each person was equally likely to know a Rose, then this would be equivalent to asking if they know each person on a list of the half a million Roses in the US.[2] If we were to take all half a million of these Roses and put their names on a list, then each respondent would have the same chance of knowing each of these half a million individuals if knowing someone named Rose were entirely random. That is, each respondent on each Rose is a Bernoulli trial with a fixed success probability proportional to the size of this respondent's network size. Network structure makes these types of independence assumptions invalid. For example, since Rose is most common amongst older females and people are more likely to know individuals of similar age and the same gender, older female respondents are more likely to know a given Rose than older male respondents. Statistical models are needed to understand how these responses change based on homophily, as in this example, and on more complicated network properties. Ignoring social network structure induces bias in the individuals' responses. Since estimates of hard-to-count populations are then constructed using responses to ARD questions, the resulting estimates are also biased (Bernard, Johnsen, Killworth, & Robinson, 1991; Killworth et al., 1998).

In addition to the applications of the scale-up method using ARD described in the previous section, two substantial steps in modeling ARD will influence our proposed method. Zheng, Salganik, and Gelman (2006) began by noting that under simple random mixing the responses to the "How many *X*'s do you know?" questions would follow a Poisson distribution with the rate parameter determined by the degree of the respondent and the network prevalence of the subpopulation. Here, the network prevalence is the proportion of ties that involve individuals in the subpopulation and should match the proportion of the population comprised of members of the given subpopulation. Under

---

2 This also assumes that one could recall their acquaintanceships with complete accuracy. This assumption is often not valid and we will discuss the issue in further detail in subsequent sections.

this assumption, for example, the expected number of Roses known by a respondent with degree equal to 500 would be 500 × (500,000/280 million) ≈ 1. They apply their method to data from McCarty *et al.* (2001) and find that many of the questions in the data did not follow a Poisson distribution. In fact, most of the responses show overdispersion, or greater-than-expected variance. We can interpret the overdispersion as a factor that decreases the frequency of people who know exactly one person of type X, as compared to the frequency of people who know none. As overdispersion increases from its null value of 1, it is less likely for a person to have an isolated acquaintance from that group. For example, consider the responses to the question: "How many males do you know incarcerated in state or federal prison?" The mean of the responses to this question was 1.0, but the variance was 8.0, indicating that some people are much more likely to know more than one individual in prison than others. To model this increased variance, Zheng, Salganik, and Gelman (2006) allowed individuals to vary in their propensity to form ties to different groups. In a multilevel model, this corresponds to assuming that these propensities follow a gamma distribution with a shape parameter determined by the overdispersion. The responses then can be modeled as a negative binomial distribution so that the expected number of alters known by a respondent in a given subpopulation is the degree of the respondent times the network prevalence, as under the simple model, but now scaled by the overdispersion parameter to estimate the variation in individual propensities to form ties to people in different groups.

23.3 Statistical methods for ARD

In this section, we discuss methods for extracting network properties using ARD collected using survey questionnaires. The discussion is organized according to the network features under study.

23.3.1 *Estimating personal network size*

The scale-up estimate

Consider a population of size N. We can store the information about the social network connecting the population in an adjacency matrix $\Delta = \left[\delta_{ij}\right]_{N \times N}$ such that $\delta_{ij} = 1$ if person i knows person j. Though the methods discussed here do not depend on the definition of know, throughout this chapter, we will assume the McCarty *et al.* (2001) definition of know: "that you know them and they know you by sight or by name, that you could contact them, that they live within the United States, and that there has been some contact (either in person, by telephone or mail) in the past 2 years." The personal network size or degree of person i is then $d_i = \sum_j \delta_{ij}$.

One straightforward way to estimate the degree of person i would be to ask if she knows each of n randomly chosen members of the population. Inference could then be based on the fact that the responses would follow a binomial distribution with n trials and probability $\frac{d_i}{N}$.

In a large population, however, this method is extremely inefficient because the probability of a relationship between any two people is very low. For example, if one assumes an average personal network size of 750 (as estimated by Zheng *et al.*, 2006), then the probability of two randomly chosen Americans knowing each other is only about 0.0000025, meaning that a respondent would need to be asked about millions of people to produce a decent estimate.

A more efficient method would be to ask the respondent about an entire set of people at once through ARD type survey questions. For example, asking "How many women do you know who gave birth in the last 12 months?" instead of asking the respondent if she knows 3.6 million distinct people. The scale-up method uses responses to ARD questions of this form ("How many X's do you know?") to estimate personal network size. For example, if you report knowing three women who gave birth, this represents about one millionth of all women who gave birth within the last year. We could then use this information to estimate that you know about one millionth of all Americans,

$$\frac{3}{3.6\ million}(300\ million) \approx 250\ people.$$

The precision of this estimate can be increased by averaging responses of many groups yielding the scale-up estimator (Killworth *et al.*, 1998) of the degree of person i

$$\hat{d}_i = \frac{\sum_{k=1}^{K} y_{ik}}{\sum_{k=1}^{K} N_k} N$$

where y_{ik} is the number of people that person i knows in subpopulation k, N_k is the size of subpopulation k, and N is the size of the population. One important complication to note with this estimator is that asking "How many women do you know who gave birth in the last 12 months?" is not equivalent to asking about 3.6 million *random* people; rather, the people asked about are women, probably between the ages of 18 and 45. This creates statistical challenges that are addressed in detail in subsequent sections. To estimate the standard error of the simple estimate, we follow the practice of Killworth *et al.* (1998) by assuming

$$\sum_{k=1}^{K} y_{ik} \sim \text{Binomial}\left(\sum_{k=1}^{K} N_k, p = \frac{d_i}{N}\right).$$

The estimate of the probability of success, $p = \frac{d_i}{N}$, is

$$\hat{p} = \frac{\sum_{k=1}^{K} y_{ik}}{\sum_{k=1}^{K} N_k} = \frac{\hat{d}_i}{N} \tag{23.1}$$

with standard error (including finite population correction; Lohr, 1999)

$$SE(\hat{p}) = \sqrt{\frac{1}{\sum_{k=1}^{K} N_k} \hat{p}(1-\hat{p}) \frac{N - \sum_{k=1}^{K} N_k}{N-1}}.$$

The scale-up estimate $\hat{d}_i$ then has standard error

$$SE(\hat{d}_i) = N \cdot SE(\hat{p}) = N \sqrt{\frac{1}{\sum_{k-1}^{K} N_k} \hat{p}(1-\hat{p}) \frac{N - \sum_{k-1}^{K} N_k}{N-1}} \approx \sqrt{\hat{d}_i} \sqrt{\frac{1 - \frac{\sum_{k-1}^{K} N_k}{N}}{\frac{\sum_{k-1}^{K} N_k}{N}}}.$$

For example, if we asked respondents about the number of women they know who gave birth in the past year, the approximate standard error of the degree estimate is calculated as

$$SE(\hat{d}_i) \approx \sqrt{\hat{d}_i} \sqrt{\frac{1 - \frac{\sum_{k-1}^{K} N_k}{N}}{\frac{\sum_{k-1}^{K} N_k}{N}}} \approx \sqrt{750} \sqrt{\frac{1 - \frac{3.6\,\text{million}}{300\,\text{million}}}{\frac{3.6\,\text{million}}{300\,\text{million}}}} \approx 250$$

assuming a degree of 750 as estimated by Zheng *et al.* (2006). If, in addition, we also asked respondents the number of people they know who have a twin sibling, the number of people they know who are diabetics, and the number of people they know who are named Michael, we would have increased our aggregate subpopulation size, $\sum_{k=1}^{K} N_k$, from 3.6 million to approximately 18.6 million and in doing so decreased our estimated standard error to about 100. In Figure 23.1 (adapted from McCormick, Salganik, & Zheng, 2010), we plot $\frac{SE(\hat{d}_i)}{\sqrt{\hat{d}_i}}$ against $\sum_{k=1}^{k} \frac{N_k}{N}$. The most drastic reduction in estimated error comes in increasing the survey fractional subpopulation size to about 20 percent (or approximately 60 million in a population of 300 million). Though the above standard error depends only on sum of the subpopulation sizes, we will show that there are other sources of bias that make the choice of the individual subpopulations important as well.

As we increase the fraction of population represented by survey subpopulations, the precision of the estimate improves, with diminishing improvements after about 20 percent.

Issues with the scale-up estimator

The scale-up estimator using "How many X do you know?" data is known to suffer from three distinct problems – transmission errors, barrier effects, and recall problems (Killworth, McCarty, Bernard, Johnsen, Domini, & Shelley, 2003; Killworth, McCarty, Johnsen, Bernard, & Shelley, 2006) – when the ARD questions are chosen arbitrarily. *Transmission errors* occur when the respondent knows someone in a specific subpopulation, but is not aware that they are actually in that subpopulation. For example, a respondent might know a woman who recently gave birth, but might not know that she had recently given birth. These transmission errors likely vary from subpopulation to subpopulation depending on the sensitivity and visibility of the information. These errors are extremely difficult to quantify because very little is known about how much information respondents have about the people

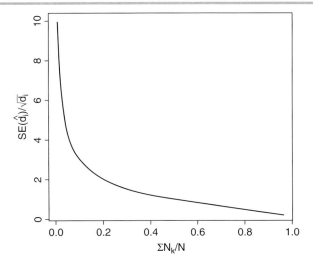

Figure 23.1   Standard error of the scale-up degree estimate (scaled by the square root of the true degree) plotted against the sum of the fractional subpopulation sizes

they know (Killworth *et al.*, 2006; Laumann, 1969; and Shelley, Killworth, Bernard, McCarty, Johnsen, & Rice, 2006). *Barrier effects* occur whenever some individuals systematically know more (or fewer) members of a specific subpopulation than would be expected under random mixing, and thus can also be called nonrandom mixing. For example, since people tend to know others of similar age and gender (McPherson, Smith-Lovin, & Cook, 2001), a 30-year-old woman probably knows more women who have recently given birth than would be predicted just based on her personal network size and the number of women who have recently given birth. Similarly, an 80-year-old man probably knows fewer than would be expected under random mixing. Therefore, estimating personal network size by asking only "How many women do you know who have recently given birth?" – the estimator presented above in Equation 23.1 – will tend to overestimate the degree of women in their 30s and underestimate the degree of men in their 80s. Because these barrier effects can introduce a bias of unknown size, previous researchers have avoided using the scale-up method to estimate the degree of any particular individual. A final source of error is that responses to these questions are prone to recall error. For example, people seem to underrecall the number of people they know in large subpopulations (e.g., people named Michael) and overrecall the number in small subpopulations (e.g., people who committed suicide) (Killworth *et al.*, 2003; Zheng *et al.*, 2006). If people were answering such questions consistently, we would expect a linear relationship between the size of the subpopulation and the mean number of individuals recalled. That is, if the size of the subgroup doubled, the mean number recalled should also double. This is not the case, as can be seen in Figure 23.2 (adapted from McCormick *et al.*, 2010), which plots the mean number known in each subpopulation as a function of subpopulation size for the twelve names in the McCarty *et al.* (2001) data. The figure shows that there was overrecall of small subpopulations and underrecall of large subpopulations, a pattern that has been noted previously (Killworth *et al.*, 2003; Zheng *et al.*, 2006).

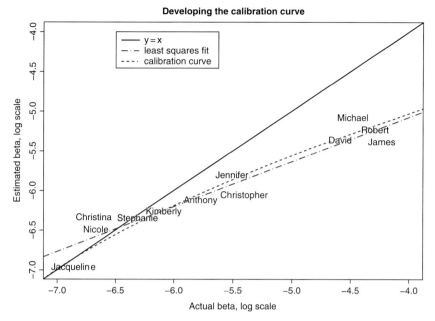

Figure 23.2   Mean number recalled as a function of subpopulation size for twelve names

If respondents recall perfectly, then we would expect the mean number recalled to increase linearly as the subpopulation size increases. The best-fit line and less curve show that this was not the case, suggesting that there is recall error.

Reducing bias in degree estimates

In this section, we review design recommendations for reducing bias in degree estimates described in Section 23.3.1. The intuition behind the recommendations we describe is that the names asked about should be chosen so that the combined set of people asked about should be easy to recall, with perfect transmission of traits being asked (first names), *and* is a *scaled-down* version of the overall population. For example, if 20 percent of the general population is females under 30, then 20 percent of the people with the names used must also be females under 30.

In ARD, respondents are conceptualized as *egos*, or senders of ties in the network. As discussed in McCormick *et al.* (2010), we divide the egos into groups based on their demographic characteristics (males (20–40 years old, for example). The individuals who comprise the counts for ARD are the *alters*, or recipients of links in the network. The alters are also divided into groups, though the groups need not be the same for both the ego and the alter groups. The scaled-down condition was motivated by the *latent nonrandom mixing* model in McCormick *et al.* (2010) that assumes an expected number of acquaintances for an individual i in ego group e to people in group k,

$$\mu_{ike} = E(y_{ike}) = d_i \sum_{a=1}^{A} m(e,a) \frac{N_{ak}}{N_a}.$$

Here, $m(e,a)$ is the *mixing matrix* as in McCormick *et al.* (2010). The mixing matrix accounts for the propensity for individiuals to know more respondents in some demographic groups than others (a young female respondent will likely know more young females than older males, for example). On the other hand, the scale-up estimator assumes

$$E\left(\sum_{k=1}^{K} y_{ike}\right) = \sum_{k=1}^{K} \mu_{ike} = d_i \sum_{a=1}^{A} m(e,a) \left[\sum_{k=1}^{K} \frac{N_{ak}}{N_a}\right]$$

$$\equiv d_i \frac{\sum_{K=1}^{K} \sum_{a=1}^{A} N_{ak}}{N}, \forall e.$$

(23.2)

Equation 23.2 shows that the Killworth *et al.* (1998) scale-up estimator is in expectation equivalent to that of the latent non-random mixing if either

$$m(e,a) = \frac{N_a}{N}, \forall a, \forall e,$$

(23.3)

or

$$\frac{\sum_{k=1}^{K} N_{ak}}{\sum_{k=1}^{K} N_k} = \frac{N_a}{N}, \forall a.$$

(23.4)

In other words, the two estimators are equivalent if there is random mixing (Equation 23.3) or if the combined set of names represents a scaled-down version of the population (Equation 23.4). Since random mixing is not a reasonable assumption for the acquaintances network in the United States, we need to focus on selecting the names to satisfy the scaled-down condition. That is, we should select the set of names such that, if 15 percent of the population is males between ages 21 and 40 $\left(\frac{N_a}{N}\right)$, then 15 percent of the people asked about must also be males between ages 21 and 40 $\left(\frac{\sum_{k=1}^{K} N_{ak}}{\sum_{k=1}^{K} N_k}\right)$. In actually choosing a set of names to satisfy the scaled-down condition, we found it more convenient to work with a rearranged form:

$$\frac{\sum_{k=1}^{K} N_{ak}}{N_a} = \frac{\sum_{k=1}^{K} N_k}{N}, \forall a.$$

(23.5)

In order to find a set of names that satisfy Equation 23.5, it is helpful to create Figure 23.3 (McCormick *et al.*, 2010) that displays the relative popularity of many names over time. From this figure, we tried to select a set of names such that the popularity across alter categories ended up balanced. For example, consider the names Walter, Bruce, and Kyle.

These names have similar popularity overall, but Walter was popular from 1910 to 1940, whereas Bruce was popular during the middle of the century and Kyle near the end. Thus, the popularity of the names at any one time period will be balanced by the popularity of names in the other time periods, preserving the required equality in the sum in Equation 23.5.

When choosing what names to use, in addition to satisfying Equation 23.5, we recommend choosing names that comprise 0.1 to 0.2 percent of the population, as these minimize recall errors and yield average responses from 0.6 to 1.3. Finally, we recommend choosing names that are not commonly associated with nicknames in order to minimize transmission errors.

Selecting the number of names

For researchers planning to use the scale-up method, an important issue to consider in addition to which names to use is how many names to use. Obviously, asking about more names will produce a more precise estimate, but that precision comes at the cost of increasing the length of the survey. To help researchers understand the tradeoff, we return to the approximate standard error under the binomial model presented in Section 23.3. Simulation results using six, twelve, and eighteen names chosen using the guidelines suggested above agree well with the results from the binomial model in Section 23.3 (results not shown). This agreement suggests that the simple standard error may be reasonable when the names are chosen appropriately. To put the results of Equation 23.1 into a more concrete context, a researcher who uses names whose overall popularity reaches 2 million would expect a standard error of around $11.6 \times \sqrt{500} = 259$ for an estimated degree of 500 whereas with $\sum N_k = 6$ million, she would expect a standard error of $6.2 \times \sqrt{500} = 139$ for the same respondent. Finally, for the good names, $\sum N_k = 4$ million, so a researcher could expect a standard error of 177 for a respondent with degree 500.

23.3.2 Estimating nonrandom mixing

In this section, we introduce a missing data perspective for ARD and propose an estimator based on the EM algorithm (Dempster, Laird, & Rubin, 1977).

If for a given respondent, i, we could take all the members of the social network with which i has a link and place them in a room, we would compute the mixing rate between the ego and a given alter group, $a = (1, \ldots, A)$, by dividing the room in A mutually exclusive sections and asking alters to stand in their respective group. The estimated mixing rate would then be the number of people standing in a given group divided by the number of people in the room. We could also perform a similar calculation by placing a simple random sample of size n from a population of size N in a room. Then, after dividing the alters into mutually exclusive groups, we could count y_{ia}, or the number of alters respondent i knows in the sample who are in each of the a alter groups. Since we have a simple random sample, we

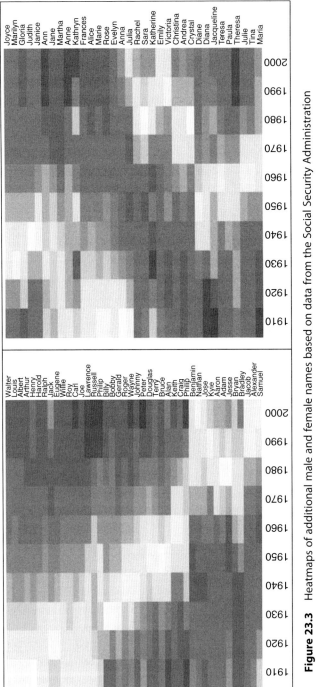

Figure 23.3 Heatmaps of additional male and female names based on data from the Social Security Administration

Note: Lighter color indicates higher popularity.

can extrapolate back to the population and estimate the degree of the respondent, $\hat{d}_i$, and the within alter group degree, $\hat{d}_{ia}$, as

$$\hat{d}_i = \sum_{a-1}^{A} \frac{y_{ia}}{n/N} \quad \text{and} \quad \hat{d}_{ia} = \frac{y_{ia}}{n_a/N_a}.$$

Given these two quantities, we can estimate the mixing rate between the respondent and an alter group by taking the ratio of alters known in the sample who are in alter group a over the total number known in the sample. This computation is valid because we assumed a simple random sample and, thus, (in expectation) the demographic distribution of alters in our sample matches that of the population. In ARD, the distribution of the hypothetical alters we sample depends on the subpopulations we select. If we only ask respondents about sub-populations which consist of young males, for example, then our hypothetical room from the previous example would contain only the respondent's young, male alters. Estimating the rate of mixing between the respondent and older females would not be possible in this situation. Viewed in this light, ARD is a form of cluster sampling where the subpopulations are the clusters and respondents report the presence/absence of a tie between all alters in the cluster. Since the clusters are no longer representative of the population, our estimates need to be adjusted for the demographic profiles of the clusters (Lohr, 1999). Specifically, if we observe y_{ika} for subpopulations $k = (1, \ldots, K)$ and alter groups $a = (1, \ldots, A)$, then our estimates of $\hat{d}_i$ and $\hat{d}_{ia}$ become

$$\hat{d}_i = \sum_{k=1}^{K} y_{ik} / \left(\sum_{k=1}^{K} N_k/N \right) \quad \text{and} \quad \hat{d}_{ia} = \sum_{k=1}^{K} y_{ika} / \left(\sum_{k=1}^{K} N_{ak}/N_a \right).$$

where N_k is the size of subpopulation k and N_{ak} is the number of members of subpopulation k in alter group a. To estimate the mixing rate, we could again divide the estimated number known in alter group a by the total estimated number known. Under the scaled-down condition, the denominators in the above expressions cancel and the mixing estimate is the number known in the subpopulations that are in alter group a over the total number known in all K subpopulations. In the examples above, we have assumed the alters are observed so that y_{ika} can be computed easily. This is not the case in ARD, however, since we observe only the aggregate number of ties and not the specific demographic makeup of the recipients. Thus, ARD represent a type of cluster sampling design where the specific ties between the respondent and members of the alter group are *missing*. If we ignore the residual variation in propensity to form ties with group k individuals due to noise, we may assume that the number of members of subpopulation k in alter group a the respondent knows, y_{ika}, follows a Poisson distribution. Under this assumption, we can estimate m_{ia} by imputing y_{ika} as part of an EM algorithm. Specifically, for each individual define $y_{ik}^{(com)} = (y_{ika}, \ldots, y_{i1A})^T$ as the complete data vector for each alter group. The complete data log-likelihood for individual i's vector of mixing rates, $m_i = (m_{i1}, \ldots, m_{iA})^T$, is $\ell\left(m_i; y_{i1}^{(com)}, \ldots, y_{iK}^{(com)}\right)$, which has the form

$$l\left(m_i; y_{i1}^{(com)}, \ldots, y_{ik}^{(com)}\right) = \sum_{k=1}^{K} \sum_{a=1}^{A} \log\left(Poisson\left(y_{ika}; \lambda_{ika} = d_i m_{ia} \frac{N_{ak}}{N_a}\right)\right). \quad (23.6)$$

Using Equation 23.6, we derive the following two updating steps for the EM:

$$y_{iak}^{(t)} = y_{ik} \left(\frac{m_{ia}^{(t-1)} \frac{N_{ak}}{N_a}}{\sum_{a=1}^{A} m_{ia}^{(t-1)} \frac{N_{ak}}{N_a}} \right)$$

$$m_{ia}^{(t)} = \frac{\sum_{k=1}^{K} y_{ika}^{(t-1)}}{\sum_{k=1}^{K} y_{ik}}.$$

If one sets $m_{ia}^{(0)} = N_a/N$, which corresponds to random mixing in the population, and runs one EM update, this would result in the following *simple ratio estimator* of the mixing rate for individual i:

$$\hat{m}_{ia} = \frac{\sum_{k-1}^{K} y_{ik} \left(\frac{N_{ak}}{N_k} \right)}{\sum_{k-1}^{K} y_{ik}} \tag{23.7}$$

In our simulation studies (details not shown), this simple estimator produces estimates very close to the converged EM estimates. Additionally, it is easy to show that the simple ratio estimate, $\hat{m}_{ia}$, is unbiased if $N_{ak}/N_a \neq 0$ for only one alter group a and that for any a there exists a subpopulation, k, such that $N_{ak} = N_a$. We refer to this condition as *complete separability*. Therefore, Equation 23.7 constitutes a simple estimate for individual mixing rate and can be used to estimate average mixing behaviors of any ego group.

23.3.3 Estimating demographic profiles of hard-to-survey groups using ARD

In this section, we describe a model presented by McCormick & Zheng, (2012) for estimating latent demographic profiles for hard-to-reach groups. This method will provide information about the demographic makeup of groups which are often difficult to access using standard surveys, such as the proportion of young males who are infected with HIV. Under the set-up of ego groups and alter groups discussed in Section 23.3.1, members of hard-to-survey groups are one type of alter. Thus, the alter groups defined determine the demographic characteristics that can be estimated for the hard to survey. The McCormick and Zheng (2012) method combines estimation and survey design strategy, making it well suited for researchers who intend to collect ARD. First, one needs to use ARD questions satisfying the scaled-down condition in McCormick *et al.* (2010) for selecting subpopulations to reduce bias in the estimates of respondent degree discussed in Section 23.3.1 and derive the mixing matrix estimates as in Section 23.3.3.

The estimates for respondent degree (Section 23.3.1) and mixing estimates (Section 23.3.3) rely on latent profile information from some "known" populations. Using these estimates, we now further develop a regression-based estimator for unobserved latent profiles. Define $h(a,k)$ as the fraction of alter group a made up of members of group k. For each respondent and each unknown subpopulation we now have

$$y_{ik} = \sum_{a=1}^{A} \hat{d}_i \hat{m}_{ia} h(a, k). \tag{23.8}$$

If we denote the matrix $X_k = \hat{d}\hat{m}_{\cdot k}$ and the vector $h(\cdot, k) = \bar{\beta}_k$, then Equation 23.8 can be regarded as a linear regression equation, $\bar{y}_k = X_k' \bar{\beta}_k$, with the constraint that coefficients, $\bar{\beta}_k$, are restricted to be nonnegative. Lawson and Hanson (1974) propose an algorithm for computing these coefficients. Since the $\hat{m}_{\cdot k}$ sum to one across alter groups, the columns of X_k are collinear. This could produce instability in solving the quadratic programing problem associated with finding our estimated latent profiles. In practice, we have found our estimates perform well despite this feature.

Simulation experiments

Here, we present simulation experiments to evaluate our regression-based estimates under four strategies for selecting observed profiles. First, we created profiles which are *completely separable* (defined in Section 23.3.3). Second, we constructed profiles for the names satisfying the scaled-down condition presented in Section 23.3.1 using data from the Social Security Administration. These names provide insights into the potential accuracy of our method using actual profiles. As a third case, we include the names from McCormick *et al.* (2010) which violate the scaled-downed down condition and are almost exclusively popular among older respondents. For the fourth set of names, recall from Section 23.3.3 that the mixing matrix estimates are identifiable only if the matrix of known profiles, $H_{A \times K}$, has rank A. To demonstrate a violation of this condition, we selected a set of names with uniform popularity across the demographic groups, or nearly perfect collinearity. There is some correlation in the scaled-down names since several names have similar profiles. The degree of correlation is substantially less than in the flat profiles, however. In each simulation, McCormick and Zheng (2012) generated 500 respondents using the latent nonrandom mixing model (see McCormick *et al.*, 2010) with each of the four profile strategies. Mixing matrix estimates were calculated using the simple estimate derived from the first step of the EM algorithm in Section 23.3.3. We compare our mixing matrix estimates to the estimated mixing matrix from McCormick *et al.* (2010), which we use to generate the simulated data. We evaluate the latent profiles using six names with profiles known from the Social Security Administration. We repeated the entire process 1,000 times.

The vertical axis is the sum of the errors across all eight alter groups. We generated 500 respondents using the four profile structures then evaluated our ability to recover the mixing matrix estimated in McCormick *et al.* (2010), and the known profiles of six additional names. We repeated the simulation 1,000 times. In both cases, the ideal profile has the lowest error, followed by the scaled-down names.

Figure 23.4 (adapted from McCormick & Zheng, 2012) presents boxplots of the squared error in mixing matrix and latent profile estimates. In both cases, the ideal, completely separable, profiles have the lowest error. The scaled-down names also perform well,

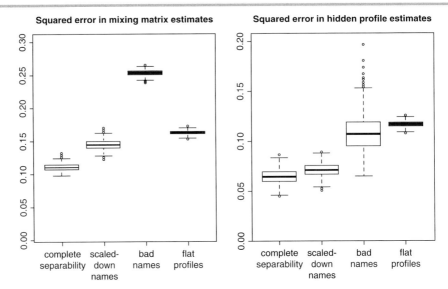

Figure 23.4   Total mean squared error across all elements of the mixing matrix and latent profile matrix

indicating that reasonable estimates are possible even when complete separability is not. The flat profiles perform only slightly worse than the scaled-down names for estimating mixing but significantly worse when estimating latent profiles. The names which violate the scaled-down condition produce poor estimates of both quantities.

23.4   Conclusion and discussion

In this chapter, we present methods for estimating features of hard-to-reach populations using indirectly observed network data. ARD are easy and cheap to collect using standard survey mechanisms. This means that the information needed to estimate sizes of some hard-to-reach populations can be collected using existing surveys designed for other topics. We have focused particularly on survey designs which lead to reliable, but simple, estimates. We belive that the design conditions we propose are critical to the performance of these simple estimators. In cases where data have already been collected, or when it is not possible to develop survey questions in accordance with these guidelines, we suggest using model-based strategies proposed in McCormick *et al.* (2010) and McCormick and Zheng (2012). We also note that there are many open areas of research in this challenging problem, with contributions to be made both in improving estimation methods as well as verifying and calibrating currently proposed techniques.

References

Bernard, H. R., Johnsen, E. C., Killworth, P. D., McCarty, C., Shelley, G. A., & Robinson, S. (1990). Comparing four different methods for measuring personal social networks. *Social Networks*, 12, 179–215.

Bernard, H. R., Johnsen, E. C., Killworth, P. D., & Robinson, S. (1991). Estimating the size of an average personal network and of an event subpopulation: some empirical results. *Social Science Research*, 20, 109–21.

Dempster, A. P., Laird, N. M., & Rubin, D. B. (1997). Maximum likelihood from incomplete data via the EM algorithm. *Journal of the Royal Statistical Society: Series B (Methodological)*, 39(1), 1–38.

Freeman, L. C., & Thompson, C. R. (1989). Estimating acquaintanceship volume. In M. Kochen (ed.), *The Small World* (pp. 147–58). Norwood, NJ: Ablex Publishing.

Goel, S., & Salganik, M. (2009). Respondent-driven sampling as Markov Chain Monte Carlo. *Statistics in Medicine*, 28(17), 2202–29.

Heckathorn, D. (1997). Respondent-driven sampling: a new approach to the study of hidden populations. *Social Problems*, 44(2), 174–99.

(2002). Respondent-driven sampling II: deriving valid population estimates from chain-referral samples of hidden populations. *Social Problems*, 49(1), 11–34.

Killworth, P. D., & Bernard, H. R. (1978). The reverse small-world experiment. *Social Networks*, 1(2), 159–92.

Killworth, P. D., Bernard, H. R., & McCarty, C. (1984). Measuring patterns of acquaintanceship. *Current Anthropology*, 23, 318–97.

Killworth, P. D., Johnsen, E. C., Bernard, H. R., Shelley, G. A., & McCarty, C. (1990). Estimating the size of personal networks. *Social Networks*, 12, 289–312.

Killworth, P. D., McCarty, C., Bernard, H. R., Johnsen, E. C., Domini, J., & Shelley, G. A. (2003). Two interpretations of reports of knowledge of subpopulation sizes. *Social Networks*, 25, 141–60.

Killworth, P. D., McCarty, C., Bernard, H. R., Shelley, G. A., & Johnsen, E. C. (1998). Estimation of seroprevalence, rape, and homelessness in the U.S. using a social network approach. *Evaluation Review*, 22, 289–308.

Killworth, P. D., McCarty, C., Johnsen, E. C., Bernard, H. R., & Shelley, G. A. (2006). Investigating the variation of personal network size under unknown error conditions. *Sociological Methods & Research*, 35(1), 84–112.

Laumann, E. O. (1969). Friends of urban men: an assessment of accuracy in reporting their socioeconomic attributes, mutual choice, and attitude agreement. *Sociometry*, 32(1), 54–69.

Lawson, C. L., & Hanson, R. J. (1974). *Solving Least Squares Problems*. Englewood Cliffs, NJ: Prentice Hall.

Lohr, S. L. (1999). *Sampling: Design and Analysis*. Boston, MA: Duxbury Press.

McCarty, C., Killworth, P. D., Bernard, H. R., Johnsen, E. C., & Shelley, G. A. (2001). Comparing two methods for estimating network size. *Human Organization*, 60, 28–39.

McCormick, T. H., & Zheng, T. (2012). Latent demographic profile estimation in hard-to-reach groups. *Annals of Applied Statistics*, 6, 1795–813.

McCormick, T. H., Salganik, M. J., & Zheng, T. (2010). How many people do you know? Efficiently estimating personal network size. *Journal of the American Statistical Association*, 105, 59–70.

McPherson, M., Smith-Lovin, L., & Cook, J. M. (2001). Birds of a feather: homophily in social networks. *Annual Review of Sociology*, 27, 415–44.

Milgram, S. (1967). The small world problem. *Psychology Today*, 1, 62–67.

Pool, I., & Kochen, M. (1978). Contacts and influence. *Social Networks*, 1, 5–51.

Shelley, G. A., Bernard, H. R., Killworth, P. D., Johnsen, E., & McCarty, C. (1995). Who knows your HIV status? What HIV+ patients and their network members know about each other. *Social Networks*, 17, 189–217.

Shelley, G. A., Killworth, P. D., Bernard, H. R., McCarty, C., Johnsen, E. C., & Rice, R. E. (2006). Who knows your HIV status II? Information propogation within social networks of seropositive people. *Human Organization*, 65(4), 430–44.

Zheng, T., Salganik, M. J., & Gelman, A. (2006). How many people do you know in prison?: Using overdispersion in count data to estimate social structure. *Journal of the American Statistical Association*, 101, 409–23.

24

Link-tracing and respondent-driven sampling

STEVE THOMPSON

24.1 Introduction

For studies of hidden and hard-to-reach human populations, often the most effective way of obtaining a sample is to use link-tracing methods. Conventional designs, such as a random stratified household sample, tend to produce a very small yield of very rare subpopulations and an even smaller yield of subpopulations with stigmatized or socially marginalized behaviors, such as illegal drug use or commercial sex-related activities. The usual frames used in surveys, such as landline and cell-phone numbers and household addresses, lead to underrepresentation of subgroups, such as persons who are homeless, traveling, or in institutionalized settings. Undocumented workers may be hard to survey because of geographic mobility and uncertain legal status. Social network connections can in some cases provide access not easily obtained by other means.

For some studies, it is important to understand the network structure of a population as well as the individual characteristics of the people in it. This is especially true in the case of epidemics of contagious diseases. The epidemic of the human immunodeficiency virus (HIV) has compelled societies throughout the world to try to understand sexual and drug-using behaviors and reach at-risk, hidden populations in an effort to understand and alleviate the spread of the disease. More broadly, individual behaviors and social connections are related, and understanding of social network structure is necessary for the understanding of each. Link-tracing sampling designs provide a natural means for studying and understanding socially structured human populations.

Link-tracing methods have long been used for studying hard-to-survey populations. Recently, the statistical properties of link-tracing designs have become better understood, and improved inference methods for data from such designs have become available. At the same time, increasingly effective methods for carrying out such designs have emerged.

24.1.1 Background

One of the earliest descriptions of methods of probability-based inference from link-tracing designs was a set of strategies called network sampling or multiplicity sampling, introduced

The author would like to thank the National Science and Engineering Council for support of this work.

503

by Birnbaum and Sirken (1965), with further developments in Sirken (1972a, 1972b). It was initially motivated by a problem in studying the characteristics of people with a rare disease, based on samples of medical records. A person with the disease might be treated at more than one medical center. The more medical centers a person was linked to (the multiplicity of that person), the higher the probability of that person showing up in the sample. Design-unbiased estimators were derived along with estimators of variance. One type of estimator was of the Horvitz–Thompson form with probabilities based on link multiplicities obtainable from the sample data. A simpler estimator, termed the "multiplicity estimator," used a reasoning similar to that involved in the Hansen–Hurwitz estimator but with the difference that selection units, the medical centers, were selected without replacement, though a person from the rare population could show up more than once in the sample through the links from the centers to the individual. A considerable literature in network sampling based on this idea emerged, mostly in the 1970s and 1980s (a review of this literature can be found in Thompson, 2012), developing the method for more elaborate design situations and a variety of applications.

Frank (1971, 1977a, b, 1978a, b, 1979) conceptualized the problem as sampling in a graph. That is, the population is a mathematical graph or network, with nodes represented by circles and undirected links or edges represented by lines between pairs of nodes or directed links represented by arrows. A sample of nodes was obtained from this graph by some probability design, such as simple random sampling or unequal probability sampling, and information of one kind or another on the links between, from, or to sample nodes was observed or estimated. He and his co-authors developed many results on design-based estimators of population characteristics, including average degree or density of the graph. In addition, some of this work assumed stochastic graph models and developed some model-based methods. Issues in link-tracing designs were discussed in Snijders (1992) and Spreen (1992). Frank and Snijders' (1994) paper was ground-breaking in using this type of reasoning to estimate the size of a hidden population of heroin users from a one-wave snowball sample.

Klovdahl (1989) described the use of a random walk to obtain a sample from a social network. Reviews of the properties of random walks or Markov chains in graphs can be found in Aldous and Fill (2002), Boyd, Diaconis, and Xiao (2004), Heckathorn (1997, 2002), and Lovasz (1993). Heckathorn (1997, 2002) introduced the methodology of respondent-driven sampling using coupons for organization and incentive for respondents to recruit additional respondents in studies of hard-to-reach populations. Salganik and Heckathorn (2004) describe the respondent-driven sampling methodology in most wide-spread current use, including a generalized ratio estimator with sample unit degrees as inverse weights. The motivation for the estimator is the limiting distribution unit selection probabilities in a with-replacement random walk in a connected, undirected graph. Magnani, Sabin, Saidel, and Heckathorn (2005) review this method for surveillance of behaviors related to HIV spread in hard-to-survey populations. Volz and Heckathorn (2008) examine further considerations in estimation with these designs. Examinations of the statistical properties of the prevailing respondent-driven sampling methodologies and suggestions for improvements are found in Gile and Handcock (2010) and Goel and Salganik (2010).

Targeted random walk designs are described in Thompson (2006a). In these designs, an additional screening step in the sampling procedure can produce a sample having specified limiting selecting probabilities, such as equal probability for each unit or a target such as people with certain risk-related characteristics having twice the selection probability of other units. The asymptotic probabilities are exact for the with-replacement case. Their approximation to the desired probabilities in the without-replacement case was studied through simulation.

A more flexible class of link-tracing sampling designs, adaptive web sampling, is described in Thompson (2006b). Design-based estimators of population characteristics and variance were obtained based on initial sample selection properties and Rao–Blackwell improvement of initial estimators. Model-based estimators for these designs were described in Kwanisai (2005, 2006). Variations of these designs in which links have weights affecting the link-tracing probabilities are described in Thompson (2011).

24.2 The sampling problem

For sampling in a network, the situation is conceptualized as follows. A population of interest has N units or nodes. The population has network structure, so some pairs of nodes are connected by a link in one or both directions and, assuming the network is not completely connected, some pairs of nodes are not connected by a link. A sample of n nodes is selected from this population by some design. The sampling design could be a conventional one such as simple random sampling or area sampling. But, in addition, we consider designs in which links are traced from sample units to add more units to the sample. In this way, a sample of nodes and a sample of pairs of nodes is obtained. For nodes in the sample, we observe node characteristics of interest. For example, in studies regarding the spread of HIV, a node represents a person and a characteristic of interest might be the result of a test for infection, the presence or absence of a risk-related behavior, or the time spent in a specified activity. A pair of nodes would be two people and a characteristic of interest might be whether they have a sexual relationship or other type of social relationship. We say that pair is in the sample if through interviews we determine that the two have the specified relationship or do not have the relationship. If we do not know one way or the other whether the relationship exists, we say that pair of nodes is not in the sample, even though both individuals may be. This is an important distinction to maintain for purposes of inference.

The sampling problem is that we are interested in characteristics of a wider population or community, but we can obtain, even with link-tracing, only a sample from the population. The characteristics of interest might include a population mean or total, such as the prevalence of injection drug use in the community. It may be of interest to estimate characteristics associated with links or population network structure, such as the prevalence of links over which an epidemic spreads or the connectedness between components of the population.

A sampling strategy consists of a sampling design for selecting the sample and an inference procedure for using the sample data to estimate population characteristics as well as estimating statistical properties of the procedure. The design problem concerns what is the best way to select the sample. The inference problem considers how to use the sample observations to estimate the characteristics of the wider, hard-to-reach population of interest.

24.3 Link-tracing designs

Examples of link-tracing designs include snowball sampling, multiplicity sampling, random walks through networks, targeted walks, adaptive web sampling, and related procedures. Some of these procedures are described below.

24.3.1 Snowball designs

A complete snowball design works as follows. A set of units is selected from the population using random sampling with replacement, unequal probability sampling with replacement, or some other initial design. At the first wave, every link out from the initial sample is traced and the unit it leads to is added to the sample. A one-wave snowball design stops here, but in general a snowball design can be followed for any desired number of waves.

24.3.2 Random walk designs

In a random walk design, an initial unit is selected at random, or with probability proportional to degree, or with an unequal probability design based on some other procedure. One of the links out from that unit is selected at random and followed to the next unit. In turn, one of the links out from the next unit is selected at random. This process continues for a desired number of waves.

  If the sampling is carried out with replacement, this sampling process can continue indefinitely and is a Markov chain having current state equal to the identity of the current unit being visited. If the links in the network are symmetric and the network consists of only one connected component, the stationary distribution of the chain has probabilities proportional to the degrees of the nodes. If there is a positive probability of not moving at one of the wave steps, the random walk is referred to as "lazy." If the network has more than one component, a walk that starts in one component cannot reach any other component unless an additional feature is added to the design, such as having a small probability at each step of making a random jump to any other unit in the population. If the random walk is carried out without replacement, it loses its Markov chain properties. Those properties are sometimes used as an approximation for without-replacement walks.

24.3.3 Targeted walk designs

Suppose we want the limiting distribution of a random walk to have specified probabilities instead of those resulting naturally from the link pattern in the population. We can use a Markov chain Monte Carlo accept–reject procedure at each step in the chain to induce those probabilities. In the simplest case, where there are no random jumps in the sampling process, the acceptance probability is based on the number of links out from the current node, and the number of links out from the tentatively selected next node, in relation to the desired stationary probabilities. With random jumps also, the acceptance ratio probabilities incorporate the random jump probabilities into the calculation as well. The random jump component of the design prevents the sampling from being stuck in any component and improves the mixing properties of the chain. The selection step, in which a candidate link is followed, is equivalent to a screening interview. The candidate needs only to be queried about its number of links out or some variable related to the desired target probability, whereas all variables of interest are measured on an accepted node.

A targeted walk design can also be carried out without replacement. The Markov properties of the with-replacement design can serve as an approximation to the properties of the without-replacement design and studied with simulation. An example target distribution would be equal limiting probabilities for each node, so that step by step, the selection probabilities become more uniform for different nodes. An example of an unequal target distribution would be to seek a sample in which members of a hidden population with a risk behavior of interest would tend to be selected with twice the probability as members without that behavior.

24.3.4 Adaptive web sampling

Adaptive web sampling is a class of link-tracing designs with flexibility in design features. In the simple case, a random sample of initial nodes is selected. At the first step beyond that, a single link is selected at random from all the links out from the initial sample, and the unit it leads to is added to the sample. At the next step again a single link is selected from all the links out from the current sample, which is now larger. This process can be continued for a given number of waves. Additionally at each step, a small probability is allowed that the next unit, instead of being, selected from the links out from the current sample, is selected at random from the units not in the sample. Note that this version of adaptive web sampling is without replacement. The small probability of random selection of a node at each step prevents the sample from being stuck in any component of the population and provides an escape if at some step there are no links out from the current sample. The random jump probability also provides a way to control the tendency of the design to spread out over the whole population versus focusing on the more highly connected components of the population. Choosing the size of the initial sample in relation to the chosen final sample size is another way to allocate effort between the adaptive link-tracing and the random spreading out of the sample.

Adaptive web sampling can be carried out instead with unequal selection of the initial sample and with unequal selection probabilities for different links out from the sample. For example, one may want to trace links with higher probability from people having a high-risk behavior in relation to a disease. Additionally, sampling may be carried out in waves, with different numbers of units added per wave or step, instead of one unit per step. Instead of a fixed sample size or number of waves, the procedure can be carried out until there are no more links to follow out from the current sample, so that intersected components of the population are traced out completely and total sample size is a random variable.

The more general idea in adaptive web sampling is to have an "active set" of units that is a subset of the current sample, and links are followed out from the sample only from units in the active set. A random walk design is an extreme case, in which only the most recently selected unit is in the active set.

An adaptive web sampling design can also be carried out with replacement.

24.3.5 Weighted-link methods

A random walk design can be generalized so that links in the population have different weights, amounting to link variables of interest, and at each step link selection is proportional to link weight. The with-replacement version is a Markov chain in a network. Properties of the without-replacement versions can be studied with simulation and compared with the Markov chain properties, such as the limiting distribution of the with-replacement weighted walk. If weighted links are involved in a targeted walk design, the link weights need only be incorporated into the acceptance calculation. The adaptive web sampling designs and inference methods are already set up to handle unequal probabilities of following links, whether the link weight is based on a variable of interest associated with the link, a variable of interest associated with the originating sample node, or a variable of interest of the destination node that is observed in a screening interview.

24.4 Respondent-driven sampling

In this chapter the term "respondent-driven sampling" will be used in its precise sense, meaning a link-tracing sampling design in which members of the hidden population are enlisted to do the actual sample recruitment based on their social connections. This usage is both more narrow and wider than the way "RDS" has come to be used in practice. It is more narrow in that we are restricting the term to describe who does the actual selection of subpopulation members, rather than including the inference method used. It is wider in that we can use the term with any link-tracing sampling design whatsoever so long as study participants from the population are enlisted in finding subsequent study participants.

24.4.1 Coupon designs

Any of the above designs can be carried out using coupon methods and, in the coupon-based designs actually used in practice, lead to interesting sampling properties. The basic method is to select an initial sample or set of "seeds" from a hard-to-reach population by some design or convenience procedure. Subject to satisfying screening interview criteria, each seed is given some number of coupons to use in recruiting new members of the hard-to-reach population to the sample. The recruiter gives the coupons, one each, to members of the target population known to him or her. In this way, the coupons are tracing links. A coupon carries a double incentive. If the potential recruit comes in to be interviewed and satisfies the screening criteria, he or she receives a monetary incentive. In addition, the recruiter is given a monetary reward for the recruit coming in to the sample. Any of the recruits may in turn be given a set of coupons with which to recruit additional members of the population to the sample, and the process may be continued for a desired number of waves or target sample size.

In an idealized view, the selection of seeds could be a simple random sample, and at each step the recruits are selected as a random sample of the recruiter's acquaintances. Selection of seeds with probabilities proportional to their degrees (number of acquaintances) may be assumed instead. With one coupon per recruiter to hand out and the person given the coupon invariably coming in to be interviewed, the process is a random walk. In practice, the sampling is usually done without replacement and some number of coupons greater than one is given to each recruiter. A common number of coupons is three, but the use of other numbers of coupons per recruiter have been investigated. With three coupons, the sampling process could be idealized as a variation on adaptive web sampling in which, once the recruiter has passed out all three coupons, he or she moves from the active to inactive subset of the sample. It is also known that of those potential coupons offered by a recruiter, some decline to accept them and of those who accept a coupon, only some come in to be interviewed. In this way, the design includes selection properties at different steps and these selection processes are the subject of continuing interest and investigation. These investigations of these sampling properties are important because the coupon methods appear to be the most cost- and time-effective methods currently available for the carrying out of sampling in many hard-to-reach populations.

24.4.2 Researcher engagement in respondent-assisted link-tracing

In studies of hidden and hard-to-reach human populations, a variety of research methods and practices have been developed over a number of decades to enable better understanding of the individual behaviors and social dynamics of the community of interest. The approaches developed include enabling the researcher to become an active and trusted participant in the community under study and the members of the community to become active participants in the research, helping the study in ways that include introducing the researcher to other members of the community. Through this process, recruitment methods have evolved that trace social links or relationships in the community, allowing the researcher to penetrate more deeply and become more substantially integrated with the community. In one study, a research participant might take a researcher directly to meet members of the subpopulation that are normally more deeply hidden and hard to reach than those met in the initial part of the study. In another study, a community member might give sufficient information for the researcher to find the person referred to. With these types of studies, the underlying sample selection methods are not well understood. The insights and understanding that have emerged from studies of this kind, however, have been very useful in developing statistical methodologies for sampling and inference in networks giving access to hidden populations. The field workers engaged in these studies emerge with remarkably good understanding of what is going on in the population. Studies of this type could be carried out on respondent-driven sampling itself for better insight into what sort of selection processes occur as coupons pass from one participant to another in the community, something that normally takes place outside the view of researchers. In principle at least, if one could understand the underlying selection procedures, one could very effectively use the design- and model-based inference methods described in the next section.

24.5   Inference approaches

Once a sample has been selected and the data obtained, the sample data can be used to make inferences about population characteristics. When the sampling design uses link-tracing or other adaptive procedures in selecting the sample units, some care is required in making and interpreting inferences. Link-tracing designs often have a tendency to bring in units that are more highly connected than average to other units in the population. Because there are more network paths to these units than others, the more connected units are selected with higher probability than other units. This results in a sampling design having unequal selection or inclusion probabilities for different units.

The most effective inference methods developed so far for data from link-tracing designs have been design-based and model-based ones. These approaches will be described below. For perspective, it is worth noting some advantages and importance of very simple methods of inference with such designs.

Simple methods are of value for situations in which field workers want to make estimates on the fly on which to base decisions. These must be done often under adverse conditions in which advanced computing resources are not available.

24.5.1 Simple methods

One very simple approach is to estimate a population mean or proportion with a sample proportion. The bias of such estimates with a link-tracing design will depend not only on the specific design but on population network characteristics such as the evenness of the degree distribution. These properties can be investigated with simulation studies and sensitivity analyses.

Another quite simple estimation method of a population mean or proportion is the generalized ratio estimator in which each unit value in the sample is divided by the unit's degree. The sample sum of those reciprocally weighted values is in turn divided by the sample sum of the reciprocals of the unit degrees. This is an estimator that has design-consistency properties when used with a random walk design in a connected, undirected network population, when the design is carried out with replacement. The asymptotic unbiasedness of this estimator is lost with other types of link-tracing designs and other types of populations. But for many of these situations, it is still the case that units having high degree have higher inclusion probabilities than units having low degree. For this reason, simulation studies show that the bias with the generalized ratio estimator is in many, but not every, situation less than the bias of a sample mean or proportion.

Another type of simple inference that can be of high importance in studies using link-tracing sample selection is simple detection of a condition or behavior of interest in the population. For instance, investigators may be monitoring for the emergence of a disease or a risk behavior in a region or social setting. Finding even a single case establishes the presence of the condition in the subpopulation, and finding a number of cases establishes a minimum number of cases for the population. When the object of inference is presence in the population, inference from the sample data is simple. For an effective sampling strategy in this situation, the need is to find a design that has a high probability of finding units with the condition of interest. For this purpose, link-tracing designs are often highly effective.

24.5.2 Design-based inference methods

Much of the earlier work in inference methods used primarily design-based approach. Probabilities of finding units by following links from an initial sample were figured out and design-unbiased estimators obtained for estimating mean node characteristics in the population. For some link-tracing designs, it is not possible to calculate these probabilities from the sample data. For example, unit inclusion probabilities can be derived for a one-wave snowball sample starting from an initial simple random sample. But if the sampling continues for more than one wave, or if the links are directed, then the inclusion probabilities cannot be obtained from the sample data.

For some designs such as these for which the inclusion probabilities are not computable for every unit in the sample, design-unbiased estimators are still possible. One way is to obtain a simple, if inefficient, unbiased estimator using only the initial sample and the design probabilities with which it was selected. This initial estimator can then be turned into a more efficient one using the Rao–Blackwell method. The improved estimator is the conditional expectation of the initial estimator given a sufficient statistic. For many sampling situations, including many of the link-tracing design problems, the Rao–Blackwell method amounts to considering every reordering of the sample data, calculating the initial estimator, which typically will be different for different reorderings, weighting that by the probability of selecting the sample in the given order, which also will typically be different for different reorderings of link-tracing samples, and computing the average. Except for small samples, the number of reorderings is too large for exact computation. A Markov chain Monte Carlo method for approximating the Rao–Blackwell estimator is described in Thompson (2006b).

The usual sufficient statistic in sampling is the unordered set of distinct units in the sample together with their associated variables of interest (Basu, 1969). In a number of sampling problems associated with link-tracing designs, this statistic is no longer sufficient. In particular, this can happen in situations where the population size is unknown and must be estimated, and it can also happen from the uncontrolled way in which the initial sample may be selected (Vincent and Thompson, 2012).

24.5.3 Inference methods that are design-based under model assumptions

What about an estimator that under a certain set of assumptions about the population has a known limiting distribution for the unit selection probabilities? This is the case with the use of the generalized ratio estimator based on degree, described earlier used with random walk type designs with replacement (Salganik & Heckathorn, 2004; Thompson, 2006a). Is the inference in this case design-based or model-based? The population is assumed fixed, as in the usual design-based case. The limiting unit selection probabilities on which the estimator is based, and a property of the estimator such as being asymptotically unbiased, depends on the way the sample is selected, not on an assumed stochastic population model. But the effectiveness of some of the estimators used with these types of designs does depends on assumptions made about the population. For the estimator most commonly associated with respondent-driven sampling, those assumptions are that the population network is an undirected graph consisting of a single connected component. That is, by following links, any unit can be eventually reached from any other unit by some path, and links are symmetric. If either of those population assumptions are not realistic, the asymptotic unbiasedness of the estimator is lost.

It can be said that such a procedure uses a combination of design-based and model-based considerations. In contrast to the usual model-based situation, it does not necessarily assume a statistical model for the population, of which the population being sampled is a particular realization. Or if it does, then every realization possible under the model must satisfy the assumptions of connectedness and symmetry for the asymptotic properties to hold unconditionally. With the population being fixed, strong assumptions are required about the characteristics of the population, in contrast to the usual design-based situation. The situation here also differs from the usual "model-assisted" inference situation, in which the form of an estimator is guided by optimality criteria under an assumed model but modified by incorporating design-induced probabilities, resulting in a strategy that might not be optimal under the assumed model but has robustness against departures from model assumptions.

24.5.4 Model-based inference approaches

Felix-Medina and Thompson (2004), Frank and Snijders (1994), and Felix-Medina and Monjardin (2006) used combinations of design- and model-based methods for estimating the size of a hidden population sampled with a link-tracing design. A more general approach to model-based inference for link-tracing designs was presented in Thompson and Frank (2000), who described the general approach and obtained maximum likelihood estimators of population quantities for a link-tracing design under an assumed stochastic graph model. Among model-based approaches, likelihood-based methods are preferred, because for many, though not all, link-tracing sampling situations the design is ignorable, in the sense of Rubin (1976), for likelihood-based inference but not for other types of model-based approaches.

Bayes inference in particular appears to offer the most practical approach to model-based inference methods with link-tracing designs. Exact Bayes inference methods with link-tracing were used in Chow and Thompson (2003). Computational Bayes inference for adaptive web sampling using Markov chain Monte Carlo is described in Kwanisai (2005, 2006). Computational Bayes methods with link-tracing designs have been further developed in Handcock and Gile (2010), under an exponential random graph model. Gile (2011) and Gile and Handcock (2011) develop methods of this type for use with data from existing respondent-driven sampling programs. Handcock, Gile, and Mar (2012) use this approach, in a case in which the design in nonignorable for the Bayes inference, to estimate an unknown population size from respondent-driven sampling data.

Model-based methods of inference for link-tracing designs has been helped by continuing development of stochastic networks. Reviews of network models include Goldenberg, Zheng, Fienberg, and Airoldi (2009) and Kolaczyk (2009), who also includes some discussion of sampling designs.

24.5.5 Simulation

At the other end of the spectrum from simple to complex, simulation studies which incorporate design and population features can be viewed as being often the most appropriate inference method for complex situations. The ideal simulation may be that provided by the computational Bayes methods that sample from the predictive posterior distribution given the sample data, which in the process integrate the known and estimated design and model features of the situation. Sampling from the posterior is carried out using either Markov chain Monte Carlo, approximations to the posterior distribution, or exact independent samples from the posterior distribution where possible.

Parametric bootstrap methods are similar in spirit. Estimates of population characteristics may be based on maximum likelihood or other parametric method, and simulations are carried out sampling from the estimated population model using the design actually used in the field.

In the most complex situations, it is often necessary to obtain estimates of population values from many different sources of data and published estimates. Simulation studies provide perhaps the most effective available approach to inference about population characteristics as well as about alternative sampling designs for such situations. The design- and model-based methods of inference for network data as described here are beginning to have an impact in scientific simulation studies such as the dynamics of the HIV epidemic. The dynamic network simulation methods presented in Goodreau, Cassels, Kasprzyk, Montano, Greek, and Morris (2012) provide an example.

24.6 Discussion

In this chapter, link-tracing designs for sampling in hard-to-reach populations have been described. Respondent-driven and respondent-assisted methods for carrying out the sampling have been discussed. A range of inference methods available for data obtained using link-tracing sampling methods have been described. Each of these topics are areas of active research. This continued research is crucial to the need for effective survey methods for hard-to-reach and underrepresented populations and to understanding and alleviating emerging epidemics.

References

Aldous, D., & J. Fill. (2002). *Reversible Markov Chains and Random Walks on Graphs* [online draft book]. Retrieved from www.stat.berkeley.edu/~aldous/RWG/book.html.

Basu, D. (1969). Role of the sufficiency and likelihood principles in sample survey theory. *Sankhya A: Mathematical Statistics and Probability*, 31(4), 441–54.

Birnbaum, Z. W., & Sirken, M. G. (1965). Design of sample surveys to estimate the prevalence of rare diseases: three unbiased estimates. *Vital and Health Statistics*, Ser. 2, No. 11. Washington, DC: US Government Printing Office.

Boyd, S., Diaconis, P., & Xiao, L. (2004). Fastest mixing Markov chain on a graph. *SIAM Review*, 46(4), 667–89.

Chow, M., & Thompson, S. K. (2003). Estimation with link-tracing sampling designs: a Bayesian approach. *Survey Methodology*, 29(2), 197–206.

Felix-Medina, M. H., & Monjardin, P. E. (2006). Combining link-tracing sampling and cluster sampling to estimate the size of hidden populations: a Bayesian-assisted approach. *Survey Methodology*, 32(2), 187–96.

Felix-Medina, M. H., & Thompson, S. K. (2004). Combining link-tracing sampling and cluster sampling to estimate the size of hidden populations. *Journal of Official Statistics*, 20(1), 19–38.

Frank, O. (1971). *Statistical Inference in Graphs*. Stockholm: ForsvaretForskningsanstalt.

(1977a). Survey sampling in graphs. *Journal of Statistical Planning and Inference*, 1(3), 235–64.

(1977b). Estimation of graph totals. *Scandinavian Journal of Statistics*, 4(2), 81–89.

(1978a). Estimating the number of connected components in a graph by using a sampled subgraph. *Scandinavian Journal of Statistics*, 5(4), 177–88.

(1978b). Sampling and estimation in large social networks. *Social Networks*, 1(1), 91–101.

(1979). Estimation of population totals by use of snowball samples. In P. W. Holland and S. Leinhardt (eds.), *Perspectives on Social Network Research* (pp. 319–47). New York: Academic Press.

Frank, O., & Snijders, T. (1994). Estimating the size of hidden populations using snowball sampling. *Journal of Official Statistics*, 10(1), 53–67.

Gile, K. J. (2011). Improved inference for respondent-driven sampling data with application to HIV prevalence estimation. *Journal of the American Statistical Association*, 106 (493), 135–46.

Gile, K. J., & Handcock, M. S. (2010). Respondent-driven sampling: an assessment of current methodology. *Sociological Methodology*, 40(1), 285–327.

(2011). *Network Model-Assisted Inference from Respondent-Driven Sampling Data.* arXiv:1108.0298 [Cornell University Library].

Goel, S., & Salganik, M. J. (2010). Assessing respondent-driven sampling. *Proceedings of the National Academy of Sciences*, 107(15), 6743–47.

Goldenberg, A., Zheng, A. X., Fienberg, S. E., & Airoldi, E. M. (2009). *A Survey of Statistical Network Models.* arXiv:0912.5410 [Cornell University Library].

Goodreau, S. M., Cassels, S., Kasprzyk, D., Montano, D. E., Greek, A., & Morris, M. (2012). Concurrent partnerships, acute infection and HIV epidemic dynamic among young adults in Zimbabwe. *AIDS and Behavior*, 16, 312–22.

Handcock, M. S., & Gile, K. J. (2010). Modeling social networks from sampled data. *Annals of Applied Statistics*, 4(1), 5–25.

Handcock, M. S., Gile, K. J., & Mar, C. M. (2012). *Estimating Hidden Population Size Using Respondent-Driven Sampling.* arXiv:1209.6241 [Cornell University Library].

Heckathorn, D. D. (1997). Respondent-driven sampling: a new approach to the study of hidden populations. *Social Problems*, 44(2), 174–99.

(2002). Respondent-driven sampling II: deriving valid population estimates from chain-referral samples of hidden populations. *Social Problems*, 49(1), 11–34.

Klovdahl, A. S. (1989). Urban social networks: some methodological problems and possibilities. In M. Kochen (ed.), *The Small World* (pp. 176–210). Norwood, NJ: Ablex Publishing, 176–210.

Kolaczyk, E. D. (2009). *Statistical Analysis of Network Data: Methods and Models.* New York: Springer.

Kwanisai, M. (2005). Estimation in link-tracing designs with subsampling. Unpublished doctoral dissertation, Pennsylvania State University.

(2006). Estimation in network populations. In *Joint Statistical Meetings Proceedings, Survey Research Methods Section* (pp. 3285–91). Alexandria, VA: American Statistical Association.

Lovasz, L. (1993). Random walks on graphs: a survey. In D. Miklos, D. Sos, & T. Szoni (eds.), *Combinatorics, Paul Erdos is Eighty* (vol. II, pp. 1–46). Keszthely: Janos Bolyai Mathematical Society.

Magnani, R., Sabin, K., Saidel, T., & Heckathorn, D. (2005). Review of sampling hard-to-reach and hidden populations for HIV surveillance. *AIDS*, 19 (Suppl. 2), S67–S72.

Rubin, D. B. (1976). Inference and missing data. *Biometrika*, 63(3), 581–92.

Salganik, M. J., & Heckathorn, D. D. (2004). Sampling and estimation in hidden populations using respondent-driven sampling. *Sociological Methodology*, 34(1), 193–240.

Sirken, M. G. (1972a). Stratified sample surveys with multiplicity. *Journal of the American Statistical Association*, 67(337), 224–27.

(1972b). Variance components of multiplicity estimators. *Biometrics*, 28(3), 869–73.

Snijders, T. A. B. (1992). Estimation on the basis of snowball samples: how to weight. *Bulletin Méthodologie Sociologique*, 36(1), 59–70.

Spreen, M. (1992). Rare populations, hidden populations, and link-tracing designs: what and why? *Bulletin de Méthodologie Sociologique*, 36(1), 34–58.

Thompson, S. K. (2006a). Targeted random walk designs. *Survey Methodology*, 32(1), 11–24.

(2006b). Adaptive web sampling. *Biometrics*, 62(4), 1224–34.

(2011). Adaptive network and spatial sampling. *Survey Methodology*, 37(2), 183–96.

(2012). *Sampling* (3rd edn.). New York: John Wiley & Sons.

Thompson, S. K., & Frank, O. (2000). Model-based estimation with link-tracing sampling designs. *Survey Methodology*, 26(1), 87–98.

Vincent, K., & Thompson, S. (2012). *Estimating Population Size with Link-Tracing Sampling*. arXiv:1210.2667 [stat.ME] [Cornell University Library].

Volz, E., & Heckathorn, D. D. (2008). Probability based estimation theory for respondent driven sampling. *Journal of Official Statistics*, 24(1), 79–97.

PART V

Data collection strategies for the hard to survey

25

Use of paid media to encourage 2010 Census participation among the hard to count

W. DOUGLAS EVANS, A. RUPA DATTA, AND TING YAN

25.1 Introduction

This chapter describes a relatively uncommon approach, paid media campaigns, to encourage participation of hard-to-survey populations. Specifically, we discuss the paid media component of the 2010 Integrated Communication Campaign conducted by the US Census Bureau as part of its 2010 Decennial Census effort in the United States.

Why, from a methodology perspective, might one want a paid media campaign to encourage survey participation? The conceptual model of survey participation laid out by Groves and Couper (1998) suggests that respondents' decision to participate in a survey request is based on several factors – the social environment, respondent characteristics, survey design features, interviewer characteristics, and the respondent–interviewer interactions at the point of survey request. The first two factors are usually out of the control of survey organizations; in other words, survey organizations are not able to manipulate or change who respondents are and where they live. However, the context in which a survey request is presented, received, and perceived can be changed to facilitate a favorable participation outcome from respondents. We consider a paid media campaign a useful means for changing the survey-taking climate.

A paid media campaign could include a wide variety of communication modes, including television, radio, and print advertisements, Internet pop-up or banner ads, billboards, or other out-of-home advertisements, such as park benches or coffee-cup sleeves. Paid media, especially when pervasive, can lend legitimacy to the survey effort and alter the survey environment in which the survey request is made. Paid media campaigns can also prime individuals to receive the survey request favorably in an amplification of the effect that an advance letter prior to a survey request might typically have. Another advantage of deploying paid media is the ability to reach individuals with particular characteristics without knowing their exact location. For example, we may know that 20 percent of residents of a metropolitan area belong to a certain ethnic group, but unless we know their exact addresses,

This work was partially supported by funds from the US Census Bureau for the 2010 CICPE contract. Views expressed in this chapter are those of the authors and do not represent the US Census Bureau.

we cannot directly mail them targeted survey information. If a medium such as a radio station is known to have high listenership among the targeted group, we can reach that group without knowing how to reach any individual member.

Paid media has historically been unaffordable for most surveys. Mass media advertising has been expensive, and because it reaches everyone, requires spending to reach many non-targeted individuals for each targeted individual. The rise of micro-media outlets that use inexpensive technologies and the narrowly defined audiences of some media mean that the price of advertising to reach rare populations is declining, while the ability to reach targeted individuals through advertisements is increasing. For these reasons, paid media may increasingly be attractive for surveys of rare populations, even those with relatively limited budgets.

A common alternative for this type of outreach would be to use existing organizations or other social networks to reach individuals, but paid media may reach many more individuals, and the survey agency has much greater control over message delivery in the paid media context. As it happens, the campaign we discuss in this chapter employed both paid media and a partnership program[1] which enlisted existing organizations and social groups in encouraging survey participation among their constituents.

In this chapter, we present a particularly ambitious example of a paid media campaign to enlist survey cooperation among hard-to-reach groups. In the next section, we review the literature on recent public service media campaigns. We then turn to the specific case of the 2010 Integrated Communication Campaign (ICC), discussing its goals, implementation, and evaluation. In the fourth section, we present the conceptual model that underlays the campaign evaluation and presents four associated hypotheses. The fifth section reviews the evidence pertaining to these hypotheses. We conclude with general remarks about possible paid media campaigns for other survey efforts.

25.2   Review of recent media campaigns

We define media campaigns as mass communications and social marketing designed to change specific behaviors. For example, campaigns may seek to promote health and well-being, encourage energy conservation, increase financial literacy, or increase survey or civic participation (Bertrand, Mullainathan, & Shafir, 2006; Evans, Davis, & Farrelly, 2008; World Bank, 2012). Media campaign evaluation is distinct from other forms of program evaluation in that it focuses specifically on behavior change through communicating messages, marketing, and promotion of targeted behaviors, or avoidance of behaviors (Evans, 2008).

There is a growing body of evidence, especially from public health subject areas such as tobacco control, nutrition, and physical activity, and HIV/AIDS, to suggest that social marketing can change behavior and is a broadly effective social change strategy that can be applied to modify behaviors across multiple subject areas (Abroms & Maibach, 2008; French, Blair-Stevens, McVey, & Merritt, 2010). A recent systematic review by the US Preventive Services Taskforce of twenty-two campaigns that used products (e.g., helmets)

---

1 See Chapter 29 for details about the 2010 Census Partnership Program.

to promote health and prevent disease and injury concluded that communication and social marketing was an effective practice (Robinson, Tansil, Elder, Soler, Labre, Mercer *et al.*, n.d.).

There is also growing evidence that social marketing can be used for other types of behavior change, from increasing energy conservation (McKenzie-Mohr & Oskamp, 2010) to promoting community participation (Dutta-Bergman, 2003). The best evidence of social marketing effectiveness comes from media campaign evaluations, typically studies of large mass media campaigns or laboratory experiments where messages are tested under controlled conditions (Evans, Uhrig, Davis, & McCormack, 2009; Snyder & Hamilton, 2002). Recently, however, mobile phones, social media, and other new technologies have been studied for behavior change as well (Abroms, Padmanabahn, & Evans, 2012).

25.2.1 Mass media

Recent evidence reviews indicate that social marketing through mass media is effective in changing health behaviors on a population level. In general, these studies show that social marketing has been effective in changing health behavior, such as smoking, physical activity, and condom use, and behavioral mediators, such as knowledge, attitudes, and beliefs, related to these behaviors. However, most of these studies have shown effect sizes of less than 10 percent (Snyder & Hamilton, 2002).

In their widely cited study of forty-eight US social marketing campaigns based on mass media, Snyder and Hamilton (2002) found that the average campaign accounted for about 9 percent of the variation in health risk behavior outcomes but with heterogeneous results. A study of seventeen recent European media campaigns on a range of topics including promotion of HIV testing, myocardial infarction admissions, immunizations, and cancer screenings found similar effects in the range of 5 to 10 percent (Grilli, Ramsay, & Minozzi, 2002). Evans (2006) points out that single- or few-time behaviors can be easier to promote than behavior requiring repetition and maintenance over time. Some behaviors that do not require long-term maintenance, such as Vitamin A promotion and switching to 1 percent milk, have shown greater effect sizes and generally appear to have higher rates of success (Hornik, 1997; Reger, Wootan, & Booth-Butterfield, 1999). Media campaigns have thus been used to modify both complex behaviors, including those involving multiple lifestyle risk factors such as HIV risk behavior, as well as simpler behaviors such as choosing a food product. Because of the wide applicability of media campaigns to assess behavior modification, it may be that such an approach would be effective in changing civic behaviors such as mailing back a census form.

The most effective mass media campaigns have generally been those with substantial financial resources and thus the ability to generate high levels of audience exposure and recall or recognition of messages and advertising executions. For example, among the most successful media campaigns to change health behavior have been tobacco counter-marketing campaigns aimed at preventing youth smoking initiation, such as the American Legacy Foundation's (http://legacyforhealth.org) *truth* campaign. Legacy spent several hundred million dollars in the campaign's early years, from 2000 to 2002. Farrelly, Davis, Haviland, Messeri, and Healton (2005) showed that from 1999 to 2002, US youth smoking prevalence declined from 25.3 percent to 18.0 percent, and *truth* accounted for approximately 22 percent of that decline. While this is a relatively small effect size by clinical standards, it demonstrates that media campaigns can have a big impact on population-level health. For example, in the case of *truth*, the campaign-attributable decline in youth smoking equates to some 300,000 fewer youth smokers, and thus millions of added life years as well as tremendous reductions in health care expenditures and other social costs.

There is evidence that media campaigns are effective in targeting other behaviors, such as financial education and literacy. The Mediae Financial Education project in Kenya aimed to improve knowledge, attitudes, behaviors, and practices in terms of financial capability (World Bank, 2012). This initiative focused on banking, budgeting, savings, and investments to increase levels of financial education in the country. The campaign's primary objective was to encourage people to manage their finances in a sustainable manner more likely to lead to financial security. The basic approach integrated financial education content into an entertaining television program, Makatuno Junction, featuring characters that people could identify with. Outcome evaluation was conducted through a pre- and post-intervention cross-sectional survey of viewers and nonviewers. Prior to the airing of the episodes involving financial topics, 57 percent of the baseline survey respondents claimed to have "seen/heard information about the four target financial topics from sources in their environment" – this number jumped to 67 percent after the show among viewers. For nonviewers there was no increase in awareness or knowledge, suggesting a treatment effect of Makatuno Junction (World Bank, 2012).

25.2.2 New technologies

Randomized trials of text messaging programs have shown behavioral effects among adolescents and adults, minority and nonminority populations, and across nationalities (Cole-Lewis & Kershaw, 2010). With mobile phones, the majority of published research has been on short message service (SMS), or text messaging. There is evidence that supports text messaging as an effective behavior change strategy in smoking cessation, weight loss, physical activity, and diabetes management (Cole-Lewis & Kershaw, 2010; Fjeldsoe, Marshall, & Miller, 2009; Whittaker, Borland, Bullen, Lin, McRobbie, & Rodgers, 2009), and, to a lesser extent, for STD prevention and treatment (Lim, Hocking, Hellard, & Aitken, 2008) and in treating hypertension (Logan, McIsaac, Tisler, Irvine, Saunders, Dunai *et al.*, 2007). Very little is known about the utility of smartphones and their associated applications (or "apps") for health promotion. Recent reviews of the literature found no studies that examined the efficacy of smartphone apps for health promotion or disease management, although a few studies have evaluated the quality of apps for smoking cessation (Abroms, Padmanabahn, Thaweethai, & Philips, 2011), weight loss (Breton, Abroms, & Fuemmeler,

2010), and diabetes self-management (Ciemens, Coon, & Sorli, 2010), as well as their usability for diabetes self-management (Rao, Hou, Golnik, Flaherty, & Vu, 2010).

In summary, media campaigns have been shown to be effective across a wide range of subject matter, with the majority of evidence coming from health and health care. Because media campaigns have been effective in affecting a range of behavior changes – including complex hard-to-change health behaviors and simpler knowledge and awareness raising and consumer choices – the collective evidence suggests that they may be effective in promoting survey participation and civic behaviors such as returning census forms as well. The 2010 ICC is perhaps the largest example of a paid media campaign designed to promote participation in a census.

25.3   Implementation and evaluation of the 2010 Integrated Communication Campaign

25.3.1 The 2010 Integrated Communication Campaign

Accuracy and coverage evaluation research conducted by the US Bureau of the Census for the 2000 Decennial Census indicated net undercounts of non-Hispanic Blacks, Hispanics, renters (as opposed to homeowners), and males ages 18–49. In addition, mail return rates to the 2000 Decennial Census were particularly low for renters in non-Hispanic Black Hispanic, Native Hawaiian, and Other Pacific Islander, and off-reservation American Indian and Alaska Native race/ethnic origin categories (US Census Bureau, 2003). These groups were thus high priority for targeted outreach in the 2010 Census, both to improve data quality (through reduction of differential undercount) and to reduce costs (through increased mail return and improved cooperation with enumerators).

The US Census Bureau implemented the 2010 ICC to encourage participation in the 2010 Decennial Census, including coordinated delivery of targeted outreach to specific subpopulations. Components of the 2010 ICC included paid media advertising; an expansive grass-roots Partnership Program that engaged organizations, such as churches, civic groups, and local leaders; a census in schools program for students in elementary and secondary schools; and earned media, such as news and features coverage in traditional and digital media outlets. Outreach to households for the 2010 ICC began in late 2009, with peak paid media and partnership activities taking place from January through June 2010. The goals of the 2010 ICC were to increase mailback of the census form, improve cooperation with enumerators, and reduce differential undercounting. The 2010 ICC was indeed integrated, with a high degree of coordination in materials, images, and themes across the different components of the campaign. The campaign was also pervasive. The paid media campaign was one of the nation's most ubiquitous television advertising efforts in the early part of 2010 – between January and June of 2010, census television advertising was ranked fourth behind McDonald's, Walmart, and Geico.

The lion's share of paid media dollars were spent on television advertising. (Television advertising is expensive, but clearly enjoys the largest audiences of the various media outlets.) Partly because of the structure of American television ratings data and how advertisement placements are sold, targeting of populations was largely done based on race/ethnic origin definitions (as opposed to homeownership, for example). The 2010 ICC was a major investment of public dollars and occasionally became a point of political contention among critics of public spending.

Advertisements for the 2010 ICC were customized in twenty-eight languages and for as many race/ethnic origin groups. Some of the variation in advertisements involved conveying standard messages (such as the low burden of completing a census form) through creative executions that were culturally specific (including through dress, music, and even style of rice cooker). Others involved messages tailored to the particular concerns of the target group, for example, fears of contact with government agencies among Muslim-Americans. Target ads almost exclusively used non-English languages common to each target group (except for non-Hispanic Blacks). As a result, many native-born or long-term immigrants who may not have frequented in-language media outlets received only the nontargeted general population messages that ran in the mainstream English-language media. The Census Bureau conducted a survey in 2008 to better understand Americans' perceptions of, knowledge of, and attitudes toward the decennial census. Analyses of the data from this survey informed development of themes for the 2010 ICC and the mapping of themes to population subgroups (Bates, Conrey, Zuwallack, Billia, Harris, Jacobsen *et al.*, 2009). Focus groups and other qualitative research helped to refine themes and creative material, especially for small subgroups who were not well represented in the 2008 survey.

The paid media component of the 2010 ICC was conducted in three phases: an awareness phase in January and February of 2010, a motivation (to return the census form by mail) phase in March and April of 2010, and a Nonresponse Follow Up (NRFU) phase to encourage cooperation with census enumerators, who would be visiting neighborhoods to enumerate households that had not returned their forms. The awareness phase themes sought to increase knowledge of the census, particularly that its results are used to allocate Congressional representation and that confidentiality of census data is protected by law.

In the motivation phase, emphasis was given to the low burden involved ("10 questions, 10 minutes"), messages that suggested that census participation was a civic duty and reflected pride in one's community, additional factual information about the distribution of public funds based on census results ("$400 billion dollars over the next 10 years"), and the legal requirement to participate in the census ("It's the law"). For some groups, the motivation phase advertisements informed individuals that not returning the form would result in a personal contact from an enumerator. Another group-specific message emphasized confidentiality for undocumented individuals or others who might fear reprisal from honest responses to the census questions. In the NRFU phase, a single theme was varied for all target groups encouraging cooperation with enumerators if they came to the door, with tips on how to know that an enumerator was legitimate.

25.3.2 The 2010 Census Integrated Communication Program Evaluation

The 2010 Census Integrated Communication Program Evaluation (CICPE) was sponsored by the US Census Bureau and conducted by NORC at the University of Chicago to evaluate the full 2010 ICC, including the paid media campaign. The objective of the study was to assess the extent to which the 2010 ICC achieved its goals of increasing mail returns and increasing cooperation with enumerators. The evaluation was also structured to investigate some of the mechanisms through which the campaign might or might not have succeeded in affecting people's census-related knowledge, attitudes, and behavior. The principal data source for the 2010 CICPE was a set of three nationally representative household surveys conducted between October 2009 and August 2010 to capture knowledge, attitudes, and exposure to the campaign. To increase the ability to understand person-specific response to the campaign, the surveys included a panel sample in which the same individuals were interviewed in each of the three waves.

Survey data collection for the 2010 CICPE took place at three points: (1) Wave 1 was conducted mid-September 2009 through mid-January 2010, during early partnership activity (and prior to the launch of the paid media effort), to assess baseline levels of all measures of public attention and intentions that were the focus of the 2010 Census ICC; (2) Wave 2 took place January 19 through March 18, 2010, during the peak of the paid media campaign and partnership activities, but before census forms were distributed to households; and (3) Wave 3 was conducted during the NRFU period from mid-April through mid-July 2010 when people had made their decisions about participating in the mailback phase and had been exposed to the full course of the main paid media and partnership campaigns.

Mirroring the structure of the paid media component, the 2010 CICPE also focused on race/ethnic origin groups. Specifically, survey samples included approximately equal numbers of individuals from five hard-to-count groups (Hispanics, non-Hispanic Blacks, American Indians and Alaska Natives, Asians, and Native Hawaiians and Other Pacific Islanders); for comparison purposes, all others were included as a sixth group. Table 25.1 provides (unweighted) completed case counts by race/ethnicity and wave. (See Datta, Yan, Evans, Pedlow, Spencer, & Bautista, 2012, for survey details.)

The 2010 CICPE interviews were conducted with sampled individuals by telephone or, if needed, in-person. Panel respondents in the latter two waves were first invited to complete by mail or web, then pursued using telephone and finally in-person modes for nonresponse follow up. Items on census knowledge, attitudes, and intention to participate were adopted from earlier surveys where possible to enhance comparability across census years and with the 2008 survey that informed development of 2010 ICC messages and strategy. The questionnaires also collected detailed information on individuals' self-reported exposure to 2010 ICC components. Operational data on actual 2010 Census participation were combined with survey data to determine households' actual census behavior.

Table 25.1 *2010 CICPE completed cases by race/ethnicity group*

Race/ethnicity	Total cases completed		
	Wave 1	Wave 2	Wave 3
Hispanic	461	369	539
Non-Hispanic Black	377	384	526
Non-Hispanic White	404	358	472
American Indian	457	392	529
Asian	542	410	548
Native Hawaiian	430	350	494
Total	2,671	2,263	3,108

Note: The non-Hispanic White category includes all non-Black, non-Hispanic individuals, including Asians, Native Hawaiians and Other Pacific Islanders, and American Indians and Alaska Natives. This category, together with the Hispanic and non-Hispanic Black categories, constitutes a nationally representative sample of all Americans in households. The remaining three categories – Asians, Native Hawaiians and Other Pacific Islanders (NHOPIs), and American Indians and Alaska Natives (AIANs) – are independent supplemental samples fielded in order to collect adequate numbers of interviews from rare populations.

25.4   CICPE conceptual model and research hypotheses

The 2010 CICPE design did not support estimation of a "total" effect of the campaign. Rather, the evaluation analyses sought to determine the relationship, if any, between increased "dosage" of campaign exposure and changes in interim or final outcomes such as knowledge, attitudes, beliefs, or census mailback behavior.

Figure 25.1 below, the CICPE conceptual model,[2] visually depicts relationships between campaign exposure, the outcomes of primary interest, and other relevant factors. The conceptual model provides a framework within which to consider the objectives for the 2010 CICPE, and provides a basis for hypotheses to be tested in analysis of outcome data.

The model reflects well-supported theoretical assumptions from health communication (Evans *et al.*, 2009). The reception phase involves exposure to the campaign, campaign message recall, and message receptivity (MR). Three types of exposure are assumed in the model, through paid and earned media, partnership and school activities, and word of mouth and other social interactions. In this chapter, we focus on the paid media component.

Our hypothesis (H1) is that exposure intensity affects message recall and receptivity, which we measure with questionnaire items.

Following exposure, we hypothesize that there is a degree of receptivity to 2010 ICC messages. MR is a construct that represents rational and affective reactions to messages

---

2 The 2010 CICPE conceptual model was authored by Bob Calder of Northwestern University.

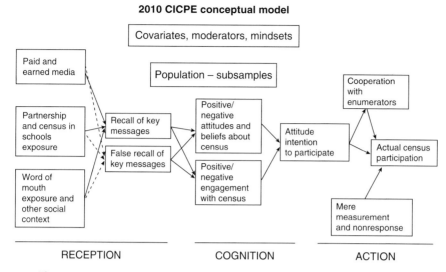

Figure 25.1 2010 CICPE conceptual model

(Evans, Davis, Umanzor, Patel, and Khan, 2011). A number of studies in health communication have established measures of "receptivity" to public service advertising (PSA) that capture audiences' subjective appraisals of message persuasiveness, believability, and other aspects of cognitive processing (Bruner, 1998; Dillard, Shen, & Vail, 2007). These measures are often used as proxies of ad effectiveness. They have been shown to predict changes in attitudes toward the social issues and other subject matter of PSAs (Davis, Nonnemaker, Farrelly, and Niederdeppe, 2011). Such measures can be used to assess effectiveness of campaign messages during development and prior to implementation. They can also be used as mediators to test the theory of change underlying a campaign during and after implementation (Evans *et al.*, 2009).

The Cognition phase involves the processing of the received messages and their integration into views held by the individual regarding the census in particular and the public good more generally. Knowledge and attitudes targeted by the 2010 ICC advertising should increase as a function of exposure and receptivity to census messages. We hypothesize (H2) that the specific targeted knowledge attitudes, and intent promoted in 2010 ICC advertising will be higher among respondents who have higher exposure, and among those who have higher MR, compared to those with lower exposure or lower MR.

The Cognition phase of the model has two elements that measure the effect of messages on attitudes toward and knowledge of and engagement with the census, respectively. The former (attitudes and knowledge) covers inherent positive or negative aspects of participating in the census, such as the time required or the potential invasion of privacy. The latter (engagement with) pertains to the motivations for participation that stem from the individual's broader views about the public good. For example, one belief measured in the 2010 CICPE is that "Answering and sending back the census matters for my family and community." These two elements then inform intention of the individual to participate.

However, intention alone does not entail census participation. In the Action phase, individuals translate their attitudes and beliefs about the census and the public good into concerted behavior. We have a record of actual participation behavior from the Census Bureau. Hypothesis (H3) holds that increased knowledge of or positive attitudes toward the census will translate to increased likelihood of census participation.

Spanning the full conceptual model, we further hypothesize (H4) that greater exposure to 2010 ICC advertising will be associated with greater census participation as measured both by self-report and by Census Bureau records.

Finally, while we do not present specific tests of mediation in this chapter, the model specifies mediating variables between 2010 ICC exposure and census participation. Specifically, we hypothesize that MR, census attitudes, and knowledge targeted in 2010 ICC advertising, and intentions to participate each mediate the pathway from exposure to participation.

We derived and examined four research questions in the light of the conceptual framework:

(1) Did exposure to the 2010 ICC, including group-specific advertising, lead to improved reception of census messages?
(2) Did improved reception of census messages lead to more positive knowledge, attitudes, and intentions to participate?
(3) Were more positive knowledge and attitudes associated with greater observed census participation?
(4) Did more exposure to the ICC have direct impact on the observed census participation?

25.5 Results

25.5.1 Hypothesis 1: Did exposure to the ICC, including group-specific advertising, lead to improved reception of census messages?

To address the first hypothesis, we created an MR index using only Wave 3 data. In Wave 3, each respondent was asked whether they remembered seeing or hearing three specific advertisements – an advertisement designed for the general population (called "diverse mass"), a target population-specific advertisement (i.e., one intended for the respondent's racial/ethnic group), and an NRFU ad (i.e., one implemented late in the campaign to encourage individuals to cooperate with enumerators going door-to-door). The ads[3] were selected primarily because they received a substantial fraction of air time during the 2010 ICC, but also because testing during questionnaire development indicated that the chosen

---

3 Note that each respondent was asked about one of six different population-specific ads (e.g., Hispanic respondents reported on the Hispanic-targeted ad, Native Hawaiians on an ad targeting that group, etc.). Thus, tabulations for the "population-specific" ad are actually aggregate indicators across six different advertisements that share the attribute of being very culturally and linguistically specific.

ads were easier to describe and recognize than other ads in the campaign that ran with similar frequency.[4] For each ad, three messaging items were included in the survey:

- Would you say the ad grabbed your attention? (YES, NO)
- Would you say the ad gave you good reason to mail back your census form? (YES, NO)
- During the past ninety days, how often have you seen this advertisement? Would you say never, once or twice, 3–15 times, 16 to 30 times, or 31 times or more?

We recoded the first two questions so that 1 is YES and 0 is everything else. For the third question, never is recoded as 0, once or twice as 1, 3–15 times as 2, 16 to 30 times as 3, and 31 times or more as 4. Based on the above item coding, we calculated an MR index (MR score) at the ad level for each respondent by summing up the recoded responses to the three messaging items. We calculated an overall MR index at the respondent level by summing up the MR scores across the three ads. Table 25.2 below displays descriptive statistics and reliability analysis of the MR index.

Exposure to the 2010 ICC is measured through a survey question in Wave 3 asking the number of times a respondent saw or heard anything about the census in the past ninety days. We did a median split based on this exposure measure and show the MR scores for each group. As shown in Table 25.3, higher mean MR scores within a cell indicate the row variable is correlated with higher MR for the ad in that column. We found that by ad, higher

Table 25.2 *Descriptive statistics and reliability analysis of MR index*

Item	Mean	SE	Factor loading	Item-scale correlation	Inter-item correlation	Alpha
This ad was attention grabbing	0.12	0.01	0.94	0.90	0.85	0.82
Ad gave good reasons to mail	0.13	0.01	0.92	0.88	0.81	0.85
How often have you seen this ad?	0.29	0.02	0.89	0.94	0.75	0.90
MR index (summary of the 3 variables)	0.54	0.04	—	—	—	—

Table 25.3 *Mean and standard error of MR to census ads, by exposure*

	Diverse mass ad mean (SE)	Population-specific ads mean (SE)	NRFU ad mean (SE)
Above median W3 total campaign exposure (n=1,285 cases)	0.65 (0.07)	0.72 (0.08)	1.12 (0.14)
Below median W3 total campaign exposure (n=1,823 cases)	0.25 (0.06)	0.27 (0.04)	0.53 (0.07)

4 Other items in the questionnaire that measured exposure included "confirmed awareness" items, in which respondents verify self-reported exposure to advertisements by providing confirmatory details about the ads, as well as use of visual and aural clips from referenced ads to cue respondents. In Datta, Yan, Evans, Pedlow, Spencer, and Bautista (2011), we find consistent results across the various self-report measures.

MR was correlated with higher scores on the total campaign exposure measure. Thus, higher MR is consistently correlated with more exposures to the 2010 ICC by ad.

25.5.2 Hypothesis 2: Did improved reception of census messages lead to more positive knowledge, attitudes, and intentions to participate?

We next estimated the effects of messaging on knowledge, attitudes, behavioral intention, and the actual behavior through multivariate regression models. Knowledge of the census is measured by counting, for each respondent, the number of correct answers to the eight knowledge questions asked in Wave 3. To measure respondents' attitudes towards the census, an exploratory factor analysis was performed on eleven attitudinal questions asking respondents' attitudes towards the census. Two factors were extracted; one factor is only loaded on a question about burden and the other factor is loaded on the other ten questions. So we used the second factor, which we label an "attitude factor," as the dependent variable in the models. Behavioral intent is measured via a survey question included in Wave 2 asking the likelihood that respondents would return their census form.

We regressed each interim and final outcome (knowledge score, attitude factor, and census participation intent) on MR as noted earlier. These analyses controlled for the same set of respondent characteristics, such as education, homeownership, whether the respondent speaks or understands another language other than English, and race and ethnicity of the respondents. We initially calculated a full model including all covariates. Then we calculated a reduced model including only those covariates found statistically significant in the full model. These included education level, home ownership, and non-English-speaking status. As presented in Table 25.4 (reduced main effects model), we found that both the knowledge score and attitude factor were positively and significantly associated with a higher MR score. There was, however, no relationship observed between MR and census participation intent.

As a follow up, we examined differences in relationships between MR and 2010 ICC outcomes for each of the major subpopulations targeted in the campaign for which 2010 CICPE had adequate analysis sample. We developed similar multivariable regression models for each subpopulation and used the same covariates as in previous analyses. We estimated a reduced model as before and report those results here. Due to co-linearity, the reduced model excluded non-English-speaking status for subgroup analyses of Hispanics who speak Spanish.

Table 25.4 *Predicting knowledge, attitude factor, and intent, using MR*

	Knowledge score		Attitude factor		W2 intent	
	n=2,401		n=1,888		n=924	
Outcome	Coefficient	*p*-value	Coefficient	*p*-value	Coefficient	*p*-value
MR index	0.16	<0.01	0.03	<0.01	0.02	0.09
R-squared	0.24		0.14		0.27	

Table 25.5 presents the effects of MR on knowledge for various subgroups. Overall, MR has a positive significant effect on knowledge scores for all subgroups.

Table 25.6 shows the relationship between MR and positive attitudes towards the census for various respondent subgroups. Overall, we found that the relationships between MR and knowledge scores and attitudes index were generally similar across subpopulations – significant associations with some variation in magnitude. One exception was no significant relationship observed between MR and the attitudes index for Asians.

Table 25.7 presents the association of MR with self-reported intent to complete and mail back a census form. This set of analyses was conducted on panel respondents who completed both Waves 2 and 3. Thus, the sample size is much smaller. MR has a positive significant association with intent for non-Hispanic Blacks and Native Hawaiians, but negative significant relationship for Asians. No other significant associations between MR and outcomes were observed in the subpopulation analyses.

Table 25.5 *Predicting knowledge scores using MR index by race/ethnicity*

Respondent Pool	Hispanics n=530		Non-Hispanic Blacks n=511		Non-Hispanic Whites n=465	
	Coefficient	*p*-value	Coefficient	*p*-value	Coefficient	*p*-value
MR index	0.18	<0.01	0.12	0.03	0.15	<0.01
R-squared	0.25		0.18		0.24	
Respondent Pool	AIANs n=521		NHOPIs n=487		Asians n=541	
	Coefficient	*p*-value	Coefficient	*p*-value	Coefficient	*p*-value
MR index	0.09	0.04	0.20	0.01	0.11	0.02
R-squared	0.17		0.24		0.23	

Table 25.6 *Predicting positive attitude factor using MR index by race/ethnicity*

Respondent Pool	Hispanics n=441		Non-Hispanic Blacks n=382		Non-Hispanic Whites n=366	
	Coefficient	*p*-value	Coefficient	*p*-value	Coefficient	*p*-value
MR index	0.04	0.01	0.05	<0.01	0.01	<0.01
R-squared	0.10		0.12		0.07	
Respondent Pool	AIANs n=382		NHOPIs n=370		Asians n=389	
	Coefficient	*p*-value	Coefficient	*p*-value	Coefficient	*p*-value
MR index	0.03	0.04	0.04	<0.01	0.01	0.20
R-squared	0.15		0.09		0.04	

Table 25.7 *Predicting (Wave 2) intent to return census form using MR index*

Respondent Pool	Hispanics n=172		Non-Hispanic Blacks n=194		Non-Hispanic Whites n=189	
	Coefficient	*p*-value	Coefficient	*p*-value	Coefficient	*p*-value
MR index	0.02	0.26	0.06	<0.01	0.02	0.53
R-squared	0.13		0.32		0.06	
Respondent Pool	AIANs n=209		NHOPIs n=164		Asians n=205	
	Coefficient	*p*-value	Coefficient	*p*-value	Coefficient	*p*-value
MR index	0.00	0.81	0.06	0.05	-0.05	0.01
R-squared	0.09		0.12		0.21	

Overall, higher MR is associated with higher census-related knowledge and more positive attitudes. This is consistent with the 2010 CICPE evaluation conceptual model and previous research on MR. Some population subgroups have higher MR and for those groups higher MR is associated with higher knowledge and more positive attitudes.

25.5.3 Hypothesis 3: Were greater knowledge and more positive attitudes associated with greater observed census participation?

We further examined whether there is a relationship between knowledge and attitudes and actual census participation. Tables 25.8 and 25.9 define mail return as having occurred prior to April 18, before the start of the NRFU effort. These tables show the results of a multivariate logistic regression model with the dependent variable being actual census mailback behavior and knowledge and attitudes count as independent variables. Note that in contrast to the analyses associated with Hypothesis 2, attitudes here are represented by a simple count of positive (negative) attitudes expressed, rather than an attitude factor. We see in Table 25.8 that, when we include all cases in a simple main effect model, higher knowledge scores and the more positive attitudes are both associated with increased likelihood of mail return, holding everything else constant in the model.

Among race/ethnicity groups as shown in Table 25.9, a higher knowledge score is significantly associated with increased mail return for every group except Hispanics. Among Hispanics, none of the knowledge, positive attitudes, or negative attitudes are significantly associated with mail return. Among non-Hispanic Whites, American Indians, and Native Hawaiians, positive attitudes are also associated with mail return, but a larger number of positive attitudes increases the likelihood of mail return among the first two groups and decreases the likelihood of mail return among Native Hawaiians. The count of negative attitudes is not statistically significant for any group, although it is very close to significant among Native Hawaiians, for whom more negative attitudes are associated with lower likelihood of mail return. Knowledge and attitudes seem to explain almost a third of

Table 25.8 *Predicting mail return using knowledge and attitudes*

	All cases
	Odds ratio (*p*-value)
Knowledge scores	1.18 (0.01)
Positive attitudes count	1.24 (0.01)
Negative attitudes count	1.32 (0.13)
Pseudo-R-squared	0.06
Max.-rescaled R-squared	0.09

Table 25.9 *Predicting mail return using knowledge and attitudes by race/ethnicity*

Variable	Hispanic	Non-Hispanic Black	Non-Hispanic White	AIAN	Asian	NHOPI
	Odds ratio (*p*-value)	Odds ratio (*p*-value)	Odds ratio (*p*-value)	Odds ratio (*p*-value)	Odds ratio (*p*-value)	Odds ratio (*p*-value)
Knowledge score	0.87 (0.43)	1.19 (0.04)	1.21 (0.04)	1.12 (<0.01)	1.26 (0.01)	1.28 (0.05)
Positive attitude count	0.99 (0.94)	1.23 (0.17)	1.31 (0.02)	1.61 (<0.01)	1.10 (0.38)	0.83 (<0.01)
Negative attitude count	1.36 (0.46)	1.05 (0.82)	1.36 (0.15)	0.94 (0.93)	0.68 (0.19)	0.70 (0.11)
Pseudo-R-squared	0.01	0.04	0.31	0.01	0.02	<0.01
Max.-rescaled R-squared	0.02	0.07	0.31	0.14	0.08	0.04

the variation in mail return among non-Hispanic Whites, but for all other groups, this model has minimal explanatory power.

In sum, we found evidence supporting the conceptual model. Increased media exposure is associated with higher MR, which in turn is associated with greater knowledge, more favorable attitudes, and greater intention. Better knowledge and more favorable attitudes predict higher observed census participation.

25.5.4 Hypothesis 4: Did more exposure to the ICC have direct impact on observed census participation?

Tables 25.10 and 25.11 demonstrate the direct link between exposures and actual census participation. Survey respondents reported whether or not they had heard or seen something

Table 25.10 *Predicting mail return using exposure*

	All cases
Variable	Odds ratios (*p*-value)
Exposed to paid media	1.69 (0.31)
Exposed to partnership	1.62 (0.12)
Exposed to census in schools	0.86 (0.61)
Exposed to earned media	1.21 (0.55)
Exposed to word of mouth	0.46 (0.01)
Frequency of total exposure	1.05 (0.39)
Pseudo-R-squared	0.05
Max.-rescaled R-squared	0.06

recently about the 2010 Census through different channels. For this analysis, we created binary exposure measures based on survey responses to indicate whether or not respondents were exposed to each of the components of the ICC campaign.[5]

Table 25.10 shows results for all cases; we see one statistically significant effect for word of mouth exposure. Since these are odds-ratios, we interpret the 0.46 coefficient on word of mouth to mean that having any word of mouth exposure is associated with a lower likelihood of mail return than having no word of mouth exposure, all other exposure measures held constant. In Table 25.11, we see that different groups respond differently to the campaign. For Hispanics, we see no statistically significant effects for any of the exposure measures, which is not surprising given that MR, knowledge, and positive attitudes have no impact on mail returns for this group (see Tables 25.7 and 25.9). For non-Hispanic Blacks, we see positive partnership and negative word of mouth effects when everything else in the model is held constant. The negative word of mouth result also appears for non-Hispanic Whites. American Indians and Native Hawaiians have positive effects for both earned media exposure and frequency of total exposure, although the coefficients are about one third the size for the latter group controlling for other variables in the model. American Indians also exhibit a negative partnership effect. Asians seem to have only a positive (increased mail return) response to the total count of ICC exposures and, again, a reduced mail return rate associated with having word of mouth exposure.

Tables 25.10 and 25.11 indicate limited evidence consistently connecting 2010 ICC exposure to mail return.[6] These results are somewhat difficult to square with the findings in Tables 25.8 and 25.9, which suggest that increased knowledge and greater positive attitudes toward the census are both strongly associated with increased likelihood of census

5 Components of the 2010 ICC included paid media advertising, partnership efforts in local communities, a census in schools program for outreach to students in elementary and secondary schools, and earned media in traditional and digital media outlets. We also include whether or not individual respondents reported any word of mouth activity about the census, noting that this component falls within and outside of the ICC.

6 Separate analyses using paid media ratings and other administrative data about 2010 ICC implementation also failed to link exposure to census participation. Those analyses can be found in Datta *et al.* (2012).

Table 25.11 *Predicting mail return using exposure by race/ethnicity group*

Variable	Hispanic Odds ratio (*p*-value)	Non-Hispanic Black Odds ratio (*p*-value)	Non-Hispanic White and other Odds ratio (*p*-value)	AIAN Odds ratio (*p*-value)	Asian Odds ratio (*p*-value)	NHOPI Odds ratio (*p*-value)
Exposed to paid media	1.11 (0.90)	1.30 (0.64)	1.82 (0.40)	0.95 (0.95)	1.59 (0.38)	0.43 (0.18)
Exposed to partnership	1.36 (0.48)	2.16 (0.01)	1.68 (0.20)	0.43 (0.07)	1.33 (0.36)	0.92 (0.90)
Exposed to census in schools	1.35 (0.30)	1.44 (0.60)	1.16 (0.85)	1.20 (0.73)	0.78 (0.48)	1.01 (0.98)
Exposed to earned media	1.00 (1.00)	1.56 (0.38)	1.13 (0.80)	3.38 (<0.01)	1.13 (0.64)	1.62 (0.07)
Exposed to word of mouth	0.58 (0.13)	0.30 (0.06)	0.44 (0.05)	1.73 (0.43)	0.54 (0.10)	0.81 (0.50)
Frequency of total exposure	0.98 (0.75)	1.10 (0.42)	1.12 (0.16)	1.33 (0.05)	1.24 (0.02)	1.16 (0.07)
Pseudo-R-squared	0.01	0.06	0.24	0.01	0.01	0.01
Max.-rescaled R-squared	0.02	0.11	0.24	0.13	0.04	0.03

Table 25.12 *Mean correct knowledge and positive attitude counts by race/ethnicity group*

Race/ethnicity group	Count of correct knowledge (out of 8)			Count of positive attitudes (out of 5)		
	W1 (SE)	W2 (SE)	W3 (SE)	W1 (SE)	W2 (SE)	W3 (SE)
Hispanic	3.8(0.2)	4.5[a](0.3)	5.3[b](0.2)	3.4 (0.3)	3.9 (0.2)	4.4[b](0.0)
Non-Hispanic Black	3.2(0.4)	3.9(0.3)	4.4[b](0.2)	3.0 (0.3)	3.5 (0.3)	3.8[b](0.1)
Non-Hispanic White and other	4.6(0.2)	4.9(0.2)	5.4[b](0.1)	3.4 (0.1)	4.0[b](0.1)	4.0[b](0.1)
AIAN	3.6(0.1)	4.3[b](0.2)	4.7[b](0.3)	3.1 (0.1)	3.8[b](0.2)	3.9[b](0.3)
Asian	3.1(0.2)	4.2[b](0.2)	4.5[b](0.3)	2.5 (0.2)	3.5[b](0.2)	3.5[b](0.2)
NHOPI	3.2 (0.3)	4.2[b](0.1)	4.7[b](0.2)	2.9 (0.3)	3.9[b](0.1)	3.8[b](0.2)

[a]Indicates statistically significant changes relative to Wave 1 among the relevant group at $p < .10$ level.
[b]Indicates statistically significant changes relative to Wave 1 among the relevant group at $p < .05$ level.

participation. In fact, over the course of the 2010 ICC, both knowledge and positive census attitudes increased markedly. Although we are unable to connect these increases directly to 2010 ICC exposure using the available data, it would nonetheless appear that efforts that succeed in increasing knowledge and positive attitudes can lead to increased census participation. Table 25.12 documents the increases observed in knowledge and positive attitudes before, during, and after implementation of the 2010 ICC. Both knowledge and positive attitudes increased significantly across waves for all groups. Thus, it is possible that exposure may increase mail return through its impact on MR and increased knowledge and attitudes.

25.6 Discussion

We found that greater MR to a subset of 2010 ICC ads is associated with greater knowledge, attitude, and intent to participate for most groups. When we use self-reported frequency of paid media (across all ads, not just a subset), we mostly fail to find a relationship between paid media exposure per se and census knowledge or attitudes, but we do find that total recalled exposures to the campaign are associated with increased knowledge or attitudes for multiple groups. This association does not extend to directly linking exposure to census participation – there was no direct effect of self-reported paid media exposure on mail return. As noted in Tables 25.10–11, we do find effects of exposure to other nonpaid media components of the campaign and census return. Given the integrated and pervasive nature of the 2010 ICC as well as the extremely high rates of census participation, it is difficult to know how much measurement error or other confounding factors are masking any underlying relationship.

While the mail return results are inconclusive, the MR results have important practical implications for efforts to promote survey and civic participation. First, both general population advertising and efforts to reach hard-to-enumerate groups (those that census media campaigns are intended to motivate) need to use messages to which audiences are receptive and lead to positive attitudes and beliefs about participation. Subgroups, such as Hispanic Americans, who primarily speak Spanish, Native Americans, and Native Hawaiians, are among the groups with traditionally low survey and census participation, but for whom MR was a significant predictor. Creating messages with high MR is especially important for them. Future media campaigns should be designed to maximize MR.

These and other 2010 CICPE results are discussed further elsewhere (see Datta *et al.*, 2012), but we note here that several features of the 2010 ICC made it nearly immune to rigorous evaluation. A few of these limitations are inherent to almost any paid media campaign to increase survey participation among hard-to-reach populations. First, the types of media outlets that cater to rare (often hard-to-reach) groups typically use technologies that are difficult to measure consistently, such as low-viewership cable television stations, Internet-only newsletters, or community-produced radio and print publications. Secondly, hard-to-reach groups may have very variable media coverage and may be almost idiosyncratic in their presence across locations. For example, media outlets covering the Native Hawaiian population are almost nonexistent outside of Hawaii, although a sizable fraction of this ethnic group lives in other states. This inconsistency across locations again complicates efforts to evaluate campaign activities rigorously with survey outcomes without having results swamped by confounding factors.

25.7 Conclusions

In this chapter, we have described an ambitious paid media campaign to increase census participation among hard-to-reach groups. Feasibility of conducting a paid media campaign is an important issue for smaller sample surveys. Although mass media advertisements remain prohibitively expensive, online and other "narrowcast" advertisements can be considerably less expensive than direct mail outreach or securing endorsements, two common communications methods for many surveys. The evolution of micro-targeting communications mechanisms (such as satellite television channels, social-networks or otherwise narrowly targeted websites, or online radio stations) makes paid advertising more cost-feasible for hard-to-reach populations than for the general population. For example, keyword-based online advertisements can be purchased for less than 10 cents per advertisement viewed.

Broadcast television advertisements can be very costly outreach mechanisms for the typical household survey since very few audience members will be in the survey sample. Population-specific surveys of hard-to-reach populations, however, have three advantages. First, these groups may have quite narrowly targeted media outlets. Second, because the media serve quite small audiences, their advertising rates are quite inexpensive. Third, these surveys may sample relatively high fractions of individuals within specific subgroups, so that the likelihood that audience members are in the survey sample is nontrivial. Surveys of individuals in low prevalence ethnic or linguistic groups, particular disease or disability conditions, or sharing uncommon characteristics such as homelessness or international adoption experience may find that today's media options offer lower-cost outreach through advertising than traditional survey outreach methods such as direct mail or endorsements from relevant community groups.

Implementing a paid media campaign with highly customized messaging and executions for each type of hard-to-reach respondent requires appropriate media outlets catering to each specific subpopulation of interest; there must also be sufficient information about the audiences of these media outlets so that well-informed purchasing of paid media is possible. Finally, media campaigns require sufficient budgets to generate relatively high levels of audience exposure to messaging. In the case of national-level campaigns, the budget requirements will be relatively large, as reflected in the examples discussed in Section 25.2 and evidenced by the ICC.

Survey practitioners will have recognized in the 2010 ICC paid media messaging (Section 25.3.1) the same themes typically used in survey brochures, refusal conversion letters, or interviewer scripts to increase survey cooperation even in the absence of a paid media campaign. Paid media campaigns are another delivery vehicle for the survey pitch, but the content may not be very different. One exception may be that advertisements can include more humor and creative license than the typical survey document. The use of such techniques may help to frame participation in surveys as beneficial or desirable for the individual. The framing of messages in terms of a "gain" or "benefit" has been shown to predict positive receptivity and in many cases participation in interventions (Scheufele, 1999).

References

Abroms, L., & Maibach, E. (2008). The effectiveness of mass communication to change public behavior. *Annual Review of Public Health*, 29, 16.1–16.16.

Abroms, L. C., Padmanabhan, N., & Evans, W. D. (2012). Mobile phones for health promotion. In S. Noar and N. G. Harrington (eds.), *Interactive Health Communication Applications: Promising Strategies for Health Behavior Change* (pp. 147–66). New York: Routledge.

Abroms, L. C., Padmanabhan, N., Thaweethai, L., & Philips T. (2011). iPhone apps for smoking cessation: a content analysis. *American Journal of Preventive Medicine*, 40(3), 279–85.

Bates, N., Conrey, F., Zuwallack, R., Billia, D., Harris, V., Jacobsen, L., *et al.* (2009). Messaging to America: results from the Census Barriers, Attitudes and Motivators Survey (CBAMS). In *Joint Statistical Meetings Proceedings, Survey Research Methods Section* (5807–5821). Alexandria, VA: American Statistical Association.

Bertrand, M., Mullainathan, S., & Shafir, E. (2006). Behavioral economics and marketing in aid of decision making among the poor. *Journal of Public Policy & Marketing*, 25(1), 8–23.

Breton, E., Abroms, L. C., & Fuemmeler, B. F. (2010). Weight loss iPhone applications and their adherence to best practices for weight loss: a content analysis. Unpublished manuscript.

Bruner, G. C. (1998). Standardization and justification: do ad scales measure up? *Journal of Current Issues and Research in Advertising*, 20(1), 1–18.

Ciemens, E., Coon, P., & Sorli, C. (2010). An analysis of data management tools for diabetes self-management: can smart phone technology keep up? *Journal of Diabetes Science and Technology*, 4, 958–60.

Cole-Lewis, H., & Kershaw, T. (2010). Text messaging as a tool for behavior change in disease prevention and management. *Epidemiologic Reviews*, 32(1), 56–69.

Datta, A. R., Hepburn, P., Yan, T., & Evans, W. D. (2011, July). Have you really seen this ad? Using confirmed awareness to correct estimates of self-reported exposure. Paper presented at the Joint Statistical Meetings in Miami Beach, FL.

Datta, A. R., Yan, T., Evans, W. D., Pedlow, S., Spencer, B., & Bautista, R. (2012). *2010 Census Integrated Communications Program Evaluation: Final Report*. Prepared for the US Department of Commerce, Bureau of the Census. Chicago: NORC at the University of Chicago.

Davis, K. C., Nonnemaker, J., Farrelly, M. C., & Niederdeppe, J. (2011). Exploring differences in smokers, perceptions of the effectiveness of cessation media messages. *Tobacco Control*, 20(1), 26–33.

Dillard, J. P., Shen, L., & Vail, R. G. (2007). Does perceived message effectiveness cause persuasion or vice versa? 17 consistent answers. *Human Communication Research*, 33(4), 467–88.

Dutta-Bergman, M. (2003). Demographic and psychographic antecedents of community participation: applying a social marketing model. *Social Marketing Quarterly*, 9, 17–31.

Evans, W. D. (2006). How social marketing works in health care. *British Medical Journal*, 332, 1207–10.

(2008). Social marketing campaigns and children's media use. *Future of Children*, 18(1), 181–203.

Evans, W. D., Davis, K. C., & Farrelly, M. C. (2008). Planning for a media evaluation. In D. Holden and M. Zimmerman (eds.), *A Practical Guide to Program Evaluation Planning*, Thousand Oaks, CA: Sage Publications, Inc.

Evans, W. D., Davis, K. C., Umanzor, C., Patel, K., & Khan, M. (2011). Evaluation of sexual communication message strategies. *BMC Reproductive Health*, 8(15). Published online May 20, 2011. Retrieved at www.ncbi.nlm.nih.gov/pmc/articles/PMC3117765/.

Evans, W. D., Uhrig, J., Davis, K., & McCormack, L. (2009). Efficacy methods to evaluate health communication and marketing campaigns. *Journal of Health Communication*, 14(3), 244–54.

Farrelly, M. C., Davis, K. C., Haviland, M. L., Messeri, P., & Healton, C. G. (2005). Evidence of a dose-response relationship between "truth" antismoking ads and youth smoking. *American Journal of Public Health*, 95(3), 425–31.

Fjeldsoe, B. S., Marshall, A. L., & Miller, Y. D. (2009). Behavior change interventions delivered by mobile telephone short-message service. *American Journal of Preventive Medicine*, 36(2),165–73.

French, J., Blair-Stevens, C., McVey, D., & Merritt, R. (2010). *Social Marketing and Public Health: Theory and Practice*. Oxford: Oxford University Press.

Grilli, R., Ramsay, C. R., & Minozzi, S. (2002). *Mass Media Interventions: Effects on Health Services Utilisation*. Cochrane Database of Systematic Reviews, Issue 1, Art. No. CD000389, http://onlinelibrary.wiley.com/doi/10.1002/14651858.CD000389.

Groves, R., & Couper, M. (1998). *Nonresponse in Household Interview Surveys*. New York: John Wiley & Sons.

Hornik, R. C. (1997). Public health education and communication as policy instruments for bringing about changes in behavior. In M. Goldberg, M. Fishbein, and S. Middlestadt (eds.), *Social Marketing: Theoretical and Practical Perspectives* (pp. 45–58). Mahwah, NJ: Lawrence Erlbaum Associates.

Lim, M. S. C., Hocking, J. S., Hellard, M. E., & Aitken, C. K. (2008). SMS STI: a review of the uses of mobile phone text messaging in sexual health. *International Journal of STD & AIDS*, 19(5), 287–90.

Logan, A. G., McIsaac, W. J., Tisler, A., Irvine, M. J., Saunders, A., Dunai, A., *et al.* (2007). Mobile phone-based remote patient monitoring system for management of hypertension in diabetic patients. *American Journal of Hypertension*, 20(9), 942–48.

McKenzie-Mohr, D., & Oskamp, S. (2010). Psychology and sustainability: an introduction. *Journal of Social Issues*, 51(4), 1–14.

Rao, A., Hou, P., Golnik, T., Flaherty, J., & Vu, S. (2010). Evolution of data management tools for managing self-monitoring of blood glucose results: a survey of iPhone applications. *Journal of Diabetes Science and Technology*, 4(4), 949–57.

Reger, B., Wootan, M. G., & Booth-Butterfield, S. (1999). Using mass media to promote healthy eating: a community-based demonstration project. *Preventive Medicine*, 29, 414–21.

Robinson, M. N., Tansil, K. A., Elder, R. W., Soler, R. E., Labre, M. P., Mercer, S. L., *et al.* (n.d.). Guide to Community Preventive Services. Health communication and social marketing, www.thecommunityguide.org/healthcommunication/index.html. Retrieved on January 31, 2014. *American Journal of Preventive Medicine*.

Scheufele, D. A. (1999). Framing as a theory of media effects. *Journal of Communication*, 49, 103–22.

Snyder, L. B., & Hamilton, M. A. (2002). Meta-analysis of U.S. health campaign effects on behavior: emphasize enforcement, exposure, and new information, and beware the secular trend. In R. Hornik (ed.), *Public Health Communication: Evidence for Behavior Change* (pp. 357–83). Hillsdale, NJ: Lawrence Erlbaum Associates.

US Census Bureau. (2003). *Technical Assessment of A.C.E. Revision II*. March 12, 2003. Washington, DC: author. Retrieved from www.Census.gov/dmd/www/pdf/ ACETechAssess.pdf.

Whittaker, R., Borland, R., Bullen, C., Lin, R. B., McRobbie, H., & Rodgers, A. (2009). Mobile phone-based interventions for smoking cessation. *Cochrane Database of Systematic Reviews*, 4, 1–22.

World Bank. (2012). *Africa Regional Dialogue on Financial Literacy and Capability: Final Report*. Washington, DC: World Bank.

26

The hard to reach among the poor in Europe: lessons from Eurostat's EU-SILC survey in Belgium

IDES NICAISE AND INGRID SCHOCKAERT

Every year the European (and Belgian) authorities publish figures concerning poverty and precariousness, based on the EU Surveys of Income and Living Conditions (EU-SILC). These surveys are carried out jointly by the statistical offices of the member states and coordinated by Eurostat. From these, it can be seen that the *at-risk-of-poverty rate* (AROP) in the EU for the year 2011 was 16.9 percent (European Commission, 2013). The income threshold used to define the AROP rate is set separately for each member state at 60 percent of the median equivalized disposable income in the country,[1] and the EU average is weighted by the population size. Despite widespread consensus on the validity of this AROP rate, new problems arose with the extension of the EU in 2004. In the new member states from Central and Eastern Europe, the *average* standard of living was so low that the 60 percent norm looked unrealistically low.[2] Therefore, two additional poverty criteria were introduced, namely, a material deprivation index (based on a list of necessities) and joblessness at household level. Households meeting any of the three criteria are called "at-risk-of-poverty-and-social-exclusion" (AROPE). Incorporating these criteria, the extended poverty rate for the EU was 24.1 percent in 2011, affecting 119.5 million people (European Commission, 2013). All three criteria are measured by means of EU-SILC. The importance of these indicators is also reflected in the Europe 2020 strategy, which aims (among other targets) to reduce poverty (based on the AROPE criterion) by 20 million individuals.

Apart from the three key indicators discussed above, EU-SILC produces data for a wider set of indicators relating to education, housing, health, etc. (the so-called Laeken indicators), which allow for a multidimensional comparison of poverty and living conditions (see, e.g., European Commission, 2013). Moreover, the survey is a "rotating panel," with one quarter of the sample being renewed every year. In other words, every household forms part of the sample for between one and three years, which allows limited longitudinal analyses to be performed.

Research funded within the context of the AGORA research program of the Belgian Federal Science Policy Office (BELSPO) and at the request of the Combat Poverty, Insecurity, and Social Exclusion Service.

1 Equivalized income is the income per consumption unit, using the modified OECD equivalence scales to make income comparable across household types.

2 The average disposable income in countries such as Bulgaria or Romania is barely one third of the average in rich Western member states.

Despite the wealth of information that can be extracted from the EU-SILC, further problems arise with the poverty measures, which are attributable to the difficulty in reaching the poor in general. For this reason, the Belgian Combat Poverty Service[3] commissioned research on the gaps and potential quality improvements in these poverty statistics for Belgium. The purpose of this research can be summarized in three main points: (1) an analysis of the selective nonresponse from groups that are included in the EU-SILC; (2) an identification of groups with a relatively high poverty risk that for various reasons were not included in the EU-SILC; and (3) a complementary pilot survey on the living conditions of some of those "forgotten groups of poor people."

26.1 Selective nonresponse in the EU-SILC

Are poor households hard to reach? The answer to this question is complex and ambivalent. Some research suggests that it is easier to gain cooperation from poor populations than from the wealthy, especially at the initial contact – they are more compliant, willing to cooperate with authorities. Yet, De Keulenaer and Levecque (2004), Groves and Couper (1998), and Heerweegh, Abts, and Loosveldt (2007) found enhanced nonresponse rates among low-income groups, due to characteristics that correlate with poverty rather than low income per se (immigrants, single persons, single parents, inner city inhabitants, and tenants). Using Tourangeau's typology in Chapter 1, this volume, we would argue that poor households are not hard to sample or hard to contact in general. However, some specific subgroups, such as homeless people, are hard to *sample*; others are also hard to *contact*, such as undocumented immigrants; still others may be hard to *interview*, due to language barriers (newly arrived immigrants) or low literacy (low-educated people).

The first objective of our research was to examine in greater detail the determinants of selective nonresponse in the EU-SILC survey, particularly among poor households. This nonresponse has various levels and forms:

- As in most cross-section surveys, a basic distinction is made between *unit nonresponse* (a household that does not respond) versus *item nonresponse* (no answer to specific questions).
- Unit nonresponse may be attributable to *unreachability* (e.g., because the address is incorrect or the household is repeatedly absent), *refusal*, or to *interruption or uselessness* of the interview (e.g., too many missing values, inconsistencies, etc.).
- As EU-SILC is a rotating panel, a further distinction can be made between *initial nonresponse* (at first contact) versus *attrition* (nonresponse during a subsequent wave as part of the panel).

In the EU-SILC, little is known about the bias that may be associated with nonresponse in the first wave. The overall nonresponse rate was approximately 40 percent; slightly less than

---

3 The full name is Service for the Fight against Poverty, Insecurity, and Social Exclusion (www.combat poverty.be). This service, created by law, supports a permanent dialogue between all stakeholders in the fight against poverty and produces recommendations and evaluations of the policies conducted in this field.

half of this was attributable to refusals. We assume the nonresponse rate among poor households is higher, in part because of language barriers among immigrants and also for the reasons mentioned above. The potential bias in the first wave of EU-SILC has not yet been fully examined by the Belgian statistical office (ADSEI). Although only limited information is available for analyzing this issue, it appears to be possible and desirable to examine the data that could shed light on bias. For all households, ADSEI has access to (a) basic information from the National Register[4] (age, sex, nationality, occupation, civil status, etc.) and (b) an address. ADSEI calculated nonresponse rates based on the variables included in the National Register only. However, addresses could have been linked to socioeconomic profile data about the statistical sector (neighborhood) in which this address is located. In this way, patterns of nonresponse by socioeconomic background could have been mapped in a better way. Unfortunately, due to a combination of restricted access to National Register data and understaffing of ADSEI, we were unable to carry out this analysis during our research project.

However, we are able to analyze *attrition* in detail because this involves households that have participated during a given wave but no longer participated in a subsequent wave for some reason. One may obviously speculate why some households (including the poor in particular) would start participating in a panel and drop out later. In the initial sample, overall nonresponse is typically higher than in subsequent waves, but we see no reason why the *patterns* of nonresponse would differ between waves. On the contrary, we can learn a lot about selective nonresponse from the analysis of attrition, because very detailed information is available from the previous wave about these households. We can also study the determinants by "type" of nonresponse (unreachability, refusal, or interruption of the interview). Table 26.1 shows overall nonresponse in Wave 2 by type, and Table 26.2 shows the results of our logistic regression models.

The most striking finding in Table 26.1 is the relatively high rate of *break offs* during the interviews (14.4 percent), compared to other CAPI surveys. This may be attributable to the long duration of interviews and complexity of the questionnaires. The section devoted to

Table 26.1 *Overall attrition in EU-SILC Wave 2 (2005) by type of nonresponse*

	n	%
(Repeated) attempt at contact[a]	4052	
Contact failure (Household unreachable)	38	0.94
Refusal	495	12.33
Interrupted interview, unreliable answers	506	12.61
Successful interview	3013	75.06

[a] The number of missing values for this variable was substantial (98 observations).

4 The samples for EU-SILC are drawn from the National Register.

Table 26.2 *Selective attrition in Wave 2: results of the logistic regression analysis*

	Model 1: Noncontact Ref: respondents from Wave 1 n = 38/4052		Model 2a: Refusal Ref: successful contacts n = 495/4014		Model 2b: Failed interview Ref: participants n = 506/3519		Model 3: Overall nonresponse Ref: resp. Wave 1 n = 1039/4052	
	Coeff.	St. err.	Coeff.	St. err.	Coeff.	St. err.	Coeff.	St. err.
Age group								
–25 years	1.053^a	0.460	–0.027	0.249	0.033	0.224	0.094	0.170
25–34 years	0.523	0.356	0.267^a	0.124	0.360^b	0.114	0.313^b	0.088
35–44 years	0.188	0.384	0.142	0.117	0.068	0.116	0.091	0.086
64+ years	–0.520	0.457	–0.131	0.124	–0.187	0.125	-0.193^a	0.092
Ref: 45–64 years								
Educ. level of hh head								
Low	0.034	0.288	0.396^b	0.074	–0.018	0.078	0.193^a	0.057
Intermediate	–0.335	0.301	-0.128^c	0.075	0.072	0.071	–0.041	0054
Ref: high								
Household type								
Single	1.422	45.821	–0.324	0.219	–0.146	0.218	–0.222	0.177
Couple with children	1.643	45.822	–0.308	0.217	–0.328	0.217	-0.300^c	0.176
Single with children	0.586	45.827	-0.519^a	0.270	-0.536^a	0.269	-0.539^b	0.212
Other	–6.132	183.3	1.369^c	0.755	1.110	0.749	1.175^c	0.626
Ref: couple, no kids								
Housing status								
Tenant	0.296	0.231	–0.100	0.063	0.124^a	0.060	0.023	0.046
Ref: owner								
Region								
Brussels	0.633^a	0.288	0.469^b	0.094	0.182^c	0.099	0.346^b	0.072
Flanders	-0.867^b	0.320	-0.185^b	0.071	-0.176^a	0.074	-0.204^b	0.054

Ref: Wallonia								
Subjective poverty								
Yes	−0.252	0.217	0.028	0.055	0.033	0.056	0.025	0.042
Ref: No								
Financial poverty								
Yes	0.447[a]	0.228	−0.075	0.075	−0.106	0.078	−0.067	0.056
Ref: No								
N° of working adults								
0	0.852[b]	0.303	−0.018	0.128	0.24[a]	0.117	0.160[c]	0.090
1	−0.025	0.286	0.004	0.095	−0.123	0.094	−0.073	0.070
Ref: 2+								

[a] $p < .05$
[b] $p < .01$
[c] $p < .10$

income in particular requires extensive information based in principle on households' tax declarations of the previous calendar year (to be combined if necessary across different subunits in the household). Whenever respondents raise objections against these questions or cannot retrieve the requested information, they may stop collaborating.

Which factors explain differences in response behavior between groups? *Financial poverty* has a significant effect on "unreachability." In addition, a separate analysis of the probability of moves between Waves 1 and 2 (not reported in detail here) showed that poor households move more frequently, which increases the risk of unreachability.[5] Note, however, that this is the only type of nonresponse for which the effect of financial poverty is significant, and moreover the number of unreachable households was low (thirty-eight cases). The overall direct effect on attrition is negligible. Nevertheless, it does seem that other determinants of poverty such as the *absence of income from employment*, a low level of *education* of the household head, and *residential status* (tenant as opposed to owner) are significantly correlated with one or more of the nonresponse types.

For a better understanding of these findings, two focus groups were held with experienced interviewers from ADSEI. Most interviewers had extensive experience in various surveys organized by ADSEI. They also received a manual and an extensive briefing before the start of each EU-SILC wave. For our focus group interviews, four interviewers were selected from each region in Belgium (Flanders, Wallonia, and Brussels); two-thirds of them had more than four years' experience with EU-SILC.

According to the interviewers, nonresponse in poor households is related to the following factors:

- General mistrust by low-educated individuals;
- The complexity of the questionnaire (as explained above, the questions about income constitute major stumbling blocks);
- Tenants more often live in apartments or studio flats, where contact via an intercom leads to refusal more often than face-to-face contact at the door.[6]

The combination of statistical analyses with qualitative information from the focus groups can also contribute to a better preventive and remedial approach to nonresponse. Nonresponse can be partly avoided by (a) simplifying the questionnaires (e.g., by offering respondents encountering difficulties the possibility of skipping certain questions); (b) further refining the interviewer manual and providing better training concerning complex items (especially relating to sources of income); and (c) enlisting experienced interviewers to assist in the training of new colleagues. Experienced interviewers have developed a certain proficiency in anticipating nonresponse, in their way of making contact and their

---

5 This appears to be in line with other surveys. The US Census produces data on mobility rates by income and age of householder. Housing instability is much higher among the young, the poor, and couples in child-rearing.
6 One may wonder why such households cooperated in the first wave and no longer in the second wave. This may be attributable to the fact that in the latter case they already knew more about the contents and duration of the interview.

presentation style as well as in their skill in maneuvering through difficult sections in the questionnaire.

Obviously, some degree of selective nonresponse and attrition is unavoidable. To a certain extent, nonresponse can be remedied by adjustment weights. Weights have been developed for the EU-SILC datasets, but there is still substantial room for improvement in the estimation methods, including using individual estimation models for nonresponse by wave.

26.2 Population groups with a high risk of poverty that are not included in the EU-SILC surveys

A second goal of our research was to examine which groups with an elevated risk of poverty were excluded from the EU-SILC *at the outset*. We identified a number of at-risk groups and, based on existing studies, assessed their risk of poverty. To begin with, the EU-SILC sample was drawn from the National Register, excluding collective households. Hence, some groups are explicitly not covered in the sampling frame, specifically "collective households" and households that are not included in the National Register.

Collective households include homes for elderly people, institutions, prisons, and convents/monasteries. The number of people living in such institutions is known: figures can be retrieved from the population census or from occasional publications focused on specific groups. Approximately 1.4 percent of the Belgian population live in collective households, and four-fifths of this group are elderly people. With the exception of monasteries, we can safely assume that these groups have an increased risk of poverty. Some of them may be hard to interview, but the main reasons for their exclusion are (a) that the people concerned do not live in their original (private) household, and (b) that the EU-SILC questionnaires were not designed to measure living conditions in collective households.

People who are *not listed in the National Register* (or related registers) are mainly undocumented immigrants, who are presumed to have a (very) high risk of poverty but their numbers are unknown. Following the 2000 regularization campaign in Belgium, the Ministry of Employment estimated the number of undocumented immigrants at 87,000 (0.8 percent of the population). Djajić (2001) mentions an estimate of 100,000, whereas Delaunay and Tapinos (1998) published the highest figure (140,000 or 1.3 percent of the population).

In addition to groups that are not covered by the sampling frame, some groups rarely or never stay at their legally registered address and cannot be reached at the address where they live.[7]

This group includes rough sleepers and other homeless people (living in shelters, homes, or temporary dwellings), as well as caravan dwellers and itinerant groups:

---

7 Note that, in addition to official residence address lists, interviewer assignments include updated addresses provided by the municipal administration or (in the case of panels) updates signalled by the respondents themselves. They receive instructions regarding flexible timing of the interviews and – if the household no longer lives at the indicated address – use of informal information sources to track households.

- 10,000 travelers, circus people, and bargees are known to ADSEI. In addition, Gypsies supposedly account for more than 10,000 people.
- The number of permanent camping dwellers is estimated at 10,000 in the Walloon Region and 4,300 in the Flemish Region. However, these figures are not up to date and serious efforts are being made to transfer these households into regular housing.
- As regards homeless people, the ETHOS typology (European Typology of Homelessness) distinguishes between "rough sleepers" (who sleep in open air or in public spaces), homeless people living in shelters, households in insecure housing, and households in inadequate housing. In 2003, the European Federation of National Organizations working with the homeless estimated that the two former categories (which would not be reached by EU-SILC) accounted together for 17,000 people in Belgium. There is a widespread impression that this number has increased since 2003.

Taken together, all the aforementioned groups constitute between 2.6 and 3 percent of the Belgian population. The impact of these groups on the overall (financial) risk of poverty in Belgium could lie somewhere between 0.6 and 1.7 percentage points.[8] Apart from their quantitative significance, some groups are also important because of their specific living conditions (e.g. caravan dwellers) or their extreme poverty (e.g., rough sleepers or undocumented immigrants).

26.3 Complementary survey among hidden groups of poor people

Due to the budget constraint on this research, we had to confine our complementary pilot survey to two selected population groups that either do not form part of the sampling frame of the EU-SILC or do not live at their official residence: rough sleepers and homeless people and undocumented immigrants. These groups were selected because of their high level of obscurity, their relative size, and their unusually high level of deprivation. The aim of our exercise was not to count them, but rather to collect data that would allow us to compare the living conditions of these groups with those of other poor households and with the cross-section of Belgian households.

26.3.1 *Methodology*

Organization of the field work

Our survey was carried out in the spring of 2010. The strategy for the pilot relied on collaboration between the research team, a specialized interview office, advocacy groups,

---

8 The lower bound assumes an enhanced poverty risk (AROP definition) only among the homeless and unauthorized immigrants (72 percent among homeless people and 96 percent among undocumented immigrants – see Section 26.4) and is based on the lowest estimated number of undocumented people. The upper bound assumes a poverty risk of 30 percent among the other excluded categories and the highest estimated number of undocumented people.

and social services working with the homeless and/or undocumented immigrants. The survey was part of a long and carefully planned process in several steps:

- We started with a study of existing (though fragmented) *evidence* concerning the profile and living conditions of the selected groups, particularly in the Belgian context.
- *Negotiation of the purpose* of statistical data collection with advocacy groups and social services was important to the success of the survey. These organizations can increase the efficiency of the data collection through feedback on the draft questionnaires and by mediating between interviewers and (potential) respondents. By the same token, they act as gatekeepers who decide to collaborate based on the perceived utility of the research (see also Olson, Vargas, and Williams, Chapter 29 in this volume). Our previous experience showed that social workers tend to be skeptical about research in general and statistical research in particular. Their participation in the survey development stage improved its relevance and helped avoid mistakes, but also helped the research team overcome prejudices and resistance vis-à-vis the planned research. Overall, sixty-two organizations from the social sector (service providers, advocacy groups, and street corner workers) collaborated in the research.
- Although the content and method of the survey needed to stick as closely as possible to the design of EU-SILC, there was extensive *consultation* with field workers about adaptations to the questionnaire (language issues, rephrasing of questions, deletion of complex items, addition of target-group specific modules), the sampling method, and the contact procedure for the interviews.
- The team of the Combat Poverty Service carried out a *"pre-pilot survey"* with thirty individuals and households in order to test the revised draft of the questionnaire and to evaluate the contact procedure with respondents. This resulted in a second revision of the questionnaire and procedures. In particular, it appeared already from this pre-pilot survey that homeless people are much more accessible to interviewers than undocumented immigrants, and men more than women. We also learned that random sampling of respondents within organizations would not be feasible, due to the absence of registers and interference of language, psychological, and mental problems (such as addiction or depression).
- For the proper survey, IPSOS (the market research company which was responsible for the field work) *selected interviewers* with considerable experience and good social skills and offered them a specific training coorganized with the research team. Ethnic background was not a criterion for interviewer selection.
- During the *field work* for the proper pilot survey, the interviewer team was continuously backed by the researchers. An extensive *interviewer debriefing* collected their opinions about and experience with the questionnaire and the data collection process (see below).
- The research team made a *preliminary analysis* of the data, both from a methodological and a substantive point of view. The main findings from this analysis are presented below.
- Finally, in order to encourage ownership of the research by stakeholders, *feedback* was provided to all participating parties through seminars and presentations at various locations.

Table 26.3 *Anticipated/achieved number of interviews, homeless people*

Flanders			Brussels			Wallonia		
91 / 141			71 / 68			88 / 68		
Men		Women	Men		Women	Men		Women
61 / 89		30 / 52	57 / 41		14 / 27	64 / 38		24 / 30
Rough sl.		Shelter	Rough sl.		Shelter	Rough sl.		Shelter
13 / 19		78 / 120	11 / 19		60 / 49	13 / 26		75 / 42
< 30	30–50	>50	< 30	30–50	>50	< 30	30–50	>50
47 / 50	31 / 66	13 / 21	30 / 15	29 / 37	12 / 16	37 / 17	36 / 39	15 / 10

Sampling and response

The target was to interview 250 homeless people and 250 undocumented immigrants. The two-stage sampling process, beginning with a selection of intermediaries, obviously involved a risk of missing the most marginalized people in our target groups – particularly rough sleepers. Therefore, 15 percent of the interviews were conducted in the street, in stations, or abandoned buildings, and another 5 percent of the respondents were contacted through a snowball method. On the other hand, we opted for collaboration with third-sector organizations because in this way we expected to have easier access to a sufficient number of respondents, especially among undocumented immigrants who appeared to be the hardest to reach. Our expectations were met on this point, because the overall "nonresponse" is attributable to the unreachability of targeted persons rather than refusals or failed interviews. Of all individuals contacted for an interview, 70 percent completed the interview.[9]

Quotas were set per region on the basis of different sources that provided approximate information: for homeless people, we benefited from registers of the associations of shelters, while for undocumented immigrants we assumed that their profile would be comparable to that of asylum seekers. Tables 26.3 and 26.4 give an overview of the anticipated and achieved quota per cell for each of the target groups.

As can be seen from the tables, the achieved numbers deviate from the anticipated figures. Homeless people appeared easier to reach in Flanders, while undocumented immigrants were hard to reach in all three regions. The female and young homeless were (presumably) underrepresented as well, whereas Asians and Eastern Europeans are poorly represented among the undocumented immigrants. Nevertheless, it remains uncertain whether the anticipated quota should be taken as reliable.

This survey can serve as a model for similar complementary surveys in the future. The following key lessons could be drawn from this experience:

---

9 Rates of (un)reachability could not be measured as interviews mainly occurred on the spot, in the buildings of collaborating organizations.

Table 26.4 *Anticipated/achieved number of interviews,*
undocumented immigrants

		Flanders 110 / 88	
Africa 28 / 49	America 5 / 2	Asia 40 / 30	Europe 37 / 6
		Brussels 68 / 30	
Africa 18 / 22	America 2 / 1	Asia 25 / 3	Europe 23 / 4
		Wallonia 72 / 50	
Africa 19 / 33	America 3 / 0	Asia 26 / 8	Europe 24 / 11

- Three-way collaboration between the research team (watching over the scientific nature of the survey), the survey team (carrying out the hard field work), and social sector services (validating the questionnaires and liaising with respondents) is in our view an absolute condition for effectively reaching the intended target groups. The research also benefited from the mediation by the Combat Poverty Service, which has great authority among all stakeholders and facilitated collaboration.
- Admittedly, compromises were made in survey methodology. A balance was sought in the sampling between scientific criteria and practical feasibility. For example, the researchers' initial protocol to interview every *nth* person on a list, or every *nth* person entering a shelter, was soon modified to a more realistic procedure whereby persons under the influence of drugs or alcohol or with severe psychological disorders were screened out, because this would lead to incoherent patterns of response. An alternative approach using the snowball method appeared to produce only a limited return. In the case of homeless people, snowballing was redundant because there was enough direct access to other respondents; as regards undocumented immigrants, anxiety and distrust probably explain why respondents did not refer the interviewers to their peers.
- The interviewers themselves must also be psychologically counseled so that they can cope well when faced with consequences of extreme poverty or social exclusion. Some interviewers were so overwhelmed by their respondents' misery that they wanted to provide emergency assistance; others were faced with suicide, crime, police intervention, and expulsion (see also Chapters 6, 7, and 8 in this volume). Admittedly, such incidents were insufficiently anticipated.
- Undocumented immigrants appear to be particularly hard to reach – partly as a result of language barriers and partly as a result of their fear of being caught and expelled from the

country. In many cases, we first needed to identify the sampled person's native language and by the time an interpreter was found the person had disappeared or refused to collaborate. The field work also coincided with a regularization campaign, which may have involved some tension and may explain the reluctance of interviewees.

The questionnaire

As mentioned earlier, the questionnaire (which was produced in Dutch, French, and English) had been carefully adapted in order to strike a balance between comparability with EU-SILC statistics and feasibility and relevance for our target groups. The challenge appeared to be greater than expected. Very poor people seem to have such a different life experience that for them a survey tuned to the average household can become surprisingly hard to answer. Many basic concepts do not exist or have a different meaning in the context of marginalized groups:

- In EU-SILC, the *household* is defined as a unit consisting of one or more persons, usually forming a family, who live at the same address and share their income and/or expenses. "Living at the same address" and "sharing income and/or expenses" are ambiguous concepts for homeless people, as their situation just before and after becoming homeless may differ radically (see Chapter 9, in this volume). This leads to different ways of reporting household composition. Similar difficulties arise with (undocumented) immigrants who may have different households in their home and host countries.
- As undocumented immigrants come from different parts of the world, it is not obvious how their *educational degrees* fit into the European classifications.
- Patterns of *income* are blurred for different reasons: a homeless person may be entitled to a benefit but may be unable to obtain it, because s/he cannot provide proof of his/her official address; people may receive income from informal activities which may be hidden (moonlighting) or simply not foreseen in the list of income sources (begging, remuneration in kind, recycling).
- Even the definition of work is not straightforward in a context of extreme poverty. One in five male rough sleepers and homeless people and one in five undocumented immigrants have worked in the previous month. The fact that most of them still live below the poverty line not only demonstrates the precarious nature of that work (agency work, part-time, low-paid, or temporary work), but also that the link between work and pay is far from obvious. Particularly among undocumented immigrants, who are legally denied access to the labour market, work is often unpaid or remunerated in kind.

In Chapter 28 in this volume, Pan and Lubkemann elaborate on similar issues from the point of view of linguistic and cultural minorities.

Apart from interpretation problems, some questions appeared to trigger quite emotional reactions among respondents:

- Questions about household composition (and children in particular) remind respondents about situations of family breakdown, institutionalization, separation linked with migration, etc.;

- Checklists of consumption items (TV, Internet access) used to measure material deprivation lead to 100 percent deprivation among the homeless and are met with cynicism;
- Questions relating to administrative procedures can make respondents afraid that the survey will turn into police interrogation;
- Interviewers believe that questions about some sensitive health-related behaviors (e.g., the use of alcohol or sleeping pills) are not always answered truthfully.

All these issues demonstrate the importance of a well-conceived interviewer training, extensive written guidelines, and scientific as well as psychological support for the interviewer team.

On the other hand, the adaptation of the questionnaire also provided opportunities to include specific questions that are particularly relevant for the selected target groups. For homeless people, we included a few questions about mental health and access to sanitary accommodation. The survey revealed lack of access to potable water, a toilet, or a shower in their place of residence, as well as problems of lack of sleep, loneliness, and anxiety related to the use of alcohol or narcotics. As for undocumented immigrants, a specific module was included concerning their administrative and legal status, contacts with police, etc.

26.4   Lessons for EU-SILC

Given the importance attached to EU-SILC as an instrument to monitor the effectiveness of antipoverty policies, the key message from our research is that this instrument overlooks some of the most excluded groups and underestimates overall poverty rates, due to a combination of sampling and content issues. The underestimation of the poverty rate in Belgium may be as large as 1.7 percentage points (not including the nonresponse bias). Moreover, our complementary survey among homeless people and undocumented immigrants illustrates that these excluded groups are likely to experience the most severe forms of deprivation. Not only do the vast majority of these households live below the at-risk-of-poverty threshold (72 percent of rough sleepers and homeless people and 96 percent of undocumented immigrants) but most of them live far below it. Financial income is extremely low, especially among undocumented immigrants. Both target groups also show material deprivation indices of 100 percent.

Several types of measures are needed to remedy these sources of bias: re-weighting, extension of the sampling frame, and adaptations to the questionnaires.

Re-weighting is probably the simplest part of the correction. We showed how selective nonresponse in the initial sample as well as selective attrition can be corrected for. The extension of the sampling framework to hard-to-survey groups is more difficult, simply because register data on some groups is missing. We would therefore recommend conducting specific small stratified surveys among hard-to-reach groups with an enhanced poverty risk and integrating the results with the "mainstream" survey by means of a weighting procedure. Our complementary survey points to the feasibility of such specific additions to the EU-SILC. The fact that this has worked in two target groups that are very hard to reach suggests that it might also work with other target groups. Obviously, such additional surveys involve serious efforts and fairly high marginal costs. Policymakers need to decide whether it is preferable to invest in yearly additional surveys or in periodic ad hoc modules. We recommend at least (a) that this type of survey also be carried out among the other population groups that currently fall outside the EU-SILC samples (those in "collective households," caravan dwellers, itinerant populations, etc.); (b) that such surveys should take place periodically, so as to allow for systematic monitoring of progress made; and (c) that the methodology should be replicated at EU level for the purpose of cross-national comparisons.

Another lesson from our nonresponse analysis relates to the contents of the EU-SILC survey: there are strong indications of a tradeoff between the extent and precision of the collected information and the representativeness of the survey for population groups with an enhanced risk of poverty. The underrepresentation of poor households appears to be due at least partly to the complexity of the questionnaire. Hence, it may be desirable to include simplified modules, particularly in relation to income data, for respondents who lack the skills (or indeed the tools) to analyze their yearly household income in detail – even in face-to-face interviews with support from experienced interviewers.

Furthermore, our experience showed that even a well-designed standard questionnaire may lose a lot of its transparency when used in exceptional circumstances. Basic concepts, such as household, income, educational attainment, housing, and work, need to be clearly defined and adapted to all circumstances. Interviewers need to receive clear guidelines and adequate training in order to minimize nonresponse or biased answers.

References

De Keulenaer, F., & Levecque, K. (2004). Mood and socio-economic status bias in survey non-response: results from an 11-wave panel. In C. van Dijkum, J. Blasius, & C. Durand (eds.), *Proceedings of the 6th International Conference on Social Science Methodology: Recent Developments and Applications in Social Research Methodology* (pp. 1–21). Amsterdam: Netherlands Institute for the Social Sciences (SISWO).

Delaunay, D., & Tapinos, G. (1998), *La mesure de la migration clandestine en Europe, vol. I: Rapport de Synthèse*. Eurostat Working Papers: Population and Social Conditions. Luxembourg: Eurostat.

Djajić, S. (2001). Illegal immigration: trends, policies and economic effects. In S. Djajić (ed.), *International Migration: Trends, Policies and Economic Impact* (pp. 37–61). London: Routledge.

European Commission. (2013). *Social Europe. Current Challenges and the Way Forward. Annual Report of the Social Protection Committee (2012)*. Brussels: Directorate – General Employment and Social Affairs.

Groves, R. M., & Couper, M. P. (1998). *Nonresponse in Household Interview Surveys*. New York: John Wiley & Sons.

Heerweegh, D., Abts, K., & Loosveldt, G. (2007). Minimizing survey refusal and noncontact rates: do our efforts pay off? *Survey Research Methods*, 1(1) 3–10.

27

Tailored and targeted designs for hard-to-survey populations

MARIEKE HAAN AND YFKE ONGENA

27.1 Introduction

Obtaining survey data has become a challenging task, as response rates have decreased over the years in the United States and Europe (Atrostic, Bates, Burt, & Silberstein, 2001; de Heer, 1999). Collecting data from hard-to-survey populations is even more difficult; they are either hard to reach or known for low cooperation rates (for a more extensive discussion, see Tourangeau, Chapter 1 in this volume).

Complete lists covering many hard-to-survey populations do not exist (Sudman & Kalton, 1986) and there is no simple method to define these groups (Lin & Schaeffer, 1995; Smith, 1983). Nevertheless, researchers have made an attempt to identify character- istics of typical nonrespondents (e.g., Caetano, Ramisetty-Mikler, & McGrath, 2003; Gannon, Northern, & Carroll, 1971; Shahar, Folsom, & Jackson, 1996). Many nonresponse characteristics found in these studies are sample-specific and therefore not useful for other investigations. While most surveys cannot produce response rates by population group, use of inclusion rates (i.e., a ratio of the estimate in a survey to an official estimate) can provide useful information (Griffin, 2012). Hard-to-survey groups also possess characteristics that have demonstrated barriers to participating in many studies.

Based on a literature review of Stoop (2005), the following sociodemographic groups are hard to contact or reluctant to cooperate:

- *Inhabitants of highly urbanized cities* may be reluctant to let strangers enter their homes and their attitude towards survey research can be more negative (Campanelli, Sturgis, & Purdon, 1997; Goyder, Lock, & McNair, 1992).
- *Small households* can be harder to reach than large households since there are fewer contact persons.
- *Elderly people* may not be able to participate because of health issues (Cohen & Duffy, 2002). However, when willing or able, they cooperate more than younger aged households (Groves & Couper, 1998).
- *Full-time workers* can be difficult to contact because of their at-home pattern. However, when contacted, they are generally willing to participate (Goyder, 1987).

This research is part of a project that was funded by the Netherlands Organization for Scientific Research (NWO), grant #471-09-002.

- *Less-educated persons* may be reluctant to cooperate, although this is not found in every study (Brehm, 1993; Groves & Couper, 1998).
- *Ethnic minorities* are often thought to be difficult, perhaps because of their lower socioeconomic status. However, in some studies, only their contact rates are low, perhaps because of periods spent abroad (Blohm & Diehl, 2001), but they can have higher cooperation rates than natives (Feskens, 2009; Feskens, Hox, Lensvelt-Mulders, & Schmeets, 2007).

Sociodemographic characteristics cannot always explain why sample members are hard to contact or reluctant to cooperate. According to Stoop (2005), social involvement of sample members plays an important role in the decision to participate in a survey. Sample members can, for instance, differ in social responsibility (Groves, Cialdini, & Couper, 1992), values of privacy (Cialdini, Braver, & Wolf, 1991, 1993; Cialdini, Braver, Wolf, & Pitts, 1992), and their trust in government and survey organizations (Hoopman, Terwee, Muller, Öry, & Aaronson, 2009).

Researchers have tried to adjust their survey designs to address the data collection difficulties among hard-to-survey populations. However, Groves *et al.* (1992) warned against applying universal survey designs; approach techniques should be carefully chosen depending on the sample. With hard-to-survey populations, so-called tailored or targeted approaches should be developed to obtain contact and cooperation. Some of these approaches involve targeted incentives (Singer, 2002), increasing the number of contact attempts (Feskens, 2009), and tailoring and maintaining interaction (Groves & McGonagle, 2001; Maynard & Schaeffer, 2002).

This chapter begins by introducing the concepts of tailoring and targeting. We then discuss their application in the data collection process. Subsequently, we assess the emergence of responsive designs, in which response propensities are tracked before and during the data collection process in order to target subsample populations and develop data collection strategies to maximize response rates or to minimize cost and errors. Next, we discuss several panel studies that have been successful in retaining sample members over time by being flexible and innovative. After that, we explore mixed-mode designs and emphasize the importance of mode preferences for future targeted approaches. The closing part of the chapter offers some general recommendations to enhance tailoring and targeting techniques in the future.

27.2   Tailoring or targeting?

The term "tailoring" or "tailored approach" is used in a variety of ways in many areas of research. Tailoring techniques are often used in health education studies in which materials are developed for individualized intervention (Bauer, 2008). In these fields, tailoring is defined as "any combination of information or change strategies intended to reach one specific person, based on characteristics that are unique to that person, related to the outcome of interest, and have been derived from an individual assessment" (Kreuter, Farrell,

Olevitch, & Brennan, 1999). This definition highlights the fact that tailored approaches are aimed at reaching individuals and not groups of people. According to Kreuter (2003), creating a particular technique for a specific subgroup of a population should be called targeting. However, the terms tailoring and targeting often are used interchangeably as the line of demarcation between individual attributes and group attributes can sometimes be vague (Bauer, 2008).

Since the beginning of the 1990s, the term "tailoring" has been used within survey research. In their theory stressing the importance of tailoring and maintaining interaction, Groves *et al.* (1992) defined tailoring as "the use of different dress, physical behaviors, words, and strategies of persuasion for different sample persons." Groves and his colleagues (1992) focused on the respondent's decision to participate. In addition, they tried to describe specific interviewer behaviors that might reduce the likelihood of sample members ending the discussion prematurely. The combination of tailoring and maintaining interaction should lead to higher cooperation rates and higher overall response rates.

Groves and Couper (1998) continued working on the concept of tailoring and developed a conceptual framework of survey participation based on psychological premises about the decision-making process of sample members being contacted. An important aspect of their framework is the tailoring technique interviewers use to overcome concerns of sample members relating to the prospective interview. Groves, Singer, and Corning (2000) extended this conceptual framework by introducing the leverage-saliency theory of survey participation. The leverage refers to the importance and attractiveness of a survey feature to a sample member (e.g., duration of the interview). Saliency refers to the emphasis interviewers give to the attributes of the interview (e.g., when time is a concern, it is made salient the interview is short).

In addition, the survey design can be adjusted to entire hard-to-survey groups instead of only focusing on individuals. For example, people with full-time jobs could be contacted evenings and weekends, whereas elderly people can be contacted during office hours. Models can be used to predict the likelihood of contact at each call (Durrant, D'Arrigo, & Steele, 2011). In line with the work of Kreuter and colleagues (1999), we refer to changing the survey design for a subgroup of the population as "targeting."

27.3 Tailoring and targeting possibilities in the survey process

The survey participation process basically consists of two steps: contacting the respondent and obtaining cooperation. Consequently, hard-to-survey populations can be divided into hard-to-contact sample members and those who are reluctant to cooperate (although see Chapter 1 in this volume for a more elaborate view). Three stages can be distinguished: contactability, initial decision, and final decision (Groves, Fowler, Couper, Lepkowski, Singer, & Tourangeau, 2004). In surveys where the preferences of hard-to-survey sample members are known, design features can be targeted to them (Schouten, Calinescu, & Luiten, 2011). Table 27.1 provides a summary of the features mentioned by Groves *et al.* (2004) and Schouten *et al.* (2011), and shows our comments on the possibilities of making

Table 27.1 *Survey design features affecting response*

---

1. Contactability

Survey mode or sequence of survey modes	The possibilities for targeting contact strategies depend on the available contact information; contact can be made via personal visit, phone call, mail, or email. Choosing the right contact mode when approaching sample members can save resources. Sample members may differ in the extent to which they open their mail, answer their phone (e.g., use call screening), or open the door to strangers. For example, young people may be less likely contacted by phone, but more easily reached through email, mail, or mobile short messaging service (Holbrook, Green, & Krosnick, 2003).
Length of data collection period	The data collection period could be adjusted to hard-to-reach subgroups. Response differences were found for several demographic variables in experiments with two data collection procedures; five-day period vs. eight-week period (Keeter, Miller, Kohut, Groves, & Presser, 2000).
Number and timing of calls	In interviewer-administered modes, the moment when contact is made can be vital. Approaching sample members at several different times can be effective (Cunningham, Martin, & Brick, 2003). With hard-to-survey populations, adaptive designs are likely to be useful. For example, people with full-time jobs could be contacted evenings and weekends, whereas elderly people can be contacted during daytime hours. Models can be used to predict the likelihood of contact at each call (Durrant *et al.*, 2011). In addition, the scheduling of contact attempts may be adjusted based on the sequence of preceding attempts (Kreuter & Kohler, 2009).
Interviewer workload	A high interviewer workload reduces response rates by limiting the interviewer's ability to make call-backs (Botman & Thornberry, 1992). In addition, long or tedious interviews and extended travel time result in vigorous physical interviewer effort and can therefore affect response rates (Japec, 2008). Interviewers contacting hard-to-reach subgroups should have enough time to contact the sample members and their workload should be low.
Interviewer observations	Interviewer observations of household characteristics (e.g., presence of children or pensioners) can be used to adapt strategies for contacting specific groups (Durrant & Steele, 2009). However, the use of interviewer observations for nonresponse adjustments and survey targeting should be performed with care, since observations may be subject to measurement error (Olson, 2013; West, 2012).

Table 27.1 (*cont.*)

---

2. Initial decision

Pre-notification

An advance letter or email pre-notifying sampled households of the upcoming survey can increase response rates (de Leeuw, Callegaro, Hox, Korendijk, & Lensvelt-Mulders, 2007; Dillman, Clark, & Sinclair, 1995). Literature on tailored pre-notifications shows mixed results; tailored texts can have positive effects on response rates (Kaplowitz, Lupi, Couper, & Thorp, 2012) or no effects (Callegaro, Kruse, Thomas, & Nukulkij, 2009).

Sample member selection

If there are more adults in a household, it is easier to obtain data since there are more potential sample members (Groves & Couper, 1998). When contacting hard-to-survey populations, response rates could be increased by allowing alternative sample persons in the household to participate. Allowing for proxy reporting is another possible strategy to increase response rates (Moore, 1988). Furthermore, interviewer training focused on tailoring skills to avert refusal could improve cooperation rates (Groves & McGonagle, 2001).

Request

The actual wording of a request to participate can have a major influence on participation rates (Pondman, 1998). For example, when the loss involved as a consequence of not completing the survey is emphasized in the request, response rates can increase (Tourangeau & Ye, 2009). Also, compared to scripted request texts, interviewers who are given more freedom can obtain higher response rates (Morton-Williams, 1993).

Respondent burden

The time sample members need to finish the questionnaire and their level of enthusiasm might affect cooperation rates. First, pretesting of questionnaires can decrease data collection difficulties (Forsyth, Rothgeb, & Willis, 2004). Furthermore, subgroups that have negative attitudes towards long surveys could be offered a shorter questionnaire (Feskens, 2009; Kreuter, 2013). A self-response option might also be offered so respondents can choose to complete at their own convenience.

Sponsorship

Sponsorship can influence response rates. The effects of sponsorship may differ across subgroups, depending on whether sample members have prior experience with the sponsor (Groves & Peytcheva, 2008). Therefore, it may be useful to adjust the salience of the sponsor in survey materials (e.g., by highlighting or dropping sponsor logos).

Incentives

Incentives have an effect on response rates (types and level), and the amount of the incentive can be varied across subgroups (Singer, 2002). Prepaid incentives have been shown to be an effective strategy in telephone surveys (Singer, Van Hoewyk, & Maher, 2000), while both conditional and unconditional monetary incentives are routinely used in longitudinal surveys (Laurie & Lynn, 2009).

Table 27.1 (*cont.*)

Interviewer behavior	Increasing response rates entails tailoring and maintaining interaction (Groves & Couper, 1998). For example, an interviewer may postpone asking for participation when a sample member provides discouraging cues in the interaction (Maynard, Freese, & Schaeffer, 2011). Durrant, Groves, Staetsky and Steele (2010) and Groves *et al.* (1992) recommend using interviewers experienced with the subpopulation and adjusting interviewing training to the subpopulation and situation (Groves & McGonagle, 2001). It can be worthwhile to employ interviewers who can show empathy towards the sample members and who are confident (Durrant *et al.*, 2010; Porter, 2004).
Householder/interviewer match	Characteristics of interviewers, such as age and race, may influence response rates. This effect may depend on characteristics of sample members. For example, response rates for female sample members are higher with female interviewers than with male interviewers (Nealon, 1983).
3. Final Decision	
Two-phase sampling	Responsive designs can use data from a previous phase to create a subsample of the remaining cases to improve representation of reluctant sample members (Axinn, Link & Groves, 2011).
Response mode switch	Response rates in the US have declined in the past ten years and the decrease is larger in telephone than in face-to-face surveys (Brick & Williams, 2013). A reluctant sample member might prefer another mode of survey administration (Joshipura, 2008). Offering the preferred mode can lead to higher response rates (Olson, Smyth, & Wood, 2012).
Reminder (persuasion letter)	In some circumstances, reminders or additional reminders can have positive effects on response rates (Chesnut, 2010; Kaplowitz, Hadlock, & Levine, 2004). There is hardly any literature on the contents of persuasion letters. A study of Olson, Lepkowski, and Garabrant (2011) has shown that tailored reminders seem not to affect response rates.
Interviewer switch	After an initial refusal, a different interviewer may have more success (for example, because of interviewer matching). Conversion of reluctant sample members is important in increasing response rates (Billiet, Philippens, Fitzgerald, & Stoop, 2007), but it is only useful to contact these cases using the best interviewers, possibly with bonus arrangements, and to offer reluctant sample members large incentives. However, as Billiet *et al.* (2007) have pointed out, such re-contacts can be very difficult because of privacy regulations. In some countries, sample members' contact information must be removed from the contact list after initial reluctance is communicated.

adjustments for hard-to-survey populations. Differences exist in the possibilities of targeting across modes, partly due to differences in information available of sample members.

27.4 Responsive design

In 2006, Groves and Heeringa introduced the term "responsive survey design." This approach involves targeting. Response propensities are tracked before and during the data collection process in order to target subsample populations and develop data collection strategies that maximize the response, achieve more precise estimates, and are cost-effective. Key elements of the responsive design are:

(1) Pre-identification of design features that can have an effect on key survey estimates,
(2) Identification of indicators of those design features affecting the estimates,
(3) Monitoring of indicators during the data collection process,
(4) Adjusting features of the survey in subsequent phases based on the monitoring results, and
(5) Combining (para)data from the separate phases for statistical evaluation.

The responsive survey approach is mainly focused on the phases of a design; a phase is "a time period of a data collection during which the same set of sampling frame, mode of data collection, sample design, recruitment protocols and measurement conditions are extant" (Groves & Heeringa, 2006, p. 440). Another important aspect of the responsive approach is the notion of phase capacity. According to Groves and Heeringa (2006), phase capacity is reached when certain key survey estimates are stable. For example, the effect of numbers of calls on reaching sample members can be measured. These measures give an indication of the necessary number of calls to achieve stable estimates with an acceptable, cost-effective response rate. On the basis of these indicators, targeted phase decisions can be made to reach the highest number of sample members cost-effectively.

The data collection process in a responsive design encompasses two or more phases. The first phase of data collection in a responsive design is not very different from data collection under normal survey designs. Sample members are approached and often little is known about them. However, before the whole process begins, possible costs and errors are mapped. Then, the data collection starts and sample members are contacted. The paradata gathered from this first phase (e.g., time spent on calling or visiting households, success of advance letters, and effects of incentives on response rates) forms the basis for the design choices made in the second phase. In the second phase, an optimal balance should be found between survey quality and cost-effectiveness. After the second phase, the newly obtained paradata is analyzed again to control for costs in the third and (often) final phase of the process "while attaining desirable non-response error features for key statistics" (Groves & Heeringa, 2006, p. 441). Finally, the data of the three stages is combined for the final statistical inferences.

In 2008, Wagner introduced the term "adaptive survey design." In the adaptive approach, the notion of "treatments" is used instead of "design features." The treatments (e.g., the contact mode, time of approach, and incentives) are targeted to subgroups of the population.

The combination of treatments with the highest probability of success is the optimal adaptive survey design. Schouten *et al.* (2011) distinguished two forms of adaptive design: "static adaptive design" and "dynamic adaptive design." Both make use of data of previous studies on specific populations in order to target those populations with fixed combinations of treatments. However, only dynamic adaptive designs take into account the information gathered during the data collection, which can be used for new phases in the survey process.

According to Couper and Wagner (2011), the terms responsive design and adaptive design can be used interchangeably as they share the same idea. They take the definitions of both designs as being less strict; they see "treatments" as targeting of groups of individual cases that share some common set of features, and they relax the notion of explicit phases. This chapter adopts the viewpoint of Couper and Wagner (2011). The term "responsive design" will be used in the remainder of this section.

Only a few household-based surveys have taken the responsive design approach. Statistics Canada has used the 2009 Household and the Environment Survey (HES) to test the effects of a responsive design in a computer-assisted telephone interview (CATI) survey (Laflamme & Karaganis, 2010). This survey used a subsample drawn from the Canadian Community Health Survey (CCHS). A four-phase responsive design was adopted for the HES 2009. In the first phase, the data collection strategies were planned. Data of a previous data collection cycle (HES 2007) were analyzed to improve HES 2009 in terms of productivity, costs, and response propensities as well as responding potential of outstanding cases. In the second phase, the initial data collection, data was collected using CATI with two new features. A maximum number of twenty-five call attempts was imposed, and, after twenty attempts, the sample members that had not been reached were combined for further analyses to determine how to contact them in the final five attempts. The second feature added was the renewing of time slice settings (i.e., distributions of contact attempts). Paradata from HES 2007 was used to implement a new time slice strategy "to improve the distribution of attempts and collect more informative paradata" of sample members (Laflamme & Karaganis, 2010, p. 5). Furthermore, during the second phase, key indicators (e.g., response rate, costs, and productivity) and the response potential of in-progress cases were monitored. In the third phase, paradata from the previous phases and data from the CCHS (which was used for the selection of the HES sample) was used to model the response probability for each outstanding case. During the third phase, all in-progress cases were categorized each day, the response probability of each case was calculated, and the sequence of calls was registered. Based on the results coming from the paradata of the third phase, the fourth phase was executed in some Regional Offices (ROs). The main goal of this phase was to reduce the variance of response rates in the different ROs. Although the response rates still varied by RO, the researchers expect that in the future responsive designs will improve data collection monitoring, maintain or increase response rates, reduce costs, and increase data quality.

The National Survey of Family Growth (NSFG) has also adopted a responsive design. Long before the actual responsive design term was created, similar phased data collection techniques were already used in Cycle 2 of the NSFG (Grady, 1981). Axinn et al. (2011) studied the use of the responsive design for Cycle 6 of the NSFG using computer-assisted personal interviewing (CAPI). They especially focused on the representation of reluctant sample members. The NSFG field work comprised two phases: an initial data collection and a new recruitment protocol adopted in the last month of field work. During the first phase, paradata were collected and monitored (e.g., timing of call attempts, interviewer performance, and neighborhood and housing unit indicators). Next, response propensity models were built. Based on the results of the models, the survey continued with a responsive phase subsample. The subsample was selected by stratifying sample segments (blocks or block-like areas) according to the number of cases that were still active and the total expected response propensities for active cases. Segments with a high total propensity to be interviewed *or* with a large number of active cases were retained in the final phase. In that phase, the recruitment protocol was changed to reach reluctant sample members. Only the most productive interviewers were used, more proxy informants were allowed, and increased prepaid and additional incentives were offered. In the end, the overall response rates were increased by changes made to the protocol.

27.5 Targeting in panel studies

Panel surveys offer even greater opportunities for targeting efforts to subgroups in later waves (see also Chapters 26 and 30 in this volume.). Sample members can fail to respond in later waves temporarily (i.e., miss one or more intermediate waves, but re-engage in later waves) or drop out permanently. Problems in contacting and gaining cooperation can increase nonresponse in later waves. In panel surveys, geographical mobility combined with failure to trace moving panel members and panel fatigue are two major reasons for attrition (Laurie, Smith, & Scott, 1999). Panel fatigue is likely to occur after several waves of participation, when sample members lack motivation or interest in the survey (Groves *et al.*, 2000).

Information obtained about the sample members in earlier waves enables researchers to examine the characteristics of nonsample members at later waves and determine the differences between sample members and nonsample members at later waves. Indeed, many studies have investigated those differences, focusing on demographics, attitudinal measures, and experiences during earlier interviews (for an overview, see Olson and Witt, 2011). Information collected in earlier waves also allows implementation of additional design features in later waves. For example, the design of survey materials can be adjusted to specific subgroups with low response rates in previous waves. Tailored approaches can benefit from the information collected in the first waves of a panel study. This information can be used to predict the sampled units' specific reasons for refusal and help interviewers to anticipate their reactions (Lipps, 2012).

As Watson and Wooden (2011) have shown, the decision to re-engage in a panel survey is very different from the decision to continue participation. They studied re-engagement of sample members who failed to respond in a previous wave, examining data from three national household panel surveys (i.e., the Australian Household, Income, and Labour Dynamics Survey, the British Household Panel Survey, and the German Socio-Economic Panel). Six key findings were presented. Four of them were as expected: sample members who refused to participate in a previous wave are less likely to rejoin the survey than other type of nonrespondents; face-to-face interviewers are more successful in persuading to rejoin than telephone interviewers; re-engagement tends to become less likely after more successive waves of nonparticipation; and a change in interviewer seems mostly beneficial for re-engagement. This latter finding indicates that, although interviewer experience and continuity are beneficial for continuation in a panel, the chances of recruiting nonrespondents back into the panel are better for a different interviewer who is also new to the study. Two surprising findings in Watson and Wooden's study were that changes in interview mode appeared to have no benefit or even harmful effects, and that nonrespondents from households where only some of the eligible family members participated were less likely to respond at future waves than nonrespondents from households where none of the eligible family members responded. The only survey in which this effect was not found appeared to pay a bonus if all members of the household were interviewed.

Experimental studies investigating the effects of design features on subgroups expected to have low cooperation rates at later waves are rare. The most commonly studied subgroup in targeting experiments is nonresponding sample members from a previous wave. Laurie and Lynn (2009) report several studies in which incentives were targeted based on response at previous waves. For example, in an experiment in the Survey of Income and Program Participation (SIPP), prepaid incentives were targeted at nonresponding households from a previous wave (Martin, Abreu, & Winters, 2001). Among a group of sample members who had refused at an earlier wave, response rates at conversion were higher for people who received incentives ($20 or $40) than people who received no incentive. In another experiment, in the Health and Retirement Study (Rodgers, 2011), an incentive of $50 appeared to be more effective than a $20 or $30 incentives for two targeted groups (sample members having poor health at a previous round and sample members not interviewed at a previous round) as well as for nontargeted households. This was not the case for another targeted group – sample members for whom proxies reported in a previous round.

Other experiments focus on panel members' lower response propensities, making greater effort to contact them between waves in order to keep addresses up to date (Fumagalli, Laurie, & Lynn, 2013; McGonagle, Couper, & Schoeni, 2011). McGonagle *et al.* (2011) conducted an experiment in the Panel Study of Income Dynamics (PSID) with treatments designed to increase cooperation to a request for contact information. Within the experiment, they tried to identify subsamples for which different effects of the experimental treatments might be found. These subsamples were panel members likely to move and panel members requiring more than four calls before cooperation in a previous wave. For likely movers, the most effective treatments were a prepaid incentive, a mailing closer to the previous wave, and a post-paid incentive like the ones used in previous rounds. For the subsample that required more effort in the previous wave, the same features, as well as mailing a newsletter between waves, appeared to be effective.

In the experiment of Fumagalli *et al.* (2013) on targeted designs, survey data from previous waves was used to adapt the content of a between-waves brochure. The brochure was designed for two subgroups with relatively low cooperation rates – younger and busy people. Targeting the between-wave respondents appeared to increase response rates at a subsequent wave. Fumagalli and colleagues (2013) suggest that targeted designs may be even more effective in other situations, such as when sample members are likely to be less committed (i.e., the early stage of a longitudinal survey). However, the need for reducing panel attrition due to motivation is also more likely to be higher in a later stage, due to panel fatigue. In the experiment of Fumagalli *et al.* (2013), young people were selected based on the ample evidence of previous studies showing lower response rates and higher attrition rates for this group (Behr, Bellgardt, & Rendtel, 2005; Lillard & Panis, 1998; Stoop, 2005; Uhrig, 2008; Watson & Wooden, 2009). In addition, it is expected that this group has lower commitment or loyalty due to a lower number of years of eligibility (and as a consequence participated in fewer waves than older sample members).

McGonagle *et al.* (2011) argue that targeted designs for panel members likely to attrite may facilitate contact with these panel members. However, when sample members are treated differentially (for example, giving incentives to high-effort panel members only), related sample families of different households may expect to be treated similarly. Nevertheless, a study in which the effect of disclosure of differences in incentives on later response was tested (Singer, Groves, & Corning, 1999) showed that there were no significant differences in response rates between sample members who were informed about the difference in payments and those who were not, even though the informed sample members perceived the inequality as unfair.

27.6 Mode targeting

As Marsden and Wright (2010) have argued, new modes and combinations of modes can be used to enhance data collection. Previous research has shown that sample members may have preferences for different modes of contact (Dillman, West, & Clark, 1994), or they may favor different modes of responding (Groves & Kahn, 1979). Therefore, mode preferences can be used to target sample members as it may increase their willingness to participate in the survey.

Hoffer, Grigorian, and Fesco (2007) studied the effects of offering sample members their preferred mode in panel studies. A question in which sample members could indicate their mode preference for future surveys (i.e., self-administered paper questionnaire, CATI, web, or no preference) was included in the 2003 Survey of Doctorate Recipients (SDR). Next, sample members who indicated a preference were assigned to their preferred mode in the 2006 SDR, those without a preference or who did not answer the question were assigned to the mode they finished in the 2003 SDR. Overall, higher response rates were found for sample members who were assigned to their preferred mode. In addition, assigning sample members to their preferred mode was cost-effective as the data collection period was shorter than when they were assigned to the original 2003 SDR response mode.

Olson *et al.* (2012) studied the effects of mode preference on response, contact, and cooperation rates. First, sample members of the Nebraska Annual Social Indicators Survey (NASIS) 2008 were asked questions about their willingness to participate in future surveys, and on their mode preferences. Those sample members who indicated in NASIS 2008 to be willing to participate in future surveys were approached again for NASIS 2009 conducted by CATI, and in addition a random sample was contacted in this first follow-up survey. Higher cooperation rates were found for sample members who indicated in NASIS 2008 they preferred the telephone response mode. However, the contact rates were only marginally higher. 'In a second independent follow-up survey, the willing NASIS 2008 sample members were randomly assigned to a single-mode (mail only or web only) or a sequential mixed-mode design (mail with web follow-up or web with mail follow-up) in the Quality of Life in a Changing Nebraska Survey (QLCN). Overall, it appeared that sample members who indicated they preferred the web and were then assigned to the web only mode had higher response rates than the other sample members in the single-mode design. In the sequential mixed-mode design, no differences were found in response rates between the sample members who immediately received their preferred mode and those who received their preferred mode later. Although Hoffer *et al.* (2007) and Olson *et al.* (2012) did not focus on hard-to-survey populations, based on these results, it could be interesting to offer hard-to-survey subgroups their preferred mode to increase response rates and reduce survey costs.

To find out more about mode preferences, sample members can be offered mode choices within a single survey (de Leeuw, 2005). Researchers have been using either a sequential design with mode choice (e.g., Tancreto, Zelenak, Davis, Ruiter, & Matthews, 2012) or a concurrent design (e.g., Haan, Ongena & Aarts, 2014). In a concurrent design, sample members are offered a choice of modes during the first contact. In the sequential design with choice, sample members are offered one mode to respond during the first contact. If there is no response, the sample member is approached again and is offered an additional mode next to the main mode.

In the 2000 Census, using a concurrent design, higher response rates were found for sample members who were offered a choice of modes than for those who were not given a choice (Schneider, Cantor, Malakhoff, Arieira, Segel, Nguyen, & Tancreto, 2005). Participants who responded by web were more likely to be younger, male, White, non-Hispanic and non-Black than the ones responding by mail. In addition, higher response rates were found for households in dense coverage areas than in low coverage areas but no effect was found between the area and the mode choice.

Tancreto *et al.* (2012) attempted to determine the best method to present the Internet mode to increase self-response in the American Community Survey (ACS). The study investigated two concurrent choice panels that allowed respondents to select a paper questionnaire or the Internet survey. Choice panels included a nonprominent strategy where the Internet mode was mentioned but not highlighted and a prominent panel where the Internet was noticeably featured. In addition, a "push Internet" approach was tested using a sequential design where sample members first received instructions on how to participate via the Internet before later receiving a paper questionnaire in a nonresponse follow-up mailing. The control group received the survey by mail with the regular ACS reminders. Results from these experiments showed that response rates were almost alike between the choice strategies and the mail only strategy. The highest self-administered response rates were found for the push strategy. In the push strategy condition, more people responded by Internet than in the choice condition, and, within the choice conditions, more people responded by Internet in the prominent choice condition than in the non-prominent choice condition. Internet sample members were more likely to be younger, Asian, non-Black, "other" race, with higher education, living in larger households, and speak a non-English language than mail sample members.

Haan, Ongena and Aarts (2014) developed a concurrent mixed-mode design within an additional round of the European Social Survey (ESS) to study mode preferences of hard-to-survey populations and the impact of offering a choice of modes on response rates. They studied various difficult groups, including young adults, households with more than one full-time worker, ethnic minorities, and big city inhabitants. Forty municipalities of the Netherlands were selected (with varying levels of urbanization). Newly built houses and low-income neighborhoods were oversampled in an effort to include more members of the hard-to-survey groups. First, the sample members received a letter explaining the goal of the survey and their selection in this study. Next, the sampled units were approached. The first group (contacted face to face) could choose between CAPI and a web survey, the second group (contacted by telephone) between CATI and a web survey. The third group was randomly assigned to a mode after being contacted by telephone. The address-based sampling technique was successful for contacting the full-time workers, young adults, and big city inhabitants. However, only a very small number of ethnic minorities participated. Supported by a marginally significant difference, full-time workers were more likely to choose the web response mode when contacted face to face than other sample members. Young adults were also more likely to choose web over CAPI when contacted face to face compared to the other sample members, and here the difference was significant. When sample members were contacted by telephone, no significant differences were found. Also, no significant effects were found for mode choice on the willingness to participate.

27.7 Discussion

This chapter has given an overview of tailored and targeted data collection strategies to increase response rates of hard-to-survey populations. Tailoring and targeting possibilities in the survey process seem to be numerous. Nevertheless, approach techniques should be carefully chosen depending on the sample (Groves *et al.*, 1992). Some features that allow interpersonal interactions, such as interviewer behavior, typically call for tailoring (focusing on individuals), whereas other features only allow targeting (focusing on groups of sample members). Innovative approaches, such as using responsive designs, panel designs based on information from previous waves, and mixed-mode designs that find out more about sample members' mode preferences, could improve the data collection process and increase response rates when surveying hard-to-survey groups.

However, the approaches described in this review need further exploration. Only a few household-based surveys have adopted the responsive design approach. An evaluation of the reviewed studies (see Section 27.4) suggests this particular design is not easily executed. A rigorous communication plan, survey paradata, real-time monitoring, and other resource requirements are essential to complete a survey successfully with this methodology. Looking at previous studies on targeting design features in panel surveys, the opportunities in this field are great; information collected in earlier waves can be used when sample members fail to respond in later waves. Unfortunately, experimental studies investigating the effects of design features on contacting hard-to-survey populations and their willingness to cooperate are rare. Mode preference experiments have shown discrepant results regarding the effects of mode choice on response rates. Choosing a mode might be too complex for sample members and may distract them from actually participating in the interview (Tancreto *et al.*, 2012). If so, once the mode preference of a group is known, only the preferred single mode should be offered instead of offering response mode choices. However, taking into account the positive results of mode choice experiments, the number of choices could possibly affect respondent behavior. Sample members might feel overwhelmed when many mode choices are offered (Gillian, Loosveldt, Lynn, Martin, Revilla, Saris, & Vannieuwenhuyze, 2010), therefore it would be interesting to experiment with the number of modes offered to sample members. In panel surveys, a change in mode appears not to improve or even worsen response rates. In addition, Internet response modes are often offered as the alternative to the main mode, which is frequently mail. It is possible that other combinations of modes, such as CATI and web, result in a more positive effect of choice on response rates.

The need to tailor or target design features for surveying difficult populations appears to be essential. Such features should be carefully designed for the target subgroup. Research is necessary to find out more about the effects of mode choice; for example experimenting with other response modes than Internet and mail. Currently, the usefulness of targeting design features in panel surveys to decrease attrition is undervalued. Learning more about effective treatments for difficult populations in panel surveys will probably lead to better data collection quality and higher response rates in the future. Unfortunately, experimenting with innovative techniques is expensive, and it often is a great challenge to develop accurate designs. However, once these designs are optimized, the benefits of increased cooperation among hard-to-survey populations can outweigh the invested time and costs.

References

Atrostic, B. K., Bates, N., Burt, G., & Silberstein, A. (2001). Nonresponse in U.S. government household surveys: consistent measures, recent trends, and new insights. *Journal of Official Statistics*, 17(2), 209–26.

Axinn, W. G., Link, C. F., & Groves, R. M. (2011). Responsive survey design, demographic data collection, and models of demographic behavior. *Demography*, 48(3), 1127–49.

Bauer, J. E. (2008). Tailoring. In P. J. Lavrakas (ed.), *Encyclopedia of Survey Research Methods* (pp. 874–76). Thousand Oaks, CA: Sage.

Behr, A., Bellgardt, E., & Rendtel, U. (2005). Extent and determinants of panel attrition in the European Community Household Panel. *European Sociological Review*, 21(5), 489–512.

Billiet, J., Philippens, M., Fitzgerald, R., & Stoop, I. (2007). Estimation of non-response bias in the European Social Survey: using information from reluctant sample members. *Journal of Official Statistics*, 23(2), 135–62.

Blohm, M., & Diehl, C. (2001). Wenn Migranten Migranten befragen, Zum Teilnahmeverhalten von Eindwanderern bei Bevölkerungsbefragungen. *Zeitschrift für Soziologie*, 30(3), 223–42.

Botman, S., & Thornberry, O. (1992). Survey design features correlates of non-response. In *Joint Statistical Meetings Proceedings, Survey Research Methods Section* (pp. 309–314). Alexandria, VA: American Statistical Association.

Brehm, J. (1993). *The Phantom Sample Members: Opinion Surveys and Political Representation*. Ann Arbor, MI: University of Michigan Press.

Brick, J. M., & Williams, D. (2013). Explaining rising nonresponse rates in cross-sectional surveys. *ANNALS of the American Academy of Political and Social Science*, 645(1), 36–59.

Caetano, R., Ramisetty-Mikler, S., & McGrath, C. (2003). Characteristics of non-sample members in a U.S. national longitudinal survey on drinking and intimate partner violence. *Addiction*, 98(6), 791–97.

Callegaro, M., Kruse, Y., Thomas, M., & Nukulkij, P. (2009, May). *The Effect of Email Invitation Customization on Survey Completion Rates in an Internet Panel: A Meta-Analysis of 10 Public Affairs Surveys*. Paper presented at the Annual Conference of the American Association for Public Opinion Research, Hollywood, FL.

Campanelli, P., Sturgis, P., & Purdon, S. (1997). *Can You Hear Me Knocking: An Investigation into the Impact of Interviewers on Survey Response Rates*. London, United Kingdom: Survey Methods Centre SCPR.

Chesnut, J. (2010). *Testing an Additional Mailing Piece in the American Community Survey, Final report*. Washington, DC: US Census Bureau.

Cialdini, R. B., Braver, S. L., & Wolf, W. S. (1991). *A New Paradigm for Experiments on the Causes of Survey Nonresponse*. Paper presented at the Second International Workshop on Household Survey Nonresponse, Washington, DC.

(1993, September). *Predictors of Non-Response in Government and Commercial Surveys*. Paper presented at the Fourth International Workshop on Household Survey Nonresponse, Bath.

Cialdini, R. B., Braver, S. L., Wolf, W. S., & Pitts, S. (1992, September). *Who Says No to Legitimate Survey Requests? Evidence from a New Method for Studying the Causes of Survey Non-Response*. Paper presented at the Third International Workshop on Household Survey Nonresponse, The Hague.

Cohen, G., & Duffy, J. C. (2002). Are sample members to health surveys less healthy than sample members? *Journal of Official Statistics*, 18(1), 13–23.

Couper, M., & Wagner, J. (2011, August). *Using Paradata and Responsive Design to Manage Survey Non-Response*. Invited paper presented to the World Statistics Congress of the International Statistical Institute Conference, Dublin.

Cunningham, P., Martin, D., & Brick, M. (2003). An experiment in call scheduling. In *Joint Statistical Meetings Proceedings, Survey Research Methods Section* (pp. 59–66). Deerfield, IL: American Association for Public Opinion Research.

de Heer, W. (1999). International response trends: results of an international survey. *Journal of Official Statistics*, 15(2), 129–42.

de Leeuw, E. D. (2005). To mix or not to mix data collection modes in surveys. *Journal of Official Statistics*, 21(2), 233–55.

de Leeuw, E. D., Callegaro, M., Hox, J., Korendijk, E., & Lensvelt-Mulders, G. (2007). The influence of advance letters on response in telephone surveys. *Public Opinion Quarterly*, 71(3), 413–43.

Dillman, D. A., Clark, J. R., & Sinclair, M. A. (1995). How prenotice letters, stamped return envelopes, and reminder postcards affect mailback response rates for census questionnaires. *Survey Methodology*, 21(2), 1–7.

Dillman, D. A., West, K. K., & Clark, J. R., (1994). Influence of an invitation to answer by telephone on response to census questionnaires. *Public Opinion Quarterly*, 58(4), 557–68.

Durrant, G. B., D'Arrigo, J., & Steele, F. (2011). Using paradata to predict best times of contact, conditioning on household and interviewer influences. *Journal of the Royal Statistical Society: Series A (Statistics in Society)*, 174(4), 1029–49.

Durrant, G. B., Groves, R. M., Staetsky, L., & Steele, F. (2010). Effects on interviewer attitudes and behaviors on refusal in household surveys. *Public Opinion Quarterly*, 74(1), 1–36.

Durrant, G. B., & Steele, F. (2009). Multilevel modeling of refusal and non-contact in household surveys: evidence from six UK government surveys. *Journal of the Royal Statistical Society: Series A (Statistics in Society)*, 172(2), 361–81.

Feskens, R. C. W. (2009). *Difficult Groups in Survey Research and the Development of Tailor-Made Approach Strategies*. Utrecht: University of Utrecht.

Feskens, R. C. W., Hox, J. J., Lensvelt-Mulders, G. J. L. M., & Schmeets, J. J. G. (2007). Non-response among ethnic minorities: a multivariate analysis. *Journal of Official Statistics*, 23(3), 387–408.

Forsyth, B., Rothgeb, J., & Willis, G. (2004). Does pretesting make a difference? An experimental test. In S. Presser, J. M. Rothgeb, M. P. Couper, J. T. Lessler, E. Martin, J. Martin, & E. Singer (eds.), *Methods for Testing and Evaluating Survey Questionnaires* (pp. 525–46). Hoboken, NJ: John Wiley & Sons.

Fumagalli, L., Laurie, H., & Lynn, P. (2013). Experiments with methods to reduce attrition in longitudinal surveys. *Journal of the Royal Statistical Society: Series A (Statistics in Society)*, 176(2), 499–519.

Gannon, M. J., Northern, J. C., & Carroll Jr., S. J. (1971). Characteristics of nonsample members among workers. *Journal of Applied Psychology*, 55(6), 586–88.

Gillian, E., Loosveldt, G., Lynn, P., Martin, P., Revilla, M., Saris, W., & Vannieuwenhuyze, J. (2010). ESS Prep6 – Mixed-Mode Experiment. Final Mode Report. Unpublished research report. London: Centre for Comparative Social Surveys, City University.

Goyder, J. (1987). *The Silent Minority. Nonsample Members on Sample Surveys*. Cambridge: Polity Press.

Goyder, J., Lock, J., & McNair, T. (1992). Urbanization effects on survey non-response: a test within and across cities. *Quality and Quantity*, 26(1), 39–48.

Grady, W. R. (1981). National Survey of Family Growth, Cycle II: Sample design, estimation procedures, and variance estimation. Data Evaluation and Methods Research, Series 2, Number 87. DHHS Publication No. (PHS) 81–1361. Hyattsville, MD: US Department of Health and Human Services, National Center for Health Statistics.

Griffin, D. H. (2012). *Evaluating Response in the American Community Survey by Race and Ethnicity. Final Report*. Washington, DC: US Census Bureau.

Groves, R. M., Cialdini, R. B., & Couper, M. P. (1992). Understanding the decision to participate in a survey. *Public Opinion Quarterly*, 56(4), 475–95.

Groves, R. M., & Couper, M. P. (1998). *Nonresponse in Household Interview Surveys*. New York: John Wiley & Sons.

Groves, R. M., Fowler, F. J., Couper, M. P., Lepkowski, J. M., Singer, E., & Tourangeau, R. (2004). *Survey Methodology*. Hoboken, NJ: John Wiley & Sons.

Groves, R. M., & Heeringa, S. G. (2006). Responsive design for household surveys: tools for controlling survey errors and costs. *Journal of the Royal Statistical Society: Series A (Statistics in Society)*, 169(3), 439–57.

Groves, R. M., & Kahn, R. L. (1979). *Surveys by Telephone: A National Comparison with Personal Interviews*. New York: Academic Press.

Groves, R. M., & McGonagle, K. A. (2001). A theory-guided interviewer training protocol regarding survey participation. *Journal of Official Statistics*, 17(2), 249–66.

Groves, R. M., & Peytcheva, E. (2008). The impact of non-response rates on non-response bias: a meta-analysis. *Public Opinion Quarterly*, 72(2), 167–89.

Groves, R. M., Singer, E., & Corning, A. (2000). Leverage-saliency theory of survey participation. *Public Opinion Quarterly*, 64(3), 299–308.

Haan, M., Ongena, Y. P., & Aarts, C. W. A. M. (2014). Reaching hard-to-survey populations: mode choice and mode preference. *Journal of Official Statistics*, 30(2), 1–25.

Hoffer, T., Grigorian, K., & Fesco, R. (2007, July). *Effectiveness of Using Respondent Mode Preference Data*. Paper presented at the Joint Statistical Meetings of the American Statistical Association, Salt Lake City.

Holbrook, A. L., Green, M. C., & Krosnick, J. A. (2003). Telephone vs. face-to-face interviewing of national probability samples with long questionnaires: comparisons of respondent satisficing and social desirability response bias. *Public Opinion Quarterly*, 67(1), 79–125.

Hoopman, R., Terwee, C. B., Muller, M. J., Öry, F. G., & Aaronson, N. K. (2009). Methodological challenges in quality of life research among Turkish and Moroccan ethnic minority cancer patients: translation, recruitment and ethical issues. *Ethnicity & Health*, 14(3), 237–53.

Japec, L. (2008). Interviewer error and interviewer burden. In J. M. Lepkowski, C. Tucker, J. M. Brick, E. D. de Leeuw, L. Japec, P. J. Lavrakas, M. W. Link, & R. L. Sangster (eds.), *Advances in Telephone Survey Methodology* (pp. 187–211). Hoboken, NJ: John Wiley and Sons.

Joshipura, M. (2008). *2005 ACS Respondent Characteristics Evaluation: Evaluation Report.* DSSD American Community Survey Research and Evaluation Memorandum Series Chapter #ACS-RE-2. Washington, DC: US Census Bureau.

Kaplowitz, M. D., Hadlock, T. D., & Levine, R. (2004). A comparison of web and mail survey response rates. *Public Opinion Quarterly*, 68(1), 94–101.

Kaplowitz, M. D., Lupi, F., Couper, M. P., & Thorp, L. (2012). The effect of invitation design on web survey response rates. *Social Science Computer Review*, 30, 339–49.

Keeter S., Miller, C., Kohut, A., Groves, R. M., & Presser, S. (2000). Consequences of reducing nonresponse in a national telephone survey. *Public Opinion Quarterly*, 64(2), 125–48.

Kreuter, F. (2013). Facing the nonresponse challenge. *ANNALS of the American Academy of Political and Social Science*, 645(1), 23–35.

Kreuter, F., & Kohler, U. (2009). Analyzing contact sequences in call record data. Potential and limitations of sequence indicators for non-response adjustments in the European Social Survey. *Journal of Official Statistics*, 25(2), 203–26.

Kreuter, M. W. (2003). Tailored and targeted health communication: strategies for enhancing information relevance. *American Journal of Health Behavior*, 27(Suppl. 3), 227–32.

Kreuter, M. W., Farrell, D., Olevitch, L., & Brennan, L. (1999). *Tailored Health Messages: Customizing Communication with Computer Technology.* Mahway, NJ: Erlbaum.

Laflamme, F., & Karaganis, M. (2010, December). *Implementation of Responsive Collection Design for CATI Surveys at Statistics Canada.* Paper presented at the Symposium on Recent Advances in the Use of Paradata in Social Survey Research, London.

Laurie, H., & Lynn, P. (2009). The use of respondent incentives on longitudinal surveys. In P. Lynn (ed.), *Methodology of Longitudinal Surveys* (pp. 205–33). Hoboken, NJ: John Wiley & Sons.

Laurie, H., Smith, R., & Scott, L. (1999). Strategies for reducing nonresponse in a longitudinal panel survey. *Journal of Official Statistics*, 15(2), 269–82.

Lillard, L. A., & Panis, C. W. A. (1998). Panel attrition from the Panel Study of Income Dynamics: Household income, marital status and mortality. *Journal of Human Resources*, 33(2), 437–57.

Lin, I., & Schaeffer, N. C. (1995). Using survey participants to estimate the impact of nonparticipation. *Public Opinion Quarterly*, 59(2), 236–58.

Lipps, O. (2012). Using information from telephone panel surveys to predict reasons for refusal. *Methoden – Daten – Analysen*, 6(1), 3–20.

McGonagle, K., Couper, M., & Schoeni, R. F. (2011). Keeping track of panel members: an experimental test of a between-wave contact strategy. *Journal of Official Statistics*, 27(2), 319–38.

Marsden, P. V., & Wright, J. D. (2010). *Handbook of Survey Research*. Bingley: Emerald.

Martin, E., Abreu, D., & Winters, F. (2001). Money and motive: effects of incentives on panel attrition in the survey of income and program participation. *Journal of Official Statistics*, 17(2), 267–84.

Maynard, D. W., Freese, J., & Schaeffer, N. C. (2011). Requests, blocking moves, and rational (inter)action in survey introductions. *American Sociological Review*, 75(5), 791–998.

Maynard, D. W., & Schaeffer, N. C. (2002). Refusal conversion and tailoring. In D. W. Maynard, H. Houtkoop-Steenstra, N. C. Schaeffer, & J. van der Zouwen (eds.), *Standardization and Tacit Knowledge: Interaction and Practice in the Survey Interview* (pp. 219–39). New York: John Wiley & Sons.

Moore, J. (1988). Miscellanea, self/proxy response status and survey response quality: a review of literature. *Journal of Official Statistics*, 4(2), 155–72.

Morton-Williams, J. (1993). *Interviewer Approaches*. London: Dartmouth Publishing Company.

Nealon, J. (1983). The effects of male vs. female telephone interviewers. In *Joint Statistical Meetings Proceedings, Survey Research Methods Section* (pp. 139–141). Alexandria, VA: American Statistical Association.

Olson, K. (2013). Paradata for nonresponse adjustment. *ANNALS of the American Academy of Political and Social Science*, 645(1), 142–70.

Olson, K., Lepkowski, J. M., & Garabrant, D. H. (2011). An experimental examination of the content of persuasion letters on nonresponse rates and survey estimates in a nonresponse follow-up study. *Survey Research Methods*, 5(1), 21–26.

Olson, K., Smyth, J. D., & Wood, H. M. (2012). Does providing sample members with their preferred survey mode really increase participation rates? *Public Opinion Quarterly*, 76(4), 611–35.

Olson, K., & Witt, L. (2011). Are we keeping the people who used to stay? Changes in correlates of panel survey attrition over time. *Social Science Research*, 40(4), 1037–50.

Pondman, L. M. (1998). *The Influence of the Interviewer on the Refusal Rate in Telephone Surveys*. Amsterdam: Free University of Amsterdam.

Porter, S. R. (2004). Raising response rates: what works? *New Directions for Institutional Research*, 121, 5–21.

Rodgers, W. (2011). Effects of increasing the incentive size in a longitudinal study. *Journal of Official Statistics*, 27(2), 279–99.

Schneider, S. J., Cantor, D., Malakhoff, L., Arieira, C., Segel, P., Nguyen, K., & Tancreto, J. G. (2005). Telephone, internet and paper data collection modes for the census 2000 short form. *Journal of Official Statistics*, 21(1), 89–101.

Schouten, B., Calinescu, M., & Luiten, A. (2011). *Optimizing Quality of Response Through Adaptive Survey Designs. Discussion Paper (201118)*. The Hague/Heerlen: Statistics Netherlands.

Shahar, E., Folsom, A. R., & Jackson, R. (1996). The effect of nonresponse on prevalence estimates for a referent population: insights from a population-based cohort study. *Annals of Epidemiology*, 6(6), 498–506.

Singer, E. (2002). The use of incentives to reduce nonresponse in household surveys. In R. M. Groves, D. A. Dillman, J. L. Eltinge, & R. J. A. Little (eds.), *Survey Nonresponse* (pp. 163–178). New York: John Wiley & Sons.

Singer, E., Groves, R. M., & Corning, A. (1999). Differential incentives: beliefs about practices, perceptions of equity, and effects on survey participation. *Public Opinion Quarterly*, 63(2), 251–60.

Singer, E., Van Hoewyk, J., & Maher, M. P. (2000). Experiments with incentives in telephone surveys. *Public Opinion Quarterly*, 64(2), 171–88.

Smith, T. W. (1983). The hidden 25 percent: an analysis of nonresponse on the 1980 General Social Survey. *Public Opinion Quarterly*, 47(3), 386–404.

Stoop, I. (2005). *The Hunt for the Last Respondent. Non-Response in Sample Surveys*. The Hague: Social and Cultural Planning Agency.

Sudman, S., & Kalton, G. (1986). New developments in the sampling of special populations. *Annual Review of Sociology*, 12, 401–29.

Tancreto, J. G., Zelenak, M. F., Davis, M., Ruiter, M., & Matthews, B. (2012). *2011 American Community Survey Internet Tests: Results from First Test in April 2011. Final Report*. Washington, DC: US Census Bureau.

Tourangeau, R., & Ye, C. (2009). The framing of the survey request and panel attrition. *Public Opinion Quarterly*, 73(2), 338–48.

Uhrig, S. C. N. (2008). *The Nature and Causes of Attrition in the British Household Panel Study. Working Paper 2008–05*. Colchester: Institute for Social and Economic Research, University of Essex.

Wagner, J. R. (2008). *Adaptive Survey Design to Reduce Nonresponse Bias*. Ann Arbor, MI: University of Michigan Press.

Watson, N., & Wooden, M. (2009). Identifying factors affecting longitudinal survey response. In P. Lynn (ed.), *Methodology of Longitudinal Surveys* (pp. 157–81). New York: John Wiley & Sons.

Watson, N., & Wooden, M. (2011). *Re-Engaging with Survey Non-Respondents: The BHPS, SOEP and HILDA Survey Experience. Working Paper Series No. 2/11*. Melbourne: Melbourne Institute of Applied Economic and Social Research, University of Melbourne.

West, B. T. (2012). An examination of the quality and utility of interviewer observations in the National Survey of Family Growth. *Journal of the Royal Statistical Society: Series A (Statistics in Society)*, 176(1), 211–25.

28

Standardization and meaning in the survey of linguistically diversified populations: insights from the ethnographic observation of linguistic minorities in 2010 Census interviews

YULING PAN AND STEPHEN LUBKEMANN

28.1 Introduction

Long a destination for millions of immigrants, the United States has included significant groups of non-English speakers in its population throughout most of its history. It therefore showcases many of the challenges that linguistic and cultural differences increasingly pose to survey methodologists in a globalizing world. This chapter draws upon an empirical field study of the 2010 US Census Nonresponse Follow-up (NRFU) interview that was conducted with respondents with limited (or no) English proficiency (LEPs) in seven immigrant communities. The goal of the study was to examine how linguistic and cultural differences affected access to LEP respondents and the quality of the responses they provided.

In the US context, non-English speakers are likely to be harder to reach and enumerate than their English-speaking counterparts for several reasons. Most obviously, language barriers impose hurdles to effective communication and thus to access. Some LEPs are recent arrivals who may be less familiar or comfortable with survey practices than English-speaking respondents. Others are reluctant to interact outside of their native community because they have tenuous legal status or distrust government authorities. It is reasonable to assume that limited English proficiency makes respondents relatively harder to reach for surveys in the US.

In this chapter, we discuss select findings from our field study that highlight some of the primary difficulties interviewers confront in their effort to achieve "communicative success" in interviews with LEP populations. We use the term communicative success to refer to the ability of interviewers to obtain the information from respondents that the questionnaire and interview protocol were designed to elicit.

In our field study, we observed how linguistic and cultural differences affected the following four tasks, all of which are necessary components of communicative success in cross-linguistic survey contexts.

(1) Achieving comparability, ensuring that concepts in the questionnaire convey the same meaning in target languages that they convey in the source language (i.e., English). Our findings suggest this is a particularly acute challenge for concepts that are susceptible to significant cross-cultural variation in their social construction (such as race).

(2) Ensuring "speaker–listener correspondence" with respect to an utterance's meaning. This refers to the extent to which recipients understand an utterance to mean what the speaker intends it to mean, or, as per Braun and Harkness (2005), that "perceived meaning" corresponds to "speaker intended meaning." Any overlap between this task and that of achieving comparability is at best partial. Speaker–listener correspondence includes several other possible sources of "discursive dissonance." Discursive dissonance refers to situations in which a question or utterance conveys a meaning to an LEP respondent that is different from what the interviewer intended.

(3) Securing "question-focused responses," responses that are formulated with narrow reference to the (intended) terms of the questions themselves, and not to other concerns. As we will discuss, there may be a heightened risk of "ulterior signaling" in cross-linguistic interview contexts, where the particular terminology, structure, or context of the question inadvertently raises respondent suspicions that other forms of information are being sought. These other forms might serve some ulterior motive (usually assumed by the respondents to be undesirable). Respondents often provide responses to what they believe is the (unstated) "real question" rather than to the actual question as stated.

(4) Negotiating and maintaining access to respondents. While survey methodologists have usually treated negotiating initial access and maintaining access as separate tasks, we view access as a status that remains under continuous negotiation (and thus always potentially at risk of failure) throughout the course of the interview. In this respect, we treat the interview in the same terms used for any other form of social interaction. This approach implies that the negotiation of access cross-cuts, and thus interacts with, the other three tasks, all of which are primarily concerned with comprehension of meanings conveyed in utterances. Most obviously, securing and maintaining access is a necessary prerequisite for accomplishing the other tasks. Yet, as we observed in our field study, these other tasks also reciprocally affect the ongoing negotiation of access. At the same time, many factors other than the questions themselves also inform the negotiation of access as a *social* (and not merely communicative) process, i.e., a process of defining and enacting roles, rights, and obligations that set the expectations about social interaction in the interview context.

This chapter highlights some of the primary difficulties that NRFU interviewers confronted in meeting these four requirements of communicative success when interviewing LEP respondents during the 2010 Census. Our analysis draws heavily upon observations of the strategies devised and improvised by bilingual enumerators to cope with those challenges.

Rather than viewing these merely as problematic deviations from protocol that undermined these tasks, we explore how those deviations contributed to communicative success by preempting or repairing the problems generated by a NRFU questionnaire and protocol that did not adequately account for sociocultural and linguistic differences. In our conclusions, we explore the theoretical implications of these observations for how to understand, define, and achieve "standardization" in surveys that target multilingual populations and in survey research in general.

28.2   Theoretical background and objectives

28.2.1 Issues and debates in survey standardization and translation

The observations we discuss in this chapter provide a specific point of entrée into the broader theoretical discussion of what survey standardization can and should mean and how it might be methodologically operationalized. The broader debate over the problems, merits, and tradeoffs involved in survey standardization has a long and fascinating history (Conrad & Schober, 2000; Dykema, Lepkowski, & Blixt, 1997; Fowler, 1991; Fowler & Mangione, 1990; Kovar & Royston, 1990; Schaeffer, 1991; Schaeffer & Maynard, 2002; Schober & Conrad, 1997; Smit, Dijkstra, & van der Zouwen, 1997; Suchman & Jordan, 1992; for particularly useful overviews, see Beatty, 1995; Platt, 2002; and Singleton & Straits, 2002). However, this debate has largely evolved with reference to monolingual populations in the North American context and has not engaged with parallel debates about translation and cross-cultural and cross-national survey practice (Fitzgerald & Jowell, 2010; Harkness, 1998; Harkness, Edwards, Hansen, Miller, & Villar, 2010; Harkness, van de Vijver, & Mohler, 2003; Jowell, Kaase, Fitzgerald, & Eva, 2007).

Our findings substantiate a number of important critiques that have gained traction in the cross-national and comparative survey research literature and explicitly underscore their relevance to the North American context. This is particularly true with respect to critiques of the predominant models and assumptions that guide most survey translations. Generally speaking, survey organizations (including the US Census Bureau) have sought to address the challenges of linguistic diversity within a population of respondents through translation and/or interpretation. Thus, in its effort to enumerate non-English-speaking households accurately in the 2010 Census, the Census Bureau developed a comprehensive language assistance program, including, among other efforts, translating the 2010 Census form into five primary non-English languages (Spanish, Chinese, Korean, Russian, and Vietnamese), and language assistance guides into fifty-nine languages (see Kim & Zapata, 2012).

These translations followed the approach used in most multilingual and cross-national survey work, which Harkness has termed the "Ask-the-Same-Question" (ASQ) model (2003, p. 35). This approach generally assumes that terminological correspondence between and across languages, though at times difficult, is nevertheless virtually always possible to achieve. Survey researchers guided by this perspective thus tend to view translation as primarily a matter of finding the terminological equivalents in different languages and "plugging these in" to a question whose phrasing should be otherwise minimally altered. Their premise is that retaining the phrasing and structure of the question and response categories from source to target languages is desirable in order to achieve standardization.

In this chapter, we support the critiques of the ASQ translation model (Braun, 2003; Harkness, 2003; Harkness & Schoua-Glusberg, 1998; Harkness, Villar, & Edwards, 2010; Schwarz, 2003; Smith, 2003). We demonstrate that its problematic effects are particularly pronounced when surveys conducted in multilingual populations utilize, or even inquire about, concepts that lack cross-linguistic equivalency. Our study suggests that in the 2010 Census the ASQ model proved particularly inadequate and problematic for concepts that refer to forms of social identity (such as race or ethnicity) that are socially constructed in highly culturally specific, and thus culturally variable, ways.[1] However, our field research also demonstrates how even concepts that seem fairly obviously universal (such as "age") can be susceptible to cross-cultural/linguistic conceptual variance.

To address some of the problems of the ASQ translation model, a group of survey researchers (e.g., Behling & Law, 2000; Harkness, 2003; Harkness *et al.*, 2010; Harkness & Schoua-Glusberg, 1998; McKay, Breslow, Sangster, Gabbard, & Reynolds, 1996) has proposed an alternative *adaptation* approach to survey translation. This school of thought advocates using a source questionnaire from an original language as a base, but then allowing survey questions to be significantly modified to make them more easily comprehensible in a different target language. The modifications this approach allows can take several forms, including the provision of supplemental explanations of terms, adjustments to grammatical rules that are language-specific, and some accommodation of language-specific conventions and sensitivities (such as indicators of politeness or gendered language rules). However, by and large, the adaptation approach remains squarely focused on the reformulation of question wording, structure, and to a lesser extent sequencing.

In this chapter, we seek to extend the adaptation approach's critique of the ASQ translation model in several ways, while also more fully exploring some key theoretical implications of that critique for the broader debates about survey standardization. In particular, we suggest that from a sociolinguistic and anthropological perspective, the adaptation approach in actual practice deploys a theoretically inadequate notion of language that is excessively narrow in its analysis of how the meaning of any given utterance is understood. It remains almost exclusively focused on the wording and structure of questions themselves, while paying very little attention to the process of asking those questions, or what might be termed the "performative" aspect of communication. Thus, despite acknowledging in theory (e.g., Braun, 2003; Harkness, 2003; Schwarz, 2003) the importance of "pragmatics" in giving utterances their meaning, in practice the adaptation approach still tends to treat words as the predominant determinants of meaning conveyance in verbal communication.

---

[1] There is an extensive anthropological and sociological literature that discusses the ways in which various forms of social identity – including race and ethnicity – are constructed in highly variable ways in different sociocultural contexts. For a basic review, see Eriksen (2002).

Such a minimally contextualized view of language ignores the role that a host of culturally specific referents inevitably play in providing words with the specificity of meaning required to render verbal communication successful. Even a seemingly straightforward and mundane term, such as "April 1" in the census questionnaire, can invoke very different interpretations depending on the social or contextual factors that affect its use in any given community of language. Thus, when this question is posed in communities whose own communicative conventions eschew such specificity the question can come across as not merely "odd" or "unclear," but as potentially a trojan horse that masks some other "real question" that is unknown to the respondent. In short, we will argue that effective translation cannot be achieved without fully addressing the pragmatic/performative aspects of language, which are specific to communities of language, in conjunction with linguistic code itself.

28.2.2 Defining the survey as a communicative and a social event: the census interview encounter

In this chapter, we also highlight a second deficit in the current debate about survey translation, namely that it does not examine factors, other than overt communication, that influence meaning conveyance. We argue that this deficit also applies to larger debates about survey standardization. Both debates presume that standardization of meaning in surveys revolves around the referential or informational content of the questions being asked (Harkness *et al.*, 2003; Johnson, 1998; Schaeffer, 1991; Schaeffer & Maynard, 2002; Suchman & Jordan, 1992). In this, they tend to make unwarranted assumptions about the *social definition of the situation*, i.e., about how the interview itself is defined or "framed" (Braun, 2003; Goffman, 1974; Tannen, 1993) as a form of social interaction. In particular, they assume that interview subjects largely share the same understanding that interviewers and survey designers themselves have of what the interview as a social encounter is "about."

Thus, to the survey interviewer or designer it might seem self-evident that the survey is first and foremost a situation that conveys information related to the questions that are being asked. Certainly from the perspective of the Census Bureau, the purpose of the NRFU interview is quite clearly defined: to obtain accurate information from respondents about a limited set of variables that have been pre-defined in very specific ways. The interview protocol that NRFU interviewers were instructed to follow was meant to maximize the extent to which respondents also accepted this definition of the situation.

Yet, in this chapter, we illustrate how LEP respondents often quite simply did *not* read from the same script as their interviewers in terms of how they define the "Census Interview Encounter" (CIE) as a social interaction. As we will elaborate further, these differences are derived from different historical experiences in both their respective lands of origin and as immigrants in the United States.

Our main objective in this chapter is to argue for the need for a far more robust notion of language in surveys than the one that currently informs the adaptation approach to translation and the standardization debate as a whole. More than linguistic code alone, true translation must address other meta-communicative factors (Briggs, 1986) that sociolinguistic and linguistic anthropological research has amply demonstrated to be indissolubly intertwined with linguistic code and indispensable to the conveyance of all spoken meaning and communicative interaction.[2]

28.3   Description of data and methodology

Field work and data

We use data drawn from a field study conducted in seven distinct communities of language using ethnographically informed direct observation of 2010 Census NRFU interviews. Every decade, the Census Bureau undertakes the decennial census to enumerate the US population. A census form was mailed out to every housing unit with a valid mailing address in April 2010. Residents of housing units were asked to fill out the census forms and mail them back. When no census form was returned from an address, the 2010 Census attempted to collect these missing data through NRFU interviews. During the NRFU operation, a census enumerator visited households that had failed to return their census forms and sought to collect their data through a personal interview.

The current study focused specifically on NRFU interviews conducted with non-English-speaking households. More specifically, 586 live NRFU interviews were observed by ethnographer teams in seven communities of language (Arabic, Chinese, Korean, Portuguese, Russian, Spanish, and Vietnamese).

Research teams and sites

Teams consisted of two sets of researchers: (1) a Census Bureau coordinating research group led by an in-house sociolinguist and anthropologist; and (2) a bilingual field research group for each community of language (a senior ethnographer and two to four assistant ethnographers), comprised of ethnographers drawn from several disciplines, including anthropology, sociology, and sociolinguistics. Their previous long-term socially immersive research had provided them with linguistic fluency and equipped them with the knowledge that allowed them to both interpret the communicative events and understand the social interactions in the CIEs they observed.

The field sites in which research was undertaken were selected using purposive criteria. We sought to match geographic areas that had high concentrations of speakers of the seven

---

2 In any communicative event (Hymes, 1972), the transmission, comprehension, interpretation, and meanings of verbally conveyed information is profoundly affected by, and actually depends upon, communicative conventions that differ significantly across – and sometimes even within – communities of language. Such conventions encompass implicitly understood rules about how to ask for and provide information, understandings of how verbal and nonverbal inflections signal different interpretations of specific words or phrases, and culturally specific understandings about what the purpose of specific genres of conversation may be. Surveys tend to reflect the meta-communicative repertoire of their originators' community of language. This is reflected in both the wording of particular questions and in the ways in which survey protocols prescribe specific ways to pose questions and interact with respondents.

Table 28.1 *Language teams and research sites*

Language teams	Research sites
Arabic	Michigan
Chinese	Maryland, New York, and Virginia
Korean	Maryland, New York, and Virginia
Portuguese	Massachusetts, Rhode Island
Russian	Ohio, New York
Spanish	Illinois
Vietnamese	California

target languages (based on the ACS 2007 data) with ethnographers who met the aforementioned qualifications. During the process, nine states were selected as the research sites (see Table 28.1).

Observation protocol

We developed a common observation protocol and debriefing questions. The following steps were followed by all seven teams in their field work:

(1) Over a two-week period, each ethnographer accompanied one enumerator throughout any given day and observed NRFU interviews. Some enumerators shared the language of non-English-speaking respondents; others were monolingual English speakers. Enumerators were observed interviewing both LEP and English-speaking households.

(2) Ethnographers obtained consent for audiotaping interviews from respondents, following the guidelines specified by the Census Bureau. If respondents did not agree to be audiotaped, ethnographers took detailed notes of the interview.

(3) Immediately following their observation of the NRFU interview, ethnographers conducted a post-enumeration debriefing with the respondent whose NRFU interview they had just observed. These were conducted on an individual basis (apart from the enumerator). The ethnographers sought to understand better how respondents had understood and experienced the NRFU interview process, their knowledge and awareness of the US Census, and their experience with surveys and censuses in their country of origin.

(4) Ethnographers conducted at least one debriefing with each enumerator whose NRFU interviews they observed.

Data analysis

Data included taped interviews, ethnographers' observational notes, respondent debriefings, enumerator debriefings, focus group discussions, and in-depth interviews for each language team. Two levels of analysis were performed in each community of language: first, by individual language teams and, second, by the Census Bureau research team. Both levels utilized a common analytical framework to identify how linguistic and sociocultural factors affected the census interview as both a communicative event (Hymes, 1972) and as a form of social interaction (Briggs, 1986), two interrelated aspects of the CIE.

A third level of analysis led by the Census Bureau research team sought to compare the findings from the seven field studies. At this level, the analytical framework was further refined to focus on comparing the mediating effect of sociolinguistic factors on the four componential tasks of communicative success. At all levels of analysis, we paid particular attention to two axes of comparison: that between bilingual and monolingual (English-speaking) enumerators, and that between LEP monolingual and English-speaking mono-lingual respondents.

28.4   Findings

In this section, we illustrate the ways in which differences in linguistic code (narrowly construed) and in meta-communicative repertoires affected the four tasks that NRFU interviewers had to attend to in their efforts to achieve communicative success when interviewing LEP respondents.

28.4.1 Defining the situation in the "census interview encounter"

As noted earlier, negotiating and maintaining access is a prerequisite for the other three tasks and cross-cuts them. For interviews with both English-speaking and LEP respondents, interviewers must negotiate and maintain access to persons who, by definition, are likely to be unaware of, disinterested in, or reluctant to participate in the census process in the first place (see Chapter 1 in this volume). The challenge of access is amplified in situations where the interview subjects live in households where English is not spoken or not the primary language. We contend that in part this is because the prescribed census protocol reflects assumptions grounded in a set of experiences and cultural knowledge specific to the US social context which non-English-speaking immigrants quite often simply do not share.

The prescribed protocol for the survey interview conforms to a particular frame (definition of the situation) familiar to most English speakers in the US: that of the official standardized interview. The social register (Agha, 2006; Biber & Finegan, 1994; Ferguson, 1982) for this particular type of interaction establishes a series of expectations about interaction and information transmission within the CIE, including:

(1) social interaction should be largely limited to the narrow task of information exchange.
(2) The relationship between participants should be confined to the performance of the task at hand (i.e., "question asker" or "question answerer").
(3) The length of the relationship should be confined to the length of the task.
(4) This type of personal information is largely unremarkable and inoffensive to collect.

(5) The collection of such information is a matter-of-fact task of government.
(6) The information will be utilized in the manner explicitly claimed.
(7) Such personal information is typically and acceptably collected by strangers.
(8) The identification of a stranger as a government authority safeguards the transmission of personal information that would not otherwise be acceptable to convey to a stranger.

These expectations are themselves premised on a broad array of culturally constituted understandings about sociality, authority, and governance that are particular to a Western or US democratic social milieu. These expectations are clearly reflected in the design of the Census NRFU protocol.

The 2010 Census NRFU interview protocol outlines the steps in opening the interaction as:

(1) Greeting and introduction of self.
(2) Verification of address.
(3) Introduction of topic and emphasis on the short amount of time needed for the interview.
(4) Assurance of confidentiality.

Our field observation showed that the NRFU interviewers followed this protocol much more closely and far less problematically with English-speaking respondents than tended to be the case with LEP respondents. Many assumptions that informed how English-speaking respondents framed the CIE were simply not shared by LEP respondents from other social and cultural backgrounds and whose own status and social experience in American society differed in important ways from that of English speakers. Accordingly, many of the interactional guidelines prescribed by the protocol not only failed to secure and sustain access to needed information but in fact often inhibited it.

All of our research teams reported that the bilingual enumerators drew upon tacit knowledge of social interaction norms that were appropriate and specific to their particular language community in order to reframe the CIE in an alternative social register. This helped them build and maintain the rapport and trust with LEP respondents that was necessary to secure and maintain access, and that allowed them to obtain the information which the NRFU questionnaire and protocol had been designed (but often failed) to elicit effectively.

Knowledge of these norms influenced the communicative conventions that bilingual interviewers deployed, often resulting in significant question or item rewording and reordering and even in significant changes in how the tasks of asking questions and explaining the interview were approached. Table 28.2 summarizes some strategies that proved particularly successful in engaging LEP respondents.

As we observed it, the conventions bilingual enumerators used in many ways directly contravened the NRFU protocol's efforts to define the CIE as a very low context, highly impersonal information exchange. However, for LEP populations, interviewers found that only after a certain degree of personal connection and in-groupness had been established, could they effectively proceed with the rest of interview. In other words, in almost every LEP community of language, respondents required a far more detailed initial explanation to the questions "Who are you?" and "Why are you here?" than the NRFU protocol provided.

Table 28.2 *Effective meta-communicative conventions used by bilingual enumerators*

Language group	Conventions used
Arabic	Reframing interview as a "social" (rather than "official") visit. Using terms like friend or uncle to invoke forms of culturally specific forms of social connection that suggested their trustworthiness. Accepting invitations to enter homes and occasionally share a meal. Great attention paid to respecting expectations about gender appropriateness in all interaction.
Chinese	Using culturally appropriate politeness strategies and terms of respect for interaction with strangers. Repeating the respondents' answers at almost every turn to signal attentiveness and respect.
Korean	Using honorifics (such as "Grandmother") that signaled deference; less-fluent enumerators positioning themselves as "learners" and respondents as "teachers."
Portuguese	Seeking to identify common connections (based on shared neighborhood, institutions, acquaintances, knowledge of places of origin) to establish a sense of shared community and identity. Employing a casual, intimate conversational style, using humor, and showing interest in personal topics and welfare. Taking a supplicant approach (i.e., asking respondent for help). Accepting invitations to enter home.
Russian	Initially emphasizing authority and legal requirements of the census. Subsequently, seeking to reframe interview as a social visit, accepting invitations to enter home. Occasionally providing personal contact information.
Spanish	Emphasizing indirectness, informality, politeness. Actively seeking to preempt respondent concerns about the confidentiality of the census. Avoiding any references to census as a government activity. Persistent emphasis on usefulness of getting interview "over with" to avoid future visits.
Vietnamese	Taking age, gender, and social status into account in deploying a range of honorifics, often being hyper-polite. Using culturally appropriate jokes.

Moreover, the responses that enabled access were ones that signaled trustworthiness in terms that were largely community-specific.

Thus, for example, the Arabic enumerators sought to reframe the CIE in terms that stressed as close a social relationship as they could identify and assume vis-à-vis their respondents. This process started through a linguistically and behaviorally enacted effort to identify what would imperfectly translate as the most proximate "level of ethnicity" the enumerator shared with the respondent. This allowed the interviewer to establish the CIE as an interaction that could be dictated by the culturally prescribed expectations that would govern those among members of a shared social group rather than among strangers. This strategy was reinforced through a range of specific communicative conventions, including the use of terms that metaphorically invoked certain kinds of obligations and interactional possibilities based on trust and intimacy through the use of deferential kinship terminology.

Witness the following transcript/field note excerpts from one interview observed by our Arabic field team.

In the interview, the enumerator referred to the elderly respondent as "uncle," "brother," and "father." Enumerators also, regardless of national origin, often used Arabic phrases to adhere to cultural norms designating respect. For instance, a respondent reported his age (78), and the enumerator responded with a culturally appropriate phrase, "Oh, wow, may He [God] extend your age."

By way of contrast, an enumerator who was not of Arab-speaking national origin took a different approach – more in line with the prescribed protocol – by attempting to secure access in Arabic based on the signaling of authority and by framing the CIE as a legal transaction. The following field notes illustrated how the approach used by this enumerator made it difficult to carry out interviews with Arabic speakers:

> respondent's son tried to get excuses to avoid the interview himself by saying that he is only visiting, had to leave soon, and not sure if he will provide us with the right information, etc. Enumerator assured son that interview will take only 10 min. and that they have to complete this interview. It was hard at times to get son to continue with the interview.

The Spanish and Russian cases contrasted dramatically in the forms of social register that proved most successful. In the Spanish case, enumerators sought to establish a social register that emphasized indirectness, informality, and respect, while de-emphasizing the official, authoritative, or legal aspects of the census. To accomplish this, they relied on communicative conventions that conveyed politeness and on a nonthreatening demeanor (using kind facial expressions, smiling, dressing casually, listening patiently to what respondents had to say even if not directly related to the census, and being willing to chat with respondents). In the frequently observed situations in which respondents signaled they were reluctant to participate and were pressed for time, enumerators effectively conveyed respect by stating directly the purpose of the visit, repeatedly emphasizing how little time the interview would require, and by suggesting that "taking care of this now" would prevent (presumably undesirable) future visits.

Our field research team concluded that the most successful enumerators in the Spanish context were those who were patiently adamant, went to extra lengths to ensure that the confidentiality issue was understood, and who were particularly careful never to underscore that participation was a legal requirement or to frame participation as a matter of "compliance with authority."

In stark contrast, our Russian-language field research team noted that the most effective way to induce participation from Russian speakers was for enumerators bluntly to underscore at the very outset of an interview that participation in the CIE was required as a matter of legal compliance. They specifically noted the exceptional effectiveness of one enumerator who clearly seemed to sway reluctant Russian respondents by knocking loudly on their doors and announcing in a clear loud voice, "United States Federal Government, Census Bureau!" After having announced himself, he would then say his name and bring his badge closer for the respondent to see. Whereas less imperious enumerators often failed to gain access to Russian respondents (heard talking behind unopened doors), in every case Russian respondents opened the door for this particular enumerator. In the view of our Russian ethnographic team, the effectiveness of this imperative social register in securing participation from Russian respondents reflected that particular group's social conditioning in Russia about the importance of at least appearing to be responsive to government authority.

However, they also noted that while an authoritative framing proved effective in securing initial access, maintaining access and securing reliable information required skillful modulation and renegotiation of the social register during the course of the interview. Thus, after initially asserting their authority, bilingual enumerators usually sought to demonstrate personal interest in the respondent, and to reframe the interview in culturally recognizable ways as a visit (inspiring confidence and truthful responses) rather than an official interrogation (inviting evasiveness and deception). Accomplishing this required deviation from established NRFU protocol rules (e.g., accepting invitations to enter the respondent's house and visit).

In Korean and Vietnamese cultural contexts it is important to use the appropriate terms of address in social interaction when there are significant age differences. Using culturally specific honorifics can establish a form of deference that invites reciprocal assistance from the study subject. Bilingual Korean enumerators adjusted their use of various titles (such as "Teacher") in ways that culturally signaled forms of respect. Such deference placed participants in a culturally recognized didactic role that was consistent with providing the information being requested. Knowledgeable bilingual enumerators were also very careful to use kinship terms such as "Mother" or "Grandmother" followed by appropriate honorific suffixes, along with the respondent's full name followed by an honorific suffix (also often used in official settings) to convey appropriate forms of politeness to more elderly respondents.

Amongst Chinese-speaking respondents, conveying politeness and respect depended on altogether different communicative conventions. In this community of language, politeness can be signaled through repetition of what another protagonist has already said, demonstrating the attentiveness and interest of the listener (Pan & Kádár, 2011). Following is an example of this strategy:

Example 28.1   Interaction between a bilingual census enumerator (E) and a Chinese-speaking respondent (R)

> **E:** Did you live here on April 1st?
> **R:** This is the situation: we just … we just bought this house. Just moved in.
> **E:** Ah, you just moved in.
> **R:** It hasn't even been ten days.
> **E:** Ah, it hasn't even been ten days? Based on what you just said, what about April 1st? Where were you living on April 1st?
> **R:** Not here, on April 1st I was in a different place, I was …
> **E:** Ah, on April 1st you were in a different place.

R: We … we just moved here on May 1st.
E: Ah, you just moved here on May 1st.
R: Correct. Correct.

In this interaction, repetition was used as a rhetorical device to probe deeper, as a means to extract and verify information, and as a means of transitioning to another question. Interestingly, this form of continuous repetition proved highly dysfunctional when this same Chinese–English bilingual enumerator used it with native English speakers, who tended to respond with frustration, exasperation, and passive-aggressive expressions of anger. They often interpreted it as a sign of linguistic incompetency:

> A white middle-aged female, visibly frustrated when asked to re-spell her name, voiced complaints about the inefficiency of census, and her tone verged on sarcasm. Ethnic issues were clearly an unspoken background aspect of this interaction; the Chinese–English bilingual enumerator carefully repeated each answer, which led the respondent to say twice, "Yes, that's what I said!" Other comment: "How long will this take?" – Respondent was visibly agitated, looking at her watch, sighing loudly, even grimacing.

This example illustrates how even seemingly minor communicative conventions that extend beyond wording per se (such as repetition) may play a decisive role in constructing meaning and in affecting communicative success when participants hail from different communities of language.

Although we have only provided a few illustrative examples, the overall conclusion from our observations is that both tacit knowledge of norms in communication and culturally specific reference frameworks contributed to what sociolinguists would term the "meta-communicative competence" (Briggs, 1986) of enumerators in ways that often proved crucial in their efforts to define the CIE as a social encounter. The meta-communicative competence of enumerators clearly affected their ability to negotiate a social register that could secure and maintain access to respondents. These social registers also framed the act of questioning and the questions themselves in ways that often affected the more specific tasks associated with managing the conveyance of uttered meaning which we discuss in the next section.

28.4.2 Striving for comparability

While negotiating access is an obvious prerequisite for communicative success, it is insufficient by itself. Another critical interviewer task was achieving comparability (Johnson, 1998; Mohler & Johnson, 2010; van de Vijver, 1998). Comparability across languages can be achieved when a social practice or construct exists in both a source and a target language. A social practice is a chain of mediated actions that have a history within a particular group of social actors and within the cognitive development of the individuals socialized within that group (Scollon, 2001). If there is no comparable social practice or construct in two different language communities, the translation is likely to be highly problematic. Our researchers observed that comparability problems were particularly pronounced in the 2010 NRFU questions about the English-language concepts of ethnicity (i.e., Hispanic origin) and race. Problems with these two questions were pervasive in five of the language groups and in the other two – Korean and Chinese – enumerators omitted those questions altogether.

Race and ethnicity are forms of social categorization that have developed under sociohistorical circumstances quite specific to the United States. Immigrants to this country learn and appropriate those categories to quite varying degrees (see, for example, Halter, 1993). In several communities, it was readily apparent that answers conformed closely to the categories of identity prevalent in the immigrants' countries of origin and that those categories differed substantially from those which prevail in American society. For example phenotype (skin color) has historically played a central role in American conceptions of race but does not factor prominently in Russian categorizations of social identity. However, Russians in the Union of Soviet Socialist Republics (USSR) were often assigned a "nationality" that designated a sense of "peoplehood" signified by a combination of religion, native language, and location of birth. Yet, neither Russian nor Jewish (both nationalities in the USSR) are recognized as a racial or ethnic category in mainstream American parlance.

Similarly, in the Arabic-speaking community, the Hispanic origin question was variously confused with language spoken or national origin – and sometimes first as one and then the other as in the following case:

Example 28.2   Arabic interview

E: "Now, are you Hispanic [stated in English], Latino [stated in English], Spanish [Espagne in Arabic]?"
R: "French."
E: "No, not the language you speak, for example, what's your origin?"
R: "Lebanese."

After the enumerator asked the Hispanic origin ethnicity question, he followed up by asking the respondent to look at the response card (which was in English, and the respondent could not read English): "It says here, look at List C. Are you from Mexican, Puerto Rican origin from your grandparents?" The respondent further stated: "No. No. Lebanese. The father and mother are Lebanese."

While race and ethnicity raised comparability problems that arguably surpass the problems documented with these concepts in the census research of the English-speaking population (e.g., Childs, Terry, & Jurgenson, 2011; Gerber & Crowley, 2005), our study also identified problems with seemingly far more universal concepts, such as age. The question "What was (name's) age on April 1, 2010" was asked for every household member. Yet, in contrast to ages that start from zero at birth, Korean ages start from 1 at birth, and then change every New Year's Day, rather than on every specific calendar birthday. This way of reckoning Korean age is a cultural practice rather than an official system but is likely to have affected responses, particularly those of more elderly LEP respondents. Enumerators provided no clarification that "American" rather than Korean ages were being sought.

Finally, our field teams noted occasions in which imperfect comparability threatened to undermine rapport and therefore the task of maintaining access itself. Thus, for example, the term *raza* which was used to translate race into Spanish, is the same term that is used in certain Spanish-speaking contexts to also denote the concept of *species*. Our field teams observed that the use of this term in the race question invited indignant responses from some Spanish speakers, who felt insulted when they incorrectly perceived that they were being asked about their species (and thus implicitly questioned about their very humanity).

28.4.3 Overcoming discursive dissonance and ulterior signaling

The tasks of achieving "speaker–respondent correspondence" and "question-focused responses" proved most elusive for interviewers of LEP respondents on one particular census question: "Did you or anyone in this household live or stay here on April 1, 2010?"

In some of these cases the problem was primarily one of "discursive dissonance," an utterance was understood by the interview subject to mean something different from the meaning that the interviewer intended to convey. This difference could result from word structure and terminology or from the inadvertent reference to a different social context. For example, in the Spanish-speaking context, the question about whether respondents were living in a house on a specific day proved somewhat incongruent with a cultural notion that living in a household necessarily implied a relatively long timeframe that precluded short-term habitation. The responses of some monolingual Spanish-speaking respondents demonstrated this form of misinterpretation:

Example 28.3   Spanish interview

>   **R:**   I have been living here since November of last year, November.
>   **E:**   November? 2009?
>   **R:**   Yes.
>   **E:**   How about April 1? Were you living here on April 1?
>   **R:**   No, November.
>   **E:**   Okay, yes.

Even greater confusion about this question was often evident among Arabic respondents. Most initially misunderstood this as a question about the length of time they had lived at that location and rather than about where they were living on a particular date.

In other cases, "ulterior signaling" occurred. Ulterior signaling happens when the particular terminology and structure of the question, or the context and mode of its asking, inadvertently trigger respondent suspicions that the question serves some ulterior (usually undesirable) motive. Thus, the specificity of the April 1 date not only led to the forms of misunderstanding of the question altogether amongst Arabic speakers (as noted above), but when insisted upon was often reinterpreted as a probe for information about some (unstated) event of significance or importance associated with that specific date. Reading this as a question about how they might be associated to a still unidentified event of interest to government officials led some Arabic respondents to take evasive discursive action as they sought to identify what that event might be and understand why they were being asked about it.

The same question also elicited evasiveness from many Russian-speaking respondents. Debriefings revealed that elderly Russian respondents living in government-subsidized housing were apprehensive that this question might be hinting that they were suspected of hiding another resident (and thus violating the law). This concern led them to focus on a different aspect of the question: the *number of* residents. As with Arabic speakers, both the directness of the question and the specificity of the date also represented a departure from everyday communicative conventions typical of commonplace discourse, invoking instead a form of "marked speech" they associated with threatening official interrogation. In both of these cases, the wording of question invoked different forms of ulterior signaling when deployed in communities with different meta-communicative conventions. Enumerators confronted a challenge in securing responses to the questions they actually asked, as respondents offered evasive responses to the questions they believed they were "really" being asked about.

28.4.4 Contending with inadvertent social affront

Finally, one of the thorniest challenges to communicative success occurred when a question itself, rather than its wording per se, proved provocative or offensive to members of a particular community of language in ways that would not usually be the case for American English speakers. Here, we illustrate the interactional difficulties occasioned by one question (about adoption) in two different communities.

The question about whether a child was adopted proved particularly awkward in the Korean-language context. Deeply influenced by Confucian tradition, blood ties are viewed as essential to family organization in Korean culture. As Kim and Ryu (2005) put it, "Korean families have a clear boundary as to who is 'in' and who is 'out'" (p. 352). A very rigid view of family boundaries has made Koreans extremely reluctant to adopt orphaned children, a culturally informed orientation that has led to the infamous image of Korea as a sender of adoptees to foreign countries ever since the Korean War. Even asking if a child is adopted is potentially quite offensive. While some bilingual Korean enumerators simply omitted this question altogether, those who asked it inevitably added a form of excuse to the question, such as: "That question was not appropriate for Koreans, but I had to ask because it's on the form."

Discomfort with this question among Russian respondents stemmed from different reasons altogether. In Russian society, there is a stigma attached to parents'– especially women's – infertility. Thus, adopting a child remains a rare and highly secret act (Isurin, Pan, & Lubkemann, 2013). Adopted children are not usually informed about their status. The extent of adoption's social stigma in Russian society is evident by the lengths to which the Soviet-era government went in order to protect it as a secret. Thus, despite acute housing shortages, adoptive parents were usually given new housing in order to ensure neighbors remained ignorant of the adoption. Given this history, a census question about whether a child is biological or adopted is almost inconceivably offensive to most Russians. Knowledgeable of this fact and reluctant to endanger the progress of the NFRU interview, most Russian-speaking enumerators skipped this question altogether in Russian language interviews.

28.5 Discussion

We recognize that the issues we have raised here – problems of comparability, differences in communicative conventions, and the differences in social conventions that inform how interviews are framed by respondents – have also been noted in populations that share the same language. Indeed, the bulk of the debate over the tradeoffs and implications of standardization has been based on observations of variance within such monolingual populations (Beatty, 1995; Conrad & Schober, 2000; Schaeffer, 1991; Schaeffer & Maynard, 2002; Schober & Conrad, 1997; Suchman & Jordan, 1990). However, we agree with Harkness (2003) that the forms of variance across communities of language are not only significantly more acute but of a qualitatively different order altogether than those within communities of language.

One of the essential roles of language is to enable interaction among socially differentiated actors in the same community. The historical development of a language (including its meta-communicative conventions) reflects this imperative. However, by definition languages were not developed to overcome comparable challenges with speakers of *other* languages. Thus, communicative conventions, social framing rules, and to at least some extent concepts are likely to differ significantly *across* communities that do not share a linguistic code.

From this perspective, the adaptation model does not go nearly far enough in what it targets for "translation." Our research suggests that any effective effort to address the four tasks we have described as constituent of communicative success in cross-linguistic contexts requires far more than attending to matters of equivalence in linguistic codes or even the structure of utterances. Rather, translation must equally account for differences in meta-communicative conventions and for other social and cultural factors that impinge on the definition of the interview as a social situation. Things that will almost certainly require significant modification include not only wording and question sequencing, but often the extent of background information and explanation provided, as well as many other substantial aspects of survey protocol.

To date, survey researchers have viewed minimizing variance in all of these (save linguistic code and to some extent question structure) as a sacrosanct requisite for safeguarding standardization. Yet, as our findings highlight, in the 2010 Census enumeration communicative success with different LEP populations often *depended upon* the capacity of bilingual enumerators to *deviate* from established protocol in many respects in order to accomplish its four constituent tasks.

Such deviations from the script are typically treated as a significant methodological problem that undermines the integrity of standardization. However, as we observed it, most of these deviations represented informal, ad hoc, and implicit efforts to cope with differences in meta-communicative and social conventions in order to achieve commensurable *communicative effect*. From this perspective, the *deviation* from protocol of bilingual enumerators should thus be treated more as a source of insight into solutions for maximizing standardization, than as a threat to it.[3]

Based on this observation, we conclude with the following propositions for re-thinking survey translation and the broader theoretical understanding of standardization:

(1) An incisive differentiation must be made between two forms of standardization that hitherto have typically been conflated in most theoretical debates: between the standardization of stimulus *input* (the question or utterance verbalized by the interviewer) and the standardization of stimulus *output* (the information received by the respondent or communicative effect).

(2) The relationship between stimulus input and output must be the subject of empirical investigation rather than merely being assumed. It is a fallacy to *assume* that the standardization of the stimulus *input* will result in the standardized stimulus *output*.

(3) Differentiated stimulus *inputs* at some level are *methodologically indispensable and actually required* in order to achieve commensurable stimulus *outputs* across all segments of a population that includes monolingual speakers of different languages. The key question is not about whether stimulus inputs should be differentiated, *because they must be*, but rather about "in what ways" and "at what level"? We reiterate that the answer to this question must be based on the methodological deployment of a more theoretically robust notion of language itself that includes meta-communicative conventions as well as linguistic code.

(4) The standardization that ultimately matters is that of stimulus *outputs* (i.e., communicative effects) rather than the stimulus *inputs* per se. Leading proponents of adaptation in translation have lamented what they take to be the undermining of standardization because wording and question structure (stimulus input) are modified for specific communities of language: "A further drawback for some purposes is that adapted items provide limited scope for statistical analysis, since only statistical tools accommodating partly dissimilar instruments can be used" (Harkness *et al.*, 2003, p. 27). In our view, this mistakenly confuses and conflates the variance in stimulus input with variance in stimulus output.

(5) Our fifth and final point highlights a more specific theoretical and methodological quandary posed by certain cases of noncomparability across languages. Different solutions have been proposed by survey researchers to address conceptual equivalency challenges. "Front-end" approaches attempt to identify analytical constructs that exist across all communities of interest in order to incorporate these into initial questionnaire design (e.g., Harkness *et al.*, 2010; Howell, 2010; Smith, 2003; Thornton, Achen, Barber, Binstock, & Garrison, 2010). "Back-end" approaches seek to construct scales

---

[3] The improvisational aspect of these deviations introduces interviewer variance that can be addressed at the intra-language level.

post facto that harmonize the answers of respondents from different communities of language (e.g., Billiet, 2003; Hox, de Leeuw, & Binkhuis, 2010; Mohler, Smith, & Harkness, 1998). What might be termed "concessionary approaches" (Howell, 2010) accept the possibility that some initial concepts may not actually exist in different languages and selectively exclude such questions as a result. Of course, this last strategy ultimately concedes the possibility of noncomparability altogether – which may be problematic if the behaviors of concepts of core interest happen to fall in this domain.

In our view, both of these approaches are limited in their ability to address many of the comparability issues we observed. Front-end approaches presume a level of negotiability for survey categories that simply does not exist in the environment in which the US Census operates. The bureaucratic and political dynamics of that environment are far more potent than methodological concerns in determining how certain forms of categorization (such as race) will operate.

Many comparability problems are not merely a matter of different metrics being used to measure the same construct, but rather involve incompatibility between substantially different constructs altogether. It is difficult to imagine what sort of *post facto* scale could harmonize English-speaking American responses about "race" with those of Russian Jews who think in terms of nationality. Front-end approaches are also unlikely to offer much methodological respite inasmuch as they are likely to find conceptual commonality across communities of language only at levels of very broad and abstract generalization (i.e., "group identity"). At that level, the construct often loses the specificity needed for analysis and may become susceptible to new forms of variance error because it can be interpreted to refer to so many different things even within the same community (i.e., group identity could easily be taken to refer to ethnicity, citizenship, race, or any number of other forms of groupness in the American English-speaking context).

Such forms of substantive noncomparability pose a choice that, in our view, uniquely differentiates linguistically diversified populations from monolingual ones. In particular, they force a methodological choice between providing an explanation of a concept that is largely alien to the respondent's experience or functional understanding, or deferring to a concept that is meaningful to the respondent but at best has only partial (or sometimes virtually no) overlap with the concept the survey intends to measure. Drawing from our findings, an example of the concretization of such a choice might be whether to attempt an extensive explanation of the American concept of ethnicity to a Russian speaker, or conversely to accept an answer (such as "Jewish" or "Russian") that reflects their understanding of nationality.

Either option introduces problems to any analysis that strives for comparability. The first protects the instrument's intended construct but at the expense of a response that is hypothetical and largely divorced from the experiential basis whose relationship to behavior surveys are supposedly designed to measure and ascertain; whereas the second reflects an experiential basis that informs real behavior but introduces a variance error by ensuring the same question is actually measuring a fundamentally different phenomenon. The methodological adjudication of this choice may well depend on several empirical factors, including the actual concept and question itself as well as on theoretical formulations. It may also introduce tensions between tasks necessary for achieving communicative success and the goal of ensuring standardized communicative effect. Thus, whereas utilizing a construct that is recognizable and "unmarked" to respondents may better serve purposes of negotiating access, the explanation of a concept that is alien to them but reflective of the constructs that operate in the mainstream may better ensure the standardization of "stimulus output."

Ultimately, for our present purposes, we merely highlight the fact that, absent an awareness of this choice, and of a deliberate methodological decision embodied in explicit protocol to opt systematically one way or the other, both are likely to occur simultaneously as a result of the individual choices and improvisations of enumerators, as we certainly observed in our study. This introduces uncertainty about the source of variance error. Explicitly making this choice can improve analytical comparability by ensuring error consistency, which can more readily be accounted for in *post facto* analysis.

28.6 Conclusion

How linguistic difference is theorized and methodologically addressed is relevant to survey research, which is increasingly undertaken in linguistically diversified contexts. Within the US, LEP groups already comprise a significant proportion of the population of interest to standardized survey researchers. It is a crucial methodological task to ascertain that the survey response differences among LEPs, and between LEPs and English speakers reflect genuine sociological differences rather than potentially avoidable forms of measurement error. This is certainly a central concern for the US Census Bureau given its mandate and the wide-ranging political and socioeconomic implications of the census results for the American body politic. It should be of equal concern to the American survey research community that utilizes US Census data in academic and policy research, particularly in studies that focus on immigrant minorities. Even more broadly, the challenges we have discussed here apply to most cross-national survey research in which the population of interest includes linguistically differentiated communities and in which research aims to make comparisons among these groups.

References

Agha, A. (2006). Registers of language. In A. Duranti (ed.), *A Companion to Linguistic Anthropology*. Oxford: Blackwell Publishing.

Beatty, P. (1995). Understanding the standardized/non-standardized interviewing controversy, *Journal of Official Statistics*, 11(2), 147–60.

Behling, O., & Law, K. S. (2000). *Translating Questionnaires and Other Research Instruments: Problems and Solutions*. London: Sage.

Biber, D., & Finegan, E. (eds.). (1994). *Sociolinguistic Perspectives on Register*. New York: Oxford University Press.

Billiet, J. (2003). Cross-cultural equivalence with structural equation modeling. In J. A. Harkness, F. J. R. van de Vivjer, & P. Ph. Mohler (eds.), *Cross-Cultural Survey Methods* (pp. 247–64). Hoboken, NJ: John Wiley & Sons.

Braun, M. (2003). Communication and social cognition. In J. A. Harkness, F. J. R. van de Vivjer, & P. Ph. Mohler (eds.), *Cross-Cultural Survey Methods* (pp. 57–68). Hoboken, NJ: John Wiley & Sons.

Braun, M, & Harkness, J. (2005). Text and context: challenges to comparability in survey questions. In J. P. Hoffmeyer-Zlotnik & J. A. Harkness (eds.), *Methodological Aspects in Cross-National Research* (pp. 95–107). Mannheim: ZUMA.

Briggs, C. (1986). *Learning How to Ask: A Sociolinguistic Appraisal of the Role of the Interview in Social Science Research*. Cambridge: Cambridge University Press.

Childs, J. H., Terry, R., & Jurgenson, N. (2011). Measuring race and Hispanic origin: cognitive test findings searching for "truth." *Bulletin de Méthodologie Sociologique*, 111(1), 26–42.

Clark, H. H., & Schober, M. F. (1992). Asking questions and influencing answers. In J. A. Tanur (ed.), *Questions about Questions: Inquiries into the Cognitive Basis of Surveys* (pp. 15–48). New York: Russell Sage.

Conrad, F. G., & Schnober, M. F. (2000). Clarifying question meaning in a household telephone survey. *Public Opinion Quarterly*, 64(1), 1–28.

Dykema, J., Lepkowski, J. M., & Blixt, S. (1997). The effect of interviewer and respondent behavior on data quality: analysis of interaction coding in a validation study. In L. Lyberg, P. Biemer, M. Collins, E. D. de Leeuw, C. Dippo, N. Schwartz, & D. Trewin (eds.), *Survey Measurement and Process Quality* (pp. 287–310). New York: John Wiley & Sons.

Eriksen, T. H. (2002). *Ethnicity and Nationalism: Anthropological Perspectives*. London: Pluto Press.

Ferguson, C. A. (1982). Simplified registers and linguistic theory. In L. K. Obler & L. Menn (eds.), *Exceptional Language and Linguistics* (pp. 49–66). New York: Academic Press.

Fitzgerald, R., & Jowell, R. (2010). Measurement equivalence in comparative surveys: the European Social Survey (ESS) from design to implementation and beyond. In J. A. Harkness, M. Braun, B. Edwards, T. P. Johnson, L. E. Lyberg, P. Ph. Mohler, B.-E. Pennell, & T. W. Smith (eds.), *Survey Methods in Multinational, Multiregional, and Multicultural Contexts* (pp. 485–96). Hoboken, NJ: John Wiley & Sons.

Fowler, Jr., F. J. (1991). Reducing interviewer-related error through interviewer training, supervision and other means. In P. P. Biener, R. M. Groves, L. E. Lyberg, N. A. Mathiowetz, & S. Sudman (eds.), *Measurement Errors in Surveys* (pp. 259–78). Hoboken, NJ: John Wiley & Sons.

Fowler, Jr., F. J., & Mangione, T. W. (1990). *Standardized Survey Interviewing: Minimizing Interviewer-Related Error*. Newbury Park: Sage.

Gerber, E. R., & Crowley, M. (2005). *Report on Cognitive Testing of a Shortened Sequence of Hispanic Origin, Race and Modified Ancestry Questions: Content Development for the 2005 National Content Test.* Suitland, MD: US Census Bureau.

Goffman, E. (1974). *Frame Analysis: An Essay on the Organization of Experience.* New York, NY: Harper and Row.

Halter, M. (1993). *Between Race and Ethnicity.* Champaign, IL: University of Illinois Press.

Harkness, J. A. (ed.) (1998). *ZUMA-Nachrichten Spezial N. 3. Cross-Cultural Survey Equivalence.* Mannheim: ZUMA.

(2003). Questionnaire translation. In J. A. Harkness, F. J. R. van de Vivjer, & P. P. Mohler (eds.), *Cross-Cultural Survey Methods* (pp. 35–56). Hoboken, NJ: John Wiley & Sons.

Harkness, J. A., Edwards, B., Hansen, S. E., Miller, D. R., & Vilar, A. (2010). Designing questionnaires for multipopulation research. In J. A. Harkness, M. Braun, B. Edwards, T. P. Johnson, L. E. Lyberg, P. Ph. Mohler, B.-E. Pennell, & T. W. Smith (eds.), *Survey Methods in Multinational, Multiregional, and Multicultural contexts* (pp. 33–58). Hoboken, NJ: John Wiley & Sons.

Harkness, J. A., & Schoua-Glusberg, A. (1998). Questionnaires in translation. In J. A. Harkness (ed.), *ZUMA-Nachrichten Spezial No. 3. Cross-Cultural Survey Equivalence* (pp. 87–127). Mannheim: ZUMA.

Harkness, J. A., van de Vijver, F. J. R., & Mohler, P. P. (2003). Questionnaire design in comparative research. In J. A. Harkness, F. J. R. van de Vivjer, & P. P. Mohler (eds.), *Cross-Cultural Survey Methods* (pp. 19–34). Hoboken, NJ: John Wiley & Sons.

Harkness, J. A., Villar, A., & Edwards, E. (2010). Translation, adaptation and design. In J. A. Harkness, M. Braun, B. Edwards, T. P. Johnson, L. E. Lyberg, P. Ph. Mohler, B.-E. Pennell, & T. W. Smith (eds.), *Survey Methods in Multinational, Multiregional, and Multicultural contexts* (pp. 117–40). Hoboken, NJ: John Wiley & Sons.

Howell, D. A. (2010). Enhancing quality and comparability in the comparative study of electoral systems (CSES). In J. A. Harkness, M. Braun, B. Edwards, T. P. Johnson, L. E. Lyberg, P. Ph. Mohler, B.-E. Pennell, & T. W. Smith (eds.), *Survey Methods in Multinational, Multiregional, and Multicultural Contexts* (pp. 525–34). Hoboken, NJ: John Wiley & Sons.

Hox, J. J., de Leeuw, E., & Binkhuis, M. J. S. (2010). Analysis models for comparative surveys. In J. A. Harkness, M. Braun, B. Edwards, T. P. Johnson, L. E. Lyberg, P. Ph. Mohler, B.-E. Pennell, & T. W. Smith (eds.), *Survey Methods in Multinational, Multiregional, and Multicultural Contexts* (pp. 395–418). Hoboken, NJ: John Wiley & Sons.

Hymes, D. (1972). Models of the interaction of language. In J. J. Gumperz & D. Hymes (eds.), *Directions in Sociolinguistics: The Ethnography of Communication* (pp. 35–71). New York: Holt, Rinehart, & Winston.

Isurin, L., Pan, Y., & Lubkemann, S. (2013). *Observing Census Enumeration of Non-English Speaking Households in the 2010 Census: Russian Report.* Center for Survey Measurement Research Report. US Census Bureau.

Johnson, T. P. (1998). Approaches to establishing equivalence in cross-cultural and cross-national survey research. In J. A. Harkness (ed.), *Cross Cultural Survey Equivalence* (pp 1–40). Mannheim: ZUMA.

Jowell, R., Kaase, M., Fitzgerald, R., & Eva, G. (eds.) (2007). *Measuring Attitudes Cross-Nationally: Lessons from the European Social Survey*. Thousand Oaks, CA: Sage.

Kim, B. C., & Ryu, E. (2005). Korean families. In M. McGoldrick, J. Giordano, & N. Garcia-Preto (eds.), *Ethnicity and Family Therapy* (pp. 349–62). NY: Guilford Press.

Kim, J., & Zapata, J. (2012). 2010 Census: Language Program Assessment Report. 2010 Census Program for Evaluations and Experiments. 2010 Census Planning Memoranda Series #204.

Kovar, M. G., & Royston, P. (1990). Comment on "interactional troubles in face-to-face survey interviews." *Journal of the American Statistical Association*, 85(409), 246–47.

McKay, B., Breslow, M. J., Sangster, R. L., Gabbard, S. M., & Reynolds, R. W. (1996). Translating survey questionnaires: lessons learned. *New Directions for Evaluation*, 70, 93–104.

Mohler, P. Ph., & Johnson, T. J. (2010). Equivalency, comparability and methodological progress. In J. A. Harkness, M. Braun, B. Edwards, T. P. Johnson, L. E. Lyberg, P. Ph. Mohler, B.-E. Pennell, & T. W. Smith (eds.), *Survey Methods in Multinational, Multiregional, and Multicultural Contexts* (pp. 17–32). Hoboken, NJ: John Wiley & Sons.

Mohler, P. Ph., Smith, T. W., & Harkness, J. A. (1998). Respondents ratings of expressions from response scales: a two country, two language investigation on equivalence and translation. In J. A. Harkness (ed.), *Cross Cultural Survey Equivalence* (pp. 159–184). Mannheim: ZUMA.

Pan, Y., & Kádár, D. Z. (2011). *Politeness in Historical and Contemporary Chinese*. London and New York: Continuum.

Platt, J. (2002). The history of the interview. In J. F. Gubrium & J. A. Holstein (eds.), *Handbook of Interview Research* (pp. 33–54). London: Sage.

Schaeffer, N. (1991). Conversation with a purpose – or conversation? Interaction in the standardized interview. In P. P. Biemer, R. M. Groves, L. E. Lyberg, N. A. Mathiowetz, & S. Sudman (eds.), *Measurement Errors in Surveys*. New York: John Wiley & Sons.

Schaeffer, N., & Maynard, D. W. (2002). Occasions for intervention: interactional resources for comprehension in standardized survey interviews. In D. W. Maynard, H. Houtkoop-Steenstra, N. C. Schaeffer, & J. van der Zouwen (eds.), *Standardization and Tacit Knowledge: Interaction and Practice in the Survey Interview* (pp. 261–80). New York: Wiley.

Schober, M., & Conrad, F. (1997). Does conversational interviewing reduce survey measurement error? *Public Opinion Quarterly*, 61(4), 576–602.

Schwarz, N. (2003). Culture-sensitive context effects: a challenge for cross-cultural surveys. In J. A. Harkness, F. J. R. van de Vijver, & P. Ph. Mohler (eds.), *Cross-Cultural Survey Methods* (pp. 93–100). Hoboken, NJ: John Wiley & Sons.

Scollon, R. (2001). *Mediated Discourse: The Nexus of Practice*. London and New York: Routledge.

Singleton, Jr., R. A., & Straits, B. C. (2002). Survey interviewing. In J. A. Holstein & J. F. Gubrium (eds.), *Handbook of Interview Research*. Thousand Oaks: Sage.

Smit, J. H., Dijkstra, W., & van der Zouwen, J. (1997). Suggestive interviewer behaviour in surveys: an experimental study. *Journal of Official Statistics*, 13(1), 19–28.

Smith, T. W. (2003). Developing comparable questions in cross-national surveys. In J. A. Harkness, F. J. R. van de Vivjer, & P. Ph. Mohler (eds.), *Cross-Cultural Survey Methods* (pp. 69–92). Hoboken, NJ: John Wiley & Sons.

Suchman, L., & Jordan, B. (1990). Interactional troubles in face-to-face survey interviews. Journal of the American Statistical Association, 85(409), 232–41.

(1992). Validity and the collaborative construction of meaning in face-to-face surveys. In J. M. Tanur (ed.), *Questions about Questions: Inquiries into the Cognitive Bases of Surveys* (pp. 241–70). New York: Russell Sage.

Tannen, D. (1993). *Framing in Discourse*. Oxford: Oxford University Press.

Thornton, A., Achen, A., Barber, J., Binstock, G., & Garrison, W. (2010). Creating questions and protocols for an international study of ideas about development and family life. In J. A. Harkness, M. Braun, B. Edwards, T. P. Johnson, L. E. Lyberg, P. Ph. Mohler, B.-E. Pennell, & T. W. Smith (eds.), *Survey Methods in Multinational, Multiregional, and Multicultural Contexts* (pp. 59–74). Hoboken, NJ: John Wiley & Sons.

van de Vijver, F. J. R. (1998). Towards a theory of bias and equivalence. In J. A. Harkness (ed.), *ZUMA-Nachrichten Spezial No. 3. Cross-Cultural Survey Equivalence*. Mannheim: ZUMA.

29

Mobilizing hard-to-survey populations to participate fully in censuses and surveys

TIMOTHY P. OLSON, ARTURO VARGAS, AND JEROME D. WILLIAMS

29.1 Introduction

Conducting an accurate census or survey requires active public participation. Without complete participation from all population segments, particularly among those who are hard to count, results will be skewed and not reflect the resident population's reality. "Hard-to-count" populations are those who are less likely to participate than others in a national census or survey. Hard-to-count populations often include immigrants, those who speak a language other than the nation's dominant language, renters, people or households living in poverty, and people who feel marginalized or abused by the prevailing society or government (see Chapter 1 in this volume). This chapter discusses how an active public engagement campaign through grass-roots community organizations can ignite participation among those least likely to participate.

29.2 Why a grass-roots campaign is critical

According to Rice and Atkin (2013), public communication campaigns are defined as purposive attempts to inform or influence behaviors of large audiences within a given time period using an organized set of communication activities and featuring an array of mediated messages in multiple channels to produce noncommercial benefits to individuals and society. In assessing the impact of public communication campaigns, they note that most experts conclude that such campaigns tend to have a modest rather than strong impact, notably on the health behaviors. There can be a multitude of factors that contribute to the limited impact of these campaigns. For example, Rice and Atkin suggest meager dissemination budgets, unsophisticated application of theory and models, poorly conceived strategic approaches, and promoting complex or difficult behaviors are among the key contributors. They also note that the difficult task of targeting resistant audience segments can be a significant factor. When considering the challenges of reaching hard-to-count population segments in the context of a

This report is released to inform interested parties and encourage discussion of work in progress. The views expressed on statistical, methodological, and operational issues are those of the authors and not necessarily those of the US Census Bureau.

census public communication campaign, this latter point certainly is a critical consideration, and for this reason alone, it makes sense to have a strong focus on grass-roots efforts.

Within hard-to-count population segments, which are disproportionately by members of racial and ethnic minority groups, the preferred sources of information tend to be different than the general population, and, as such, these sources can be highly effective in overcoming resistant attitudes. High credibility is given especially to members and leaders of the community, and grass-roots efforts can be highly effective in tapping into these leaders with high source credibility. The role of culture in African-American and Hispanic/Latino communities make greater distinctions between insiders and outsiders, compared to the general population (Williams & Tharp, 2002). Furthermore, there is a long tradition of respect for oral communication within these communities. In addition, members of these communities tend to talk more with family and friends about products, companies, and advertising than the general population. Also, members of hard-to-count population segments will be more responsive to communications campaigns that use local media outlets from within their community, and engage with social organizations and institutions from their communities. Grass-roots campaigns that play off of these cultural characteristics can be highly effective in overcoming resistant attitudes.

It may seem obvious, but treating members of hard-to-count population segments with dignity and respect is the first principle of any successful public communication campaign targeting these communities. This is especially important for members of racial and ethnic minority groups because historically they have been "invisible" and "ignored" by commercial marketing campaigns, and, when they are included, the depictions often are stereotypical, negative, and unflattering. In addition, members of these population segments frequently have faced incidents of racial prejudice and discrimination in the marketplace (Williams & Henderson, 2012). As a result, a public communication campaign that treats these segments with dignity and respect and has a grass-roots appeal by including credible sources can have a significant positive impact on message receivers.

Community engagement is critical to the success of any public communications campaign targeting hard-to-count population segments. Kramer, Schwarte, Lafleur, and Williams (2013) discuss the importance of community engagement to achieve positive changes in a community. They point out that a community engagement approach is based on the premise that efforts to achieve changes in a community are more likely to be effective and sustainable if the community is directly involved in the effort. Community is broadly defined to include community members and youth, community-based organizations, advocacy organizations, public institutions, and businesses. This involvement is usually initiated through use of community organizing strategies to raise awareness and understanding of the issue and ultimately develop support for policy change. A community engagement approach then builds on this support by developing in residents the capacity to act as advocates for change.

In addition to focusing on community engagement, there are a number of other factors that distinguish public service campaigns that can contribute to their success in effectively reaching hard-to-count population segments. Paisley (2001) identifies several character-istics that are notable in this regard. For example, he distinguishes between "public service versus advocacy" campaigns. In the former, goals are generally supported by a broad array of stakeholders, while, in the latter, goals are controversial and challenged by significant stakeholders. In the case of communication about the census, the general population may be more inclined to view the campaign as a public service, in which the goals of having high participation by all segments of society is a laudable goal, whereas a significantly larger percentage of the hard-to-count segment may have a higher degree of skepticism about the benefits of participating in a census, hence requiring more of an advocacy approach.

Another distinguishing characteristic of public communication campaigns that Paisley (2001) mentions is "strategies of change." Strategies may be different for the general population, where emphasis might be on educating and reinforcing positive attitudes about the benefits of completing the census form, versus hard-to-count segments, where there may be a greater emphasis required on changing behaviors and attitudes that are more negative and resistant to census cooperation.

Paisley also mentions "individual or collective benefits." For hard-to-count population segments, there may be a different perception of the benefits of the census compared to the general population, based on cultural values. For example, the United States is generally recognized as an individualistic culture; however, many members of hard-to-count seg-ments tend to be more collectivistic. The individualism/collectivism construct (I/C) is associated with a broad pattern of differences among cultures, and persuasive appeals in messages often reflect a culture's standing along this dimension. For example, a study by Han and Shavitt (1994) suggests that messages consistent with the underlying cultural themes of collectivism are more persuasive with members from collectivistic cultures. For example, they found that respondents from an individualist culture found ads to be more appealing and persuasive that emphasized individualistic benefits, whereas respondents from a collectivistic culture found ads to be more appealing and persuasive that emphasized in-group benefits, such as harmony and family integrity. Such a cultural contrast between hard-to-count population segments and the general population provides an interesting context in which to examine the efficacy of public communication campaign messages targeting these respective communities, based on their respective individualistic versus collectivistic cultural orientations.

As noted by Rice and Atkin (2013), another critical aspect of any public communication campaign includes understanding the audience. They note that campaign designers typically emphasize three basic types of audiences, namely, focal segments, interpersonal influencers, and societal policymakers, all of which are important in focusing on hard-to-count popula-tion segments.

Focal segments are audiences grouped by levels of risk or illness, readiness, income, and education, and other factors such as sensation-seeking. Hard-to-count segments typically display a lower level of readiness to engage in completing a census and tend to be lower in income and education than the general population.

Interpersonal influencers are opinion leaders, media advocates, peer and role models, who can mediate the campaign (positively or negatively) and help set the public agenda. For hard-to-count segments, the interpersonal influencers are going to be significantly different than for the general population. For example, celebrities may be much more effective for some hard-to-count segments. Williams and Qualls (1989) point to research by ethnic and social psychologists that characterize the cultural script of racial/ethnic minorities as being largely influenced by interpersonal interaction, affiliation, group orientation, peer acceptance, and feeling orientation. These characteristics suggest that hard-to-count members may be more responsive to individuals who are perceived as likeable and attractive, as opposed, for example, to individuals who may be perceived as more of an expert. Williams and Qualls suggest that celebrity advertising is generally associated with referent social power, and referent social power is closely associated with the characteristics of the cultural script of racial/ethnic minorities, who make up a large proportion of hard-to-count population segments. However, research conducted by the National Association of Latino Elected and Appointed Officials (NALEO) indicates that celebrities, who represent one type of referent social power, are less effective messengers within the Latino community than spokespersons who represent other types of referent social power and with whom the target audience can also identify. For example, NALEO focus groups show that teachers, nurses, firefighters, and individuals of the same ethnic group in military uniform, all rank as more credible than celebrities or athletes (National Association of Latino Elected and Appointed Officials Educational Fund, 2003).

Societal policymakers affect the legal, political, and resource infrastructure, such as through regulations on media messages, environmental conditions, safety standards, and social action. The most influential policymakers for the hard-to-count population will be different than for the general population, as they will tend to be more vocal on issues of greater importance and priority to the hard-to-count segments, e.g., issues related to immigration, discrimination, voting rights, and taxation on lower income groups. Atkin (2001) has argued that campaigns may want to develop a *product line* or continuum of intended outcomes, so that audiences with different levels of receptivity or resistance can find their comfortable location in the campaign mix. This would be particularly appropriate for the hard to count, as they would be much more receptive to messages and societal policymakers that resonate with them based on their circumstances and issues, compared to those of the general population.

29.3   Examples of noncensus engagement campaigns

According to Paisley (2001), the success of social marketing campaigns depends on their ability to become an important and enduring part of the public agenda and to obtain first-party entitlement for significant stakeholders. A significant challenge is elevating the campaign agenda items in the eyes of hard-to-reach populations. Items on the public agenda of the campaign may not be high or salient priorities to these segments and, in fact, may pale in comparison to more important concerns. For example, a public health campaign to promote healthy diets and exercise may be low on the list of priorities in hard-to-count communities where reducing neighborhood crime, obtaining affordable housing, and meeting financial obligations are far more pressing. Rice and Atkin (2013) delineate a number of topics that rise and fall over time, such as energy conservation, global warming, busing, endangered species, cancer, HIV/AIDS, drugs, drunken driving, tobacco, starvation due to famine, abortion, and civil rights. They note that one challenge in campaigns is to understand and try to shape these agenda items and to cut through the cluttered set of public agenda items that compete for people's attention and understanding. This becomes a significant challenge in reaching hard-to-count populations. Below are brief descriptions of several noncensus engagement campaigns that were successful, or not successful, by applying, or not applying, some of the principles described above.

Kramer *et al.* (2013) point out two examples where the community engagement model was used as an effective tool in the public health arena. The first case is Healthy Eating Active Communities (HEAC) and the Central California Regional Obesity Prevention Program (CCROPP), which, together, pioneered multisector initiatives focused on obesity prevention in low-income, ethnically diverse communities. Community and youth engagement were instrumental to achieving a variety of recent policy and environmental change successes, such as removal of soda from school campuses, acceptance of government assistance electronic debit cards at farmers markets, and parks renovation to ensure access to physical activity opportunities. In another case, community engagement was influential in a successful campaign to improve physical education in the Los Angeles Unified School District (LAUSD), the second largest school district in the nation, serving more than 675,000 students, 90 percent of whom are students of color and three-quarters of whom qualify for free/reduced price meals. A 2007 community organizing campaign provided fliers, online videos, news articles, speakers, and other messaging that mobilized the community to become involved in improving physical education for LAUSD students. These efforts were critical to bringing the community on board and forging a diverse and effective alliance between parents, teachers, health advocates, community activists, and lawyers.

Williams and Kumanyika (2002) discuss two examples where well-intended social marketing campaigns were not effective until they tailored the message and approach to reflect the priorities and agenda of the target audience. The first example was a campaign geared toward getting normally sedentary members of the African-American community more involved in physical activity. The key was associating exercise with the cultural interest and values of the community by conducting a 5K race along the path of the old Underground Railroad in the Baltimore area. The campaign shifted its focus by incorporating an educational component of understanding the legacy and historical significance of the path of the race, and this contributed to the successful outcome of the social marketing campaign among the targeted segment. In a second example, a social marketing campaign to promote increased milk consumption among African-Americans unleashed criticism from those who asserted that higher dairy product intake is inappropriate or unnecessary for African-Americans. These critics noted that long-term health implications of low dairy product consumption may not be as unfavorable for African-Americans as would be assumed on the basis of data for Whites (Bertron, Barnard, & Mills, 1991). Therefore, the campaign had to shift its focus based on the priorities and agenda of the targeted segment.

29.4   Strategies used by other data collection organizations

Many data collection organizations employ public engagement campaign principles as the basis for reaching both the population at large and hard-to-count populations. While this chapter includes many examples from the 2010 Census conducted by the US Census Bureau, the authors are familiar with community engagement campaigns used by other statistical agencies, such as Statistics Canada, the Australian Bureau of Statistics, and Mexico's Instituto Nacional de Estadistica y Geografia (INEGI).

Statistics Canada partners with Federal government agencies, municipalities, businesses, and many cultural and ethnic organizations to help local residents understand the importance of their national census and actively participate every five years. This partnering effort is reflective of the community engagement approach advocated by Kramer *et al.* (2013) and described above. The Australian statistical agency works closely with community-based organizations to engage aboriginal populations during their national census. This effort drew upon the peer and interpersonal influence of the aboriginal population, which proved more persuasive, likeable, and appealing to other in-group aboriginal group members.

INEGI uses the following guiding principles to generate active participation by the public in their census (Instituto Nacional de Estadistica y Geografia, 2011):

(1) Deploy a massive communication campaign that includes paid advertising, public relations, and engagement with schools throughout the nation;

(2) Use all communication channels to create an awareness effect among all populations; and

(3) Ensure people hear the same census message from a variety of sources encountered in their daily lives.

INEGI used print and electronic messaging during their most recent 2010 Census in nontypical locations, such as cement bags, egg cartons, and pizza coupons. They also used social media for the first time to reach certain segments of their population. These novel approaches increase the effectiveness of the message by employing media that play off cultural values of the communities they are trying to reach and influence. Teachers became central communicators to students and their families to encourage active participation, representing virtually all elements of communications campaign principles. As noted above, high credibility is given to members and leaders of the community, and teachers are perceived by many as being key influencers in this regard, especially in their role of being entrusted with the care and educational nurturing of the community's children.

The US Census Bureau implemented an unprecedented communications campaign during the 2010 Census that incorporated paid advertising in twenty-eight languages, extensive public relations, social media, and an energetic partnership campaign with more than 257,000 local and national organizations. Nearly 4,000 partnership staff, with linguistic capabilities in 146 languages, reached deep into hard-to-count communities throughout the fifty states, the District of Columbia, and Puerto Rico. They relied on communication campaign principles to influence the general population and hard-to-count populations into active participation in their national census.

29.5 Underpinnings of the 2010 Census engagement campaign

The United States census is conducted every ten years. Public participation has declined significantly since 1970 (see Table 29.1), reaching an all-time low in 1990 (US Census Bureau, 2003). "Mail return rate" reflects the percentage of occupied housing units that returned questionnaires in time to avoid door-to-door enumeration during nonresponse follow-up. Beginning in 2000, extensive public outreach and paid advertising were introduced into the census process, helping stem previous declines. The 2010 Census experienced a slight increase in mail returns from occupied housing units, reflecting the approximately $600 million spent to conduct the Integrated Communication Campaign (US Census Bureau, 2012a). Half of that amount was spent on grass-roots community engagement through the partnership program, helping reduce the differential undercount and maintain participation among all populations residing in the US.

Increasing diversity within many nations contributes significantly to the challenge of achieving an accurate census. Immigration status, language barriers, housing disparity, poverty and economic well-being, and levels of educational attainment are all factors that are frequently at play with increasingly diverse societies.

During the 2010 Census in the United States, non-Hispanic Whites were overcounted by 0.08 percent, whereas American Indians and Alaska Natives living on reservations were undercounted by 4.9 percent. When some groups are disproportionately undercounted, policy decisions and funding allocations based on census data may not accurately reflect population reality. In short, real lives are negatively affected and marginalized if individuals or families are part of an undercounted population.

Table 29.1 *US Census mail return rates since 1970*

Census year	Mail return rate
1970	87.0%
1980	81.3%
1990	74.1%
2000	74.1%
2010	75.8%

Table 29.2 *US Census over/undercount since 1990*

Population group	1990 Over/ undercount	2000 Over/ undercount	2010 Over/ undercount
Non-Hispanic White	−0.68%	+1.13%	+0.84%
Black	−4.57%	−1.84%	−2.07%
Asian	−2.36%	+0.75%	−0.08%
American Indian on reservation	−12.22%	−0.88%	−4.88%
American Indian off reservation	−0.68%	−0.62%	+1.95%
Native Hawaiian or Pacific Islander	−2.36%	−2.12%	−1.34%
Hispanic	−4.99%	−0.71%	−1.54%
Overall census accuracy	−1.61%	+0.49%	+0.01%

29.5.1 Understand who is undercounted

Census overcount and undercount data for the past three decennial censuses in the United States are illustrated in Table 29.2 (US Census Bureau, 2012b). Percentages with positive symbols indicate an overcount, and those with negative symbols reflect an undercount. Overall, the 1990 Census experienced a 1.61 percent overall undercount, whereas both the 2000 and 2010 Censuses had slight overcounts.

From a statistical perspective, the over/undercounts experienced in 2010 are viewed as indications of a high-quality census. In previous US Censuses, particularly in 1990, some populations were undercounted as high as 12.22 percent. Though 2010 undercounts among Black, Hispanic, and American Indians living on reservations were slightly higher than in 2000, without extensive grass-roots engagement it was expected these undercounts would have been much higher.

29.5.2 Engagement efforts ("partnership") within context of overall census budget and plan

The majority of funds used to conduct censuses and surveys are operational in nature and used to develop an address frame, conduct the enumeration, and then capture the data and tabulate results. Very little proportionally is spent on outreach or communications. During the United States' Census 2000 Partnership Program, approximately 2 percent of the total census budget was spent on community outreach. Similarly, during the 2010 Census, slightly more than 2 percent of the total census budget was spent on grass-roots community outreach. Though relatively small percentages are spent on public outreach, we believe an engagement campaign is critical to an accurate census, particularly among hard-to-count populations.

The partnership and marketing plan for the US Census Bureau's Census 2000 Partnership Program was based on the rationale that conducting a complete and accurate census is dependent on the involvement of trusted and respected tribal, state, and local governments, community groups, and businesses that can persuade and motivate people to respond to the questionnaire (US Census Bureau, 1998). More than 140,000 national and local organizations partnered with the Census Bureau during Census 2000. Partner organizations and partnership specialists distributed written promotional materials and promotional items, organized activities, and supported operations, such as identifying and providing sites for Be Counted/Questionnaire Assistance Centers (BC/QAC) and enumerator testing and training sites. From October 1997, when the first partnership positions were hired, through September 2000, the Census Bureau spent approximately $142.9 million on the Partnership Program, which was approximately 2 percent of the estimated $6.5 billion allocated for the 2000 Census. At its peak, the program was staffed with 594 full-time positions, more than triple the 181 Partnership positions of 1990 (US Census Bureau, 2001).

The 2010 Census built upon the success of the 2000 Census and expanded outreach efforts to trusted community leaders seven-fold with nearly 900 professional outreach workers and 2,900 partnership assistants. Nearly 4,000 partnership staff developed partnerships with more than 257,000 local and national organizations. These organizations became active census partners and collectively contributed more than $1.3 billion in pro-bono services and promotional materials to the census effort. Total cost to the Census Bureau for this program was approximately $300 million, slightly more than 2 percent of the total 2010 Census lifecycle budget.

29.6 Structural barriers to participation

Hard-to-count populations have lower self-response rates than other populations (see Figure 29.1), as experienced during the US Census 2000 (US Census Bureau, 2003). Data collection organizations should identify why certain populations avoid self-participation and then determine strategies to overcome those barriers.

Many developed nations use a mailout/mailback methodology to conduct their national census. This methodology is less costly than traditional personal visit enumeration and studies prove that data quality is better when households complete their own form (Hansen & Taeuber, 1964; US Census Bureau, 1966). But residents without mail delivery or those who live in "hidden housing units" (e.g., separate living quarters that are not

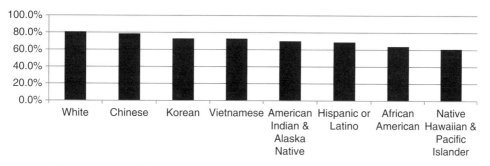

Figure 29.1   Mail Self-Response by Race/Ethnicity during U.S. Census 2000

obvious, such as add-on living quarters, rental basement units, divided homes, or garages converted into living quarters) may never receive a form. This creates a need to provide additional self-response options. Options may include the availability of census forms at public libraries, post offices, and other public gathering places, online forms, specialized outreach into neighborhoods where some housing units may not be on the master list, or phone response options. The public engagement campaign should include messaging about alternate self-response options, particularly in hard-to-count areas.

Complex household composition presents difficulties regarding who should be included on the census form, potentially affecting census coverage and accuracy. Most census forms are based on the premise of one family residing in each housing unit. On the contrary, one housing unit can often include multiple families at the same address, a mix of unrelated individuals and/or families, children that alternate living with parents that do not reside together, households with temporary college or university students, or households with temporary residents that frequently move between locations based on work or personal situations. Because most censuses ask one person to complete the form on behalf of all persons living within the housing unit (i.e., the "householder"), there can be confusion regarding who should be included on the form. Public engagement campaigns can provide information that articulates census residence rules regarding who to include on each household's form. In the 2010 US Census, specialized messaging and paid advertising were developed and targeted to individuals displaced by Hurricane Katrina to ensure they were counted where they lived during the census.

29.7   Attitudinal and other barriers to participation

Most censuses are conducted by each nation's statistical agency on behalf of the national government. In the US in recent years, favorability toward the Federal government has significantly declined, contributing to a negative view by residents toward the census. Participation in Presidential elections has also declined 10.1 percent since 1964 (US Census Bureau, 2012c). Overall public trust in government has declined from 75 percent in 1958 to less than 25 percent in 2010 (Pew Research Center for the People & the Press, 2010). This association between the Federal government and the national census creates an attitudinal barrier that inhibits participation. Identifying and communicating public benefits and tangible political rights as a result of the census are important messages to help overcome this growing negative view of government. For example, emphasizing the benefits to the community and the family, such as better schools and better community facilities, are messages that will resonate more with individuals from collectivistic cultures, which tend to be overrepresented in hard-to-count populations.

Some population groups do not want to participate in national censuses because they fear what might happen to them as a result. Recent immigrants who may or may not have legal status are particularly hesitant to participate, fearful of deportation. Others who live in overcrowded or illegal housing units may also be fearful of reporting their personal information, worried that information on their form might lead to eviction or a criminal fine. Laws governing the statistical agency's confidentiality pledge should be communicated to help alleviate these fears.

Increasing diversity also frequently means increased language diversity. In the United States, the number of persons who speak a non-English language at home increased from 23.1 million in 1980 to 57.1 million in 2010 (Shin & Ortman, 2011). The foreign-born population in the US increased nearly three-fold from 4.7 percent in 1970 to 12.9 percent in 2010 (US Census Bureau, 2012d). This means that many US residents have difficulty understanding English-based communications about the census and also have trouble understanding the English-language census form. Providing information and census forms in languages other than the nation's dominant language is critical to achieve an accurate count with full participation from all population groups.

29.8 Core strategy – engage and equip partners to motivate their constituents to participate

Considering the barriers encountered by hard-to-count populations, these groups must be motivated individually or as a community to improve participation.

Questions that may assist planners in identifying what motivates hard-to-count groups include:

(1) Are there tangible benefits that groups receive as a result of being counted?
(2) Do specific populations respond favorably or unfavorably to legal mandates?
(3) Is community empowerment a motivating factor for a population?
(4) Are there political benefits to participating?
(5) What barriers inhibit participation?
(6) Are people motivated primarily through personal or communal gain?
(7) Does it really matter if some individuals or groups do not participate in the census?

Once motivators for the general and hard-to-count populations are identified, a communication plan can be developed to deliver these motivational messages in an effective manner. In the United States, motivation is often tied to benefits resulting from an accurate count, such as better decision-making related to new retail business locations, funding for schools, public safety improvements, and transportation infrastructure improvements. Because improvements do not immediately occur after the census, it can be difficult to make a convincing argument that census participation is tied to community benefits. However, in the case of the US Census, communicating the message that more than $400 billion in federal funds is disbursed each year to states and local communities based, in part, on census data, helped make a tangible connection between being counted and the resulting benefits.

One primary strategy that helps motivate people to participate includes asking community-based organizations that already have the trust of their constituents to serve as liaisons. In short, rather than government officials functioning as the sole source of census communications, trusted community leaders and local organizations motivate their populations to be counted. We call these organizations and community leaders "census partners."

29.8.1 Multiyear campaigns by partner organizations that focus on civic engagement

Organizations that focus on civic engagement through ongoing campaigns are ideally suited to serve as census partners. Examples include organizations that focus on voter engagement, human rights, healthcare, neighborhood concerns, and educational initiatives. These organizations already work closely with populations to encourage civic involvement through a "be heard, be valued" organizational culture. For these organizations, the message can become, "The census is our next opportunity to be heard and valued as part of our organization's ongoing civic engagement campaign."

An example of this phenomenon is the multifaceted, multiplatform media messaging and direct service campaign coordinated by several national Latino organizations and Spanish-language media companies, all of which enjoy significant name and brand recognition among the US Latino immigrant population. The campaign "*ya es hora*" ("It's Time") was coordinated by the NALEO Educational Fund, the National Council of La Raza, Mi Familia Vota, SEIU (for a portion), and Univision, Entravision, and Impremedia. The campaign began in 2007 in Los Angeles as an effort to motivate large-scale numbers of legal permanent residents to apply for US citizenship.

This first component of the campaign was branded "*ya es hora CIUDADANIA!*" ("It's Time, Citizenship!"). This campaign entailed consistent messaging on television, radio, print, and online platforms about the importance of becoming a US citizen. The messaging included extensive promotion of a toll-free bilingual phone hotline and a website where individuals could receive information on where to acquire assistance in the process. Only those service organizations that agreed to a set of service delivery and quality standards were branded as "*ya es hora*" centers and received referrals from the campaign. The Los Angeles campaign proved so successful that within months it was replicated by Univision and Entravision in dozens of other media markets across the country.

The media companies incorporated the citizenship message in every component of their original programing, including morning, mid-day and evening newscasts, morning news shows, and public information programs. Once the campaign became national, the messaging was incorporated by the national Univision network in all of its original programing as well, including major entertainment weekend programs. By the end of 2007, the campaign contributed to encouraging an historic number of citizenship applications from Latin American origin immigrants.

The model proved so effective that the campaign evolved under two additional brands in 2008, "*ya es hora REGISTRATE!*" ("It's Time, Register!") and "*ya es hora VE Y VOTA!*" ("It's Time, Go and Vote!"). The campaign was credited with motivating record numbers of US citizen Latinos who consumed Spanish-language media to participate in the 2008 election cycle. The campaign continued the strategy of consistent and persistent messaging around civic engagement themes, supported by a national network of national, statewide, and local service organizations that were prepared to provide information and assistance to individuals motivated to register to vote and to vote.

In 2009, the campaign developed a fourth brand to promote the 2010 Census, *"ya es hora HAGASE CONTAR!"* ("It's Time, Make Yourself Count!"). The campaign coordinators were able to secure support from foundations to fund a broader and more extensive service network to provide information and assistance to individuals seeking to be counted in the census. After four years of a consistent drumbeat of *"ya es hora,"* the Latino Spanish-speaking immigrant community had been primed for the census message. The campaign effectively developed a desire by this population to want to be counted, and thus take the proactive steps necessary to participate in the 2010 Census, including proactively looking for a census form in the mail, calling information assistance hotlines to request forms, completing "Be Counted" forms, and other steps.

29.8.2 Partner with trusted and relevant representatives and community groups

Similar in impact to the national organizations cited above, local community-based organizations and representatives can also serve as census partners. Typically, these organizations exist to provide direct services or represent a small (or large) group of people with similar concerns. Because these organizations are usually respected by their constituents, they usually have more legitimacy and are able to call members to action. Community organizations may include groups that focus on legal assistance, housing, health services, youth associations, neighborhood councils, or immigration. Other entities that can be effective in communicating a census message include local and tribal governments, schools, and religious groups that have extensive communications networks with local residents.

The following questions may prove helpful when determining which organizations can be the most effective as census partners:

(1) Do local organization(s) exist that represent a particular hard-to-count population?
(2) Does the organization have the respect and trust of the hard-to-count group?
(3) Does the organization have easily engaged communications networks with their constituents?
(4) Does the organization have existing networks with other like-minded organizations?
(5) Can the organization be motivated to become a census partner by emphasizing a tangible benefit for constituents?

Individuals hired by the organization to conduct the community engagement campaign should be trusted by the local community and possess appropriate linguistic and cultural skills. During the 2010 Census, nearly 4,000 partnership staff were hired that collectively had linguistic skills in 146 languages. They were hired locally, trained and supervised by the Regional Census Centers, and usually had recent experience working as a volunteer or professional within the various hard-to-count communities in their assigned area. Preferred skill sets included community organizing, public speaking, event planning, or campaign management. Two of the key attributes to evaluate for each person who is hired for community mobilization include (1) whether the person is trusted by the community they will motivate and (2) whether they will be able to represent the statistical agency and census message effectively while reaching out to their own community.

29.8.3 Integrate partnership engagement with all segments of overall communications campaign

Many data collection organizations implement a multi-pronged public engagement campaign during their national census that incorporates some level of paid or donated advertising, public service announcements, public relations efforts, social media, and local partnership efforts. When multiple elements contribute to one campaign, it is critical that overall campaign timing, messaging, and emphasis are integrated so there is one consistent message given to all population groups at the right time. As campaigns become more complex with multiple moving parts, this is difficult to achieve. With potentially thousands of community-based organizations serving voluntarily as census partners, the need for consistent messaging and campaign timing is even more important.

During the 2010 Census, the US Census Bureau spent several years planning and conducting research for their Integrated Communication Campaign. This joint venture within the agency included the decennial, communications, and field directorates working closely together to map out campaign strategies, delivery vehicles, timelines, and messaging. External advisory groups participated extensively throughout the campaign and provided significant input.

The following suggestions may assist organizations in fully integrating community outreach into their overall census communications campaign:

(1) Develop a written plan that outlines all campaign elements (advertising, social media, public relations, partnership, and/or other elements) and describe how each element interfaces, compliments, and contributes to the overall campaign. Within the plan, interface with operational managers to ensure that the communications campaign is fully integrated with census operational timelines, questionnaire messaging, and recruitment operations for temporary census workers.

(2) Develop a campaign timeline that articulates each phase and what each element's role is during that phase. Include the specific role that community outreach will have during each phase.

(3) Establish a senior-level program management team that oversees the overall campaign.

(4) Identify potential risks and mitigation strategies. Manage risks and respond accordingly.

(5) Develop promotional materials for community use that reflect the national campaign's theme and "look and feel."

(6) Establish an easy-to-navigate public website designed for census partners that provides turnkey materials, such as campaign messaging, timelines, training, and promotional materials.

Organizations that agree to partner with the data collection organization do so voluntarily but need support in order to effectively engage and motivate their constituents. The data collection organization should provide promotional materials that partners can use with their constituents. Examples of promotional materials include awareness and action posters, brochures that describe why someone should be counted, youth-oriented promotional materials, public event fliers, banners, and other materials that can be used in direct engagement with populations. Materials should be created in languages that hard-to-count populations use in their daily lives and, for many societies, this will mean creating materials in multiple languages.

Partners should have access to electronic templates of promotional materials on the data collection organization's website. Partners can tailor the materials with images of the geography and populations served and insert the organization's logo and name alongside the data collection organization's name. This affords partners instant access and also permits the data collection organization to roll materials out as they are developed, avoiding long printing or mailing times. Many smaller nonprofit community organizations with limited funding increasingly rely upon the Internet (websites, email, social media apps) as a communications tool because this vehicle is less costly than using paper or mail. Examples of promotional materials from the US 2010 Census can be found at www. census.gov/2010census/partners/.

The authors are not aware of any data collection organization, particularly national statistical agencies, that "pays" organizations to become partners. The premise behind this strategy is that organizations voluntarily participate because they are motivated to make sure their population groups are accurately counted. But in some instances, the data collection organization may be able to provide some form of tangible support beyond the usual census posters and printed literature that helps partner organizations effectively reach their constituents. During the 2000 and 2010 Censuses, the US Census Bureau used limited funds to purchase organization-specific promotional materials for organizations that served hard-to-count populations. This "Partner Support Program" permitted the Census Bureau to purchase up to $3,000 of specialized promotional materials for qualified partner organizations as long as the purchased materials were specifically for census promotion. Though difficult to administer, and with a ceiling on the amount of available funds, this program did provide needed help to organizations that could not otherwise have effectively promoted the census among their constituents. Some organizations received specialized street banners, printed promotional materials, online videos, event handouts, and door-to-door flyers that promoted the census within their communities. Many of these materials were created in non-English languages.

Although the data collection organization may not be in a position to become a grant-making organization (legally or otherwise), it is possible that established grant-making organizations may adopt the nation's census as an important project for support. During the 2000 and 2010 US censuses, several philanthropic organizations adopted the census and provided a mechanism to provide direct funding to partner organizations. In 2000, the State of California committed $24.7 million to statewide outreach through community organizations and the mail return in California experienced a significant increase over expectations (State of California, 2001). In 2010, several large philanthropic organizations such as the Joyce Foundation, Bill and Melinda Gates Foundation, and the Ford Foundation provided grant assistance totaling $35.9 million to organizations that served minorities, children, and other populations to actively promote the census (Crews, 2011). In each of these instances, the Census Bureau provided technical information to the donor agencies about the census process, but did not get involved with the grant-making process.

29.8.4 Making partnerships actionable

An engagement campaign is much different than an awareness campaign. An awareness campaign simply raises people's awareness with the hope that this new or revitalized knowledge will change how they think or motivate them to do something. An engagement campaign goes beyond awareness and has a "call to action." In the case of the US Census, the action is simple and clear – fill out your census form and mail it back. Census public engagement campaigns often include three phases: (1) raise public awareness that the census is coming and why it's important; (2) heighten motivation to participate (self-response); and, (3) urge cooperation with door-to-door interviewers during the nonresponse follow-up phase. Canada, Mexico, Australia, and the United States rely on these phases to engage their populations during their national censuses.

The authors suggest that planners identify actionable activities to engage their populations. For example, community partners can communicate the importance of the upcoming census in sermons or publicize locations where constituents can receive help completing their forms (i.e., questionnaire assistance centers). Survey sponsors should specify whether organizations should send emails, write letters, make speeches, knock on doors, hold festivals, talk to other leaders, or make phone calls. Determining a simple action campaign helps organizations tailor the campaign to their constituents.

The best action example we can think of during the US 2010 Census is the "National March to the Mailbox" campaign. During this event, 25,000 partner organizations mobilized approximately 300,000 volunteers in 6,000 pre-identified hard-to-count census tracts literally to march in neighborhoods, shouting out to their neighbors to "fill it out and mail it back." Live news coverage dominated this event throughout the nation and more than 900 local news stories were written or aired covering this national event taking place in local neighborhoods. On April 10, 2010, census parades and action marches took place in some of the US's most difficult-to-enumerate neighborhoods. Each march carried the same large census banner, wore the same white t-shirts with red census lettering, and carried the same signage urging people to mail their forms back. Marchers used air horns to announce their presence and shouted census chants to drive home their message. Between April 10 and April 19, 2010, there was a 4.8 percent increase in the official mail return rate, saving US taxpayers approximately $408 million in nonresponse follow-up costs (US Census Bureau, 2012a). While there were many other contributing factors that helped increase the mail return during this period (such as continued paid advertising), the localized publicity generated by March to the Mailbox reminded millions of people that it was not too late to fill out and return their form (Morello, 2010).

As mentioned earlier, it is important to have a risk mitigation strategy in case negative publicity surfaces that could decrease participation in the data collection. Because most censuses affect national politics and funding decisions, census activities are highly scrutinized and public relations crises can affect public perception and self-response. While the data collection organization must own and respond actively to each publicity crisis, it can be helpful to engage key census partners to address the crisis publicly. Throughout the US 2010 Census, several issues emerged that threatened to derail the census and negatively affect self-response, including the Evangelical Hispanic census boycott, the "Gay the Census" campaign, and the use of "Negro" on the census form. In each of these situations, key census partners became conduits to respond publicly to the crisis in ways that the Census Bureau could not. National partners responded to the Evangelical Hispanic census boycott by rallying census supporters to denounce the boycott and urge census participation within the Hispanic community. During the "Gay the Census" campaign, national and local lesbian, gay, bisexual, and transgender (LGBT) leaders used this campaign to urge LGBT participation in the census (Our Families Count, 2010). One politically sensitive anticensus campaign emerged when those opposed to the US President linked a national census partner, Association of Community Organizations for Reform Now (ACORN), to the 2010 Census, claiming the census would be used to promote the President's agenda at the expense of other political parties. In this instance, several influential national census partners with ties to both political parties countered this threat by expressing strong support for the 2010 Census and helping the Census Bureau publicly end its partnership with ACORN (*New York Times*, 2009).

29.8.5 Continue partnerships after the census

Once census activities conclude, it is helpful to thank organizations that made public cooperation possible. Delivering thank you certificates, distributing online thank you videos, and providing insights into data products are great ways to thank partner organizations. Maintaining relationships with partners after the census is important. Use of email and social media to announce census data releases, data collection job opportunities, and data presentations can be a powerful tool to keep the relationships alive. Use of virtual meeting technology permits subject matter experts from the data collection organization to conduct data information meetings with large audiences located remotely.

Involving partners in planning for the next census helps them stay informed and engaged. Some partners may agree to serve as official members of the organization's advisory committee. Asking for help communicating about ongoing surveys in specific geographic areas through organizational newsletters, websites, and other communication methods can also help partner organizations stay involved between censuses.

29.9 Summary

Motivating hard-to-count populations to participate in a national census or survey can be achieved through an active engagement campaign that engages trusted leaders and community organizations. This chapter summarized current literature explaining principles of community engagement campaigns, provided examples from noncensus campaigns, illustrated the US Census Bureau's experience in community mobilization during the 2000 and 2010 Censuses, and described the National Association of Latino Elected and Appointed Officials' experience in mobilizing the Latino population during the 2010 Census.

We recommend that community engagement campaigns be built around three phases:

Awareness – Action – Appreciation

When planning and implementing a community mobilization designed to engage and motivate hard-to-reach populations we suggest:

(1) Give careful consideration to the *identification and selection* of partners;
(2) Inform partners about action phase plans and activities at the *beginning of the campaign*;
(3) Provide *simplified materials* that are clear, compelling, and relevant;
(4) Where appropriate, provide *carefully translated in-language* materials;
(5) *Manage expectations* between partner organizations and the data collection organization.

References

Atkin, C. K. (2001). Theory and principles of media health campaigns. In R. E. Rice, & C. K. Atkin (eds.), *Public Communication Campaigns* (3rd edn.) (pp. 49–68). Thousand Oaks, CA: Sage Publications.

Bertron, P., Barnard, N. D., & Mills, M. (1991). Racial bias in federal nutrition policy, part I: The public health implications of variations in lactase persistence. *Journal of the National Medical Association*, 91(3), 151–57.

Crews, K. (2011). *Philanthropic Support for 2010 Census*. Washington, DC: Funders Census Initiative. Retrieved from www.funderscommittee.org/files/2__Overview_of_Grants_Awarded_by_Kim_Crews-_final.pdf.

Han, S., & Shavitt, S. (1994). Persuasion and culture: advertising appeals in individualistic and collectivistic societies. *Journal of Experimental Social Psychology*, 30(4), 326–50.

Hansen, M., & Taeuber, C. (1964). A preliminary evaluation of the 1960 Censuses of population and housing. *Demography*, 1(1), 1–14.

Instituto Nacional de Estadistica y Geografia. (2011). INEGI's 2010 Census communications campaign. *13th International Regional Directors Conference*, Miami, FL.

Kramer, K., Schwarte, L., Lafleur, M., & Williams, J. D. (2013). Targeting marketing of junk food to ethnic minority youth: fighting back with legal advocacy community empowerment. In J. D. Williams, K. E. Pasch, & C. Collins (eds.), *Advances in*

Communication Research to Reduce Childhood Obesity (pp. 389–405). New York: Springer.

Morello, C. (2010, April 10). Census volunteers will pile on the pressure Saturday. *Washington Post*. Retrieved from the *Washington Post*: www.washingtonpost.com/wp-dyn/content/article/2010/04/09/AR2010040902745.html.

National Association of Latino Elected and Appointed Officials Educational Fund. (2003). *Community Empowerment Project – Voter Engagement Focus Groups Supporting Voces del Pueblo Program*. Los Angeles, CA: author.

New York Times. (2009, September 11). Census Drops ACORN From 2010 Effort. Retrieved from www.nytimes.com/2009/09/12/us/politics/12acorn.html.

Our Families Count. (2010). Census 2010 – Lesbian, Gay, Bisexual, and Transgender Visibility. Retrieved from http://ourfamiliescount.org/.

Paisley, W. (2001). Public communication campaigns: the American experience. In R. E. Rice, & C. K. Atkin (eds.), *Public Communication Campaigns* (pp. 3–21). Thousand Oaks, CA: Sage Publications.

Pew Research Center for the People & the Press. (2010). *Public Trust in Government: 1958–2010*. Retrieved from www.people-press.org/2010/04/18/public-trust-in-government-1958–2010.

Rice, R. E., & Atkin, C. K. (2013). Theory and principles of public communication campaigns. In R. E. Rice, & C. E. Atkin (eds.), *Public Communication Campaigns* (4th edn.) (pp. 3–19). Thousand Oaks, CA: Sage Publications.

Shin, H. B., & Ortman, J. M. (2011). *Language Projections: 2010–2020*. Paper presented at the Federal Forecasters Conference. Washington, DC. Retrieved from www.census.gov/hhes/socdemo/language/data/acs/Shin_Ortman_FFC2011_paper.pdf.

State of California. (2001). *Counting All Californians: An Analysis of Outreach Effectiveness*, ed. S. Maria Contreras-Sweet. Retrieved from California Business, Transportation, and Housing Agency: www.sdcbidc.iupui.edu/sharing/ccc.html.

US Census Bureau. (1966). *1960 Censuses of Population and Housing – Procedural History*. Washington, DC: US Government Printing Office.

(1998). *Census 2000 Partnership and Marketing Program Master Plan*. Retrieved from www.census.gov/dmd/www/pdf/operational2000.pdf.

(2001). *2000 Census Review of Partnership Program Highlights for Best Practices for Future Operations*. Retrieved from www.census.gov/procur/www/2010communications/library.html.

(2003). *Census 2000 Mail Return Rates*. Retrieved from www.census.gov/pred/www/rpts/A.7.b.pdf.

(2012a). *2010 Census Mail Response/Return Rates Assessment Report*. Retrieved from www.census.gov/2010census/pdf/2010_Census_Mail_Response_Return_Rates_Assessment.pdf.

(2012b). *2010 Census Coverage Measurement Results*. Retrieved from http://2010.census.gov/news/pdf/20120512_ccm_newsconf_slides.pdf.

(2012c). *Voting and Registration*. Retrieved from www.census.gov/hhes/www/socdemo/voting/index.html.

(2012d). *The Foreign Born Population in the United States: 2010*. Retrieved from www.census.gov/newsroom/releases/pdf/20120512_foreignborn_webinar_slides.pdf.

Williams, J. D., & Henderson, G. R. (2012). Discrimination and injustice in the marketplace: they come in all sizes, shapes, and colors. In D. Mick, S. Pettigrew, C. Pechmann, & J. Ozanne (eds.), *Transformative Consumer Research for Personal and Collective Well Being: Reviews and Frontiers* (pp. 171–89). Boca Raton, FL: Taylor & Francis Group.

Williams, J. D., & Kumanyika, S. K. (2002). Is social marketing an effective tool to reduce health disparities? *Social Marketing Quarterly*, 8(4), 14–31.

Williams, J. D., & Qualls, W. J. (1989). Middle-class black consumers and intensity of ethnic identification. *Psychology and Marketing*, 6(4), 263–86.

Williams, J., & Tharp, M. (2002). African Americans: ethnic roots, cultural diversity. In M. Tharp (ed.), *Marketing and Consumer Identity in Multicultural America* (pp. 165–211). Thousand Oaks, CA: Sage Publications.

30

Finding the hard to reach and keeping them engaged in research

KIRSTEN BECKER, SANDRA H. BERRY, NATE ORR, AND
JUDY PERLMAN

30.1 Introduction

Many types of survey respondents are difficult to access, to locate, and (in longitudinal research) to stay in contact with throughout the course of a study. These types of respondents fall into two main categories. The first category includes people who are difficult to reach by nature, such as young adults whose lives are in transition, the mentally ill, the homeless, and drug users. These population groups are extremely mobile and, in some cases, less likely to maintain close ties with relatives who might serve as a means of locating or contacting them. The second category includes people who are consciously avoiding being located in an attempt to avoid contact with the justice system, immigration authorities, debt collectors, stalkers, or others. People falling into either of these two categories may lack fixed addresses, or be "cell phone only," with episodic cell service and numbers that change frequently, or list residences or phones in the name of another person.

The hardest subjects to reach in a target population group might provide fundamentally different responses than members of the group who are relatively easier to find and survey (Groves, Fowler, Couper, Lepkowski, Singer, & Tourangeau, 2004). Not including certain segments of a population leads to nonresponse bias, which threatens the quality of survey statistics and the validity and generalizability of research findings (Cottler, Compton, Ben-Abdallah, Horne, & Claverie, 1996). The goal of maximizing power and minimizing potential nonresponse becomes even more difficult when the study population by definition is hard to reach. Researchers face a trifecta of challenges to data reliability when such studies are longitudinal: maximizing power, minimizing systematic nonresponse, and maintaining the respondent pool over time. Tracking efforts can minimize these threats by maximizing participation among sample members (Brown & Nederend, 1997), minimizing nonresponse among respondents with certain characteristics or reflecting sample subpopulations (Teitler, Reichman, & Sprachman, 2003), and reducing subject attrition in research requiring multiple waves of data collection (Cottler *et al.*, 1996).

In this chapter, we will outline methods for locating hard-to-reach respondents, including online resources, public records searches, mail techniques, phone lookups, calling third-party

The authors would like to acknowledge and thank Julie Brown, Director of RAND's Survey Research Group, for her insightful review of chapter drafts and for her expert consult and guidance.

contacts, and field techniques. These techniques could be applied to difficult cases in a list-based sample or to individuals lost in the course of follow-up on a longitudinal study. Next, we discuss techniques used to stay in touch and minimize attrition over time such as interim contacts, monetary and in-kind incentives, social media, newsletters, and establishment of a field office. Finally, we present a framework of factors to consider to help guide researchers in selecting the most effective and efficient tracking protocol for their particular research effort. These considerations include knowledge of the study population, appropriate staffing and training, budget and cost, project timeline and number of follow-up waves, and human subjects issues. Since each targeted research group has different tendencies and traits, and study designs vary so widely, it would be imprudent to advocate for a "one-size-fits-all" approach to tracking. Our goal in this chapter is to provide a set of considerations that will help researchers make effective choices about tracking methods that are most practical and effective for particular target groups and research objectives given timeline and budgetary considerations.

30.2   Strategies for locating respondents

Generally, tracking and locating protocols for hard-to-reach populations need to be multi-pronged and multilayered. It is unlikely that a single strategy will be sufficient in locating respondents. Strategies should be used in concert and ordered in a thoughtful population-specific way. Survey researchers typically approach tracking with a cost vs. yield approach, starting with the cheapest methods and then working outward so that most expensive strategies are used for the smallest number of cases. It is suggested that projects start with the easiest cases – those that can be located quickly with one of the free or low-cost strategies described below, such as vendor address/phone matching or national change of address records. Cases that are not located via these mechanisms should then be tried using a strategy that is more moderate in cost, such as case-by-case searching in databases such as Lexis Nexis, leaving only the most difficult cases to try using the more expensive strategies, such as field tracking. Another strategy might be to start by identifying cases that will be noncompletes. For example, particularly in high mortality groups, it might be prudent to spend time during the pre-field period searching the Social Security Death Index to identify deceased cases in order to limit time and money spent tracking them with higher-cost efforts such as phone or field attempts. If the project timeline is short, the researchers might not have the luxury of working step-by-step and might choose to work in a model where multiple low and moderate cost activities are performed simultaneously in order to favor saving time in the tradeoff with reducing costs.

Table 30.1 lists some of the possible methods that might be used to locate individuals either for a single wave study or a longitudinal one. Costs vary over time and are dependent on institutional rates and structures, study population, sample size, and geography. It is difficult to associate a specific dollar amount to each tracking method. We have categorized the cost of these methods into free, low, moderate, or high.

Table 30.1 *Summary of strategies for locating respondents*

Method	Cost	Access	Relevant populations	Resources
Address and phone updating				
Online free records searches	Free	Public	All	Broad search engines such as Google and person-locator specific sites such as www.pipl.com, www.spokeo.com, or www.whitepages.com.
Address service requested	Free	Public	All	Printed on outgoing mail. Updated address is returned through the post office.
National address server	Free	Public	All	Partial/incomplete addresses can be searched at www.cedar.buffalo.edu/adserv.html.
United States Postal Services National Change of Address database (NCOA)	Free/Low	Public, but account required with vendor	All	Accessed through vendors only. A list of approved vendors is available from the United States Postal Services at www.nationalchangeofaddress.com/.
Online paid records searches	Low	Account required; access varies by sector and purpose	All	Paid record searches include Lexis Nexis and Intelius. Additionally, credit information can be searched using Equifax or Experian.
Vendor address/phone matching and crisscross directories	Low	Public, but account required with vendor	All	Phone appending, address matching, reverse directory look-ups, adjacent address/phone info. Can be conducted by numerous companies such as Relevate, Haines & Company, Crisscross & Woodard Information Services.
411/Directory assistance	Low	Public	All	Listed phone numbers can be searched by dialing 411. Also available online.
Administrative and vital records				
Jail and prison searches	Free	Public and online in most states and many counties	Probationers and parolees, substance users, gang involved, homeless	The Federal Bureau of Prisons, Vinelink.com, County Sheriff's websites, State Department of Corrections websites and inmate locators.

Table 30.1 (*cont.*)

Method	Cost	Access	Relevant populations	Resources
Death records and obituaries	Free	Public	All, particularly high mortality groups	Social Security Death Index (SSDI), Obitfinder, www.legacy.com.
Other vital records (marriages, divorces, births)	Free in some states and low in others	Varies by state, often public	All	Local or State Departments of Health, Department of Vital Statistics websites, www.vitalrec.com, online genealogy searches, such as www.ancestry.com or www.ancestorhunt.com.
Administrative records (e.g. DMV, court records, voter registration)	Free in some states and low in others	Varies by state, often public	All	State Department of Motor Vehicles, County Registrar, or County Courthouses.
Other methods				
Social media	Free	Public	All	Facebook, Twitter, Tumblr, MySpace, LinkedIn, etc.
Calling third-party contacts	Moderate	Public	All, particularly young adults in transition, homeless	Calls to family, friends, or known service providers.
Field tracking	High	Public	All, particularly substance abusers, mentally ill, homeless	In-person field visits.
Private investigators	High	Public	All	Hiring a professional private detective to track respondents.
Building community relationships	High	Public	Substance abusers, victims of domestic violence, homeless	Establishing and maintaining contacts at known local service providers, such as shelters, group homes, and treatment facilities.

Note: The examples mentioned here are resources the authors have used over time. Inclusion as an example in this table does not indicate endorsement. Examples provided in this table are valid as of the writing of this chapter and may change over time.

- Generally speaking, "free" methods make use of public information available for no cost. However, many of these methods require individuals to be searched one-by-one, case-by-case rather than in batch mode, so investment of staff time could be significant if the "hit rate" is low or the sample size very large. Still, these methods produce information very quickly that could lead to the individual and do not require staff with highly specialized skills.

- "Low"-cost methods typically allow searching in batches for a fee and can be done quickly within a day or two. There can be fairly high yield in a short period of time.

- "Moderate" costs are attributed to those methods which would be done on a case-by-case basis and might involve staff time, but it is time that could be done in the office as a centralized activity, often by phone or online. Staff typically need special skills in building rapport, explaining the study, and maintaining confidentiality. Outside of staff time, there is little operational cost to these methods. Generally, it will take some time to yield results.

- "High"-cost methods are activities like field tracking that require investment in staff with a special skill set, staff time, and a generous timeline to allow for multiple visits and rapport building, mileage, and training costs.

The third column of Table 30.1 describes the access level or availability of using each method of tracking. Access to many of these records varies by state and/or purpose of the search. The fourth column highlights the populations each method might be most relevant to. The final column of the table provides a short description and, where possible, some examples of applicable websites, offices, or organizations.

The most effective method for hard-to-reach populations will vary by population, geography, staff skills, and respondent characteristics. The evidence for success of these strategies alone or in various combinations and orders has been largely anecdotal and experiential, passed down within organizations as part of the institutional knowledge. While there is descriptive literature around tracking strategies, especially for certain populations like the homeless or substance users, there has been little empirical evidence (to our knowledge) testing the outcomes of various tracking protocols and methods within specific hard-to-reach populations. Table 30.2 lists some specific hard-to-reach populations and tracking strategies that have been employed in cross-sectional studies and longitudinal studies with relative success. What is clear in the literature is that while vendor look-ups and online resources can be very useful in improving contact rates, for hard-to-reach populations, researchers should expect that at least a portion of cases will require moderate and high-cost tracking strategies. For groups that are sometimes considered the most difficult to locate, such as the homeless or the seriously mentally ill, substantial investment in high-cost activities, such as field tracking and building community relationships will be necessary for successful locating.

For longitudinal projects, authors are clear that respondent-provided re-contact information is the most important resource for success. Section 30.3 discusses collection of re-contact information as well as other strategies for staying in touch and minimizing attrition over the course of a longitudinal study.

Table 30.2 *Strategies used with certain hard-to-reach groups*

Population	Strategies	Sample reference
Young adults in transition	• Mailings with address service requested • Contacts to parent, family, friends • Online database look-ups • Social media	McCuller, Sussman, Holiday, Craig, & Dent (2002)
Low-income/ public assistance	• CD-ROM phone and address directory • Vendor phone matching • Calls to neighbors identified in criss-cross directories	Brown & Nederend (1997)
Victims of sexual assault	• Vendor look-ups for updated address • Building relationships with DV shelters • Contacts to parent, family, friends	Rumptz, Sullivan, Davidson, & Basta (1991)
Criminal justice	• Jail and prison searches • Building relationships with parole, probation, other facilities • Contacts to family/friends	Edelen, Slaughter, McCaffrey, Becker, & Morral (2010) Menendez, White, & Tulsky (2001)
Homeless	• Building relationships with homeless shelters • Local field office • Field tracking	Cohen, Mowbray, Bybee, Yeich, Ribisl, & Freddolino (1993)
Substance users	• Online searching of public records including jails/prisons and death records • Contacts to family/friends • Building relationships with treatment facilities • Building a presence and "face" in the local drug markets • Field tracking	Cepeda, & Valdez (2010) Corsi, Van Hunnik, Kwiatkowski, & Booth (2006)

30.3   Strategies for staying in touch for longitudinal studies

With longitudinal studies, attrition is of primary concern, particularly when the studies involve hard-to-reach and highly mobile populations. In such studies, the researcher has the opportunity to be proactive to minimize the need for intensive tracking and maximize contact and completion rates (Burgess, 1989).

   The methods described in this section will not alone solve the problem of "lost" respondents. Tracking strategies must be employed in combinations with creativity, reactivity, and thoughtfulness all with an eye to building rapport with the respondents. Maintaining contact throughout the entire study period and remaining "present" to the respondent through positive interactions which instill trust and demonstrate respect and appreciation is essential. These begin with the study management and design of the study, as well as the interactions within the community, the hiring and training of interviewers, and the availability of and willingness to provide information about the study. Also essential is the demonstration to the sample population that the project staff understands the importance of protecting confidentiality both in verbal communication and through their actions. Coen, Patrick, and Shern (1996) indicate that conveying the importance of the research, the value of continued participation, and respect for the respondents through verbal communications and staff actions are key.

The following section discusses some of the many strategies for staying in touch over the course of a longitudinal study including:

- Respondent provided re-contact information;
- Incentives and reminder gift items;
- Interim contacts;
- Social media;
- Newsletters;
- A field office, toll-free number, study website;
- Providing phone cards, cell phones, or other devices; and
- Study branding.

All tracking efforts should be carefully documented in a tracking system or database in order to make best use of information gleaned and maximize utility of efforts. A tracking database can allow for tracking case status, housing and allowing access to contact information from all sources, triggering of interim contacts or other project activities, and provision of easy access to operational and production reports (Hunt & White, 1998).

30.3.1 The re-contact form: the respondent as the source of information

Perhaps our best resource for minimizing attrition for follow-up interviews with hard-to-reach populations is the respondent him or herself. Researchers have the opportunity at the baseline interaction (and at every follow-up wave or interaction) to ask directly for contact information and for permission to use it for locating at follow-up.

The re-contact form almost certainly should ask for full name, date of birth, home address, phone, cell, email, workplace (if applicable) and job title, work address and phone. With permission from a research ethics review board, it is also important to ask for contact information for two or more individuals who will best know how to reach the respondent. For each contact person, name, relationship to the respondent, phone, cell phone, address, and email should be collected. For certain populations, additional questions might include the following: any aliases, nicknames, hangouts, check cashing locations, service providers, parole or probation officers, regular treatment locations, administrative records ID, military ID number, social security number (SSN), and use of social networking sites like Facebook or Twitter. If a respondent is unable to provide exact contact information, interviewers should collect whatever information is available. For example, in developing countries, rural areas of the US, or in homeless encampments, participants may be unable to provide an address, but they may be able to describe how to get to the contact address, draw a map, or offer a description (Hill, 2004). Think creatively and ask the respondent for any key contact data that might be useful in locating him/her at follow-up.

For some populations, like the homeless or parole violators, photographs might even be useful. On a study with homeless women in Los Angeles that was directed by the author, 77 percent consented to a photo at baseline. These photos were included in field tracker assignment sheets and were used to help confirm identity when a respondent was located and help prevent the situation where a nonrespondent claimed to be the woman in question in order to earn the incentive amount. Photos could also be presented at shelters and meal lines to gather locating information from facility staff who might know that woman only by a street name.

The amount of re-contact information collected might vary depending on the anticipated difficulty of follow-up, the amount of time available to elicit information from a respondent, and other sensitivities. In general, the more information collected the better. The number of unique contacts that researchers collect matters. Anecdotally, we saw this confirmed on a recent study (Community Partners in Care conducted by RAND in partnership with UCLA, Healthy African-American Families, and QueensCare) in which clients were screened for depression at social service agencies and transitional housing. If eligible, individuals were asked to complete a contact form with full name, date of birth, gender, preferred language, address, two personal phone numbers, email address, and information for two people who would know how to reach the respondent. The interviewer reviewed the contact form on the spot for completeness and legibility and probed for more complete information. Interviewers were trained to try to get four different contacts for each participant. Respondents were then contacted by phone for interview. Response rates varied dramatically by the number of phone numbers that were collected on the contact form. While we were able to complete interviews with 53 percent of respondents who provided no phone numbers on the contact form, we achieved an 88 percent response rate with individuals who provided four (or more) phone numbers. Of course, the quantity and number of contact numbers might also be an indication of the traits of the participant or their life, resulting in their being more difficult or easier to find.

Researchers might encounter reluctance to provide contact information. Generally, reluctance stems from concerns about confidentiality and how the information will be used. Respondents should be informed that they will be tracked. Without this information, respondents and those who are contacted might be surprised, suspicious, and upset by tracking efforts (Hill, 2004). If a respondent is made aware that the information is for study follow up and a monetary incentive will be provided for future participation, then it is more likely they will be cooperative (Grandone & Moritz, 2010).

Respondents are not always the ones hesitant about providing contact information. Sometimes interviewers are reluctant to ask for contact information, perhaps fearing damage to rapport or being seen as "pushy." However, this is an essential skill for interviewers to develop. Interviewer confidence, experience, and attitudes have been demonstrated to be associated with respondent participation rates (Durrant, Groves, Staetsky, & Steele, 2010) and, similarly, it has been the authors' experience that new interviewers are especially reluctant to probe for more contacts. This can then affect a project's ability to contact sample members for follow-up, particularly in the first cohort due for follow-up. Role plays eliciting contact information during training provide practice for the interviewer. Continued feedback from the supervisor at team meetings regarding average numbers of contacts collected by interviewers can motivate the interviewers to gather more information.

30.3.2 Incentives and gift items

The effectiveness of incentives in improving response rates is well documented. Numerous studies and experiments have been conducted to assess the impact of varying amounts of payment, timing of payment (pre- vs. post-survey completion), and mode of payment (cash vs. gift, number and denomination of currency in a cash incentive, use of a lottery) including experiments involving the hard to reach (Singer & Kulka, 2002). Research ethics review boards may have particular rules regarding provision of incentives as a tool to promote participation in hard-to-reach populations. For example, some may limit or prohibit the payment of cash to certain populations (the homeless, known drug users, individuals receiving public assistance), requiring an incentive in the form of a food voucher or gift card. In this chapter, we focus on the use of incentives as a tool to keep hard-to-reach populations engaged in a study over time.

In-kind incentives

In-kind incentives labeled with the study logo, name, and a toll-free number can be a useful way to "brand" the study for respondents and keep them in touch with the study. Examples include pens, refrigerator magnets, personal hygiene kits, healthy child kits, and other items printed with the study name, logo, and toll-free number. The appropriateness of each type of incentive will vary by population. A magnet can be useful for studies of families or households, a personal hygiene kit is appreciated by respondents who are homeless, a kit of items to promote child health can be useful for a study of children or mothers. The goal is to provide an item that is useful to respondents that they will be likely to keep and use and that reminds them of the study and how to keep in contact. Additionally, these items can help develop rapport and good will by both providing something useful while indicating to respondents that the project understands their particular needs (Gregory, Lohr, & Gilchrist, 1992; Hough, Tarke, Renker, Shields, & Glatstein, 1996; Marmor, Oliveria, Donahue, Garrahie, White, Moore, *et al.*, 1991). Willimack, Schuman, Pennell, and Lepkowski (1995) conducted an experiment where half of the sample addresses in the Detroit Annual Survey were mailed a gift pen with the pre-notification letter for a face-to-face interview while half were mailed no gift item. The total incremental additional cost for the pen

(pen plus postage) was $3.98. The Pen group had a 5 percent higher response rate over the No Pen group, showing an apparent increase in willingness in the Pen group. Additionally, nonviable addresses were confirmed at a higher rate in the Pen group; one theory to explain this difference is the increased likelihood of mail carriers to return to sender larger mailing envelopes with more substantial contents (the pen).

Progressive incentives

As evidenced by Singer, Groves, and Corning (1999), it is not necessary to pay a large incentive for the first interview in a longitudinal study. What can be useful is communicating an incentive schedule that increases the incentive for subsequent waves of data collection ($10 for the first interview, $20 for the second, and $30 for the third). There is no substitute for building rapport with study participants but provision of a progressive incentive can minimize attrition.

Additional incentives

A tool the authors commonly use in studies of adolescents, the homeless, and other hard-to-reach populations is providing an additional incentive for respondents who initiate contact prior to the next wave of data collection. Most multiwave studies provide respondents with an appointment reminder card noting the month and year of their next interview. The authors include the reminder that contacting the study to schedule an interview prior to the date noted on the card will result in an additional incentive (ranging from $2 to $5) (Couper & Ofstedal, 2009; Wright, Lampton Allen, & Devine, 1995). Another strategy might be incentivizing the number of third parties or other contacts the respondent provides with confirmed valid contact information (e.g. $5 per third-party contact provided).

30.3.3 Interim contacts

If the interval between interviews is substantial and/or the risk of mobility is high, then investing in between-interview contacts can be essential. Interim contacts can be done in multiple modes; most of the literature we reviewed that involved longitudinal research with a difficult population employed one or more mechanisms for staying in touch between waves (Cepeda & Valdez, 2010; Gwadz & Rotheram-Borus, 1992; Leonard, Lester, Rotheram-Borus, Mattes, Gwadz, & Ferns, 2003; Rumptz, Sullivan, Davidson, & Basta, 1991; Scott, 2004). Staying in touch by mail, email, phone, social networking, or even text message serves three purposes. First, it serves as an opportunity point to update contact information for the respondent and their third-party contacts. Secondly, it allows early identification of "problem" or "lost" cases via returned mail, undeliverable emails, and disconnected phone numbers. And, lastly, but certainly not least important, is the additional opportunity for relationship and rapport-building with the respondent. Interim contact efforts can be low-cost/effort, such as mail or email, or high-cost/effort, such as field visits, but either way, it is sometimes more cost-effective in the long run to invest the effort in the intersurvey period when contact information is more up to date than wait for follow-up when contact information is old and more intensive tracking will be required (Burgess, 1989).

Interim contacts can include:

- Regular activities, such as monthly letters/calls or quarterly newsletters to respondents;
- Event-related contacts, such as mailing of birthday or holiday cards;
- Opportunity-related contacts, such as visits to respondents (for example, when they are re-incarcerated);
- Scheduled activities at intervals between waves – for example, at six months if the first follow-up interview is scheduled at one year post-baseline; and
- Targeted efforts for those most likely to need tracking at future waves – for example, cases with previously disconnected phone numbers, previously returned mail, or cases with bounced back emails.

Fumagalli, Laurie, and Lynn (2013) recently tested several methods for updating address records between survey waves. Individuals in the British Health Panel Survey were randomized to one of three conditions: (1) asking only those individuals who have moved to return a provided change-of-address card, (2) asking only those individuals who have moved to update the project of changes to address without provision of an update card, and (3) asking all individuals to provide confirmation of address via an address-confirmation card. The authors found that provision of a change of address card with a conditional incentive upon return of the card upon move was both the most effective and the most cost-effective method for reducing the number of cases not found at follow-up.

The frequency and scope of interim contacts will be largely dependent on the mobility and difficulty of the population, the interval between waves, and on the budget. In order to allocate tight resources best, another option to consider would be scheduling interim contacts and tailoring materials for the most difficult cases who are most likely to be lost at follow-up.

30.3.4 Social media

Social media includes a broad range of Internet communication tools: chat forums, blogs, wikis, podcasts, content communities (e.g., YouTube, Pinterest), social networking services, gaming communities (e.g., World of Warcraft), and virtual or simulated communities (e.g., Second Life). These services allow individuals with shared interests to communicate, share contact, or interact via the Internet. In this chapter, we focus on one form of social media – social networking services – and its use as a tool for staying in touch with respondents in longitudinal studies.

Social networking services (SNS) provide a means for users to communicate with friends and family, and find individuals with similar interests. There are dozens of SNS sites but five more commonly used sites include Facebook, Twitter, LinkedIn, MySpace, and Google+ (eBizMBA, 2012). Of course, access to these networks will vary by population, but these sorts of accounts are often more stable than address, phone, and work contacts, and stay with respondents through multiple moves. Homeless youth, for example, often use Facebook (Young & Rice, 2011). Use of SNS is still an emerging and developing tool for reaching out to respondents, but several studies have demonstrated its usefulness as a tool to minimize sample attrition (Rhodes & Marks, 2011). One site in the Longitudinal Studies of Child Abuse and Neglect (LONGSCAN) consortium found follow-up using Facebook and MySpace identified profiles for 23 percent of young adult subjects not located through mailings and public Internet searches; 20 percent of these subjects then agreed to participate, reducing the overall number of subjects lost to attrition by 4.6 percent (Nwadiuko, Isbell, Zolotor, Hussey, & Kotch, 2011).

Ways in which SNS are used to keep in touch with respondents include:

- Direct communication (nonpublic messages) to respondents including those who cannot be located at address or telephone number of record;
- Direct communication (nonpublic messages) to a contact previously identify by the respondent; and
- Obtaining updated contact information on respondents through public posting of city of residence, email address, or even phone number.

SNS can also be used to create an identity for or publicize a longitudinal study through the creation of a study-specific Facebook page or Twitter account to update respondents and post reminders of upcoming data collection. Additionally, these pages can provide a means for respondents to communicate with the project directly (nonpublic communication) about changes in location or contact information. Because social media and social networking sites are an emerging method for respondent contact, there are no best practices or common standards for its use within the social science and public policy research community. This creates some ambiguity in how best to communicate with respondents using SNS tools. What is clear is that all communication with respondents via SNS should be private (e.g., email, direct messaging) not public (e.g., posting to a public comment page or wall) and that study staff should not engage in a social relationship with respondents by "friending" or "following" them on SNS sites.

30.3.5 Maintaining a field office, project toll-free number, study website

As important as it is for the study to have a way to contact respondents, it is also critical that respondents have a reliable and convenient way to contact study staff. Three possibilities to facilitate respondents contacting the study are (1) maintaining a conveniently located storefront or field office, (2) maintaining a dedicated project telephone line, and (3) maintaining an interactive study website.

If the project is based in a single geographic location, a field office/storefront can serve multiple purposes. As Conover, Berkman, Gheith, Jahiel, Stanley, Geller *et al.* (1997) note, a field office should be "user friendly for both participants and staff." Staff can use the space to store materials, conduct interviews, and leave messages for and receive messages from respondents. Respondents can drop by the office to check on the due date for their next interview, update their contact information, or just to say hello. If possible, small items such as toiletries, snack bars, resource guides, or Internet access, for example, might be provided here to encourage respondents to visit the space. In order to be most useful, the field office should be regularly staffed and the office hours posted clearly. A local field office also proves useful in promoting visibility of the study in the community as a whole.

One example is the Downtown Health Project, a study on hepatitis and HIV in homeless adult shelters and using meal lines in the Skid Row area of Los Angeles (Gelberg, Robertson, Arangua, Leake, Summer, Moe *et al.*, 2012). The study involved a baseline interview, blood draw for hepatitis and HIV testing, one week notification of blood test results, and referral and follow-up interviews. Data collection staff maintained a field office stationed at a large shelter in the center of Skid Row. The field office was staffed five days a week by interviewers working in shifts. The office quickly became a place for participants to drop in to receive their blood test results and referrals, complete follow up interviews, or to pick up a payment for a follow-up interview conducted by phone. Ultimately, this project was able to enroll 92.7 percent of those sampled with 92 percent of those returning for blood test results and treatment referrals, and 91.3 percent of those eligible completing a one month follow-up interview. Cepeda and Valdez (2010) made use of a field office on their study with Mexican-American noninjecting heroin users in Texas. The office was located in an established community-based agency known throughout the community. They note that respondents "felt comfortable visiting our field office given its association with the agency." Project branding is important and when a project occurs with a limited geographical scope, researchers have an opportunity to ensure that the study brand has high recognition and visibility locally (Calderwood, 2012). Field offices/storefronts can help maintain visibility and study identity within the targeted neighborhoods to help legitimize and brand the project in the community.

Toll-free project telephone numbers are necessary for longitudinal studies. Respondents should be encouraged to call in with updates to their contact information and with study-related questions. Some researchers find that it is useful to incentivize respondents calling in with small monetary amounts, lotteries, or other services (Wright *et al.*, 1995). Though a message line is somewhat helpful, the literature suggests a project staffed toll-free number is best. In this case, staff members have "real-time" access to the caller's next interview date and the name of the interviewer assigned (Gregory *et al.*, 1992). In addition to providing necessary information to respondents and taking down contact updates, this interaction by a project staffer provides another opportunity to develop rapport. When the phone line cannot be staffed, it is important for the outgoing voicemail message to be clear and ask respondents to identify themselves by full name or other predetermined unique study identifier (like ID number). Quick response to voicemail left also helps to maintain rapport. The toll-free line is only useful to respondents if they have easy access to the phone number. The number should be distributed freely on printed study materials, mailings, a wallet-sized reminder card, and even on gift items, such as mugs, notepads, magnets, etc.

Interactive project websites can also be a useful tool in longitudinal studies, allowing respondents to update contact information, look up information about future interviews, and even schedule appointments. Additionally, information can be made available to third-party contacts, providing some authentication to the project and reassuring them of the project's legitimacy. It is important for these webpages to be updated and well-maintained and for any respondent questions or emails to be returned promptly in order to maintain positive relationships.

30.4   Designing a tracking protocol: important issues to consider

We now turn to considerations that will help guide researchers towards selecting the most appropriate techniques for finding and tracking hard-to-reach study populations. It is ideal to plan a strategy before data collection begins to create procedures dependent on the population studied and be prepared to adapt the plan and modify it as necessary throughout data collection. Scott (2004) suggests a model of tracking, for example, emphasizing congruency between population characteristics and follow-up techniques, a clearly defined careful tracking infrastructure, and a system to monitor the details of tracking participants. There is no one formula that can be applied to all hard-to-reach populations and no one method that will work. Rather, designing a tracking and locating plan involves drafting a multi-pronged, organized, population-specific approach, given the available budget, staffing and resources, study design, human subjects issues, and project goals.

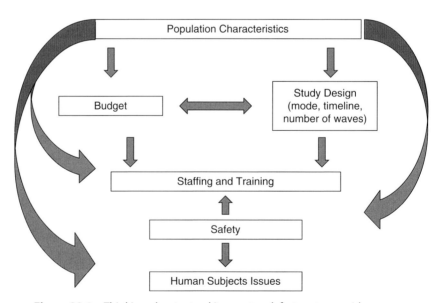

Figure 30.1   Thinking about a tracking protocol: factors to consider

30.4.1 Budget and cost

Budget is one of the primary decision factors affecting tracking and locating options. *What percent of the budget is allocated toward data collection?* Things to consider include direct costs, such as mileage or printed flyers, postage, telephone costs, maintaining a toll-free respondent project line, and vendor costs, but also staff training, staff time, and management time.

In order to make decisions about various tracking techniques researchers must evaluate the cost relative to the benefit. *What is the possible yield of this technique? Will the extra cost of employing a survey technique be worth it for this study?* Besides overall response rates, researchers also need to consider whether there are types of subjects that will be missed if a particular mode of tracking or data collection is not used. *Will employing this technique help reach respondents the study cannot access another way? Will analyses be affected by higher rates of nonresponse?* If subgroups missed through phone-only outreach, for example, might have had systematically different responses than phone responders, this is where concerns about nonresponse bias come into play.

Teitler *et al.* (2003) conducted a study with unwed fathers of newborns. They employed a mixed-mode approach – first attempting to approach fathers at the hospital as soon as possible after the child's birth, secondly reaching out by telephone when hospital-based interviews were not possible, and thirdly attempting interviews via in-person visits to telephone nonrespondents. By adding telephone and in-person follow-up, the researchers increased completion rates from 68 percent to 80 percent, thereby making the final sample more representative. Approximately 65 percent of the data collection budget was spent on hospital completes representing 85 percent of completed cases; 20 percent of the budget was spent on phone completes yielding 12 percent of the completes; and 15 percent of the budget was spent on field completes yielding only 3 percent of completed cases. They found, however, that after about a 75 percent response rate there were diminishing returns – cases completed with very high levels of effort were quite similar to those where a moderate level of effort (and cost) and they were poor proxies for the nonrespondents.

In the Andresen, Machuga, Van Booven, Egel, Chibnall, and Talt (2008) study of workers with low back injuries, tracking consisted of three steps: batch tracking with use of the US Postal Service's national change of address (NCOA) database; searching in Internet white pages, reverse directories, and national phone directory software; and, finally, credit bureau and paid people searches such as Intelius. Costs were about 69 percent higher for cases completed via hands-on paid people search as opposed to batch look-ups only cases. They found that more intensive tracking efforts were able to improve the representativeness of their study by reaching more minorities and women. The pool of individuals completing after more intensive tracking were more comparable to those claimants not located as compared to those completed after less-intensive tracking efforts. That said, $98,000 was spent tracking 1,027 individuals who were never located.

The cost/benefit issue is a very tricky one, and there are no easy answers. Rather, our goal here is ensure these sorts of issues are discussed and considered when thinking about developing a tracking strategy.

30.4.2 *Appropriate staffing and training*

"Individuals assigned to the demanding task of locating participants in panel studies are the cornerstone of the data collection effort" (Ribisl, Walton, Mowbray, Luke, Davidson, & Bootsmiller, 1996). Choice of staff becomes an early and important part of the success of any research effort (Coen *et al.*, 1996; Leonard *et al.*, 2003). There are generally three models for staffing the tracking effort:

(1) Using the interviewer/tracker model where the same staff who interview are also responsible for tracking efforts. In this case, it is important to select individuals who can both collect valid and reliable data in an interview, as well as possess the persistence, creativity, enthusiasm, and attention to detail that is required to track and locate individuals. This method tends to work best for smaller projects. "Using the same interviewer to track participants over time demanded less coordination than using several trackers for the same participant and was therefore generally more efficient" (McKenzie, Tulsky, Long, Chesney, & Moss, 1999). Additionally, consistency over time leads to more investment on the part of the interviewer and more knowledge of the individual's network, service providers, and patterns, increasing likelihood of locating. The reverse is also true – by assigning the same tracker/interviewer over time, the participant has the opportunity to develop trust and comfort with the study staff, and a personal investment in the research, making tracking success more likely (Cohen, Mowbray, Bybee, Yeich, Ribisl, & Freddolino, 1993; Conover *et al.*, 1997; Hough *et al.*, 1996).

(2) Using a central core group of trackers. This allows specialization and efficient investment in development of tracking skills for staff and a focus on use of less costly tracking strategies, such as phone and online efforts. This can be particularly useful and efficient for very large or geographically diverse projects and enables cases to be worked in batches.

(3) A combination of the above where either cases are initially worked centrally and then only the most difficult cases are sent to field tracking by interviewer (this is often cost-effective) or cases are initially attempted by field staff, but if attempts fail, the cases get routed to a core group of tracking experts. This strategy requires high levels of communication to ensure a case is not being worked by multiple trackers at once. Clear case ownership is essential for maximizing efficiency of this strategy.

In their review of studies involving tracking and follow-up with marginalized populations, McKenzie *et al.* (1999) noted that traits stressed across studies included "friendliness, like-ability, ethical conduct, and attentiveness to detail." They also note in their review that study authors "emphasized that diversity in race, ethnicity, gender, and sexual orientation increased staff sensitivity." This is not to say it is necessary to match interviewers to respondents.

Training is essential for project staff interacting with respondents and third parties (Freedman, Thornton, & Camburn, 1980; Ribisl *et al.*, 1996). They should be trained not only on the research interview and survey protocols, but on project basics like how to describe the project briefly and confidently to respondents, to third parties, and to service providers, establishing rapport, maintaining confidentiality, and on basic tracking methods. These skills should be modeled and practiced just as interview administration is. All tracking staff needs to be able quickly and convincingly to communicate the reason for the call or visit and disassociate with any group the respondent might be avoiding. This speaks to the need to spend time crafting a solid but brief survey description and answers to frequently asked questions about the goals and nature of the study. Adequate training and practice time as well as ongoing supervision and re-training is needed.

Another important aspect of training is to make clear how far one should go in seeking to gain a complete survey. *How many attempts should be made? Should staff attempt in-person tracking, phone tracking, or both, and in what sequence? Are personal visits on different times of day on different days of the week an expectation?* Researchers need to communicate the answers to these questions to staff before cases are worked. This is especially important for field tracing as this mode is very expensive comparable to other modes. The field costs tend to accumulate quickly and be less easy to control with staff working more independently.

30.4.3 Study design issues: timeline and follow-up waves

How long is the project field period? Sometimes one of the most important determinants of successful tracking is allowing enough time for efforts to lead to completes. While results from vendor and batch look-ups can be obtained quickly, certain tracking methods take time to yield a complete. Phone attempts often require multiple calls varying the times of day and days of the week as do field visits to respondents' homes or homes of third-party contacts or potential informants. Understandably, the demands of a short research timeline can tempt researchers to increase the pacing of search and tracking efforts. However, researchers should avoid a pacing that will antagonize respondents or third-party contacts. Phoning the parent of a respondent every day for a week is likely to make that person angry and uncooperative; on the other hand, waiting weeks between attempts or waiting until a person returns a call is not ideal either.

Is this a single-wave study or longitudinal study with multiple survey waves? How mobile will the study population be during this interval? Single-wave studies with outdated or poor quality list samples might invest time in administrative records searching, paid online databases, and criss-cross directories, while longitudinal studies should plan to collect contact information from respondents at each interview, carefully consider rapport development activities, and develop community and service-provider relationships, as able. *For longitudinal studies, what is the interval between survey waves? How will this interval affect staffing and consistency?* Several studies (Scott, 2004) have cited the importance of interim contacts via mail, phone, or in person as one of the primary factors improving response at follow-up waves. Cepeda and Valdez (2010) found with Mexican-American noninjecting heroin users in Texas that 80 percent of respondents said the main reason they participated in the follow-up interview was because of personal reminders between the interview waves from outreach specialists. The frequency of interim contacts will be affected by the length of the follow-up interval as well as budget.

30.4.4 Human subjects issues

What contact information exactly will the project be collecting? How will the project protect respondents' contact information? Tracking respondents raises many human subjects issues: data safeguarding, consent to contact, project naming, third-party interactions, administrative records access, and legal issues to name a few.

Deciding what information to collect can have significant impact on data safeguarding procedures. For example, SSNs can be very useful in accessing certain administrative or financial records. However, should this information be disclosed accidentally, consequences can be severe. Very careful data safeguarding protocols must be in place to ensure disclosure does not occur. If these sorts of administrative records will not be accessed, perhaps only partial SSN could be collected. Sometimes, gathering too much information might damage rapport; in a longitudinal study with adult women sexual assault survivors, Ullman (2011) notes that the decision was made not to collect SSNs, Department of Motor Vehicles (DMV) information, and contact information on collaterals (third-party contacts), given the safety and confidentiality concerns of their respondents. They realized there was a potential risk in failing to collect this information, but felt the benefit of the confidence of the women and maintenance of rapport outweighed the risk, given there were only two waves of data collection.

When designing systems for collection and storage of re-contact and historical tracking information, data safeguarding should be of primary concern. Electronic data collection can often be more secure than paper; however, project considerations in budget, scale, and logistics might make paperless collection unfeasible. These are important issues to weigh and consider. Additional thought should be given to the storage of contact information and length of time the researchers will retain it. Storing tracking data separately from survey responses is considered good practice and can ease some ethical concerns. Training interviewers on protection protocols is essential, particularly for field interviewers. In the United States, researchers might wish to pursue a Certificate of Confidentiality from the Department of Health and Human Services to protect the project from forced disclosure of respondents' information (both contact information and survey data) even under court order or subpoena (Hough *et al.*, 1996).

What information will be disclosed to third parties who are contacted? Are there any permissible use restrictions relevant to administrative data requests? Tracking protocols and training plans should always be reviewed and approved by a research ethics review board in advance of data collection. Even the study name can be of issue – it is important to select a study name that does not disclose sensitive information about a respondent if study participation was disclosed. For example, naming a project "The Heroin-Users Health Project" would disclose the respondent's status as a heroin user to anyone who viewed printed materials, such as flyers or mailing letters, or heard voicemail messages. Thoughtful consideration on naming and project branding is suggested. If the study is longitudinal, when collecting contact information, it is important to inform the respondent why the information is being collected and how it will be used and to build appropriate language into informed consent documents. The use of administrative records for tracking should be stated, and, where necessary, a signed written consent should be obtained. For example, tracking residents of a substance abuse treatment facility after they leave treatment using treatment facility records or probation records might require signed written consent in order to access those files legally (Grandone & Moritz, 2010).

Similarly, respondents should be informed when third-party contacts, service providers, and probation officers, for example, might be contacted and that confidentiality will be maintained. Generally, communications with third parties should describe in only the most general terms what the research entails. For example, a study about HIV risk with needle injectors might be described as "a health project he or she is taking part in." Information should be gathered from informants while maintaining the confidentiality at all times of the respondents. McKenzie *et al.* (1999) cautions us to think carefully about employing individuals such as service providers and probation or parole officers to assist with tracking efforts. Though these individuals might be able to provide good locating information or be used to pass along a message from the study, efforts should be taken to ensure their assistance is not considered coercive to the respondent and threats or implied punishment for nonresponse should not be tolerated.

Although researchers' tracking and interviewing staff should be striving to obtain the number of survey completes to make findings valid, tracking needs to be done in a legal and ethical fashion. Researchers should not misrepresent themselves by pretending to be someone they are not, such as law enforcement representatives or lottery officials, and coercion should be considered unacceptable (Coen *et al.*, 1996). Staff training is crucial in this area to ensure compliance with ethical and legal standards particularly when compensation is linked in any way to the number of cases located or completed. Again, staff should be highly motivated to track and find survey respondents, but not so motivated or pressured that they break the rules. Consistently communicating this to staff and implementing quality control measures, along with support and supervision, are key. Phone monitoring, validation of interviews or call records, and direct field supervision by research managers and supervisory staff can also help prevent instances where tracking and interviewing staff crosses ethical or legal red lines.

30.5 Conclusions

Of primary concern in survey research is our ability to collect quality data and minimize nonresponse bias (Ribisl *et al.*, 1996). Next to refusal to participate, failure to find respondents (either from list samples or in longitudinal studies) is the most common cause of nonresponse, so thoughtful consideration of tracking strategies in research is essential. This is particularly relevant in data collection with hard-to-reach populations, such as the homeless, runaway youth, migrant workers, probation or parole violators, or substance users, who by their very definition and characteristics will prove challenging to locate. Extra and special efforts must be put towards issues of minimizing nonresponse in these groups. Cottler *et al.* (1996) suggest that "a comprehensive tracking strategy as well as persistence and creative teamwork are the most important determinants of the rate of success of a follow-up investigation."

The general literature on survey locating and tracking is very sparse. Quite a few articles describe various tracking protocols in specific populations, particularly in longitudinal studies with the homeless and with substance users. While some describe observed effectiveness of these efforts on a given project or "hit rates" of various strategies, few discuss unit cost of efforts. There are relatively few scholarly articles that report any locating or tracking experiments, attempt to randomize respondents to tracking conditions, or more rigorously explore relative effectiveness within a population or across populations. This is an area for more research.

Though this chapter discusses and provides examples from certain subsamples of these difficult populations, we have provided a framework of basic principles that are applicable to any and all difficult populations, with options for a variety of budgets, timelines, and modes. No matter the group, forward thinking of a comprehensive, multi-pronged, organized strategy is a must. The approach should be tailored to the population, cognizant of project budget and resources, appropriate for the project timeline, and sensitive to human subjects and safety issues. Tracking protocols should combine multiple strategies, be creative, and remain flexible where possible. As Wright *et al.* (1995) so perfectly sum up, "Our impression is nothing works well for everyone but that everything works for some subset of the client base."

References

Andresen, E., Machuga, R., Van Booven, M., Egel, J., Chibnall, J., & Talt, R. (2008). Effects and costs of tracing strategies on nonresponse bias in a survey of workers with low-back injury. *Public Opinion Quarterly*, 72(1), 40–54.

Brown, J., & Nederend, S. (1997). *Locating and Surveying Medicaid and AFDC Beneficiaries: CAHPS Field Test Experience to Date*. DRU-1664-AHCPR. Prepared for Agency for Health Care Policy Research. Santa Monica, CA: RAND Corporation.

Burgess, R. D. (1989). Major issues and implications of tracing survey respondents. In D. Kasprzyk, G. Duncan, G. Kalton, and M. P. Singh (eds.), *Panel Surveys* (pp. 52–74). New York: John Wiley & Sons.

Calderwood, L. (2012). Tracking sample members in longitudinal studies. *Survey Practice*, 5(4). [e-journal: http://surveypractice.org/index.php/SurveyPractice/article/view/34/html.]

Cepeda, A., & Valdez, A. (2010). Ethnographic strategies in the tracking and retention of street-recruited community-based samples of substance using hidden populations in longitudinal studies. *Substance Use and Misuse*, 45(5), 700–16.

Coen, A., Patrick, D., & Shern, D. (1996). Minimizing attrition in longitudinal studies of special populations: an integrated management approach. *Evaluation and Program Planning*, 19(4), 309–19.

Cohen, E., Mowbray, C., Bybee, D., Yeich, S., Ribisl, K., & Freddolino, P. (1993). Tracking and follow-up methods for research on homelessness. *Evaluation Review*, 17(3), 331–52.

Conover, S., Berkman, A., Gheith, A., Jahiel, R., Stanley, D., Geller, P., *et al.* (1997). Methods for successful follow-up of elusive urban populations: an ethnographic approach with homeless men. *Bulletin of the New York Academy of Medicine*, 74(1), 90–108.

Corsi, K., Van Hunnik, B., Kwiatkowski, C., & Booth, R. (2006). Computerized tracking and follow-up techniques in longitudinal research with drug users. *Health Services and Outcomes Research Methodology*, 6(3–4), 101–10.

Cottler, L., Compton, W., Ben-Abdallah, A., Horne, M., & Claverie, D. (1996). Achieving a 96.6 percent follow-up rate in a longitudinal study of drug abusers. *Drug and Alcohol Dependence*, 41(3), 209–17.

Couper, M., & Ofstedal, M. (2009). Keeping in contact with mobile sample members. In P. Lynn (ed.), *Methodology of Longitudinal Surveys*. Chichester: John Wiley & Sons.

Durrant, G., Groves, R., Staetsky, L., & Steele, F. (2010). Effects of interviewer attitudes and behaviors on refusal in household surveys. *Public Opinion Quarterly*, 74(1), 1–36.

Edelen, M., Slaughter, M., McCaffrey, D., Becker, K., & Morral, A. (2010). Long term effect of community based treatment: evidence from the Adolescent Outcomes Project. *Drug and Alcohol Dependence*, 107(1), 62–68.

Freedman, D., Thornton, A., & Camburn, D. (1980). Maintaining response rates in longitudinal studies. *Psychological Methods & Research*, 9(1), 87–98.

Fumagalli, L., Laurie, H., & Lynn, P. (2013). Experiments with methods to reduce attrition in longitudinal surveys. *Journal of the Royal Statistical Society*, 176(2), 499–519.

Gelberg, L., Robertson, M., Arangua, L., Leake, B., Sumner, G., Moe, A., *et al.* (2012). Prevalence, distribution, and correlates of Hepatitis C virus infection among homeless adults in Los Angeles. *Public Heath Reports*, 127(4), 407–21.

Grandone, M., & Moritz, K. (2010). Strategies for client tracking and follow-up, Global Appraisal of Individual Needs Training Manual, Normal, IL. Retrieved from www.gaincc.org/_data/files/Posting_Publications/Strategies_for_Tracking_and_Followup_Manual.pdf.

Gregory, M., Lohr, M.J., & Gilchrist, L. (1992). Methods for tracking pregnant and parenting adolescents. *Evaluation Review*, 17(1), 69–81.

Groves, R., Fowler, F.J., Couper, M., Lepkowski, J., Singer, E., & Tourangeau, R. (2004). *Survey Methodology*. Hoboken, NJ: John Wiley & Sons.

Gwadz, M., & Rotheram-Borus, M.J. (1992). Tracking high-risk adolescents longitudinally. *AIDS Education and Prevention*, Fall Supplement, 69–82.

Hill, Z. (2004). Reducing attrition in panel studies in developing countries. *International Journal of Epidemiology*, 33(3), 493–98.

Hough, R., Tarke, H., Renker, V., Shields, P., & Glatstein, J. (1996). Recruitment and retention of homeless mentally ill participants in research. *Journal of Consulting and Clinical Psychology*, 64(5), 881–91.

Hunt, J., & White, E. (1998). Retaining and tracking cohort study members. *Epidemiologic Reviews*, 20(1), 57–70.

Leonard, N., Lester, P., Rotheram-Borus, M., Mattes, K., Gwadz, M., & Ferns, B. (2003). Successful recruitment and retention of participants in longitudinal behavioral research. *AIDS Education and Prevention*, 15(3), 269–81.

McCuller, W., Sussman, S., Holiday, K., Craig, S., & Dent, C. (2002). Tracking procedures for locating high-risk youth. *Evaluation & the Health Professions*, 25(3), 345–62.

McKenzie, M., Tulsky, J. P., Long, H., Chesney, M., & Moss, A. (1999). Tracking and follow-up of marginalized populations: a review. *Journal of Health Care for the Poor and Underserved*, 10(4), 409–29.

Marmor, J., Oliveria, S., Donahue, R., Garrahie, E., White, M. J., Moore, L., *et al.* (1991). Factors encouraging cohort maintenance in a longitudinal study. *Journal of Clinical Epidemiology*, 44(6), 531–35.

Menendez, E., White, M. C., & Tulsky, J. P. (2001). Locating study subjects: predictors and successful search strategies with inmates released from a U.S. county jail. *Controlled Clinical Trials*, 22(3), 238–47.

Nwadiuko, J., Isbell, P., Zolotor, A., Hussey, J., & Kotch, J. (2011). Using social networking sites in subject tracing. *Field Methods*, 23(1), 77–85.

Rhodes, B., & Marks, E. (2011). Using facebook to locate sample members, Survey Practice (2011, October 24). Retrieved April 16, 2012 from http://surveypractice.wordpress. com/2011/10/24/using-facebook-to-locate-sample-members/.

Ribisl, K., Walton, M., Mowbray, C., Luke, D., Davidson II, W., & Bootsmiller, B. (1996). Minimizing participant attrition in panel studies through the use of effective retention and tracking strategies: review and recommendations. *Evaluation and Program Planning*, 19(1), 1–25.

Rumptz, M., Sullivan, C., Davidson, W., & Basta, J. (1991). An ecological approach to tracking battered women over time. *Violence and Victims*, 6(3), 237–44.

Scott, C. (2004). A replicable model for achieving over 90% follow-up rates in longitudinal studies of substance abusers. *Drug and Alcohol Dependence*, 74, 21–36.

Singer, E., Groves, R. M., & Corning, A. (1999). Differential incentives: beliefs about practices, perceptions of equity, and effects on survey participation. *Public Opinion Quarterly*, 63(2), 251–60.

Singer, E., & Kulka, R. A. (2002). Paying respondents for survey participation. In M. Vander Ploeg, R. A. Moffitt, & C. F. Citro (eds.), *Studies of Welfare Populations: Data Collection and Research Issues* (pp.105–28). Washington, DC: National Academy Press.

Teitler, J., Reichman, N., & Sprachman, S. (2003). Costs and benefits of improving response rates for a hard-to-reach population. *Public Opinion Quarterly*, 67(1), 126–38.

Ullman, S. (2011). Longitudinal tracking methods in a study of adult women sexual assault survivors. *Violence against Women*, 17(2), 189–200.

Willimack, D., Schuman, H., Pennell, B.-E., & Lepkowski, J. (1995). Effects of a prepaid nonmonetary incentive on response rates and response quality in a face-to-face study. *Public Opinion Quarterly*, 59(1), 78–92.

Wright, J., Lampton Allen, T., & Devine, J. (1995). Tracking non-traditional populations in longitudinal studies. *Evaluation and Program Planning*, 18(3), 267–77.

Young, S., & Rice, E. (2011). Online social networking technologies, HIV knowledge, and sexual risk and testing behaviors among homeless youth. *AIDS Behavior*, 15(2), 253–60.

Index